MENTAL RETARDATION
Nature, Needs, and Advocacy

MENTAL RETARDATION
Nature, Needs, and Advocacy

DONALD F. SELLIN
Western Michigan University

ALLYN AND BACON, INC.   Boston   London   Sydney   Toronto

*Photo credits: on pp. 1, 67, 85, 211, and 369—Kalamazoo Association for Retarded Citizens; on pp. 19, 45, 249, 287, and 325—Berrian Intermediate School District; on p. 137—*Kalamazoo Gazette; *on p. 109—Michigan Special Olympics; and on p. 405—FAR Conservatory of Performing Arts.*

470 Atlantic Avenue, Boston, Massachusetts 02210

LIBRARY OF CONGRESS CATALOGING IN PUBLICATION DATA

Sellin, Donald F., 1934–
Mental retardation.

Includes bibliographies and index.
1. Mental deficiency. 2. Mentally handicapped—Case and treatment. 3. Mental retardation services. I. Title. [DNLM: 1. Mental retardation. WM300.3 S467m]
RC570.S44 362.3 78-12012
ISBN 0-205-05989-9

Printed in U.S.A.

Dedicated
to
My wife Lucy and children, Elizabeth, Philip, Francis, John, and Andrew.
Their understanding made this text possible.

Contents

Preface

This book was *not* prompted by a disenchantment with existing tests, but by a perception of the need for an activist text to describe the what is and the what can be. Although the book explores historical roots, the main concern is contemporary influences and their implications for the future. It is activist in the sense of describing problems and presenting a variety of possible solutions.

This text is organized around three main themes: nature, needs, and advocacy. The first four chapters reflect what is known and understood about the *nature* of mental retardation; they establish its etiology and ecology. The next four chapters examine the *needs* of mentally retarded citizens. Chapter 5 reviews intelligence and learning, with an emphasis upon the need for enlightened views of human potential. Chapter 6 outlines the significance of early childhood learnings and the need for attention to physical activity and fitness. Chapter 7 is a discussion of language and adjustment. In chapter 8, the structure and function of comprehensive, coordinated services are described. Attention is given to concept and process of social action.

The third theme is *advocacy,* and the next five chapters relate to practice, standards, and examples. Chapter 9 identifies three interrelated service needs associated with supportive services. Chapter 10 outlines alternatives for definition design, implementation, and evaluation of responsive environments. Chapter 11 relates to the services of education and vocational preparation. Chapter 12 is devoted to the nature and tasks of the advocate relationship. Chapter 13 concerns the nature of helping relationships. It is believed that both chapters give guidance and structure to implement a protege relationship. Chapter 14 identifies a way of thinking about and valuing the future.

The concept of *advocacy* may be misleading. I believe that advocacy equates with the western tradition of *stewardship* and the marshaling of resources and information to improve the quality of life. This view of advocacy recognizes that decision making and practice are based upon valuing people. One must initiate change on the basis of informed opinion and be open in evaluating one's efforts and accomplishment. The science of evaluation is one tool by which the goals of a service system are realized. This text was prompted by a need to assemble opinion and evidence that identify or imply: worthy goals, the present circumstances, and options for consideration.

The intended readership of this text is open, since the field of mental retardation should include all interested persons and all sources of support and information. The term *practitioner* is inclusive rather than exclusive. Teacher, social worker, psychologist, counselor, physician, therapist, paraprofessional, parent, researcher, administrator, and advocate are but a few of those who practice in this field. Promoting self-esteem, learning, communication, and competence are shared tasks of a team. This text can be one rallying point to organize and discover common interests.

This text was also designed for both preservice and inservice educators. The assumption is that such persons will have taken an introductory survey course in exceptional children and will later experience a curriculum and methods sequence. This text is intended to bridge the initial and culminating experiences by reviewing initial learnings and providing a frame of reference for a course on educational philosophy, curriculum, and method. I believe this text does no violence to noncategorical approaches to curriculum and method in teacher preparation.

I hope that a sense of optimism, excitement, and mastery have been communicated and that the text encourages a sense of learning beyond the period of formal preparation and beyond a mere text. Lifelong learning can enrich and refresh one's own practice and development.

This text emphasizes environment as an important source of performance. I have been fortunate to experience helpful environments. Appreciation is expressed to Dr. Joseph Eisenbach, head of the Department of Special Education, Western Michigan University, for his reactions, encouragement, and support, and to Dr. James Bosco of Western Michigan University for technical assistance. The Michigan and Kalamazoo Associations for Retarded Citizens have provided a sense of family and a set of life experiences for the concerns of this text. Feedback from undergraduate and inservice teachers has encouraged me to pursue the concerns of advocates in this type of text. Their reactions have confirmed the interest of these future educators in the understanding of common and shared tasks. Of particular encouragement was their perceived need to understand the resources of allied agencies and disciplines. Allyn and Bacon, with the activist interest of R. Curtis Whitesel, has provided a responsive publishing environment. Numerous parents of retarded persons have influenced me by their belief in potential and by their excitement in their accomplishments. Finally, my family has been a source of encouragement and help. The actual writing required their patience and understanding. After looking through a seven-hundred-page text in my library, one of my children remarked wistfully to his brother, "I wonder how many summers that book messed up for his kids?" That there was patience and tolerance of fatherly absence is proven by the existence of this text.

The typing of this text required also significant effort and dedication. Words do not express the debt to Mrs. Sharon Flickinger, Mrs. Mary Redford, Mrs. Joan Khaled, and especially Ms. Connie Ketcham.

I would also like to thank those who reviewed the manuscript and offered valuable suggestions and, finally, the organizations who graciously gave permission to use materials from their publications: the American Association on Mental Deficiency, the Council for Exceptional Children, the National Association for Retarded Citizens, the Michigan Association for Retarded Citizens, the Michigan Department of Mental Health, The Berrian Intermediate School District, the Kalamazoo Valley Intermediate School District, the Kalamazoo Association for Retarded Citizens, the American Institute for Mental Studies, Grune & Stratton, Inc., Prentice-Hall, Inc., Charles C Thomas, Publisher, and *The Philadelphia Inquirer*.

A Note to the Reader

The Preface has outlined certain features of the intention and the organization of the text. This note is intended to give suggestions for relating to the text.

Each chapter is organized in a similar format of Synopsis, Objectives, Chapter Content, Summing Up, and On Location. The Synopsis and Objectives portions provide an orientation toward what is to come, while the Summing Up is a concise résumé. The orientation and résumé are intended as aids to learning and retention. The On Location selections are designed to lift the reader out of the world of the text and into the world of the retarded citizen. Hopefully, these selections will enrich the chapter discussions and create a sense of involvement through these discussions. Summative tables and figures have been included as an additional aid and resource.

This text should be understood as an initial step in one's preparation. Hopefully, it will engender a resolve for life-long learning as one indication of commitment to service. The nature of advocacy on behalf of the mentally retarded reflects the need for competent people.

DFS

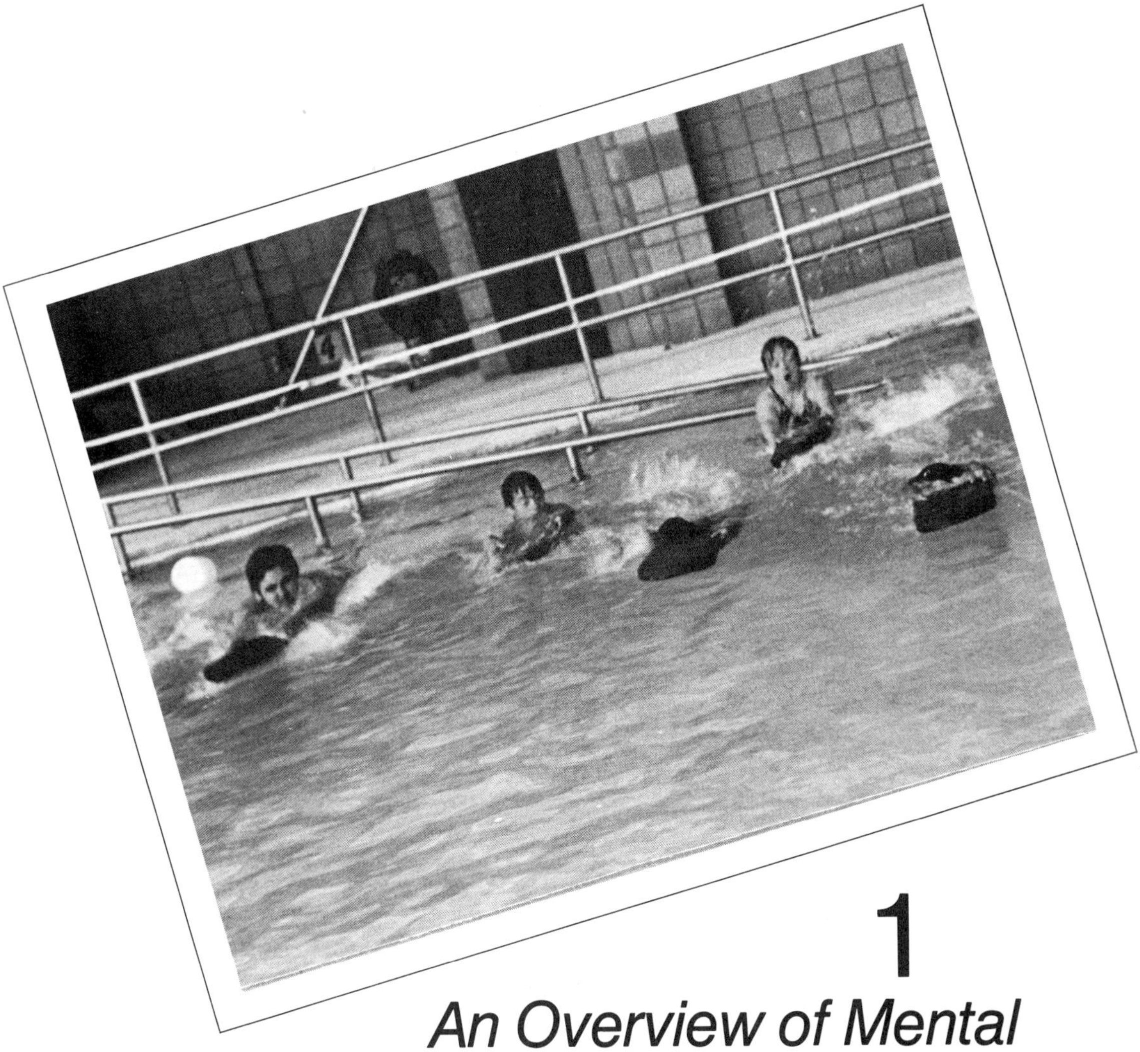

1
An Overview of Mental Retardation and the Mentally Retarded

SYNOPSIS

This chapter discusses the components or elements necessary to assess retardation and presents a resumé of the characteristics of the mentally retarded.

OBJECTIVES

ATTITUDES

1 To formulate a personal definition of mental retardation that suggests reasonable, positive expectations for the retarded.
2 To view mental retardation as a dynamic condition worthy of public attention.

UNDERSTANDINGS

1 To compare and contrast various perspectives surrounding a definition of mental retardation.
2 To describe the components of a complete definition of mental retardation.
3 To specify the dynamics that affect mentally retarded persons.

SKILLS

1 To describe mental retardation to one's own peers.
2 To differentiate mental retardation from other conditions.

THE SCOPE OF A DEFINITION OF MENTAL RETARDATION

A precise definition of mental retardation is essential in formulating a basis for services founded upon the unique characteristics of the retarded. Historically, mental retardation has been defined in terms of *social competence*. In medieval times, the test of mental retardation centered around work situations, recognizing one's name, counting money, etc. *Physical appearance* and *physical development* have also been significant gauges. The advent of *mandatory school attendance* brought a focus on school performance, and the emergence of *psychological testing* has added another dimension. All of these factors suggest that retardation is defined in terms of a group of diverse behaviors. The search for a uniform definition has centered around identifying descriptors that encompass the complex variations associated with this condition. Different definitions have stressed various combinations of:

1 Criteria of conformity to social-cultural norms of behavior, especially independent adult behavior;
2 estimates of vocational-occupational adequacy;
3 estimates of ability to profit from educational opportunities, especially in literacy-oriented tasks;
4 criteria of ultimate mental potential in comparison with individuals of similar age;
5 specification of etiological factors (causation) as sources of impaired functioning;
6 determination of the possibility of remediation, restoration, or even outright cure;
7 sufficient specificity to differentiate mental retardation from other conditions which also exhibit difference in functioning; and
8 a formulation of standards for service.

A CURRENT VIEW

As a result of the leadership of the American Association of Mental Deficiency (AAMD), a definition of mental retardation has been formulated which encompasses helpful dimensions of what this term has come to mean in the United States. Grossman (1973, p. 11) summarizes the efforts of his group:

> Mental retardation refers to significantly subaverage general intellectual functioning existing concurrently with deficits in adaptive behavior, and manifested during the developmental period.

Compare the previous definition adopted by the same group under the leadership of Heber (1960, p. 3):

> Mental retardation refers to subaverage general intellectual functioning which originates during the developmental period and is associated with impairment in adaptive behavior.

Both definitions emphasize the developmental period, general intellectual functioning, and the notion of adaptive behavior. Missing from both are assumptions of cause and potential.

The principal components of these two definitions specify a condition that is usually discovered in childhood (birth to age eighteen) and may persist throughout a lifetime; requires a complex diagnostic inference involving concurrent intellectual behavioral observations; requires individual differential intellectual assessment with either the Wechsler Scale for Children (WISC) or the Binet to determine intellectual functionality; and implies that adaptive behavior involves maturation, learning, and the capability of economic independence. Thus, one can also state that mental retardation is *not* an IQ score alone; social deviance alone, applicable to children alone; or the province of one discipline, professional affiliation, or service system alone.

Polloway and Payne (1975) have compared the Heber and Grossman reports. These authors note these meaningful differences:

1 The Grossman definition eliminates approximately 13.6 percent of the population eligible for classification as retarded. Hence, 2 to 3 percent of the general population would be considered mentally retarded.

Table 1–1 COMPARISON OF TERMINOLOGIES TO DESCRIBE MENTAL RETARDATION

Generic Terms	*Descriptors*
Mentally retarded	status term, involves four levels, involves behavior and measured intelligence.
Feebleminded	of British origin but also a traditional American term which emphasizes physical criteria and potential adult performance.
Mentally handicapped	in the United States a term employed to describe school populations; also a legal term descriptive of nonresponsibility for contracts.
Mentally subnormal	a world, or UN, term to describe discrepancy between actual performance and age appropriate norms.
Mentally deficient	a term once popular in the U.S. to suggest that observable damage or impairment to the brain is the principal explanation of socially inappropriate behaviors.
Mentally restored	a term in limited usage to describe individuals once thought to be in need of special services, supervision, or guardianship, but who have been judicially restored to legal independence.
Mentally impaired	a term in some vogue to emphasize cognitive process (as opposed to overt brain injury) as the source of behavioral manifestations.

2 The Grossman definition extends the developmental period from sixteen to eighteen.
3 Adaptive behavior becomes, in the Grossman report, a separate, distinct factor, a converging set of variables that operate with intelligence. In the prior view, there was the inclination to view intelligence as causing adaptive behavior.
4 The concepts of adaptive behavior have been further refined in the Grossman report into a greater variety of behaviors.
5 While the medical section has been little changed, another major shift has been to virtually eliminate borderline, cultural-familial mental retardation.

Mental retardation is the preferred term. Since the original interest in the United States (circa 1848), continuing through the present, this term has survived its competitors. At present, it appears to be the most accepted descriptor to parents, federal agencies, and professional organizations, although other terminology lingers on or strives to replace it. Table 1–1 attempts to place these various terminologies in perspective. While this summary may be overly simplified, one can observe the different perspectives involved. Again, it should be emphasized that *mental retardation* is a simple term to describe a complex population.

BEHAVIORAL DIMENSIONS OF MENTAL RETARDATION

As has been noted, the behavior, or performance, of the person is the central reference. One might conclude, therefore, that intelligence and behavior are not necessarily separate entities, only separable. Intelligence is a tool, or means, to adjustment. This view suggests an interaction effect (figure 1–1). The upper-right square represents an optimal pattern of adjustment where the behavior of the person is facilitated and/or rewarded by a responsive environment. The lower-left square illustrates paucity of behavioral responses in a basically hostile or neglectful environment. The remaining squares suggest a balance of either personal or social compensation required for adjustment.

The AAMD reports of Heber and Grossman agree that intellectual functioning (one dimension only) is inferred by measured intelligence. In the United States, the concept of measured intelligence is usually equated with the scores obtained from either Wechsler or Stanford-Binet instruments. While the results of these tests have come to be expressed in global scores such as intelligence quotients and mental ages, their emphasis is on controlled sampling of certain behaviors (chapter 5). These behaviors encompass factors such as:

Figure 1–1 *Illustrative Diagram of Personal-Social Influences Upon Human Development*

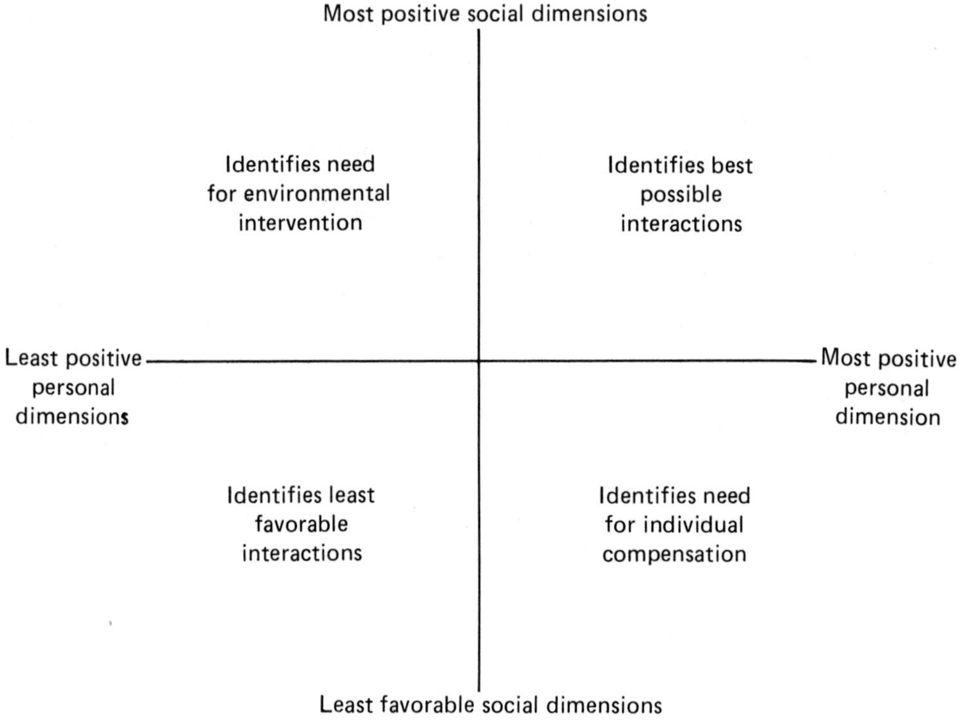

1 *memory,* both immediate recall, such as recitation of digits, as well as recognition of familiar terms, events, and objects;
2 *evaluation-judgment,* including the commonsense choice in a practical situation, estimate of a numerical solution, and selection of an appropriate theme;
3 *motor skills,* such as manipulation of objects into patterns, assembly of objects, and motor coordination;
4 *associative strategies,* including skills in classifying materials into common properties and in recognition; and
5 *perceptual relationships,* including relationships in space and positional concepts of directions.

This listing is by no means exhaustive. The point, however, is that intellectual functioning describes behaviors of a particular type. There is considerable debate as to whether these instruments measure *innate capacity* reflective of an efficient nervous system, or if the measure is in reality a complex achievement score reflecting an *advantaged environment*. The most helpful viewpoint is that any "score" is a *current* estimate to be evaluated with other data. The future intellectual status of a person is open-ended.

It is, however, *adaptive behavior* that commands the attention of the practitioner, especially the educator. This concept describes the person's present status and possible future goals, especially curriculum outcomes. The Grossman report (p. 123) defines adaptive behavior as

> the effectiveness or degree with which the individual meets the standards of personal independence and social responsibility expected of his age and cultural group. Three aspects of this behavior are: (1) maturation; (2) learning; and/or (3) social adjustment. These three aspects of adaptation are of different importance as qualifying conditions of mental retardation of different age groups.

Maturation is seen as those performances that result from physiological change and are not directly associated with practice. *Learning* is the acquisition and retention of knowledge with reference to the amount of time required. In this sense, learning is a rate concept. *Social adjustment* is seen as conformity to reasonable community standards and attainment of vocational competence. This was essentially the Heber view. The Grossman report identifies behavior that accompanies certain ages: infancy and early childhood (the maturation period, encompassing sensory-motor, communication, self-help, and interacting with others); childhood and early adolescence (the period of learning school tasks, including academic skills, mastery of the environment, and engaging in activities with others); and vocational and social responsibilities (especially in areas of employment and independent living).

While these listings may seem vague and general, measurement is possible. These behaviors, descriptive of adaptive behavior, provide the basis for curriculum goals appropriate for specific age groupings. The adaptive behavioral focus assumes that coping skills can be identified.

DISTINGUISHING MENTAL RETARDATION FROM OTHER CONDITIONS

Often the retarded have been perceived as behaviorally disordered, with the result that their educational and vocational needs have been neglected. The learning disabled often have been educated as if their learning styles were equivalent to that of the mentally retarded. For example, even today one encounters behaviorally disordered children enrolled in programs for the moderately retarded. The argument is that since there is no program for these learners, this arrangement is a reasonable compromise. However, the new Public Law 94–142 *mandates* the establishment of meaningful programs for all exceptional learners.

The Grossman (1973) report offers a model for an operational distinction between conditions based upon the dual criteria of measured intelligence and behavior (table 1–2). This model shows that *both* impairment in intellectual functioning and adaptive behavior must be evident in order to apply the label of mental retardation. For example, the model suggests that intellectual functioning may be adequate for the behaviorally disordered person, but his or her adaptive behavior must be remediated. When adaptive behavior is within acceptable limits, but intellectual functioning is impaired, further explanations must be sought. For the retarded, there is a presumption that consequences will be for *prolonged* periods of time and will require a carefully planned *developmental* sequencing of programs to maximize diminished potential. For the behaviorally disordered, however, there is a presumption for restoration of "normal" potential. Hence, duration of treatment may be less.

In summary, exceptional learners are first noticed by comparison of a given learner to age-appropriate norms. Usually the comparison yields a discrepancy of performance less than age-appropriate expectations. Depending upon measured intelligence *alone,* or upon adaptive responses (maturation, learning rates, or social adjustment) *alone* would constitute imperfect, imprecise, and probably illegal diagnostic and placement conditions. Increasingly, placement based upon IQ alone is being viewed as a violation of rights. In summary the distinctions are:

1 Intelligence-normal/behavior-normal defines an individual of at least adequate development.
2 Intelligence-normal/behavioral-retarded defines an individual of adequate potential for independence. This individual may be thwarted by in-

Table 1–2 A MODEL FOR THE COMPARISON OF MENTAL RETARDATION AND MENTAL ILLNESS

Adaptive Behavior	*Intellectual Functioning*	
	Retarded	*Nonretarded*
Retarded	Mental Retardation	Learning Disabilities Behavioral Disorder
Nonretarded	Further Study Indicated	"Normal"

SOURCE: Adapted from the Grossman (1973) Report.

efficient cognitive perceptual process (learning disabled), unsuspected sensory impairment, or self-defeating response patterns (behaviorally disordered).

3 Intelligence retarded-behavior normal could define imperfections of methods of assessment, lack of tolerance for culturally different life-styles, and unsuspected sensory impairment.

GROUPINGS OF THE MENTALLY RETARDED

How many groupings exist within the generic group of mental retardation is a fascinating question. The answer reflects the advances in knowledge and practice and the increasing complexities of American society. Residential facilities that served court-committed clients have expanded in this country from severely limited clients (the idiot, mid 1800s) through the imbecile (late 1800s) to the milder forms (early 1900s, especially World War I). Conversely, the public schools have progressed from the more capable clients (the educable, early 1900s) through the trainable (late 1950s and early 1960s) to the severely retarded (1970s). The reasons for these shifts are complex and varied and will be dealt with elsewhere. The main lesson is that both understanding (knowledge) and effort (doing) have been required to produce change. Table 1–3 summarizes the major groupings of mental retardation. These descriptors are somewhat overly concise and require the further amplification found in this text. The purpose of this table is to provide an initial concept about mental retardation. Note that:

1 One term denotes groups of persons.
2 Each group may possess an implied, or hypothetical, potential (as expressed in psychometric data).
3 The ultimate potential (as expressed in behavior) is dependent upon the appropriateness of program procedures.
4 Criteria for identification may be different as a function of age.
5 Services will be necessary for adult populations.

The thoughtful reader of the Grossman and Heber reports will note that measured intelligence and adaptive behavior may be independent, rather than interdependent. IQ alone does not predicate motivation, persistence, adequacy of programming, helpful parents, responsive personnel, and the host of factors presented by Dybwad. (chapter 2)

The preferred terminology in the United States would appear to be *mild, moderate, severe,* and *profound. Educable, trainable,* and *severe* enjoy a vogue

Table 1–3 RESUMÉ OF MAJOR TREATMENT GROUPINGS OF THE MENTALLY RETARDED

Terminology	*Psychometric Descriptors*	*Behavioral Descriptors*
Mild, Educable, Moron. Approximately 83 percent of the service population.	IQ 50 to 75, with mental age approximately one-half to three-fourths of actual chronological age.	Growth and development will seemingly approximate normalcy. Capacity for attainments is in literacy areas to fourth- and sixth-grade levels by late teens. Capable, with special education training, of self-sufficiency as an adult. Usually able to manage vocational and social standards. May require support services in times of crisis. Likely to be unrecognized in preschool and adult years.
Moderate, Trainable, Imbecile, Mentally Defective. Approximately 13 percent of the service population.	IQ 30 to 50, with mental age approximately one-third to one-half of actual chronological age.	Growth and development, especially language, will provide the basis for identification during the preschool years. May be potential for literacy attainments, especially reading, given a highly structured approach. Traditional emphasis has been upon functional literacy. Capable of productive employment *if* structured learning is followed. Traditional vocational emphasis has been upon noncompetitive employment. Will require guardianship and supervision for management of adult affairs.

Table 1–3 (continued)

Terminology	*Psychometric Descriptors*	*Behavioral Descriptors*
Severe, Idiot, Custodial. Approximately 4 percent of the service population.	IQ below 30, with mental age approximately one-fourth of chronological age.	Growth and development, especially motor development, will provide basis for early infant and toddler recognition. Responsive to program intervention. Capable of basic self-care and language skills. Capable of economic productivity provided sufficient structure and supervision of tasks. Requires extensive guardianship and advocacy.
Profound.	IQ may be untestable in the conventional sense. Opportunity to participate in a program will be the basis of distinction between severe and profound mental retardation.	Similar to the severe group. Much needs to be known before a statement can be written.

among educators. One might argue that a distinction between *educable* and *trainable* is not altogether as helpful as it once might have been. The complexity of teaching tasks, the creativity of teaching styles, and the diversity of curricular goals are equal in all instances. The problem with the term *trainable* has been the implication of less capability on the part of the learners, with less required of the teacher.

DEVELOPMENTAL CHARACTERISTICS OF THE MENTALLY RETARDED

Figure 1–2 portrays the four groupings of the mentally retarded across basic age groupings (three to past fifteen) and eight levels of complexity. It suggests that the

Figure 1–2 *Illustrative Rates of Developmental Manifestation of Adaptive Behavior for Four Groupings of Mentally Retarded Persons*

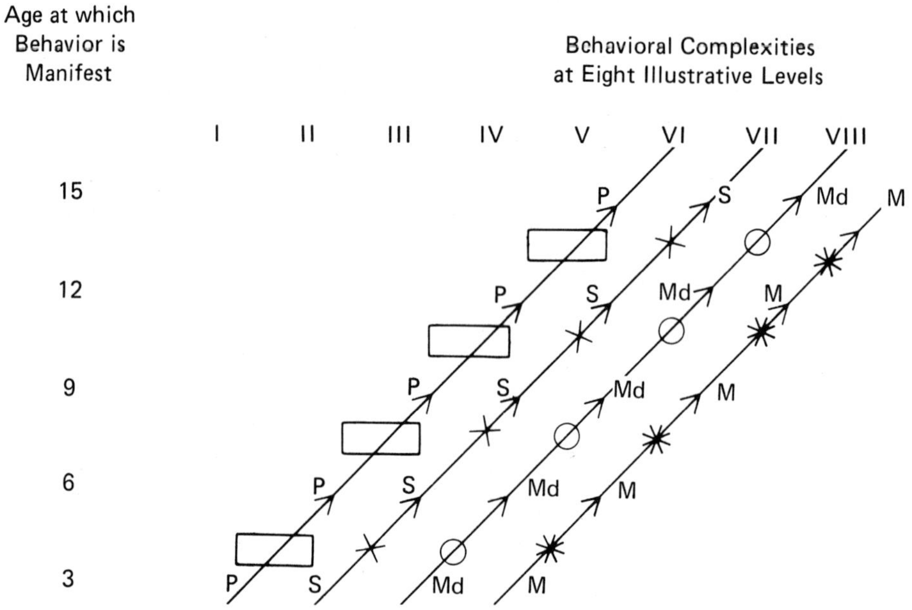

P = Profound
S = Severe
Md = Moderate (Trainable)
M = Mild (Educable)

"curve" of development is similar, but that the upper limits may be dramatically different for ultimate attainments. The graph is meant only to be illustrative, not a final statement. The attempt is only to set certain guidelines, not ultimate expectations.

The remainder of this section contains material adapted from Grossman which identifies common behaviors identified with these four main groupings. It should be remembered that these data reflect *current* opinion and research. Mental retardation is a dynamic condition about which opinions and knowledges change. New technologies and new information modify current notions.

Table 1–4 presents a resumé of the largest grouping, the mildly (educable) mentally retarded. It has been this group around which controversies regarding special education placement have centered. Traditionally, these persons have not been institutionalized. At present the majority of community programming has stressed preschool intervention, school programming, and vocational programming.

Table 1–4 REPRESENTATIVE ADAPTIVE BEHAVIORS ILLUSTRATING HIGHEST LEVELS FOR THE MILDLY MENTALLY RETARDED

Independent Functioning	*Physical Development*	*Communication*	*Social Development*	*Economic Development*	*Occupation*	*Self-Direction*
self-care and grooming adequate help in purchasing of clothes help and reminders in obtaining health and personal care	move about freely in hometown help in out-of-town travel use of complex equipment	telephone simple letter writing complex conversations emphasis upon concrete personal experiences; may be restricted in abstractions	rapid, complex, or involved, preplanned activities may not be as enjoyed as simple recreation seeks group membership involved in local recreation and church membership	some guidance for money management accurate in change, but does not necessarily use banking facilities errands to several stores for several items without notes	can engage in unskilled or semiskilled job everyday household chores cook and prepare simple meals	conscientious and responsible for work, but may require guidance in complex situations may require guidance in care of others attending to tasks for more than 15–20 minutes

Table 1–5 REPRESENTATIVE ADAPTIVE BEHAVIORS ILLUSTRATING HIGHEST LEVELS FOR THE MODERATELY MENTALLY RETARDED

Independent Functioning	*Physical Development*	*Communication*	*Social Development*	*Economic Development*	*Occupation*	*Self-Direction*
adequate self-care select daily clothing iron and store clothes care of hair	good body control good gross and fine motor coordination	read simple prose and signs with comprehension use of complex sentences	cooperative and competitive activities	errand without notes two-to-four item purchases without notes	do simple household tasks prepare simple foods which require mixing	initiate own directions attending to tasks for more than 15–20 minutes conscientious

The major controversy concerning these learners is whether they are most effectively helped by special class placements or by service delivery more in the mainstream of education. The guidelines posed in table 1–4 may seem to underestimate the size of the group. This is because the more conservative definitions imposed by court decisions have altered the population base. With a trend toward an upper-limit IQ of 70 (Polloway and Payne), significant numbers (in some communities almost half) of school-age persons previously defined as retarded have been reclassified. Consequently, those who remain have not necessarily been placed on single-criterion grounds.

The moderate, or trainable, mentally retarded have become a recognized group for public school programming (table 1–5). In the past, these persons have been community-oriented residents, with about 50 percent being institutionalized either during early childhood or in later adulthood. It is remarkable that so many persisted in the communities despite the lack of services in the 1950s and 1960s. Today, institutionalization is not viewed as a permanent placement, especially by those associated with residential facilities. The design of community services incorporates living and working arrangements for these persons.

The severely mentally retarded is the newest group to receive the rights of education by both legal decisions and enlightened voluntary compliance (table 1–6). Programs for this group have shifted from "day-care" units to "day-training" units. The shift, in part, represents a current emphasis upon instructional goals and directed intentions. With increased educational orientations, the possibilities for attracting personnel and financial support greatly improves their prospects.

The profound mentally retarded are the fourth group (table 1–7). Much remains to be done for such persons. In instances of diagnostic uncertainty, current practice suggests a trial enrollment in a day-training unit. The most functional diagnosis between severe and profound retardation would be the opportunity to be enrolled in a program. Presently, programs of sensory stimulation and adaptive physical development are indicated.

The profound, severe, and moderately mentally retarded are, and will be, community residents. This is no ideological statement, simply realistic. At present, the search is for living facilities in the community, not permanent placement in a residential facility. The residential facility of the present and the future will serve as a human development center to provide special services for specific, special clients and for a limited period of time.

SUMMING UP

This chapter has reviewed the key points that provide a basis for programs.

1 Mental retardation is what people believe it to be.

Table 1–6 REPRESENTATIVE ADAPTIVE BEHAVIORS ILLUSTRATING HIGHEST LEVELS FOR THE SEVERE MENTALLY RETARDED

Independent Functioning	*Physical Development*	*Communication*	*Social Development*	*Economic Activity*	*Occupation*	*Self-Direction*
adequate self feeding	throw ball and hit target	complex sentences	friendship choices over months	simple errands and purchases with a note	can assist with simple household tasks, empty cleaning, carrying	ask if there is "work"
can put on clothes (including buttons and zippers)	run, hop, skip, etc.	two or three step directions	simple competitive games (i.e., tag	knows money has value, but not the values of money	clear and set table	attending to task for 10 minutes
bath with supervision	sled and skate	understand but and because	self initiated group activities		prepare sandwich	makes effort to be dependable and responsible
wash hands without help		recognizes signs and reading without comprehension				

2. In the United States, this condition is judged on *both* intellectual and behavioral criteria.
3. The attitudes, beliefs, and opinions of a majority act as either facilitators or obstacles to behavioral adjustment. There is evidence to suggest that these factors can be changed in positive directions.
4. Practitioners need to examine their own assumptions about the retarded to ensure that they are a facilitating source in their expectations and services.
5. Comprehensive data is required from a variety of disciplines, and consumers should be intelligent and open-minded.
6. Mentally retarded children should be perceived as future *adults* who are capable of participation in a community setting.
7. An implied role of the practitioner is that of advocate for the mentally retarded.
8. The concept of adaptive behavior represents one helpful source for the design of programs and program outcomes.
9. The retarded have *rights* by virtue of citizenship, among which is the right to an education that prepares them for adulthood.

ON LOCATION

The selection illustrates the impact of the human meaning of mental retardation and has been an enduring favorite of the author. Although written in prose, it is almost

Table 1–7 REPRESENTATIVE ADAPTIVE BEHAVIORS ILLUSTRATING HIGHEST LEVELS FOR THE PROFOUND MENTALLY RETARDED

Independent Functioning	*Physical Development*	*Communication*	*Social Development*
feed self with spoon and fork	hop and skip	300-word vocabulary	simple games and group activities (house, store, etc.)
partially toilet-trained	climb stairs with alternating feet	many gestures	expressive art and dance
assistance with clothing	ride bike or tricycle	follow one-step directions	
assistance with bathing	play dance games	recognize simple signs and advertising (STOP EXIT, etc.)	
	climb trees or jungle gym	relate experiences in simple language	
	throw ball and hit target		

like a poem in blank verse. The author is unknown, but Lowell (1961) has preserved this selection for us. The Empty Shell reminds us that while mental retardation can be defined and its characteristics understood, there remains the important quality of interaction.

The Empty Shell

It lay between them on the beach, the pink-and-white shell. Like a barrier, it staked out limits between the little boy and girl and the two mothers who watched their children and furtively weighed each other.

The little boy raced along the beach, yelling and flinging out his arms. Sometimes he flew like a gull along the sand, whirling his arms and calling; sometimes he held his arms stiffly like the wings of a plane and made engine noises in his throat as he turned and banked against the summer sky.

The little girl was quiet. For the most part she sat with her face lifted, smiling vacantly as the wind brushed her hair, now and then patting the sand with an aimless hand. Only when the noisy little boy whirled toward her did her eyes light. The little girl was mentally retarded.

The mother of the little boy saw. She caught her small son by the arm. "Hush!" she said distractedly. In her heart she said, "We are in the presence of disaster. How does one behave? Can I speak? What would I say? I will not intrude. One should be silent in the face of tragedy."

"Hush!" she said again to her child. "Be quiet." And she turned away.

The little girl's mother turned away, too, and her heart broke again with bitterness and envy and with despairing love for the child who sat too quietly on the shore. "The day is spoiled," she said in her heart. "We will leave this hateful place." And she began to gather the tin pail and shovel, the towel, and sunglasses.

The little boy's mother was gathering a tin pail, towel and sunglasses, too. "We will leave them alone," she said in her heart. "We will not spoil their day."

But the little boy had found the shell. He put it to his ear, hearing again the far-off echo of the sea. Then he saw the little girl, standing now, looking at the water. Carefully he carried the shell. Carefully he put it to her ear. "Listen!" he said.

She stood very still, hearing the voice but not the words, listening not to the whisper of the shell but to that of the little boy's heart. Then her toes curled, her starfish hands stretched in ecstasy, and she laughed her low throaty chuckle.

The mothers looked up quickly, and their eyes met across the sand where the shell no longer lay. They smiled . . . at the little boy's gentleness, the little girl's delight, at the sun-drenched summer day, and the eternal music of wind and water and the laughter of children. They then gathered towels, tin pails and children and walked together from the shore.

The little boy carried the shell. It was quite empty. But it could be filled with sand or sound or with the waters of the heart which make their own tides.

To many parents of retarded children who have emptied themselves of hate and bitterness and have shared with us their sorrow and despair, their hopes and aspirations, we give our gratitude. To those parents of normal children, and especially to those with no children at all, who have emptied themselves of superstition and prejudice concerning the retarded, we acknowledge an eternal debt.

REFERENCES

Grossman, H. J. (ed.) *Manual on Terminology and Classification in Mental Retardation.* Washington, D. C.: American Association on Mental Deficiency, 1973.

Heber, R. *A Manual on Terminology and Classification in Mental Retardation,* 2nd Edition. Willimantic, Connecticut, American Association on Mental Deficiency, 1960.

Lowell, R. The Empty Shell. *Span,* 1961, 4, 3–4.

Polloway, E. and Payne, J. Comparison of AAMD Heber and Grossman Manuals. *Mental Retardation,* 1975, 13, 12–14.

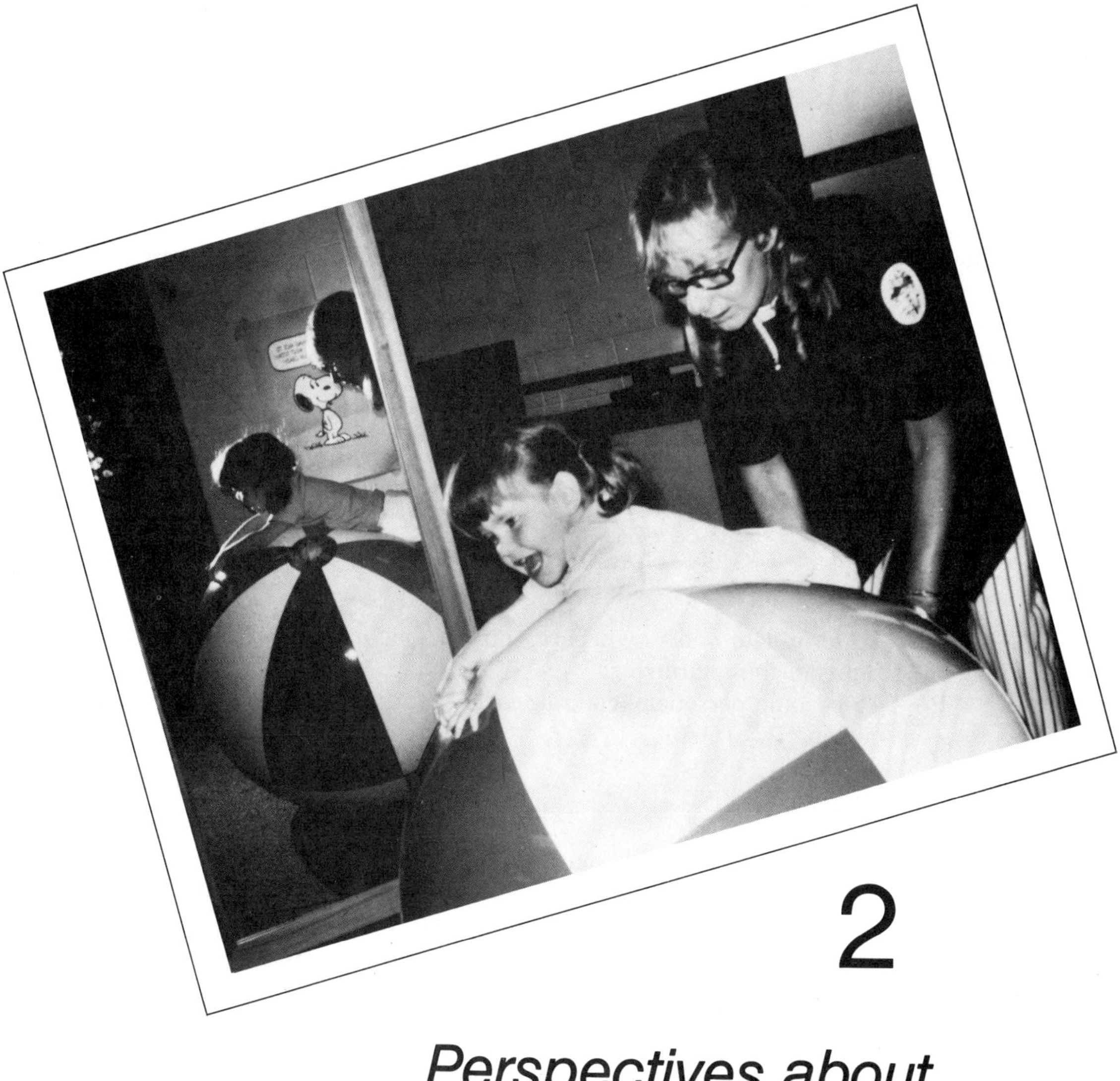

2

Perspectives about Mental Retardation

SYNOPSIS

This chapter reviews both the historical and contemporary viewpoints that have influenced professional thinking on mental retardation. Mental retardation is a dynamic condition; factors within the retarded person resulting from the condition and factors external to the person both influence the individual's potential. Individual factors such as cerebral functioning, attention, motivation, cognition, memory, and coping skills are discussed, as are external factors such as label, public attitude, and prejudice. The chapter concludes with a third perspective centering on the concept of rights.

OBJECTIVES

ATTITUDES

1. To formulate one's own perspective about mental retardation and the rights of the retarded.
2. To become personally committed to securing the rights of the retarded citizen.

UNDERSTANDINGS

1. To view mental retardation from different perspectives.
2. To realize that there is no universal view of mental retardation, but a variety of searches for the significant factors for treatment.
3. To identify at least four perspectives: cerebral, significance, dynamic-social, and rights.
4. To define elements of retardation and retarded behavior perceived as significant.
5. To identify models or concepts of the retarded person which have influenced public opinion.

SKILLS

1 To describe the qualities of retarded persons that should receive priority consideration.
2 To describe the qualities of professional persons that should receive priority consideration.
3 To look consciously beyond a label in determining treatment.

THE STRUCTURE AND FUNCTION OF THEORY

VanDalen (1966) has clarified the function of theory and practice: theory is an explanation about events and circumstances; it seeks to develop relationships among those events or circumstances.

To be valid, according to VanDalen, theory must perform one of the following functions:

Identification of relevant facts. The deductive approach may suggest that A precedes B so that a C should be logically assumed to follow. Consequently, there may be testing to confirm the speculation.

Classification of data. This function serves at least two purposes. First, theory serves to assemble data into related sets or classes of information. Second, the retrieval of data is greatly assisted by associated groupings.

Formulation of constructs. A construct may be also termed a logical construct, a hypothetical construct, or intervening variables. This function deals with events or circumstances not directly experienced. Nevertheless, the consequence does exist. VanDalen uses the example of reading readiness. This concept is not directly manifest, but is indirectly inferred.

Summation of facts. This use of theory enables the sorting of information for a particular practice.

Prediction of future facts, events, or circumstances. This is the ultimate test of theory's validity. One test is the ability to predict unanticipated information. Another critical use is the ability of theory to predict consequences of action.

Identification of needed research. This function notes gaps in information and suggests the means to secure necessary data.

In the field of mental retardation the normalization principle, citizen advocacy, and precision teaching are valuable products of theory building. The formulation of goals and the evaluation of learner-clients involves theorizing. Goals are based upon one's consideration of relevant information. The practitioner seeks activities, experiences, or materials that have validity for both goals and learner capabilities.

The lament "It sounds fine in theory, but it won't work in practice" is an obvious distortion of the function of theory. The validity of any theory depends upon its effectiveness in practice. If the theory does not work (predict consequences, identify new needs, etc.), it must be refined or abandoned.

This chapter is concerned with selected theories, labeled perspectives, which influence current thinking about the treatment and management of the mentally retarded. A rich and varied range of opinion exists. While they may appear to differ, all theories have the common goal of assimilating data into a framework to guide and evaluate practice. The variety of experience and perceptions of proponents contributes to the diversity of opinion. The reader is directed to two perspectives in particular: the historical and the legal. Historical tradition provides a context in which to judge present efforts and future intentions. The legal perspective focuses on the mentally retarded as a citizen. Increasingly, the retarded person is viewed as a citizen who has rights. Consequently, services are not charities but a birthright. The perspectives of the mentally retarded as a citizen may be remembered as the hallmark of the 1970s.

THE RETARDED PERSON IN HISTORICAL CONTEXT

The purpose of this section is to capture a sense of the events and persons that have provided the cultural context for present practice. The goal of this section is to enable the reader to identify the traditions that have influenced this field of service and to create an awareness that mental retardation is a field with its own sense of the past and future.

The Retarded as Eminent Persons

Case and Cleland (1975) have identified those retarded persons who have achieved eminence. This trait was "measured" by examination of standard reference works in the mental retardation literature. Among the most famous were:

1. Victor, the "Wild Boy of Averyon," was the pupil of Itard, a physician, who undertook to normalize the "wolf child" found wandering in the forest. Victor is by far the most eminent person in the literature, but his fame appears to be dependent upon his association with Itard rather than upon any special or unique skill.
2. J. H. Pullen, the "Genius" of Earlswood Asylum, constructed a steamship

model that contained over a million handmade parts and required three years to complete.

3 Gottfried Mind, the "Cat's Raphael," won fame as a painter and sketcher.

4 Blind Tom could play two tunes on a piano at the same time.

Other persons have emerged, but they have not acquired wide reknown in the literature. For example, Nigel Hunt, a Down's syndrome person, wrote his own autobiography, *The Diary of a Mongoloid Youth,* and Kiyoshi Yamashita, the "Van Gogh of Japan," has won fame for his paintings, which achieved a certain commercial success in Japan and the United States.

While Victor was judged the most eminent, the others attained a certain status because of *accomplishment*. The term *idiot savant* usually denotes persons of perceived intellectual limitations who possess a skill of *genuine* merit. (This concept is explored in chapter 5.) These historical figures show that the retarded are capable of genuine achievement.

A Time Line

Figure 2–1 presents a historical time line regarding events, circumstances, and persons influencing the development of services for mentally retarded persons. The listing is only partial, and someone's favorite event may be excluded.

A number of historical commentaries are available for the thoughtful reader: Doll (1962), Kirk and Johnson (1951), Kanner (1967), Cruickshank (1975), Hewett (1974), Kirk (1962), Hutt and Gibby (1976), Kauffman and Payne (1975) and Jordan (1972). The subsequent discussion and interpretation of figure 2–1 constitutes a synthesis of these sources.

Persons and Events

These sources make little mention of the status of the retarded during the colonial period of American history, and scant attention is given to the years before the middle 1840s. Edmond Seguin, a Frenchman, had the most profound effect in this country and was active continuously until his death near the turn of the century. Seguin was inspired by the experiment of Itard, a French physical educator.

In 1799, a twelve-year-old boy was found living in a wild state in the province of Aveyron. His parents were unknown. Between 1801 and 1806, Itard sought to train and civilize this youngster. The design was that systematic sensory stimulation would train the intellect and/or faculties of the mind. After one year, Itard reported progress regarding sensory learnings and associations. Space does not permit a

Figure 2–1 *A Historical Timeline in Mental Retardation*

Years	Period	Organizations	Services	Science	Involvement of Federal Programs	People and Events
Before 1845		European Influences of Itard				
1845–1860	Institution Movement		• Origins of institutions	• Death of Victor		• Seguin comes to U.S. • S. G. Howe advocates for services of education
1860–1875	Institution Movement					• Dorothea Dax and reform
1875–1890	Institution Movement	• AAMD		• Dugdale's *Jukes*		
1890–1905	Institution Movement		• Origins of special class	• Cattell's concept of mental age • Dewey emerges • Binet begins work		• Origins of college training in M.R.
1905–1920	Day School and Special Classes		• Colony concept oriented to work production	• Goddard's *Kallikaks* • Terman version of Binet test		• Montessori gains recognition • Goddard's concept of moron
1920–1935	Day School and Special Classes	• First ARC Unit-Ohio • CEC		• Dall's Vineland Social Maturity Scale	• Vocational Rehabilition • Supreme Court upholds sterilization • White House Conference	• Origins of Eugenics movement • Emergence of "unit" method • Ingram establishes unit method
1935–1950	Day School and Special Classes	• UCPA • NARC	• Occupational education • Emergence of classes for moderate	• Wechsler produces WAIS Wechsler produces • WISC	• Crippled Children's Commission • WPA child care • VR extended to civilians	• Elizabeth Fannell establishes concept of clinical special class • Emergence of Hungerford's occupational education • Schmidt's IQ articles • P. Buck's *Child Who Never Grew*
1950–1965	Special Classes	• President's Panel • CEC-MR	• Delaware and Michigan classes for severe MR	• Kornberg and DNA • PKU controlled • ITPA emergence	• PL 85-926 • PL 88-164 • Elementary and Secondary Act	• Emergence of Strauss and Orton procedures • Emergence of SERB's project on behavior modification • Kirk's *Early Education* • Johnson's Paradox article • Medicare and Medicaid
1965–1975	Mainstreaming/ Community Placement	• President's Commission	• Origins of resource room • Origins of Citizen Advocate-Nebraska		• Vocational Rehabilitation for MR • Developmental Disabilities • Pennsylvania Decision • Maryland's Career Educ.	• Dunn's article • Normalization and the Developmental Model • Revision of 1960 AAMD definition of MR

recounting of his teaching method; however, one is struck by his use of discrimination and association learnings. For example, the darkening of a room so that his student would attend to color; the blindfolding of the eyes to heighten sound recognition.

Itard's work was an attempt to demonstrate the radical French notion of human equality through educational intervention. Victor, as the youngster was called, did attain a modest vocabulary and minimal literacy gains, but in 1805 the experiment was terminated. It is believed that with the onset of puberty Victor's behavior became uncontrollable. He lived out his days with a governess until his death in 1830.

It is commonly agreed that Itard achieved a major feat, and in 1806 the French Academy of Science honored him for his work, the first recognition for a purely educational experiment. By the standards of the world, Itard had made a difference in the life of Victor; by his own standards, Itard felt deep disappointment and considered himself a failure. What has endured is the recognition of Itard as the man who demonstrated that change could be effected, and although our perspective is confined to American events, Itard remains a significant historical figure. One wishes that he could know of his continuing stature and recognition.

Edmond Seguin is regarded as a historical figure second only to Itard, but his philosophy of treatment and his boundless energy have endured beyond his specialized physiological method. It was his belief that residential facilities should be centers for special training leading to eventual return to the community. These facilities should construct a total responsive environment for the continuous training of the retarded. His writings stress his belief that affective traits such as mercy, compassion, and empathy could be fostered by humane, compassionate, and emphatic adults. His thinking anticipates modern techniques of modeling and is remembered for his emphasis upon the personality-affect of the responsible adult. He founded nearly a dozen residential institutions. Apparently he was more patient and tolerant of his clients than of those colleagues unwilling to share his optimism. He was the first president of the organization that became the American Association of Mental Deficiency (AAMD). His technique of using sensory perception as a basis for mental development was an elaborate formula for its time. It is generally agreed, however, that the success of his approach depended upon his unique personality and insight. Binet acknowledged Seguin's pioneer efforts, but was skeptical of his scientific objectivity.

The 1800s through 1900 saw the establishment of residential facilities, which were transformed gradually from training sites into more custodial purposes. There were other important developments:

1. During 1900, community-based educational efforts emerged.
2. The advent of scientific measurement of intelligence affected the field. Its premise was to create a scientific basis for treatment.

3. During the First World War, numerous men were rejected for service as mentally unfit, even those judged competent by their communities. This heightened interest in testing and in eugenics as a means of prevention.

4. The 1930s saw the first involvement of the federal government in health and welfare programs for large numbers of citizens. The unit method emerged as one example of the application of learning principles to education.

5. The emergence of professional societies has been a helpful source and resource to professionals and to clients. Organizations such as the AAMD and the Council for Exceptional Children provided encouragement during those times when vocations in this field were not so fashionable. They also encouraged the pursuit of research to organize an objective basis for treatment.

6. In 1950 what is now known as the National Association for Retarded Citizens (NARC) was founded. The NARC is usually credited with competent education of the general public, effective efforts in legislation, demonstration of program innovation, and the rallying of parents and concerned citizens. The 1950s saw the first direct expenditure of federal funds for research and personnel training in mental retardation under P.L. 85–926.

7. The 1960s was a period of aggressive attack on the problem. P.L. 88–164 extended federal efforts to many aspects of health, education, employment, and social services. Moreover, there was the trend to include the exceptional learner in general legislation as well. The central theme was an almost military response, with themes such as mobilizing, combating, organizing, etc. Emphasis was upon planning and action. During this time, behavior modification as directly applicable to the severely retarded received significant attention. The pioneering research in DNA and RNA as building blocks of genetics became a part of popularized treatments. The conquering of polio inspired confidence in medical research to solve social problems.

8. Little has yet been written about the 1970s. This period may be remembered as the period of advocacy, both legal and service. Legal recourse to protect rights appears a dominant theme. Concepts such as normalization, mainstreaming, least restrictive alternative, and the developmental model are examples. The emergence of the citizen advocate program suggests that the language of combat has been replaced by the language of the retarded person as a citizen and as a person significant for friendships. Passage of P.L. 94–142 may prove to be the fruition of these efforts.

Another dominant theme of the 1970s has been the emergence of noncategorical approaches for mildly handicapped learners, regardless of etiology. There is a prevailing assumption that differences in one limited area do not constitute the basis for complete segregation in all areas of human activity. As will be seen elsewhere in this chapter, the retarded person's commonality with the human condition is the primary consideration. The central aim is to facilitate inclusion.

HISTORICAL DETERMINANTS

Hewett (1974) concluded that four historical determinants have shaped attitudes toward the handicapped and their treatment. These determinants suggest a certain evolution of social response. Hewett describes this evolutionary sequence as survival, superstition, science, and service.

The survival period lingered until about the late eighteenth century. Many handicapped were deliberately exposed to the harsh elements to die, and survivors were ignored. The handicapped were described as weak and poor.

The period of superstition overlapped the survival period. The handicapped were seen as scapegoats or objects for self-indulgent exploitation. A dominant response was fear and avoidance of the unknown, and ignorance ascribed an evil connotation to the handicapped.

Hewett describes science as the attempt to explain the unknown, the process of resisting superstition. Its outcome has been to formulate predictable and helpful courses of action. The nineteenth and twentieth centuries have been marked by the application of the rigors of science to the study of the human condition.

Hewett believes that the optimistic attitude of service is characteristic of our times. His review traces service from its emphasis on refuge to programs based upon enlightened belief and knowledge. Today we do not promise cure, but there is the assumption that service does make a difference by maximizing potential.

In summary, the historical perspective indicates a meshing of persons and events in an evolutionary striving for progress. The view of the retarded as a threat has faded into a perception of them as citizens and human beings with potential.

A CEREBRAL PERSPECTIVE

Deficiency of the nervous system has been the traditional explanation for both cause and consequence of retarded mental development. The human brain, often characterized as the most complex of computers, is the mechanism by which one responds to the environment, learns from responses, and imposes one's own responses upon the environment. The brain may be likened to an encyclopedia, computer, dictionary, or other reference system which has systems for receiving, storing, retrieving, evaluating, associating, and expressing data.

Application to Mental Retardation

Benoit (1959, p. 551) and (1960) has evolved a comprehensive view of mental retardation which correlates biological and psychosocial factors. He acknowledges his debt to the work of Hebb, who views neuropsychological adjustment as the imprinting of data into nerve cell assemblies for specific tasks. The Benoit definition:

> Mental retardation may be viewed as a defect of intellectual function resulting from the various intrapersonal and/or interpersonal determinants, but having as a common proximate cause a diminished deficiency of the nervous system (beginning with impaired irritability and further involving a lowered capacity for impulse transmission and for developing primitive and integrating cell change through interfacilitating interneuronal connections), thus entailing a lessened general capacity for growth and conceptual integration and consequently in environmental adjustment.

For Benoit, the emphasis upon integrity becomes an important focus for both diagnosis and treatment. The treatment advocated centers around approaches that emphasize motor learning as antecedents as well as reinforcers of task acquisition.

This perspective has significant implications for prevention of primary and secondary consequences of mental retardation. Treatment based upon neurological damage, especially behaviorally oriented treatments such as education, remains to some degree controversial. Research studies comparing behavioral performance of known brain damaged persons with persons presumed to be free of organicity have been inconclusive at best. While this perspective may not be universally accepted, this definition does support the AAMD view of retarded behavior as the product of internal and external factors. Benoit appears to focus upon the interaction of the person's nervous system as the focal point of acquiring adaptive behaviors.

An associative outcome of this approach is a concern with those factors that influence cerebral development. Leland (1972), writing from a humanist tradition, identifies specific consequences of American life which influence all of us, and the retarded in particular. Leland notes that program possibilities for the adolescent and adult retarded must receive continuous effort. Factors that must bind all citizens and the retarded citizen together are the effects of: malnutrition; the psychology of poverty; sensory inundation; social and racial prejudice; environmental pollution; and a greater emphasis on mild mental retardation, rather than more moderate, severe, or profound levels.

One of the implications of the Leland resumé is that those interested primarily in a *treatment* service have responsibilities for *prevention* as well. Much of retardation is caused by factors or dynamics over which parents have little control. Birch and Gusson (1970), for example, have assembled data on the consequences of nutrition, health care, poverty, and intellectual level which strengthen the Leland position.

SOCIAL-DYNAMIC APPROACHES

While the traits, abilities, and potential of the person are relevant concerns, there are those who suggest that other people have a greater impact upon the person. Thus, an individual may be "trained" for community living to criteria of success. The willingness of the neighborhood to accept the newcomer is ultimately decisive. Some argue that the label *retarded* and response to the label may be more handicapping than the condition itself. This viewpoint does not minimize the impact of the condition, but it does recognize the importance of the attitudes of people upon the retarded.

Factors of Influence

Dybwad (1964) has provided a concise summary of events that affect the retarded. (Since parent organizations were responsible for public interest in programs for the mentally retarded, it should be noted that the efforts of Drs. Dybwad and Ignacy Goldberg helped organize and focus parent effort.) Dybwad identifies the following: individual factors, social factors, cultural factors, the effect of concepts upon the development of the child, some sources of confusion, and levels of intelligence.

Individual factors include the elements of a complex personality which do not remain static. Progress is seen as dependent upon the attitudes and resultant actions of society, the home, and eventually one's own attitudes and actions.

Social factors are the relationship between demands, expectations, and level of functioning. Values, employment levels of the economy, and developmental expectations are identified. For example: the public meaning of the condition may affect a family's reaction to it; the economic health of the community will determine the adult independence of the retarded; incidence studies illustrate that at preschool ages the difficulties of identification are greater than during the school years.

Cultural factors are links between the aspiration level of the individual and his willingness to attain goals. To paraphrase Dybwad, vocational independence may be dependent upon the extent to which an individual's striving is rewarded by people in his environment.

Dybwad's discussion of *how concepts affect the development of children* and of *sources of confusion* brings the previously discussed factors into focus. His most cogent point is that what passes for information, scientific evidence, and objective data is as destructive as the myths of everyday culture. He notes the confusion between diagnosis and service recommendation with the illustration of the consequences of terms such as "crib case, vegetable, custodial." The terms suggest the levels of service to be given. Psychometric data is also persistently misused in two ways: First, the concept of mental age is abused when a retarded adult with a mental age of five is treated like a five year old. Second, groups established on the basis of one criteria should not be maintained for other purposes. For example, one might establish groups for instructional purposes, such as "trainable," and perpetuate it through adulthood in spite of the different purposes of adulthood. Dybwad stresses flexibility of grouping.

Levels of intelligence represent another area of scientific imprecision. Dybwad notes that such data are often expressed in what the person *cannot* do without concurrent statements of what he *can* do. He endorses the AAMD system. Dybwad's message is that the concept or view one has of mental retardation can and will affect both practitioner and the retarded person.

Implications

Certain models that illustrate the relationship of social dynamics to practice have been advanced by Jordan (1972) and Wolfensberger (1969). These discussions illustrate the social-dynamic hypothesis or perspective, which assumes that the viewpoint of a condition affects practice.

Wolfensberger (1969) has identified six models that have influenced the operation of program environments for retarded persons. One would suspect that these models have counterparts in a variety of service settings. The models are summarized in table 2–1. This summary follows the naming of the model, overt indicators of the model in operation, and implications of the model for the person.

Table 2–1 A SYNOPSIS OF MODELS FOR SERVICES FOR THE MENTALLY RETARDED, AS PER WOLFENSBERGER

Name	*Indicators*	*Implications*
Sick Person	1. Administrative dominance by medical persons 2. Terminology such as: patients, charts for records, treatments, etc. is likely to dominate 3. Personnel tend to model after medical roles, no matter how inappropriate	1. MR is viewed as a disease 2. Preoccupation with personal hygiene 3. Decision making is focused upon only physical needs
Subhuman Organism	1. Views the retarded as an unmanageable animal 2. Construction of the facility uses indestructible material 3. Wire screens and wire fences to protect property 4. Segregation by sex	1. Retarded persons are seen as without right to privacy, treatment, or communications 2. Emphasis on "keeping" or confinement 3. Emphasis upon staff efficiency rather than client needs

Table 2–1 (continued)

Name	*Indicators*	*Implications*
Menace	1. Similar to the subhuman model 2. Preoccupation with sexual deviates and control of sexual behaviors	1. Emphasis upon protecting the normal from the retarded 2. Staff may feel the retarded requires punishment to cast out sinful behavior
Object of Pity	1. Person is described as suffering and being aware of it 2. Person is viewed as an "eternal child" 3. Lack of accountable standards for the retarded person's behavior	1. A sheltering against injury and risk 2. Makes few demands for personal growth, development, and responsibility
Burden of Charity	1. Charity extended to victims who have been punished 2. Service must be rendered as an unescapable duty, a burden	1. Contempt rather than sympathy for the person by the responsible person 2. Emphasis upon "bare essentials" for survival
Holy Innocent	1. Views the retarded person as a "harmless childlike entity" 2. Emphasis upon protection	1. Benevolence invokes dependence. 2. Protects the retarded from the normal
Developing Person or Developmental Model	1. Perceives the retarded person as more like than unlike others 2. Rights to privacy and possessions 3. The physical facilities resemble a "family-home" atmosphere	1. Emphasis upon human dignity 2. Optimistic emphasis upon compensation, or minimizing deviance, rather than its "control." 3. Relating to the retarded to promote independence

Wolfensberger (1969) identifies the *developmental model* as the most promising for the retarded person.

Models of professional practice have their counterparts to the program models identified by Wolfensberger. Jordan (1972, pp. 559–60) has identified four nonhelpful models that may persist even today.

1 The *bucket model* views the learner as literally a cerebral bucket to be filled with information. It is the teacher's task to fill up this bucket.
2 The *garden model* views learners as tender plants to be cultivated and nourished. This view portrays the teacher as a magical fertilizer.
3 The *love model* believes that loving learners enough will cause them to love you; and loving you will cause them to learn; and in turn you will love them, and so it goes.
4 The *trainable beast model* views the "organism" as a series of responses to be manipulated by and through modification.

A listing, somewhat complimentary and overlapping to Jordan's, can be found in a summation of teaching models identified by Harmin and Gregory (1974). These authors are in agreement regarding the bucket and garden models. Their additional models would be said to include:

1 The *lamplighter model* views learners as bulbs to be ignited. Learners are seen as persons in darkness needing to be shown the light by superior persons.
2 The *personnel manager model* views learners as units to be processed. The preoccupation is with keeping students busy, efficient, and industrious.
3 The *muscle-builder model* views the mind as a flabby blob to be "exercised." This view concentrates upon the use of subject to stimulate operation of function.

Harmin and Gregory agree with Jordan that education is an outcome for the learner rather than an object to be manipulated. The Harmin and Gregory position is that the interaction between practitioner and learner is that of *meaning-maker*. In the preceding models the mind is to be variously "cultivated," "filled," "trained," "exercised," and/or "lighted." These authors proposed the concept of meaning-maker. This view has a subtle *duality*. It implies that what is to be learned involves the making of meanings by *both* learner and practitioner. That is to say, the practitioner attempts to influence meaning, and the learner attaches meanings to learnings. Implications of the model of meaning-maker are:

1 Reactions to learnings do not necessarily proceed from "things" around the person, but as the result of internalizing learnings.
2 Learning arises from previous experience.
3 Learning requires *active* participation from the learner.
4 While presentation may be standard, each learner will perceive, experience, and respond in a unique way.
5 Learning is also a function of the language and linguistic categories available to the learner.

The Harmin and Gregory discussion demonstrates that conceptions about the retarded may have their origins in views of intelligence. The views of intelligence exposed by Jordan, Harmin, and Gregory, coupled with the Wolfensberger exposition, lead one to suspect that persons perceived to be limited in mind are consequently perceived to be limited in all areas of functioning. A view of mind as *a thing* may reinforce a passive view of treatment. A common theme of all these discussions is the emphasis upon the multiple variables of perception, experience, effort, and language required by both practitioner and learner.

SIGNIFICANCE PERSPECTIVES

Psychologists and educators have attempted to identify the behavioral consequences of retarded mental development. The search has been for those variables that should influence service delivery systems. In a landmark series of articles within one volume, Milgram (1969), Zigler (1969), Ellis (1969), and Leland (1969) outline rather specific perspectives relevant for the practitioner. All four agree that mental retardation has dimensions other than measured intelligence. Their investigations are directed toward identifying traits with significant implications for treatment procedures. All recognize that mental retardation has two reference points for comparison: chronological age (CA) norms and mental age (MA) norms. One essential question, for professionals, is how to blend these two reference points with other data in order to prescribe expectations, implement programs, and evaluate results. (It may be of some help to say that the younger the learner, the more mental age applies, while the older the learner, the more chronological age applies.) At issue is: Given the discrepancy between MA capacities and CA demands, what are significant reference points to prepare retarded persons for an adult world?

Cognitive

Milgram emphasizes a *cognitive* approach, which favors study of individuals of similar IQ, but varying on MA levels. This cognitive view postulates that abilities such as verbal mediation are developmental and hence not necessarily a persistent *defect* of the retarded. Milgram (p. 531) further states:

> One of the applications of cognitive research has been to recommend techniques to shore up relatively inefficient cognitive abilities by special training or to circumvent the relatively weak abilities and capitalize on the stronger ones by packaging the stimulus input or teaching methods so as to permit retardates to achieve a desired result by alternate routes that are more readily available to them.

Developmental

Zigler (1969) states his perspective as a *developmental*-cognitive approach. To Zigler, MA, as a global measure of cognitive function, allows for a developmental exploration of similarities between the retarded and the normal. Zigler notes that intellect, as opposed to IQ, are processes that flourish and increase with age and experience. The relevance of Zigler's research to practice may be summarized as a recognition that a cognitive system is one aspect of mediation between the person and the environment; a notion that "retarded behavior" is not explained by exclusive reference to cognitive inefficiency; and a recognition that life's experiences affect *motivation* to perform (aspiration, in the Dybwad [1964] sense). Zigler is most critical of studies that generate "knowledge" to explain retardation by comparing an institutionalized retarded sample with a noninstitutionalized normal sample. Consumers of research should include incentives for the sample to respond and comparable residential modes of the sample as criteria for judging a study's validity. A large sample size and sophisticated statistical techniques may create illusions of learnedness. As Zigler (p. 547) concludes: "Due to their many failure experiences, retarded individuals are distrustful of their own solutions to problems, and, thus, tend to look for cues or solutions provided by others in their problem solving efforts."

Zigler also stresses the identification of attention. This trait, which is subject to multiple influences (brain damage, cultural incentives, previous experience, etc.), does have a common consequence of acquisition of learning as related to attending to presentations.

Difference

Ellis identifies a case for a *difference* approach, which he feels is the same as a developmental approach. His approach tends to reject *etiological* factors, since "rarely have behavioral differences characterized different etiological groups" (p. 561). Much investigative effort has not attended to solution of practical problems, systematic testing of theory, the "logic" of their designs, a clear expression of the relationship of design to purpose, and how varied (i.e., heterogeneous) any sample of the retarded will be. Ellis (p. 563) advocates a comparison based upon CA match, since "it is directed to the primary characteristic of mental retardation. It is the differences in adaptive behavior of persons of similar chronological age that define retardation." Ellis reminds us, however, that to say a person has low adaptive behavior because of low intelligence is not explaining the consequences of low intelligence; rather, it is saying that one test score posits a relationship to another. He suggests that the significance of retardation probably lies in the short-term memory system. Studies of this trait might lead to a more general understanding of intelligent behavior.

Habilitation

Given Milgram's emphasis upon cognitive behavior and Zigler's emphasis upon motivation and attention, Leland postulates what might be termed a *habilitation* approach. The question of what is retarded about retarded behavior is discussed from a community adjustment frame of reference. Leland rejects classification systems that rest exclusively on psychometric data of MA and IQ, for, he (p. 503) notes:

> Intellectual functioning is a product of an interaction between a variety of social and personal forces. . . . Successful coping can be described as intelligent behavior. Unsuccessful is less than intelligent behavior, and . . . is on a continuous line so that there is no absolute measure of what would be called successful.

At this point, Leland (pp. 534–535) provides a synthesis of the biological, psychological, sociological, and the AAMD definition of mental retardation:

1. . . . mental retardation is essentially a social definition and . . . the IQ becomes merely a convenient handle on which to hang an individual already defined as maladaptive.
2. . . . in terms of impairment of adaptive behavior, the inability of the individual, regardless of etiology, to learn to cope successfully with the natural and social demands of his environment is the element which makes him socially visible and thus liable to labeling.
3. Thus, the real test of a classification scheme must be based on how well it serves the individual being classified. If it tends to merely label him, or even worse, to keep necessary services away from him, it must be considered as a false scheme.

SYNTHESIS

Consequently, for the practitioner, the perspectives of mental retardation are varied. Low IQ is not a sole explanation for subaverage performance. Factors such as internal mediation, motivation, attention, and memory are individual differences which affect an individual's coping skills. Additionally, identification and labeling as a retarded person is helpful only as an aid for special service delivery. Labeling becomes an additional cross to bear if the reactions to the labeled person are irrelevant or rejecting of needs.

MENTAL RETARDATION AS A LABEL

Acceptance

Mental retardation, as a label, has received widespread attention. This interest demonstrates that this condition has internal as well as external consequences.

Guskin (1963) and Bartel and Guskin (1971) have identified a considerable body of literature that investigates social acceptance of mental retardation. Both sources note studies in which the perceptions of normals were altered by labeling children as "retarded" or "nonretarded." Bartel and Guskin also identify certain studies to illustrate how teacher expectations, and hence pupil achievement, were altered by differential labels. Both research reviews focus on the theory of the self-fulfilling prophecy, which postulates that an assumption of dependent behavior leads to actual dependent behavior. They further discuss dimensions that affect parents, the person's self-concept, and eventual careers.

One of the most ambitious and sophisticated studies ever attempted to assess public awareness and understanding was undertaken by Gottwald (1970). The study used a variety of interview techniques on a national sample systematically selected to represent a reasonable cross section of religion, education, age, sex, etc. Of special interest was the isolation of the "image" of the retarded person. The retarded person is generally seen as a child, a male, inferior to the normal on desirable traits, economically dependent, and should be put away some place. On the positive side was that those persons acquainted with a retarded person were usually better informed. Additionally, people did seem to be influenced in positive directions by media campaigns. Their perception of positive traits and willingness to support special services increased. However, their inclination for greater personal contact did not increase in a similar fashion.

Bartel and Guskin (1971) identify four strategies for the social acceptance of handicapped citizens: minimize the segregation of the disabled; eliminate diagnostic procedures that do not prove themselves useful for successful treatment attempts; eliminate categorical treatment services whenever these services are proven ineffective; and convince social groups of the advantages of retaining disabled persons within the group. Subsequent research experience will ultimately isolate which one, or combinations of these strategies, will prove to be the most helpful.

CHANGING REACTIONS

Inspired by Cleland and Chambers (1959) and Cleland and Cochran (1961), Sellin and Mulchahay (1965) demonstrated that under proper supervision and preparation, the tour of a residential facility for the retarded can have positive and relatively lasting effects on the attitudes of the nonretarded. Dingman, Cleland, and Schwartz (1970) remind us of the folklore about retarded persons which passes for wisdom and how such folklore serves as a shield against change. Bransford and Brooks (1972) suggested that attitudes can be modified. Harth (1973), in a comprehensive review of the literature concerning attitudes and attitude change, offers many notes of encouragement. Attitudes toward retarded people are a part of a person's larger philosophy of life, but attitudes can be modified. Harth warned that mere physical contact may not be altogether sufficient. As noted before, planning and follow-up are required. Consequently, while the retarded (and practitioners) will encounter prejudice, these attitudes can be modified. This capacity to change is one of the great promises and challenges of the 1970s.

RIGHTS AND CITIZENSHIP

The concept of a right implies that the citizen has guarantees by virtue of citizenship. Qualification for the exercise of the right is usually viewed as protected by government with a minimum of effort by the person. A privilege, by contrast, must be earned. A privilege is extended to the person by government, but the granting is not necessarily mandated or required. For example, voting is a right, while driving is a privilege. In American society, a remarkable fact and a source of pride has been the transformation of elementary and secondary schooling from the status of a privilege to that of a right. For the most part, however, services for the retarded have existed at a privilege level, dependent upon enlightenment, good-will, and available revenues. Expansion and installation of services have historically followed strategies of voluntary compliance and acknowledgement of need. This attitude is changing. Today there is steady and determined movement, often through the courts, to extend to the retarded the same rights enjoyed by all citizens. Mandated compliance through laws and court decisions are being initiated to provide a rationale and a system for the funding and sponsorship of services.

The magnitude of court decisions in the 1960s and 1970s suggests that the rights the retarded should enjoy by virtue of American citizenship needed the reaffirmation of judicial intervention.

Basic Rights

Weingold (1973) has proposed six basic rights that require legislative protection so that in the absence of good-will, the retarded person will not be slighted. He identifies *freedom from involuntary servitude* as necessary for the retarded in the 1970s, with reference to institutional placement and so called "therapeutic" work situations. Legal rights include *competency to stand trial* and *equal protection under law*. The former relates to the need to distinguish the retarded from the mentally ill; a label of mental retardation must not create an atmosphere of guilty until proven innocent. The latter identifies the anomaly that while the law guarantees benefits to all citizens free of charge, the mentally retarded must pay for residential services, while the blind and deaf do not. Weingold itemizes a host of necessary reforms under *right to work*. He outlines how vocational services, adequate housing, and life insurance may be denied citizens by virtue of the label. Educators will be pleased to observe that *right to education* is included. Weingold is especially critical of exclusion under vague provisions of "no longer able to profit from further instruction." The implication is that the onus should be upon the system, not the learner. Finally, *right to services* addresses the discrepancy between the costs of services and the quality of services, as well as the discrepancy between better benefits for staff than for clients.

Rothstein (1971, pp. 58–59) has excerpted a declaration of rights for the retarded adopted by the International League of Societies for the Mentally Handicapped in 1968. These rights were said to include the right to:

1 the same guarantees as all citizens,
2 services regardless of disability and costs,
3 economic security and a decent standard of living,
4 residential living with his family or in a family-like atmosphere,
5 a qualified guardian,
6 freedom from abuse or exploitation, and
7 periodic review of all decisions when rights have been modified by virtue of disability.

The league concludes that the mentally retarded person above all has the right to respect.

Encompassed in both these statements is the protection of dignity and respect.

We must see the retarded as people, not labels. Smith (1973) reminds us that when people become an abstraction, such as the "final solution," "slaves," or an ethnic derogation, things are done to that abstraction that would not be done to human beings. Human beings would not be allowed to languish in a basement classroom, but the "retards" would. A human being would not be allowed to starve for want of medical attention, but a "mongoloid" would. The ultimate right is to recognize the humanity in all of us regardless of measured intelligence. The ultimate right to bestow on the retarded is treatment according to how we would be treated if our roles were reversed.

A statement of program-service rights might include:

1 due process in using comprehensive data for placement,
2 experiences relevant to living a normalized life in our communities,
3 exposure to the best and most competent practitioners available to the agency,
4 a program responsive to developmental expectations,
5 an environment that expects the best and most from clients,
6 the involvement of parents as a full partner in planning,
7 the orderly transition from one program element to another, and
8 a program that prizes the uniqueness of each individual.

INTEGRATION

This chapter has presented perspectives regarding historical, cerebral, social dynamic, significance, labeling, and rights of mentally retarded persons. If these positions were to be assimilated into management/treatment strategies, they might furnish a basis for the formulation of criteria for judging and evaluating the validity of intentions and efforts.

An *historical* perspective serves to remind practitioners of our tradition of service. The retarded person is an "historical" person in the sense that history provides a cultural context for beliefs and practice. Additionally, practice and progress has emerged as a quest for knowledge. Helpful efforts have originated, in part, because of scientific understanding. It is hoped that commitment to acquisition of information is still a valid trait of the practitioner. The validity of programs should reflect a sound underpinning in knowledge gained through inquiry and research. Programs should remain open to continuing evaluation.

A *cerebral* perspective acknowledges the central nervous system as a source of human function. A major implication of this position is that prevention is an essential emphasis, especially the reduction of etiologies that can be countered through adequate diet, health care, stimulation, and redress of economic disadvantage.

A perspective concerning mental retardation as a *label* identifies both positive and adverse consequences. One implication is that accuracy of diagnosis is an urgent concern, not an ideal. Concurrent with this premise is the requirement that diagnosis should be specific enough to formulate a unique, individualized plan of management. This specification should be a program standard.

A view of mental retardation in a *social-dynamic* context identifies the impact of people and their beliefs and values upon the retarded person. Certain views have tended to reduce the retarded person to the status of an entity less than human. Programs can be evaluated as to their adherence to the principles of the developmental model as well as to those of the meaning-maker model.

If one were to assimilate the consequences of the *significance* perspectives into treatment modes, the resulting plan might be quite different from the usual. The implications of the four positions might also serve as guidelines for program emphasis, method, and evaluation. The following are possible applications:

The *habilitative* position would emphasize coping with social demand. Its focus would be upon immediate concerns and needs of the person. Great stress would be placed upon future vocational implications of current instruction. An important learning principle would be the transfer of learnings to other situations.

The *difference* position would judge training activities in terms of short-term memory considerations. The practitioner would insure sufficient practice, reduction of anxiety, and active repetition to enable the learning to be transformed from the short-term to the long-term system.

The *cognitive* approach would stress facilitating the increase of complex behavior. Attention would be given to areas of judgment and discovery of relationships. Systematic activities would concentrate upon the use of memory and manipulation of ideas to solve tasks. Moreover, the ability of the person to function according to a helpful sequence would be stressed as an aid to recall and retention.

The *developmental* position would require sensitivity to incentives for performance. A person should have a reason for responding. Motivation would be seen as the handmaiden of attention. Additionally, attention would be heightened by clarity of presentation, approach sequence, careful orientation of the learner as to expectations, and subsequent feelings of success.

For the practitioner, the following constitute certain criteria by which to judge one's own plan of professional activity:

1 Does the plan enable the person to function in the ordinary circumstances of his or her community?
2 Does the plan address itself to some immediate concern or goal of the person?
3 Does the plan have any merit with respect to employment or economic productivity?

4 Does the plan increase the complexity of responses of the person?
5 Does the plan use positive incentives in training activities?
6 Does the plan encourage the giving and maintaining of attention?
7 Does the plan reflect the application of transfer of training, memory, and motivation?

Finally, programs should stress both prevention of civil disenfranchisement as well as the more positive guarantee of protection and extension of rights.

SUMMING UP

While there is current consensus as to a definition of mental retardation, there is variation as to what is significant about persons with, or believed to possess, this condition. This chapter has identified four broad perspectives. Implications of these perspectives would reinforce the AAMD focus upon intellectual performance and adaptive responses to the environment. Summary generalizations of this chapter might be:

1 Intelligence is a tool with which to cope with an environment.
2 Poverty, environmental paucity, hunger, and lack of health care are symptoms of neglect, indifference, and prejudice which affect intellectual potential.
3 Attitudes toward people and attitudes toward labels affect individuals, and these attitudes can be modified.
4 While the significance of nerve cell damage may be in debate, attending, motivation, cognition, short-term memory, and adequate coping are behaviors that require attention.
5 Society must learn to adapt to the needs of the retarded citizen.
6 There is a justified and reasonable optimism regarding assisting the retarded.
7 The retarded deserve legal safeguards and protections of their human rights. The ultimate rights are dignity and respect as a person, with an individual identity beyond a label.

ON LOCATION

As an illustration of the relative influence of individual factors and social factors, Lowell (1958) provides an imaginary visit to two contrasting worlds. One earnestly hopes that one of them will be different for the future.

The Two Lives of Kimo

Kimo was born on an anonymous island in the South Seas. He was a fat, good-natured baby, content to ride his mother's hip as she went about her work, or to lie blinking in the sun under a coconut palm.

He was slow in learning to talk, but eventually he learned enough words for his needs. Besides, Kimo very early showed that he could do something far more important than talk. Fibre mats were used on the island for everything from plates to beds. This was a job assigned to women and children. Most of them soon grew tired of the monotonous task. Kimo had remarkable staying power, and, while it took him longer to learn to weave than the others, it was not long before he could turn out more mats in a day than anyone else. His mother took great pride in his accomplishment, and so, at a very young age, Kimo became valuable to the community.

Later, he took to spending long hours at the shore with the netmaker. The old man laughed and nodded as he watched the boy knotting the tough fibre into miniature nets with which he could catch the small fish that darted near shore. He laughed, but he taught Kimo all he knew. It took a long while, but there was no hurry, and what Kimo once learned, he never forgot.

Today, Kimo is chief netmaker. Since the economy of his island depends upon fishing, Kimo is an important member of his community. He can make a net strong enough to catch a boatload of fish or one delicate enough to be handled by a single man from his perch on a rock. He can mend a net, too, so skillfully that only the keenest eye can tell that it was ever torn. Yes, Kimo is a man among men.

He sits all day along the shore with his nets. Those who go out in the boats greet him as they leave in the early morning, and he receives the first news of the day's catch when they return in the evening. He is a quiet man who speaks little, but he smiles a great deal. Because he is important to his community, he is important to himself. Kimo is a happy man. Yet, in terms of our culture, Kimo would be classed as mentally retarded.

It is not that Kimo's island is more acceptant of the problem of retardation than our own community. It is not, contrary to popular belief, that life on the island is an easygoing, catch-as-catch-can existence. Life on the island is precarious and everyone has to do his part. It is just that there happens to be an important part for Kimo.

For a moment let us transfer this same Kimo to Michigan and see what might happen. First of all, his slowness in learning to talk will probably become an almost immediate source of anxiety to his parents. Before long, Kimo begins to have a vague anxiety about himself. He uses his hands well, and could be happy for long hours at useful but monotonous tasks such as pulling out basting threads as his mother sews. But there is no satisfaction in this for Kimo, for he has learned that he can please others only when he does what is most difficult for him . . . when he uses words well. He tries harder, fails, and becomes irritable and difficult to manage.

At somewhere near the appropriate age, he tries school. Here again the same measure of Kimo's worth is applied. To earn a place in this society, he must again use words, only now the task of qualifying is more difficult. He must learn to read and write, and this he cannot learn. The fact that only a fraction of the economy of this culture demands such clerical skills makes no difference. Society states that in order to be admitted, he must read and write. To escape the censure of his fellows and their cries of "dumb" or "stupid," he uses his clever hands to strike back. He is sent home, a failure before he is ten years old, and he knows himself to be just that.

No one will ever know what this Kimo might have learned. We know only that he could not learn to read or write. Somewhere a factory owner searches in vain for a solution to the problem of turnover in a job which is both monotonous and important. Kimo might have been the answer. We will never know.

In the light of Kimo of the Island, we cannot even be sure just how retarded Kimo of Michigan really is. For who can say how much of his failure is the result of his biological condition and how much the result of his conditioning to a society which has no room for him? In another time and another place, he might have been chief netmaker of his island. More important still, he might have been a happy man.

REFERENCES

Bartel, N., Guskin, S. An Handicap as a Social Phenomenon, in *Psychology of Exceptional Children and Youth,* Cruickshank, W. (ed.). Englewood Cliffs, New Jersey: Prentice-Hall, 1971.

Benoit, E. P. Application of Hebb's Theory to Understanding the Learning Disability of Children with Mental Retardation. *Training School Bulletin,* 1960, 57, 18–23.

Benoit, E. P. Toward a New Definition of Mental Retardation. *American Journal of Mental Deficiency,*1959, 63, 550–565.

Birch, H., and Gusson, J. *Disadvantaged Children, Health Nutrition, and School Failure.* New York: Grune and Stratton, 1970.

Case, J., and Cleland, C. Eminence and Mental Retardation as Determined by Cattell's Method. *Mental Retardation.* 1975, 3, 20–21.

Cleland, C., and Chambers, W. Experimental Modification on Attitudes as a Function of an Institutional Tour. *American Journal on Mental Deficiency,* 1959, 64, 124–130.

Cleland, C., and Cochran, I. The Effects of Institutional Tours on Attitudes of High School Seniors. *American Journal on Mental Deficiency,* 1961, 65, 473–481.

Cruickshank, W. The Development of Education for Exceptional Children, in Cruickshank, W., and Johnson, G. O. (ed.). *Education of Exceptional Children and Youth.* Englewood Cliffs, N.J.: Prentice-Hall, 1975.

Dingman, H., Cleland, C., and Schwartz, J. Institutional "Wisdom" as Expressed Through Folklore. *Mental Retardation,* 1970, 8, 2–8.

Doll, E. E. A Historical Survey of Research and Management of Mental Retardation in the United States, in *Readings on the Exceptional Child,* P. Trapp and L. Himmelstein, (eds.). New York: Appleton-Century-Crofts, 1962.

Dybwad, G. *The Dynamics of Mental Retardation.* Washington, D.C.: U.S. Department of Health, Education, and Welfare, 1964.

Ellis, N. A Behavioral Research Strategy in Mental Retardation: Defense and Critique. *American Journal of Mental Deficiency,* 1969, 73, 557–566.

Gottwald, H. *Public Awareness About Mental Retardation.* Washington, D.C.: Council for Exceptional Children, 1970.

Guskin, S. Social Psychologies of Mental Deficiencies, in *Handbook on Mental Deficiency,* Ellis, N. (ed.). New York: McGraw-Hill, 1963.

Harmin, M., and Gregory, T. *Teaching Is . . .* Chicago: Science Research Associates, 1974.

Harth, R. Attitudes and Mental Retardation: Review of the Literature. *The Training School Bulletin,* 1973, 69, 150–164.

Hewett, F. (with Fomess, S.). *Education of Exceptional Children.* Boston: Allyn & Bacon, 1974.

Hutt, M., and Gibby, R. *The Mentally Retarded Child: Development, Education, and Treatment* (3rd ed.). Boston: Allyn and Bacon, 1976.

Jordan, T. E. *The Mentally Retarded* (3rd ed.). Columbus, Ohio: Charles Merrill, 1972.

Kanner, L. *A History of the Care and Study of the Mentally Retarded.* Springfield, Illinois: Charles C. Thomas, 1967.

Kauffman, J., and Payne, J. *Mental Retardation: Introduction and Personal Perspectives.* Columbus, Ohio: Charles Merrill, 1975.

Kirk, S. *Educating Exceptional Children.* Boston: Houghton Mifflin, 1962.

Kirk, S., and Johnson, G. O. *Educating the Retarded Child.* Boston: Houghton Mifflin, 1951.

Leland, H. Review of *An Introduction to Mental Retardation. American Journal of Mental Deficiency,* 1972, 76, 604–605.

Leland, H. The Relationship Between "Intelligence" and Mental Retardation, *American Journal of Mental Deficiency,* 1969, 73, 533–535.

Lowell, R. The Two Lives of Kimo. *Span,* 1958, 1, 8–10.

Milgram, N. The Rationale and Irrational in Zigler's Motivational Approach to Mental Retardation. *American Journal of Mental Deficiency,* 1969, 73, 527–532.

Rothstein, J. *Mental Retardation: Readings and Resource,* (2nd ed.). New York: Holt, Rinehart, and Winston, 1971.

Sellin, D., and Mulchahay, R. The Relationship of an Institutional Tour Upon Opinions About Mental Retardation. *American Journal on Mental Deficiency,* 1965, 60, 566–567.

Smith, D. *Report From Engine Co. 82.* New York: Pocket Books, 1973.

VanDalen, D. *Understanding Educational Research.* New York: McGraw-Hill, 1966.

Weingold, J. Rights of the Retarded. *Mental Retardation,* 1973, 11, 50–52.

Wolfensberger, W. The Origin of Our Institutional Models, in *Changing Patterns in Residential Services,* Kugel, R. and Wolfensberger, W. (eds.). Washington, D.C.: The President's Committee on Mental Retardation, 1969.

Zigler, E. Developmental Versus Difference Theories of Mental Retardation and the Problem of Motivation. *American Journal of Mental Deficiency,* 1969, 73, 536–556.

3

The Etiology of Mental Retardation

SYNOPSIS

This chapter reviews the basic biological correlates of mental retardation. The causes, or etiology, of mental retardation are relevant for nonmedical personnel, since prevention depends upon public understanding and support. While efforts are underway to search out and eventually prevent the condition, advances in the world of medicine pose social choices.

OBJECTIVES

ATTITUDES

1. To associate with and participate in programs of treatment and prevention.
2. To recognize that the ultimate goal of mental retardation programs should be prevention as well as treatment.

UNDERSTANDINGS

1. To see that the causes of mental retardation can be classified by the time of onset, origin of trauma, and extent of severity.
2. To realize that sterilization, institutionalization, and other similar deprivation strategies are less effective approaches to prevention than the search for fundamental agents of cause.

SKILLS

1. To incorporate causation data into helpful record-keeping procedures.
2. To formulate a personal philosophy regarding the consequences of advances in medical science.

AN OVERVIEW OF ETIOLOGICAL FACTORS

The Grossman report updated the original Heber report by identifying the medical components associated with mental retardation. While medical data might suggest an exclusive interest in intrapersonal variables and trauma, it should be understood that etiological data involve interpersonal, environmental variables as well.

The etiology and ecology of mental retardation as reflected in the Grossman-AAMD system revolve around the following variables:

1 The *where:* Did the trauma manifest itself prior to, during, or following birth?
2 The *how:* What were the origins of trauma upon various components of the nervous system, or what impact did environmental factors have upon the nervous system?
3 The *what:* Are associated disabilities present in addition to, or concurrent with, retarded mental development?
4 The *when:* What is the prognosis and estimate of current function with respect to the four levels, or degrees, of mental retardation?

Table 3–1 portrays these elements. These data represent a universe of sources that would constitute both diagnostic and perspective inferences. The potential benefit of the Grossman-AAMD medical system would be to develop uniform reporting systems and case protocols for interdisciplinary staffing.

THE RELEVANCE OF ETIOLOGICAL AND ECOLOGICAL FACTORS

The goals of understanding and mastery of the interpersonal and intrapersonal factors associated with mental retardation are:

1 to identify those factors that could be *prevented* through environmental and/or medical intervention, so that persons and families could be spared needless incidence of mental retardation;
2 to identify those factors that could be *remediated* through appropriate interventions so that the individual's full potential can be realized;
3 to guarantee that a complete and comprehensive diagnosis is rendered so that the determination of mental retardation is valid;
4 to formulate a comprehensive basis for program management based upon an individual's identity rather than upon group membership;

5 to identify one's own area of professional competence and appropriate sphere of influence;
6 to develop genuine respect and utilization of the competencies of other members of a service team, including parents;
7 to assess present and future service needs; and
8 to recognize the influence of one's own beliefs and values regarding professional behavior.

Table 3–1 SUMMARY OF MEDICAL FACTORS

Primary Classification Categories	*Additional Medical Information Categories*	*Supplemental Data*
Intoxications and Infections	Genetic Component	Obstetrical History
Metabolism or Nutrition	Secondary Cranial Anomaly	Apgar Rating
Gross Brain Damage (Postnatal)	Impairment of Special Senses	Nutritional Status
Unknown Prenatal Influence	Disorders of Perception and Expression	Birth Weight
Chromosomal Abnormality	Convulsive Disorder	Maternal Diabetes
Gestational Disorders	Psychiatric Impairment	Conditions and Length of Labor
Post-Psychiatric Disorder	Motor Dysfunction	Delivery Method
Environmental Influences		
Other Conditions		

The Grossman report, in keeping with current trends, suggests a systems-management model that can be applied to the retarded. The model places diverse, but necessary, elements into a reasonable Gestalt to facilitate communication, cooperation, and mutual effort.

Figure 3–1 conveys the scope and sequence of events necessary to gather data and translate that data into a plan of action. The chart is an approximation found in the Grossman report, as amended by the present writer, and includes the following stages:

1 The *discovery* period, or process, which leads a concerned adult to suspect a discrepancy within their child.
2 Identification and *referral,* which defines the engaging of the means to begin assessment procedures.
3 The *diagnostic* process, which involves correlation of presenting symptoms of the referred person (adaptive behavior) with suspected etiologic and ecological factors. At this point, the individual may exit out of the retardation system if other explanations can be found.
4 The *prescriptive-intervention* process, which specifies the disciplines and/or professionals to be involved relative to priorities and/or focus of behavior-medical needs.
5 The *implementation* and *delivery* stage, which formulates mobilization of necessary resources to achieve prescriptive intentions. Here the means, the procedures, and the appropriate setting must be carried out.
6 The *evaluative* stage describes a multiphased enterprise including: client outcomes, professional values and performances, and the circumstances in which the program operates.

This presentation is intended to suggest that more is involved in the management of a retarded person than accurate diagnosis. A critical factor is responsible follow-through (prescriptive-implementation) and follow-up (evaluation). Client outcomes are but one aspect of evaluation; the values and skills of involved professionals are equally important.

Examples of the advantages of correlating educationally and medically significant data are numerous. For instance, the cumulative record of a nine-year-old noted: "This mentally retarded child sits in the back of the room and talks to her friends." This impression was tragically repeated by the second-grade and third-grade teachers. The latter recommended retention, since "this mentally defective child has failed to acquire the fundamentals of the primary grades," but the child's next third-grade teacher recommended a visual examination. She was found to have a visual acuity of 20/100 correctable to 20/70. An individual psychological examination revealed a Binet IQ of 125. She was immediately promoted to fourth grade, with

Figure 3–1 *Sequence and Scope of the Relevant Data Diagnosis and Management*

Discovery and/or
Suspect Discrepancy State

↓

Identification and Referral

↓

Diagnostic Stages
Correlation and collaborating of presenting symptoms with known etiological and ecological factors.

↓

Prescriptive-Intervention Stages
Selection of behavioral and intrapersonal priorities for management. Selection and assembly of relevant data.

↓

Implementation and Delivery Stages
Specification and mobilization of personnel; facilities (medical, residential, instructional, etc.); program (age, level, setting, etc.); sponsoring or responsible agent or agency; method or approaches; and materials.

Evaluative Stages

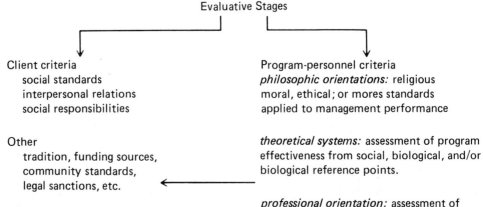

Client criteria
- social standards
- interpersonal relations
- social responsibilities

Other
- tradition, funding sources, community standards, legal sanctions, etc.

Program-personnel criteria

philosophic orientations: religious moral, ethical; or mores standards applied to management performance

theoretical systems: assessment of program effectiveness from social, biological, and/or biological reference points.

professional orientation: assessment of program effectiveness from professional perspective of service, research, treatment-administrative, legal, etc.

placement in a resource room for the visually impaired. Without the intervention of that alert third-grade teacher, one can only speculate as to the child's future. It can become easy to accept a diagnostic label without question. In summary, the educator must maintain close communication with medical personnel and other professionals to validate diagnostic and prescriptive recommendations, especially in the prescribing of drugs and the monitoring of their effects (chapter 11).

PERSISTING MYTHS ABOUT THE CAUSES OF MENTAL RETARDATION

Mythology about the causes and physical characteristics of mental retardation significantly hampers professional and public understanding. Among others, Polonsky (1961) and Blatt (1960) have identified those that persist even in the Gottwald report (table 3–2). Themes of these myths are: mental retardation has a single cause (inheritance); mental retardation is basically a constitutional defect (intellectual damage is the only problem); the mentally retarded are all alike in appearance and capabilities; and repressive social controls are acceptable for this group.

Most of these themes are readily discounted by an appeal to reason and the professional literature. Recognition that the term *mental retardation* applies to a diverse, rather than a single population suggests the unfounded nature of these myths. Moreover, there still tends to be an equating of the clinical types in the public mind, ignoring the vast numbers of the mildly mentally retarded.

Table 3–2 PERSISTING MYTHS ABOUT THE CAUSES AND PHYSICAL NATURE OF MENTAL RETARDATION

From the Polonsky article	*From the Blatt article*
Mental retardation can be cured like many mental diseases.	Mental retardation is basically a physical or constitutional defect.
Mental retardation is always inherited.	Mental retardation exists from birth, or early age . . . is incurable and irremediable.
Sterilization of the mentally retarded is the best solution to the problem.	40 to 50 percent of mental retardation is due to inheritance.
The mentally retarded are all equally defective.	The mentally retarded are less liable to physical defects and illness and lack physical stamina of the normal.
The mentally retarded are readily recognizable as such.	

Blatt offers counterevidence of these myths, as does Polonsky's earlier article. Sterilization for genetic control has been a failure. For example, PKU, a metabolic disorder with a heredity basis, could never have been eliminated by sterilization or institutionalization, because victims generally do not possess a sexual drive for reproduction, lack the reproductive adequacy for procreation, and do not survive into the childbearing age if untreated. The "best" solution to the problem was to discover the basic protein deficiency and institute dietary control. Extensive brain damage is thus prevented, and the person can expect a life of normal growth and development. Families can be spared the trauma of retardation. There are difficulties however. The diet is expensive and, during the preschool years, may be unappetizing. The diet must be monitored to avoid a possible state of malnourishment. Moreover, the PKU person must be alert to the possibility of this trait in his or her children and must insist on testing at birth. Sterilization and institutionalization, however, could never have been thorough enough to eradicate this genetic trait.

One is familiar with the myth of the retarded man big in muscle and short in mind, the childlike giant who creates mischief and mayhem as does Lennie in Steinbeck's *Of Mice and Men*. Blatt recognized that the reality, even for the mildly retarded, is quite the reverse. There is a greater incidence of disability and vulnerability to disease. One explanation is that certain causal agents do not stop with injury to the nervous system alone. Cerebral palsy, an orthopedic disability caused by damage to the motor cortex of the brain, is an example. Associated with such trauma can be also damage to other areas of the brain responsible for such functions as language and memory. A toxic agent may cause both. Despite this recognition, one might assume that mental retardation and physical defect are necessary correlates. One might accept these correlates as a "fact of nature" and passively accept the status quo. Blatt forcefully reminds us that these two conditions, especially among the mildly retarded, may be the result of an environmental factor or factors. Standards of health and health care, nutrition, housing, parental attitudes, and economic income may all contribute to both. The implication for management and services is to be alert to the preventable nature of mental retardation. Advances in early detection, surgical intervention, antibiotics, nutritional supplements, and family guidance can alter this pattern.

THE SCOPE OF RELEVANT ETIOLOGICAL DATA

Stevens (1962) identified the relevant somatopsychological attributes of body disorder (table 3–3). The Stevens summation provides a helpful base for the planning and the delivery of services. These attributes offer a continuing checklist for ap-

Table 3–3 RESUME OF EDUCATIONALLY SIGNIFICANT ATTRIBUTES, AS PER STEVENS

Major Emphasis	*Associated Concerns*
Epidemiology	incidence (as a percent of the population) and prevalence (an actual or estimated count), sex differences, and possible contagion
Temporal	age of onset and duration chronicity, or levels, or degree recurrence and periodicity
Symptomatology	degree or severity course and sequelae
Therapeutic	amenability and prognosis duration of treatment elimination and amelioration prosthetics styles and communications
Psychological	behavioral manifestations behavioral symptoms behavioral traits and characteristics
Social	legal provisions rules and regulations
Cultural	attitudes beliefs mores

praisal. Stevens offers numerous examples of the ways in which these data might be useful. This information can be used to anticipate needed services (epidomology); to decide when to install services (temporal); to identify criteria of identification (symptomology); and to recommend necessary support services (therapeutic). The Stevens model can be applied to the operation and evaluation of services with reference to reactions of the client (psychological); the use of expert opinion and judgment (cultural); and standards of existing legal and regulatory provisions (social). As one examines existing programs with reference to these data, new resources can be identified. Comparison of known incidence and prevalence figures to one's own community can be a useful index. If one's actual count is below a national standard, that case-finding procedures possibly should be examined. If the actual count is significantly high, one might question the presence of adverse environmental factors. Incidence and prevalence figures can have dramatic impact. For example, cretinism, once a significant contributor to mental retardation, was found to be excessively distributed in particular areas of the world (western and midwestern United States and central Europe) and only minimal elsewhere. Examination uncovered a thyroid defect that could be remedied with iodized salt. It was the original comparison and resulting curiosity which led to this discovery.

The etiologies of mental retardation, according to the Grossman report, can be:

1. infection and intoxication (cytomegalic defects, rubella, syphilis, toxoplasmosis, etc.);
2. trauma, or physical agent (prenatal injury, mechanical injury at birth, asphyxia);
3. metabolism or nutrition (carbohydrates, galacrose, amino acid, mineral, and endocrine defects among others;
4. gross brain damage after birth (Von Recklinghausen's disease, Sturge-Walker, Bounnerville's syndrome);
5. unknown origins (microcephaly, hydrocephalus, etc.);
6. chromosomal disorder (Down's syndrome is the principal example, although the American Academy of Pediatrics notes research may eventually identify certain conditions previously thought to have another cause);
7. premature birth (defined by weight and estimated time of arrival);
8. psychiatric disturbance (following retardation, but no cerebral dysfunction present); and
9. environmental (including sensory deprivation).

A CONSTELLATION OF ETIOLOGIES

It should be recognized that the majority of clinical etiological factors remain unknown. While damage to the nervous system is a suspect, exact determination of the trauma may remain unclear.

Gellis, Feingold, and Rutman (1968) have prepared a helpful atlas of the syndromes of mental retardation. The American Academy on Pediatrics (1971) and Covert (1964) sponsored by the American Medical Association, have produced enlightening and comprehensive discussions of these syndromes (table 3–4). To understand what a brief summary this table represents, it should be pointed out that the American Academy on Pediatrics lists forty-eight known metabolic disorders alone. *Mental Retardation, Its Biological Factors* (1966) provided the rationale for the selection of the listed syndromes. The table is meant to give an overall impression of the wide constellation of etiological sources. Inspection of this table should

Table 3–4 CONSTELLATION OF SYNDROMES

Identification	*Symptomatology/ Temporal*	*Social Psychological*	*Therapeutic Aspects*
Apert (acrocephalosyndactyly)	evident shortly after birth, syndactyly of hands and feet, "smashed," depressed facial features; sporadic and no presumed genetic problem	varying degrees of retardation; true incidence is unknown	surgical intervention for webbing of hands and feet; surgical intervention for skull is controversial
Bounnerville (tuberocus sclerous)	genetics varies from autosomal dominant to recessive, distinct skin coloration	varies in severity, but usually severe	control of seizures
Cri du Chat (cry of the cat)	distinctive cat like cry present at birth which may persist beyond five months of age, undersized compared to normal	severe to moderate retardation, other motor involvement	none
Cretinism	rarely genetically linked; goiter, skin is coarse and dry; lack of thyroid	severity of retardation varies with age of discovery	thyroid treatment is strongly indicated; preventable
Crouzon (craniofacial dysostesis)	expophthalmus of the eyes, dwarfism in stature, beaked nose; an irregular genetic transmission	mental retardation not necessarily present unless there is intracranial pressure	surgery to relieve intracranial pressure
De Lange	microcophbrachyencephalic; in third percentile for height and weight; upturned nose; genetics unknown	usually severe mental retardation	extreme care to avoid infections and caution in feeding
Down (mongolism Trisomy 21)	simian line of the palm, slanted eyes, tongue thrust, coarse hair, no known genetic component, nondysfunction of chromosome 21 or translocation of chromosome	considerable range of mental abilities, usually moderate but some reports of normal range	correction of circulation defects, caution to prevent respiration and weight problems; parents require counseling for management; normalized environment is indicated.

Table 3–4 (continued)

Identification	*Symptomatology/ Temporal*	*Social Psychological*	*Therapeutic Aspects*
Hurler (gargoylism)	may be autosomal recessive; early demise; coarse features with broad flat features	usually severe	symptomatic relief if indicated
Hydrocephalus	generally not a genetic defect; increased head size, affects motor and visual performance; ventricals to the brain are blocked	severity depends upon extent and degree of blockage	surgical procedures and valve to reduce and minimize obstructions
Kernicterus	Rh incompatibility between mother and fetus; risk increases with each pregnancy; can affect vision and hearing as well	great variation in severity	exchange transfusions; careful monitoring of mother and fetus; preventable
Laurence-Moon-Biedel	generalize obesity; variety of visual defects; poly- and syndactyly; broad, coarse features; autosomal recessive	varies from normal range to severe retardation	visual problems require correction; careful management to ensure a "normal" intelligent person is not mistaken for a retarded person
Lowe (oculocerebrorenal)	X-linked traits; rare among females; elongated features, normal head size, repetitive movements; progressive	usually severe	correction of visual defects; caution regarding infections, vitamins
Microcephalus	autosomal recessive, although other factors contribute; skull does not expand in normal fashion, sloping forehead with distinct ears and mouth	may be normal development during preschool, usually terminates in moderate to profound retardation	none known
Niemann-Pick (sphingimlelm-lipidosis)	autosomal recessive, frequently in Jewish families; protrusion	severe and progressive demise usually by size although sur-	none

Table 3–4 (continued)

Identification	*Symptomatology/ Temporal*	*Social Psychological*	*Therapeutic Aspects*
	of stomach, deformities of the skeletal system	vival may be into adulthood	
Sturge-Walker (encephalotrige minalonglomatosis)	portwine blotches of skin, seizures, calcium deposits near cortex, head asymetrical	mental retardation is present	treatment of seizures, cosmetic treatment for skin disorders; removal of cortex affected may be rarely done
Von Reckinghausen (neuro ofibromatosis)	multiple tumors which affect all parts of the body, especially the central nervous system, autosomal	tumors of the central nervous system may cause death before retardation becomes manifest	no known treatment except secondary consequences of tumors
Wilson (hepatolenticular degeneration)	autosomal recessive, set facial expression with open mouth and teeth exposed into apparent smile; muscle contractions, especially of the wrist	mental retardation; progressive deterioration may result in motor and speech patterns	food high in copper to be avoided; family members should be checked to institute therapy
Rubella	infectious virus during first trimester, exposure to measles; attacks nerve tissue with resulting damage to vision and hearing; not an inherited condition	severe to no mental retardation present	preventable by vaccine; surgery to correct lesions

convey the inadequacy of describing mental retardation as a disease entity. It is not contagious; there is no single cause; its effects are lifelong; and it encompasses more than a single population.

UNLOCKING GENETIC CODES

Traditionally, heredity has been viewed as the primary cause of retardation. Views of genetics, however, are changing. First, structures of genetic transmission may be subject to alteration. That is to say, eventually, there may be the capability to tamper with existing heredity. Second, environmental forces, such as virus and nutritional level, can alter human heredity. Introduction of greater abundance of food sources and changes in life-styles have produced dramatic, apparently permanent changes in physicial stature and weight.

The Grossman report outlines three basic patterns of inheritance: autosomal dominant, autosomal recessive, and X-linked factors. Each cell in our bodies has a performance function and a program function to reproduce itself. Within each cell body lie chromosomes, which in turn contain genes. The gene, in turn, carries a set of instructions that links with similar genes to make up the genetic structure of each individual. The trait or traits transmitted to the newborn can be expressed in probabilities, or odds (i.e., one in four).

In the *autosomal dominance* pattern, a trait is reproduced regardless of whether it is matched by like or unlike genes. The trait is usually found in one parent, regardless of sex, and there is fifty-fifty chance of its appearing in both sons and daughters. In the *autosomal recessive* pattern, both parents must have the trait. The transmission odds are one in four for affliction, one in four for normalcy, and one in two for the trait to be autosomal dominant. In the *X-linked* pattern, the dominance pattern can be either/or for the female, but will be manifested in the male. Referring to the AAMD classification system, one notes that the trait can be as specific as an enzymatic defect, or as extensive as dysfunction of an organ of the body or an entire system of the body.

Implications for management and/or prevention are becoming known. Tay-Sach's syndrome appears to be a clear-cut heredity pattern of a recessive type. By the process of amniocentesis (a drawing of fluid from the uterus), the likelihood of this syndrome can be predicted. This development, coupled with greater precision in determining the sex of the unborn, could mean that if the fetus were male, there would be a high probability of the syndrome, while the reverse would be true for the female. Therapeutic abortion then may be considered, with due consideration of psychological and physical factors.

As well as internal genetic transmission between two people, there is now increasing evidence of external environmental influences as well. These influences alter the genetic make up in directions other than what the genetic heritage of the parents would have predicted. For example, there is evidence that LSD alters genetic codes. Research indicates that Down's syndrome may be the result of a virus similar to the virus causing hepatitis. Industrial pollutants affect nerve cells if ingested by the mother and radiation has been shown to have adverse effects on genetic make up. Thus, the benefits of technology, which has brought about improved standards of living and education, must be balanced against potential genetic hazards.

THE STRUCTURE AND FUNCTION OF THE NERVOUS SYSTEM

It is obvious to state that the source of intelligent behavior is the human nervous system. As yet there is no valid (accurate), reliable (consistent), or direct assessment of brain function and intellectual function. Until the advent of direct cerebral measurement, observation and standard measures remain the only criteria.

The human nervous system remains a subject of fascination. A consideration of the nervous system may seem irrelevant to the practitioner oriented to symptoms and manifestations of the nervous system, but awareness may prove relevant to assessment of certain treatment systems that purport to encompass patterning and motor education of the brain (chapter 6). Only the essentials will be considered.

Certain texts that attempt to communicate essential neurological information for practitioners, especially teachers, as well as to parents center around certain common themes:

1 The nerve cell is the building block of the entire system.
2 The nervous system can be divided according to structure and responsible function.
3 The brain can be similarly divided.
4 Human abilities are complex interactions of the system as a whole, not of localized sections.
5 Consequences of insult, trauma, and/or toxication have differential effects depending on origin, extent, duration, and age of the person.

The human brain is understood as the location and origin of the humanness of human beings, especially of speech and language. While the brain is likened to a complex computer, the similarity has its limits, since the most complex computer fades in comparison with the intricacies of the human brain.

The central nervous system of the human is a delicate, interlocked system which includes the spinal cord, with its branches of nerve endings throughout the body, and the brain itself, which in turn is divided into special areas. Current agreement and research suggest that the nervous system is a composition of interdependent functions rather than independent functions.

Gellner (1959) as well as Stevens, Sellin, and Gray (1964) identify the nerve cell as the basic building block or unit of the nervous system. The humble individual cell, in combination with over 100 billion of its counterparts, elaborates into the nervous system. There are different cells for different purposes, according to Guyton (1972), such as motor, sensory, and perceptual functions. Each cell has three essential components, the cell body as well as dendrites and axons. The last two structures serve as receivers and expressors of electrical transmissions, called the synapse, among the nerve cells. Nerve cells cluster together in ganglion to form a localized arrangement for neurophysiological activities. Nerve cells, like other cells, are formed during the prenatal period by cell division. Within the chromosomes, which program genetics, are genes activated by physiological codes, or material, abbreviated as DNA. This in turn affects a more minute substance knows as RNA. Whilc the exact procedure is still not completely understood, it is known that a protein synthesis is involved. Thus, the nerve cell is a complex structure with responding and response functions. The synaptic process, which transmits impulses from nerve to nerve, is the basis of the neural activity called human thought. The cell is protected by a sheathlike tube, called the myelin which is necessary for the focus and direction of neural activity.

The brain is not one structure but at least four: the pons, the cerebellum, the cerebrum, and the medulla. In a similar fashion, the nervous system may be divided into two systems according to function: the autonomic and the reflexive. Many of the functions necessary to maintain life (i.e., respiration and circulation) are automatically regulated without "conscious" thought. Responses to temperature and light, for example, are reflexes completed in thousandths of a second without effort, and we respond by blinking our eyes or putting on a sweater. The human infant is the most helpless of life forms and could not begin to duplicate the construction capabilities of the ant or the beaver. However, "natural" law appears to be that the longer the period of dependency, the greater will be the complexity of the responses. This explains why human beings exist all over the world while ants and beavers exist in only specific environments.

Figure 3–2 portrays a representation of behavioral functions of the brain. The intent is *not* to present a neurological map, but to show that a single human act is the interaction of various parts of the brain, not a localized section. Furthermore, human beings "feel," "see," and "hear" with the brain. The eyes, ears, and skin are sensors that transform environmental data into particular neuroelectrical data. These impulses are conducted along particular pathways toward the brain. It is the brain, especially the cerebral cortex, which makes interpretation and recall possible. Inspect a set of Chinese characters and one notes the difference between sensation (receiving) and understanding meaning (perception). With increased experience these precepts (initial impressions) formulate concepts, or labels, which become the data base for problem solving. The brain, consequently, serves as the basis for human learning based upon short-term and long-term memory. Furthermore, the brain "stores" our associations with learning, especially feeling tones of pleasure and pain. Thus, it is not only what happens but how we feel about that learning experience that influences subsequent learning. Thus, a given event may cause one person to subsequently avoid further contact, while the other person will be drawn to approach.

Baker (1970), among others, reminds us that the brain is divided into two

Figure 3–2 *Representation of Brain Function*

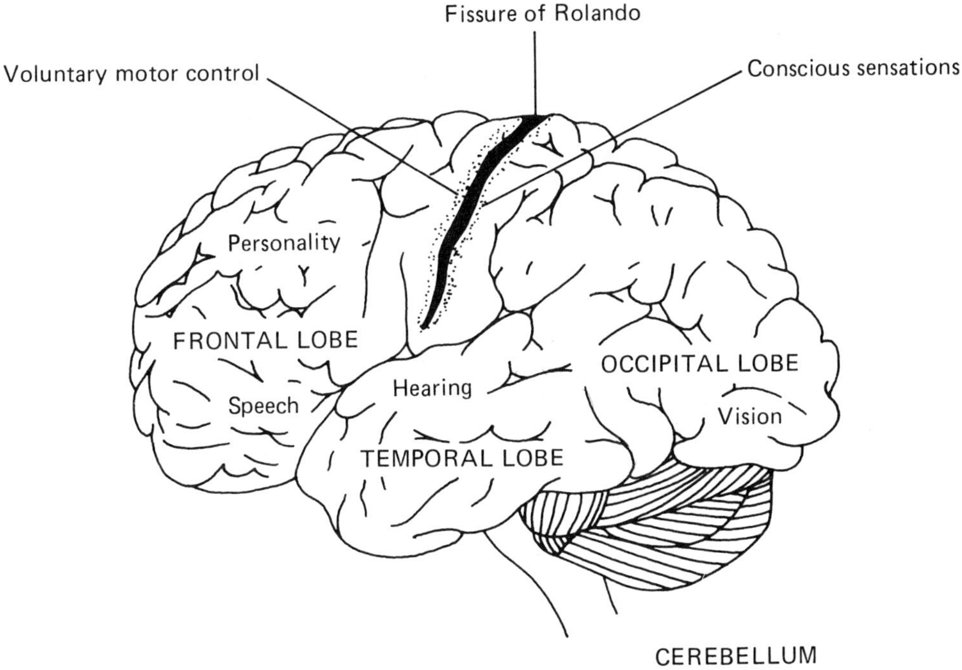

hemispheres that are separated anatomically but connected by nerve fibers. Each sphere has fairly defined functions, and one will be dominant over the other. In the left-sided person (i.e., an observed preference for the left foot, eye, and hand), there is a crossover effect which is observed in the dominance of the right side of the brain. In general, the dominant hemisphere is responsible for essentially human functions, while the other hemisphere is responsible for more automatic functions. For some learners, it is hypothesized that if dominance is imperfectly established then "messages" (i.e., nerve impulses) may be routed into inappropriate areas and retrieval of data may be impaired.

While there are billions of nerve cells, there is no one nerve cell for each bit of data. The process of learning encompasses many related centers widely scattered throughout the cortex. *Time* (1974) cites Eigen to the effect that as many as 100,000 neurons may be involved in the transmitting of information that results in as simple an action as stepping back to avoid being struck by an oncoming car. The entire process occurs in less than a second.

The three and one half pounds that constitutes the brain is well protected. The hair, scalp, skull, and linings below the skull are defenses from outside trauma. However, nerve tissue, once damaged, does not regenerate itself as does a skin injury. Thus, the brain is highly vulnerable to insult from within and without.

BEYOND THE GENETIC CODE

If cerebral functioning were exclusively nerve activity dependent upon the unfolding of genetic codes contributed by the biological parents, mental retardation would be a stable field. For example, if neuron process is dependent upon protein synthesis; imagine the consequences of restrictions in nutritional level of the mother on the fetus. This has led the Massachusetts Association for Retarded Citizens (1975) to develop materials to alert parents concerning nutrition and medical care. Among the points made:

1 Expectant mothers are feeding themselves and their babies too.
2 Poor and imbalanced nutrition may cause a baby to be born with various handicaps. The health of a mother before and after pregnancy is very important in safeguarding an unborn baby.
3 Something should be eaten every day from the four basic food categories: the milk and milk products group; the meat, fish, and egg group; the fruits and vegetable group; and the bread and cereal group.
4 Blood and urine specimens should be laboratory tested to determine whether or not a newborn baby has a metabolic disorder.
5 A child should be medically examined regularly.
6 Proper nutrition is important to insure that the young child reaches his full mental and physical development.
7 Immunizations that will protect a child from infectious diseases should be given at recommended times.
8 Preventing accidents and poisoning is an essential part of early childhood care. This includes locking up medicine and dangerous materials as well as using appropriate automobile restraint devices.

Bray (1969) advanced a neurological viewpoint and perspective that views the mentally retarded as composed of two groups, the pathologic and the physiologic. The pathologic group exhibits specific and overt symptoms and neurological defects. The physiologic are those without evidence of either general or neurological defect. From a medical standpoint, the physiologic group outnumbers the pathologic ten to one. In general, according to Bray, the physician is likely to overestimate the developmental rate for the physiologic group and underestimate the pathologic group. Symptoms of neurological impairment which lead to suspicions of mental retardation include delays in basic reflexes (sucking, swallowing), lack of muscle tone, and vision and hearing coordination, and absence of speech at two years. A complete pediatric history is then necessary.

1 Complete family history is seen as the most essential element.
2 Metabolic screening as well as the search for other problems may identify a specific syndrome.
3 EEG examinations are seen as helpful in treatment recommendations. A main problem is that these measures of brain activity may be insensitive to partial functioning.
4 A developmental history of the person is taken, with a primary focus upon the acquisition of developmental landmarks.

Bray recognizes that one of the primary roles of the physician is family counseling and management. The delicate balance is between honest recognition that a problem exists and avoiding a sense of hopelessness. Figure 3–3 presents a com-

Figure 3–3 *Representations of Development*

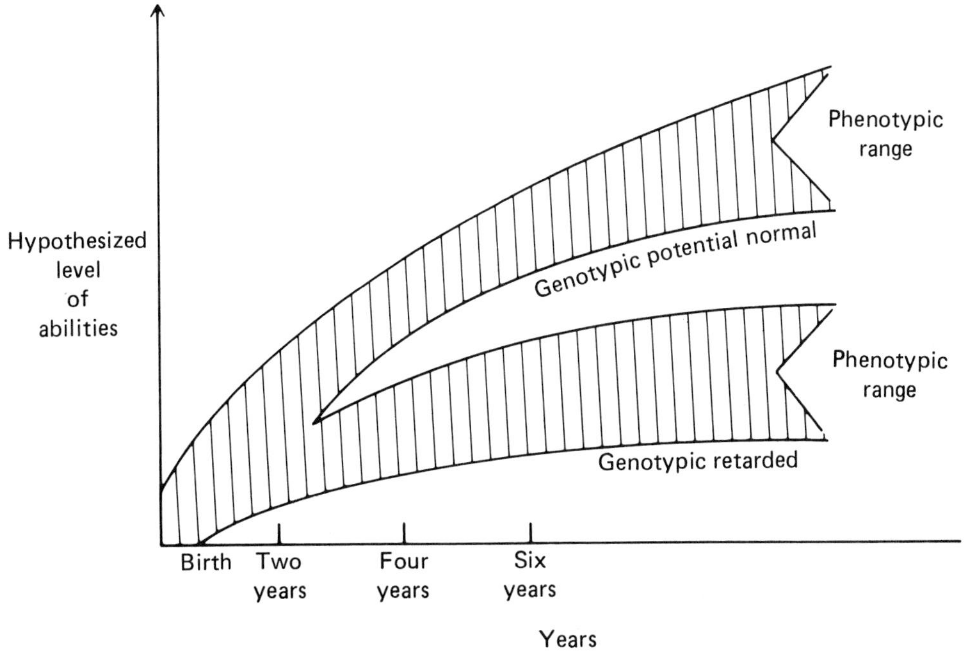

parison of a hypothesized normal child and of a retarded child. While there are similarities between the two, gaps will widen and increase with age. Bray notes that this illustration also conveys the retarded person's capacity for progress. The balance of counseling is directed toward establishing realistic goals consistent with developmental attainments.

SUMMING UP

This chapter has attempted to dispel the myths about the physical nature of the retarded. It has tried to convey that initial diagnosis should be directed toward physical symptoms which must be viewed in collaboration with comprehensive evaluation. An attempt was made to illustrate the correlation and integration of diagnostic-medically oriented data into a comprehensive treatment plan. A resumé of the nervous system and the dynamics of genetics was intended to convey the complexities of the transmission of human qualities. It should be obvious that since there is no single cause, or single transmission pattern, then single solutions such as sterilization beg the question of meaningful prevention. Mental retardation is not a nature vs. nurture proposition; it is both nature and nurture.

ON LOCATION

A possible risk in a review of the biological correlates of mental retardation, however brief, may be a detachment from the humanness of the people involved. The affected individuals may be reduced to "clinical types." The following account from the *Philadelphia Inquirer* illustrates that one community has not fallen into this pitfall.

Two Little Girls Full of Love

Mary Ann is a two-and-a-half-year-old girl with a nature as sweet as June roses. When you walk through her front door, she holds her arms out for a hug and says, "Hi, dear!"

This is true even if you have caterpillar eyebrows, a nose hooked enough to hang a teacup from and a history of grumpy introductions. She'll love you anyway, because that's her way of living.

Joycie, almost five, who was in this column eight months ago, is just as unjudging and affectionate.

These two little girls, who are both waiting for adoption, have another thing in common. They have Down's Syndrome, also known as mongolism. This is a congenital ailment occurring in approximately one birth in a thousand, but the chances of producing a mongoloid child increase with the mother's age.

The affected child has 47 chromosomes instead of the normal 46. All children with this condition experience some retardation but, while there is no known cure for the ailment, there is a wide range of behavior and achievement.

Many Down's Syndrome children can be taught to be useful in society and to function in a limited way. Unless afflicted by heart ailment, they can live a normal life.

Mary Ann is a good listener. No matter where she is in the house, if you call her name you'll hear a tippity-tap of small shoes. And she'll round the corner wearing a smile.

She's recently learned to walk, but needs help up and down stairs. Other children are a delight to her. Whether it's rocking baby dolls or building four-block towers, she'll go along with whatever games they want to play.

Joycie is doing many of the things that Mary Ann will soon be taught to do. The emphasis with any retarded child must always be toward independence and self-reliance.

Knowing her church shoes from her sneakers and even identifying the color of her clothes has been a recent job well done.

A child study team says in September Joycie can go to special education classes in a public school.

This summer she's in camp for four hours of happy learning each day. They sit and splash in a wading pool, pick up leaves, feel the bark on tree trunks, and just stop and smell the flowers in peaceful content.

Children with Down's Syndrome must be constantly stimulated to be aware of things we take for granted. A family considering adoption will need great patience and kind understanding. For though rewards in returned love are great, it is a job to be considered with much thought.

In the event of the parents' death, there is always a worry of how the child will be taken care of financially. The Association of Retarded Citizens now has a very reasonably priced insurance plan.

It looks hopeful that some day Mary Ann and Joycie will obtain enough measure of independence to be placed in a sheltered workshop atmosphere.

They are not related and are in today's *Inquirer* together only because there are many other Down's Syndrome children on the DARE Exchange. They need separate adoptive homes.

REFERENCES

American Academy on Pediatrics. *The Pediatrician and the Child with Mental Retardation.* Evanston, Illinois: A.A.P., 1971.

Baker, A. B. *An Outline of Applied Neurology.* Dubuque, Iowa: Kendall-Hunt, 1970.

Blatt, B. Some Persistently Recurring Assumptions Concerning Education of the Mentally Retarded. *Training School Bulletin,* 1960, 57, 46–59.

Bray, P. F. *Neurology in Pediatrics.* Chicago: Yearbook Medical Publishers, 1969.

Butterfield, E. C. A Provocative Case of Over-Achievement by a Mongoloid. *American Journal of Mental Deficiency,* 1961, 66, 444–448.

Covert, M. *Mental Retardation: A Handbook for the Primary Physician.* Chicago: American Medical Association, 1964.

Gellis, S., Feingold, M. and Rutman, J. *Atlas of Mental Retardation Syndromes.* Washington, D.C.: U.S. Department of Health, Education, and Welfare, 1968.

Gellner, Lise. *A Neurophysiological Concept of Mental Retardation and Its Educational Implications.* Chicago: Dr. Julian D. Levinson, Research Foundation for Mentally Retarded Children, 1959.

Guyton, A. *Structure and Function of the Nervous System.* Philadelphia: W. B. Saunders, 1972.

Hurley, R. *Poverty and Mental Retardation: A Causal Relationship.* New York: Random House, 1969.

Massachusetts Association for Retarded Citizens. *Proper Nutrition for Your Unborn Baby.* Newton Upper Falls, Massachusetts, no date.

Mental Retardation, Its Biological Factors, Hope Through Research. Washington, D.C.: National Institute of Neurological Diseases and Blindness, 1966.

Philadelphia Inquirer. Two Little Girls Full of Love. August 1975.

Polonsky, A. Beliefs and Opinions Concerning Mental Deficiency. *American Journal of Mental Deficiency,* 1961, 62, 12–17.

Stevens, G. D. *Toxonomy in Special Education for Children with Body Disorders.* Pittsburgh: Department of Special Education and Rehabilitation, University of Pittsburgh, 1962.

Stevens, G. D., Sellin, D., and Gray, G. *The Human Brain.* Pittsburgh: Department of Special Education and Rehabilitation, 1964.

Time. Inside the Brain, 14 January 1975, 50–59.

4

The Ecology of Mental Retardation

SYNOPSIS

This chapter summarizes certain known environmental correlates of mental retardation and discusses the recently renewed debate on the purported genetic transmission of intelligence. Two prime ecological correlates, labeling and poverty, are presented. The chapter concludes with a brief summary of the status of current prevention efforts, both etiological and ecological.

OBJECTIVES

This chapter is concerned with:

ATTITUDES

1. To make a commitment to eliminate known environmental correlates that have adverse effects upon development.
2. To recognize that education has a role in prevention of adverse ecological factors.

UNDERSTANDINGS

1. To summarize the relative importance of nature and nurture.
2. To formulate guidelines for intervention strategies.

SKILLS

1. To identify appropriate elements in a high-school curriculum relative to secondary prevention.
2. To describe the range of efforts being undertaken to eliminate environmental factors.

DIMENSIONS OF NATURE AND NURTURE

The individual's environment is an important determinant of behavior. The early efforts of services for the retarded in this country pioneered by E. Seguin were founded upon a rehabilitation concept. There was the belief in curing, or at least in sufficient training to restore the retarded to community life. Vigorous training in sensory-motor development was seen as the key to unlocking the faculties of the mind. Demonstration schools in New England and the eastern states showed great promise. Legislators reflected amazement at "idiots" who could talk and who responded with the "airs of gentle folk." Education promised much.

Then a reaction and backlash set in. The middle of the nineteenth century saw the dream of community adjustment centers give way to institutions committed to avowed custodial retention. By the turn of the century, the success of the science of education held out the promise that fundamental "principles of pedagogy" could be applied to the retarded. World War I mass testing and rejection of significant numbers of males for mental defects, coupled with the publication of the *Jukes* and *Kallikaks*, seemed to demonstrate the inherited nature of feeblemindedness.

It should be noted that by today's standards both studies would not be considered scientific. From the vantage point of modern times one may observe a major flaw of these studies. In the standard social order of the seventeenth and eighteenth centuries one inherited an environment, social status, and privilege *as well as* a body. Examination of existing institutional enrollments, *in retrospect,* tended to ignore the one-only family member resident and tended to concentrate on only multisibling members. Accordingly, the first quarter of this century witnessed a strong eugenics movement, climaxing in a 1929 Supreme Court decision permitting involuntary sterilization so that society could protect itself from a genetic menace. Again institutions were forced into custodial roles.

In the 1950s there were reports from Chicago of dramatic increases of IQ through special education. Articles in popular magazines cited data and proof of a cure. Debate raged between Kirk (1948) and Schmidt (1948) regarding educable-level pupils. This debate was never entirely resolved, owing in large part to the fact that the data base never became fully available. One consequence of the popularization of the argument was the formation of the National Association for Retarded Citizens in 1950. Parents of moderate-level children, largely ignored by public schools, began to ask themselves, "If education is good for the educable, why not for our children?" Consequently, local groups sponsored private day schools, which were eventually absorbed by public, tax-supported efforts.

The 1960s witnessed the active involvement of New Frontier and Great Society programs directly applied to the retarded. Great studies were made in prevention and service delivery efforts. Great promise was held out for special education and improved funding for residential facilities. A principal lesson learned was that optimism must be balanced with reality. The retarded tend to suffer as much from zealous claims as from repressive beliefs.

At present, the nature-nurture debate looms again. It had appeared that after the rapid pace of the 1960s, there would be calm attention to study of relative intervention efforts. Not so. Thc discussion has again been revived in the context of the genetic base of the IQ score, with particular emphasis upon certain ethnic groups. The debate centers around IQ as the reference point.

The work of Dobzhansky is often cited. Mental retardation specialists such as Sarason (1973), Smith (1968), and Birch and Gussow (1970) have applied his concepts. This application centers around constructs of *genotype* (a supposed innate potential) and a *phenotype* (an actual attainment) mediated by environmental influences. For example, the person's genotype can be expressed as a wide *range* of potential, and a person's phenotypic behavior is viewed as within this range. (figure 3–3) One interpretation of these constructs is to search for the appropriate environment for maximizing potential. Another interpretation has been to suggest that genotypic inferences remain unaltered. There have been searches "to prove" the genotypic superiority of certain groups over others so as to justify certain environments. Others have argued that environmental interventions offer the promise of altering genotypic performance beyond expectations.

One definitive study of environmental intervention has been the investigation of Kirk (1958), which still stands as a model. Four groups of educable mentally handicapped (i.e., mild mental retardation) from community and institutional settings were divided into experimental and contrast groups. In general the findings supported the experimental groups (community or institution) over the contrast group regardless of setting. An intriguing note was that children who evidenced overt central nervous system impairment reflected progress, but less than that of pupils from disadvantaged backgrounds. Heber (1963, p. 81) has commented:

> This is perhaps the study of greatest significance in the education of the mentally retarded which has been conducted in the past several years. Kirk has demonstrated the importance of providing early enriched environmental opportunities for the mentally handicapped, particularly for children being reared under subcultural conditions.

If life were simple, research and practice might have progressed toward the basic question of the genotype–phenotype interaction. The basic inquiry is to understand the reciprocal interchange between heredity and environment. On the one hand would be the search for understanding of the process of genetics and for ways to manipulate it, to eliminate traumatic biological agents. On the other hand would be the search for optimum environments to maximize potential.

Jensen, Hermstein, Shockley, and Eysenck advanced IQ deficit as a correlate associated with ethnic groups. The doctrine of genetic equality was seriously questioned. Rice (1973) has detailed the pattern of events that transformed a question of scientific inquiry into a popularized and politicized issue. The claim has been made that those who differ with the genetics of intelligence position are acting out of rigid, liberal self-interest to maintain vast educational organizations. Supporters of the genetic position view themselves as brave minds daring to think the unthinkable. There is no dispute that those who espouse academic freedom have been less than tolerant of those who propose the genetic position. Such persons have not served as models for reasoned dissent. It is regrettable that with so much available information there has to be a preoccupation with the ethnic, genetic origins of intelligence.

The basic premise is that on measures of intelligence, blacks consistently are one standard deviation below whites on intellectual groupings. Evidence pointing to the supposed failures of intervention programs is cited to prove that genotype cannot be altered. The elaborated argument is that IQ differences (as measured by standard tests) are real, and efforts to intervene are — and have been — nonproductive.

Jensen (1973) suggests his position has been misunderstood because his work refers to group differences, not to all individuals. He believes that heredity versus environment is still an open question and acknowledges the superiority of some blacks over some whites. His position seems to be that the distribution of intelligence is different for different groups. In support of his position, Jensen suggests:

1. The hereditability of intelligence is demonstrated consistently by statistical analysis of scores of the groups.
2. Tests are culturally loaded rather than culturally biased. Tests of "culture-fairness" do not predict much, and blacks do better on the standard tests than the "fair" ones.
3. Tests are color blind, because the same validity and reliability obtains for both groups. While there is recognition of differences within cultures (i.e., geography and sex), differences between groups still maintain themselves.
4. The effect of the tester, according to Jensen, is of minimal effect. His own research indicates that language differences and race differences have no impact on the scores of black children.
5. Verbal deprivation is a myth according to Jensen, since his studies of the most deprived of all learners, the deaf, showed adequate performance. Jensen refutes the teacher-expectation hypothesis as a source of deprivation.
6. Jensen is of the opinion that comparing blacks and whites of similar economic, occupational, and demographic backgrounds is merely a sampling tactic to draw biased samples.
7. Malnutrition is viewed as a world problem. Jensen sees no evidence of this condition in this country. He cites the Netherlands experience of World War II to suggest that even in a period of undernourishment, intelligent, normal children were produced.

Jensen, as others, pleaded for the opportunity to continue their research free from the political hysteria engendered by the media. Their search, they claim, is for the further understanding of racial-ethnic origins of intelligence.

Birch and Gussow (1970, p. 265) responded to the genetics of intelligence proponents:

> The conclusions we believed would be drawn from the relative failure of compensatory programs have been drawn, and scientists such as Shockley and Jensen are now arguing that educational failure in socially disadvantaged children, especially among those classified as non-white, must be viewed as deriving from an underlying genetic incompetence. . . . We noted in the opening passages of this book . . . that the genetic argument might be used to bolster the notion that we should accept a lower level of achievement from disadvantaged children.

Birch and Gussow (1970, pp. 265–266) cite Dobzhansky to offer the geneticist's view regarding the genetics of genotypes and phenotypes:

> The geneticist is constantly forced to remind his colleagues, especially those in the social sciences, that what is inherited is not this or that particular phenotypic trait, or character but a genotypic potentiality for an organism's developmental response to its environment. Given a certain genotype and a certain sequence of environmental situations, the development follows a certain path. . . . A given genotype might well develop phenotypically along different paths in different environments. Identical genetic constitutions, in other words, will result in different products when their development takes place under different environmental conditions.

PERSISTING MYTHS ABOUT THE SOCIAL NATURE OF MENTAL RETARDATION

Blatt (1960) and Polonsky (1961) have also identified certain socially oriented myths about mental retardation (table 4–1). Again certain themes emerge: the ability to benefit from educational efforts; the menace aspect; and the criminality aspect.

One can speculate that the common viewpoint is that "bad genes" beget "bad" behavior, "inferior" people gravitate toward "inferior" environments, and inferior people do not recognize their plight anyway (chapter 7). The potential of the educational enterprise as an ecological factor is very much open to question. Effectiveness is not the only issue. The primary issue is the setting. That is to say, the debate centers around whether to place the retarded in sheltered, contained environments especially designed for them or in more open, normal settings. This same debate occurs in regard to residential and vocational services as well. The belief at present, as reflected in court decisions concerning educational and residential services, is that special services presumably give effective benefits. (chapters 11 and 14)

Table 4–1 PERSISTING MYTHS ABOUT THE SOCIAL NATURE OF MENTAL RETARDATION

From the Blatt article	*From the Polonsky article*
Mental retardation results in the inability of the individual to profit from ordinary schooling. . . . a different educational program suited to his needs can make him more capable of facing the world which lies ahead.	Mental retardation is a mental disease.
Eighty-five percent of delinquents and criminals are mentally retarded.	The mentally retarded are a menace and should all be kept in institutions.
	The mentally retarded are unteachable and a total loss to society.
	The mentally retarded have no feelings and do not realize their condition.

ECOLOGICAL FACTORS

A resumé of the ecological factors of mental retardation is, in reality, an examination of the manipulation of environment for mediation of genotype and phenotype. Intervention, at present, is being executed on many levels, including efforts on behalf of the mentally retarded and the economically disadvantaged. The overlap between the retarded and the disadvantaged has centered upon the mildly retarded. Smith (1968) and the Group for the Advancement of Psychiatry (1967) have identified the mildly retarded as *two* somewhat distinct populations rather than one homogeneous group (table 4–2). Group B may be viewed as genuinely mentally retarded by the current Grossman definition. Group A learners are considered less likely to be mentally retarded, since these learners tend to reflect appropriate adaptive behavior except in academic situations. These are the learners that the President's Committee on Mental Retardation (1969) defined as the "six-hour retarded child."

> We now have what may be called a 6-hour retarded child — retarded from 9–3, five days a week, solely on the basis of an IQ score, without regard to his adaptive behavior, which may be exceptionally adaptive to the situation and community in which he lives (p. 2).

Intervention strategies for the mildly mentally retarded have involved legal, political, and educational efforts. Rice (1973) reports that in one state Spanish surname learners and black learners outnumber white learners in special classes for the retarded by between 300 to 400 percent. Further disquietude is created by the Johnson (1962) and Dunn (1968) reports of the seeming ineffectiveness of special education classes for the mildly retarded. These two reports offer counterevidence to Jensen's claim of nonrelevance of such sources of performance as tester effects and teacher expectations. Some coping strategies are the current emphasis upon

Table 4–2 COMPARISON OF TWO GROUPS OF THE MILDLY MENTALLY RETARDED

Trait	*Group A*	*Group B*
Organic, Central Nervous System Involvement	found less frequently	found more frequently
Family-Ecological	broken home; family present oriented; medical care unknown-unavailable; fewer financial resources for coping; other siblings may reflect similar levels.	intact family, future oriented; resources for financial coping; medical care is sought; family life significantly affected by child; other comparable children rare in family.
Educational	personal experience in school may have been punitive; view schools as another agency; will require time to gain trust.	family views schools and schooling as positive; personal experience has been helpful and rewarding; have immediate trust of schools.

mainstreaming (a system of regular classroom inclusion of the learner with support from either a resource room or an itinerant specialist) *and* the dramatic increase in programs for the learning disabled. Interestingly, reexamination of the data cited by Johnson and by Cassidy and Stanton (1963) suggested that Group B type learners were overrepresented on the experimental group (special class) and underrepresented in the contrast groups (regular class). When it is said that regular class placement is as effective as special class, it must be noted that neither placement has demonstrated the capacity to enable achievement of mental age potential.

At present, there is agreement that environmental intervention, usually in the form of learning-education interventions, requires continued study and research support. For the moderately and severely retarded, efforts have been directed toward improving phenotypic performance in upward directions. Part of the motivation for depopulation of institutions has been to create more normalized community settings for phenotypic development.

The intelligence test, especially the Stanford-Binet and the WISC, have come under severe criticism in the recent decade. It is not so much that these tests (called individual tests since they are administered on a one-to-one basis) are challenged. It is the use of their results that is questioned. The case history literature of mental retardation has reflected the tragic injustice of false diagnosis of retardation. It should be noted that an examination of the case history in the field of the mentally advanced shows a different trend. In some instances a gifted person was considered retarded until individual examination showed otherwise.

The original intention of Binet was to develop a diagnostic tool to identify strengths and weaknesses so as to prescribe an exact teaching strategy. As described by Kirk and McCarthy (1961) and Kirk (1962), Binet was commissioned to identify children in need of special help. His beliefs dictated his approach. The concept of *mental age* was used to establish standards that would be met by a majority of children of a given age, "failed" by younger children, and surpassed by older ones. Thus, it could be said that passing certain tasks and failing others indicated a performance approximate to children of a given level of development. Binet was persuaded that there was an educability of intelligence. Mental age was seen as an indicator of present, not necessarily future, intelligence. The IQ, a later development, was seen as a measure of the velocity of development or as an index of development. Thus, dividing mental age by chronological age yielded a kind of percentage or rate of growth, and today manuals provide exact tables for computation to avoid mathematical errors. IQ is seen as a rough indicator for the future. Furthermore, with the importation of psychometric testing to this country from Europe, there was the trend to use these tests as classification or categorical tools. (For a more complete discussion see chapter 5.) Because countless learners have been labeled as mentally retarded on IQ scores alone, there has been a severe reaction. It is appropriate to understand the appropriate limits of such tests. Bane and Jencks (1973), have proposed five helpful guidelines based upon a review of the research literature.

1. IQ tests are not the exclusive measure of human intelligence. Intelligence tests do measure school performance, but prediction of vocational success may be open to other variables.

2. IQ does not predict the effects of discrimination in future economic standings. Numerous studies were cited drawn from IQ data from the armed services. For whites and minority males of equal measured intelligence, the latter had consistently lower paying jobs attributable to employment discrimination.

3. IQ is not a function of genetic endowment. Research indicates that most intervention strategies have not included a multienvironment approach (health, nutrition, job training, and schooling).

4. Low IQ is not associated with "bad" genes. Comparable studies of similar social-economic groups across ethnic groupings reflect minimal differences. IQ accounts for only a partial amount of income gaps. Studies of certain regions reflect significant increase in IQ with mobility.

5. Improving the quality of the schools will go a long way toward decreasing IQ differences. Improving quality is not a bad idea as far as it goes. These authors isolate the effects of racial and economic segregation as prime targets. There is the need to eradicate these barriers as well as to improve opportunities.

Hurley (1969) offers documented testimony of the overall effects of economic poverty, particularly in health services. In one city, he cites an infant mortality rate of 41.3 per thousand, while the state average was 23.9, the national was 25.3, and the lowest rate in the state was 15.9. Similar rates of prematurity were also cited. Pediatric services were available to only 12 percent of low-income families, while available to over 30 percent of middle-income families.

Birch and Gussow (1970), after an intensive study, summarize their impression by a "flow chart" of economic disadvantagement (figure 4–1). The impression is of a repeated economic cycle that influences the person. The cycle can inculcate a psychology among program staff which assumes that people are what they are with little potential for improvement and may create feelings of hopelessness among those affected. The cycle originates with lessened opportunities for vocational development, which promotes early parenthood, which may increase the chances for high-risk infants, which involves lessened maternal and infant care, which . . . . The cycle, however, can be broken.

Birch and Gussow (1970) have noted that compensatory education has not failed as much as been inadequately applied. They note an urgent need to improve prenatal care and recommend that intervention adopt a dual focus upon both the parent's economic status *and* the delivery of intervention services.

In summary, it is apparent that IQ as a measure of genetic, innate aptitude is a violation of the function of the instrument itself. The psychometric score has been employed to explain a biological fact when it was intended to be a developmental inference. It would be like measuring blood pressure with a yardstick. The geneticist viewpoint ignores the AAMD proposition that intelligence is but one attribute of the person. The genetic view of the hereditability of intelligence reinforces single-criterion diagnosis based upon one measure. As Sarason (1973) says, if a puppy were mistreated by a person with an IQ of 160, one would search for an explanation. If the person is found to have an IQ of 60, his behavior is ascribed to his low IQ

TARGETS OF PREVENTION EFFORTS

With respect to prevention, Begab (1974, p. 519) has noted:

> The dynamic nature of mental retardation denies the long-cherished bromide of once retarded always retarded. Failure to induce changes early in life and thus prevent retardation in its primary sense will doom an individual to a lifetime of maladaptation. For certain categories, particularly the so-called cultural-familial group, cure through behavior therapy or change is possible.

While prevention may be possible, Begab warns that measuring the effectiveness of prevention is difficult and cautions against a "numbers" game approach. Two main

Figure 4–1 *Hypothesized Relations Between Environmental Factors and Effects of Poverty*

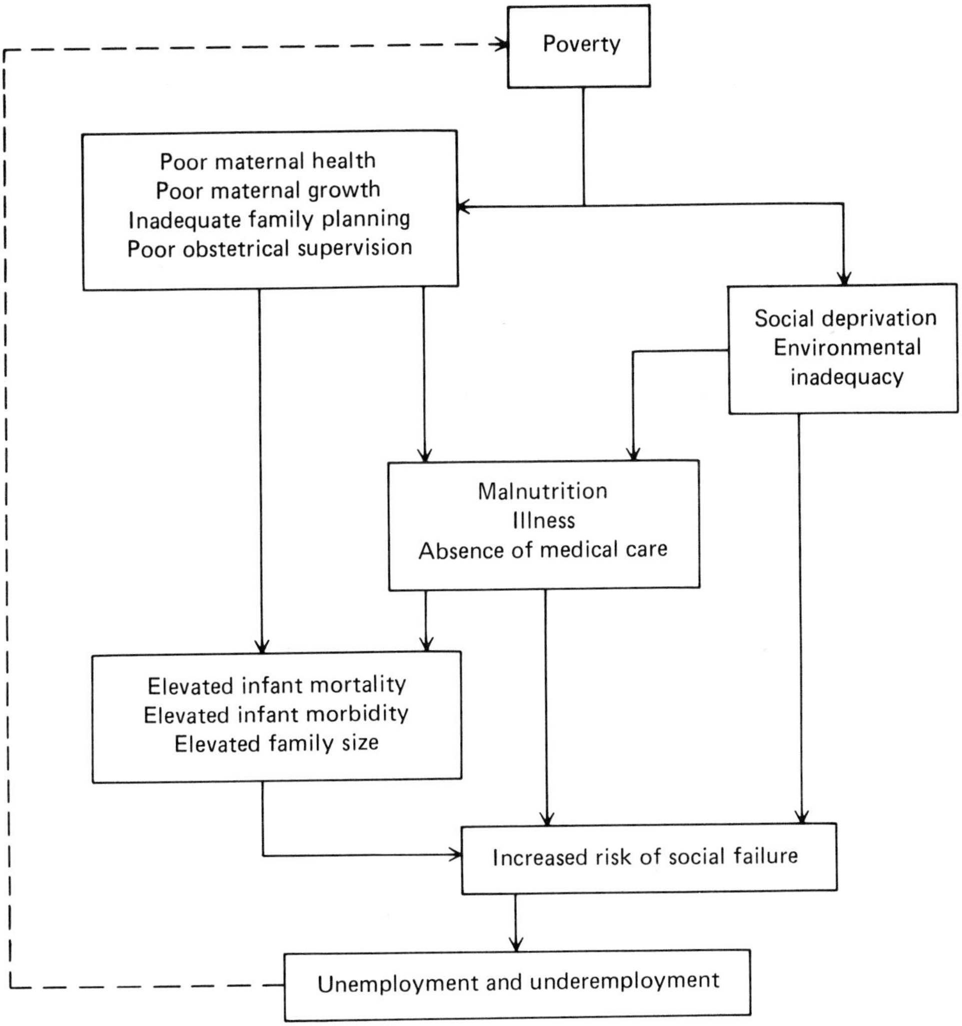

SOURCE: Birch and Gussow (1970, p. 268)

obstacles to evaluation were identified. First, while certain clinical conditions such as PKU and Down's syndrome are apparent, there is insufficient historical trend data to form a baseline to form a comparison regarding present efforts. Second, within certain communities, psychometric data such as IQ (when an upper limit of 70 is used) has yielded estimates of wide variance of incidence.

Despite these limitations, Begab (p. 521) does note: "Some observations can be made on factors that affect the incidence of mental retardation and inferences can be drawn regarding our progress in prevention."

Table 4–3 outlines two main classes of factors that contribute to an increase in mental retardation. One notes the consistency between the Begab discussion and the AAMD system presented earlier. One set of factors revolves around the primary physical agents concept, and the other centers upon secondary environmental factors.

STATUS OF PREVENTION EFFORTS

Begab identifies four major dimensions concerning our knowledge of prevention: genetic, prematurity, nutrition, and social environmental factors. Table 4–4 summarizes the first three dimensions of knowledge related to prevention. Begab notes that known genetic errors constitute about 10 percent of institutional population and that Down's syndrome constitutes the largest single category of genetic, clinical types. It was noted, however, that the death rate among certain etiologies precludes an accurate estimate of incidence. Much emphasis is laid upon prenatal diagnosis and abortion, coupled with programs to inform vulnerable mothers, which could effectively reduce mental retardation.

As will be pointed out elsewhere in this text, abortion is no easy solution. Abortion, like previous efforts at sterilization and excessive institutionalization, must be considered from philosophical standards and not be based exclusively upon scientific data. The author is of the opinion that people should have choices. Consequently, abortion requires guidance and counseling. It should never be mandated.

Birth weight as a function of various factors and malnutrition were seen by Begab as associated with the consequences of poverty, especially nutrition. There is sufficient knowledge about minimal nutrition levels for sound human development. Only social action is necessary to utilize this knowledge.

Begab recognizes that social environmental factors are probably most applicable to the mildly retarded. There must be an interactive function between the person and the surroundings. He notes (p. 526):

> How much each contributes to the variance between individuals, however, is a matter of quite diverse opinion. . . . Suffice to say that the role of environmental factors is of

Table 4–3 FACTORS AND CONSEQUENCES THAT AFFECT THE INCREASE OF MENTAL RETARDATION

Biological Factors that Contribute to the Increase of Incidence of Retardation		*Social-Environmental Factors that Contribute to the Increase of Incidence of Retardation*	
Factors	*Consequences*	*Factors*	*Consequences*
Addictive Drugs (LSD) Tobacco	Chromosomal abnormalities, prematurity, and low birth weight	Industrialization	Increased stress upon greater complexes of adaptive behavior than in less complex social orders.
Pollution air, water, food (lead and mercury)	encephalopathy, mercury contamination, and fetal toxication	Social change and economic standards of living housing health services education nutrition	lead paint poisoning infections and failure of remediation lack of preschool programs, lethargy, lack of stamina, and induced brain damage
Radiation X-rays	brain damage		
Disease and Infection syphilis bacteria meningitis rubella	damage to the fetal nervous system and prematurity		
Obstetrical Practices	Unknown, but damage to the skull and nervous system		

SOURCE: Adapted from Begab

Table 4–4 SUMMARY OF KNOWN APPROACHES TO PREVENTION

Dimensions					
Genetic Disorders and Inborn Errors of Metabolism		*Prematurity and Low Birth Weight*		*Malnutrition*	
Circumstance and Consequence	*Possible Solution*	*Circumstance and Consequence*	*Possible tebon*	*Circumstance and Consequence*	*Possible Solution*
Tay-Sachs syndrome PKU, (phenylketonuria), Cystinosis, Wilson's disease, Down's syndrome, galaciosemia tuberous sclerosis	dietary restriction to reduce effects of metabolic disturbance must be balanced against possible effects of malnutrition	survival of low-birth-weight infants because of advances in medical technologies	alert attention to blood supply to the uterus though prenatal care	reduction in nerve cell size and number	improved nutrition for expectant mothers
	amniocentesis	malnourishment *in utera*	increased health education	reduction of protein synthesis	improved nutrition for infants and toddlers toddlers
	organ transplants as in liver and kidney disorders; at present very risky	toxenima	family planning information should be available	severe neurochemical, electrical and structural changes in the brain	may be a consequence of poverty
	introduction of DNA virus to modify misprogrammed cells; still requires much effort	behavioral consequences of hyperactivity, autism, and disorganization	use of food stamps	apathy, lassitude, appetite loss	some slight evidence that early nutritional and sensory stimulation may offset early malnourishment
	genetic counseling	impairment in language and academic and motor behavior	attention hygiene standards	kwashiorker or marasmus symptoms	
	utilization of "therapeutic" abortion	high correlation as consequence of low income, poverty and lack of adequate medical delivery system to the indigent	counseling and services for unmarried teenage mothers	lowered motor, social, academic, physical stature performance	
	education of high-risk groups i.e., mothers over thirty-five			stillbirths and natural abortions	

> sufficient magnitude that dramatic changes in a child's daily experiences can alter his intellectual status.

Begab suggests that, while early intervention is better, promising results can be obtained as late as adolescence. The effects seem to be most beneficial in enriching, stimulating, and motivating behavior rather than in increased IQ scores.

Particular attention is given to the Milwaukee project reported by Heber, Garber, Harrington, and Hoffman, as cited by Begab. One special population was families in a poverty area where the parents appeared disadvantaged economically and intellectually. The program consisted of direct services to the child *and* the family. The child's program was described as full day and year long, emphasizing achievement motivation, sensory and language stimulation, problem solving, and interpersonnel skills. The mothers' program emphasized child-care skills, homemaking, literacy acquisition, and on-the-job training. Comparison between the experimental and contrast groups reflected mean IQs of 125 for the former and 92 for the latter. The differences have been consistent. Behaviorally, the experimental group has been far superior in language skills.

Major implications from Begab's discussion are that instructional programs for adolescents must emphasize: nutrition and the significance of well-balanced, low-cost meals; child-care skills that emphasize conversations promoting self-esteem, self-concept, and positive aspirations; financial management skills to conserve one's financial resources; and knowledge of helpful community agencies in times of crisis. In this respect, educators and other practitioners of the behavioral sciences have a significant role in prevention. Begab (p. 529) concludes:

> Undoubtedly, we have much still to learn about mental retardation, but in certain aspects of the problem at least, we have only to apply what we already know. We can indeed significantly reduce the incidence and prevalence of mental retardation. Shall we?

The answer would seem obvious, except that there are certain obstacles. Begab notes:

1 There is no concentrated, focused, cooperative effort.
2 Our knowledge may be only a beginning.
3 Economic and attitudinal factors related to social action thwart initiation of programs, especially nutrition and food distribution.
4 Economic and attitudinal factors toward spending discourage intervention at preschool levels.
5 Difficulties in locating and trust building among multiproblem families need to be overcome.
6 Information relating to family planning, spacing of children, and maternal care must be disseminated and accepted.

7 Research and development in genetics, nutrition, and family intervention are costly and must be financed.
8 There must be examination, antenatal detection, and abortion coupled with sufficient information for high-risk mothers.

Adequate health care and intervention programs are indeed costly, but such programs are also investments in the future. The author recalls an initial opposition to statewide PKU testing at a cost of $200,000 to $300,000. The objection was that only between one to three such persons might be identified, yet at that time, the average cost of lifetime institutionalization for one person was approximately $200,000.

SUMMING UP

1. The causes of mental retardation are a complex interaction between the biological and environmental.

2. The etiologies of mental retardation can be classified according to the time of onset and the locus of trauma.

3. There is great promise that etiological factors relating to errors of metabolism and genetic transmission will be eventually controlled.

4. The ecologies of mental retardation can be understood as those influences that should serve to activate and stimulate the nervous system *as well as* those influences that promote positive self-concept as a capable person.

5. There is great promise that family-centered intervention during the period of infanthood and toddlerhood can alter adverse patterns of development (chapter 6).

6. The study of cause should lead to humane, considerate patterns of prevention.

7. Intelligence is not a single genetic trait, nor is IQ transmitted like eye color.

8. Intervention efforts must be viewed with a patient time frame. At present, there is not sufficient baseline data to appropriately judge the time span necessary to judge change.

9. One must be alert to advances outside of one's field, as well as within, so that new knowledge can be applied toward prevention.

10. The identification and development of the genetic and birth technologies will have social implications, especially with respect to choices involving life and the quality of life. There is a need to develop a public policy that supports informed choice.

11. School curricula should emphasize preparation for adulthood, including child-rearing practices, nutrition, prenatal care, and personal hygiene. Also, there should be emphasis upon what can be accomplished through prevention.

ON LOCATION

The President's Panel Report (1962, p. 200) quoted its charge from President John F. Kennedy. His remarks convey the spirit of prevention in mental retardation as well as the urgent need for these efforts.

> Much of the world's population still struggles for mere survival; others for domination of the weaker. Our aim is individual and national dignity. Our fortune is scientific and technological ability. Our obligation is to search for the secrets of the human mind and to share our knowledge throughout the world. Discoveries of the wheel, the internal combustion engine, and principles of thermodynamics have liberated mankind from much physical labor. Two hundred years ago man demonstrated through the discoveries of Lavoisier and Harvey that human life is governed by universal physical laws. Major progress in science and medicine can be measured from that date. Until the last two decades, however, little research was concentrated on the nature of the living cell and its reproduction. But great strides have been made in that direction through the understanding of the chemical basis of genes and chromosomes and their governing role in life itself.
>
> The future belongs to those who can forward these achievements. It is now possible to attack the causes and prevention, as well as the treatment of mental retardation. This will require new breakthroughs, but it will pay enormous dividends in knowledge about ourselves, for the function of the brain represents an almost completely uncharted frontier. . . . Exploration and discovery in this field may uncover the secrets of life and man's capacities, and the answers to many mysteries of social behavior. Perhaps even more important, an understanding of the motivation and effect of human behavior offers the hope fostering the rational behavior of nations.

REFERENCES

Bane, M. J., and Jencks, C. Five Myths About Your I.Q. *Harpers*. February 1973, 28–41.

Begab, M. The Major Dilemma of Mental Retardation: Shall We Prevent It? (Some Social Implications of Research in Mental Retardation.) *American Journal of Mental Deficiency*, 1974, 78, 519–529.

Blatt, B. Some Persistently Recurring Assumptions Concerning Education of the Mentally Retarded. *Training School Bulletin*, 1960, 57, 46–59.

Cassidy, V., and Stanton, J. *An Investigation of Factors Involved in the Educational Placement of Mentally Retarded Children*. Columbus: Ohio State University, 1969.

Dunn, L. M. Special Education for the Mildly Retarded — Is Much of It Justifiable? *Exceptional Children,* 1968, 35, 5–22.

Group for the Advancement of Psychiatry. *Mild Mental Retardation, A Growing Challenge to the Physician.* New York: The Group for the Advancement of Psychiatry, 1967.

Heber, R. The Educable Mentally Retarded, in Kirk, S. and Weiner, B. *Behavioral Research on Exceptional Children.* Washington, D.C.: Council for Exceptional Children, 1963.

Hurley, R. *Poverty and Mental Retardation: A Causal Relationship.* New York, Random House, 1969.

Jensen, A. The Differences Are Real. *Psychology Today,* December 1973, 80–86.

Johnson, G. O. Special Education for Mentally Handicapped — a Paradox. *Exceptional Children,* 1962, 19, 62–69.

Kennedy, J. F. Statement by the President Regarding the Need for a National Plan in Mental Retardation, in President's Panel on Mental Retardation, *A Proposed Program for National Action to Combat Mental Retardation.* Washington, D.C.: U.S. Government Printing Office, 1962.

Kirk, S. An Evaluation of the Study of Berardine G. Schmidt, Entitled "Changes in Personal, Social, and Intellectual Behavior of Children Originally Classified as Feebleminded." *Psychological Bulletin,* 1948, 45, 321–333.

Kirk, S. *Educating Exceptional Children.* Boston: Houghton Mifflin, 1962.

Kirk, S., and McCarthy, J. The Illinois Test of Psycholinguistic Abilities: An Approach to Differential Diagnosis. *American Journal of Mental Deficiency,* 1961, 66, 399–412.

Kirk, S. A. *Early Education of the Mentally Retarded.* Urbana: University of Illinois Press, 1958.

Masland, R. Conclusion in *Etiologic Factors in Mental Retardation.* Columbus, Ohio: Ross Laboratories, 1957.

Polonsky, A. Beliefs and Opinions Concerning Mental Deficiency. *American Journal of Mental Deficiency,* 1961, 62, 12–17.

President's Committee on Mental Retardation and the Bureau for the Education of the Handicapped. *The Six Hour Retarded Child.* Washington, D.C.: U.S. Department of Health, Education and Welfare, 1969.

Rice, B. The High Cost of Thinking the Unthinkable. *Psychology Today.* December 1973, 89–93.

Sarason, S. Jewishness, Blackishness, and the Nature-Nurture Controversy. *American Psychologist.* November 1973, 962–971.

Schmidt, B. Changes in Personal, Social, and Intellectual Behavior of Children Originally Classified as Feebleminded. *Psychological Monograph,* 1948, 5, 60.

Skeels, H., and Dye, H. A Study of the Effects of Differential Stimulation on Mentally Retarded Children. *American Journal of Mental Deficiency,* 1939, 44, 114–136.

Smith, R. M. *Clinical Teaching, Methods of Instruction for the Retarded.* New York: McGraw-Hill, 1968.

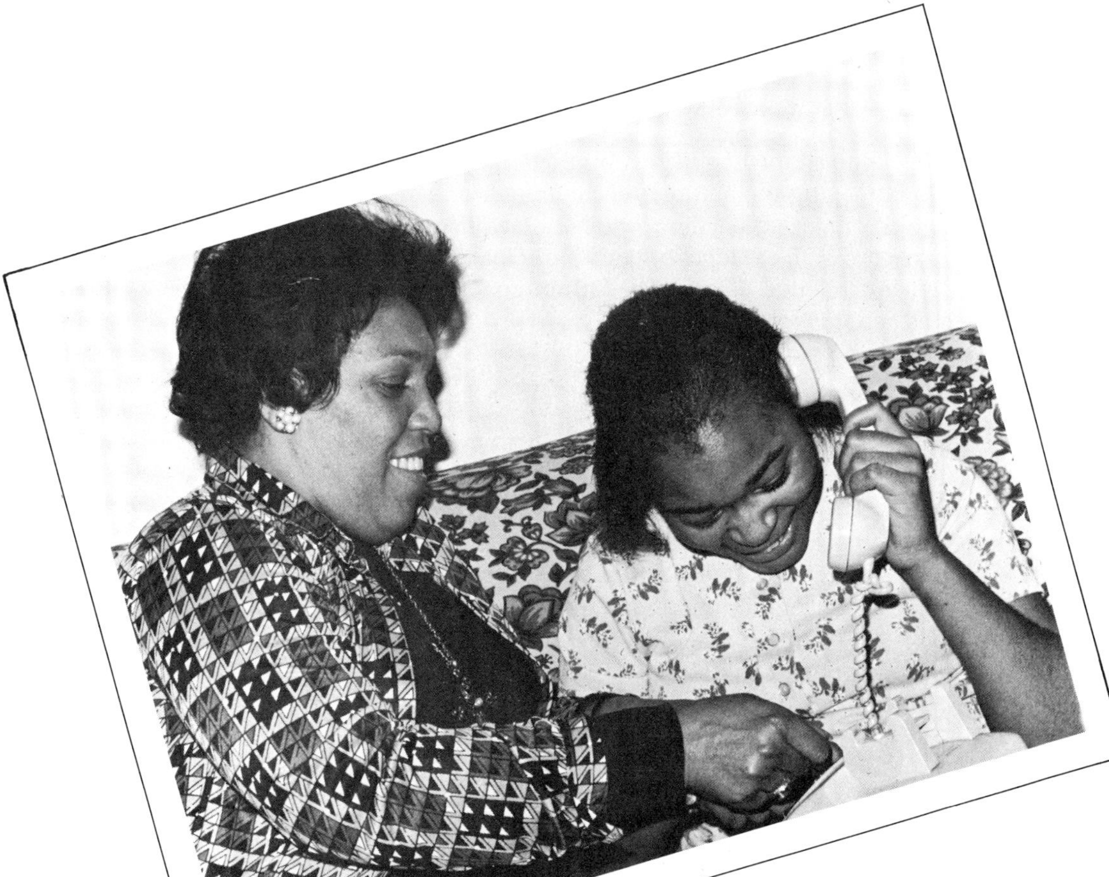

5

Intelligence and Learning

SYNOPSIS

Learning, as an adaptation to environment, has emerged as a primary arena of investigation. Managing the nature and conditions of learning is viewed as a pathway for assisting the retarded person toward the acquisition of skills, knowledges, and attitudes necessary for effective social participation. One must, however, distinguish between intelligence as *measured* through psychometric techniques and intelligence as *development*.

OBJECTIVES

ATTTITUDES

1 To explore the contributions of Bruner, Guilford, and Piaget.
2 To engage in and relate to research studies.
3 To examine teaching preferences in relation to the learning styles of learners.

UNDERSTANDINGS

1 To study Bruner, Guilford, and Piaget and their value as guidelines for developing environments for cognitive development.
2 To view learning as a purposeful act involving three main outcomes.
3 To define prototypes of learning.
4 To summarize variables that affect performance.
5 To distinguish learning and teaching as based upon emotional and sociological correlates.

SKILLS

1 To define variables that describe rate, retention, and transfer of learning.
2 To use psychometric data as an estimate of learning.

3 To formulate guidelines to assess one's own performance in facilitating learning.
4 To identify the applications of teaching-learning principles to instructional/training situations.

THE NATURE OF INTELLIGENCE

Rowland (1972) has related views of intelligence to views of mental retardation. In his opinion, intelligence has evolved from philosophical and speculative study to the level of direct observation and measurement of cognitive abilities. (See the following section.) Rowland observed that intelligence, at least in Western thought, is defined as a *developmental* sequence of increasing complexity of adaptation. All sources — Aristotle, Bruner, or Piaget — agree that intelligence is adaptation and response to environment, and that it is developmental, passing through stages, or levels, of attainment over time.

The *first* level of learning is linked to the environment, which dominates response. "I" is the reference point for learning. The *next* level involves cause-and-effect learnings associated with increasing accuracy of judgment. At this level, the person has a sufficient data base to explore the environment with reasonable safety. At the *third* level, logic emerges. This type of intelligence generates propositions, conclusions, decisions, and statements of the probable and the possible. However, Rowland noted, the most brilliant thinker can be dominated by environment when the milieu either fails to provide stimulation, indoctrinates "ignorant" assumptions, prizes superstition, demands conformity, and/or contains inadequate facilities.

Thinking about mental retardation can reflect the dominance of a limiting environment, according to Rowland. The I-Thou relationship and hypothesis testing about the possible could be considered the most advanced stage of thinking about mental retardation. Thinking about the possible, especially about intelligence, is evident in the field of mental retardation. The concept of cognitive capacity and cognitive competence has been discussed by Bortner and Birch (1970). They emphasized that this distinction has existed since Itard, Seguin, Pinel, and Esquirol. Their distinction is that capacity is the potential, the possible resources of response, while competence is the *current*, available, measurable, and expressed performance. This view has been expressed by Throne (1972) as "predicting versus production." Blatt and Garfunkel (1967) and Ross (1972) illustrate the limitations of a single measure, the IQ, to explain the full range of intelligence. These authors appear to agree with the Jordan (1973) interview of Blatt, who acknowledged that people can change. According to Blatt, the focus should be upon conditions that foster learning. The effect of perspectives, deeds, and approaches is illustrated by the investigation of Balla, Butterfield, and Zigler (1974). This study covered two and a half years and involved four institutions and 103 children. The results indicated that institutionalization is *not* a single treatment, since growth among the residents was independent of size and cost. The Bortner and Birch (1970) discussion confirmed these citations with observations that: measurements are fragmentary indicators of capacity; possessed potentialities flourish under conditions of training and task demands; and facilitation of cognition (i.e., intelligence) will depend upon the ingenuity with which responsive environments are identified and implemented.

Models of Intellectual Development and Cognition

In 1966, the American Association on Mental Deficiency (AAMD) issued a special summary of cognitive models and development in mental retardation. Three models were identified as specially applicable to the study of mental retardation. The purpose of the monograph was to describe applicability of these three models to mental retardation. The Guilford model was discussed by Myers and Dingman (1966). The Piaget model was discussed by Wohlwill (1966). The Bruner model was discussed by Oliver (1966). A summation was presented by Garrison (1966), the editor. These articles possess a certain historical significance: they establish a benchmark by which to gauge the evolution of application to this field; they identify three approaches for consideration; and they suggest formulations for application.

Garrison observed that these systems remain descriptive systems, not necessarily treatment systems. He also recognized the necessity of alternative systems in order to spur further effort. He identified two possible approaches to the study of cognitive development. One line of inquiry is to try to understand the operations and content of mental functioning, including mental retardation. This method seeks an evolutionary view of development. A second effort attempts to understand how and why a person comes to the attention of others. In a sense, to what extent is attention a function of discrepancy in development, a deficit in culturally prized operations, and/or an interaction function? At one level, an understanding of development or evolution of cognition will devise effective diagnostic and prognostic procedures. This understanding of development will also enable the design of optimal conditions for growth. Garrison suggested that both efforts are necessary.

Bruner

Oliver (1966) identified the Bruner concept of *levels of representation* as applicable to the mentally retarded. He believed that techniques can be tailored to individual characteristics. The assumption is that growth is dependent upon the unlocking of capacity by techniques that arise out of the cultural environment. The implication is to deemphasize diagnosis of an "inner-capacity" and to stress the educational nature of environment. Obviously such intervention is to be timed to development.

Levels of representation, described by Oliver, related to four aspects of cognitive development and functioning: the interaction of thought and language, the storing and retrieval of information, the roles of the senses in acquiring information, and the development of complexities of information. These four aspects can be explained by the emergence of competence in *representation* and *integration*. The former describes ways of coding and processing past information. The latter describes techniques of organizing separate sets of information into increasingly complex problem-solving efforts. Techniques are viewed in terms of the efficiency and success of the environment, not as inner structures.

Representation, according to Oliver, is not a narrow view of memory. Representation is the storage *and* retrieval of relevant (needed and useful) information in usable form. This process exists at three levels: *enactive, iconic,* and *symbolic*. Enactive representation describes events and objects as coded by motor actions. At this level, the person can offer a gesture display of a word although unable to speak. One observes in children a higher stage of receptive understanding than of encoding or verbal expression. In iconic representation, the person utilizes images as the basis for response. Recall and/or recognition involves the association of image and symbol-image. The symbolic level involves arbitrary symbols to represent previous associations of images and actions. At this level, for example, the symbol *Kalamazoo* does not at all resemble the city-county it represents or describes. The emerging child has learned to assemble significant clusters of data around this symbol. Representations are viewed as chained into increasing complexities, from enactive through symbolic. Integration describes the strategies or rules for relating various representations.

The work of Bruner was cited by Sattler (1974) as having made at least three contributions: measurement of infants' intelligence, an objective-based challenge to deficit theory, and encouragement of an educational model based upon motivation of the child to transfer skills already known to skills or tasks at hand rather than imposing "new" intellectual structures.

Guilford

In 1966, Myers and Dingman identified five potential contributions of Guilford to the field of mental retardation. One was the reduction of redundancy of testing for ability factors so as to isolate common factors. Second, progress could be made in the comparative assessment of retarded and normal persons to establish or direct goals for prevention and intervention. Third, Guilford showed that the elements of intellect need to be understood so that differentiation of abilities can be understood. A fourth matter involved the development of instrumentation to guide new program practices. Finally, the developmental emergence of abilities can be understood.

The Myers and Dingman summary of the Guilford approach reflects a disposition toward understanding human intelligence as a set of abilities rather than as a single unitary factor. These abilities, as identified by Guilford, allow for classification of adaptive responding. IQ tests may be an appropriate *sampling* of behaviors, but they do not describe the underlying process accounting for adaptation. Guilford's elements of intelligence can be viewed as descriptive of *five* operations, *six* products, and *four* contents, for a total 120 separable factors. The Guilford model was devised to account for adult behavior with about half these abilities fully identified in childhood.

Myers and Dingman emphasize that the model is an interaction of *operations* times *products* times *content*. Operations have reference to what the person *does* to information. Products are descriptive of forms or *types of information*. Contents is a term used to describe the *elements* of information.

The *content* of information can be understood as involving elements of figural — sensory data organized around images; symbolic — signs and sounds with limited meanings; semantic — the use of words and language; and behavioral — verbal or nonverbal information which is the basis for empathy. One observes an ordering in this description.

Products were described by Myers and Dingman in a presumed order of least complex to most complex. These products were said to include: units — response related to "things" and attention to surface, obvious details; classes — grouping of items according to a common property; relations — the ordering of data by reference to classes; systems — descriptive of an organized mode for grouping which reflects a communicable logic; transformations — changing known data in forms appropriate for use, a preemergence of problem solving; and implications — interpretation of information necessary for such acts as predicting, consequence testing, cause and effect, and other forms of inference.

The notion of *operations* for Myers and Dingman constitutes a valued locus of interest. Operations are viewed as: memory — retention in relation to the conditions under which information was learned; cognition — discovery, awareness, etc. in acts of comprehension and understanding; divergent thinking — responding to a given object, fact or event and generating varieties of possibilities; convergent thinking — generating from varied data an outcome judged as reasonable; and evaluation — judgment and selection from alternatives and consequences according to pragmatic or idealistic criteria.

Convergent and divergent thinking are sometimes grouped under the general heading of *productive thinking*. Evaluation, especially for personal/social situations, was described as the most complex operation of the five. It was inferred by these authors in reference to development that memory and cognition precede other operations; figural content precedes semantic and behavioral content; symbolic content emerges last; and unit-class products emerge first, with transformations and implications being the most mature.

Some positive examples of the application of Guilford's work might be the teaching of evaluation of judgment skills, especially social judgment (Kubena, 1971); facilitation of productive thinking skills (Tisdall, 1962); facilitation of the transfer of convergent thinking beyond the immediate training situation (Kolstoe and Hirsch, 1974); and analysis of instructional materials with reference to their properties of operations, products, and contents (Brown, 1974).

Piaget

The *direct* application of Piaget's work to mental retardation, according to Wohlwill, has centered around four processes: acquisition of skills and/or concepts that fulfill biological drives toward equilibrium; the abilities of concrete operations; consequences of developmental lag (discrepancy between performance and expectations); and identification of the nature of cognitive functioning of the mentally retarded.

Cognitive development is the maintenance of balance between the internal and the external world of the person. Cognition (the product of development) emerges in an invariant sequence according to developmental laws that have been identified. These "laws" identify successive stages of complexity. These stages can be defined as a minimum of three to five depending upon the interpretation of Piaget and one's own interpretation of research. Consequently, there may be said to be a minimum of three stages of cognitive development in a sequence of sensory-motor, concrete operations, and formal operations. Various interpretations place a transitional period between sensory-motor and concrete; within concrete operations; or between concrete and formal operations.

Piagetian specialists, including Wohlwill, cite the concept of stage as crucial to an understanding of cognitive development. The precision of Piagetian language can interfere with understanding, Wohlwill noted, since one must unlearn old meanings for terms in order to replace them with new ones. A stage describes a period for formulation of *structures*. Such structures are starting points for later structures, which are the basis for identifying stages. Structures are mental processes, observed as characteristic behaviors. A stage, according to Wohlwill, is characterized by five criteria: its sequence is invariant; prestructures are incorporated into new structures; behavior (adaptation) is consolidation and preparation; a framework of integrated behaviors emerges: and there is stable equilibrium prior to preparation and after consolidation. Strictly speaking, stages are not age specific. As will be seen in the subsequent chapter on maturation, emergence is at an individual rate, while sequence is applicable and descriptive of the human condition.

The first stage is usually viewed as lasting from birth until between age eighteen months to twenty-four months. It is termed the *sensory-motor stage*. This period is dominated by movement from simple reflexive responses to coordinating reflexes into simple causality and into intentional patterns associated with the initial appearance of language. The *concrete operations* stage emerges from around age two to about ages seven to nine, although full elaboration is usually acquired by ages eleven to twelve. In this period one's reactions are dominated by immediate experience, especially perceptual interpretation. This stage can be described by progression of irreversible thought to reversible thought. For example, a child will divide a lump of clay into two equal parts. One part will be divided into a long, narrow sausage shape and the other will be formed into a small ball. Typically, the child will label the ball as having less clay. The same response pattern is also observed in pouring equal amounts of water into a tall, narrow glass and a wide, short glass. At the conclusion of this period one is able to anticipate the results, even though his or her concrete sensory perceptual input might deny the direct evidence. The period of *formal operations* emerges at adolescence. It is characterized by reference to systematic hypothesis testing, "rules" of logic, and the use of symbols to represent ideas, processes, etc.

Stephens (1971) updated the Wohlwill presentation. It would appear that current informed opinion identifies four stages. These would be described as sensory-motor, preoperation, concrete, and formal. Based upon research and observation, the *preoperation* stage has emerged as consistent with the Wohlwill criteria. This stage, as described by Stephens, usually emerges at age two to four and extends to about age seven. This period can be described by characteristic behaviors. One is termed *preconceptual* (descriptive of ages two to four), and the other is termed *intuitive* (descriptive of ages four to seven). At the preconceptual level, speech emerges as a reference point for images and information. The reference point for reasoning is one's self, described as egocentric. Attention is given to surface details. As Stephens observed, a white piece of chalk is treated as similar to a cigarette. This primitive reasoning is termed *transductive,* neither inductive, nor deductive. Intuitive thinking is characterized by elaboration of language to process information. Inferences about quantity are drawn from physical properties rather than by the use of logic. Egocentricity is still evident.

For specialists in mental retardation, the conception of these various stages possess great utility. The sensory-motor period identifies fundamental operations for curriculum for the severely retarded. Preoperation has its greatest potential for preschool programming. Concrete operation offers a data base for mastery of school tasks.

Another contribution to mental retardation, according to Wohlwill, has been the concept of equilibrium, which is the balance between *assimilation* and *accommodation*. This balance is between one's internal scheme and environmental events. The person organizes thought into a structure called a *scheme*. A learned scheme represents one's internal stability. Changing environment *and* increasing physical-neurological complexity requires continuing reevaluation of new information sources. Assimilation describes the impact of new data upon old scheme. Accommodation is the internalized process of rearranging these data into perceptions and conceptions of reality. The equilibrium between assimilation and accommodation is the Piagetian concept of *adaptation*. The stages of development can be characterized by the relative dominance of assimilation and accommodation at younger ages, while the adaptation is more evident in formal operations. It is to be noted that adaptation is a *lifelong* process. It should also be noted that adaptation is compatible with contemporary theories of adjustment, which emphasize motivation/need as the reduction of tension between internal and external demands.

Piaget's theory and worldwide research is not confined to cognition and language acquisition. One *principal* contribution of Piagetian concepts in the United States has been in the area of what is labeled *moral development*. The development of conscience, of empathy, and of sensitivity to the needs of others follows the principles of evolutionary stages.

There have been numerous recommendations regarding the application of Piaget's work to the field of mental retardation. Some representative examples include *at least:*

1 Arrangement of Piagetian-related school tasks which involve conservation and logic with reference to mental age, as reflected by the WISC (Stephens, Manhaney, and McLaughlin, 1972).
2 Use of the equilibrium model for understanding thought processes underlying mental retardation in comparison to behavior disorders (Schmid-Kitsikis, 1973).
3 Teaching mathematical skills to the moderately retarded based upon a Piagetian defined sequence and involving nonverbal aspects of concrete operations (Kiraly and Morishima, 1971).
4 Development of spatial directions and spatial orientation skills (Kershner, 1973).
5 Identification of prerequisites of expressive language for the profoundly retarded (Kahn, 1975).
6 Development of measurement of Piagetian scales appropriate for the severely and profoundly retarded (Silverstein, Brownlee, Hubbell, and McClain, 1975).

7 Understanding of the relative and differential effects of mental age and chronological age upon acquisition of Piagetian rules of logic (Cherkes, 1975).
8 Predicting arithmetic achievement by reference to Piagetian tasks (Melnick, Bernstein, and Lehrer, 1974).
9 Statement of goals and sequence of goals based upon stages (Kaya, 1961).

Commentary

Explanations of the nature of human intelligence and its developmental sequence are of interest to practitioners in mental retardation. This interest is multifaceted. Regardless of theoretical position, describing the boundaries of intellectual function may expand our present views and our view of the mentally retarded. At present these theories have a certain influence in: language orientation, emphasis on early childhood programming, rediscovery of the sensory perceptual processes of learning, and the elaboration of learning theory.

The following section presents a psychometric view of intelligence. At present it is this view which is implied in the AAMD definition of intelligence.

MEASURED INTELLIGENCE

Concepts Related to Measurement of Intelligence

McLaughlin, Hinojosa, and Trlica (1973) found 23 concepts to be the most frequently used in the literature of mental retardation (table 5–1). The terms have been rearranged in increasing order of difficulty. The first seven items were passed by a sample of 122 students in special education. Two terms, standard deviation (SD) and percentile, were of middle difficulty for the group. The remaining fourteen concepts reflected difficulty extremes of 51 percent failing the item, level of significance, to 94 percent failure for r_{rho}. The most commonly found percentage for failure on these items was in the 70s to 80s. McLaughlin et al. speculated that noncomprehension of these terms would interfere with the practitioner's role as consumer of research and measurement data. English and English (1965) were cited as sources for the definitions. In this table we will adopt that source and the references for the remainder of this section for the functional definition sources.

These twenty-three items do identify the *logic* of both measurement and learning research. This logic is the scientific basis for the measurement of human abilities. Procedures of data collection and analysis must establish *validity* and *reliability*.

Table 5–1 MOST FREQUENTLY ENCOUNTERED MEASUREMENT CONCEPTS

Term	*Use*	*Functional Definition*
1. Median	Descriptive-summative	That score which has exactly half the cases below it and half the cases above. Also the 50th percentile. Symbolized as Mdn.
2. Range	Descriptive-variation	A statistical concept. The result of subtracting the lowest score from the highest score. Gross descriptor of variability. Appropriate as estimate. Standard deviation is usually preferred.
3. Hypothesis	A statement to be proven	In statistical terms a statement to be proven by reference to levels of significance. The practice is to state a null hypothesis, that is, to state there is no difference. If there is level of significance, one rejects the null and "accepts" the initial hypothesis.
4. Mean	Descriptive-summative	Unless qualified, refers to statistical or arithmetical mean. Expressed as M or X. Calculated by adding all scores and dividing by the number of persons.
5. Correlation	Association	Not cause and effect. Tests if two traits are so related so that change in one is related to change in another. Expressed as percent with range from −.99 to +.99. Negative and positive is not good or bad, only direction of relationship. Unless otherwise specified, refers to Pearson Product approach.
6. Validity	An approach to accuracy of measurement	Relates to the extent a test measures what it claims to measure. In testing, this involves some procedures that are correlation and some that are analysis of variance. See discussion in text.
7. Reliability	An approach to stability of measurement	In testing, the property of a test which describes its stability, consistency, trustworthiness, and/or accuracy. Usually involves correlation analysis. See discussion in text.
8. Standard deviation	Descriptive-variation	Expressed as SD. Relates to position in relation to the mean of a distribution. Ranges from 0.00 to plus scores and from 0.00 to minus scores. Usually one speaks of one, two, and three SDs. Between +1 and −1 will contain 68 % of cases; −2 SD is 13 % and within +2 is 13 %. SD of 3 (+ or −) is 3 % each for "normal" distribution.

Table 5–1 (continued)

Term	*Use*	*Functional Definition*
9. Percentile	Descriptive-variation	Can be from one to 99. Describes a position on a distribution of ranked scores. Scores are correlated from low to high. If 30 persons take a test and one's score is the 10th highest, the percentile would be 20 divided by 30, or a percentile of 66. This means that the score would be 66 % better than most and only be exceeded by 33 % of the group.
10. Level of significance	Inference about results	A statistical concept. Describes a result as different from chance results. In behavioral sciences significance is set .05, .01, and .001. A .05 result functionally means that there are only 5 chances in 100 of being in error. A .01 means 1 chance in 100 of being in error.
11. $P < .05$ $P < .01$	Symbols for significance	P is a symbol for probability. The .05 and .01 describe level of significance. The remaining symbol is "less than"; reversed it would be "greater than."
12. Mode	Descriptive-summative	The most frequent score in a distribution. Of all the scores, the most popular one.
13. Analysis of variance	Comparison of differences	A statistical method used to assess difference between three or more groups on a dependent variable. Uses the F test, sometimes termed ANOVA. Can be used for two-group comparisons, but usually the t test is used. Can be separate groups or same people tested pre vs. post.
14. N	A symbol for the number of persons, items in a study	The total number of cases in a study; N usually describes the number within a subgroup.
15. F	The symbol for significance of analysis of variance	The symbol for the F test or analysis of variance. Relates to number obtained by the analysis of variance (ANOVA) which determines significance. In rare circumstances, describes frequencies.
16. Covariance	Related to techniques of comparison of differences	In comparison of two groups, tests differences between groups. To focus upon differences, a third is controlled so that the variable under focus can be fully understood. It controls effect of third variable.

Table 5–1 (continued)

Term	*Use*	*Functional Definition*
17. df	A basis of judging significance	Symbol for degrees of freedom. Relates to restrictions of sampling in that statistical tests are based on the number in a sample minus one.
18. r	A symbol for correlation	May be expressed as r_{xy} to relationship between variable x and variable y. Unless otherwise noted, relates to Pearson Product correlation.
19. Regression	Related to procedures of association	Describes the tendency of scores on a post to return to the mean of the sample. Based upon correlation techniques to enhance prediction about the future in probable, not real, attainments.
20. r_{rho}	A correlation technique	Sometimes expressed rho or Spearman rho. A measurement of correlation based upon raw scores converted into ranks. Assesses the correlation for ranked data.
21. Factor analysis	A technique for association	A statistical procedure involving correlation. Usually test scores from different tests are compared against one another to isolate a common trait or traits said to be the factor. Subtests may also be analyzed to make sure each test measures a separate trait.
22. Interaction	A concept used in ANOVA related to comparison of differences	A statistical concept. A reciprocal effect between two or more variables or treatments. Describes a change beyond chance variation. In a study a factor x and factor y may not be significant, but the effect of both produce a change, result of interest.
23. Chi-square	Can be used for differences or association problems	Expressed as ^{2}. A statistical test based upon categories rather than pure numbers. Can test differences between categories or can be a test of relationship between categories. Used in testing position above and below median. Describes results as different from chance.

Any number of texts are available on the logic and procedures of test development. The purpose of the following discussion is to convey a sense of the time, effort, expense, caution, and extensiveness that undergirds test construction in order for the reader to formulate a personalized criteria for the selection of test instruments. The topic of measurement of human abilities has been approached from perspectives of: assessment by application of scientific procedures (Aiken, 1976); assessment of theoretical constructs (Sattler, 1974); relationship to exceptional learners (Gearheart and Whillenberg, 1970); and the relationship to mental retardation (Hutt and Gibby, 1976).

The general notion of *validity* relates to a "truth" question, or the extent to which a test measures what it purports to measure, relates to the population for which it is intended, and is relevant to situations or task demands.

Validity is judged in four ways. *Construct* validity is inferred by the content of a test in relation to a description of its intended use. *Content* validity is inferred by

Table 5–2 REPRESENTATIVE TASKS OF THE STANFORD-BINET—1960

Age Groupings	*Sample Tasks*	*Guilford Operation*
Two to four	Identifying parts of the body	cognition
	Repeating two digits	memory
	Copying a circle	convergent
	Sorting buttons	convergent
	Identifying picture similarities and differences	cognition and evaluation
Five to seven	Folding paper triangle	cognition and convergent
	Copying diamond	evaluation and convergent
	Maze tracing	cognition
	Similarities—two things	cognition
	Repeating five digits	memory
Eight to ten	Naming the days of the week	memory
	Memory for designs	memory
	Paper cutting	cognition and evaluation
	Block counting	cognition, convergent, divergent
	Repeating six digits	memory
Twelve to fourteen	Picture absurdities	evaluation
	Repeating five digits reversed	memory
	Memory for sentences—level III	memory
	Copying bead chain from memory	memory and convergent
	Reconciliation of opposites	convergent

reference to the appropriateness of items to a given construct and also relates to appropriate styles of measurement. For example, content validity may be inferred if a group of experts in a field agree that test items do measure that skill or knowledge. By contrast, construct validity is inferred if the test is a reasonable (from its author's documentation) measure of that skill or knowledge related to theoretical constructs. *Concurrent* validity is a statistical examination of the relationship/correlation between scores on the test under consideration and the scores obtained on an existing test of known merit. Usually, the same persons take the two tests and scores are compared. The new test is said to be valid if it measures a common factor. *Predictive* validity describes procedures designed to assess the extent to which a test has prognostic utility. Common approaches involve: obtaining test scores in the present and obtaining evidence as to subsequent success-failure, and identifying competent versus noncompetent groups to compare on the test. In this latter situation, scores on the test should discriminate between successful, more expert persons and the less successful, less expert. The usual sequence in validation would be for the developers to define and document the constructs, identify content of items and styles of measurement, conduct concurrent studies, and establish utility as to predictiveness, especially accuracy. All four steps are the hallmark of quality in test development.

A parallel concern of the test developer is the *reliability* of a test. Does the test yield scores that are either "free" of error or that allow for known error, and does it possess items that contribute to the overall score. The inference of reliability involves consistency of results.

There are four main procedures for determining reliability. *Item analysis* is the statistical assessment of the correlation of *each* item to the total test. Items are retained or excluded on the basis of their contribution. *Split half* methods involve computing a score for odd-numbered items and for even-numbered items. Correlation between the two scores is said to signify consistency. *Test-retest* procedures involve administering the test at one point in time and after a minimal interval of two to four weeks engaging in a second testing. Consistency is inferred if there is a high correlation between scores of the two testings. In order to minimize the effects of test wisdom acquired through exposure, reliability of measurement can be increased if there are *alternate forms* available. Two or more forms should follow the process of validation.

Information gained from tests and testing is usually summarized in numerical forms and supplemented by narrative interpretation unique to the person. There are concepts that assist this summarization. A person's performance can be compared to norms judged appropriate for the purpose for which the test was designed. The *mean* serves as a reference point for an *initial* evaluation. The *standard deviation* serves as another reference point; a given score will fall in some range away from the mean in high or low directions. Since a standard deviation is not always of great communication value, concepts such as the *percentile* are helpful to express the person's standing; his or her score represents a point at which x percent of a comparable population fall above and y percent fall below. Measures other than percentiles have their advocates. The *standard error of measurement* is another significant factor for the consumer and users of testing. In general terms, this describes the degree to which an obtained score is a true score. Thus, in reality, an IQ is not really *a* score but a range. For example, if the error term in a hypothetical test is 10, then an obtained score of 69 *would* range from 59 to 79. Different variables affect error, even for the same test. For example, a decrease in known error in test manuals occurs with increasing age. The concept of standard error applies only to the statistical standardization of the test. Examiner competence, testing situation, rapport, motivation of the examinee, etc. can alter the error of the test beyond its statistically known limits (table 5–3).

An approach to reduction of error has been the emergence of *deviation* scores to replace *ratio* scores. For example, IQ was usually computed as a ratio between mental age (MA) divided by chronological age (CA). While this procedure has had

Table 5–3 COMPARISON OF SUBTEST STRUCTURES OF THE WECHSLER PROCEDURES

Subtest Name	*WAIS*	*WISC-R*	*WPPSI*
Information	V	V	V
Comprehension	V	V	V
Arithmetic	V	V	V
Similarities	V	V	V
Vocabulary	V	V	V
Block Design	P	P	P
Object Assembly	P	P	—
Picture Completion	P	P	P
Digit Span	V	(V)	—
Digit Symbol	P	—	—
Picture Arrangement	P	P	—
Coding	—	P	—
Mazes	—	(P)	P
Animal House	—	—	P
Animal House Retest	—	—	(P)
Geometric Design	—	—	P
Sentences	—	—	(V)

— = Not present V = Verbal
P = Performance ( ) = Supplementary test

its utility, it is subject to computational error, and increasing age of the person results in questionable results. The deviation IQ, by contrast, involves converting a raw score to a fixed distribution with a mean of 100 and a standard deviation, 16, for example, on the Stanford-Binet and 15 for the Wechsler tests. Increasingly, test companies are including deviation score tables to avoid the problems of error associated with ratio approaches.

Psychometric Models

It will be recalled from chapter 1 that the AAMD definition included measured intelligence as one of two criteria for defining mental retardation. The measurement, assessment, and diagnosis of intellectual functioning is termed *psychometrics*. This technique is predicated upon the belief that through observation and validation, samples of human behavior can be isolated. These isolated samples can form a reliable picture of a person's present competence and future potential.

In the United States, according to Sattler (1974), a psychometric model of intelligence clusters around the measurement themes of the Stanford-Binet or Wechsler approaches. This has come about because subsequent testing procedures are compared against either of these two approaches as an index of validity. Consequently, Sattler concluded that other testing procedures are approximations of these two approaches. In general, the cognitive content of these two approaches has possessed a certain utility in predicting school achievement, although these models also reflect a certain vulnerability. Psychometrics reflect a premise that qualitative impressions can be supplemented by numerical data for convenience of communication. The use of numerical summation is based upon the concept of mental age and an index of functioning expressed as intelligence quotient. MA is a present-oriented measure, while IQ is an estimate about the future.

Sattler concluded, after a review of the literature, that the cognitive functions underlying the obtained IQ have both limitations and advantages. Their limitations may be any one or several of the following: (1) errors in predicting job success, (2) errors in predicting nonacademic skills, (3) errors in assessment of innate potential, (4) undue emphasis upon product rather than process, (5) penalizing of unconventional responses, and (6) inaccurate long-range predictions. The use of psychometrics (the Stanford-Binet or Wechsler approaches) may have merit with respect to: (1) demonstrable correlation with known school tasks, (2) suggesting initial reference points for intervention, (3) yielding inferences about environmental effects, (4) rendering a positive view of capacities and abilities, and (5) contributing insight about a person in the context of other relevant data.

This section will describe what is known and understood about the Stanford-Binet and Wechsler approaches. The source of understanding the cognitive properties of these approaches is founded upon the assumptions of factor analysis. Although sophisticated in nature, this technique has its limitations, for the analysis is always tied to results of the population sample. For this reason, results vary from investigation to investigation.

The Stanford-Binet

The Stanford-Binet (S-B) procedure views cognitive functioning as "g" trait with universal applicability. Aiken (1976) estimates the correlation between S-B results and school performance as between .40 to .75, which is moderate, but may be more accurate than subjective human judgments.

Sattler (1974) has summarized the available literature regarding factor analysis of the S-B, 1960 version. He cautioned that the g factor underlying the construction and refinement of the S-B rather defies factor analysis. Furthermore, one should recognize the age construct of this scale; items vary as to content and response mode depending on the age level assessed. With these points considered, Sattler noted that studies generally find a factor loading around verbal fluency and reasoning at upper age levels and more diverseness at lower age levels. Specific factors associated with the S-B are said by Sattler to include:

1 *language* (vocabulary recognition and definition plus reasoning);
2 *conceptual thinking* (classifying, "as if" responses, and categorical thinking);
3 *memory* (rote and attention span);
4 *reasoning* (absurdities of logic and relationships);
5 *numerical reasoning* (generalization from numerical data);
6 *visual motor* (dexterity, coordination, and imagery);
7 *social intelligence* (while interrelated to reasoning, this factor involves maturity and judgment).

Guilford's constructs may be found in the S-B, according to Sattler. By percentage, the Guilford operations may be said to include: cognition (37), convergent thinking (23), memory (16), evaluation (15), and divergent thinking (9).

Wechsler Approaches

Aiken outlined the three Wechsler procedures as the Wechsler Adult Intelligence Scale (WAIS), the Wechsler Intelligence Scale for Children — Revised (WISC-R), and the Wechsler Preschool and Primary Scale of Intelligence (WPPSI). Age ranges for these scales were described as sixteen years plus for the WAIS, between six to sixteen for the WISC-R, and age four and a half to six for the WPPSI. All three Wechsler procedures are founded upon a similar factor concept and approach to measurement based upon verbal and performance criteria. All three procedures can yield a verbal IQ, a separate performance IQ, and a combined full-scale IQ.

The most salient factor loadings of the WPPSI were for visual perception, with a more modest loading for motor perception. Although the WPPSI has two scales, investigation reflects a high similarity between them. With reference to Guilford's model, *cognition* is the most frequent factor, while *memory, divergent thinking,* and *evaluation* are present only half as much.

By its very age grouping, the WISC-R has been the most widely reported in the mental retardation literature. Both Sattler (1974) and Aiken (1976) agree that the WISC-R is a convenient reference point for understanding the Wechsler procedures. Factor loadings should be interpreted cautiously, given the wide age spread of the scale. In general, five primary factors have emerged:

1 *verbal comprehension I,* verbal knowledge imparted or transmitted by education;
2 *perceptual organization,* visual perception against a time limit;
3 *freedom from distractability,* an attention, or attending factor;
4 *verbal comprehension II,* a factor involving judgment for new situations;
5 a factor labeled *quasi-specific,* which appears to be an undifferentiated cluster.

Cognition, convergent thinking, and memory are the principal Guilford operations.

According to Aiken, the WAIS scale has properties similar to that of the WISC-R. In very general terms, the WAIS does distinguish between verbal loadings and performance loadings. Certain verbal subtests, however, and certain performance subtests load on a general verbal factor, and the same is true for the performance factor. The WAIS will usually reflect higher functioning for mentally retarded adults than the S-B, while the reverse is true for the mentally advanced.

Anatomy of Intelligence Tests

Sattler and Aiken have described the items and tests of the S-B. Table 5–2 is an adaptation of their discussions. Items within Piagetian stages, representative of school tasks and illustrative of Guilford operations, were selected. The labeling of a task with respect to Guilford is attributed to Sattler.

Wechsler Procedures

The structure of the Wechsler procedures as identified by both Aiken and Sattler is summarized in table 5–3. This illustrates the areas of comparability and areas of emphasis among the three procedures.

Consumer Concerns

The primary concerns of consumers of testing services are: predictions about behavior, psychometrics and vocation decisions, group procedures, and information helpful to parents.

Predictions about Behavior

Klein (1972A), as well as Sattler, observed that the competence of the psychologists and the use of comprehensive data to develop a plan will increase accuracy more than a particular testing procedure or approach. Sattler and Aiken described the potential of Wechsler procedures to identify "evidence" of organic brain damage and "evidence" of behavior disorders. This identification is different for age groups and is *not* the difference between verbal IQ and performance IQ. Rather, it is a known pattern of certain verbal and performance subtests as against other patterns.

The utility of psychometric procedures in prediction remains an essential question, especially in the prediction of adaptive behavior. Advocates of caution in overreliance on a single test score tend to be deeply committed to S-B and Wechsler procedures. These same persons tend to be the strongest proponents of study and inquiry beyond the test profile. Some partial illustrations of the wisdom of analysis beyond the protocol results of a mentally retarded person can be illustrated.

1. Ambiguity of procedures to predict subsequent school achievement of minority group children exists, although they are adequate for nonminority children. With both groups, combined predictive validity increases (Goldman and Hartig, 1976); (Schwartz and Cook, 1971); and (Matheny, 1971).

2. The composition of items passed to achieve a MA may be different for retarded and normal persons. Thus, a retarded person and a normal person may have an equal MA, but owing to *scatter* effects (the differences between basal age and ceiling age is based upon items passed), retarded persons pass more concrete-type items. Consequently, the MA of the retarded may be different in composition than that of the normal person (Achenbach, 1971 and 1970).

3. Differentiation between able readers who are mildly retarded and nonachieving readers of equated intellectual range has low validity based upon scatter profiles, even though when normal high ability and low achievers are pooled the same results are obtained (Ramanauskus and Burrow, 1973) and (Black, 1971).

Psychometrics and Vocational Decisions

Wesman (1956) notes that any test can be misused and misinterpreted, although intelligence tests have a higher probability than most. He suggests that test selection should center around two questions: What inferences do I want/need to make? What information do I need to make those inferences?

Doppelt and Bennett (1967) have compared the pros and cons of the use of testing of vocational aptitude among disadvantaged groups. The arguments against testing are usually: anxiety in the testing situation, improper interpretation of test norms (given that the standardization sample is usually not disadvantaged), and lack of relevance of test items to job tasks. The authors acknowledged a certain validity of these criticisms, and they also point out that tests and testing reflect and register the consequences of disadvantagement.

From a *vocational* perspective, Doppelt and Bennett suggested four modifications in test administration and use. For the relief of *anxiety,* these specialists recommend that there should be practice and orientation sessions to reduce fear of the unknown. They see this as more effective than allowing continuous retakes. They suggest that any test will reflect a culture-laden factor because job performance exists in a given culture. They conclude that testing for vocational purposes should be "criterion-related" to the job. Thus, the content of test items must demonstrate suitability for job performance. Interpretation of *norms* suggest that certain items in any given test may have more weight in prediction of job success than others. Consequently, a weighting system might be helpful. *Appropriateness* of use of test scores was also considered from two vantage points. One was that of an employer seeking applicants with a view to future promotion to more complex jobs. A complex test battery could be defended on the basis of selection of the person(s) most likely to succeed. However, these authors also note that actual on-the-job training is a type of test as well. Skills and knowledges can be imparted to motivated people. These authors recommend and encourage this process. Testing and training are viewed as basic to assist employers (and presumably vocational preparation specialists) to select the best possible workers.

Group Procedures

Kopatic, Canale, and Kopatic (1972) assessed group tests of intelligence, individual tests of intelligence, and measures of academic achievement. Their test batteries utilized the Otis Alpha and Beta Tests of Intelligence, the California Test of Mental Maturity, the WISC, the Stanford Achievement Test, and the Raven Coloured Progressive Matrices. Data from these tests were compared over a two-to-three-year longitudinal period. The study was based on the hypothesis that the test makers' claims of validity and reliability will not hold up when applied in the schools. This hypothesis was supported by comparison of Otis performance from second grade to fourth grade and CTMM from third grade to fifth grade. Fifty percent of those tested reflected stability of IQ, while 33 percent "changed" one full standard deviation, and 11 percent reflected two. Correlations among tests of intelligence and achievement were found to be substantially lower than in test manuals. The findings of these authors can be summarized:

1. Group intelligence tests do not show the same validities and reliabilities in manuals when administered in the schools. This discrepancy can be accounted for, in this study, by student motivation, difficulties with the English language for rural children, and poor reading ability. Subtests also may not be consistent or equally difficult, and the time span between tests may be so long that children lose the "set" for responding to tests.

2. Teacher and administrator variables, in all likelihood, constitute a factor. The most frequent factor was the teachers unevenness in training, administration, and scoring. Mistakes of adding points were common. Using MA scores as IQ scores, giving assistance to the child during the test, and giving directions over the school intercom were observed, although not common.

The authors advocated that test companies should supply trained psychometricians to administer tests; or the state department of education should provide this service; or teachers should be certified to administer test instruments. There were additional recommendations for: feedback to companies concerning the performance of their tests; selection of tests in accordance with school goals as well as school conditions, especially teacher attitude toward testing and pupil characteristics; and expansion of test content beyond numerical and visual symbols.

These researchers concluded that test makers are not deceptive, but erroneously assume that the testing conditions present in the standardization process are present in the testing situation. Where this is not the case, interpretation of results will be imprecise at best and unjust at worst. Also, group tests are a global measure of performance, which must be supplemented by classroom observation. Their finding was that the test score was taken as the estimate of actual performance. As one example, one boy was found to be illiterate, although his score reflected fifth-grade achievement based upon a personalized design pattern for his answer sheet. The consistent theme of these authors was not to abandon testing, but to supplement group results with individualized observation and testing. Test content was not defended; the use of a group procedure to yield judgments about an individual was questioned. One can only speculate about the propriety of assigning children to various tracking systems on the basis of group tests alone, and also question the ethics of maintaining tracks without periodic assessment of pupils.

LEARNING ABOUT LEARNING

Perspectives

Bayles (1960) offered a *philosophical* perspective regarding learning which can be related to practice. After a review of research, Bayles contrasts the role of the teacher and the role of the learner, and emphasizes that both elements must be considered by practitioners. The premise of the Bayles analysis is that human beings behave for basically rational and predictable *reasons*.

Learning variables were identified as those conditions and circumstances that the learner utilizes to change behavior. Teaching is viewed by Bayles as the actions of the responsible adult to achieve *transfer of learning* by the learner. He suggested that acquisition is not sufficient; there must be the application of learnings.

Learning, according to Bayles, involves three conditions: goals, insight, and confronting situations. Teaching involves three parallel actions: an opportunity, a sense of opportunity, and a disposition to make use of opportunity.

Goals describe the aspirations and motives that impel a person to take or not take an action. *Insight* relates to the skills and knowledges to approach-avoid goals. *Confronting situation* involves the physical and psychological environments that possess facilitating influences or obstacles. Concerns with learning would require assessment of these three components. Transfer requires certain actions by the teacher. *Opportunity to transfer* suggests that the teacher creates the appropriate confronting situation for application. The *sense of opportunity* involves the direct utilization of insights and skills within the confronting situation. Finally, *disposition to respond* involves the recognition that responding is compatible with one's own personal motives.

A more purely *psychological* viewpoint is that of Gagne (1965), who has offered a historical perspective concerning American views of learning. His perspective coincides with prevailing opinion of learning as a behavioral change resulting from practice and instruction. The Gagne contribution applies to the identification of types of learning and the arrangement of these types along a logical continuum. He suggests that his perspective has several implications for practice.

1. Identification of the *conditions of learning* is concerned with the *internal* factors the learner possesses. These involve *prior capabilities* (previous experience) and *initial capabilities* (intellectual capacity).
2. *Planning for learning* involves the arrangement of the learning structure. In turn, learning structure involves a knowledge of the learner's readiness for a given task with its attendant prerequisites for learning. The ultimate objective for the practitioner is to specify the sequence of tasks to be presented.
3. *Managing learning* is viewed by Gagne as central to the functions of the teacher. The management functions are said to include decisions pertinent to motivating the person to begin and continue learning, guiding learner effort and interest, and assessing learner outcomes.
4. *Instruction* involves the external arrangement to be presented to the learner. One must insure that previous learning is *retained* for subsequent learning and that such learning can be *transferred* or applied to other situations.
5. *Selecting media for instruction* relates to modality as well as resource of presentation. The former involves oral, visual, print, and similar modalities. The latter describes concrete objects, films, etc.
6. Identification of the *prerequisites to learning* suggests that all learning is *not* alike. Consequently, a learning task can first be identified by its necessary prior

attainments. The practitioner then has the basis of a task analysis for teaching and learning.

7. *Integration of specific learning and competing theories of learning* suggests that certain individuals have advanced theories to account for all learning with associated recommendations for practice.

It is Gagne's notion that teaching involves knowing the *conditions* of learning and of a particular learner, from which decisions can be made with respect to instructional implications. More specifically, the practitioner's function appears to be an assessment of the learner's prior and initial capabilities in relationship to the demands of a given type of task. Based on such analysis, the practitioner formulates decisions regarding planning, managing, instructing, selecting media, and selection of a teaching-learning strategy.

Table 5–4 SUMMARY OF GAGNE'S PROTOTYPES OF LEARNING

Learning Prototypes, Arranged from Most Complex to Least Complex	*Descriptors Involved in the Prototype*	*Examples*
8 Problem solving	Said to involve thinking that combines two or more principles into a higher order principle	The highest order, the achievement of a solution, combines related principles and knowledges such as career choices, decision making which leads to new behaviors. Constitutes the content of formal education.
7 Principle learning	A chain of two or more concepts to generate a rule to guide behavior	Involves application of a consistent idea, i.e., adding *s* to a noun makes it say more than one; i.e., *i* before *e* except after *c*.
6 Concept learning	Involves a response to a group of stimuli that differ significantly among themselves	Selecting the "middle" block; involves a property of inner language to classify and group.

Table 5–4 (continued)

Learning Prototypes, Arranged from Most Complex to Least Complex	*Descriptors Involved in the Prototype*	*Examples*
5 Multiple discriminations	Involves responding differently to different stimuli which may differ significantly.	Learning the names of all the models of automobiles for the new year. Involves knowing that the label applies to a particular car and no other.
4 Verbal association	Involves the chaining of verbal stimuli to a variety of responses.	Connecting two words for the same object, *kitty* and *cat* for the same animal; the connection of a word for an object.
3 Chaining	A pairing, or arrangement in series of two or more stimulus-response connections.	Learning to say "Please" upon seeing food; involves inhibition of urge to take it.
2 Stimulus Response	Involves a precise response to a discriminated stimulus, often termed a *connection*, a *discriminated operant*, or an *instrumental response*.	Learning to stop or go on a verbal command, a light, or hand signal.
1 Signal Learning	Involves a general, diffuse response to particular event or stimulus. Describes classical conditioning.	Learning that "No!" means a painful consequence if action is continued.

Table 5–4 portrays the Gagne analysis of eight prototypes of learning. Inspection of this table suggests that learning can be conceptualized as the linkage of successive types from the basic signal learning through problem-solving behavior. One

observes from Gagne's presentation that language and the use of linguistic labels becomes increasingly necessary for more complex learnings.

Utilization of the Gagne system implies the need for careful observation of the learner by the practitioner. For example, rote recall of multiplication facts (a prototype 5) should be distinguished from the ability to solve 3 × 5 = 15 by knowing that 15 is the result of adding 5 three consecutive times (a prototype seven). Should one proceed to prototype eight, mistaking a type-five for a type-seven attainment, the potential for frustration becomes obvious.

Typically, in the public-school context learning is viewed as a rate concept expressed as the acquisition of skills within a specified period of time. This view is the basis of the grade concept of the schools. Learning is described as a percentage of content acquired. The Gagne discussion is a reminder that *retention* and *transfer* are two additional correlates to teaching and learning.

Since the publication of the original Gagne text, Gagne and Briggs (1974) have proposed an environmental design for learning. Lathey (1975) has proposed that the Gagne model has applicability to programming in mental retardation. While the Lathey article was speculative, the possibilities are of interest: each prototype could be the basis of assessment and prescription; learning tasks could be classified as to prototypic dimensions; understanding the competencies of learners to demands of tasks could be facilitated; and a basis for program evaluation might be established. In this last connection, program effectiveness could be inferred by movement within prototype as well as gain of a more complex prototype. Lathey observed that this movement might be more relevant to the life situation of the learner than increase in test scores.

Scope and Trends of Learning Research

Heal (1970) suggested that research in mental retardation from the perspective of learning theory may arise from: a desire to understand the condition from developmental vs. difference models (chapter 2); a desire to understand the effects of motivation; and a genuine interest in this population for its own sake. The Menolascino and Heal (1974) article outlined the research priorities of the NARC as: preventive behavior research, preventive biomedical research, home training techniques, residential model evaluation, and organizational (i.e., volunteerism) dynamics. The dominant themes in this NARC report were an emphasis upon prevention of loss of self-esteem and prevention of the atrophy of potential.

The Tynchuk (1970) summary reflected that research regarding exceptional children and youth was: general descriptions (35 percent), etiology (14 percent), diagnosis (17 percent), treatment (27 percent), and effects of treatments (5 percent). The Cleland, Watson, and Whitten report (1975) summarized research efforts in nonmedical aspects of mental retardation. In developmental topics, mental processes (including learning) was the largest category, with the two categories of social-emotional and psychodiagnostics having a combined total equal to the first. Physical attributes were a distant fourth.

The scope of learning research in mental retardation has been documented by Gardner and Salinger (1971). This article identified eight categories of persistent interest in the field. These included: classical conditioning, verbal learning, discrimination learning, motor learning, generalization, reinforcement, applied behavior change, and miscellaneous. The latter grouping described efforts aimed at theoretical and/or experimental studies for which inclusion of retarded persons was incidental.

Verbal learning was said to include primarily associative, serial, and concept formation. Interest in *discrimination* was said to focus upon reversal, oddity, set, and cue. Reaction time and maze learning appear to be the prime concerns of *motor* learning. *Generalization* was said to include transfer, rigidity, and transposition. *Reinforcement* and *incentives* have been studied with respect to delay, schedules, magnitude, secondary, and social aspects. Behavior modification and programmed instruction have been major concerns of *applied behavior chance*. These authors observed that since the 1950s there has been a dramatic rise in learning studies, and an article by Ellis (1963) was credited by Gardner and Salinger (1971) for a dramatic change in patterns of research and programming. Ellis detailed the use of behavior modification which preceded the establishment of federal support of improvement of services and staff development in residential facilities. It was estimated that the Ellis article generated literally thousands of reports.

The use of research information by practitioners has been discussed by Altman and Meyen (1975). They argue for clarity and communication by researchers and urged practitioners to overcome their reluctance or inability to relate to research. Warren (1975) recognized that this is not always easy, but she observed that the retarded person has the right to knowledgeable, competent practitioners.

Dimensions of Learning Research

McCarthy and Scheerenberger (1966) and Smith (1974) suggest that research efforts, regardless of learning type in the Gagne sense, are usually directed toward one or more of three possible outcomes: rate, retention, and transfer (table 5–5). An essential purpose of investigations is to identify factors that influence any of these outcomes.

Three main factors have dominated learning research. These are *meaningfulness* of the material to be learned, *attention,* and *mediation*. *Meaningfulness* relates to the degree to which the stimulus has associative power. Nonsense syllables are

Table 5–5 SCOPE OF STUDIES IN LEARNING PERFORMANCE

Areas of Interest	*Themes*		
	Rate	*Retention*	*Transfer*
Measurement	Serial learning Paired associates	Recall Recognition	Recall Recognition Demonstration
Factors	Meaningfulness Attention Mediation	Meaningfulness Short term Long term Overlearning	Meaningfulness Retroactive inhibition Proactive inhibition

popular because their meaningfulness has been verified over the years. For example, a paired associate of TEX to MEX would be considered high in meaning while TZA to HBF would be more difficult. *Attention* can be manipulated by creating distraction or reducing its effects. Qualities of the stimulus in terms of clarity, contrast, etc. may be studied. *Mediation* may include external forms of feedback or knowledge of results to the person. It also may be internal, in that the person has utilized (or is "taught" to use) some device, strategy, or rule to organize material.

Retention arises as a logical consideration of rate. While acquisition is of concern, it would also appear that having the learned material available for use is equally important. Studies of retention usually involve a design of rate (i.e., acquisition) with a time interval for retesting. Retention over time is usually related to short term (testing within 60 seconds) or long term (any interval beyond short term).

Measurement may take two forms, either savings or error scores. Savings scores involves a passage of time. The person is given opportunities to relearn the task, and the "score" is based on the trials necessary to regain mastery. The second approach, error *scores,* involves testing the person without practice after an interval of time. Testing may be of two types, recognition or recall. The first, less difficult for the person, is to indicate if the stimulus were present or not present. A multiple-choice item is an example of recognition. In the recall procedure, the person will be asked to say or write previously learned items.

Priority factors of interest have been *meaningfulness* similar in rate studies and *overlearning.* This latter concept usually follows this design. Overlearning involves additional practice beyond one successful performance. Those who practiced after attainment are compared at some later interval to those who did not have such opportunities.

It is not uncommon to find an individual study that involves both rate and retention. Increasingly, the use of positive incentives to influence knowledge of results has aroused significant interest.

With transfer the central task is to understand how learning in one situation generalizes, or transfers, to other situations or tasks. While retention is the verification of memory, transfer involves the study of: application of "old" (previous) learnings to subsequent learnings, interference of new learning with previous learning, and interference of prior learnings upon acquisition of new learnings.

The measurement of transfer is related to choice of approach. In general, the approach is to select variable A as primary. A reference variable B is then selected. Investigation would be undertaken to discover if training in A relates to performance in B. A hypothetical study would have one group trained in A to some success level and after an interval of time tested in performance B. It used to be common practice to have one group take a B pre- and/or posttest to compare with another group that received training in A. Currently, the use of comparison groups (sometimes termed as control or contrast) has been enlarged to include one presample and a separate postsample.

Two themes dominate transfer studies. These are termed *retroactive inhibition* and *proactive inhibition*. Both are characterized by experience, or learning. Primary interest is in the degree to which old learning facilitates or interferes with new learning. Similarly, there is interest in the degree to which new learning assists in the strengthening of previous learning and the extent to which it may interfere with it.

Retroactive inhibition relates to the degree to which new learning interferes with old. In this approach, the person learns A. In an interval, instruction of various types may be given. Then there is testing in A. There may be a contrast sample without intervention. If performance in A post is less than previously attained performance, allowing for retention effects, then interference is inferred.

Proactive inhibition refers to old learning interfering with new learning. To measure this effect a person is trained in A and subsequently trained and tested in B. The usual contrast sample(s) may be present. If acquisition or rate of B is less, and/or if post performance of B is less, then A may be inferred to be an inhibition.

It is not uncommon for a study to involve all three outcomes. Transfer is a primary goal of programs and services. There is an implied assumption that program efforts should enable a person to generalize beyond an immediate situation to subsequent situations.

Examples

McCarthy and Scheerenberger (1966) and Smith (1974) identified dimensions that can be illustrated by representative examples from the research literature. These examples demonstrate that a given investigation may reflect more than one dimension.

Moreland (1976) investigated the relationship of learning rate to intrapersonal variables and task variables. The sample was composed of normal and mildly retarded persons matched on MA. One portion of the sample was divided into a MA-matched group between six and eight and into another MA group of eight to ten. The task was to recognize visual symbols; performance was measured by accuracy and reaction time. Task dimensions included trial blocks varied by interruption intervals. While the findings were complex, Moreland's data suggested that MA, rather than IQ groupings, was associated with learning rate. This pattern was also evident for increased trials, although gains were also associated with increase in practice time-trials.

Ullman and Routh (1971) explored the Zeaman and House (1963) attention hypothesis, which suggests that learning rate increases as a function of the task's relevancy (meaningfulness) to the learner. Mildly retarded persons of MA six were matched to MA six normal children. The latter required less trials to reach criterion. The retarded achieved eventual mastery of the task. As relevancy was added to the discrimination task (adding one to four clues progressively), their performance gained.

The influence of affective reactions and learning rate has been reported by Schuster and Gruen (1971). They compared MA-matched and CA-matched mildly retarded and normals. The participants were exposed to experimentally induced success (easy word lists) and failure (hard word lists). The authors concluded that the retarded and normal were similar in their reactions to success and to failure. The findings indicated that success experiences increased learner expectations in approaching other tasks. Failure preceding success had a variable effect on attitude and subsequent performance. IQ level did not explain the attitude. These authors strongly recommended examination of a retarded person's life history regarding attitude toward learning.

Learning rate, reaction time, and accuracy of response were investigated by Terry and Samules (1976). These authors used a CA match of normal and mildly retarded persons. Their findings indicated that the retarded were less accurate in responses but approximated the reaction time of normals for a visual discrimination task. These authors were emphatic about the need of retarded persons for more time to orient to a task and more time for its execution. Processing, as such, was not the critical difference. This study would seem to have implications for task presentation.

Similar results were reported by Lobb (1975) in a comparison of MA-matched moderately retarded persons and nursery school children. This study examined verbal recall. Lobb concluded that differences arose because of processing strategies rather than because of a global deficiency. That is, rate of learning was more efficient for normals because of their internal inventory of "rules." In the absence of mediational strategies, the moderately retarded required more trials to achieve a criterion performance.

The influence of error in initial learning has been investigated by Lambert (1975). The learners were adolescents identified as moderate to mildly retarded. The task dealt with recognition of geometric objects under conditions of errorless acquisition (correction of mistakes prior to next task) and acquisition which involved only random feedback. Those persons who learned under errorless performance could reverse a previous "old" correct response into a "new" correct response. Those who had been allowed to acquire errors in their initial training appeared to resist extinction of error at a subsequent interval.

A study reported by Dugas (1975) offers insight into the effect of paced training on transfer. The sample was a CA match of young adults (mean CA eighteen years). One treatment was to pretrain two groups on nonsense visual stimuli while another treatment group received no pretraining. There were retarded and normal in both treatment groups. An additional dimension was self-pacing versus instructor pacing. Prior training did *not* enhance the performance of the retarded as it did for the nonretarded. This suggested a lack of a processing strategy for the retarded. However, self-pacing was found to be more effective for the retarded than an external pace set by the experimenter.

Motivation as a factor in rate and retention was investigated by Harter, Brown, and Zigler (1971). An MA-matched design of three groups of normal, institutionalized mildly retarded, and noninstitutionalized retarded was employed. MA level was eight years. Two tasks were developed. A discrimination task consisted of selecting one picture that was different from two identical ones. In an oddity task, the selection of the odd picture from three choices was a function abstracted by positive and negative renderings of similar pictures. Reinforcement conditions were either standard or social. Standard referred to the examiner positioned behind a screen with a minimum of contact. In the social treatment, the examiner engaged in no-fail games (no emphasis upon winning) prior to testing, and she maintained face-to-face contact. These authors concluded that residence was not a factor in task performance for the retarded. No differences for the discrimination task were found. The oddity task favored the normal learners, although there was significant overlap among the populations. The normal sample was more inclined to select a "Good Player Award" than candy, while the reverse was true for the retarded. However, 43 percent of the noninstitutionalized and 32 percent of the institutionalized did select the nontangible reward over candy. Institutionalized retarded persons performed better under the standard testing, while noninstitutionalized were better under social. Harter et al. concluded that motivation is an individual attribute, not a group trait.

Transfer of learning was found to be assisted by mediation, modeling, and distribution of practice by Litrownik, Franzini, and Turner (1976). The sample was a group of moderately retarded learners with a MA of nearly six. The tasks involved design completion of a marble, which could be increased in complexity. For those persons who were presented a rule to cue color of design to appropriate variables, performance was superior to those who merely observed placement without explanation. Imitation following demonstration was more helpful than passive observation. Mediation was found clearly superior for transfer to more complex tasks. Practice effects were noted by Litrownik et al. Conditions of spaced practice were more helpful in acquisition for stability of performance than massed practice. Transfer from simple tasks to three higher levels of complexity was facilitated by massed practice after distributed practice. The authors emphasized that spaced practice prior to massed practice *and* the use of mediation facilitate transfer.

Wanschura and Borkowski (1975) studied a similar population of moderately retarded persons. The task was verbal. They found training in mediation to be more significant than distribution of practice or number of items. They concluded that active participation was the significant factor in facilitating mediation.

The interplay of Gagne prototypes of learning, measures of cognitive processes, academic achievement, and IQ has been investigated by Blackman, Bilksy, Burger, and Mar (1976). The sample was 115 mildly retarded persons with a mean IQ of 62 and a standard deviation of six. Their mean CA was 14, with a standard deviation of one year. Achievement was measured by WRAT (Wide Range Achievement Test). Reading achievement, expressed as word recognition, was *not* found to be related to IQ (either S-B, or WISC-R). Measures of performance associated with paired associates learning, recall of digits, and sorting were predictive of reading skill. Blackman and his associates conducted a factor analysis that established word recognition at the Gagne level four, while arithmetic computation was established at line six. IQ, oddity learning, and digit was found related to this arithmetic task. This investigation concluded that IQ remains an overall estimate of functioning and, as such, remains a global reference point. Specific measures which are task related can be of greater utility in understanding the intellectual processes underlying achievement.

These examples illustrate the ingenuity with which scientists have approached the study of learning and the retarded. This brief resumé was intended to illustrate some of the approaches utilized. The next discussion summarizes expert opinion.

Implications of Learning Research

Given the dimensions of learning and given those variables that influence acquisition (rate), memory (retention), and application (transfer), the practitioner will be interested in applicability of learning research to areas of practice. Kolstoe (1970) and Smith (1974) have suggested that selection of learning tasks represents one dimension of application. Hutt and Gibby (1976) have emphasized the intrapersonal influences. Moss and Mayer (1975) have explored procedural variables associated with assessment and observation of the person. A summation of these sources is presented to identify certain guidelines of applicability for the practitioner. It will be noted that these citations reflect a certain consistency with the Gagne interest in both task conditions and learner conditions.

Kolstoe (1970) identified certain implications:

1 Tasks should be uncomplicated and contain highly familiar elements.
2 Tasks should be brief.
3 Proceeding from simple to complex tasks is crucial to proper sequencing.
4 No-failure learning is essential for task performances.
5 Overlearning (i.e., continuation beyond one errorless performance) is essential for task retention.
6 Tasks should be directed toward situations in the life environment to increase both meaningfulness and transfer.
7 Tasks should be within the learner's capacity to respond.
8 Tasks should recognize the learner's subjective, affective reactions to learning.

Smith (1974), independent of the Kolstoe analysis, advanced his own assessment of implications of learning research.

1 The person's task must be within his or her level of maturity to respond in a consistent and accurate fashion.
2 The person must perceive a reason to respond.
3 The consequences of responding appropriately need to be strengthened or increased.
4 Opportunities to practice and strengthen acquired skills in a variety of ways are necessary.
5 Spacing of instruction over frequent intervals is preferred to concentrated time blocks. As Smith noted, however, this principle is highly variable to the task and the student. Smith points out that there is no evidence to specify optimal length except that given either less familiar material and/or a student less motivated, spaced, distributed practice is preferred. The more motivated, attending student and/or more familiar material can be massed in terms of time.
6 Physical movement and stimulation consistent with the student's level of attention and capacity is helpful for both rate and retention.
7 Using the child's strengths should be the initial point of instruction and should precede a gradual incursion into areas of weakness. Appropriate reinforcement should accompany performance.

Hutt and Gibby (1976) have advanced their own implications.

1 Mental age is a partial index for expectation, in that the life experience (environment) is a powerful determinant.
2 Attending, memory, and discrimination influence transfer and concept formation.

3 The individual learner will display variability in capacities and potential in comparison to his or her norm group. Thus, individualization for the person is essential.

Moss and Mayer (1975) identified these implications.

1. When matched on MA in the presence of meaningful tasks, learning rates of normal and retarded approach equality.

2. Research studies (regardless of MA or CA match) reflect overlap between the retarded and the normal. Certain retarded persons surpass normals, and certain normals achieve less than the retarded. Mean scores and variance usually reflect a positive direction for the normal. Increasingly, research should emphasize the overlap in populations, especially the "successful" retarded person.

3. IQ and MA should be understood to reflect a global measure of presumed functioning. Both remain an estimate of functioning, but these measures show variation of correlation, in that low-IQ students may be high in some aspect of achievement (a negative correlate) rather than the typical pattern of low IQ and low achievement (positive). These observations confirm the need to supplement formal testing with direct observations.

4. Pre-post evaluation approaches reinforce the need for reliable scales of assessment and observation. If the assessment procedures possess wide error in results, or if this error is not controlled, differences may be inferred when none exist. Furthermore, reliability for age groups and retardation levels should be known, for reliability can vary on age and levels of retardation.

5. There is a trend to have more precise descriptions of observational procedures in order to achieve reproducability among studies for applicability. The work of Guilford and Piaget were cited as promising approaches.

SOURCES OF LEARNING POTENTIAL

Cure is not an absolute pursuit in the teaching of retarded persons. The search is for the means to enhance potential of learning. Learning potential is viewed as the maximum adaptive efficiency of the person, regardless of measured intellectual level. The search is for understanding of the circumstances that limit potential and those that enhance potential. This section discusses those circumstances.

Assessment of Learning Potential

Hamilton and Budoff (1974) identify an adapted use of Kohs Blocks (design cubes as found in the WISC-R test) as a more direct *assessment* of learning potential than is typically provided by standardized measures of intelligence and achievement data. While not rejecting these measures, these authors suggest inference of learning potential requires a controlled situation to observe the person's gains in performance following tutoring. The obtained measure is perceived as an index of learning to learn. The Kohs procedure minimizes overt verbal behavior, but requires fairly complex covert inner language behavior to complete the matching task. Hamilton and Budoff (1974) report an investigation involving forty persons within the moderate and severe range (using the Peabody Picture Vocabulary Test — PPVT) divided between contrast and trained. The gains made by the trained groups were stable and significant over one month. The authors noted the preliminary nature of their work, but it was noted that refinement will continue.

The use of this learning potential procedure was applied to evaluation of educational achievement by Budoff and Gottlieb (1976). The sample of thirty-one mentally retarded pupils (mean CA of 138 months and mean WISC IQ of 70) was randomly assigned to a special class and resource room. These pupils were "new" to the school so that labels or past reputation did not follow the child. Both groups (fourteen vs. seventeen) had equal teacher-pupil ratio of seven to one. The resource room group was assigned to regular class and attended a learning center *along with* typical children. Consequently, to the integrated student, participation in the center was not a stigma.

High and low learning potential as measured by the Budoff procedure did *not* relate to academic achievement at the conclusion of the study. The results reflected an interaction effect for high-learning-potential children in the mainstream effect. Measures of self-concept, locus of control, and aspiration were associated with more reflective behavior. Budoff and Gottlieb cited other studies that supported their findings that reentry will require at least a year for the former special student to reestablish his or her identity.

Learning Style

Learning style as a source of learning potential has emerged as an interaction factor. It may be possible, as Dunn and Dunn (1974) postulate, that learning is an outcome of teaching style. The optimal method would be to match teaching and learning styles. Thus, styles of open learning and open teaching could be matched as well as structured styles. Cegelka and Cegelka (1970) pointed out this need in their discussion of reading instruction.

Dunn and Dunn identified four major elements of learning-teaching styles, which were further subdivided into related elements.

1. *Physical environment* relates to sound, light, temperature, and design of facilities.

2 *Emotional aspects* relate to motivation, persistence, and structure.
3 *Sociological aspects* relate to preferences for orientation toward peers, authority figures, and the learning process itself.
4 *Physical aspects* would be preference for input through visual, auditory, and/or kinesthetic channels.

Some illustrations of style are found in the literature on memory. Comparisons of mildly and moderately retarded persons reflect greater similarity of the mild to the intellectually able than of the moderate to the mild on tasks of memory (Ullman, 1974). Despite a forty-point difference between the mild and typical student, as opposed to a ten-point difference between the mild and moderate, differences in rote learning were vastly greater between moderate and mild than in comparisons between the mild to average group. Sabatino and Hayden (1970) compared learning disabled and mildly retarded learners on three aspects of memory: sensory, perceptual, and cognitive. Sensory was receiving; perception was the integrative and transmittal process; cognitive described associative processes underlying expressive responses of recall and recognition. They concluded that conventional IQ tests, achievement tests, and/or teacher judgments are not altogether helpful in prescription. They recommended further exploration of the cognitive aspects of memory.

A number of investigations have identified certain variables that affect learning potential for memory which have implications for teaching style. For example, Harris and Tramontan (1973) found that merely being positive favorably affects learning. Prehm, Logan and Towle (1972) and Levy (1974) reported that social reinforcement and knowledge of results facilitated learning, especially the former. More direct evidence of the cognitive processes of memory are reflected in the studies of Stayton and Ohwaki (1971) and Riegel and Taylor (1974). Stayton and Ohwaki report that retention of words was related to their meaningfulness (familiarity) as compared to equally difficult words without associative power. The Riegel and Taylor report suggests that learning strategies for grouping of items can be acquired. The effect of this approach is to reduce the discrepancy between normal and mildly mentally retarded persons matched on CA.

Practitioner Behavior

Teacher behavior has emerged as an important variable affecting the performance of retarded learners. England, Semmel, Creenough, Krieder, Sitks, Weaver, and Van Ever (1969) explored the possible relationship between achievement of moderately retarded learners and teacher traits. During a three-year period, 657 learners and 86 teachers were involved. Pupil gains using the Cain-Levine Social Competency Scale were the measure of effectiveness. In general, pupil achievement gains were related to teacher classroom behavior. The characteristics of effective teachers were found to include:

1 physical stamina
2 active functioning rather than passive functioning
3 flexibility in adapting schedules
4 objectivity in assessing pupils
5 an overt interest in people
6 a zest for life in which teaching is one element
7 sensitivity in adjusting expectations
8 mental alertness in knowledge of pupil characteristics.

The Minnesota Teacher Attitude Inventory was helpful in identifying who was activistic and flexible in teaching style.

Blackwell (1972) compared seventy teachers of moderately retarded learners. Supervisor ratings were used to distinguish the most from the least effective. Effectiveness was judged in seven areas:

1 discipline
2 task behavior of learners
3 developing personal worth
4 guiding learning experiences
5 encouraging interactions
6 securing attention
7 encouraging verbal response.

The Edwards Personal Preference Schedule did not discriminate, while the Minnesota Teacher Attitude Scale did. (The former is a measure of needs, while the latter is a measure of tolerance for flexible practices.) Characteristics of effective teachers were found to include: women were more effective than men; preschool teachers were more effective than vocational level; and effectiveness was associated with prior training at preschool or early-elementary levels. Variables of nonsignificance were said to include:

1 academic degree
2 teaching experience
3 teaching experience in other areas of education
4 prior contact with exceptional children
5 prior occupation
6 previous teaching at secondary levels
7 years in school
8 number of hobbies.

Program Design

The teaching of reading is a central task of the schools. A previous section showed that IQ does not explain reading skills; at best, psychometric measures only demonstrate that a problem exists.

Carter (1975) compared equated groups of mildly retarded learners whose characteristics were mean scores of: CA of 9, WISC IQ of 64.8, and Iowa Reading Skills of 2.5. This group of seventy was found in regular class, self-contained class, and a resource room arrangement (partial enrollment in regular classroom). The rho statistic compared IQ and reading achievement and yielded .48 for regular class, .68 for special class, and .79 for resource room placement. Carter concluded that there was no support for a particular placement based on IQ and achievement. Given the compatability among the three groups and the variation in correlation, there appear to be factors operative in placement beyond achievement data.

Cegelka and Cegelka (1970) summarized the available literature regarding reading achievement. These authors reviewed the relative merits and findings of reading instruction based upon approaches of:

1 *remedial reading* founded upon auditory approaches;
2 *language experience* based upon chart stories and/or a unit of experience focused on language arts;
3 *kinesthetic* based upon Fernald (emphasis upon vision and motor) techniques;
4 *initial teaching alphabet* (letters correspond to sounds which precede the usual system), based upon phonic analysis;
5 *rebus*-based pictures representing word units prior to conventional reading;
6 *programmed instruction* based upon teaching machines, programmed texts, etc.; and
7 *progressive choice* methods, which involves discrimination of shapes and eventually transfer to letters, finally into the complex act of reading.

These authors concluded that while these methods appear different, they all possess: pursuit of the child's interests, conditioning for success, allowing for individual progress, novelty of approach, direct relation to reading tasks, and emphasis on transfer. No one method has emerged as *the* single best method.

Hammill, Iano, McGertigan, and Wiederholt (1972) reported the results of a resource-room intervention on behalf of a group of twenty-two learners. Their characteristics were: CA, 6–10 to 12–11 (mean 9–4); IQ 59–79 (mean 68). The sex ratio was male 3:1. Census tract data reported the group to be mostly black and economically disadvantaged. The mean reading achievement was .87 (less than first grade) with a standard deviation of .39. The resource-room "treatment" was to emphasize educational goals. It was neither a crisis room nor a placement for the delinquent. An approximation of precision teaching coupled with positive incentives was employed. Comparing the initial scores of October with those of May, the mean gain was .7 of an academic year, with an average reading score of 1.54. The authors noted certain problems in attributing the gains to the resource room exclusively. However, the authors did reflect satisfaction in noting the significant gain in seven months time.

One identifiable variable regarding the learning potential of the retarded is the phenomena of *expectancy* (Jacobs and DeGraef, 1973). The *actual,* measurable performance of children was influenced by the set, or expectations, that adults believed about them. No reasonable person believes that merely expecting more will generate dramatic results, but adult expectations are an important reference point for the learner.

Expectations about achievement are illustrated in the reports of Brown and Perlmutter (1971) and Appfel (1974). Both acknowledged the prevailing "wisdom" of discouraging reading instruction for the moderately retarded. They suggested that inability to read should be understood with reference to *conventional* methods. Both reports identified variations of selected symbol-motor response programs. In essence, this is a variation of progressive-choice methods. This approach applies task analysis to chain learning elements as per the Gagne and Briggs discussions cited earlier.

Another promising area of learning potential for the retarded would appear to be science instruction. The National Science Teachers' Association devoted an entire issue of its journal, *Science and Children,* to science education for various types of exceptional children, including the mentally retarded. Science education was discussed as a vehicle for mainstreaming the handicapped. Given an observational approach with manipulation of concrete materials, instruction in science was portrayed as presenting common ground for literate and nonliterate learners alike. Furthermore, science was observed to possess a powerful motivating force for acquisition of literacy skills. Science was also advocated as a coordinating mechanism for correlation with other activities, such as visual perception, auditory discrimination, physical education, art education, and the development of cognitive skills.

Within this special issue, Holzberg (1976) as well as Lombardi and Balch (1976) identified special considerations for the mentally retarded learner. The Holzberg paper emphasized looking beyond the label and into the individuality of the learner. He advocated science teaching as a means to increase attending, generalization production, and lessening of rigidity of classification. Lombardi and Balch emphasized science as stimulation and fulfillment of curiosity. Their paper centered upon the nontextbook possibilities of instruction to encourage greater complexity of concept formation. Science was perceived by these authorities as a means of learning to problem solve. Their recommendation was that science for the retarded should emphasize environmental awareness and coping. Suggested units were: care of pets, puberty, aviation, emotions, parenthood, and health.

A Special Kind of Potential

A special term describes the evidence of superior ability in persons labeled and/or diagnosed as mentally retarded: *idiot savant*. Spitz and LaFontaine (1973) observed that the idiot savant reflects one or more of the following explanations: undiagnosed autism, specific brain damage, compensatory response, reduction in interference from other stimuli, and the effects of social reinforcement. Their study involved eight persons whose mean age was thirty years. Individual characteristics included: a person with an IQ of below thirty who could read at sixth-grade level; two persons with IQs of 47 and 69 who had superior music talent; one person with an IQ of 48 who made intricate models of buildings he designed himself; one person with an IQ of 51 who had exceptional memory for birthdays and license plates; and three with IQs of 37, 52, and 53 who were calendar calculators. The memory for digits of this group of eight persons was superior to a "matched" sample of mildly retarded persons and to an equated group of normal persons. This possession of short-term memory was viewed as a principal explanation of these exceptional retarded persons.

Extraordinary abilities of certain retarded persons have been documented by Hoffman (1971) and Hill (1974).

1. Calendar calculation (predicting the day of the week on which a specific date has fallen or will fall).
2. Memorization of all of the numbers on all the cars of a freight train after it has passed.
3. One man who memorized: the population of every town in the U.S. above five thousand population, the population of every county seat in the U.S.; the names and location of two thousand hotels and their number of rooms; statistics regarding three thousand mountains and rivers in the U.S.; and dates and facts associated with over two thousand inventions.
4. The Genius of Earlswood Asylum (circa 1914), who constructed ship models, one of which was ten feet long and had over one million handmade parts.
5. Identification of cloth by smell.
6. The separation of a sheet of newspaper into two parts as one would peel a stamp from an envelope.
7. The ability to give the square root of any number up to four digits in four

seconds and the cube root of any number of up to six figures in six seconds.

The person cited in the last example, was presented with this problem:

> Given 64 boxes, there will be one grain of corn in the first box, two in the second box, four in the third, eight in the fourth and so on until the boxes are filled. How many grains of corn are there in the fourteenth box? the eighteenth box? the twenty-fourth? the forty-eighth? and in all sixty-four boxes?

The first three answers (8,192; 121,672; and 8,388,628) were given instantly. The fourth answer (140,737,488,355,328) was given in six seconds, while the final correct answer was given in forty-five seconds.

LaFontaine and Benjamin (1971), Morishima (1974), and Lindsley (1966) have considered possible implications for further study of the idiot savant. All three articles agree that undiagnosed autism or a specific brain damage does not "explain" the performance of such persons. LaFontaine and Benjamin argue for respect of these abilities rather than for dismissing them as oddities. They affirmed Guilford's endorsement for the study of such persons to enhance an understanding of human learning and intelligence. The Lindsley report is consistent with the previous findings of this section's sources that there are certain common factors in the *known* instances of idiots savant. These factors appear to be an initial deprivation and/or isolation coupled with the emergence of an ability as a compensatory response in the presence of social reinforcement. There appears to be a "blocking out" of other stimulation and/or a purposeful concentration on rewarding cues.

Though separated by a span of nearly ten years, the Lindsley (1966) and Morishima (1974) articles focused on two retarded persons of artistic ability who have been described as the "Van Gogh of Japan," Kyoshi Yamashita, and "another Van Gogh of Japan," Yoshihiko Yamamoto. Both had similar patterns of their abilities being discovered and encouraged by a helpful benefactor and advocate. Morishima lauds the longtime relationship of Kawasaki, the educator, mentor, advocate, and friend of Yamamoto. While Lindsley stressed the vocational potential of special skills, Morishima placed equal emphasis upon special abilities as a tool in the humanization process. Kawasaki was quoted to the effect that art was his protégé's life and spirit.

The Lindsley exposition is noteworthy in its emphasis on respect for these abilities. He deplored their dismissal as only a mysterious accident. It was his contention that these special skills may have practical value for retarded persons and the larger society. These skills should not be explained away but studied, sought after, and adapted to socially urgent needs. Lindsley observed that the life-histories of these persons reveal "accidental" discoveries of these abilities and "accidental" development by the person. Lindsley's challenge to the field is to change the pattern of accident into purposeful development.

PRACTITIONER APPLICATIONS

The Management of Learning

The application of the insights rendered by cognitive theory and learning research can be observed in the exchange between practitioner and the retarded person. One specific application of theory and research is the development and execution of a lesson plan. Any encounter between a learner and another person which has a purpose is a lesson. In this sense, all practitioners are teachers. What follows is an example of a lesson plan founded upon sources cited in chapters 2 and 5. The suggested scope of the proposed lesson plan is the writer's responsibility.

The specific content and sequence of a lesson plan may vary according to the instructional area under consideration. The most essential aspect of a lesson plan is that every lesson is a *language* lesson. One must be sensitive to how each lesson will increase or reinforce language skills. The elements of a lesson plan are:

- I Purposes, Goals, Objectives
  - A Teacher — the prescription for the learner
  - B Learners — possible incentives and/or source of interest
- II Motivation
  - A The means for gaining and maintaining attention
  - B The means for rewarding attending
- III Readiness
  - A Recall of previous experiences relating ultimately to learner purposes
  - B Introduction of new concept
- IV Development
  - A Relate new topic to previous experiences
  - B Distinguish new from old and relate new to familiar
- V Retention
  - A Practice of new skill in isolation, especially with the learner using his own terms to internalize the lesson
  - B Practice of the new skill in relation to as many situations in which the new skill *does* and *does not* apply
- VI Evaluation
  - A Practitioner's performance and suitability of goals, activities, etc.
  - B Learner's attainment of lesson goals and directions for subsequent goals

Lesson planning should not be confused with scheduling. Lesson planning is a means of translating teaching/learning principles into program practice. The plan defines an advance agenda to guide reactions and actions.

The Practitioner as Researcher

Blackman (1972) has noted an increasing shift of research efforts toward classroom settings and concerns. Altman and Meyen (1976) identified the need for information to be secured by a variety of persons, including practitioners. Swartz, Cleland, and Altman (1971) have observed that practitioners now have electronic technology for data collection and recording. They advocated the use of television as a time capsule of records. Viewing the performance on film will increase the accuracy of recollection and comparison.

Research is one tool by which curiosity is transformed into channels of knowing. This transformation for the practitioner has been described by Newland, Baer, and Simches (1961) as a six-step procedure.

1. *The situation.* State the event or conditions that prompted the original curiosity. This constitutes the background or context in which the effort is undertaken.

2. *The sample or sampling.* State the characteristics, behaviors, etc. of the persons being studied. This should also include relevant traits such as age and sex.

3. *The procedure.* State the means by which behavior is measured, including instruments, scales, and/or modes of observation. Also specify the conditions of the setting in which the study is being carried out. Finally, describe the procedure under consideration. Incentives for the "subjects" should be identified.

4. *Reporting.* State one's findings as statistically as is warranted, with due regard to cause and effect relationships, and with awareness of limitations and compromises required. Then present results, even though the results are either different from original intentions or nonsignificant.

5. *Summative.* Review how curiosity was aroused and the procedures used to satisfy it. Review only principal findings.

6. *Inference.* Statements should distinguish between what was found (results), what the findings mean (discussion), and implications for future action.

The Newland et al. discussion (1961) should be understood as a scope; circumstances may dictate alteration of the sequence.

SUMMING UP

This chapter has considered intelligence and learning. Both ideas can be measured, inferred, and investigated. Another generalization is that there is not one type of intelligence and one definition of learning. Both ideas possess common features of adaptation, of change, and of the use of experience for coping with the present and future. However, the content of this chapter reflects that there are types of intelligence and types of learning.

The Nature of Intelligence

1. The term *intelligence* is the equivalent of *cognition* in the literature. The exception is that the Guilford model places cognition as *one* operation of intellect.

2. It is generally agreed in the United States that intelligence is not a thing, but a unique, interrelated cluster of abilities. It is further agreed the intelligence is inferred with reference to adaptation of the person to his or her environment.

3. The literature related to mental retardation identifies four models of intelligence and intellectual development: the structure view of Guilford, the genetic view of Piaget, the linguistic-representation/integration view of Bruner, and a psychometric-measurement view.

4. The role of the preceding viewpoints is to describe the exact nature of abilities in development (growth), dynamic (interplay of person and environment), and eventually diagnostic terms. The latter assesses what is thought — and presently verified — to succeed in life, especially school life.

5. Theories of development agree that the age period prior to school merits respect and attention, certain skills precede others, and the sequence is similar, while individuals vary in the timing of emergence.

6. The Bruner model was found applicable to language development. The emergence of enactive, iconic, and symbolic levels within the person can formulate an ethological approach to intervention.

7. The Guilford model prizes process (how) as distinguished from product (what) in relationship to task presentation. There appears to be support for a developmental view of Guilford, since research is confirming emergence of portion of his structure prior to others.

8. The Stanford-Binet and Wechsler procedures served as the basis for identifying the elements of intelligence, defined from a psychometric model. Consistent with theorists, this model prizes verbal fluencies and prior experience. All four procedures were described with respect to available information regarding factor analysis and structure of intellect operations.

The Measurement of Intelligence

1. Basic measurement concepts helpful to practitioners were identified. These concepts are also relevant to research. Understanding *validity* and *reliability* were viewed as essential characteristics of measurement procedures.

2. The anatomy of the Stanford-Binet and Wechsler procedures was briefly considered. This description was organized around the structures and functions of the scales.

3. Information about testing/assessment was related to ideas needed by consumers of testing services, practitioners and parents.

4. Guidelines for testing procedures and inferences of potential were identified.

5. The emergence of *deviation* scores based upon formulated tables should help curtail one source of error contained in the ratio approach.

6. The use of testing still remains a matter of the competence of the examiner, knowing what is predictable and what is not, awaiting confirmation from cognitive theory for the redesign of approaches, and understanding sources of error.

Learning

1. Learning can be viewed from philosophic-psychological perspectives. These disciplines prize acquisition and transfer equally.

2. The philosophic emphasis is concerned with motives, goals, and life circumstances as the basis for learning. The psychological aspect emphasizes types of learning and sequence of learnings into more complex behavior chains.

3. The prototypes of Gagne may have promise in diagnostic-prescriptive functions as well as for evaluation. The Gagne analysis would appear to be applicable to a variety of cognitive-learning systems and theories.

4. The study of learning has been prompted by a variety of motivations, one of which is to seek prevention of learning failure and to enhance potential.

5. Priorities and areas of need for research in learning were identified.

6. Learning, in experimental studies, can be viewed, regardless of topic, as centering around themes of rate, retention, and transfer. Basic procedures of measurement and identification of factors which influence these three themes were identified, with considerations for practice.

7. The need for practitioner-produced research was discussed with suggested guidelines for reporting of results.

8. The commitment to knowledge on the part of the practitioner was emphasized.

Learning Potential

1. A unique form of learning potential was identified among the mentally retarded: the idiot savant. These persons appear to be mentally retarded in the AAMD sense, but they reflect average-to-superior ability or abilities in some area. The common features in the lives of such persons are: isolation, social reinforcement for the skill, and the presence of an advocate-benefactor. Expert opinion suggests that such persons should *not* be regarded as one of nature's curiosities. Rather, there should be efforts directed toward use of these abilities.

2. Learning potential can be assessed through controlled observation of learning from experience, or learning how to learn.

3. The study of learning documents the variability among the mentally retarded, especially among and between groupings of the moderate, mild, and average learners. Examples were presented.

4. Reading methods and the potential of science instruction for the retarded were discussed.

5. Memory acquisition was used to illustrate intervention in learning potential and performance. An illustrative study was cited to document that practitioner behavior is a source of learning potential.

6. The concept of learning style was discussed. It was shown that learning style constitutes four elements: environmental, emotional, sociological, and physical. It may be possible that learners and teachers can be matched according to preferences and strengths of both.

7. The management of learning was outlined by a summation of a prototype of a lesson plan. It was pointed out that regardless of one's role, interactions between practitioner and retarded person is a lesson.

ON LOCATION

The selection for this chapter is an excerpt from a manual designed to orient consumers of testing services and to orient those who would administer them. As the material unfolds, the reader is invited to guess the author and the date.

On the Qualifications of Psychological Examiner

The tests are the result of psychological progress, both in experimental technique and in the knowledge of facts and principles about mental processes, particularly about the mental development of children. Without this the test could not have been produced, nor can they be fully understood without this now that we have them. Is this knowledge of psychological technique, facts, and principles required in order to use the tests successfully? Considerable discussion has arisen over this question, and there is not promise of an immediate understanding. The tests themselves are very simple and devoid of much technique. The directions for applying them are easily comprehended. This simplicity seems to have led to the belief in many quarters that anyone who can follow the directions is fully qualified to use the tests. This, however, is a mistake, because in the details of the procedure in giving the tests a variety of circumstances will always arise that cannot be foreseen and provided for beforehand, and the children's responses vary in so many ways from typical forms that rules for interpretation can never be made complete. This results from the fact that in a psychological experiment or test the subject's mental make-up at the moment of the test, which determines the particular result obtained, is so complex and variable and so largely unknown and uncontrollable, a condition which the physical experiment has to deal with only in a much less degree. To adapt the procedure in the test and to give the proper interpretation of the child's response in these frequent special circumstances, and to do this reasonably well, requires the same knowledge and training that were necessary to devise the tests in the first place. In other words, it requires a full understanding of the tests. But this is not all. Scientific training alone does not give the examiner the ability to adapt himself to children's ways, which is also quite essential. The examiner should be able to get down to the mental level of the child he is examining, to adopt his attitude and childish mannerism in speech and action. This must be supplied mostly by the examiner, as it can be indicated only in a small measure with the printed words of the directions. Some can do this readily and naturally, others fail almost entirely. Nevertheless, the best trained psychologist could make only a partial success with the tests if he proceeded with the three- or four-year-old child, for example, as one would with a ten-year-old, or vice versa. In the main, he would fail to arouse the effort of the younger child and disgust the older with an attitude he has outgrown and looks down upon. Furthermore, some initial practice in the use of the tests is required in the case of any examiner. The authors do not regard one as prepared to use them until after he has examined at least twenty children.

The failure of the general public, of the school authorities and medical profession in particular, to appreciate these requirements is at present leading to an extensive misuse of the tests, which must necessarily tend to the result of depriving the tests of the general recognition of their merits and the public of the benefits of their use. There is an extraordinary demand for tests that will do what these promise to accomplish when properly used. But it is the teachers of the public schools and physicians who are chiefly called upon or tempted to use them, the latter particularly in connection with medical inspection of the schools. Neither is particularly qualified as an examiner, and on the whole would probably not do so much better than the intelligent layman. There is even a tendency to take this work out of the hands of the teacher and entrust it to the school medical inspector as the expert, whereas in the majority of cases the teacher would probably get the better results with the tests because of her better understanding of children and ability to adapt herself to their mental levels.

Kuhlmann (1912)

REFERENCES

Achenbach, T. Comparison of Stanford-Binet Performance of Non-Retarded and Retarded Persons Matched for MA and Sex. *American Journal of Mental Deficiency,* 1970, 74, 488–494.

Achenbach, T. Stanford-Binet Short-Form Performance of Retarded and Non-Retarded Persons Matched for MA. *American Journal of Mental Deficiency,* 1971, 76, 30–32.

Aiken, L. R., Jr. *Psychological Testing and Assessment* (2nd ed.). Boston: Allyn and Bacon, 1976.

Altman, R., and Meyen, E. Guidelines for the Research Implications Department. *Education and Training of the Mentally Retarded,* 1975, 10, 167–168.
Altman, R. and Meyen, E. Research Needs with Severely/Profoundly Retarded: An Interactive Model. *Education and Training of the Mentally Retarded,* 1976, 11, 147–150.
Appfel, J. Some TMR's Can Read. *Education and Training of the Mentally Retarded,* 1974, 9, 199–200.
Bayles, E. *Democratic Educational Theory.* New York: Harper and Brothers, 1960.
Balla, D., Butterfield, E., and Zigler, E. Effects of Institutionalization on Retarded Children: A Longitudinal Cross-Institutional Investigation. *American Journal of Mental Deficiency,* 1974, 78, 530–549.
Black, W. An Investigation of Intelligence as a Causal Factor in Reading Problems. *Journal of Learning Disabilities,* 1971, 4, 22–25.
Blackman, L. Research and the Classroom. *Exceptional Children,* 1972, 39, 181–190.
Blackman, L., Bilksy, L., Burger, A., and Mar, H. Cognitive Processes and Academic Achievement in EMR Adolescents. *American Journal of Mental Deficiency,* 1976, 81, 125–134.
Blackwell, R. Study of Effective and Ineffective Teachers of the Trainable Mentally Retarded. *Exceptional Children,* 1972, 39, 139–143.
Blatt, B., and Garfunkel, Q. Educating Intelligence: Determinants of School Behavior of Disadvantaged Children. *Exceptional Children,* 1967, 33, 601–608.
Bortner, M. and Birch, H. G. Cognitive Capacity and Cognitive Competence. *American Journal of Mental Deficiency,* 1970, 74, 735–744.
Brown, L. The Analysis of Instructional Materials, *Mental Retardation,* 1974, 12, 21–25.
Brown, L., and Perlmutter, L. Teaching Functional Reading to Trainable Level Retarded Students. *Education and Training of the Mentally Retarded,* 1971, 6, 74–84.
Budoff, M., and Gottlieb, J. Special Class EMR Children Mainstreamed: A Study of an Aptitude (Learning Potential) X Treatment Interaction. *American Journal of Mental Deficiency,* 1976, 81–1–11.
Carter, J. L. Intelligence and Reading Achievement of EMR Children in Three Educational Settings. *Mental Retardation,* 1975, 13, 26–27.
Cegelka, W. and Cegelka, P. A Review of Research: Reading and the Educable Mentally Handicapped. *Exceptional Children,* 1970, 37, 187–200.
Cherkes, M. Effect of Chronological Age and Mental Age on the Understanding of Rules of Logic. *American Journal of Mental Deficiency,* 1975, 80, 208–216.
Cleland, C., Watson, C., and Whitten, R. Documentation in Mental Retardation. *Mental Retardation,* 1975, 13, 22–23.
Doppelt, J., and Bennett, G. Testing Job Applicants from Disadvantaged Groups. *Test Service Bulletin,* 1967, 57, 1–5.
Dunn, R., and Dunn, K. Learning Styles as a Criterion for Placement in Alternative Programs. *Phi Delta Kappan,* 1974, 56, 275–278.
Dugas, J. Effects of Stimulus Familiarity on the Rehearsal Strategies Transfer in Retarded and Nonretarded Individuals. *American Journal of Mental Deficiency,* 1975, 80, 349–356.
England, J., Semmel, M., Creenough, D., Krieder, J., Sitks, M., Weaver, P., and Van Ever, P. An Exploratory Study of the Relationships Between the Training, Experience, and

Selected Personality Characteristics of Teachers and the Progress of Trainable Mentally Handicapped Children. Final Report Project 5–1051. Grant No. OE–5–10–022 HEW. Wayne Intermediate School District. Detroit, Michigan, 1969.

English, H., and English, A. *A Comprehensive Dictionary of Psychological and Psychoanalytical Terms.* New York: McKay, 1966.

Ellis, N. R. Toilet-Training the Severely Retarded: An S–R Reinforcement Approach, in Ellis, N. R. (ed.). *Handbook of Mental Deficiency Research.* New York: McGraw-Hill, 1963.

Gagne, R. *The Conditions of Learning.* New York: Holt, Rinehart and Winston, 1965.

Gagne, R., and Briggs, L. J. *Principles of Instructional Design.* New York: Holt, Rinehart and Winston, 1974.

Gardner, J. M., and Selinger, S. Trends in Learning Research with the Mentally Retarded. *American Journal of Mental Deficiency,* 1971, 76, 733–738.

Garrison, M., Jr. Summary. *American Journal of Mental Deficiency,* 1966, 70, 141–143. (Monograph supplement).

Gearheart, B. R., and Whillenberg, E. *Application of Pupil Assessment Information: For the Special Education Teacher.* Denver: Love Publishing, 1970.

Goldman, R., and Hartig, L. The WISC May NOT Be a Valid Predictor of School Performance for Primary-Grade Minority Children. *American Journal of Mental Deficiency,* 1976, 80, 583–587.

Hamilton, J., and Budoff, M. Learning Potential Among the Moderately and Severely Retarded. *Mental Retardation,* 1974, 72, 33–36.

Hammill, D., Iano, R., McGertigan, J., and Wiederholt, J. Retardates' Reading Achievement in the Resource Room Model: The First Year. *The Training School Bulletin,* 1972, 69, 104–107.

Harris, L. H., and Tramontan, J. Discrimination Learning of Retarded Children as a Function of Positive Reinforcement and Response Cost. *American Journal of Mental Deficiency,* 1973, 78, 216–219.

Harter, S., Brown, L., and Zigler, E. Discrimination Learning in Retarded and Non Retarded Children as a Function of Task Difficulty and Social Reinforcement. *American Journal of Mental Deficiency,* 1971, 76, 275–283.

Heal, L. W. Research Strategies and Research Goals in the Scientific Study of Mental Subnormality. *American Journal of Mental Deficiency,* 1970, 75, 10–15.

Hill, L. A. Idiot Savants: A Categorization of Abilities. *Mental Retardation,* 1974, 12, 12–13.

Hoffman, E. The Idiot Savant: A Case Report and a Review of Explanations. *Mental Retardation,* 1971, 9, 18–21.

Holzberg, R. The Educable Retarded. *Science and Children,* 1976, 13, 19.

Hutt, M., and Gibby, R. *The Mentally Retarded Child: Development, Education, and Treatment* (3rd ed.). Boston: Allyn and Bacon, 1976.

Jordan, J. On the Educability of Intelligence and Related Issues — A Conversation with Burton Blatt. *Education and Training of the Mentally Retarded,* 1973, 8, 219–229.

Jacobs, J., and DeGraef, C. Expectancy and Race: Their Influences on Intelligence Test Scores. *Exceptional Children,* 1973, 40, 108–109.

Kahn, J. Relationship of Piaget's Sensorimotor Period to Language Acquisition of Profoundly Retarded Children. *American Journal of Mental Deficiency,* 1975, 79, 640–643.

Kaya, E. A Curricular Sequence Based on Psychological Process Rather than Subject Content. *Exceptional Children,* 1961, 27, 425–428.

Kershner, J. Conservation of Vertical-Horizontal Space Perception in Trainable Retarded Children. *American Journal of Mental Deficiency,* 1973, 77, 710–716.

Kiraly, J., Jr., and Morishima, A. Developing Mathematical Skills by Applying Piaget's Theory. *Education and Training of the Mentally Retarded,* 1971, 9, 62–65.

Klein, S. Psychological Testing, Part Four. *The Exceptional Parent,* 1972A, 1, 18–21.

Klein, S. Psychological Testing, Part Three. *The Exceptional Parent,* 1972B, 1, 24–28.

Kolstoe, O. *Teaching Educable Mentally Retarded Children.* New York: Holt, Rinehart and Winston, 1970.

Kolstoe, O., and Hirsch, D. Convergent Thinking of Retarded and Non-Retarded Boys. *Exceptional Children,* 1974, 40, 292–293.

Kopatic, N., Canale, V., and Kopatic, N. A Contribution to the Study of Group Testing in Schools. *The Training School Bulletin,* 1972, 69, 121–126.

Kubena, M. *Judgment Making Skills, Can They Be Developed?* Austin, Texas: Brown Schools for Exceptional Children, 1971.

Kuhlmann, F. A Revision of the Binet-Simon System for Measuring the Intelligence of Children. *Journal of Psycho-Asthenics,* 1912, 1, 8–9.

LaFontaine, L., and Benjamin, G. Idiot Savants: Another View. *Mental Retardation,* 1971, 9, 41–42.

Lambert, J. Extinction by Retarded Children Following Discrimination Learning with and Without Errors. *American Journal of Mental Deficiency,* 1975, 80, 286–291.

Lathey, J. Gagne's Learning Types and Levels of Retardation. *Mental Retardation,* 1975, 13, 26–27.

Levy, J. Social Reinforcements and Knowledge of Results as Determinants of Motor Performance in EMR Children. *American Journal of Mental Deficiency,* 1974, 78, 752–758.

Lindsley, O. G. Can Deficiency Produce Specific Superiority — The Challenge of the Idiot Savant. *Exceptional Children,* 1966, 31, 225–332.

Litrownik, A., Franzini, L., and Turner, G. Acquisition of Concepts by EMR Children as a Function of Type of Modeling, Rule Verbalization, and Observer Gender. *American Journal of Mental Deficiency,* 1976, 80, 620–628.

Lobb, H. Effects of Verbal Rehearsal on Discrimination Learning in Moderately Retarded and Nursery School Children. *American Journal of Mental Deficiency,* 1975, 79, 449–454.

Lombardi, T. P., and Balch, P. E. Science Experiences and the Mentally Retarded. *Science and Children,* 1976, 12, 20.

Matheny, A. P., Jr. Comparability of WISC and PPVT Scores Among Young Children. *Exceptional Children,* 1971, 38, 147–150.

McCarthy, J., and Scheerenberger, R. A Decade of Research on the Education of the Mentally Retarded. *Mental Retardation Abstracts.* Vol. 3, No. 4. Washington, D.C.: U.S. Dept. of Health, Education and Welfare, 1966.

McLaughlin, J., Hinojosa, V., and Trlica, J. Comprehension of Statistic Terms by Special Education Students. *Exceptional Children,* 1973, 39, 408–412.

Melnick, G., Bernstein, J., and Lehrer, B. Piagetian Tasks and Arithmetic Achievement in Retarded Children. *Exceptional Children,* 1974, 40, 358–361.

Melolascino, F., and Heal, L. New Directions in NARC Research. *Mental Retardation,* 12, 44.

Moreland, S. IQ, Mental Age, Complexity, and Trial Blocks and the Response Latency of Retarded and Nonretarded Children. *American Journal of Mental Deficiency,* 1976, 80, 437–441.

Morishima, C. Another Van Gogh of Japan: The Superior Artwork of a Retarded Boy. *Exceptional Children,* 1974, 41, 92–96.

Moss, J. W., and Mayer, D. L. Children with Intellectual Subnormality, in Gallagher (ed.). *Application of Child Development Research to Exceptional Children.* Reston, Virginia: Council for Exceptional Children, 1975.

Myers, C. E., and Dingman, H. F. Factor Analytic and Structure of Intellect Models in Study of Mental Retardation. *American Journal of Mental Deficiency,* 1966, 70, 7–28. (Monograph supplement).

Newland, T. E., Baer, C. J., Simches, R. F. When the Teacher Researches. *Exceptional Children,* 1961, 27, 299–336.

Oliver, R. R. Bruner and the Center for Cognitive Studies. *American Journal of Mental Deficiency,* 1966, 70, 109–126. (Monograph supplement).

Prehm, H. J., Logan, D., and Towle, M. The Effect of Warm-Up on Rote Learning Performance. *Exceptional Children,* 1972, 39, 623–627.

Ramanauskus, S., and Burrow, W. WISC Profiles: Above Average and MR Good and Poor Readers. *Mental Retardation,* 1973, 11, 12–14.

Riegel, H. R., and Taylor, A. Comparisons of Conceptual Strategies for Grouping and Remembering Employed by EMR and Non-Retarded Children. *American Journal of Mental Deficiency,* 1974, 78, 592–598.

Rodee, B., and Sellin, D. Incidental Learning Performance of Retarded and Normal Children. *The Training School Bulletin,* 1973, 69, 180–184.

Ross, R. T. Behavior Correlates of Levels of Intelligence. *American Journal of Mental Deficiency,* 1972, 76, 545–549.

Rowland, G. T. From a Development Point of View. *Mental Retardation News,* 1972, 21, 5.

Sabatino, D., and Hayden, D. Information Processing Behaviors Related to Learning Disability and Educable Mental Retardation. *Exceptional Children,* 1970, 37, 21–29.

Sattler, J. M. *Assessment of Children's Intelligence.* Philadelphia: W. B. Sanders, 1974.

Schmid-Kitsikis, E. Piagetian Theory and Its Approach to Psychopathology. *American Journal of Mental Deficiency,* 1973, 77, 694–705.

Schuster, S. O., and Gruen, G. Success and Failure as Determinants of the Performance Predictions of Mentally Retarded and Nonretarded Children. *American Journal of Mental Deficiency,* 1971, 77, 190–196.

Schwarz, R., and Cook, J. Mental Age as a Predictor of Academic Achievement. *Education and Training of the Mentally Retarded,* 1971, 6, 12–14.

Silverstein, A. B., Brownlee, L., Hubbell, M., and McClain, R. Comparison of Two Sets of Piagetian Scales with Severely and Profoundly Retarded Children. *American Journal of Mental Deficiency,* 1975, 80, 292–297.

Smith, R. M. *Clinical Teaching: Methods of Instruction for the Retarded* (2nd ed.). New York: McGraw-Hill, 1974.

Spitz, H., and LaFontaine, L. The Digit Span of Idiots Savants. *American Journal of Mental Deficiency,* 1973, 77, 557–579.

Stayton, S., and Ohwaki, S. Retardates Memory for Contextually Related Words. *Training School Bulletin,* 1974, 71, 30–38.

Stephens, W. B. The Appraisal of Cognitive Development, in Stephens (ed.). *Training the Developmentally Young.* New York: John Day, 1971.

Stephens, W. B., Manhaney, E., and McLaughlin, J. Mental Ages for Achievement of Piagetian Reasoning Assessments. *Education and Training of the Mentally Retarded,* 1972, 7, 124–128.

Swartz, J., Cleland, C., and Altman, P. Time Capsules for Research in Profound Retardation. *Mental Retardation,* 1971, 9, 29–30.

Terry, P., and Samules, S. J. Comparison of Nonretarded and Mentally Retarded Children on a Perceptual Learning Task. *American Journal of Mental Deficiency,* 1976, 81, 167–171.

Throne, J. M. The Assessment of Intelligence: Towards What End? *Mental Retardation,* 1972, 10, 9–11.

Tisdall, W. Productive Thinking in Retarded Children. *Exceptional Children,* 1962, 29, 36–41.

Tynchuck, A. Recent Trends in Research with Exceptional Children, in Jordan, J., and McDonald, P. (eds.). *Dimensions.* Washington, D.C.: Council for Exceptional Children, 1970.

Ullman, D. Breadth of Attention and Retention in Mentally Retarded and Intellectually Average Children. *American Journal of Mental Deficiency,* 1974, 78, 640–648.

Ullman, D. G., and Routh, D. K. Discrimination Learning in Mentally Retarded Children as a Function of the Number of Relevant Dimensions. *American Journal of Mental Deficiency,* 1971, 76, 176–179.

Wanschura, P., and Borkowski, J. Long-Term Transfer of a Mediational Strategy by Moderately Retarded Children. *American Journal of Mental Deficiency,* 1975, 80, 323–333.

Warren, S. A. Another Right. *Mental Retardation,* 1975, 13, 2.

Wesman, A. Aptitude, Intelligence, and Achievement. *Test Service Bulletin,* 1956, 51, 4–5.

Wohlwill, D. Piaget's Theory of the Development of Intelligence in Concrete Operations Period. *American Journal of Mental Deficiency,* 1966, 70, 57–78. (Monograph supplement).

Zeaman, D., and House, B. J. The Role of Attention in Retardate Discrimination Learning, in Ellis (ed.). *Handbook of Mental Deficiency.* New York: McGraw-Hill, 1963.

6

Development and Maturation

SYNOPSIS

This chapter and the next constitute a composite of the AAMD concept of adaptive behavior. This chapter presents a task orientation as the framework for understanding human development and potential. Included in this discussion is a view of tasks encountered beyond the school years.

Maturation as sensory-motor-perceptual learning is discussed. The efforts of Doman-Delacato, Kephart, and Frostig are considered, along with the significance of physical fitness. Finally, there is a brief resumé of preschool programming.

OBJECTIVES

ATTITUDES

1 To feel motivated to seek out further information regarding early childhood.
2 To feel a commitment to support early childhood programs.
3 To respect the genuine accomplishments in this period of life.

UNDERSTANDINGS

1 To distinguish maturation as a particular type of learning.
2 To define the developmental tasks required for lifelong learning.
3 To define the developmental tasks required for various periods of life.
4 To formulate a personal resolution regarding conflicting claims of competing approaches for perceptual motor development.

SKILLS

1 To identify formal approaches for assessment of maturational development.

2 To describe goals and standards for early childhood programs.
3 To identify the social and political implications of research findings.

OVERVIEW

Development as Tasks

Muller (1969) emphasized that the development of human beings is more than a listing of "what happens." He proposed that human development should be viewed as progress toward increasingly complex behavior. His perspective was based on the examination of the *tasks* associated with increasingly complex adaptations. For Muller, these tasks constitute a dialogue between the child and the environment. He acknowledged Havighurst's efforts (1953) to identify the tasks necessary to complete the process of adaptation. To update the Havighurst model, Muller integrated "newer" sources of data, especially Piaget and Guilford. The concept of the developmental task has several advantages. *First,* it establishes a rationale for helpful management based upon the principle of critical period. In essence, the premise of critical period identifies: a time period, the central tasks to be acquired, and the consequences for subsequent developmental tasks. Certain periods of life are viewed as essential, or critical, for the timing of developmental experiences. The critical period theory postulates grave consequences if developmental tasks are not accomplished. Research cited by Muller suggests that it is difficult to retrace and/or fill in. Knowledge of tasks and their responsiveness to intervention can be helpful for the design of program goals. While the Muller discussion encompassed birth through adolescence, recent efforts by American psychologists have extended scientific knowledge of developmental tasks beyond adolescence into adulthood and midlife transition. This American effort, termed by its advocates "life cycles research," strives to bring the same rigor, precision, and information to adulthood as now exists for childhood and adolescence. Levinson, Darrow, Klein, Levinson, and McKee (1974), among others, have investigated critical periods of maturity in order to establish tasks necessary for the achievement and mastery of adulthood.

Warren (1971) has noted that observing the acquisition of developmental tasks can provide diagnostic information. Failure to acquire does not mean intellectual retardation; however, lack of acquisition does mean that subsequent intervention may be merited. Hammill and Bartel (1973) identified a prerequisite series of behaviors which appear to chain into more complex behaviors. They have reviewed the diagnostic base (formal and informal tests) which can provide the foundation for intervention. Finally, the Grossman report also noted behaviors by age groupings, which reinforces the need for intervention.

Developmental Tasks

Levinson et al. (1974), like Muller, regard developmental tasks as turning points or boundary regions, although it is recognized that there are variations among people within each period as well as tremendous variation in transitional stages. Significant in the development task approach is the concept of balance between external events and internal reactions. That is to say, *how* a person feels about events is as significant as *what* the person experiences. Certain persons respond to failure by withdrawal, while others express regret and stabilize a life pattern. Others react to these events by continued striving. Therefore, as one encounters knowledge about development, it is helpful to recall that tasks are preparation and an interplay between the person and his or her surroundings.

An examination of the Muller, Levinson et al., Warren, and the Hammill and Bartell sources confirm the AAMD notion of adaptive behavior as sequenced responses associated within identified age ranges. Table 6–1 offers a resumé of developmental tasks. Inspection of this table suggests at least seven major groupings of developmental periods, although the divisions are somewhat arbitrary. These seven divisions account for the essential tasks confronted by retarded persons, their parents, and practitioners. Certain authorities, such as Freud, Jung, and Eriksen, have divided the life span into varying numbers of epochs. The inclusion of adulthood implies a life span of services for the retarded person. This inclusion also suggests that parents and practitioners will have their own tasks to face as they simultaneously attempt to relate to others. The Levinson et al. report specifically noted that a potential implication of life cycle research would be to understand the relationship between the parents' task mastery and subsequent attitudes toward children. It could be that a parent might be so drained by certain tasks that there would be little energy for children. The behavior of practitioners might be understood as related to career effectiveness and career aspirations.

MATURATION

McMahon (1974, p. 643), in an overview of contemporary expert opinion and research, defined maturation as "the process by which the organism develops in an orderly sequence and at a fixed individual rate." Maturation was viewed as a type of learning based upon physiological change and environmental opportunity, as well as change based on increased physiological complexity. Practice or instruction were

Table 6–1 RESUMÉ OF DEVELOPMENTAL PERIODS

Age Equivalents	*Major Descriptors*	*Related Component Tasks*	*Implications and Consequences*
Infancy: birth to ages 2 to 3	Motor skills Self-care skills Emergence of language	Physiological functions: trained to conform to social demands, especially toilet-training and self-care skills. Integration of sensory data into perceptual information. Origins of independence of action from dependent care. Language is a major indicator.	Necessity for preschool programs to equalize developmental opportunities. A critical time of life for acquisition of the foundation skills of adaptive behavior. A formative period for intellectual and linguistic adaptation.
Early childhood: ages 3 to 5	Awareness of skills Sensory-perceptual stability Emergence of conscience	Elements of right and wrong emerge at this level. Perceptual data becomes integrated into basic concepts and stability of laterality and directionality. Emergence of self-concept of ability. Increasing of skills forms locus of central concepts.	Emergence of conscience and introduction to the wider social order. Learning to participate and share in group settings. A foundation period for school learning. Self-concept and self-direction values originate.
Childhood: ages 5 to 10 and 12	Concrete reasoning Common sense Physical skills Peer relationships Learning sexual role Academic skills	Transition from self-centeredness to awareness and conformity to expectations of others. Emergence of reasoning and judgment skills. Peer acceptance based upon social and physical skills is important.	The foundation for career options. A transition from childhood to pre-adolescence. Discovery of one's own sense of mastery.

Table 6–1 (continued)

Age Equivalents	*Major Descriptors*	*Related Component Tasks*	*Implications and Consequences*
Adolescence: ages 12 to 18	Coping with puberty Forming vital choices Preparatory Formal logic	Acceptance of physical limitations associated with puberty as well as acceptance of one's sex. Period of vital choices of vocation, marriage partner, and philosophic values. Leaving the family originates during this period. Relating to one's sexuality is a significant task.	A period of great transition. A constant interplay between the old and familiar and the new and unknown. The emergence of adultlike roles, but still dependent.
Young adulthood: ages 18 to late 20s	Leaving the family Entering adulthood	Separation from natural family and adult controls to acquiring independence and self-sufficiency. Establishment of career competencies and acquisition of material gains. Acquiring a dream or sense of purpose to guide one's life. Mentor is important.	A sense of vulnerableness as one progresses through career paths. Securing a mentor is a helpful resource. Continuing separation from the old values of one's family.

Table 6–1 (continued)

Age Equivalents	*Major Descriptors*	*Related Component Tasks*	*Implications and Consequences*
Adulthood: ages 30s to 40s	Becoming a valid adult and establishing one's identity	This period is as turbulent as adolescence, especially the early 30s. Period of questioning values, aspirations, and life situation, especially vocation. Recognition of one's morality. Last chance to "make it" is persistent feeling. Role of mentor to younger person.	As transitional as adolescence. Values are important. Can be the best or worst of times. A period of striving.
Transition variable	Stabilization and restabilization	Reoccuring of coming to terms with the difference between the dream and actual achievements. Valuing of life's rewards and coping with diminishing physical abilities. Concentration upon the essentials. A mellowing and relaxed period and prizing of values. Period of devotion to friends and family.	Can be resignation or renewal. Usually a period of contentment and a sense of fulfillment.

not considered. McMahon emphasized that while sequence is universal, emergence of skills occurs at an individual rate.

The question of intervention remains a persistent issue. McMahon identified the *readiness principle* as a guideline for intervention. This principle postulates that environmental manipulation should be timed to coincide with physical readiness. Development is associated with, and the product of, internal capacity and a benign environment. The readiness principle also implies a realization that even normal development is not linear. McMahon noted, for example, that by age eight the brain is 95 percent complete, the body is 45 percent complete, and the reproductive system is 10 percent complete.

Acquisition of motor and sensory-perceptual skills is considered the foundation for performance in cognitive, linguistic, and adjustment situations. Intervention for retarded persons does not necessarily seek a "cure" or restoration; intervention can also be successful if behavior is made more complex. This complexity could be the establishment of skills previously viewed by tradition as unattainable, the modification of standard treatments, and the emergence of new value systems about clients, learners, and persons.

It should be noted that environmental manipulation strategies vary, and there are many advocates for differing positions. However, all agree on the significance of one environmental variable: *nutrition.* McMahon (1974, p. 95) has noted:

> When very young children are deprived of food their growth stops; if this condition lasts for awhile, later feedings will not reverse that process, and the child will never attain normal height. Worse, during the child's first year starvation results in permanent damage to the central nervous system, including a deficiency in the number of brain cells.

In a summary of studies related to malnutrition, McMahon noted the psychological consequences of starvation: nervousness, irritability, and lack of interest in others. Winesberg (1975) has critiqued an investigation that attempted to contrast the developmental consequences of adequate versus inadequate nutrition. The study compared the intelligence test performance of Dutch males conceived during a six-month period in World War II. One group was produced in a geographical area controlled by the Allies, where there was presumably adequate nutrition, contrasted with the German-held territory, where there was suspected famine. What makes this study remarkable is its central finding that males conceived in the famine areas turned out to be the more intelligent of the two groups. Winesberg (p. 361), comments:

> Bluntly, this is one of the most unfortunate books produced in epidemiology. It is based upon a study which never should have been done since one of the basic assumptions in research was violated (i.e., that the investigator makes certain that the independent variable is administered to the experimental group in an unbiased fashion). As a consequence, we now have in our permanent literature a work by epidemiologists of the highest reputation which implies that poor prenatal nutrition produces more intelligent

> offspring. The dozens of volumes of testimony before the McGovern Committee on Nutrition and Hunger Needs — which has hundreds of reports of studies and the expert testimony of additional hundreds about the effects of starvation in this country and throughout the world — now have to contend with one which will undoubtedly be quoted by those against nutritional aid. The latter will unquestionably use it to state that we need further research before aid be granted.

Richardson, Birch, and Hertzig (1973) report an investigation typical of many similar studies. Sixty-two persons between ages six and ten who were hospitalized for malnourishment during infancy were compared with a matched sample of sixty-two persons who had adequate nutrition. Thirty-one siblings of the malnourished sample also were available. The method of comparison was achievement performance as measured by the Wide Range Achievement Test as well as teacher judgments of classroom behavior. The central finding reflected the superiority of the control persons over the malnourished group in test performance and teacher judgment. Test performance of the siblings (presumably adequate diets) of the malnourished group was superior to family members, but not to the contrast sample, although classroom behaviors of persistence, motivation, conformity, etc. were similar to the contrast group. The authors concluded that the performance of the malnourished group and their siblings could be attributed to a common environment factor: malnourishment.

The President's Committee on Mental Retardation (1970) estimated that 20 million Americans suffer from malnutrition. As suggested in chapters 3 through 5, malnutrition can have serious consequences even for those who survive it beyond the preschool period. The committee estimates that upwards of 25 million Americans, including 5 million children, live in households where the annual income is inadequate to provide proper nutrition.

THE NATURE OF SENSORY-PERCEPTUAL LEARNING

It will be recalled from the discussion on perspectives that a cerebral orientation has influenced management and treatment of retarded persons, especially young retarded persons. The central nervous system was discussed as the processing center for assimilation and accommodation of data necessary for complex stages of development.

Chalfant and Scheffein (1969) have attempted to specify the relationship of central nervous system (CNS) processes to serve as guidelines for intervention strategies. Their anlaysis of available research and expert opinion suggested that the acquisition of language and literacy skills can be related to prior sensory-motor and perceptual learnings. Sensory-motor learning was described as responding to stimulus at an instinctive and/or reflex level. Changes in light and/or noise levels, for example, will produce motor movements of avoidance or approach. With increasing maturity and favorable environments, responses involve choices. This higher level of response was described as perceptual learning. Perception is descriptive of a transitional process between sensation and conceptual-cognitive learning. Emergence of conceptual learnings is usually inferred by language performance. These authors identified a cycle of inputs, process, outputs, and feedback to correlate sensation, perception, and language. Input relates to the reception of accurate, stable sensory impressions. Output describes consistent motor-based responses of speaking, writing, movement, and the like. Feedback describes knowledge of results; it is manifested by correcting errors and perfecting responses on the basis of performance. Feedback also involves feelings of pain-pleasure and success-failure. Process refers to an internal linkage between input-receiving and output-expressing. Process was said to involve cerebral function; however, they are not directly observed or measured as much as inferred. It is the inference of observers which has dictated the various theories and practices.

The emergence of learning disabilities and its attendant interest in sensory-motor and perceptual-motor learnings, according to Hallahan and Cruickshank (1973), had its origins in the study of mental retardation. Strauss, among others, was cited as an early pioneer who perceived two groupings of mildly retarded children. His philosophy and techniques have been incorporated and refined as one of several major approaches in the treatment of learning disabilities.

The learning disability emphasis, as citizens' movements *and* development of materials, according to these authors, has led to a *renewed* (not new) interest among workers in the field of mental retardation in the perceptual foundations of learning. Cruickshank (1975), acknowledging the efforts of Rappaport (1964), has advanced a framework that serves to outline the nature of these foundations (table 6–2). The dimension of *impulse control* would relate to those areas described as haptic, or motor learnings. The dimension of *integrative* relates to perceptual learnings. The *intra* and *inter personal* describes secondary consequences of impairment in the first two areas. Cruickshank (1975) further defined management approaches as structures of: relationship, program, materials, environment, and motor training.

The three dimensions of functioning and the five dimensions of structure can be transposed into a management matrix. *Relationship structure* defines the adult's ability to assist the child in areas of impulse and intra-inter-personal functioning. A critical skill is the establishment of limitations for behavior and communication of expectations. *Environment structure* involves control of space and reduction of external stimuli. *Program structure* describes control of routine and maintaining a dependable schedule for the child's security. *Teaching materials* can be structured to counter "negative" traits and yet teach positive values. For example, completing bead designs to match the teacher's product can be a distraction into learning with use of motor activity to teach sequence abilities. *Motor training* is structured to the extent that it should be daily. Kephart and Frostig, among others, have developed formal, goal-oriented programs.

Table 6–2 SUMMATIVE COMPONENTS REGARDING THE INTER-RELATIONSHIPS AMONG PM ABILITIES, CONCEPTUAL ABILITIES, AND AFFECTIVE BEHAVIORS

Components		
Major Component	*Subcomponents*	*Descriptors*
Impulse control or regulation	Hyperactivity Hyperdistractability Disinhibition Impulsivity Perseveration Lability of affect	Excessive motor ability (e.g. always in motion); inability to focus attention. Figure-ground problems. Reacts to the moment; constant and continuous repetition of an act. Rigid in moving from tasks. Overaction to ordinary events.
	Motor dysfunctions	Fine and gross motor. Kephart abilities are descriptions
Integrative functions	Perceptual	Frostig abilities, figure-ground and disassociation (perceiving of a Gestalt) are key elements.
	Conceptual	Integration of perceptions into concepts of classification; formal, rigid behaviors of organization; inability to shift groupings into different sets.
Intra and interpersonal	Frustration tolerance	Sensitive to failure; may be extreme in attack or withdrawal.
	Flight from challenge	The overt manifestation of low frustration tolerance; all tasks may be evaded or attacked because of adversion to one.
	Overcompensation	Can be seeking or avoiding activities; intent is to defend against failure
	Control and manipulation of others	Attempt to enlist others in escape and evasion of tasks; need to assert control over others.
	Power struggle or manipulation of others	Similar to the preceding, except that emphasis is upon refusal to perform.
	Self-concept	Reaction to guilt over behavior, usually distorted and preoccupied with negative feelings.

Newman, Roos, McCann, Menolascino, and Heal (1975) observed a current emphasis upon sensory-motor training. They observed that despite considerable debate, activities and programs of training in sensory-motor areas have become an addendum to the curriculum for mentally retarded learners. This report identified procedures associated with Doman-Delacato, Kephart, and Frostig as the three major approaches that have achieved widespread acceptance.

The Doman-Delacato system rests on assumptions of neurological functioning. This system postulates that neural impairment can be *directly* treated through a process of *patterning*. This process involves physical manipulation of the person, regulation of respiration, and regulation of visual-auditory stimulation. The system involves diagnostic assessment to establish a neurological age from which treatment procedures are recommended by institute staff. The process of patterning involves the recreation of postnatal movements through the developmental stages of development. In theory, the activity creates, or recreates, neural pathways to be activated for functioning. The procedure is total, involving volunteers to assist the family in maintaining the consistency of patterning. Faber (1968), among others, has written a sympathetic account of the mission and achievements of this system.

Kephart (1964) (1971) has described his system as a perceptual-motor approach. Unlike Doman-Delacato, the Kephart program is geared toward the ambulatory child who requires structured, physically oriented activities. These activities are directed toward the establishment of bonds among motor, visual, and auditory as separable pairs and into increasing complex matches. This system has a diagnostic assessment procedure for the formulation of training procedures. The crux of the Kephart system is that motor learning and exploration is the basis for subsequent acquisition of other learnings. Thus, the motor processes of locomotion, receipt and propulsion, contact (release and grasp), and balance-posture are the initial avenues of development. Through motor exploration, vision and hearing emerge as first parallel channels and eventually as the primary sources of concepts of time, space, and distance. For example, near and far are explored through motor movement until the child learns to use vision to inspect near and far distance. Initially the hand guides the eye in seeking objects, eventually yielding to eye-hand coordination. The end product of motor learnings and the focal point for perceptual development is the attainment of *laterality* and *directionality*. Laterality involves the symmetry of the body as a reference point for relating to and classifying data. Left and right, up and down, near and far, and other precepts of such nature are judged by the position of one's body. Laterality, while egocentric, is a first means of classification, memory, and judgment. The input, process, output, and feedback cycle is initiated. Directionality resembles laterality, except it is nonegocentric. At this level, the person recognizes that the left-right of another person is different from his or hers. Near is learned as a relative concept. For either organic or environmental reasons, motor learnings and laterality-directionality (Kephart appears less committed to the pure neurological orientation of Doman-Delacato) may or may not develop as splinter skills. This latter notion suggests performance of elements of a skill without its total pattern. The Kephart system implies that specifically designed activities can develop and/or remediate necessary perceptual motor learnings. Ball (1971) has advanced support for the Kephart system as a contemporary refinement of Itard and Sequin.

The Frostig system evolved as a response to learning disabled children and gained a certain following among those interested in disadvantaged children and mentally retarded children. This system reflects a testing procedure as the single basis for training procedures. Frostig (1970) and Frostig and Horne (1964) have stressed the necessity for supplementing Frostig test data with collaboration from other sources, especially the Illinois Test of Psycholinguistics, and for supplementing the paper-pencil activities of the program with movement activities similar to those advocated by Kephart. The central core of the program clusters around five abilities pertinent to visual perception: eye-hand coordination, figure-ground, perceptual constancy, spatial relationships, and positions in space. There is a diagnostic test for these abilities and workbook exercises of increasing complexity for training. Again it should be noted that Kephart-like activities might be prescribed as a readiness program prior to transition to the workbook series. These activities, plus auditory discrimination activities, can be used simultaneously for enrichment.

A tentative support for the Frostig approach can be found in the research literature for disadvantaged learners and for retarded learners. Examples for disadvantaged students would include the reports of Alley, Snyder, Spencer, and Angell (1968) and of Gell, Herdtner, and Lough (1968). Both studies compared an experiment and control group of kindergarten students with respect to subsequent reading readiness. The results favored Frostig. The reports of Thelen (1973) and of Allen, Dickerman, and Haupt (1966) lend support to the Frostig approach for mildly retarded students. The latter study reflected the suitability of the materials, while the former study confirmed the value of the sensory-motor component.

Abbott and Sabatino (1975) compared the performance gains of a group of inner city four- and five-year-olds for visual-motor perception as a function of parent involvement. One group agreed to conduct daily twenty-minute sessions in the Frostig program. The mothers were the teachers. The control group did not use this procedure but attended sessions on parent-child interactions. The program was conducted for ten weeks. The results showed statistically significant results for the experimental group. Parent reports from the experimental group revealed that the child was perceived as more confident, a better listener, better able to follow directions, and better prepared for homework in the elementary grades. The authors concluded that inner city parents are not disinterested in education, but resent being excluded from school activities. They also concluded that this procedure may have "unexpected" outcomes in behavioral areas as well as in visual perceptual skills.

In terms of the matrix model inferred from Rappaport and Cruickshank, Doman-Delacato clearly falls within the impulse dimension. The Kephart procedure overlaps motor training of impulse and the perceptual component of integration, while Frostig would be in perceptual. These latter two approaches, as will be seen elsewhere, appear to have a positive effect upon intra-inter-personal dimensions.

THE EFFECTIVENESS OF SENSORY-PERCEPTUAL INTERVENTION

The previous section identified three major dimensions of learnings which appear to sequence themselves as motor learnings. These yield to outcomes of laterality-directionality and subsequently to five visual motor learnings and to two auditory learnings — association and discrimination (implied in Kephart and Frostig). This section summarizes current opinion and describes a fourth alternative.

The Frostig and Kephart approaches both have been discussed with respect to testing procedures and their transfer effects. The reports of Morrison and Pothier (1972), Sullivan (1972), Becker and Sabitino (1973), Flegenheimer and Birch (1973), McKibben (1973), and Buckland and Balow (1973) share certain findings. When Frostig-trained groups are compared to nongroups, there is the likelihood that attainment of skills will not transfer to beginning reading. When Kephart groups are compared to groups receiving physical activity, there is usually no difference between Kephart and activity groups. The Frostig test has been called a two-factor test rather than the five-factor test it purports to be. The Kephart testing procedure is truly a survey test without norm references. To be sure, children in the treatment groups do gain. The problem has been to understand why.

Suphier (1973), in a review of research, identified thirteen assumptions about the supposed relationship among perceptual-motor training, learning, and achievement in school subjects (table 6–3). The reader should treat this table as a "true-false" test. If the responses appear paradoxical or contradictory, Suphier notes that experts are similarly perplexed. On the basis of forty-three citations, Suphier concludes that the first seven items of the table would be true, and the next five would be false, with item 13 a "maybe."

The Suphier analysis attempts to identify a theoretical framework, test the ability of the framework to predict events, identify significant implications, examine prevailing principles, and suggest future directions. This article can provide a helpful orientation to the practitioner attempting to grasp the universe of treatment-management, which could have applications to mentally retarded persons.

From a deductive point of view, according to Suphier, one might reason that factors of perceptual motor abilities (hereafter termed PM) are well known and separable. It then follows that test batteries can be selected. From test results, it would be possible to identify behavior consequences associated with deficit.

Table 6–3 ASSUMPTIONS AND MISCONCEPTIONS ABOUT PERCEPTUAL MOTOR SKILLS AND LEARNING TASKS

	Assumption
1.	PM skills are significant in the learning process.
2.	Remediation of PM deficits can be accomplished through specific training activities.
3.	PM skills are translatable directly into identifiable kinds of competencies.
4.	A child with a PM deficit may do quite well in school.
5.	Some reading-disabled students' problems are centered around PM deficits.
6.	Tests of laterality, directionality, and dominance are unreliable predictors of school reading success.
7.	PM evaluation has a useful place in preschool programs.
8.	PM abilities correlate highly with school success.
9.	The key to eliminating learning disabilities is to remediate PM deficits.
10.	All reading problems can be traced to a PM problem.
11.	Educators know the elements of PM ability.
12.	Motoric training in laterality, directionality, balance, and body image should have low priority in the preschool curriculum.
13.	A PM deficit can be identified by a standardized test.

Examination of deficit, or pattern of deficits, should indicate valid remedial or developmental procedures. Currently, factors of PM are said to constitute: acuity, kinesthetic awareness, visual perception, auditory perception, and perceptual integration.

These five factors are viewed as sequential; acuities lead to kinesthetic awareness, to visual perception, and so on. Thus, the factors should constitute the basis for conceptual learnings necessary for speech and language as well as proficiency in literacy skills.

Common assessment devices receiving attention in the clinical and/or research literature for mentally retarded, learning disabled, or high-risk kindergarten learners were identified as the Illinois Test of Psycholinguistic Abilities (ITPA), the Wechsler Intelligence Scale for Children (WISC), the Stanford-Binet Intelligence Scale, and the Wide-Range Achievement Test. These scales are usually descriptive of a generalized pattern. These tests may be, or should be, supplemented by the following classes of tests:

1 Visual perceptual:
Frostig Developmental Test of Visual Perception
Bender-Gestalt Visuo-Motor Coordination Test
Goodenough-Harris Draw-a-Man Test
Memory for Designs Test

2 Auditory perceptual:
Wepman Auditory Discrimination Test
Test of Auditory Perception

3 Motoric, or coordination:
Purdue Perceptual-Motor Survey
Lincoln-Oseretsky Motor Development Test

Acuity evaluation refers to measures of sensory input such as might be obtained by ophthalmologists, optometrists, otologists, and by audiological examinations. *Kinesthetic* awareness may be variously described in the literature as sensory-motor performance, psychomotor competence, motor coordination, or motor planning. This awareness describes the ability to control and direct the voluntary muscles of the body. In general, subabilities would be said to include laterality, directionality, ocular pursuit, balance, and body image. *Visual perception* involves figure-ground discrimination, space relationship, visual stability, visual tracking, and constancy of visual relationship. *Auditory perception* is usually defined as abilities to discriminate between and among sounds, memory for sounds, auditory figure-ground discrimination, and resistance to auditory distraction. *Perceptual integration* describes the ability to transfer perceptual input from one mode to another mode of expression. For example, an auditory command "Stop" will require cessation of movement; the visual symbol *dog* will vocally be pronounced as "dog"; or given a tap on the back, the person selects an object from among three serving as illustrations.

According to Suphier, there may not be consistent patterns among test factors and performance consequences. She notes that given seemingly paradoxical results from questionable, but best available, tests, a new breed of professional emerges who becomes expert at interpretation. There also appear to be contradictory results of treatment. For example, mildly mentally retarded persons "trained" in sensory-motor areas appear to be better in sensory-motor abilities, but there is usually no subsequent improvement in school tasks. However, there appears enough contradiction to warrant continued effort. The overall summary of Suphier is that PM approaches have promise, but multivariant analysis (simultaneous correlation of several variables) is required. She also notes that *age* and *affect* may be critical factors for future analysis. There is the suspicion that certain materials may be helpful for specific age ranges, rather than for generalized age groups. For example, the Bender Gestalt, according to Werner, Simonian, and Smith (1967), is predictive of reading achievement from kindergarten level up to sixth grade, but is *not* a predictor if given at sixth grade.

The function of affect is viewed in two ways. *First,* the learner's difficulties may prompt a secondary reaction of feelings of inadequacy and frustration. *Second,* there is evidence to suggest that while PM training may not produce changes in learning gains, there did appear to be positive gains in feelings about self and greater confidence in self.

A statement regarding the Doman-Delacato method was issued jointly by ten organizations, including the Canadian and National Association for Retarded Children (1968). The Institute for the Study of Human Potential (ISHP) responded to the statement, which it considered unfavorable. The 1968 statement and the response of the ISHP is presented in a condensed summary in table 6–4. An inspection of this table reveals the depth of feelings about the system.

Since the 1968 statement, as Neman et al. have noted, there have been several developments. First, in 1968, the American Academy on Human Development was founded. The AAHD is represented by centers around the country whose members had been trained in ISHP procedures. The AAHD also incorporated training procedures of Kephart and Frostig in its services. The second development was the

Table 6–4 COMPARISON OF POSITIONS OF THE ISHP AND TEN ORGANIZATIONS REGARDING PATTERNING SUMMARIZED IN CAPSULE FORM

Ten Organizations	*The Response*
1. Promotional materials used by the Institute create unnecessary parental guilt about their adequacy and motivation.	1. Reject charges of pressure but reflect parent instruction. Emphasize a positive view of potential through patterning.
2. Anything less than 100 percent effort in carrying out the program will result in loss of effort.	2. True, inadequate treatment is no treatment.
3. The regimens prescribed are so rigid as to lead to neglect of other family members.	3. Could be true; however, the program can also draw the family together.
4. Restrictions are placed on the child's walking and listening by reference to unwarranted theory.	4. The restrictions derive from the theory of the ISHP.
5. Diagnosis is made on the basis of a subjective observation test-profile whose validity is unknown.	5. The test is preferable to existing tests which do not measure abilities of training.
6. Undocumented claims are made for cures.	6. The experience of the ISHP can demonstrate dramatic gains.

Table 6–4 (continued)

Ten Organizations	*The Response*
7. The theory alleges that mental retardation, learning disabilities, and behavior disorders have a single cause of brain damage associated with brain dominance and impairment in physiogenesis.	7. The theory of neurological orientation suggests a continuum of brain development, not brain damage. The theory rests upon more than dominance and physiogenesis. Thus, there is potential for improvement of the continuum of nervous system potential.
8. Gains made can be attributed to growth and development-maturation, increase in a few isolated skills, and/or the effects of stimulation.	8. The gains are real and validated by ISHP instrumentation. Clinical inference is more appropriate than sterile, statistical inferences.

willingness of AAHD to open its files and actively engage in *external* evaluation and comparison of its procedures with other procedures. The Neman et al. report reflects one such effort, as does a report by the National Association for Retarded Citizens (1973). Two additional commentaries are to be found in articles by Zigler and Seitz (1975) as well as Neman (1975).

The NARC report was a survey of 282 families who had received services from AAHD centers and *not* from the ISHP. Parents reported (expressed as percentages) the following: positive change for my child — 90; change directly related to program — 59.9; would repeat the experience — 82.5; would recommend to others — 85.8; and detrimental effects to the family — 9.5. Parents reported gains (expressed as percentages) in areas of: learning — 61.7; attention — 56.3; visual performance — 57; mobility — 51; and reduction of hyperactivity — 54.9. A few families had been made specific promises such as: learning to read — 11.7; IQ gains — 3.5; and getting well — 3.9.

The Neman et al. report conducted by the NARC covered a seven-month period for a group of sixty-six retarded persons with a mean age of 14.9 years, with a SD of 2.6 and a mean Binet IQ of 39.6, SD of 10.2. The group was below age nineteen, above 30 in IQ, and free of extreme behavior disorders, sensory impairment, and genetic pathology. Three groups were established and were found to reflect equality with respect to scores on CA, Binet MA, Peabody Picture Vocabulary Test (PPVT)-MA, ITPA Language Age, Neurological Age (a measure adapted from ISHP used by the AAHD), Frostig Perceptual Age, Lincoln-Oseretsky Motor Development Scale, WISC verbal, and WISC performance. The three groups were labeled: Experimental I, which received the AAHD version of the Doman-Delacato program; Experimental II, which received a physical activity program, personal attention, and the addition of the AAHD program in the last half of the program; and a Passive Control group to serve for baseline period. In general, both the experimental groups were superior to the Passive Control group. Caution was evident in statistical analysis to control for regression effects of measurement. Neman et al. reported the following as pertinent: *no* dramatic changes in individual improvement or in IQ were reported; comparisons between Experimental II and the Passive Control group favored the former; and the Experimental I group improved over Experimental II group on the AAHD test of neurological age.

Neman et al. and the NARC (1973) noted that the AAHD version of patterning reflects a potential merit and warrants further study. The report, however, did suggest validation of the AAHD scale. Both reports did *not* reflect endorsement, only a recommendation for further study and recognition of the need for activity-oriented programs.

An exchange between Zigler and Seitz and Neman regarding the Neman et al. and the NARC reports is significant for an understanding and exposition of the technical aspects of research-evaluation; an understanding of *social* consequences of scientific research; and an understanding of the NARC regarding its 1968 position statement.

The technical aspects of the NARC parent survey should be understood. The reported opinions of 282 families out of a possible 778 families leads one to speculate on the opinions of the other 64 percent who did not respond. The technicalities of the Neman et al. report regarding sampling, statistical inferences, and experimental biases identified validity for both the Zigler and Seitz critique and the Neman response. For example, while 66 persons may *not* be representative, they were representative of AAHD clients. The implication relates to what extent results can be generalized and advanced as proof. Sample size can relate to use of statistical procedures, and Neman defended the choice of less "powerful" techniques as appropriate if results were cautiously interpreted. Experimental contamination was a compromise between having genuine experts conduct the sensory-motor treatment (Neman) and having independent persons conduct the physical activity program. In light of the findings for the Experimental II, one would wish that the same program expertise had been available. The social consequences of research were illustrated by Zigler and Seitz's concern that the NARC report and the Neman et al. report constituted an endorsement based upon limited results. These authors observed that these procedures require significant costs in money, time, physical energy, and family interaction. The modest or slight gains would seem hardly worth the investment, especially given the seemingly equal benefits of the Experimental II approach. Neman responded that the NARC (1973) report and the Neman et al. report were sufficiently cautious and temperate in tone. Both the Zigler and Seitz article and the Neman response stated that the NARC affirmed its 1968 statement. The *historical* significance of the Neman et al. report is that with the advent of the AAHD, there is now an openness regarding genuine, independent evaluation of this procedure. The significance of the Zigler and Seitz exposition is that science does not exist in a vacuum, but that its findings can have grave as well as positive overtones.

The positive support of Experimental Group II in regard to the Neman et al. report is illustrated by the investigation of Fisher (1971). His experiment involved 102 mildly retarded children. One group received a Kephart approach, another received a physical activity program, and there was a contrast sample. There were no gains in school achievement. The motor performance and school attitude of the contrast group was clearly inferior to both treatment groups. Reviews of the research literature and personal investigation by Karl (1972) and Whitcraft (1972) reflect curriculum and measurement procedures necessary for the implementation of a systematic program of physical education and physical fitness. In general, motor skills of the retarded have been found to be lower than those of normal children but similar in sequence and sex differences; modestly related to IQ; susceptible to training; and related to task difficulty rather than to IQ. The inclusion of a systematic program as outlined by these references suggests that a physical education program can be a fourth alternative to the three systems discussed. It would appear, however, that the focus on the three systems has resulted in a certain neglect of an approach that would appear to have equal potential. Freeman (1967) has observed that while researchers argue over technique, there are children in need of assistance. Parents may feel resentment toward the person who implies that nothing can be, or should be, done until *the* method is developed. Impatience must be balanced against the raising of false hopes based upon premature or careless results.

PHYSICAL FITNESS AND ACTIVITY

Aside from a perceptual development perspective, programs oriented toward physical activity and fitness have salutary benefits for the retarded person. In an early paper, Conn (1949) discussed the importance of play in affective development, especially the development of emotions. Graveivicz (1973) has documented the psychological isolation of multihandicapped children deprived of play. Campbell (1974) and Solomon and Pangle (1967) demonstrated that physical fitness was associated with general improvement in behavior. The Campbell study revealed that positive reinforcement for activity was generally associated with more positive attitudes toward self and self-direction. The Solomon and Pangle report reflected that the supposed physical inferiority of the retarded person may be as much a result of neglect as of constitutional defects. Lawhorne (1966) reported that attainment of physical fitness inspired his pupils to maintain their achievement and to seek new goals for mastery. Masters (1968) reported a survey of state institutions which reflected agreement that physical fitness assisted in community return. Stein (1963) described an experiment in which a group of mildly retarded students received ten weeks of adaptive physical education which replaced their usual academic instruction. They were compared to a control group. Results indicated that the experimental group gained more in academic achievement as well as in physical strength. This was attributed to success experiences.

A report of the Project on Recreation and Fitness for the Mentally Retarded (1966) compiled data regarding physical fitness for the mentally retarded. This report concluded that available scientific evidence supports the following generalizations regarding physical fitness:

1 Physical functioning is one area in which the retarded are nearer the norm.
2 Physical proficiency can be trained.
3 Physical fitness gains are not necessarily associated with sociometric gains.
4 Motor proficiency and intellectual functioning are more correlated than in normal populations.
5 Neglect of physical activity leads to aggravated frustration and depressed functioning.

This report outlines a curriculum of activities involving readily available equipment, including both individual and group-related activities. Bowers (1966) has developed a curriculum of physical activities which outlines practical activities. Hayden (1964) has prepared a similar curriculum. The Hayden document, however, contains a validated inventory of skills for assessment purposes.

An added incentive for physical fitness has been the emergence of the Special Olympics, spearheaded by the Joseph P. Kennedy, Jr. Foundation. Since 1968, there have been events sponsored at local, state, and national levels. The Special Olympics are described as a new kind of joy designed to end isolation and create opportunities for recognition. A publication of the Joseph P. Kennedy, Jr. Foundation (1972) has described the process necessary for inclusion in the Special Olympics family. A more recent project of the Kennedy Foundation is the Families Play to Grow (1975) program. This program emphasizes the participation of the entire family as a unit. Completion results in a special certificate for members, as well as a sense of closeness and increased physical fitness. Family-oriented activities include: water play, hiking or cycling and nature walking, volley ball, soccer and kickball, basketball, running, bowling, baseball, rhythm and dance, and special activities for young children.

A section of chapter 9 discusses recreation. This presentation will concentrate on values, content, and program examples. Art and music have a significant role in activity programs for the retarded person. Jorgensen (1971), Madson and Madson

(1968), and Rejto (1973) have presented certain examples of helpful music-oriented activities. These research investigations suggest that music and music instruction have the potential to modify behavior and to open new channels for learning. Winklestein, Shapiro, and Shapiro (1973) and Crawford (1967) have suggested that art instruction possesses utility for language expression and self-esteem.

PRESCHOOL PROGRAMS

As was evident from the discussion regarding ecology, it would appear reasonable to engage the child and the family as early as possible. Federal legislation has prompted significant aid to the states and local communities (chapter 14). Increasingly, public schools are entering into programming for youngsters well below the traditional kindergarten age. It is now mandatory by law that careers in education will include teacher preparation at this level.

A special issue of *Exceptional Children* summarized certain issues in programming for preschool handicapped children. These included: intellectual development, materials, family involvement, preparation of personnel, research, prevention, legal considerations, resources, and curriculum. The contributors were Spicker (1971), Zimmerman and Calovini (1971), Galvert (1971), Martin (1971), Blum, Harvey, and Shepard (1971), McDonald and Soeffing (1971), Abesen, Trudeau, and Weintraub (1971), and Glassman (1971).

Models

Intellectual development and curriculum are related aspects for program planning, according to Spicker (1971). Curricular emphasis has also been reviewed by Haring, Hayden, and Nolen (1961), and Spicker, Hodges, and McCandless (1966). The Spicker discussion focused upon preschool, or early childhood, programming for disadvantaged children. His review reminds us that there were intervention efforts prior to the Head Start program of the 1960s. Four basic models for early childhood programming have gained prominence. A *traditional* model features adaptive nursery school goals of social and emotional growth through play, dramatics, crafts, creative activities, etc. A *cognitive development* soon emerged as a response for a more specific effort for disadvantaged children. There have been efforts to adapt Montessori procedures into a *perceptual-motor development model.* Finally, Spicker identified an *academic skills* development model with a direct stress upon skills necessary to succeed in literacy tasks. Comparison of these models is difficult and only tentative. Spicker concluded:

1 Highest IQ gains are associated with the cognitive and academic skills models.

2 The traditional model is effective if it is well supervised, is structured, and involves language development, especially oral language.
3 An academic skills model tends to produce rote responses rather than comprehension.
4 A curriculum based upon fine motor, memory, and language skills is more effective in later school success than an emphasis upon abstract reasoning, critical thinking, or creative thinking.
5 Home intervention is essential.
6 Perceptual-motor development models have not proven more effective.
7 Intervention begun at age three is more beneficial than intervention delayed until age four.
8 The lower the teacher-pupil ratio, the more effective the program.
9 A "teaching" paraprofessional appears associated with effective programs.

The Spicker et al. report confirmed that follow-through is required to maintain gains. This project evaluated and compared graduates of intervention groups with contrast samples. The significance of the school environment of the primary grades was established as clustering around a curriculum designed to take advantage of the child's skills, teacher competence, and teacher attitudes toward disadvantaged children.

The Haring et al. project demonstrated that contingency management can be a useful tool for structure and that staff can retain its skills after training is withdrawn.

Related Elements

The significance of family involvement was noted in the ecology section and will be discussed elsewhere in this text. In the context of early childhood education, Galvert (1971) contended that family members must be included early in planning. This involvement is viewed as beneficial to the parents' own growth as well as for the child. Radin (1969) compared children enrolled in an early childhood program with a contrast sample. The experimental children further differed from those with home contact and those with school contact. The home contact group was clearly superior. It will be recalled from the discussion on ecology that parent involvement characterized successful programs.

The prevention function of care and intervention in early childhood, as presented by McDonald and Soeffing (1971), parallels that of the ecology discussion. The preventative emphasis is *not* so much on cure or dramatic gains in IQ for early childhood as it is upon prevention of negative school experience and the prevention of negative family coping skills. Zehrbach (1975) has targeted identification of children to be served as a prime problem in implementing intervention efforts. Associated with this problem is the location of children. To stimulate referrals, contact was made with agencies, and a comprehensive identification program (CIP) outside the framework of agency solicitation was instituted. Both procedures were helpful, but the CIP procedure identified *different* preschoolers to the point that the ultimate eligible population was doubled. CIP involved location procedures including: mass mailings to home addresses listed in birth registries, which was ineffective for the most part; an open house, which drew interest but few referrals; media, involving print and electronic channels, which proved effective with middle- and upper-income families; notices sent home by children already in regular school programs, which generated between 40 to 60 percent of the referrals; and next most effective, a telephone survey asking about children and neighboring children. The media campaign had been effective in preparing a receptivity for the call. House-to-house surveys were found to be more effective than the telephone. Volunteers, supervised by professional staff, were used for locating and screening. Evaluation was a staff function.

The Blum (1971) interview of Harvey and Sheperd reflected an interrelatedness between research and training of personnel. It would appear that as programs evolve, especially under federal funding, there will be careful monitoring. A special target area will be the identification of instructional competencies. Ability to work as a team member with parents and consultants was viewed as a prime skill. Also important is the use of observational skills to yield individualized prescriptions. An attitudinal dimension of viewing the child as capable and the avoidance of overprotection has emerged. Continued study of the tasks confronted by primary-grade learners is still needed so as to provide a functional curriculum for early childhood. There is also the need for continued study of effective parent involvement.

In the context of parent involvement at early childhood levels, Anderson (1962) offered a perspective on the parent-teacher conference from the social worker's frame of reference. Antecedents of parent attitude toward the school might include: their own school experiences, which may have been pleasant or unpleasant; the general opinion of the school held by the general community and/or neighborhood; and the feelings of their own child or children. Anderson notes the ability *to listen* as a significant tool to gain insight into parental feelings and opinions (chapter 12). He noted that professionals need to be alert to their own defensiveness about their competencies. The apparent indifference of the parent may be a mask to cover personal feelings of inadequacy and a fear of seeming ridiculous. With trust will come an opening up by the parent and fuller participation. Anderson suggested that trust develops as the teacher helps the parent to recognize that the parent is the individual with the greatest responsibility, influence, and feeling for the child. The teacher should be free to share his or her personal affection and concern for the child. The sharing may help the parent to understand that the conference agenda is to help the child, not blame the parents.

The question of materials is also research related, because curriculum outcomes should dictate the choice of instruction media (Zimmerman and Galovini,

1971). These authors presented four profiles of child development for ages one through five. Materials in harmony with tasks and interest should be a major consideration. Suggested materials included common objects and events found in the average home. In addition, materials should be: attractive, inviting, well constructed, durable, safe, nontoxic, challenging, and fun. As an *educational* device, materials should have some relationship to enrichment of self awareness, social development, language skills, sensory-motor development, and/or perceptual development.

The question of resources, especially legal resources, has been discussed by Martin (1971), Glassman (1971) and Abeson, Trudeau, and Weintraub (1971) (chapter 14). Martin affirmed early childhood programming as a major priority of the Bureau for the Education of the Handicapped in areas of direct grants to states, research, personnel training, and establishment of model centers. Glassman listed federal and national agencies that have undertaken service and research missions. She presented in condensed form the resources of over 120 different organizations. The Abeson et al. review examined the legal base for early childhood programming. In 1971, they noted increased legislative activity in the states for such programs — and the trend is increasing. They suggested that legislation for early childhood should provide for:

1 parent involvement and assistance
2 earliest possible identification
3 effective evaluation of children and program
4 training of staff
5 hiring of competent staff
6 suitable facilities in design and equipment
7 transportation
8 materials of quantity and variety
9 authority for cooperative regional or other joint administrative sponsorship
10 adequate funding.

These dimensions will be expanded in subsequent chapters, and especially in the discussion of PL 94–142 found in chapter 14.

SUMMING UP

This chapter has reviewed human development as adaptive behavior. The concept of tasks implies a uniqueness for periods of life as preparation for subsequent tasks. It also implies a continuum of lifelong learning. This discussion also outlined the scope of adult tasks.

Maturation

1. This term is related to learnings due to physiological change and opportunities to practice. While theories vary, there is agreement as to the importance of nutritional adequacy.

2. Intervention during the maturation period (birth to preschool) was discussed. Efforts are or have been directed toward management of impulse, integration, and intra-inter-personal dimensions.

3. Programs advocated by Doman–Delacato, Kephart, and Frostig have gained a certain eminence. The advent of AAHD now allows for an open assessment of the Doman–Delacato method. The National Association for Retarded Citizens (NARC) and allied organizations still refuse endorsement.

4. Physical education, physical fitness, and physical activity, as defined by the American Association on Health, Physical Education and Recreation (AAHPER) appear to have utility for the retarded person, especially in personal adjustment.

5. The Joseph P. Kennedy, Jr. Foundation has developed two programs of merit for the retarded, the Special Olympics for the person, and Families Play to Grow for the family.

Preschool

1. Preschool programs vary in their emphasis but appear to have a common theme of personal development and prevention of impairment. Emphasis on *what* is to be developed varies as adjustment, cognition, perceptual skills, and/or academic skills. There seems to be common agreement of the necessity of family involvement and participation. Prevention strategies may identify school problems or enhance parental skills.

2. Model legislation was identified.

General

1. Cure, or restoration to normalcy, is not the exclusive function of intervention. Improvement of function and of self-esteem are equally important.

2. The dissemination of scientific findings poses the risk of misunderstanding. The generalization from one sample to the representative population should be of prime concern.

3. There should be an organized effort to locate children as early as possible.

4. There is a need for coordination between early childhood programs and the primary grades. Furthermore, there appears to be a need for effective involvement of parents.

5. Standards of legal resources can be identified and obtained.

ON LOCATION

A function of science is to question conventional wisdom. The wisdom of questioning conventional science has been placed in perspective by Kreider (1964). No disrespect is intended in this essay; its intention seems appropriate as a reminder that assumptions require constant examination. A healthy skepticism can furnish new insights. In light of the controversies regarding sensory-motor, perceptual-motor, and visual-perceptual training, Kreider's guidelines would seem helpful, especially the willingness to subject one's assumptions to evaluation.

The Leaf and the Stone

More than three hundred years before the birth of Christ, Aristotle watched a leaf drift slowly to earth. He tossed a stone into the air and noted that it fell much more rapidly. And so he came to the conclusion that heavier bodies fell more rapidly than light ones and that a two-pound weight would fall twice as fast as a one-pound weight.

It was not until 1585 that an unknown Dutch mathematician dropped two lead weights out of a window onto a wooden platform. The single resounding thud as they hit at the same moment exploded the Aristotelian theory of falling bodies for all time.

It is obvious that Aristotle never tested his theory. His was a simple error in logic. Why, then, did it take two thousand years to bring so simple an error to light?

Aristotle was a genius. He was a giant under whose leadership the scientific knowledge of centuries was assembled and produced in nearly a thousand volumes. The very brilliance of his scientific logic, upon which rests many of our scientific truths today, led to the blind acceptance of his scientific mistakes as well. He was too great, for he stopped the inquiring of lesser minds, the flow of question and answer, experiment and trial that measure and qualify man's conclusions about himself. Who would presume to question the simple course of leaf and stone when Aristotle himself had established the principle of their descent?

The brilliant logic of Itard led to the erroneous conclusion that the mental deficiency of the Wild Boy found in the woods at Averyon could be restored. Seguin proved the fallacy and also proved to his everlasting glory that the mentally retarded could be trained. Itard was not a scientific genius. He was a teacher of the deaf.

It was in the objective climate of scientific research that the relationship was noted between sensory perception and intelligence. In America we accepted the laboratory fact as dictum and left our mentally retarded to waste in a sea of dun-colored walls. But in poverty-stricken, postwar Europe, teachers of the retarded accepted the scientific fact as challenge and pulled, pushed, and patted the flaccid muscles of their charges into response, brightened eyes with a riot of color, and assailed dull ears with rollicking melody.

They were the innovators, the make-doers, and as important to the research as the microscope.

It is not through folly that such work goes on in many directions at once and on many levels. Progress is measured by proven failure as well as by proven success. It is the sum total of both that spells our actual knowledge of the retarded.

REFERENCES

Abbott, J., and Sabatino, D. Teacher-Mom Intervention with Academic High-Risk Preschool Children. *Exceptional Children,* 1975, 41, 207–208.

Abeson, A., Trudeau, E., and Weintraub, F. Legal Opportunities and Considerations for Early Childhood Education. *Exceptional Children,* 1971, 37, 697–701.

Allen, R., Dickerman, I., and Haupt, T. A Pilot Study of the Immediate Effects of the Frostig Home Training Program with Educable Retardates. *Exceptional Children,* 1966, 33, 41–42.

Alley, G., Snyder, W., Spencer, J., and Angell, R. Reading Readiness and the Frostig Training Program. *Exceptional Children,* 1968, 35, 68–69.

Anderson, R. J. A Social Worker Looks at the Parent Teacher Conference. *Exceptional Children,* 1962, 30, 433–434.

Ball, T. S. *Itard, Sequin, and Kephart: Sensory Education — A Learning Interpretation.* Columbus, Ohio: Charles Merrill, 1971.

Barick, L., Widdop, J., and Broadhead, G. The Physical Fitness and Motor Performance of Educable Mentally Retarded Children. *Exceptional Children,* 1973, 7, 509–519.

Becker, J. T., and Sabatino, D. Frostig Revisited. *Journal of Learning Disabilities,* 1962, 6, 180–184.

Blum, E. R. Conversations in Training and Research: Interview with Jasper Harvey and George Sheperd. *Exceptional Children,* 1971, 37, 670–680.

Bowers, L. *A Program of Developmental Motor Activities for Retarded Children.* Lafayette: University of Southwestern Louisiana, 1966.

Buckland, P., and Balow, B. Effects of Visual Perceptual Training in Reading Achievement. *Exceptional Children,* 1973, 39, 299–310.

Campbell, J. Improving Physical Fitness of Retarded Boys. *Mental Retardation,* 1974, 12, 31–35.

Chalfant, J., and Scheffein, M. *Central Processing Dysfunctions in Children.* Washington, D.C.: National Institute of Neurological Diseases and Stroke. U. S. Dept. of Health, Education, and Welfare, 1969.

Conn. J. H. The Child Reveals Himself Through Play. *Mental Hygiene,* 1949, 33, 49–70.

Crawford, J. Art of the Mentally Retarded. *The Digest of the Mentally Retarded,* 1967, 4, 24–29.

Cruickshank, W. The Education of Children with Specific Learning Disabilities. *Education of Exceptional Children and Youth* (3rd ed.). Englewood Cliffs, New Jersey: Prentice-Hall, 1975.

Faber, N. W. *The Retarded Child.* New York: Crown Publishers, 1968.

Families Play to Grow. Washington, D.C.: Joseph P. Kennedy, Jr. Foundation, 1972.

Fisher, K. Effects of Perceptual-Motor Training on the Educable Mentally Retarded. *Exceptional Children,* 1971, 38, 264–266.

Flegenheimer, B., and Birch, H. Comparison of Perceptual Training and Remedial Instruction for Poor Beginning Readers. *Journal of Learning Disabilities,* 1973, 6, 230–236.

Freeman, R. Controversy Over Patterning as a Treatment for Brain Damage in Children. *Journal of the American Medical Association,* 1967, 202, 385–388.

Frostig, M. *Movement Education: Theory and Practice.* Chicago: Follett, 1970.

Frostig, M., and Horne, D. *The Frostig Program for the Development of Visual Perception.* Chicago: Follett, 1964.

Galvert, D. Dimensions of Family Involvement in Early Childhood Education. *Exceptional Children,* 1971, 37, 655–659.

Gell, N., Herdtner, T., and Lough, L. Perceptual and Socioeconomic Variables, Instruction in Body Orientation, and Predicted Success in Young Children. *Exceptional Children,* 1968, 35, 239.

Glassman, L. Directory of Resources on Early Childhood Education. *Exceptional Children,* 1971, 37, 703–712.

Graveivicz, A. Play Deprivation in Multihandicapped Children. *American Journal of Occupational Therapy,* 1973, 27, 70–72.

Hallahan, D., and Cruickshank, W. *Psycho-Educational Foundations of Learning Disabilities*. Englewood Cliffs, New Jersey: Prentice-Hall, 1973.

Hammill, D., and Bartel, N. *Teaching Children with Learning and Behavior Problems*. Boston: Allyn and Bacon, 1973.

Haring, N., Hayden, A., and Nolen, P. Accelerating Appropriate Behaviors of Children in a Head Start Program. *Exceptional Children,* 1969, 35, 773–784.

Havighurst, R. *Human Development and Education.* New York: Longmans Green, 1953.

Hayden, F. *Physical Fitness for the Mentally Retarded.* Ontario, Canada: Metropolitan Toronto Assn. for Retarded Children, 1964.

Institute for the Study of Human Potential. *Human Potential.* Philadelphia: Institute for the Study of Human Potential, 1968.

Jorgensen, H. Effects of Contingent Preferred Music in Reducing Two Stereotyped Behaviors of a Profoundly Retarded Child. *Journal of Music Therapy,* 1971, 8, 131–138.

Joseph P. Kennedy, Jr. Foundation. *A New Kind of Joy: The Story of the Special Olympics.* Washington, D.C., 1972.

Karl, P. Motor Characteristics and Development of Retarded Children: Success Experiences. *Education and Training of the Mentally Retarded,* 1972, 7, 14–21.

Kephart, N. C. Perceptual-Motor Aspects of Learning Disorders. *Exceptional Children,* 1964, 31, 201–206.

Kephart, N. C. *The Slow Learner in the Classroom* (2nd ed.). Columbus, Ohio: Charles Merrill, 1971.

Kreider, M. C. The Leaf and the Stone. *Span,* 1964, 6, 3–4.

Lawhorne, T. W. Physical Fitness for M-R. *The Training School Bulletin,* 1966, 63, 45–48.

Levinson, D., Darrow, C., Klein, E., Levinson, M., McKee, B. The Psychosocial Development of Men in Early Adulthood and the Mid Life Transition in Ricks, D., Thomas, A., and Roff, M., (eds.). *Life History Research in Psychopathology Vol. 3,* Minneapolis: University of Minnesota Press, 1974.

Madson, C., and Madson, C. Music as a Behavior Motivation Technique. *Journal of Music Therapy,* 1968, 5, 72–76.

Martin, E. W. Bureau of Education for the Handicapped: Commitment and Programs in Early Childhood Education. *Exceptional Children,* 1971, 37, 661–663.

Masters, T. *Summary of an Investigation Into the Significance of Recreation for the Educable Mentally Retarded.* Washington, D.C.: American Association for Health, Physical Education, and Recreation, 1968.

McDonald, P., and Soeffing, M. Prevention of Learning Problems. *Exceptional Children,* 1971, 37, 681–686.

McKibben, E. The Effect of Additional Tactile Stimulation in a Perceptual-Motor Treatment Program for School Children. *Journal of Occupational Therapy,* 1973, 27, 191–197.

McMahon, F. *Psychology, the Hybrid Science* (2nd. ed.). Englewood Cliffs, New Jersey: Prentice-Hall, Inc., 1974.

Morrison, D., and Pothier, P. Two Different Remedial Motor Training Programs and the Development of Mentally Retarded Pre Schoolers. *American Journal of Mental Deficiency,* 1972, 77, 251–258.

Muller, P. *The Tasks of Childhood.* New York: McGraw-Hill, 1969.

National Association for Retarded Citizens. Results of Sensorimotor Training Study Announced. *Mental Retardation News,* 1973, 22, 1 and 4.

National Association for Retarded Children. Statement on the Doman-Delacato Treatment. *Children Limited,* 1968, 17, 6–7.

Neman, R. A Reply to Zigler and Deitz. *American Journal of Mental Deficiency,* 1975, 75, 493–505.

Neman, R., Roos, P., McCann, B., Menolascino, F., Heal, F. Experimental Evaluation of Sensorimotor Patterning Used with Mentally Retarded Children. *American Journal of Mental Deficiency,* 1975, 79, 372–384.

Project on Recreation and Physical Fitness for the Mentally Retarded. *Activity Programs for the Mentally Retarded.* Washington, D.C.: American Association for Health, Physical Education and Recreation, 1966.

Radin, N. The Impact of a Kindergarten Home Counseling Program. *Exceptional Children,* 1969, 36, 251–256.

Rappaport, S. R. *Childhood Aphasia and Brain Damage: A Definition.* Narbeth, Pennsylvania: Livingston Publishing Co., 1964.

Rejto, A. Music as an Aid in the Remediation of Learning Disabilities. *Journal of Learning Disabilities,* 1973, 6, 15–24.

Richardson, S., Birch, H., and Hertzig, M. School Performance of Children Who Were Severely Malnourished in Infancy. *American Journal of Mental Deficiency,* 1973, 77, 623–652.

Solomon, A., and Pangle, R. Demonstrating Physical Fitness Improvement in the Educable Mentally Retarded. *Exceptional Children,* 1967, 34, 177–181.

Spicker, H. Intellectual Development Through Early Childhood Education. *Exceptional Children,* 37, 9, 629–640.

Spicker, H., Hodges, W., and McCandless, B. A Diagnostically Based Curriculum for Psychologically Deprived, Preschool, Mentally Retarded Children: Interim Report. *Exceptional Children,* 1966, 33, 215–220.

Stein, J. U. Motor Function and Physical Fitness of the Mentally Retarded: A Critical Review. *Rehabilitation Literature,* 1963, 24, 230–242.

Sullivan, J. The Effects of Kephart's Perceptual-Motor Training on a Reading Clinic Sample. *Journal of Learning Disabilities,* 1972, 5, 32–38.

Suphier, J. The Relationship of Perceptual-Motor Skills to Learning and School Success. *Journal of Learning Disabilities,* 1973, 6, 56–65.

Thelen, D. A Program for Training Children in Coordination and Perceptual Development. *Exceptional Children,* 1973, 8, 29–35.

Warren, S. A. Psychological Evaluation of the Mentally Retarded. *Pediatric Clinics of North America,* 1968, 15, 953–954. Also cited in Rothstein, J. *Mental Retardation: A Book of Readings.* New York: Holt, Rinehart and Winston, 1971.

Werner, E., Simonian, K., and Smith, R. Reading Achievement, Language Development, and Perceptual-Motor Development of 10 and 11 Year Olds. *Perceptual and Motor Skills,* 1967, 25, 409–420.

Whitcraft, C. Motoric Engramming for Sensory Deprivation or Disability. *Exceptional Children,* 1972, 6, 475–478.

Winesberg, B. G. Review of *Famine and Human Development: The Dutch Hunger Winter of 1944–1945,* in *American Journal of Mental Deficiency,* 1975, 80, 360–361.

Winklestein, E., Shapiro, B., and Shapiro, P. Art Curricula and Mentally Retarded Pre Schoolers. *Mental Retardation,* 1973, 11, 47–51.

Zehrbach, L. Determining a Pre School Handicapped Population. *Exceptional Children,* 1975, 42, 76–84.

Zigler, E., and Seitz, V. On the Evaluation of Sensorimotor Patterning: A Critique. *American Journal of Mental Deficiency,* 1975, 79, 483–492.

Zimmerman, L., and Galovini, G. Toys as Learning Materials for Preschool Children. *Exceptional Children,* 1971, 37, 9, 642–652.

7

Adaptive Behaviors

SYNOPSIS

This chapter is an extension of the previous one and continues the presentation of adapting. Three dimensions will be described in this chapter: communications, personal adjustment, and social adjustment.

Communications has emerged as the universal inclusive descriptor for speech and language. The scope of speech and language is outlined, with related components described. Four approaches to language development are discussed. These include approaches based upon: sociolinguistics, psycholinguistics, behaviorism, and ethology.

The dimensions of personal adjustment discussed are: self-care, self-concept, and self-direction. Self-direction, based upon internal locus of control and moral development, could be a principal priority for the management and programming of retarded persons.

Social adjustment involves dimensions of acceptance and involvement. One contribution of the study of adult adjustment is the formulation of prognoses about retarded persons. Another implication of adult studies is the reminder of the retarded person as an *adult*.

OBJECTIVES

ATTITUDES

1. To understand that social adjustment is the ultimate goal of programming.
2. To view social adjustment as a particular form of learning.
3. To realize that principles of teaching and learning apply to adjustment.

UNDERSTANDINGS

1. To identify the prognostic implications for social adjustment studies.
2. To describe the tasks of adjustment required for the retarded adult.
3. To define the elements of language programs.

4 To compare alternatives in language training.
5 To identify behaviors defined as competent.

SKILLS

1 To describe the merits of procedures designed to facilitate aspects of language acquisition of the retarded.
2 To identify standards for programs and programming for the social adjustment of the retarded.
3 To develop the scope of a follow-up study to assess the results of one's own performance with retarded persons.
4 To define self-direction as a priority for programming.
5 To define the consequences of motivation and aspiration to performance.
6 To identify the intra-individual and environmental factors that influence and facilitate adaptive behaviors.

COMMUNICATIONS

Scope of Speech and Language Problems

England (1970) views speech as the production of sounds that form particular symbols called *words*. The definition, or designation, of a speech problem has its origins in the listener. When a listener is attending to how a person speaks and is distracted from what is being said, a speech problem exists. As a linguistic process, language involves more than grammar. Applying linguistic referents, England (p. 4) defines language as

> a human, culturally established, and voluntarily acquired means of communicating our ideas, information, emotions, and desires by means of conventionalized symbol systems. These verbal symbol systems may depend upon any of our perceptual senses — auditory, visual, or tactile — singly or in combination.

The classification of speech problems, according to England, may be according to organic origins, such as cleft palate or loss of neurological function or functional origins, which involve the emotional reactions of the person to speaking. This latter area describes events that could inhibit the person's motivation to speak. Since these two origins may be interwoven, standard practice is to emphasize the behavioral in describing speech problems. From the frame of reference of behavioral manifestations, speech problems may be defined as: misarticulation, voice, and rhythm, or fluency. Misarticulation may be understood as the omission, substitution, distortion, and/or addition of sounds. Voice problems relate to the intensity, pitch, and/or quality of the voice. Rhythm relates to the fluency of sounds and absence of hesitation or repetition. Within this category, England advocates distinguishing between cluttering and stuttering. The former describes hesitation and may be observed as a developmental trait of the preschool child. Stuttering, by contrast, is significant nonfluency, with sufficient repetition so as to inhibit the completion of conversation. England emphasizes that anxious adult reaction could transform cluttering into stuttering, since the person may begin to view speech as punishing.

Language problems, according to England, may be viewed as language delay, if the reference point is preschool and school-age persons. Chronological age is the reference point by which to compare the person's performance. England notes that the term *delayed language,* in actual clinical practice, may have two meanings. Some clinicians may use this term as a general descriptor for a discrepancy between performance and expectation. Other clinicians may use this term only *after* organic, emotional, social, and intellectual factors have been excluded. The consumer of diagnostic inferences should be aware of the clinician's orientation. England identifies five sources to account for delay of language: central nervous system impairment, sensory impairment, measured intelligence, environment, and emotional adjustment. England insists that these factors be interrelated so that thc diagnosis process does not emphasize one source to the exclusion of any other.

Central nervous system impairment is described as trauma that interferes with perception. The common examples are dysarithia (motor incoordination of tongue, lips, and jaw) and aphasia (a disruption of use of symbols). The term *aphasia* may also be a varied term. Some clinicians may apply it only *after* the other four categories have been excluded, while others may apply it when one of these categories is applicable.

While *sensory impairment* does not necessarily inhibit language acquisition, England suggests two considerations. First, unrecognized sensory impairment may prevent the person from receiving appropriate compensatory management. Second, there must be careful distinction between sensory loss and perceptual loss. England illustrates this distinction by reference to differential education of deaf learners. With conductive loss, the person can benefit from manual approaches, while a more structured approach is required for nonconductive loss. The latter may be as handicapped by sign language as by standard oral language.

Measured intelligence is identified as a correlate of language development. Mental age (MA) is viewed as an estimate of current abilities, and IQ is viewed as an index of rate of acquisition. England warns that low intelligence even to the level of mental retardation is no excuse to abandon language stimulation, and he stresses the importance of language training. Additionally, England urges careful evaluation to prevent a nonretarded child from being labeled retarded. Since other factors may account for a score, it should not be the sole index of intellectual ability.

Environmental deprivation is described as a function of experience rather than socioeconomic conditions. England identifies the ideal language environment as one that:

1 provides initial and continuing incentives for language;
2 has sufficient warmth, security and experiences;
3 is associated with language stimulation;
4 is in a setting where the child is motivated to identify and communicate with others; and
5 has responsive and reinforcing adults for the child who are important to him or her.

England targets the family and education as specific environments that have a significant influence upon language development and the desire to acquire language.

Emotional adjustment, as with environment and intelligence, may be a component of other problems related to language delay. Some children may fail to gain sufficient support for language. In extreme forms, language may be muted by inner emotional conflicts and/or trauma. This form of language delay is associated with autism. As with terms such as aphasia and delayed language, autism may be a general label to describe emotional maladjustment. It may be a specific syndrome for some clinicians. Again, England cautions the consumer to be aware of the orientation of the clinician rendering the diagnosis.

Management Alternatives

Peins (1969) has suggested the scope of speech and language problems associated with mental retardation.

1 *Speech and language behaviors,* including: development of verbal behavior, inner language ability, and acquisition and comprehension of language; types of and incidence of speech and linguistic disorders; and effects of environmental influences.
2 *Assessment,* including procedures and tools for testing, measuring, or assessing speech.
3 *Hearing,* including incidence of auditory impairments; assessment and testing of hearing; and effectiveness of procedures, including aids.
4 *Habilitation* procedures, including home training; classroom activities; clinical programs; and therapy programs.

While there are competitive approaches to the selection of behaviors, assessment, and procedures, there is agreement as to the effects of neglect. Furthermore, there appears to be agreement that emphasis should be upon *language* intervention rather than an exclusive focus upon articulation training. However, it is the nature of language training, with its attendant assessment and management procedures, which remains to be resolved by individual practitioners.

Adler (1971) has advanced a *sociolinguistic* approach. This approach is intended to resolve the discrepancy between the standard English of practitioners and the nonstandard language of certain learners. It is not that learners are necessarily "deprived," or that the learner's language is "substandard-improper." The Adler position is that nonstandard English is a different experience background and can be a foundation to more conventional language acquisition. The relationship of language, culture, and exceptionality has been discussed by Gonzalez (1974). At issue is the mixture of intellectual functioning, adaptive behavior, and community acceptance. Linguistic functioning should be regarded and assessed with reference to both measured intelligence *and* functional language behavior. Assessment by clinical procedures alone, without direct observation, can lead to tragic errors in prognosis. Gonzalez noted that language is a basis of acceptance. Emphasis should be upon linguistic function and proficiency rather than precise acquisition of a particular accent. Valletutti (1971) acknowledged the existence of conservative (adherence to standard use) and liberal (prizing all language forms) approaches. The former was viewed as inflexible, and the latter as nonhelpful for cognitive functioning. Valletutti identified the need for a certain tolerance coupled with a realistic assignment of priorities. Citations from the linguistic literature demonstrate that nonstandard English has forms, rules, and logic as complex as its standard cousin. The expressions "He busy" and "He be busy" were cited to illustrate a rule regarding time. The former indicates a brief interval, while the latter constitutes a lengthy interruption. The language of children should be assessed as to elements of: phonology (sounds, pronunciation); semantics (meanings, definitions); syntax (word order); and morphology (tense, person, number, case, and other grammatical forms). The practitioner's priority might well be upon cognitive clarity. Priorities should be upon language behavior that creates genuine misunderstanding and time should not be wasted on benign dialectical differences. For example, "baffrum" for "bathroom" would be a lesser priority than "pen" for "pin." "G'rage" for "garage" would not be as serious as the omission of a final consonant to a *ba* sound, which could be interpreted variously as bat, back, bash, bag, etc. In summary, sociolinguistics respects pluralism in language while recognizing the necessity for functioning in another language system. The application of this approach, especially in assessment, could reduce mistaken diagnosis of culturally and linguistically different children as mildly mentally retarded children.

Language as *behavior,* subject to *operant procedures,* has been discussed by Lynch and Brecker (1972), Perozzi (1972), Jeffery (1973) and Miller and Yoder (1973). Lynch and Brecker outlined the acquisition of communication skills as a process of environmental influences. Language acquisition is linear progression from primitive forms to more complex forms based upon antecedent events. These events form successive approximations of more complex skills necessary to earn more complex reinforcements. These authors concede a readiness, or maturational, view. Articulation development, use of negatives, use of tense, and question words emerge according to a defined sequence. However, neurological impairment is not a sufficient excuse for neglect. They suggested that the task analysis procedures of behaviorism can be employed to ask questions about the person and/or his environment.

Perozzi affirmed both maturational and behavioristic aspects of language. The match is to recognize indicators of readiness for more complex learning coupled with an awareness of basic language behavior to be shaped, conditioned, and/or acquired. These indicators were said to include: evidence that the opportunity to speak has been present, evidence of regularity of behavior, and evidence of opportunities to practice in the presence of reinforcing conditions. The efforts of Spadlin (1963) to translate Skinnerian concepts into assessment procedures was acknowledged. The Spadlin scale, the Parsons Language Sample, allows for both verbal and nonverbal language behaviors. The four principal behaviors defined by Spadlin were: *echoic* (repeating word or words heard, essentially imitation); *mand* (learning to request or demand an object or favor); *intraverbal* (responding to questions about personal feelings, preferences, etc.); and *tact* (naming of objects or describing function of objects). Jeffery described the conditioning of a severely retarded person to increase intraverbal responses through positive, social reinforcement.

Miller and Yoder advocated that content for language training for retarded children and shaping should follow the same sequence as for normal children. The shaping of verbal expression, for example, would follow a sequence of: (1) relational terms (*more, no, stop* and other mand concepts); (2) words (e.g., nouns in the echoic and tact sense); (3) verb-object word chains (*open door, read book*); (4) subject-object (*mommy-book, baby-juice*); (5) subject verb (*teacher read, George bring*); and (6) subject-verb-object (*Father read book*). These authors cited four principles of language instruction: create a reason, motive, or need to communicate; understanding of meaning should precede production; direct experience is essential; and use reinforcement, imitation, and modeling.

A third approach has emerged: *psycholinguistic* orientation. With its stress upon maturational readiness, environmental influences, and activist intervention, this approach shares a certain commonality with sociolinguistics and operant procedures. However, the assumptions underlying the nature of language, its assessment, and its training offer certain distinctions as well. Increasingly, a discussion of the psycholinguistic approach has become inseparable from a discussion of the Illinois Test of Psycholinguistic Abilities (ITPA), developed by Kirk and McCarthy (1961). The intent of the ITPA was to devise an instrument that would: differentiate among abilities of performance, so as to yield a profile of strengths and areas of improvement, in order that specific training procedures could be implemented for specific problem areas. There is no dispute with the intent, only with the validity of measurement and treatment.

The ITPA consists of subtests. These are designed, according to Bateman and Wetherell (1965), to assess three major functions of language use: channel or modality of language (auditory, visual, vocal); process (decoding-receiving, encoding-expressive, associative-informative); and level of functioning (meaningful and conventional as representational vs. automatic-sequential level involving rote, automatic, nonmeaningful data). At the time of their article, the authors concluded that the ITPA characteristics of mentally retarded students reflected: relatively greater strength in representational levels than in automatic-sequential; greater strength in visual-motor than in auditory-vocal channel; no differences between urban-rural populations; and utility for populations between MA three to nine.

The validity of the ITPA as a measurement instrument has been investigated by Hare, Hammill, and Bartell (1973), Newcomer, Hare, Hammill, and McGettigan (1974), and Burns (1976). The Hare et al. report used a sample of twenty-six third-grade normal pupils chosen for their similarity to the original standardization sample for the ITPA. The 1968 version by Kirk, McCarthy, and Kirk was used and limited to six subtests. The intent was to discover independence of the subtests from one another. It was believed that if there were correlation between two subtests, both were measuring one common factor rather than two. This report found genuine independence of the subtests with comparable school-like tasks. The Newcomer et al. report utilized a sample of 167 third-grade pupils as a follow-up to the previous Hare report. This study found validity for level and process, but not necessarily channel dimensions. The Burns report called the diagnostic use of the ITPA for retarded children into question. The principal concern of Burns was that standardization did not include retarded persons. Consequently, judgments about ITPA profiles as a means to distinguish retarded persons from nonretarded persons may be questionable. The ITPA hypothesis of a flat profile for the retarded and a scatter (peaks and valleys) for the learning disabled is not necessarily confirmed by actual results. Stephenson and Gay (1972) and Kirk (1972) attempted to discover if ethnic differences existed in ITPA measurement. Kirk found that the ITPA did yield different patterns for white, Mexican-American, and black learners. Kirk attributes these differences to child-rearing practices. The Stephenson and Burns reports identified differences between black and white learners, but attributed these differences to the measurement style of the ITPA.

Instruction based upon ITPA processes, related to channel, level, and/or processing has been reviewed by Hammill and Larson (1974), Minskoff (1975) and Newcomer, Larson, and Hammill (1975). Hammill and Larson reviewed the available literature on ITPA training, including fifteen studies with the mentally retarded and eighteen studies involving disadvantaged populations. They concluded that these thirty-three studies failed to demonstrate improvement for the experimental groups. Lack of support was owing to either lack of specificity of the treatment; low reliability of ITPA scores, which means that error in measurement masks gains; and the inapplicability of psycholinguistics. Minskoff advocated retention of ITPA-based instruction and advanced certain guidelines: remediation objectives should fit the behavior symptoms of the person, should be within his or her readiness level, and should be directed toward disability; teaching materials should be sequenced, directed toward individual rate of progress, used by persons specially prepared, and suitable for restructuring if mastery is not immediately evident; there should be adequate time for training-teaching, description of prescription and procedures, and services beyond remediation available to pupils; and there must be suitable fit between testing and training procedures. The Newcomer et al. (1975) report did not share Minskoff's support for ITPA training and concluded that such training has failed to demonstrate help or improvement. The practitioner was advised to remain skeptical and to base treatment on supplemental observations. For the present, one can conclude that language training for retarded persons based upon ITPA profiles is still a promise to be pursued.

Treatment Alternatives

Keane (1972) reviewed fourteen studies of the incidence of speech and language problems among over 21,000 retarded persons. In addition, twenty-seven studies relating to specific problems were reviewed, which included about four thousand retarded persons. With respect to speech and language functioning, Keane concluded:

1 There is a higher incidence of speech and language disorders among the retarded.
2 Incidence is greater for institutionalized persons than for noninstitutionalized persons.
3 In general, lower IQ ranges are associated with more frequent and more severe disorders.
4 There is not a pattern unique to the retarded, and disorders are scattered.
5 The retarded are a heterogeneous group.
6 Articulation, voice, and nonfluencies (stuttering) are the most common speech problems, in that order.
7 Language is a basis for self-sufficiency.
8 There is a need for continued research on training procedures.
9 The use of nonverbal communication through gestures and pictorial symbols should be further studied.

The response of practitioners to speech disorders of retarded persons has *not* been a passive reaction. Nelson, Peoples, Hay, Johnson, and Hay (1976) have described a multisensory approach using visual, auditory, and kinesthetic stimuli to stabilize speech sounds through operant procedures. Niswander and Kelley (1975) have shown that familiarity with words used in articulation improves performance.

Increased familiarity also improves facility in auditory memory. These reports are representative of many that have demonstrated a certain promise of operant techniques for speech production.

Language acquisition can be viewed from perspectives of sociolinguistics (the environment upon the person), psycholinguistics (the person as a learning system), and behavioristic-operant (increased complexities of imitation stimulated by reinforcement). Mahoney (1975) and Sailor, Guess, and Baer (1973), among others, have proposed an *ethological* approach to research and treatment of language disorders. In essence, this viewpoint combines all three perspectives, because language acquisition is viewed as an interaction product. The ethological approach views acquisition of communication as a synchronization between two systems — the system of the person, and the system of an adult caretaker.

There have been efforts to use language training as a basis for skill emphasis. Brown, Huppler, Pierce, Schuerman, and Sontag (1973) described a process for enhancing the recall of episodes as a form of training for increase of memory. Longhurst (1972) utilized language activities to facilitate descriptive skills. Baram and Meyer (1975) has described the use of television as both event and procedure for language training. Two reviews of the literature by Buralnick (1972) and Snyder, Lovitt, and Smith (1975) reflected both a justified optimism regarding language training for the severely retarded and support for ethological approaches. Procedures for this group emphasize shaping of response prior to production, use of reinforcers, and emphasis upon transfer of skills. According to Mahoney, it is the study of events that focus on behaviors of the person which are effective in eliciting a response from others. The advantage of this view is that it places a certain responsibility on adults to learn to communicate, instead of an exclusive onus on the retarded. Typically, investigations have focused upon the failures of the retarded, their inability to profit, and/or inefficiency of programming. Ethology attempts to reverse this pattern and to assert that adults are responsible for devising effective programs. The Sailor et al. program illustrates the structure and content of an ethological system. The structure centers around: reference, control, self-extended control, and integration. These are child-oriented outcomes. Reference refers to creating *events* that require response, such as reacting to directions, commands, signs, etc. *Control* describes learning request forms of language that teach a person that language behavior can have results. *Self-extended control* requires learning an elaboration of self-management skills. Specifically, this involves learning to seek information when confronted by lack of information — what, where, how, etc. *Integration* describes the chaining or combining of the previous three areas. The content of the program involves a six-phase sequence. The complete program involves sixty-one steps, with alternative steps. The six phases involve: persons and things, action with persons and things, possession, color, size, and relation. Within each of these six phases, the four structural elements are couched to form a matrix of structure × content. The program techniques could be transferred to materials commercially available. The basic instructional format is: receptive skills precede expressive skills; events prompt response; and response should be equated with positive outcomes.

PERSONAL ADJUSTMENT

Given the Grossman report concept of adaptive behavior and the summative data of figure 6–1, there would appear to be three essential elements of personal adjustment: self-care, self-concept, and self control and direction.

The acquisition of self-care skills (dressing, eating, toilet training, etc.) is a first step toward independence. Self-sufficiency in these tasks of personal management free the person from dependence upon others. With independence in these skills, the person is viewed as capable, and freedom from dependent care can release the person for more complex training. Acquisition of self-care skills is dependent on motivation to perform, on language skills, as well as on the integration of perceptual-motor skills.

Self-concept describes one's beliefs about one's ability to succeed. Self-concept may be task specific (one's estimate of the number of packages to be heat sealed), or it can be a generalized view of life as success or failure. Belief in one's competence is the product of messages from the environment, especially from parents, peers, and significant persons. It is also the product of testing one's self against demands of life. Messages and experience yield feelings and beliefs about striving, performing, and effort. Therefore, some persons may learn that it is "bad" to try; it is "harmful" to ever be wrong; and it is "best" to be safe. An encouraging quality of self-concept is that it is a product of learning. Thus, negative feelings can be unlearned, and positive ones can be learned. Self-concept is one of the priority goals for programs for the retarded. The facility with which self-care skills are acquired influences the origin of self-control.

A consequence of self-concept is a belief in one's ability to control one's affairs and/or destiny. The notion of *locus of control* describes the confidence to balance one's internal needs and external events. The Piagetian notions of assimilation and accommodation are helpful descriptors of environmental adaptation balanced against individual integrity.

Self-Care

The report of Ball (1971) illustrates the Muller postulates about acquisition of these developmental tasks. The Ball report demonstrated that profoundly retarded persons could acquire self-care skills, but that the acquired skills faded through neglect on the part of adults. Ball observed that responsible adults were responsive to new skills. The acquisition of self-care skills appears to depend upon physiological readiness and motivation. Self-care training must have both motive and means of response.

Haynes (1976) has adapted the work of Finnie (1968) to identify helpful procedures in self-care training. While each task of self-care training possesses its own unique traits, the Haynes and Finnie reports identified certain common features:

1. Seek consultation as to appropriateness of task demands based upon the person's physical condition, developmental level, and previous experience.

2. Make a plan in advance so as to determine the steps involved from start to finish.

3. Emphasize positive responses even if at first efforts are only an approximation. Use positive incentives, especially praise.

4. Stress attention getting so that the child knows when to perform and that he or she is expected to perform.

5. Manipulation and modeling can be useful. Placing the child on one's lap with his or her back toward the adult can help. The child can internalize the manipulation into self-directed actions.

Competence in teaching self-care skills will be increasingly necessary for teachers as programs for early childhood intervention become more common and as programs for more multihandicapped learners increase. The special education of the moderately mentally retarded offers ample precedent for the inclusion of self-care skills as curricular goals.

Self-Concept

The relationship between one's belief in one's ability to perform and actual performance has received a certain attention, although results have been inconclusive. McCoy (1963) compared academically successful and unsuccessful mildly retarded learners. Realism rather than belief distinguished between the two groups. Realism is an accurate estimate in performance rather than a view of ability to perform. Realism is usually measured by comparing one's estimate of the number of items to be done with the actual number achieved. Another approach is to have a person complete a self-concept measure of ability and to have a practitioner rate the person's ability on the same form. Agreement between the two is said to be realistic. Richmond and Dalton (1973) compared the self-ratings of one hundred mildly retarded learners with the ratings of their teachers. This study uncovered significant agreement between pupils and teachers. Furthermore, both ratings were found related to academic achievement. Aside from realism, Golow, Butler, and Gunthrie (1963) have identified self-acceptance as a variable related to performance in adjustment to community living. Acceptance describes a certain agreement of less ability when compared to others without feelings of remorse or resentment. In the

Golow et al. study, persons who accepted self-limitations were more likely to succeed in community living.

Sources of self-concept have received a certain attention. Program placement, significant others, and reinforcement have emerged as principal variables. Kahm and Garrison (1973) discovered that placement per se was not related to self-concept; consequently, self-contained class versus integrated class did not affect the self-concept, but setting did affect satisfaction with school, with a trend toward partial integration. This study used two self-concept scales, the Illinois Index of Self Derogation, popularized by Meyerowitiz (1962) and the Brookoner General Self Concept of Ability Scale, advanced by Towne and Joiner (1966). While *both* scales have gained a certain prominence as self-concept measures, correlation or agreement is only about .50. This suggests that the two scales measure different elements of the same trait. Consequently, interpretation of self-concept findings should recognize the source of measurement. Setting, self-concept, and academic achievement were investigated by Welch (1967) for a group of mildly retarded learners. A nonsegregated setting reflected more positive gains in self-concept, while the self-contained class reflected significant academic gains. The variable of *setting* reflects significant variation among studies.

The effect of reinforcement upon self-concept, as reported by Kasdin and Forsberg (1974), Piper (1971), and Sprague and Trappe (1966), has emerged as a determinant. The common theme in these studies was that immediacy of approval or reward (within one minute) improved positive feelings about performance as well as motor-task performance. It also was shown that peer encouragement was more effective than peer reprimands. Carr and McLaughtin (1973) found that attending adult education classes did not improve self-concept but did raise feelings of acceptance by peers. This study, like the others cited, did reflect a certain realism, or agreement, among self-reports, peer ratings of the person, and teachers. This aspect of realism is illustrated by the Karnes, Clarizio, and Zerbach (1964) investigation. The study attempted to discover the relationship between skill acquisition (learning to type) and self-concept. The central finding was that aptitude for typing has beneficial effects, while instruction method had minimal consequences. These authors concluded that pupil interest and readiness should be considered. Similar results were reported by Yagel (1975). Employer ratings of job performance of mildly retarded adolescents was the major concern. The study reflected employer ratings, teacher ratings (a realism measure since the person's self-report was compared to the teacher's filling out the same scale), the person's view as a capable person, and the person's view of how his friends viewed him. Yagel noted that the results of this study do identify regression (i.e., correlation) scores upon which to predict job success. The suggestion was advanced that persons might be prescreened for special help prior to job placement. The use of self-disclosure data has been discussed by Burke and Sellin (1972) in this context. Self-concept reports should represent confidential information, not a method to deny service. As Yagel noted, an honest, but devaluing response should be linked to a special source of helpfulness. Otherwise, the use of self-reports for exclusion verges on self-incrimination.

The Yagel report, as well as the Mayer (1967), Fulerton (1973) and the Neissner, Thoreson, and Butler (1967), identify adolescence as a significant factor in self-concept. These studies suggested that adolescents vary in the effect of peer and adult influence, while elementary school learners are more influenced by adult influences. Physical attractiveness and freedom from disability appear to be more significant for adolescent retarded persons than for preteens. These findings were found to be independent of socioeconomic class as well as sociometric (popularity) status. The opportunity to serve as teacher assistant and other service chores were found to be important in raising adolescents' self-esteem.

Lawrence and Winschell (1973) summarized over sixty citations regarding self-concept and mental retardation. Their principal findings were:

1. There is a significant need for longitudinal studies to discover the origins of self-concept. Most studies are retrospective and cover only a brief time span.
2. Current trends toward desegregation of programs appear justified on self-concept data.
3. The moderately retarded have been a neglected group. The emphasis of studies has been upon the mild.
4. Self-concept of ability as a teacher would be an important variable to study as a factor in the development of self-concept as a learner.
5. Continued research is necessary to standardize the various scales in use to identify common areas of measurement and differences in measurement content.
6. While performance and self-concept may be related or associated, which is dependent requires further clarification. It may be that high performance influences high self-concept, rather than the reverse.
7. Referent group is important. Investigations reflect varying results, in part because of the group with which the retarded is asked to compare himself or herself. If the comparison is to similar persons, the ratings tend to be positive and realistic. If the comparison is to normal, the ratings tend to be negative and self-derogatory.

Self-Direction

Wicker and Tyler (1975) have described the acquisition of adaptive behavior as dependent upon cognitive and affective factors. The relationship of affective factors to academic achievement and to personal adjustment has been reviewed by MacMillan (1971). This review identified three clusters of noncognitive sources of achievement. These clusters were viewed as three components of motivation and were said to include: expectancy for failure, positive and negative reaction tendencies, and outer-directedness. The first two clusters were based upon the Zigler concepts presented earlier and can be equated with self-concept. The behavioral result of these first two consequences, supported by the research literature, can be that the person comes to *expect* failure. This expectancy generalizes to responses of *avoidance* and diminished self-worth. The retarded person also establishes a pattern of a *lowered level of aspiration*. Even in a high-success environment, the person may settle for performance less than the responsible practitioner would judge to be his or her maximum level of performance. Life experiences may have taught that success has its limits. The person has learned to avoid failure *rather than* to prize success. Consequently, the person may select methods of self-control and direction that shield the self from expected failure. As a result, teachers may experience frustration when the learner does not respond to tasks within the person's range of capacity.

This situation of self-defeat and derogation is neither permanent nor hopeless. There are solutions. A prime consideration would be to include attitudinal factors as an essential element in the analysis of performance, not just cognitive factors of IQ, MA, etc. A related consideration, advanced by MacMillan, is the prescription of tasks. Helpful tasks to reverse avoidance responses should be slightly beyond the learner, but within capability; perceived as challenging and meaningful *to* the learner; and viewed as genuine mastery upon successful completion.

The third element of personal motivation was termed by MacMillan outer-directedness and has two behavioral dimensions. The first has been termed *locus of control* by Lawrence and Winschell (1975), and the second is termed *moral judgment* by Mahoney and Stephens (1974). The notion of moral judgment, as investigated by Mahoney and Stephens, is founded upon Piagetian concepts of development. Conscience, or precepts to direct one's behavior, is viewed as evolving from simple external controls to the formation of complex internal controls.

Kohlberg (1975) has been engaged in the identification of stages of moral development and judgment in the United States. The Kohlberg research has identified three levels, with two stages within each level of moral development. The first level was termed *preconvention*. This level defines good versus evil and right versus wrong in terms of hedonistic consequences of punishment, rewards, or exchange of favors. At the second level, *conventional*, morality is equated with loyalty to one's family, social group, or other reference group. The third level was termed *postconventional*. At this level, the person attempts to define morality *apart from* authority, power, and/or impositions of others. Values and principles are validated from a nonegocentric frame of reference. As stages, Kohlberg identified six orientations (two to each level), which may be said to involve orientations of morality based upon:

1. *Punishment-obedience*. Behavior is regulated by avoidance of punishment. Unquestioning deference is valued in terms of consequences, not in terms of comprehension.

2. *Instrumental relativist*. Behavior is regulated by satisfaction of needs. Actions are viewed as good if such actions bring pleasure and comfort.

3. *Good boy–nice girl.* Earning verbal approval becomes significant. One's intentions (meaning well) become as significant as the actions.

4. *Law and order.* Authority and loyalty to a fixed set of group rules is the essential theme. The guide to morality is adherence to, and earning approval of, the group.

5. *Social contract and/or legalistic.* Individual behavior is guided by awareness of the rights of others. There is recognition of a larger society that provides an agreement for the protection of individuals. There is also a sense of obligation for the protection of the individuality of others.

6. *Universal-ethical-principle.* This is the most abstract stage, where logical inferences formulate the sense of ethics. Principles at this level are internalized around abstractions that are good in and of themselves. These would include justice, reciprocity, respect, dignity, and equality. At this stage, Kohlberg observed, the Golden Rule precept is practiced without thought for gain or consequence.

While these stages do exist in a particular sequence, Kohlberg (1974) has indicated that further research is necessary to establish age norms for each stage. For the immediate future, Moore and Stephens (1974) have concluded after four years of study that retarded persons are capable of moral conduct and that conduct improves with increases in CA and MA. This competence was found most evident in self-control, as measured by refraining from temptations. Measured intelligence emerges as a necessary condition, but not sufficient explanation for conduct. Moore and Stephens concluded that with time, reasoning has more influence on conduct.

The Lawrence and Winschell (1975) discussion of locus of control reflected the relationship between behavior, conduct, and a personal feeling about one's own efforts. Locus of control is characterized by self-perception that life's rewards, successes, or reinforcements are owing to either one's own efforts (internal, inner-directedness), or to external forces such as fate, chance and luck (external, outer-directedness). They cited over thirty sources to identify differences between both normal and retarded persons with respect to internal locus versus external locus. The differences, especially in academic achievement, favored the person who possessed internal locus of control or, in even more curriculum-goal language — self-reliance, self-direction, etc. This type of person is more likely to persist in tasks, use time more wisely, have higher levels of aspiration, and be success-expectant about new situations. Locus of control among the retarded appears to be a *learned* trait. The Wicker and Tyler report, cited earlier, as well as the efforts of Mahoney and Mahoney (1976), Peterson and Peterson (1968), and Kenyon and Keogh (1974), demonstrate that intervention strategies can be effective in moving the retarded person from an external, passive, dependent, and fatalistic life position to accepting responsibility for successful and unsuccessful actions. These reports also demonstrate that the shift from external to internal is accompanied by permanent gains in skills and/or behavior. Out of these reports, typical of many, has emerged the use of contingency management applications of behavior modification and the use of self-management. Mahoney and Mahoney described self-report and self-management as an ABC approach. That is, the person, under guidance, learns to target a behavior (B) as an antecedent (A) followed by a consequence (C). Strategies for change involve manipulation of A and/or C. They reported utility and applicability for mildly retarded learners.

The Lawrence and Winschell report noted that subsequent research is needed to confirm the developmental aspects of locus of control, especially with reference to its emergence by age-related stages. They did postulate the following sequence: life events are attributed to forces beyond one's control; internal credit for success emerges, while attribution of failure to external factors begins to fade; belief in self-responsibility becomes evident; modesty for success is coupled with a "new courage" to accept responsibility for failure; and responsibility for success and failure are equally accepted. The research cited by these authors did confirm that the retarded are capable of internal locus of control; they observed, however, the necessity for careful management of the environment. Lawrence and Winschell argued that internal locus would be a requirement for mainstreaming, or inclusion in a regular class setting. One would suspect this quality would be needed in a work setting as well. They cited the need for new ways of praise and a balance between open and structured environments. It should be noted that locus of control is highly subject to regression from internal back to external. It may be concluded from these authors' commentary that open environments facilitate internal locus, while structured environments may be required to assist the person to establish a bond between effort and accomplishment.

SOCIAL ADJUSTMENT

Maladaptation to the social standards of community life has served as a principal test of mental retardation. Myths about the menace of mental retardation have perpetuated segregation of the retarded person as well as provided an excuse for the denial of the rights of citizenship.

This section considers the adjustment of retarded persons in social settings, especially program and community settings. Family adjustment will be discussed in service-related chapters. The concern of this section is identifying those variables of mental retardation which can facilitate effective integration. The central focus is a *prognostic* view of mental retardation. The study of the interaction of the retarded person in social settings can furnish a data base for the future.

Social Acceptance

Jaffee and Clark (1965) observed behaviors of seventy-five junior-high mildly retarded learners. Given the range of IQ (25 points), these authors concluded that behavior rather than IQ was associated with acceptance by normal persons. Behaviors for the high acceptance group were: attendance, kindness to others, punctuality, following directions, not borrowing, and working alone, while the unaccepted group was more unhappy than others, sought attention, and had a poor opinion of their own work. The Iano, Ayers, Heller, McGettigan, and Walker (1974) report noted essentially similar findings. Sociometric ratings (expression of popularity) were gathered for forty mildly retarded learners and eighty pupils who would qualify for special services. In general, Iano et al. found *both* "normal" and retarded pupils were accepted and rejected. The diagnostic label was *not* a significant or sufficient predictor. Academic and nonacademic classroom participation was studied by Rucker, Howe, and Snider (1969) at junior-high-school levels. In general, they found that nonacceptance was equal for both settings, but they noted that junior-high pupils were less overt in their rejection of nonretarded pupils. It was also reported that pupils sociometrically popular in the special class were also popular in regular class settings as well. The typical practice of "integration" in physical education, shop, and home economics classes was questioned. The conduct of these classes is as skill-oriented as academic classes. In fact, it was common to find a high level of literacy skills required for performance.

Certain investigations have shown that the pattern of social isolation in school settings can be modified. Jones, Marcotte, and Markham (1968) reported the positive benefits of normal fifth-graders and sixth-graders tutoring moderately retarded peers. The tutors were found to be more positive toward their retarded friends as persons, although their knowledge about the condition remained unchanged. Rucker and Vincenzo (1970) and Lilly (1971) both have demonstrated that gains in social acceptance follow intervention. Both studies involved a pairing of an unpopular pupil with a popular one around an appealing task. Unfortunately, the acceptance gains were not permanent and eventually faded. Consequently, promotion of acceptance requires rather persistent effort.

In the context of mainstreaming (inclusion of the retarded person in regular classrooms with special service support), social acceptance constitutes a significant factor for management. The Dick and Lewis (1972) report suggested an interesting variable. It is not uncommon for mildly retarded students to attend special programs in school out of the attendance area to which they would be otherwise enrolled. Their study compared attitudes of "local" students and nonlocal students toward schooling. They found that nonlocal students were more favorable and that males expressed more stigma about placement. Their interpretation was that being in special class in school and living in the same community left the pupil without recourse, while the nonlocal pupil could "pass" in his home community. Goodman, Gottlieb, and Harrison (1972) identified age and sex as variables of acceptance. They found patterns of nonacceptance to be unrelated to placement (special class, regular class, part-time special class), but that older normal males (fourth grade or older) were the sources of rejection. The Briuninks, Rynders, and Gross (1974) investigation found a developmentally understandable sex basis for elementary learners, with boys expressing preference for boys and girls for girls. This report found that urban retarded pupils received higher acceptance ratings than did suburban pupils. The urban-suburban difference was consistent for sex. Bruininks et al. recommended that sociometric studies analyze same-sex ratings rather than lumping total responses together. This report also noted that the mildly retarded are not *a* group, but subgroups whose individual traits of age, sex, placement, and residence must be considered. The challenge for mainstreaming and for research is to understand the obvious and subtle influences that facilitate acceptance within the school situation. Measured IQ is not the answer. The pairing techniques cited previously hold great promise, but other influences must be understood if gains are to remain permanent.

Community Involvement

Cleland, Swartz, McGaven, and Bell (1973) have identified voting as a demonstration of social competency in a democratic society. Voter participation is a form of social adaptation. These authors cited an interview with a forty-eight-year-old, institutionalized, mildly retarded man who was puzzled by why eighteen-year-olds could vote, and he could not. The Cleland et al. report compared the vote distribution of institutionalized retarded citizens with the vote distribution of the general electorate. The percentages were highly similar for both groups in the vote for national and state offices.

Olley and Fremouw (1974) conducted a survey of the voting rights of retarded citizens. Thirty-one states have adopted the AAMD definition. It was found that: twenty-two states have no regulations, twenty states make explicit the right to vote unless the person is adjudicated incompetent, five states have a provision of "ability to understand elections" regardless of level, and four states did not report. Five states reported organized efforts at voting registration among institutionalized citizens, while sixteen states reported no voting among institutionalized citizens. Warren and Gardner (1973) compared the knowledge of voting of mildly retarded adolescents and normal adolescents. In general, the retarded sample seemed less interested in voting and less informed about registration procedures. They urged the need for increased educational emphasis.

Eagen (1967) and Burke, Gutshall, and Hunter (1968) have compared the driving records of mildly retarded persons. The Eagen report suggested that the mildly retarded experience difficulty in judgment in quick reaction situations. The Burke et al. report reflected only minimal differences between retarded and normal drivers, especially in major violations. Attitude toward driving appeared more significant than intelligence level. A view of driving as an earned right with responsibilities rather than a view of driving as proof of adequacy and a source of pleasure appears to distinguish safe drivers from others.

A number of promising trends have emerged in the facilitation and/or measurement of community involvement of retarded citizens. The Social Learning Curriculum, prepared under the leadership of Goldstein (1974), represents an integrated media instructional program regarding personal emotions, communications, and helping/being helped by others. Dailey (1971) has described the teaching of life sciences as a vehicle for personal adjustment for the mentally retarded. Gozali and Gonwa (1973) have described a curriculum that stresses participation in political events and institutions appropriate for retarded citizens. The development of social play among severely retarded persons has been demonstrated by Strain (1975). Dramatic play techniques involving role playing paired with positive reinforcement was the principal treatment.

Edmonson (1974) has validated a pictorial inventory to measure social participation of retarded persons. This inventory allows for a nonwritten response mode to describe home and out-of-home participation to generate an index of participation. Nihira, Foster, Shelhaas, and Leland (1969) have developed a comprehensive inventory to correspond to dimensions of adaptive behavior suggested by the AAMD definition.

Rosen and Hoffman (1974), based upon an analysis of work adjustment of the retarded, have developed an Inventory of Inappropriate Behavior (IIB). The IIB appears to meet conventional standards of rater reliability (agreement among independent judges), internal consistency (items measure a common trait and subtests contribute to the total score), and predictive validity (discrimination between successful and nonsuccessful workers). IQ was found to be unrelated to IIB scores for mildly and upper-level moderately retarded persons. For those persons functioning between severe and moderate retardation, there was a modest but significant correlation (.49).

Rosen and Hoffman targeted certain clusters of behaviors whose presence is an interference with work adjustment:

1 *Overfriendliness* is reflected by touching for no appropriate reason, relating personal data without prompting to strangers, and a general lack of distinguishing between friends and strangers.
2 *Bizarre speech and actions* is reflected by speaking to one's self without reference to others, devising untrue stories, ritualized (nonorganic) behavior, and repeating movements without result to work.
3 *Socially awkward behavior* is evidenced by dependent, clinging-vine behavior, shy, passive withdrawal, and acting without regard to conventions.
4 *Poor personal appearance* is reflected in eating, grooming, and posture.

5 *Belligerence* is displayed in anger and destruction toward self, others, and property.
6 *Childishness* is reflected by reactions to frustration, criticism, guidance, and following directions.

The authors noted that these are *learned* behaviors rather than inherent traits. They suggest that the behaviors can be corrected and that work-training programs should direct efforts toward their reduction.

Zisfein and Rosen (1974) compared the utility of four measures of self-concept. Fifty-six persons were involved. One measure was a self-evaluation scale involving "How good are you?" questions. The second measure was an aspiration level procedure in which the person was asked to predict how many objects would be assembled in subsequent trials. A risk-taking procedure in which the person is to choose between two puzzles, one labeled "hard" and one labeled "easy," was the third measure. A self-comparison approach that used "true of me or not true of me" statements to problem traits was the fourth measure. All four measures were found to be highly correlated, and the resulting profile was found to be related to the Thematic Apperception Test and ratings by teachers and dormitory personnel. The self-concept measures were found to vary independently of IQ.

The relationship between personal adjustment and community involvement has been discussed by Harrison and Budoff (1972). Friendship and one's belief in forming friendships appear as a significant variable in participation. The Cutts (1947) and Buck (1956) procedure of the House-Tree-Person (H-T-P) Test still remains a helpful assessment of a personal inventory of interests, attitude, and concerns. The person is requested to draw a picture of home (representing the family), a person (the artist), and a tree (the environment). An interview schedule is used to discuss the person in the picture. If the artist and the person in the picture are same-sex and within two years of age, it can be assumed that interview responses pertain to the artist. The H-T-P technique allows for both personal assessment and assessment of the person's view of the environment.

Adult Adjustment

Windle (1962) recommended studies of adult adjustment as the scientific basis for establishing *prognostic* data. Diagnosis was viewed as a summary of the present, while prognosis was inference of future course, duration, and outcomes. Windle observed that mental retardation has often meant a rendering of prognosis at the time of diagnosis. Since incurability has been an element of definition, pessimism about the future can often be generated. Windle disputes absolute incurability as an element of definition, for it leads to unfortunate social value judgments. For Windle (p.

2) this consequence is expressed as "a philosophy of despair, a defeatist attitude that neither treatment nor investigations is worthwhile. Such pessimism is both inhumane and ultimately expensive." He suggests emphasis on amelioration, rather than on complete restoration. Furthermore, the concept of incurability reflects the perspective of one discipline imposed upon a multidisciplinary field. For Windle, prognosis of incurability tied to organic factors negates the consequences of social variables. For example, institutionalized persons can reflect later independence in a community setting.

Follow-up studies of adult adjustment are viewed by Windle as contributing to certain vital areas of decision making. These areas may be said to emphasize:

1. *Treatment.* This area involves cost factors of different treatments and the probability of outcomes following different treatments. There is the need for actuarial data as the basis for predictions about program choices.

2. *Identification of variables related to favorable outcomes.* The isolation of data would enable practitioners to further augment their influence. Moreover, there remains the great need to identify those factors associated with social and vocational adjustment.

3. *Admission and termination criteria.* This area involves knowing the length of time required for various treatments. The intent would be to select those persons who genuinely reflect the condition so as to avoid misdiagnosis and so as not to retain persons unnecessarily. Also, if certain treatment approaches were firmly established as helpful, there would be implications for physical facilities and staffing patterns.

4. *Program evaluation.* The suggestion is made that eventual client attainments could be a basis for assessing program goals. Thus, the validity of approaches that purport to achieve vocational adjustment could be assessed with reference to that criterion.

5. *Philosophy and/or theory of treatment.* The validity of either the philosophy (values structure), and/or theoretical system (integrated explanation), must depend upon its accuracy of prediction. The eventual validity of prognosis at time of diagnosis is that all variables concerning a person will account for an effective treatment plan.

6. *Base-rate data.* Windle notes that evaluation of program alternatives involves a comparison between what can be expected and the actual result. Without a knowledge of the effects of either, nontreatment or of previous treatments, it becomes difficult to attribute consequences to a "new" approach.

7. *Individualized treatment.* This area of knowledge would uncover the multiplicity of variables necessary for prediction. The current problem is that individuals similar in age, sex, and measured intelligence can differ dramatically in work adjustment. The objective of this area of inquiry would be to establish different outcomes and treatments dependent upon the implications of intervening variables between admission and graduation.

Sparks and Younie (1969) concluded, from a review of the literature, that mildly retarded persons have demonstrated capability and competence as adults. They observed that no specific type of programming and/or training procedure has emerged as clearly superior. They did, however, identify certain clusters of factors that appear associated with effective programs. In general, these factors would include:

1 *sequence:* early identification so as to provide more time for acquisition of habits and attitudes
2 *actual work experience:* direct on-the-job practice of acquired learning
3 *cooperative programming:* establishing relationships with rehabilitation agencies
4 *balanced curriculum:* equitable emphasis upon academic, social, and vocational skills
5 *community involvement:* cooperation among employing firms and industrial sites
6 *evaluation:* an openness to review and revise program outcomes.

A listing of representative follow-up studies of mildly retarded persons is presented in table 7–1. It suggests the possibilities for the retarded person as an adult. The recommendations of Windle and the scope of the Dinger (1961) report were employed to identify the elements of this figure.

Dinger (1961) has urged that studies of adult adjustment should be as interested in the *success* of retarded persons as well as in *failure.* This report still serves as a model study in light of the seven Windle criteria for follow-up studies. The sample consisted of one hundred successfully employed graduates of an occupational education class. These persons were personally interviewed by Dinger with respect to educational experience and attitudes, job histories, marital histories, financial histories, community participation, leisure activities, and employer ratings. The Binet IQ range was 50 to 85, with a mean of 76. The correlation between IQ and wages was .21 and between CA and wages was .25. The lack of relationship between IQ and indicators of adult success has been a consistent finding for mildly retarded persons, according to Sparks and Younie. The Beekman (1963) report did cite certain differences with respect to IQ. Persons within the range of 48 to 58 were found to be significantly less capable, or less well prepared, for adult roles. Both the Peterson and Smith (1960) and the Reeves-Kennedy (1966) reports attempted to compare matched normal and retarded populations. In general, both studies reflected a favorable comparison, with the exception of economic earnings. The McFall (1966), the Titus and Travis (1973), and the Milan and Bremar (1973) reports reflect a mixed picture of adult adjustment, especially in economic earnings.

Although these citations were diverse and varied, the conclusions, observations, and/or recommendations reflected a certain compatibility.

Table 7–1 RESUMÉ OF STUDIES OF THE ADULT ADJUSTMENT OF THE MILDLY RETARDED

Descriptive Variables	*Dinger (1961)*	*McFall (1966)*	*Peterson and Smith (1960)*
Sample and Treatment	100 graduates of a high-school program for mildly retarded persons.	50 graduates of a program for mildly retarded	45 mildly mentally retarded persons
Education	97% pursued training after school. 80% felt diploma was helpful in getting a job.	11 continued training after high school.	51% terminated school at age 16 to go to work. All expressed satisfaction with the school program.
Job and Military Experience	65% had service records that reflected promotion, combat, and foreign service. Military service was strongly favored. 42% earned wages greater than beginning teachers. 59% found jobs through friends or relatives and only 2% through the schools. Jobs varied but were semiskilled or unskilled.	30 were unskilled jobs. 8 were semiskilled and 12 were in skilled categories. Jobs were obtained through personal searching and/or friends and relatives.	Service jobs and unskilled jobs were the most common. Jobs were found through own initiative and/or friends/relatives. Usually change of job before present job. General satisfaction with work. 25% had served in the military, and all had been honorably discharged.

Table 7–1 (continued)

Titus and Travis (1973)	*Milan and Bremar (1973)*	*Beekman (1963)*	*Reeves-Kennedy (1966)*
38 graduates of a high-school program for the mildly retarded	216 graduates of a special high school for the mildly retarded.	200 mildly retarded graduates of a high-school program. 17 in IQ 48–58 range, 87 in IQ 60–70 group, and 96 in IQ 70–81 range.	179 mildly retarded persons enrolled in programs for the mildly retarded.
Group could be divided into two attitudes toward the school program. The satisfied group praised on-the-job training and personal adjustment classes. This group also had parents who were satisfied with the school. The unsatisfied group resented placement, and their parents did too. Both groups were critical of the math program.	Not given.	Program was major incentive to stay in school. 20% had experience after leaving school. 11% claimed multiplication and division was required, while 53% needed only counting. 24% reported no reading skills needed for work. 86% reported that diploma was helpful in getting a job.	Not given.
57% were still with first employer. Jobs varied from unskilled to skilled jobs, the latter in craft operations.	8 were in the military; 1 died in action and 1 was cited for bravery. 64% started at average salary, 61% at wages below area averages, 18% at wages above area average. Most in semiskilled jobs. None in skilled.	58% had military experience. Stabilized in job at about age 30 to 35. 48–58 IQ group reflected most job failures. IQ 70–81 has potential for even skilled jobs. Students refused admission to high-school technical classes often ended up as competent in these fields after graduation.	74% were employed, and 22% were not entirely self-supporting. 33% held skilled jobs.

Table 7–1 (continued)

Descriptive Variables	*Dinger (1961)*	*McFall (1966)*	*Peterson and Smith (1960)*
Marital	Spouse IQ was between 64 to 115. The children of the graduates had IQs between 70 to 132, with a mean of 102. Only one child had an IQ below 85. 55% were married, and 3% were divorced. Average family size was 1.5 children.	Not given.	51% were unmarried. Divorce rate was high. 10 of the 12 children were within the normal range and doing well in school. 2 were in classes for the mildly retarded.
Financial	82% were entirely self-supporting, and 15% were employed but had help from families. Financial transactions included: 51% savings, 73% medical insurance, 52% loans, and 24% checking accounts. Only 6% of the homes were rated as below average in upkeep and maintenance.	Wages tended to be at marginal levels for self-support.	5% had received unemployment benefits. Only 2 of the group were on public assistance.

Table 7–1 (continued)

Titus and Travis (1973)	*Milan and Bremar (1973)*	*Beekman (1963)*	*Reeves-Kennedy (1966)*
Not given.	67% were single and 27% married. 22% had children, 1.5 children per family. 12% were buying a home. 51% were renting.	Average family size of 3.2 children. 71% of IQ 48–68 group had children in special education. 60–80 IQ group had spouses who were higher in education levels.	Marital age higher than national average. 86% were married, 3% divorced. Lower birth rate than national average. Family size averaged 2 children. IQ groupings of children were: 4% in MR, 19% in borderline, 56% in average range, 17% in superior, and 3% in gifted. 42% reported both spouses were employed outside the home.
Majority earned wages within an adequate range and all were in minimum wage scales.	89% handle own finances, and 11% were dependent on others to handle finances. 2% on Aid to Dependents.	Wages ranged from nothing to $23,000. 72% at median income, while 16% were above median income for area. 86% of IQ 48–58 received direct aid. 14% of 60–81 IQ group were in special education groups. 70% had average homes. 59% were buying homes.	Over 50% reported homeownership. 55% lived in middle-class or above homes. 90% had insurance. 63% had bank accounts. 50% bought on the installment plan 51% had never received help from agencies. 9% received financial assistance. 69% had sought counseling and advice services. Private agencies were used most frequently.

Table 7–1 (continued)

Descriptive Variables	*Dinger (1961)*	*McFall (1966)*	*Peterson and Smith (1960)*
Community	34% voted. 80% contributed to charity. 80% belonged to a church. 20% belonged to community-improvement groups	Wages tended to be at marginal levels for self-support.	1 in 5 was a registered voter. 62% had had some contact with law enforcement agencies. Outside activity was usually a church group.
Leisure Time	60% reported newspaper subscriptions and 75% reported magazine subscriptions. 65% reported interest in local news. 75% spent leisure time visiting friends and relatives.	Not given.	Local newspaper was important, especially local news. Males favored home mechanics magazines, while females favored romance story magazines.
Employer Ratings	Only 5% of jobs required math skills. 33% of jobs required no reading. Only 31% of the jobs required high school diploma. 17% required no previous experience. 83% would not hire under age 18. 66–75% of the workers were rated as equal to normal workers, while the rest were above average.	Not given.	66% of employers rated persons as good employees.

Table 7–1 (continued)

Titus and Travis (1973)	*Milan and Bremar (1973)*	*Beekman (1963)*	*Reeves-Kennedy (1966)*
Not given.	Little recreation and/or diversion reported. Limited contacts.	78% claimed church membership. 5% had prison records. 35% belonged to labor unions. 10% were members of fraternal lodges.	88% had no arrest records, while 12% had some contact with the law. Males were more likely to have trouble than females. Organizations included: union, PTA, fraternal, veteran, church, civic, business, and social. 86% reported that they voted.
Not given.	Rather bleak social life. Relative noninvolvement in community and social groups. Few friends outside of the immediate family.	62% owned encyclopedias. 68% read the daily newspaper. 25% were involved in high school extracurricular events, usually athletics enthusiasts.	TV and radio, sports, card playing, gardening, newspaper, and magazines were favorite forms of recreation.
Most were generally satisfied, although motivation was cited as a negative trait. Recommended more school emphasis on social skills and job variety.	Not given.	Not given.	Employer compared normal and retarded workers. Retarded were *superior* in lack of absenteeism, promptness for work and speed of work. Retarded were *inferior* in learning a new job. *No differences* were reported in accuracy, judgment, and coworker relationships.

1. All were agreed that there must be close cooperation among school programs, rehabilitation agencies, and sources of employment.

2. The schools must assume an aggressive role in assisting graduates in job finding. Economic conditions require greater assistance during times of job scarcity.

3. Employment is available, even in "hard" times, for dependable and "loyal" employees. The task is to identify and match the employer's need with the worker's capabilities. Increasingly, friends and relatives must be supplemented by determined placement efforts.

4. Economic earnings may not keep pace with materialistic aspirations inspired by the media. Coping with this discrepancy should be a part of preparation.

5. Parent involvement is essential, especially to understand program intentions.

6. Consideration should be given to extending the school period beyond age eighteen. This would be helpful to those persons at the lower end of the mild range. Evidence of schooling beyond the school years would support this observation.

7. As citizens, the mildly retarded would appear to be a positive group. The delay of marriage, the low incidence of mental retardation among children, and low birth rate contradict popular myths. Dependency and criminality appear less serious than for the general public. Participation in elections follows population patterns.

8. Community involvement can be varied and active. However, a pattern of isolation does exist, except for family and church membership.

9. The influence of literacy skills appears mixed. While not job related, these skills are evident in leisure activities, especially the daily newspaper as a source of interest and information.

10. Work records are commendable. Incidence of skilled jobs is evident. Personal qualities and human relationships appear to be dominant factors in work success.

The adult adjustment of retarded persons below the mild range has received a certain attention. A resumé of these reports is found in table 7–2. The adult adjustment literature reflects a somewhat mixed picture. The Tisdall (1960) and Stanfield (1973) reports dealt exclusively with graduates of special training classes for the moderate. These reports stressed the importance of transitional assistance from school to work placement. Too often after "graduation" the parents were left with the responsibility to find and/or secure work placement. The Stabler (1974) report identified the quality and emphasis of the training program offered by a work facility. The variables that influenced work performance differed. Domino and McGarty (1972) identified a personal adjustment cluster, while Fiester and Giambra (1972) have isolated a language cluster. The former report identified personal qualities such as independence, resourcefulness, and self-confidence. The latter report identified factors associated with attending, remembering, and responding to directions.

Table 7–2 ADULT ADJUSTMENT OF MIXED LEVELS OF RETARDATION

Descriptive Variables	*Tisdall (1960)*	*Stanfield (1973)*	*Stabler (1974)*	*Edgerton and Bercovici (1976)*
Sample and Treatment	126 persons who had been in special education for the moderate.	120 graduates of a public-school program for the moderate.	248 clients of a sheltered workshop, a mixed sample of moderate and mild.	30 persons released from a state institution because of vocational competence, a mixed sample of moderate and mild.
Education	School skills were still retained.	63% of the parents reported general improvement, 4% reported life-style was worse.	Were free of negative feelings about being retarded. Accepted not being good in (1) not goofing off, (2) doing a good job, (3) getting along with others, and (4) following orders.	Externally rated as: 8 as better, 12 as the same, and 10 were worse. Self-reports: 12 were happier, and 3 said they were worse. These persons seemed no longer engaged in masking their retardation and were content to enjoy life.
Jobs and Military Experience	18% were in parent-sponsored classes or workshops	48% were in sheltered workshops. 11% were in activity centers, and 5% were in nonsheltered settings. 44% were in no postschool at all. The 5 nonsheltered employments were with family members.	41% were self-sufficient, with 48% partially self-supporting. 25% had factory jobs, and 69% had held some job.	Generally a bleak picture, with employment patterns reflecting *lack* of wage increases over a twelve-year period despite 60% rise in the cost of living.

Table 7–2 (continued)

Descriptive Variables	*Tisdall (1960)*	*Stanfield (1973)*	*Stabler (1974)*	*Edgerton and Bercovici (1976)*
Marital	None were married.	None were married. Parents reported that the person took part in home chores, and family interaction was favorable.	Not specified.	Most were married. Low divorce rate and relative contentment with one's spouse.
Financial	Largely dependent on parents, and 12% had been institutionalized.	42% of the sample came from families under $5,000/year income, and 30% were from families of over $10,000/year. Wages were $10 per week.	23% were in state institutions, 11% were dependent on others. 89% had some employment.	Most were eligible for either retirement-type benefits and/or assistance to the aged.
Community	80% remained at home 5 years after graduation.	60% were mobile in the neighborhood. 38% participated in postschool social-recreation activities.	6 had had some encounter with the law.	General decline in community activities.
Leisure	Passive and inactive.	Relative isolation from the community. Watching TV, listening to records and radio, looking at collections were examples of passive activities.	Not cited.	General increase in the quality of individual hobbies, relatives, and benefactors. Concentration on other interests besides work.
Employer	Adequate progress in sheltered workshops.	Not cited	Reliable, conscientious, eager to please and hard working. Require more reassurance and specific directions.	Not cited.

Both reported these variables were independent of programming. The Edgerton and Bercovici report (1976) has placed the study of adult adjustment within the context of *normalization*. (The concept of normalization is discussed in greater detail in subsequent chapters.) At this point the reader should understand that this concept encompasses a comprehensive philosophical movement designed to decrease the isolation of retarded citizens and to emphasize that retarded citizens should live in a manner as nearly normal as possible. This report offered thirty-nine research citations and an examination of the life experiences of thirty retarded citizens over a 12-year period to identify the importance of environmental, external factors for success to the seeming exclusion of internal factors such as measured intelligence, psychomotor skills, and adjustment factors.

These reports, representative of many, offer a certain guidance for both subsequent research and programming, especially for persons within the moderate and below range. As regards *programming* the following can be advanced:

1. Success appeared dependent upon the presence of a *benefactor*. Adaptation would seem to require a person who can provide a stable resource in times of crisis. This person has usually been a friend, a relative, and/or an employer. Edgerton and Bercovici laid great emphasis upon the presence of such a person as an external-environmental predictor of success. The concept of benefactor has become known as *advocacy*, of which the *citizen advocate* is one form.

2. Vocational-personal guidance would appear to be a significant need. These persons, according to Stabler, are often confused, bewildered, or defeated by form-related procedures such as forms for employment, income tax, welfare, employment benefits, job applications, etc. Interpersonal and human relationships in dealing with feelings and emotions would be helpful. This need will be discussed in some detail in a subsequent chapter related to helping relationships.

3. The Stanfield report, in particular, suggested a pattern of competent persons motivated and competent to work, but not enrolled. There appears to be a dire need for *coordinated* community programming. His report documented a certain lack of obligation to guarantee a transition beyond the school years. Given the possibilities for employment capabilities, there would appear to be an urgent need to upgrade services.

Research studies of the adult adjustment of the moderately retarded reflects an endorsement of the Windle concept of prognosis. The Edgerton and Bercovici report identifies certain guidelines for *research* which would be applicable to the mildly retarded as well. These guidelines are summarized as a recognition of the following:

1. The lives of retarded persons in the community are neither simple nor similar.

2. Attrition is a factor. All studies rarely include all those who would be in the sample. For example, their own study only included thirty out of forty-five possible.

An average rate of between 75 to 80 percent is usually found. Those who have "faded" may be the most competent of all.

3. Predictive efforts of social adjustment should involve attention on isolation of types of responsive environments, as well as internal factors.

4. The question of prediction is a value judgment about what should be predicted in the first place. These authors noted a significant discrepancy between their criteria and the self-reports of the sample. The implication for normalization was to listen to the retarded themselves. The decision point is to decide whose opinions to value, program persons or the person.

5. Vocational competence may not be the sole index of adjustment. For example, these authors cited marriage as a prime goal, and by reasonable criteria their sample was successful. Devotion to others and pursuit of nonwork interests may be other factors.

6. Economic conditions and the general state of the community's economy is a significant environmental factor. Productivity of the retarded person requires careful study, management, and preparation to compensate for external fluctuations of an economy.

SUMMING UP

This chapter considered three components of adaptive behaviors of retarded persons: communication, personal adjustment, and social adjustment.

General

1. The retarded person has the right to expect a reasonable adaptation to his or her capabilities as well as adapting to the demands of others.

2. Research needs to emphasize both the isolation of individual correlates of success as well as factors in the environment which are facilitative.

3. The extent of coordination of service elements has been of variable quality. Special priority would be required between school and postschool programs.

4. Adult success is defined, in part, by the person. Attention should be given to the quality of life as well as to materialistic considerations.

5. Self-concept and self-direction appear to be determinants of success, as success is a determinant of positive self-esteem and feelings of autonomy. Environment plays an important role in these dimensions.

6. Acceptance is behavior and skill, not skill alone. Normal persons are rejected for reasons similar to those for retarded persons.

7. Benefactors of retarded persons do exist in the world and do take a personal interest. There would seem to be a need for organized effort to mobilize more of these human resources.

Communications

1. Communications describes both speech and language. Mental age is only one factor that influences development. At present, there appears to be more emphasis upon language development and a shift away from speech correction.

2. Language possesses components of sound patterns (phonology), meanings and definitions (summatics), order and structure (syntax), and a sense of time and referral points (morphology). All language approaches vary in their emphasis.

3. Sociolinguistic approaches emphasize the social adaptation of language. Its emphasis is upon priorities for language as a vehicle for adaptation. Its emphasis is upon standard English and other language experiences.

4. Psycholinguistics assumes language is process, level, and channel. The ITPA has emerged as a diagnostic base for training. Advocates of ITPA-based training have yet to demonstrate utility with retarded children.

5. Behaviorism has evolved its equivalent of a language model based upon approximations, reinforcement, and imitation. Diagnostic inferences are identified through analysis of behavior.

6. Ethology is a focus upon language as the product of two systems — the child and the adult. This system places equal responsibility on both systems, but especially upon the adult. This system is a design of events to produce responses with a sequence of receptive preceding expressive language.

7. Speech and language represent a high priority for treatment.

Personal Adjustment

1. Self-care skills are a means of socialization. There appears to be sufficient literature to guide practice.

2. Self-concept is measurable, at least for the mildly retarded. Self-concept is usually assessed through interviews of a self-report nature. Self-realism is a comparison of the person's self-report to an external observation of the person. In general, there is a pattern of realism for the retarded.

3. Self-concept appears developmental; age differences do emerge. Adolescence is a vulnerable time. Peers appear to be an important source of self-concept at this period.

4. Setting of segregated versus integrated reflect a mixed picture. The reference for comparison (comparing oneself to other retarded persons or to normal persons) has not been always specified in studies. Attendance in one's own school area as opposed to outside one's area may be a factor. Urban versus suburban setting may be a factor as well. However, it appears evident that self-concept studies, regardless of flaws, have influenced the shift from self-contained classes to mainstream options.

5. Locus of control, or a belief in one's success, was explored. In general, one *learns* to approach-avoid situations based upon success-failure.

6. Locus of control can explain motivation and self-direction. There is evidence that self-concept and internal locus of control are associated with self-directed behaviors of achievement.

7. Another aspect of self-direction was identified as moral development. This refers to development of an internal sense of "good" which regulates behavior.

8. Self-direction can serve as a goal of service. Locus of control, self-concept, and moral development appear susceptible to the laws of learning, so nonhelpful consequences can be unlearned. It is of greater advantage to prevent problems.

Social Adjustment

1. The retarded person is involved in community activities. As a voter, the retarded person has been shown to reflect the patterns of his or her community. As driver, the retarded person is not a threat because of IQ. Like the normal IQ driver, attitude toward driving is the key variable.

2. Measurement procedures and instructional procedures have emerged as helpful aids.

3. Social acceptance among normal persons appears to be related to behavior, not IQ.

4. Acceptance can be achieved, although the results are not always permanent. A skill dimension appears helpful.

5. Retarded learners can be as segregated in a regular classroom as in a special class. However, genuine inclusion is possible.

6. Modification of perceptions of normal populations is possible as a basis for acceptance.

7. Adult competence is possible.

8. The sex myth of low IQ children born to low IQ parents is not supported by follow-up studies.

9. Adult adjustment for the moderately retarded appears to reflect a pattern of community residence and a lack of postschool programming to take advantage of their skills.

10. Adjustment of the mildly retarded reflects a certain optimism. It is disappointing to observe the lack of school efforts in assisting graduates in job finding.

11. The presence of a benefactor (friend, relative, or employer) emerges as a helpful environmental source for adjustment.

ON LOCATION

Language is a unitary medium between the internal, personal world of the person and the external world. Communication skills for the retarded person has its affective personal-social dimensions beyond the physical and intellectual. The selections by Burton (1973) and Butler (1975) seem a fitting culmination to a discussion of adaptive behavior. These selections, written by retarded persons, illustrates positive adaptation.

THOUGHTS AND THINKING

thoughts and thinking.
I'm here finding
thoughts float
thinking is finding the right answer
like in arithmetic.
if you have a thought
don't let it fly away
hold it
or it will go on a never ending
voyage
until it seeps in a hole
through a new mind—
you look upon our many
wonders and blunders
there you conceal yourself
in your magic world
the key is there to unlock
and bring us humans into
a new world.
yes I see and feel what's real
but like before
I must go fishing
before I catch
the answer.

—Donald Butler

UNTITLED

As the day lingers on, we start it right
Never doing things wrong.
It has a purpose just for us.
No one ever makes a fuss
I must say it sure makes
everything go very wide awake,
To step into the cold morning air,
Whether the weather is rainy or fair.
Keep happiness in your heart
And the day will be off
With a very good start!

I'd like to be a bumble bee
in a field of clover.
Maybe a little dog
By the name of Rover.
I like everything I see,
But don't know what I
really want to be.

But I am happy, just think
In the whole wide world
I am lucky that I am
Just plain little old me.
And that's just what I'll be!

—Philip Burton

REFERENCES

Adler, S. A Sociolinguistic Approach to Functional Mental Retardation. *Exceptional Children,* 1971, 38, 336–337.

Ball, T. S. Long Term Retention of Self Help Skills Training in the Profoundly Retarded. *American Journal of Mental Deficiency,* 1971, 76, 378–382.

Baram, S., and Meyer, T. Retarded Children's Perceptions of Favorite TV Characters. *Mental Retardation,* 1975, 13, 28–31.

Bateman, B., and Wetherell, J. Psycholinguistic Aspects of Mental Retardation. *Mental Retardation,* 1965, 3, 8–12.

Beekman, M. *The Retarded 200.* Lansing, Michigan: Lansing Public Schools, 1963.

Briuninks, R., Rynders, J., and Gross, J. Social Acceptance of Mildly Retarded Pupils in Resource Rooms and Regular Classes. *American Journal of Mental Deficiency,* 1974, 78, 377–383.

Brown, L., Huppler, B., Pierce, L., Schuerman, N., and Sontag, E. Teaching Young Trainable Students to Report Behavioral Events. *Education and Training of the Mentally Retarded,* 1974, 9, 15–22.

Buck, J. The H-T-P: A Projective Device. *American Journal of Mental Deficiency,* 1956, 61, 191–197.

Burke, D., Gutshall, R., and Hunter, C. An Exploratory Study of Inter-relations Among Driving Ability, Driving Exposure, and Socioeconomic Status of Low, Average, and High Intelligence Males. *Exceptional Children,* 1968, 35, 43–47.

Burke, D., and Sellin, D. Measuring the Self Concept of Ability as a Worker. *Exceptional Children,* 1972, 39, 126–132.

Burns, E. Effects of Restricted Sampling on ITPA Scaled Scores. *American Journal of Mental Deficiency,* 1976, 80, 394–400.

Burton, P. An Untitled Poem. *Mental Retardation News,* 1973, 22, 7.

Butler, D. Thoughts and Thinking. *Mental Retardation News,* 1975, 24, 8.

Carr, C., and McLaughtin, J. Self-Concept of Mentally Retarded Adults in an Adult Education Class. *Mental Retardation,* 1973, 11, 57–59.

Cleland, C. C., Swartz, J., McGaven, M., and Bell, K. Voting Behavior of Institutionalized Mentally Retarded. *Mental Retardation,* 1973, 11, 31–35.

Congdon, D. The Adaptive Behavior Scales Modified for the Profoundly Retarded. *Mental Retardation,* 1973, 11, 20–21.

Cutts, R. A Projective Interview Technique. *American Journal of Mental Deficiency,* 1947, 51, 606–610.

Dailey, R. F. Me Now—Life Sciences for the Mentally Retarded. *Education and Training for the Mentally Retarded,* 1971, 6, 127–133.

Dick, H., and Lewis, M. School Attendance Areas as a Factor in Attitudes of EMR Adolescent Students Toward School and School Related Activities. *Education and Training of the Mentally Retarded,* 1972, 7, 82–87.

Dinger, J. Post School Adjustment of Former Educable Retarded Pupils. *Exceptional Children,* 1961, 27, 353–360.

Domino, G., and McGarty, M. Personal and Work Adjustment of Young Retarded Women. *American Journal of Mental Deficiency,* 1972, 77, 314–321.

Eagen, R. Should the Educable Mentally Retarded Receive Driver Education? *Exceptional Children,* 1967, 33, 323–324.

Edgerton, R., and Bercovici, S. The Cloak of Competence: Years Later. *American Journal of Mental Deficiency,* 1976, 80, 485–497.

Edmonson, B. Measurement of Social Participation of Retarded Adults. *American Journal of Mental Deficiency,* 1974, 78, 494–501.

England, G. *Speech and Language Problems.* Englewood Cliffs, New Jersey: Prentice-Hall, 1970.

Fiester, A., and Giambra, L. Language Indices of Vocational Success in Mentally Retarded Adults. *American Journal of Mental Deficiency,* 1972, 77, 332–337.

Finnie, N. *Handling the Young Cerebral Palsied Child at Home.* New York: E. P. Dutton, 1968.

Fulerton, S. Self Concepts Changes of Junior High Students. *Journal of Counseling Psychology,* 1973, 20, 493–495.

Goldstein, H. *Social Learning Curriculum.* Columbus, Ohio: Charles E. Merrill, 1974.

Golow, A., Butler, A., and Gunthrie, G. Correlates of Self Attitudes of Retardates. *American Journal of Mental Deficiency,* 1963, 67, 549–555.

Gonzalez, G. Language, Culture, and Exceptional Children. *Exceptional Children,* 1974, 40, 565–570.

Goodman, H., Gottlieb, J., and Harrison, R. Social Acceptance of EMR's Integrated into a Nongraded Elementary School. *American Journal of Mental Deficiency,* 1972, 76, 412–417.

Gozali, J., and Gonwa, J. Citizenship Training for the EMR: A Case of Education Neglect. *Mental Retardation,* 1973, 11, 49–50.

Guralnick, M. A Language Development Program for Severely Handicapped Children. *Exceptional Children,* 1972, 39, 45–49.

Hare, B., Hammill, D., and Bartell, N. Construct Validity of Selected Subtests of the ITPA. *Exceptional Children,* 1973, 40, 13–20.

Harrison, R., and Budoff, M. Demographic, Historical, and Ability Correlates of the Laurelton Self-Concept Scale in an EMR Sample. *American Journal of Mental Deficiency,* 1972, 76, 460–480.

Haynes, U. *How To's on Dressing and Feeding.* New York: United Cerebral Palsy, 1976.

Hammill, D., and Larson, S. The Effectiveness of Psycholinguistic Training. *Exceptional Children,* 1974, 41, 5–14.

Iano, R., Ayers, D., Heller, H., McGettigan, J., and Walker, V. Sociometric Studies of Retarded Children in an Integrative Program. *Exceptional Children,* 1974, 40, 267–271.

Jaffee, C., and Clark, V. M. Observed Behavior of Educable Mentally Retarded Junior High Girls. *Exceptional Children,* 1965, 32, 113–114.

Jeffery, D. B. Increase and Maintenance of Verbal Behavior in a Mentally Retarded Child. *Mental Retardation,* 1972, 10, 35–40.

Jones, R. L., Marcotte, M., Markham, K. Modifying Perceptions of Trainable Mental Retardates. *Exceptional Children,* 1968, 34, 309–315.

Kahm, J., and Garrison, M. Self Concept Measurement and Placement of Adolescent EMR's. *Training School Bulletin,* 1973, 70, 80–83.

Karnes, M., Clarizio, H., and Zerbach, R. The Effects of Typing Instruction on the Personality and Achievement of Educable Mentally Handicapped Children. *Exceptional Children,* 1964, 31, 27–32.

Kasdin, A., and Forsberg, S. Effects of Group Reinforcement and Punishment of Classroom Behavior. *Education and Training of the Mentally Retarded,* 1974, 9, 50–55.

Keane, V. E. The Incidence of Speech and Language Problems in the Mentally Retarded. *Mental Retardation,* 1972, 10, 3–8.

Kenyon, S., and Keogh, B. Interpretation of Task Interruption and Feelings of Responsibility for Failure. *Journal of Special Education,* 1974, 8, 175–178.

Kirk, S. A., Ethnic Differences in Psycholinguistic Abilities. *Exceptional Children,* 1972, 39, 112–118.

Kirk, S. A., McCarthy, J. J., and Kirk, W. *Illinois Test of Psycholinguistic Abilities* (rev. ed.). Urbana: University of Illinois, 1968.

Kirk, S. A. and McCarthy, J. J. The Illinois Test of Psycholinguistic Abilities — An Approach to Differential Diagnosis. *American Journal of Mental Deficiency,* 1961, 66, 399–412.

Kohlberg, L. Developmental Gain in Moral Judgment. *American Journal of Mental Deficiency,* 1974, 79, 142–146.

Kohlberg, L. The Cognitive-Developmental Approach to Moral Education. *Phi Delta Kappan,* 1975, 56, 670–677.

Lawrence, E., and Winschell, J. Locus of Control: Implications for Special Education. *Exceptional Children,* 1975, 41, 483–490.

Lawrence, E., and Winschell, J. Self Concept and the Retarded: Research and Issues. *Exceptional Children,* 1973, 40, 310–318.

Lilly, M. Improving Social Acceptance of Low Sociometric, Low Achieving Students. *Children,* 1971, 37, 341–347.

Longhurst, T. Assessing and Increasing Descriptive Communication Skills. *Mental Retardation,* 1972, 10, 42–45.

Lynch, J., and Brecker, W. A. Linguistic Theory and Operant Procedures: Toward an Integrated Approach to Language Training for the Mentally Retarded. *Mental Retardation,* 1972, 10, 12–16.

MacMillan, D. The Problem of Motivation in the Education of the Mentally Retarded. *Exceptional Children,* 1971, 37, 579–585.

Mahoney, E., and Stephens, B. Two Year Gains in Moral Judgment by Retarded and Non Retarded Persons. *American Journal of Mental Deficiency,* 1974, 79, 134–141.

Mahoney, G. Ethological Approach to Delayed Language Acquisition. *Mental Retardation,* 1975, 80, 39–148.

Mahoney, M., and Mahoney, K. Self Control Techniques with the Mentally Retarded. *Exceptional Children,* 1976, 42, 338–339.

Mayer, L. Relationship of Self-Concepts and Sociometric Variables in Retarded Children. *American Journal of Mental Deficiency,* 1967, 72, 267–272.

McCoy, G. Some Ego Factors Associated with Academic Success and Failure of Educable Mentally Retarded Pupils. *Exceptional Children,* 1963, 30, 80–83.

McFall, T. Post School Adjustment: A Survey of Fifty Former Students of Classes for the Educable Mentally Retarded. *Exceptional Children,* 1966, 32, 633–634.

Meyerowitiz, J. Self-Derogation in Young Retardates and Special Class Placement. *Child Development,* 1962, 33, 443–451.

Milan, J., and Bremar, J. *Graduates of Kent Occupational High School: A Follow-Up Study: 1964–1972*. Grand Rapids, Michigan: Kent Intermediate School District, 1973.

Miller, J. F., and Yoder, D. On Developing the Content for a Language Teaching Program. *Mental Retardation,* 1972, 10, 9–11.

Minskoff, E. Research on Psycholinguistic Teaching: Critique and Guidelines. *Exceptional Children,* 1975, 42, 136–144.

Moore, G., and Stephens, B. Two Year Gains in Moral Conduct by Retarded and Non Retarded Persons. *American Journal of Mental Deficiency,* 1974, 79, 147–153.

Neissner, A., Thoreson, R., and Butler, A. Relation of Self Concept to Impact and Obviousness of Disability Among Male and Female Adolescents. *Perceptual and Motor Skills,* 1967, 24, 109–115.

Nelson, R., Peoples, A., Hay, L., Johnson, T., and Hay, W. The Effectiveness of Speech Training Techniques Based Upon Operant Conditioning: A Comparison of Two Methods. *Mental Retardation,* 1976, 14, 34–38.

Newcomer, P., Hare, B., Hammill, D., and McGettigan, J. Construct Validity of the ITPA. *Exceptional Children,* 1974, 40, 509–510.

Newcomer, P., Larson, S., and Hammill, D. A. Response. *Exceptional Children,* 1975, 42, 144–148.

Nihira, H., Foster, R., Shelhass, M., and Leland, H. *Adaptive Behavior Scales.* Washington, D.C.: American Association on Mental Deficiency, 1969.

Niswander, P., and Kelley, L. Comparison of Speech Discrimination in Non Retarded and Retarded Subjects. *American Journal of Mental Deficiency,* 1975, 80, 217–222.

Olley, G., and Fremouw, W. The Voting Rights of the Mentally Retarded: A Survey of State Laws. *Mental Retardation,* 1974, 12, 14–16.

Peins, M. *Bibliography in Speech, Hearing and Language in Relation to Mental Retardation.* Washington, D.C.: Public Health Service Publication No. 2022, Maternal and Child Health Service, 1969.

Perozzi, J. Language Acquisition as Adaptive Behavior. *Mental Retardation,* 1972, 10, 32–34.

Peterson, R. F., and Peterson, L. R. The Use of Positive Reinforcement in the Control of Self Destruction in a Retarded Boy. *Journal of Experimental Child Psychology,* 1968, 6, 351–361.

Peterson, L., and Smith, L. The Post School Adjustment of Educable Mentally Retarded Adults with that of Adults of Normal Intelligence. *Exceptional Children,* 1960, 26, 404–408.

Piper, T. Effects of Delay of Reinforcement on Retarded Children. *Exceptional Children,* 1971, 38, 139–145.

Reeves-Kennedy, R. J. *A Connecticut Community Revisited: A Study of the Social Adjustment of a Group of Mentally Deficient Adults in 1948 and 1960.* Hartford, Connecticut: Connecticut State Department of Health, 1966.

Richmond, B., and Dalton, J. E. Teacher Ratings and Self Concept Reports of Retarded Pupils. *Exceptional Children,* 1973, 40, 178–183.

Rosen, M., and Hoffman, M. An Inventory of Inappropriate Behavior. *The Training School Bulletin,* 1974, 71, 179–187.

Rucker, C., Howe, C., and Snider, B. The Participation of Retarded Children in Junior High Academic and Nonacademic Regular Classes. *Exceptional Children,* 1969, 35, 617–623.

Rucker, C., and Vincenzo, F. Maintaining Social Acceptance Gains Made by Mentally Retarded Children. *Exceptional Children,* 1970, 36, 679–680.

Sailor, W., Guess, D., and Baer, D. Functional Language for Verbally Deficient Children. *Mental Retardation,* 1973, 11, 27–35.

Snyder, L., Lovitt, T., and Smith, J. D. Language Training for the Severely Retarded: Five Years of Behavior Analysis Research. *Exceptional Children,* 1975, 42, 7–15.

Spadlin, J. H. Assessment of Speech and Language of Retarded Children: The Parsons Language Sample. *Journal of Speech and Hearing Disorders,* 1963, 10, entire issue.

Sparks, H., and Younie, W. Adult Adjustment of the Mentally Retarded: Implications for Teacher Education. *Exceptional Children,* 1969, 36, 13–18.

Sprague, R., and Trappe, L. Relationship Between Activity and Delay of Reinforcement in the Retarded. *Journal of Experimental Psychology,* 1966, 3, 390–397.

Stabler, E. Follow-Up Study of Retarded Clients From a Training Workshop. *Mental Retardation,* 1974, 12, 7–9.

Stanfield, J. Graduation: What Happens to the Retarded Child When He Grows Up. *Exceptional Children,* 1973, 39, 548–533.

Stephenson, B., and Gay, W. Psycholinguistic Abilities of Black and White Children from Four SES Levels. *Exceptional Children,* 1972, 38, 705–709.

Strain, P. Increasing Social Play of Severely Retarded Preschoolers with Socio-Dramatic Activities. *Mental Retardation,* 1975, 13, 7–9.

Striefel, S. TV as a Language Training Medium. *Mental Retardation,* 1972, 10, 27–29.

Tisdall, W. A Follow-Up Study of Trainable Mentally Handicapped Children in Illinois. *American Journal of Mental Deficiency,* 1960, 65, 11–16.

Titus, R., and Travis, J. Follow Up of EMR Program Graduates. *Mental Retardation,* 1973, 11, 24–26.

Towne, R., and Joiner, L. *The Effects of Special Class Placement in the Self Concept of Ability of the Educable Mentally Retarded Child.* East Lansing, Michigan: Office of Educational Publications Services, 1966.

Valletutti, P. Language of the Mildly Mentally Retarded: Cognitive Deficit or Cultural Deficit. *Exceptional Children,* 1971, 37, 455–459.

Warren, S. A., and Gardner, D. C. Voting Knowledge of the Mildly Retarded. *Exceptional Children,* 1973, 40, 215–216.

Welch, E. The Effects of Segregated and Partially Integrated School Programs on Self Concept and Academic Achievement of Educable Mental Retardates. *Exceptional Children,* 1967, 34, 93–100.

Wicker, P., and Tyler, J. Improving Locus of Control through Direct Instruction: A Pilot Study. *Education and Training of the Mentally Retarded,* 1975, 10, 15–18.

Windle, C. *Prognosis of Mental Subnormals.* Monograph Supplement to *American Journal of Mental Deficiency,* 1962, 66, 1–175.

Yagel, M. Measures of Self Concept Which Are Predictors of Job Success for Appalachian Adolescents with School Learning Problems. *Education and Training of the Mentally Retarded,* 1975, 10, 252–258.

Zisfein, L., and Rosen, M. Self-Concept and Mental Retardation: Theory, Measurement, and Clinical Utility. *Mental Retardation,* 1974, 12, 15–19.

8

Mobilization and Organization of Services

SYNOPSIS

Mobilization and organization of services is as essential as the prevention and treatment services themselves. The difficulties experienced by the parent, the retarded person, and the concerned practitioner may often originate from lack of services to complement an existing service, duplication that drains service resources, and a lack of jurisdiction for responsibility.

The chapter reviews expert opinion regarding the content of service goals. A proven process for mobilization has been the *change agent* model of *social action*. The tasks of social action are described in some detail to convey its scope and sequence.

Administration and coordination are the two overt functions of organization of services. The concept of developmental disabilities is presented to alert the reader to this new trend in service collaboration.

It is recognized that mobilization and organization cannot be altogether compelled and that sustained effort cannot be altogether mandated. A locus of responsibility is suggested.

One goal of this chapter is to identify the skills of the change agent. A second would be to define dimensions of the professional's program responsibilities. The third goal would be to assist the reader to formulate a personal sense of responsibility.

OBJECTIVES

ATTITUDES

1. To believe that change is possible and that one can participate in the process of change.
2. To be aware that sound programming originates with clarity of goals.
3. To want to participate with others in cooperative efforts.
4. To be open to evaluating one's own practices and strategies with retarded persons.

5 To realize that the professional is change agent, legitimizer, and active participant.
6 To wish to affiliate with citizen associations as well as professional societies in common cause.

UNDERSTANDINGS

1 To conceive the content of a plan for social action.
2 To realize one's roles as change agent, legitimizer, and active participant.
3 To understand the quality dimensions of programs and services.
4 To differentiate between administration and coordination.
5 To appreciate the incentives for legal intervention.
6 To understand the service implications of developmental disabilities.

SKILLS

1 To perform the role of change agent with respect to building relevance.
2 To evaluate one's own program.
3 To implement one's own sense of responsibility for the quality of services for the retarded.

OVERVIEW

Functions

Crosby and Taylor (1973) describe the organization of mental retardation services as centered around coordination and administration. They (p. 73) view coordination as:

> the process of bringing together all necessary resources in the appropriate sequence in order to accomplish a given objective. Coordination involves initiating, sustaining, and interrelating the various parts of the service delivery system.

Typically, coordination involves resource documentation, service advocacy, community involvement, concerns with prevention, personnel development, and volunteer services in relationship to objectives. Administration, according to Crosby and Taylor (p. 105), may be defined as the "determination of mission and purpose, and a responsibility for planning, organizing, directing, controlling, and coordinating the activities of the organization."

Administration usually involves considerations of philosophy, policies, practices (mission), internal management and external relationship to governing boards, fiscal management, personnel practices, and supervisors of standards maintenance.

Dimensions of Relevance

The practitioner who considers administration and coordination irrelevant should consider Boor's (1975) thoughtful account of Katherine, which was based on records maintained by her father. Katherine is twenty. Her IQ has floated between 70 and 90 over the years. She has been variously diagnosed as "retarded," "borderline retarded," and "borderline normal." She has been in special classes, sheltered workshops, mental hospitals, residential facilities — the listing goes on. Her file contains over twenty communications trying to find a placement for Katherine. In one instance, the family was required to complete extensive paperwork for possible admission to a school. They were denied permission to visit prior to filling out the forms. They completed the forms and eventually were turned down. At age two, the file registers a first anxiety by the parents about their child and the continuous search as each agency tells the family, "She's retarded; there is nothing to be done." At the close of the narrative, Katherine is described by Boor as twenty-one, unable to hold a job, promiscuous, unstable, happy with her guitar. Boor concludes that the service system is at war with the family, rather than striving to help.

Consider the accumulated experience of a director of an association for retarded citizens (ARC). Gorham (1975) organized her report into four categories that have implications regarding service delivery. These experiences are summarized from a parent's perspective:

Ironies

1 The responsibility for monitoring the child's progress through fragmented systems has been ours.
2 Physicians, who are viewed as expert, have only limited exposure to the total needs of the handicapped.
3 The more specialized the diagnostician, the less willing he or she is to give information to the parents.
4 We are told to institutionalize, but the institution may be the least equipped to help.
5 We are asked to release information about our child which we have not been allowed to read ourselves. [Note: The so-called Buckley amendment has now made it possible for parents and persons over eighteen to have full access to records.]
6 We are told the best place is the community, yet foster homes and group homes are hard to locate. Respite care and homemaker services are only a dream.
7 Funding has not always followed mandatory legislation for education.
8 In the past, we were made to feel guilt if we did not institutionalize. Now normalization makes us feel guilty if we do.

Effect of the Ironies

1. We are angry at finding little help from the helping professions.
2. We are still in awe of expertise.
3. We are grateful to schools for accepting our children.
4. We are accused of apathy. We have heard of so many bandwagons that we now tend to listen and decide for ourselves.
5. We plan a year at a time. The future is uncertain, and even a trust fund would not help. If my child became a ward of the state, his or her estate would become part of the state's general fund.
6. We are tired. We've been at it for so long.

Suggestions for Professionals

1. Make a management plan a part of diagnosis.
2. Be informed about community resources.
3. Prepare reports in clear, understandable language.
4. Give copies of reports to parents.
5. Help parents to understand that there is no final and unchanging diagnosis.
6. Help the parents think of life with the child as problem solving. Be there to assist. Instill confidence of coping.
7. Help the parent understand abilities and disabilities. Warn the parent that some will only emphasiee the negative. Warn about insufficiencies.

Suggestions for Parents

1. Being well informed about your child requires working with the persons who work with your child. If you meet resistance, how you handle it is important. Maintain confidence that you are a vital member of the team.
2. Learn to keep records. The evidence you collect may be persuading factors to obtain service. Ask for copies of child's records.
3. Learn the terms. Insist, if necessary, on explanations and reexplanations.
4. Locate someone who can help you coordinate the results.
5. Talk freely and openly with others. An Association for Retarded Citizens (ARC) can be helpful.
6. Stay in touch with the practitioner.
7. Listen to your child.
8. You are the primary helper, monitor, coordinator, observer, recordkeeper and decision-maker for the child. Insist you be treated as such.

The values of coordination for practitioners have been suggested by the Sellin et al. (1974) report. These values (as identified by 115 active participants) included:

1 Adequate service in client referral can be accomplished only through interagency cooperation.
2 Knowledge of agency resources is useful to enrich the programs of other agencies.
3 Interagency participation can introduce new ideas and necessary changes.
4 Interagency meetings are a means of becoming aware of other agencies which handle problems presented by our clients.
5 Being aware of how other agencies handle problems has helped my agency.
6 Changes in the programs of my agency will occur in the near future as a result of interagency planning.

DIMENSIONS OF QUALITY

Crosby and Taylor (1973) identified standards of quality for services. These included:

1. *Responsiveness*. This implies the extent a program can specify needs of persons. Emphasis should be directed toward specific developmental needs of clients. One index of this trait is early case finding so as to prevent neglect.

2. *Availability*. Comprehensive, multidisciplinary, and varied modalities of service are important. Another consideration is reference to normalization of methods of treatment as first choice, as well as an emphasis upon an orderly transition from program to program.

3. *Accessibility*. Experience has identified certain factors that limit access to available services. These may include lack of information, red tape, immobility, household responsibilities, fear, geographical or social isolation, lack of transportation, language or cultural barriers, cost, or a generalized lack of responsiveness. An implied standard favors a fixed point for information and access.

4. *Individualization*. One evident factor of normalization is that "clients" are treated as individuals. Evidence of individualization would be a personalized plan, not inclusion in a mass prescription. Other criteria for individualization would be participation of the person and/or his or her advocate in the plan. Furthermore, there should be evidence of the person and/or his or her advocate being informed of their rights and responsibilities.

5. *Records*. Information is crucial for continuing understanding of the person and for accelerated transfer from service element to service element. This standard

reflects an area of great sensitivity for the balance between what is necessary and avoiding the pitfalls of irrelevant labels.

6. *Quality Control.* Quality is the result of effort. Quality requires promotion, development, protection, and control. Evaluative procedures of relating goals to outputs, as in the McIntyre and Meirhenry discussions (1969), are evidence of effort toward quality control.

7. *Accountability.* Accountability is commitment to fulfilling goals. Accountability can be expressed as the sum total of responsiveness, availability, accessibility, individualization, records, and quality control. Evidence of accountability is the willingness to seek accreditation, which, in turn, requires willingness to declare one's service standards.

The Crosby and Taylor report also contains a manual for program assessment. Rating forms are provided for both program personnel and external judges.

Goldman (1975) reported one community's experiences in applying these standards to the design of a service. The culmination of the project was the establishment of a client decision agency. The CDA was an independent agency empowered by law to operate in an ombudsman fashion to contract for services. Furthermore, the CDA was a central clearinghouse to facilitate service delivery.

AN INTERAGENCY PERSPECTIVE

Historical Origins

PL 88–164, a direct outgrowth of the President's Panel Report, provided significant impetus to interagency service efforts at both state and community levels. Between 1963 and 1966 was a period of significant activity for the states to develop their own equivalent of the President's Panel Report.

The Guthrie report (1964) emphasized that interagency coordination originates with sound planning based upon an analysis of population needs and current resources. Planning should foster communication and cooperation. Communication establishes a commonly understood terminology and classification system. Cooperation is a learned process centered upon a mutual task. The basic tasks were summarized by Guthrie:

1 Establish mechanisms/structures at state and community levels for coordination of financial resources, consultative services, application of standards, prevention, training, research, etc.
2 Identify case-finding procedures to locate persons in need.
3 Outline a model or program of coordinated services to be achieved.
4 Define procedures for continuing reevaluation of services.

5 Provide for a regional/community approach for services.
6 Stimulate and develop public awareness.
7 Develop proposals for legislative action, based upon verified need.

Current Emphasis

The Stedman (1976) report provided an update of the state coordinating structures established in the 1960s and now known as the State Council on Developmental Disabilities. (Federal support for mental retardation planning and implementation under PL 88–164 expired in 1968.) The Developmental Disabilities Act of 1970 directed that federal funds be expended under the supervision of a state advisory council appointed by the governor of each state. Representatives from consumer groups of cerebral palsy, mental retardation, and epilepsy were to constitute a third of the membership. Stedman described the functions of the typical state council as: program evaluation; information acquisition and dissemination; resource development, either by uncovering existing resources or recommending new ones; developing alternative strategies for service deliveries; and assembling resources to carry out the preceding four functions. Stedman judged 90 percent of the councils effective, although certain problems still required ongoing attention:

1 Interagency communication is more a problem of maintenance than of jargon.
2 The size of the federal grant to be dispersed by the council should be increased.
3 Staff for the day-to-day operation of the council is inadequate in size and/or time available.
4 Some consumer participants view the state councils as a replacement of their interest group.
5 The organization of state government itself is a problem.

The last point relates to the unique status of the education system. Most state agency heads serve at the pleasure of the governor and are highly dependent upon state funds. Education, by contrast, has access to state legislators, and its head is usually appointed by an independent board, elected at large, or is not subject to influence by a governor. Also, federal funding for special education has not required an interagency plan. Consequently, Stedman noted, there has been the tendency of education to remain aloof from the mental-health rehabilitation area. Despite those troublesome factors, Stedman lauded the following states: New Jersey and California (planning and evaluation); North Carolina and Michigan (advocacy); Virginia and Colorado (resource development); New Hampshire and Florida (governmental functioning); and Virginia, West Virginia, Tennessee, Minnesota, North Dakota, and South Dakota (interstate regionalization of services).

Growth Stages

In a related report, Stedman (1975) identified four stages of growth for the interagency process. These were:

1. *Primitive*. Characterized by a plan but the staff is disorganized and without mission. Activity is fragmented and variable.

2. *Competitive*. Characterized by friction and negative interaction among members. There is a plan and some staff to assist members. Commendable effort is directed toward awarding grants to local communities to put prime services into operation.

3. *Advisory-collaborative*. This stage involves a well-defined goal-oriented plan with adequate staff and resources. The council's goals also tend to filter into the operation of participating agencies. At this stage, attention is usually directed toward establishment of a regional planning system.

4. *Affirmative-advocacy*. This stage represents a branching of emphasis. A Developmental Disabilities Council may elect to enter into the power broker phase to seek influence upon the executive and/or legislative branches of government. This activity, according to the author, can be effective if access is gained to sources of power. The pitfall, however, is that this power broker activity may distract from implementation of the plan. The other branch involves an emphasis upon communication to appropriate agencies, including the legislature and governor. In this branch, "political" activity is directed toward establishing channels of action.

Stedman concluded that stages 3 and 4, in combination, are the most effective. Stedman noted that it is possible to originate at these higher levels. He offered this stage model as a guide to assess current level and as an index for future direction.

A SOCIAL ACTION PERSPECTIVE

An Example

In one community, a high-school senior became interested in mental retardation because of a high-school psychology course. He discovered that recreation geared to adolescents and young adults was lacking, especially for the moderately retarded in the school program, in work activity centers, and for formerly institutionalized persons living in the community. His main concern was for a youth-to-youth orientation. His method of assessment was an informal survey of YOUTH-ARC members, who in turn asked their parents and friends. He also "interviewed" the directors of programs. A major obstacle was a lack of funds to finance a weekly canteen and weekend outings. The YOUTH-ARC became motivated by the young man's enthusiastic approach. Its president, another high-school senior, was positive the program was possible. She began to speculate about sources of help. The school program was willing to donate space for the canteen. Bowling alleys, skating facilities, and the like were willing to waive standard admission fees. However, the question of funding continually arose. The president and the young man decided on a Walk-A-Thon. Eventually, this event raised $10,000 from sponsors. The local ARC sanctioned the event. Promotional activities included help from two youth-oriented radio stations. Each YOUTH-ARC member recruited a member, who recruited a member in turn, and so on, to be a walker and secure sponsors. The police deputies association volunteered to provide protection at street crossings along the twenty-five-mile route. A fast-food service chain provided refreshments at the checkpoints. Student councils at high schools were enlisted to help in promotion and recruitment. Prior to the Saturday of the event, the local newspaper and the student newspaper of the local university featured editorials. The local television station agreed to furnish coverage. The mayor, members of the city council, and the local delegation to the state legislature were recruited to walk an honorary mile. The program, which the funds made possible, was an excellent example of expressive advocacy.

Although social action may seem abstract, a tool for professionals and too sophisticated to execute, these young people applied the principles in a practical way. One is struck by their intuitive sense of the organization required. Social action does not promise quick results. One of the qualities of the change agent would seem to be the ability to resist discouragement. Progress reports can be helpful to identify gains, no matter how modest.

Definition and Tasks

Beal, Payer, and Yarbrough (1965) have applied social action theory to service development for the mentally retarded and their families. Their intention was to describe approaches to gaining community support and acceptance. (It should be noted that their social action approach assumes voluntary response to human need. The 1970s, by contrast, have emphasized mandated response through the courts and legislation.) Social action, according to Beal et al. (p. 15), may be defined as "the process and the strategy by which you find, motivate, mobilize, and organize resources (individuals, groups of people, as well as physical objects) in order to accomplish a predetermined end." Tasks that relate to social action are:

1. Identification of the goal(s) to be achieved, which involves information and experience to specify what intentions are to be sought.
2. Identification of resources, human and physical, necessary to achieve goals; again, analysis is required.
3. Location of resources, which requires isolation of sources of power, influence, and control of resources.
4. Analysis of motivation, which involves the determination of cir-

cumstances that can be brought to bear to influence resources to do, or not to do, certain given things.

5 Mobilization, or the assembly of circumstances to be focused. This may involve listings of possible resources as well as the scheduling of visitations and inspections. The social action specifies its approaches.

6 Organization, which is the doing phase of implementation of the mobilization plan.

7 Goal evaluation, which describes accomplishment or lack thereof. Evaluation is a continuous activity to test the validity of assumptions, information, resources, strategies, and mobilization-organization.

Actors of Social Action

The concept of *actor* centers around doing, not doing, or opposition. There may be at least three actors. One is termed the *change agent,* or instigator. This person (or persons) performs the initial effort and provides the central organization. The change agent can be an ARC which rallies around its executive director, but is not necessarily confined to this area. A director of special education can be a change agent on behalf of learners in danger of school exclusion. The classroom teacher, in either a special class or resource room, performs as a change agent to achieve meaningful inclusion of his or her learners. The next class of actor(s) is the *legitimizers* who provide the support, guidance, authority, justification, or license to act. Legitimizers usually fall into one of two groups. One group has *authority,* a form of social power, because of a formal office or occupational role. The second form of social power is *influence.* Influence may be granted to a person because of their knowledge, past achievements, willingness to work, abilities to plan, think, and work with others, their occupation, participation in formal organizations, and their acquaintance with numerous people. In some communities a select group may possess both authority and influence. The third group is the *active participants.* These are the workers. Legitimizers approve; the active participant provides the day-to-day effort and some of the resources. Their participation may be motivated by legitimizers, or they may act from a "sense of community good."

The Social System

Social action takes place within a social system. A system exists to respond to need, to establish order and stability, to organize functions-activities, and to define time sequences in which to perform functions.

Beal et al. suggest that an analysis of a social system would include those factors that *regulate* its behavior.

1 *Goals:* What are the ends or objectives for which the agency was formed and for which it strives?
2 *Means:* What are physical, financial, and human resources, and what are the activities and programs used to accomplish goals?
3 *Norms:* What standards prescribe acceptable or unacceptable group performance?
4 *Sanctions:* What are the rewards and penalties used to attain motivation and conformity to goals and norms?
5 *Identification:* To what extent are members of the system committed to the goals?
6 *Status-role:* What is expected of the members of the system, and to what extent are those actions valued?
7 *Power:* What is the legal authority to control others, and what are the nonauthoritative means to exercise influence?
8 *Belief:* What knowledges do members hold to be true? Especially, what is thought to be true about the nature and needs of people to be served?
9 *Sentiment:* What are the feelings and attitudes members hold about belief?

Beal et al. suggest these questions can serve as a specific checklist for evaluation of the social systems in a community.

Master Processes

Analysis of a system requires an evaluation of the *processes* the system uses to *organize* and *maintain* its behavior. Beal et al. identify six questions of master processes for this analysis:

1 *Communication:* What are the means by which information, decisions, and directives filter through the system to provide data about beliefs and sentiments? How are means formed, modified, or discarded?
2 *Boundary maintenance:* What are the system's means to maintain solidarity, identity, and functions? How willing and/or capable is the system of enlargement or retraction of service boundaries?
3 *System linkage:* What are the means by which the system articulates or interfaces with other systems so as to function as a single system?
4 *Institutionalization:* What are the means by which individual performance is patterned within the system?

5 *Socialization:* What are the means of the system to persuade, educate, and/or train its membership in the ends, means, norms, beliefs, and sentiments of the social system?

6 *Social control:* What are the means by which deviation from system norms are counteracted?

The Plan of Action

Beal et al. suggest that integration of actors, social systems, and master processes can be achieved by a plan of action. The plan suggests a sequence of operations. As each step is outlined, the net effect of the planning process may be to build a sense of confidence that success is possible.

Figure 8–1 portrays a sequence of operations to execute a social action plan. The figure is an adaptation of the Beal et al. recommendations. This figure suggests ten operations. Between each operation, the change agent will evaluate the processes engaged in as a basis for subsequent operations. Involved in these ten operations are:

1. *Target group.* The focus of this operation is the recognition of the needs of the retarded person and/or the family. Attention is upon improvement for the person. At this level the change agent is convinced that a problem exists and that tentative solutions exist to resolve the situation.

2. *Analysis of social systems.* At this level, the change agent, convinced of the existence of a problem, seeks to determine *why* the problem exists and *what* needs to be changed. Within this operation, an analysis is made of agencies that conform to the nine questions of the elements of a social system.

3. *Convergence.* At this level, the change agent may discover other actors who share a similarity of interest. The interest is usually based upon a common belief about the problem and the conviction that something must be done. While convergence often is accidental, analysis may suggest visible sources of convergence.

4. *Prior social situation.* At this level, the change agent and other actors enter into a period of constructing a common strategy. Beal et al. recommend an analysis of the past and the present. Investigation centers around past experience, with special attention to understanding what was tried and why it did not work out. There also should be an analysis of the present, so that if systems have changed between the past and the present, those changes can be accounted for. Again, the elements involved in step 2 are applied. Also, at this point there may be a preliminary inventory of actors, legitimizers, and active participants who might be involved.

5. *Resolving conflict.* At some point, conflict may surface. Social-action programs will generally experience conflict around the following topics: target groups (parents versus the retarded person as the focus); creation of possible duplication (often an existing agency will feel a new service duplicates what it is currently do-

Figure 8–1 *Processes in the Implementation of a Social Action Plan*

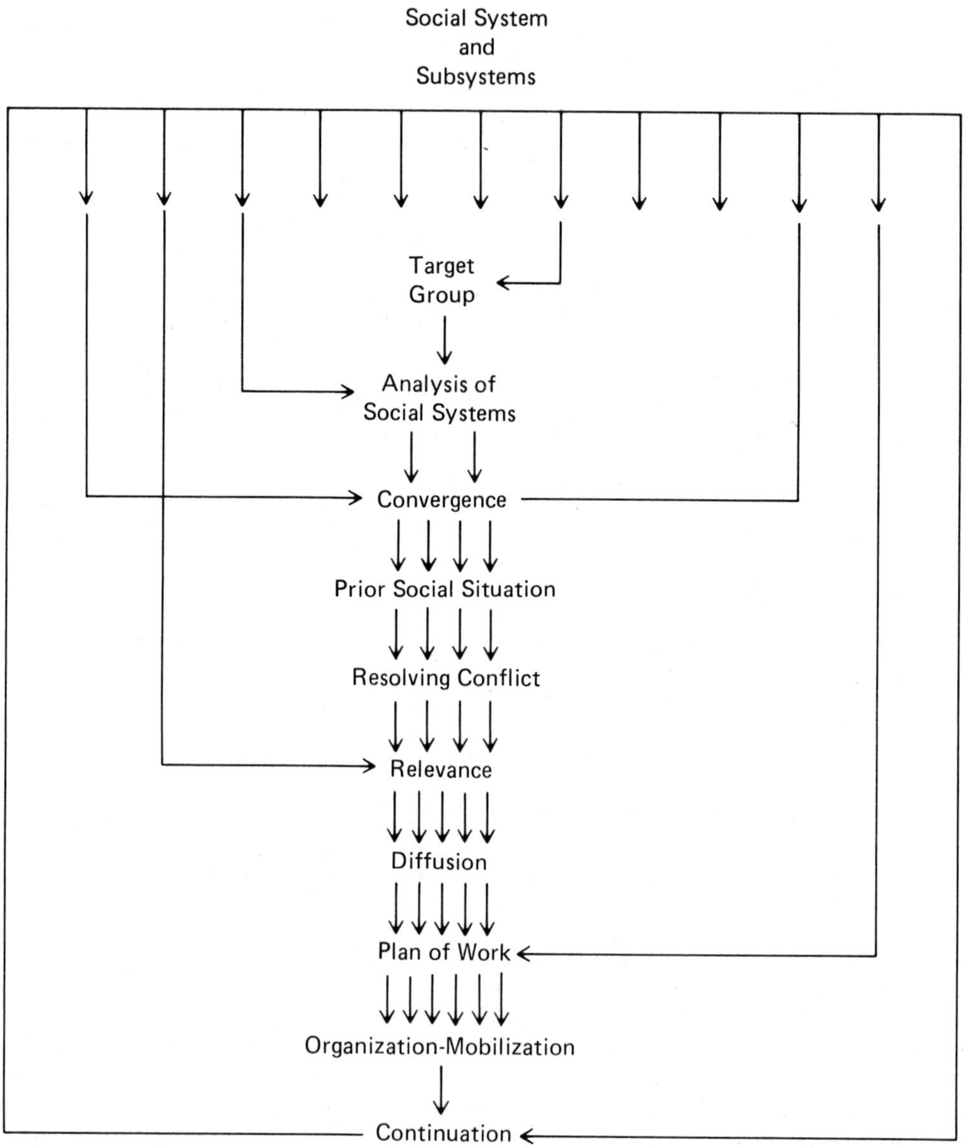

ing); and identification of legitimizers and active participants. Commonly, the debate will be around styles of communication and choices of system linkage.

6. *Relevance.* At this level, the attempt is to gain legitimization for the significance of the problem (community perception that the problem is worthy of attention) and for the feasibility of solutions. Typical appeals used to enlist legitimization include:

A *Basic education.* This approach centers upon an appeal to reason on the part of reasonable people. By mass media and direct contact, information is brought to public attention.

B *Community surveys.* While this approach is a data-gathering tool, it can be educational as well. Responding to questions may create interest in the problem.

C *Demonstrations.* Often persons cannot support a program until it is seen. Consequently, the open house, scheduled visits, and exhibits may be helpful. Another form of demonstration is for a voluntary organization to operate a program so as to persuade a public agency of its feasibility. The history of school programs for the moderately retarded reflects this approach.

D *Comparison and competition.* This approach rests upon an appeal to community pride. If the local community has been shown that other similar communities have responded, it may move to match that response. In some cases, the opportunity to be first, to pioneer, or to be a leader may have an impact. The decision to focus upon existing programs in other communities or to lead the way is a function of the community's view of itself as a trend-setter or as following proven ground.

E *Channeling complaints into action.* Vocal, passive complaints can be directed toward the media and agencies to focus attention. A helpful and successful approach to legislation has been the letter-writing campaign.

F *Building on past programs.* Often the accomplishments of a past program can justify the need for a logical extension of a new one. Sheltered workshops, for example, would be a necessary next step, following a school program.

7. *Diffusion.* This step overlaps the previous one to some extent. The previous step involved consideration of appeals to relevance. In the diffusion step, agreement is secured as to the exact strategies to be employed. Refinements would be directed toward specific groups, with special provision for how the action program relates to the goals and past activities of the target group; use to be made of power (authority vs. influence), coercion, or reciprocal obligations; and what general values (good works, concern for others, etc.) are to be emphasized.

8. *Plan of work.* Considerable time has been expended thus far. The work group has expended resources of effort. At this point, the task is to translate commitment into a plan. The essentials in a written document (which provide criteria for evaluation) would be: To what extent are goals specified? Are the persons or groups to be involved listed? To what extent does the plan identify the time expectations for specific actions to be accomplished? And to what extent are authority and responsibilities assigned to members?

9. *Organization and mobilization.* At this level, two tasks are to be accomplished: to secure resources and to carry out the program. A particular consideration is to recruit the active participants for action roles.

10. *Continuation.* The adequacy of the plan is tested against actual operations. Special attention is usually given to the extent to which resources were actually mobilized and organized. The primary concern is how the program is to be continued. According to Beal et al., programs do not develop as an integrated application of social action; they usually develop as a result of parallel sets of social actions. This should be considered in continuation questions. The basic question in continuation relates to the transfer of the program to other agencies or its retention by the change agent organization itself. The solution is an evaluation process. The process centers around *what* benefits to the target group will be gained by retention, transfer, or shared responsibility? This question relates back to the original goals identified in step 1. Comparing obtained results with likely results may suggest the appropriate alternatives.

Another activity within this step must be considered: recognition. The community and the participants observe what has been done and commend individuals for their commitments and accomplishments.

SCOPE OF SERVICE GOALS

Service Clusters

As a direct result of the PL 88–164 legislation of 1962, the states and territories of the United States were encouraged to develop equivalents of the 1962 Report of the President's Panel on Mental Retardation. This report, *A National Plan to Combat Mental Retardation,* represented the conclusions of citizens, professionals, and key political figures. (The work of the original panel was subsequently continued as the President's Committee on Mental Retardation, which was constituted by President Johnson and continues in effect at present.) The panel took note of the family as the primary "unit of care" for the retarded person. The family's basic need was to defend its retarded person. Service development was seen as the establishment of a continuum of care to parallel the life of the retarded person.

Gardner and Nisonger (1962), as an AAMD technical project, prepared guidelines for the development of services at state and community levels. This manual described service, research, professional training, legislation, and public education. This report made twenty-four recommendations for program development (table 8–1). Inspection of this material reveals certain concerns and/or priorities for planning and service delivery.

1. Concern for the early and accurate *identification, diagnosis,* and *referral* to appropriate services so as to minimize the effects of prolonged neglect.

2. Concern for an orderly system of *education* and *vocational training.* This service would provide for orderly growth and development from the preschool period through adulthood, with the ultimate objective of employability.

3. Concern for *residential programming* that emphasizes both long- and short-term provisions. This system is viewed as seeking alternatives to the traditional institution and the natural home as settings for residence.

4. Concern for parent and client support services to foster *continuous adjustment.* According to the panel, this system would support the independence of the person and the family in critical decision making.

5. The need for structurers of *coordination* at state and community levels for cooperative planning and operation. The prime objective is to conserve personnel and maximize financial resources.

6. Concern for continuing *research* so that the best available information is available to responsible persons.

7. Concern for a continuing emphasis upon *prevention.* This concern would deal with both the ecological and etiological correlates of the condition (chapters 3 and 4).

8. Concern for the periodic review of the *legal* basis of services of the retarded citizen. This would involve a focus upon the fit between the basic legal provision and what is currently believed to be accurate data. For example, the emergence of state amendments to school codes to permit and/or mandate preschool programs was based upon a recognition of the importance of the preschool period.

9. Concern for continuing *program evaluation,* which would be directed toward criteria of efficiency (cost per numbers served within defined time spans) and effectiveness (assessment of the agencies' operations with meeting defined needs of clients).

After a decade of existence, the service priorities of the President's Panel were submitted to each of the state coordinators of mental retardation planning (Luckey and Neman, 1975). The original service goals of research, preventative health, education, clinical and social services, residential care, legal protection, manpower, and public awareness were reaffirmed as necessary and relevant for the 1970s. Modifications for the future selected by the coordinators for particular emphasis were:

Table 8–1 SUMMARY AND ABSTRACT OF THE AAMD TECHNICAL REPORT ON PROGRAM DEVELOPMENT

Topic	*Guidelines for Action*
1. Prevention	Support basic research; strengthen services of health, education, and welfare that have potential for prevention; provide for early diagnosis and referral.
2. Statewide Approach	State officials to provide leadership in the assessment of needs.
3. Delineation of State and Local Government Responsibility	Legislatures to define areas of responsibility and to define relationships between local units and their state counterparts.
4. Utilization of Existing Agencies	To utilize an accepted and proven service agency as the administrative agent.
5. Early Identification	Local services are to be responsible.
6. Diagnostic Services	A state-community responsibility to develop this service, to be available regardless of where parents live.
7. Parent Counseling	To serve both long-term and short-term needs under local leadership.
8. Home-Training	To be directed toward preschool persons.
9. Education and Training	State and local boards of education are urged to expand programs.
10. Preparation for Employment	Schools and community leaders are urged to make provisions for part-time school and part-time work experience to prepare the retarded person for employment.
11. Sheltered Workshops	Community leaders should make provisions for two groups of postschool retarded persons: the deferred placement (training outside a school setting), and the sheltered employable group (a need for continuing supervised work placement).
12. Selective Placement	State and local leaders should design a system for placement, when indicated, in a setting other than the natural home.
13. Role of State Residential Facilities	State officials should plan for new facilities in light of new knowledge and in light of the expansion of community services.

Table 8–1 (continued)

14. Need for Community Residential Facilities at Community Level	Emphasis upon temporary care, but directs state and local officials seriously to plan community-based facilities.
15. State Administration	Urges state legislators and state officials to establish a position of director of services for the mentally retarded within the mental health operation. Such positions to be of appropriate authority
16. Coordination of State Services	State officials are urged to establish an interdepartmental committee for joint planning and coordination.
17. Planning and Coordination at Community Level	Community agencies and responsible leaders are urged to develop sound, orderly planning through existing councils or establish an agency for this purpose.
18. Research in Mental Retardation	State officials and research institutions should press for expanded programs, especially in the behavioral areas.
19. Professional Training	State officials and training institutions are urged to develop and/or expand programs and facilities.
20. Facilities for Research and Training	Cooperation between universities and state officials to establish necessary facilities.
21. Inservice Training	State and community leaders are urged to cooperate with universities to develop programs for professionals and voluntary personnel.
22. Nomenclature and Classification	Residential facilities and agencies are urged to develop a uniform system predicated on AAMD standards to enhance communication.
23. Statistical Reporting	Residential facilities and agencies are encouraged to cooperate in developing uniform procedures of data collection for planning and administrative procedures.
24. Legal Reform	State legislatures should conduct periodic reviews of all provisions to keep laws in line with current scientific knowledge.

1 deinstitutionalization and expansion of community services;

2 a national effort to prevent and decrease the effects of inadequate nutrition, poor housing, environmental deprivation, mandatory vaccination laws, and accessibility to health services;

3 strengthening legal rights and advocacy;
4 an emphasis on obtaining mandated educational services;
5 adequate funding of mental retardation services; and
6 a concerted effort against public apathy, including the professional community.

Age-Appropriate Clusters

The Illinois Association for Retarded Children (1966) has suggested a checklist of community services. This checklist has the dual purpose of identifying services that should exist at *community levels* as well as *chronological age* as a focus for services. The Illinois checklist is summarized in table 8–2. This checklist illustrates that there can be alternatives within the conceptualization of services.

Function-Oriented Clusters

Sellin, Clos, Deiter, Harris, Harrison, Peterson, Smith, and Zimmerman (1974) reported a survey of 115 persons involved in community-level coordination and administration of services. An adaptation of their survey form is presented in tables 8–3 and 8–4. These figures are intended to present the reader with a *minimum* checklist of services. (Participants in the original report were asked to rate each service component as good, average, poor, or don't know.) Table 8–3 summarizes the content of treatment-service, while table 8–4 summarizes the content of prevention services. Thus, services can be grouped as to overall function or intention.

A review of the sources presented within this section illustrates a certain variety in service groupings. The installation and delivery of services will vary according to the traditions and circumstances of the community.

SPECIAL CONCERNS

Permissive versus Mandated Services

There is an increased inclination for either judicial or legislative mandate for services for retarded persons. Increasingly, change agents are seeking a guarantee of services. Gilhool (1973) observed that while resort to court action is in the *same* tradition as attempts to influence legislative and executive branches, litigation is a different art. Lobbying is the art of accommodation; litigation, the art of the necessary. Gilhool suggests that citizens resort to litigation for the following reasons:

	Service Elements		
Age Groupings	*Support Services*	*Education and Preparation for Employment*	*Residential Services*
Infants and Preschoolers	Parent group Professional counseling Child welfare services Medical management	Special nursery classes Special preschool classes Home training	Home training Home nursing Trained babysitting pool Foster care
School Age	Psychiatric care Religious education Scouting Recreation Camping Speech therapy	Special classes for educable and trainable Day training for severely retarded	Homemaker services Foster home
Adolescents	Counseling at puberty Youth groups Recreation clubs Social clubs Premarital counseling Genetic counseling	Prevocational programs Vocational education Sheltered workshops Activity centers	
Adult	Recreation and social activities Legal counsel Guardianship	Vocational—evaluation, training, and placement Personal adjustment training	Supportive services: meals, housekeeping, and maintenance
Not Age Specific	Prevention programs Early diagnosis and detection Psychological evaluation Social-protective services Professional and public education Legislative action Political action Financial counseling Referral services		Adequate public and private institutional care Postinstitutional care Halfway houses

Table 8–3 SUMMARY OF PRIMARY SERVICE NEEDS

Service Cluster	*Service Components*
Identification, Diagnosis, and Remediation	Case Finding Information and Referral Diagnosis and Evaluation Therapies, O.T., P.T., and Speech
Education and Vocational Training	Education: Educable Education: Trainable Training: Day Training Centers—Severely Mentally Retarded Vocational Education Sheltered Workshops Adult Activity
Twenty-four-Hour Residential	Community Halfway Homes Regional Residential Centers Institutions
Continuous Adjustment	Income Maintenance Protective Services Homemaker Services Parent Counseling Recreation Services

SOURCE: Adapted from the Sellin et al. report

Table 8–4 SUMMARY OF PREVENTION SERVICES

Service Cluster	*Service Component*
Primary Prevention	Measles Vaccine PKU (screening and diet) Blood Exchange Holter Valve Prenatal Care
Secondary Prevention	Family Planning Early Intervention Programs for Culturally Disadvantaged Reporting Child Abuse Accident Prevention Poison Control (including lead poisoning)

SOURCE: Adapted from Sellin et al. report

1. To secure certain substantive rights such as zero-reject education — every person has a free access to education without condition.
2. To create a new forum where enforcement of rights may be gained or new rights secured.
3. To use the courts to bring to the attention of the public-at-large, legitimizers, and the ordinary citizen certain facts that have not had great exposure.
4. To petition government for redress, to express one's opinions, and to define change.

Gilhool also illustrates that litigation can protect professional integrity. He cites two different cases of social casework. In the one case, the worker refused to participate in a "raid" upon welfare recipients on a Sunday morning to uncover a "man in the house." She held this to be a violation of right to privacy. In another case, the worker, after office hours, went to a meeting of recipients to inform them that the office was not providing them with their full measure of benefits. He urged organization. Both workers were fired, and both firings were upheld by the respective state civil service commissions. In both states, however, the state supreme court overruled. In the first case, the worker was held to have the right to assert the rights of her clients. In the second case, the worker was found to have the right to respect and defend the rights of clients in the discharge of professional duties.

Rural Areas

Travelstead (1960) identified special considerations in the delivery of services to vast, sparsely populated rural areas. Service planning, according to this author, will follow the conventions of: locating and accurately identifying handicapped persons; recruiting personnel; installing personnel and retaining them; funding the program on an ongoing basis; insuring feedback to institutions of higher education for improvement of professional preparation; and certifying personnel. Transportation costs consume already scarce resources. Preferences of professionals for more urban areas becomes a problem for recruitment and retention. Also, there may be a certain cultural shock between professional and consumer over differences in language, educational levels, and philosophy of life. These problems are not insoluble, but they require thought and attention. Travelstead closes with a note of promise that a multistate regional effort, the Western Interstate Commission on Higher Education (WICHE), will be helpful in developing a coordinated approach.

Harris and Mahar (1975) observed that the noncategorical resource room is emerging as a response to programming in sparsely populated areas. According to these authors, the specialist is expected to detect eligible pupils and to create or identify resources within the system to serve them. The preparation of this person assumes a flexibility of diagnostic techniques and materials so as to serve many more learners than would be possible under a more traditional categorical arrangement. These authors note a certain financial advantage for this arrangement.

The Harris and Mahar report detailed *four* main obstacles to implementing the resource-room concept in rural areas. A fundamental consideration was identified as *lack of organizational readiness*. Related factors were the lack of complementary services, such as guidance, may be lacking; the role of the specialist may be seen as a narrow focus on testing and tutoring; and the administration may be inert to assembling resources and be content with merely hiring the person and assigning the space. The suggestion was made that preparation should precede the program by six to twelve months. *Systems shock* is another major consideration. The addition of a specialist may be a threat in a system that has not had to contend with any form of external observation of its handling of exceptional children. Consequently, role conflicts (the specialist, the guidance counselor, and the remedial reading teacher) may develop. Expectations for the program may be vague and be reflected in few referrals or a flood. Power struggles may develop between the regular classroom teacher and the specialist over questions of management, grading, discipline, methodologies, and the like. The assembly of a child-study team of school specialists might resolve role conflicts. *Interpersonal roadblocks* were the third consideration. The classroom teacher may be possessive of pupils, defensive about teaching methods, and unwilling to expand teaching methods. The specialist, on the other hand, may lack tact and patience for problem solving. These authors also note that the specialist may lack classroom teaching experience, knowledge of common materials and equipment, and experience with children of different ages and developmental levels. These factors may cause the specialist to lose credibility. Finally, there is the *competency crisis*. Rural areas may have difficulties attracting trained or experienced persons. Given the shortage of persons *trained* for this role and given legislative mandates of compliance, the rural district needs help for their personnel, not blame. Inservice and preservice recruiters should attempt to explain the advantages of teaching in rural areas. Schools, state departments of education, and colleges and universities must share a responsibility for program development to overcome those obstacles.

Carlson and Pellant (1972) described a process of integration of teacher-preparation and service to rural areas in special education. By means of video-tape, the proficiency of preservice teachers in the use of five teaching materials was "tested." These persons then served as demonstration teams in school districts.

Tarkington (1971) has reported an attempt to demonstrate that a residential facility could provide an outreach to rural communities. He noted that while the tactics involved in social action do generally apply, community centeredness and respect are essential qualities of the outreach team. In general, the effective approach is to engage existing agencies and work through their concerns rather than to attempt to "sell" prepackaged ideas.

Erdman, Wyatt, and Heller (1970) have prepared a resource text for the administration of school programs for the mildly retarded in small school districts. The report emphasizes careful development and preplanning prior to initiation of the program. No single administrative option was advocated over any other. The options were said to include:

1. *Cooperative-joint agreement programs*. Illinois was identified as an example. This arrangement enables independent school districts to enter into a master agreement for services. Consequently, learners can be transported out of the school district for a program. While problems of transportation, supervision, and diagnostics may surface, the arrangement does provide for individualization of grouping and maximizing personnel.

2. *Contract services*. The California experience furnished the basis for this example. For a district of less than 910 students, there is the option of contraction or purchase of services from private sources and/or from larger school districts.

3. *The intermediate unit*. The state of Iowa has created a service structure between the local district and the state level. The difference between this option and the first one is that the intermediate unit is a legally defined structure with geographical boundaries (county or multicounty) and with special taxing powers. Otherwise it functions in a cooperative manner.

Additional options were also identified. Oregon is experimenting with an itinerant teacher approach similar to the diagnostic prescriptive teacher model of today. Alabama and Montana use summer programs for both socialization experiences and intensive academic remediation. North Dakota was lauded for its work-study program in which the school district was the employer-trainer. Faced with a scarcity of job-training sites, the school developed needed job tasks for which students could be paid.

Public Policy

The funding of services and funding for services is the domain of public policy. Appropriations for services does represent one area of support.

Gallagher (1972) identified the special education "contract" as an agreement among the schools, parents, and the student. While labeling may have disadvantages, funds do follow labels. To minimize the alleged low expectations associated with labeling and to introduce a system of accountability, Gallagher (pp. 531–532) defined the contract as follows:

> Placement of primary school age mildly retarded as disabled or learning disabled children in a special education unit would require a contract signed between parents and educators, with specific goals and a clear time limit. This contract should be for a *maximum of 2 years* and would be nonrenewable, or renewable only under a quasi-judicial type of hearing, with parents represented by legal or child advocate counsel.

> The contract, composed after a careful educational diagnosis, would commit the special educational personnel to measurable objectives that would be upgraded on a 6-month interval.

Gallagher advanced this as a proposal for discussion, not as a finished idea. Some additional advantages were seen, such as developing parent involvement, specifying periodic review, and establishing responsibility. A key feature of the Gallagher system centered around the consequences of the contract's being broken. Gallagher advocated an "educational voucher." If the schools failed to deliver and if the parents fulfilled their options, the family would be entitled to a payment, or voucher, to purchase services elsewhere. Gallagher suggested that at present the nonquality program has little incentive to improve. He felt this system would change this.

Blatt (1972) noted that the voucher system, as a public policy, presents certain hazards. Citing the New York and Massachusetts experience, Blatt illustrates the discrepancy between intention of legislation and actual practice. In one state, the voucher system had the effect of encouraging school districts to dismantle special public programs to the point of evading responsibility. A mainstreaming program was eliminated in favor of "private" facilities. In another state, costs have risen so dramatically as to affect adversely financial support for public funding of special programs. In one of these states, the public funding of private agencies has transformed the association for retarded citizens from an advocate role into a member of the service establishment, thus robbing it of its change agent status.

Blatt advanced certain funding alternatives as public policy.

1. Statutes for funding should be written to reflect special development needs to replace the present emphasis upon defects. This approach would deemphasize the necessity of labeling as a source for funding.

2. Funding should encourage community-level programming, cooperative and joint service operation, and equalized financial support between affluent and disadvantaged districts. This approach would replace a reward system for isolated, single-service systems.

3. Each state should establish an equivalent of a state department of child development. This agency would be responsible for all functions currently scattered among the several departments of state government. The agency would serve all handicapped persons under age twenty-one. Blatt was not adamant about a single department and indicated that shared sponsorship would be acceptable.

4. Each state should establish procedures for citizen advisory councils, composed in large part of parents. A particular focus should be upon the encouragement of outreach programs to communities and to residents of residential facilities. An additional focus should also be upon the establishment of due process procedures for placement and appeal procedures.

While these alternatives were presented in the context of school services, there would seem to be a general applicability to various service elements. The contract system and funding alternatives suggested in this review therefore could be generalized to other service. While the voucher system may have drawbacks, there may be significant pressure for its adoption.

The Beal, Payer, and Yarbrough analysis (1965) identified the extension of generic (general) services to the retarded person and the family. This approach is advocated for cost-effectiveness and for the prevention of service fragmentation. Beck does concede, however, that earmarked funds have protected the interests of the mentally retarded. It is possible, she conceded, for the mentally retarded to receive low priority in the general service system. The measure of ultimate acceptance would be the inclusion of the retarded person. This can come about through broader definition of program mission, participation by parents and friends of the retarded person on community organization boards, and continuing education of general service personnel about an optimistic sense of potential of the retarded person.

Developmental Disabilities

Neisworth and Smith (1974) cite PL 91–517 to define the concept of developmental disabilities:

> The term developmental disability means a disability attributable to mental retardation, cerebral palsy, epilepsy, or another neurological condition of an individual found by the Secretary to be closely related to mental retardation or to require treatment similar to that required for mentally retarded individuals, which disability originates before such individual attains eighteen years of age, which has continued or can be expected to continue indefinitely, and which constitutes a substantial handicap to such an individual.

These authors, in turn, proposed a redefinition:

> Developmental disabilities refers to significantly deficient locomotor, communications, adjustive, or academic functioning that is manifest during the developmental period and that has continued, or can be expected to continue, indefinitely (p. 346).

Neisworth and Smith assert that their definition has greater utility for defining services and suggest existing diagnostic procedures.

Stedman (1976, p. 187) has noted:

> The concept of developmental disabilities is an administrative one and not a new syndrome. It is an organizational approach to the integration and expansion of services to the handicapped. It is an experiment in the private-public partnership to improve the quality of life for the handicapped at the local level.

Stedman suggests that this concept was intended to draw people into an initiating-advocacy relationship and away from competing for scarce resources. Neisworth and Smith have anticipated the eventuality of developmental disability becoming a *service* category, not confined to administrative practice. Consequently, their discussion merits attention.

Sluyter and Barbuto (1972) summarized one state's experience with the developmental disability concept. A total of sixty-eight grants were approved by the state council, ranging from $750 to $18,711, with a mean of $3,844. By category, mental retardation received 36 percent; cerebral palsy received 6 percent; epilepsy received 7 percent, and combined categories were allocated 31 percent. By program category, the percentages were: physical education/recreation (34), planning and surveys (28), training/education (10), inservice (7), and other (21). A collateral category such as developmental disability has both promise and problems, according to Sluyter and Barbuto. The exact incidence of cerebral palsy without mental retardation was difficult to establish but finally fixed at .35 percent. Different time schedules for agencies (fiscal year, school year, and calendar year) pose problems for concentrated action. The report concluded on a positive note that the model of a flexible definition of service need coupled with a strong advisory council has great possibilities for action.

A CONCEPT OF RESPONSIBILITY

The organization and delivery of services should allow for an orderly progression to parallel the life cycle of the person and each of the service elements should be consistent and integrated. Existing mechanisms of social action and structures of administration and coordination show that model programs can and do exist. A continuing question is the assignment of responsibility for both the operational aspects of programs *and* for effective monitoring.

Governmental Perspectives

One state's experience may be helpful. Hunter (1963) prepared a report which, in part, summarized the experiences of active participants at local and state levels regarding responsibility. This report summarized the testimony of Burgener (1963), Merelman (1963), and Coleman (1963).

Burgener (1963), a *state legislator,* observed that agencies may attempt to build empires, and agencies may, in his words, "run for the exit" when responsibility looms. He noted that lack of clarity of service goals can be destructive.

Merelman (1963) explored the concept of responsibility from the perspective of *county government.* His observations centered around resources and autonomy. To deal with the problem of resources, an inventory is required. He suggested that studies, even sidewalk surveys if necessary, should be conducted to assess the extent to which assigned responsibilities are carried out.

Coleman (1963) spoke from the perspective of a nonparent who was the president of the state ARC. He noted that his remarks were on behalf of parents, not for them. His opinion was that parents felt responsible for their child. Ordinary citizens are responsible for protection of their home from fire, but they assume there will be adequate fire protection as a resource. In a similar manner, parents expect to have resources available to assist them in their basic mission of parenting. Coleman recommends that services be nearby, so the family unit can participate and benefit. He advocated a sense of shared responsibility among the private and public sectors. He also noted that while mandated programs reflect commitment and obligation, enforcement must follow through on the promise. Two elements are helpful for responsibility: information, in order to monitor needs and resources, and a willingness for organizations to assemble a collective effort.

Another example of governmental perspective is offered by Mooring and Currie (1964). They described a "joint powers agreement" strategy for service delivery to retarded persons. The purpose was to establish an integrated, coordinated network throughout a complex county. The Gardner and Nisonger (1962) service clusters were used to identify programs of: diagnosis, treatment, medication and parent counseling; training and education; vocational habilitation and placement; day and residential care; recreation opportunities; long-term supervision and guidance; and support services of research, training, case finding, and public education. The basic concept was an extensive survey of agencies to establish needs and gaps in service. From this research, a mental retardation services board would be created. The legal authority for the board would be a joint powers agreement, signed by the participating agencies, which would designate the functions and responsibilities of participants.

Evaluation

McIntyre (1969) views evaluation as the identification of worth and value. The minimum components of evaluation include: what and when to evaluate, objectives and guidelines for action, schedule for data collection, relating budget plans to evaluation results, use of consultants, and means for disseminating results. Evaluation, according to McIntyre, can be distinguished from research by differences in sampling, controls, and hypothesis testing. The researcher is usually interested in a representative sample. The concern is the degree to which a particular sample is like other persons in other geographical areas. The evaluator is concerned with the specific persons, students, and clients under consideration. While the researcher attempts to control all variables so that the variable of interest can be examined, the evaluator operates with an existing situation, aiming at a detailed description of variables under consideration. The researcher is concerned with hypothesis testing and relating findings into a larger theoretical framework. The evaluator is concerned with investigation of immediate objectives specific to the particular program or social system under consideration.

Both researcher and evaluator use a scientific method of objectivity. The "hypothesis" of evaluation would be that *given objectives and resources (program), then these outcomes will be evident.* For example, a program may have positive self-concept as an objective. Self-concept may be operationally defined as the person's self-report of feelings of adequacy. An evaluator may compare the person's self-report on abilities with the parent's assessment of actual abilities and derive a discrepancy score. This is inappropriate. The original objective was self-concept, not self-appraisal. The current controversy regarding self-contained classroom versus resource-room program illustrates the problem. Measures applied by external evaluators may be independent of the program objectives. Consequently, either alternative may be rejected for the wrong reasons. That is, the program may be found ineffective because of errors of measurement, not errors of operation.

Meirhenry (1969), building upon the McIntyre discussion, has outlined the content of the evaluation process. The Meirhenry Gestalt includes the concepts of input, process, and output (figure 8–2). *Input* describes those values, assumptions,

Figure 8–2 *The Evaluation Cycle*

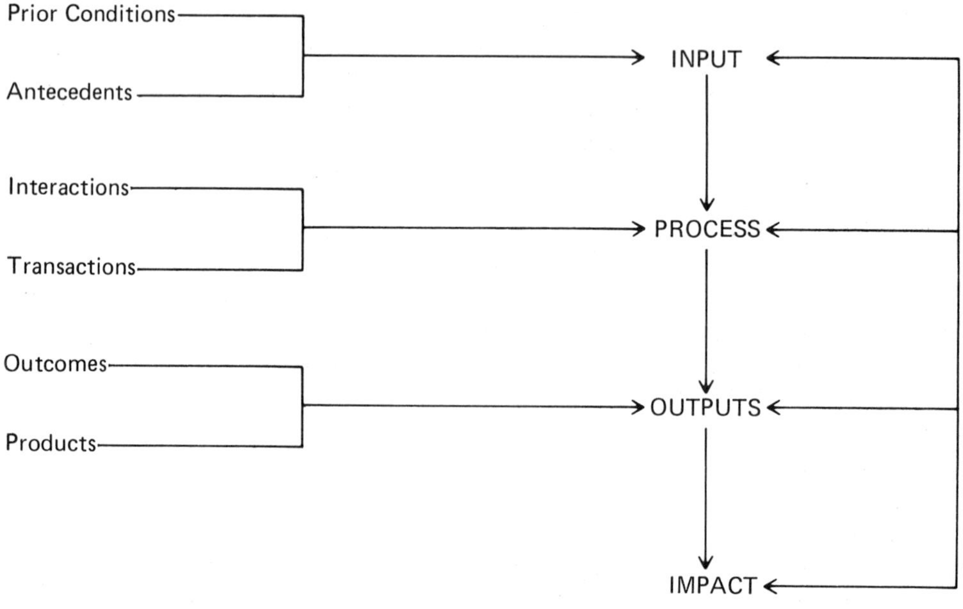

and knowledges that constitute antecedents or prior conditions that produce a sense of the need for change. From this process comes the formulation of goals and/or objectives. These statements should be descriptions of what would be acceptable as "evidence" of accomplishment. *Process* describes the resources, activities, and the like that must be assembled. *Interactions* describes what happens within the program, and *transactions* describes external relationships. *Output* describes those changes observed to happen among the target population expressed as outcomes, and with the program expressed as products. Recommendations based upon the match, or fit, among input, process, and output describe *impact*. Impact statements suggest abandonment, continuation and/or modification of either input, process, or output. Meirhenry suggests that there should be a schedule for periodic review.

Both McIntyre and Meirhenry are emphatic about using evaluation for change, not for criticism or fixing blame. The objective is to improve services to persons, not to harass staff.

Accountability

Accountability represents a powerful historical tradition in Western culture. The good steward and the faithful shepherd are symbols of the prudent use of resources. Consequently, accounting for the use of resources for program outcomes is not "new." What may be considered new is a contemporary emphasis upon specification of results based upon goals declared in advance.

Yavorsky (1975) has identified the common elements of a discrepancy model for accountability. These include:

1. *Needs assessment*. This involves a survey of population characteristics from which is deduced a statement of needs. A roster of currently available resources may also be included. The result is to identify a current status.

2. *Goals/attainments*. This involves a declaration of intentions, aspirations, and/or objectives. This accountability factor is a central focus. The degree to which goals are reached is the measure by which efforts are judged. At this level, a discrepancy between need and goals becomes the basis for subsequent steps.

3. *Service delivery*. This identifies the means by which to achieve goals. These means can include educational method, staff competencies, physical plant, etc. Current and future resources also should be inventoried.

4. *Evaluation*. By this process results/outcomes are matched to goals. Evaluation seeks to answer both attainment and circumstances of attainment.

5. *Recommendations*. The eventual objective of the accountability process is to communicate. This area, based upon evaluation, will suggest continuation, revision, and abandonment of any one of the preceding areas.

It is to be noted that research and/or evaluation procedures are tools to facilitate the accountability process. Either tool functions to enhance descriptive precision of need, intent, resource use, and results.

Examples

Lyons and Powers (1963) illustrate how evaluation can influence program quality. Their report describes 661 children and attempts to understand prior conditions and antecedents leading to exemption from school. Antecedent and condition questions included emotional maturity. IQ, grade level, and timing (school month). While the exemption rate (66 percent) was lower than the national average (10 percent), the authors were not satisfied. The two reasons for exemption were emotional immaturity and hyperactive behavior. This report closes with a series of recommendations designed for help for exempted students as well as for prevention.

Cegelka-Thomas and Tawney (1975) reported on a competency-base teacher training approach. The problem was to decrease knowledge and skill discrepancies between field supervisors of preservice teachers and university staff. The process was a teacher-center approach to reduce divergence between university and campus staff. The preservice teacher thus would receive continuity between college classroom instruction and supervision from field supervisors.

Graf and Meyers (1973) have detailed a two-year project that illustrates both the process of social action as well as a concept of responsibility. As social action, a local ARC became convinced that the residential service system required study and reform. Accordingly, the local unit voted a budget to carry out the study. The project encompassed planning phase (setting objectives, locating sources of data, enlisting participants, and informing officials of intentions); a study and recommendation phase, which involved data collection; an implementation phase concerned with shifting of data, clarifying recommendations, and involvement of the legislature, culminating in a comprehensive Community Services Act which provided major alternatives to institutionalization; and follow-up and evaluation to monitor compliance with the act. For a budget investment of $87,000 by the ARC, there was an appropriation of $1.7 million by the state to implement the act.

These diverse examples illustrate the variety of situations to which the sense of responsibility can be applied. The common theme is the evaluation of need, the specification of response-program, and the willingness to measure and test out results.

SUMMING UP

1. The content of services can be identified by reference to either the President's Panel or a technical report of the AAMD.

2. Ideally, services should be delivered as a result of community planning. Planning can center around age-appropriate concepts and/or a function-oriented basis.

3. Social action constructs may provide a helpful basis for planning, delivery, and evaluation of services.

4. Social action describes, in part, the roles of people in service. These roles include the change agent, the legitimizer, and the active participant. It is possible for a person to be all three; usually, however, different people engage in these roles.

5. The skills of the change agent may extend to an entire state or to an individual classroom teacher in a school building.

6. Building relevance is a principal method of social action. Selected techniques include: basic education, surveys and data collection, demonstration of effectiveness, use of competition, confrontation, channeling of effort, and building on the past.

7. Administration and coordination are as genuine a need as the services themselves. Services in communication and in cooperative effort are a direct benefit to parents and the retarded person.

8. Coordination is the process of assembling resources and requires sustained and interrelated effort. Administration is a mandate to accomplish a particular mission.

9. Evaluation and accountability are becoming more relevant to service operations. There is an overlap between evaluation and research.

10. Regardless of the specific program, certain common dimensions of quality exist. These baseline dimensions center around the extent and/or degree to which a program is responsive, available, accessible, individualized, and accountable.

11. The 1960s were characterized by use of social action tactics to obtain voluntary compliance for service needs. The 1970s have been characterized by legal confrontation to mandate services. This latter tactic has been to use the courts in order to secure rights, enforce rights, educate the public, and petition for redress. In these uses, legal-court intervention is an expression of social action.

12. Services in *rural* areas are possible. While delivery styles would vary, quality and sophistication are attainable.

13. As public policy, there are alternatives to the use of labels to attract funds.

14. The concept of *developmental disabilities* is both a fiscal concept and a service concept. It is an example to extend services and to protect service identity.

15. Responsibility is not passive. Responsibility is an activist obligation.

16. "Victories" are not won over a short period. There must be patience and persistence.

17. Perhaps the most difficult concept of all to grasp is the universal nature of responsibility. That is to say, all who participate in services are responsible for quality.

ON LOCATION

The selection chosen for this chapter is intended to convey some essentials regarding services. The theme of this chapter has been the managerial tools of social action, evaluation, and planning. Concepts such as system, input, impact, etc., are meant to be aids, not depersonalized entities. A recent prospectus for an evaluation of an educational system contained the phrase, "cost reimbursement unit" (CRU) as a major target for cost-effective decision making. After several pages, it became evident that the CRU notation referred to the handicapped students enrolled. CRU struck the writer as the ultimate depersonalization of a human being as well as an unwarranted abuse of management concepts.

In her letter to a state director of mental health expressing her opinions regarding service goals, Tompkins (1972), a parent, provides a perspective that puts management in balance. She provides a reminder that management systems are designed to serve people, not the other way around. Her letter also identifies human values as goals of service. Finally, service development depends upon active and interested citizens. This letter describes such a person.

Dear Sir:

This afternoon I feel a great compulsion to communicate with you. Several times this last year I have thought, sometimes very seriously, of writing to you. Especially when I would read an article making statements, comments, or giving out information which you had released to the press concerning the mentally retarded.

Now, as I am sitting in my comfortable and satisfying suburban back yard and remembering what I read in this Sunday morning's edition, I'm determined that someone, and that someone is most logically you, should know how at least one more mother sees the problem of mental retardation. Speaking for myself, it is encouraging to know that a person as fair, as concerned, and as dedicated as you seem to be is director of the Department of Mental Health.

I'll try very hard to make this letter as short and to the point as possible, omitting tears, frustrations, and gripes, although they are between almost every line. Because precepts precede specifics in the understanding of problems and developing solutions to those problems, I would like to let you know the direction in which I have been thinking.

Mental retardation is a handicap, and should be on an equal basis with every other handicap.

We have crutches, artificial limbs, and wheelchairs for the physically handicapped; glasses, white canes, seeing-eye dogs and braille for the blind; hearing aids, lip reading, and sign language for the deaf. But mankind hasn't as yet discovered or invented artificial helps or substitutes for thinking power.

How can we get the community, which is made up of human beings, to see and accept the mentally retarded as people who are also human beings, the only difference being the severity of the handicap they must live with? How can we get the average citizens to exchange their fear for an attitude of understanding?

Possibly by saying to them, "How do you think you would feel if you can imagine yourself as mentally retarded?"

Just how do you think you would feel if everyone around you were talking so fast you couldn't understand what they meant or even what they were talking about? How would you feel if every so often someone would say to you, "Hurry up! Why do you have to be so slow?" And then before long you realized that nobody wanted to wait for you, so they were doing the necessary things for you, and they kept doing them until you gave up trying.

How would you feel if every time you tried to communicate with another person, and it might be someone whom you especially wanted attention from, this person ignored you or tried only half-heartedly to listen and answer you, and then left at the very first chance available under any pretext? Would you be lonesome? depressed? or would you make yourself obnoxious trying to get recognition?

The most difficult goal for a mentally retarded person to attain is a reasonable degree of self-respect.

In the vernacular of Charlie Brown:

Self-respect is hearing someone say, "Come and walk with me."

Self-respect is having someone listen when you speak.

Self-respect is hearing someone say, "Suzie can do it."

Self-respect is having someone say, "Will you help me with this."

The answer is another person, a capable mind, who will, with love, empathy, and dedication loan X number of hours per day to be the guiding "think power" for another person handicapped by mental retardation.

The mentally retarded need help to live, to think, to enjoy, to decide, and to choose, but they also need to feel they are needed, loved, and can do something important.

A second and almost as difficult goal is a pride in ownership. This is my school, my home, my room, my doll, and my friend.

Especially for the retarded who live to reach adulthood, there is a great need for identity that also reinforces self-respect. Nice living quarters with small family-like groups, social activities with their own friends, well supervised leisure time that they can take part in planning, all these are part of a good life. This I believe the mentally retarded have a right to. All the more because they were not given a choice when handicaps were passed around.

Sunday's article was on the acceptance of the mentally retarded by the community at large. We are aware that this is the one handicap that has been hidden, hush-hushed, and given the "out of sight-out of mind" treatment in preceding generations, and for some of the very same reasons that are, today, so frustrating. Human nature being as it is, people still fear other people who are different from themselves. This difference ranges all the way from size, shape, or color of the other person to not being able to interpret or understand the action or words of the other person.

Acceptance is a give-and-take situation.

The people of any community should not be forced to accept contact with the handicapped to the point that it is annoying or intolerable. It will take more generations to build respect, friendship, and tolerance.

In the interim the answer as I see it is to keep working toward definite goals. Help the mentally retarded help themselves, for one. Make friends for the cause of the mentally retarded by educating the public.

And last but not least, be tolerant ourselves toward our fellow citizens who find it difficult to understand mental retardation.

Sincerely,
Mrs. Herbert Tompkins

REFERENCES

Adelman, H. S. The Resource Room Concept: Bigger Than a Room. *The Journal of Special Education,* 1972, 6, 361–367.

Beal, G., Payer, J., and Yarbrough, P. *Mental Retardation: A Guide to Community Action.* Des Moines: Iowa's Comprehensive Plan to Combat Mental Retardation, 1965.

Blatt, B. Public Policy and the Education of Children with Special Needs. *Exceptional Children,* 1972, 38, 537–545.

Boor, M. What's to Become of Katherine. *Exceptional Children,* 1975, 41, 517–518.

Carlson, L., and Pellant, W. Serving Teachers in Rural Areas Through a University Associated IMC. *Exceptional Children,* 1972, 39, 58–59.

Cegelka-Thomas, P., and Tawney, J. Decreasing the Discrepancy: A Case Study in Teacher Education. *Exceptional Children,* 1975, 41, 268–269.

Crosby, K., and Taylor, T. *Standards for Community Agencies Serving Persons with Mental Retardation and Other Developmental Disabilities.* Chicago: Joint Commission on Accreditation of Hospitals, 1973.

Erdman, R., Wyatt, K. E., and Heller, H. W. *The Administration of Programs for Educable Retarded Children in Small School Systems.* Arlington, Virginia: Council for Exceptional Children, 1970.

Gallagher, J. The Special Education Contract for Mildly Handicapped Children. *Exceptional Children,* 1972, 38, 527–535.

Gardner, W., and Nisonger, H. *A Manual on Program Development in Mental Retardation.* A monograph supplement to the *American Journal of Mental Deficiency,* January 1962, 66, no. 4. Willimantic, Connecticut: American Association on Mental Deficiency, 1962.

Gilhool, T. Education: An Inalienable Right. *Exceptional Children,* 1973, 39, 597–609.

Goldman, E. R. A State Model for Community Services. *Mental Retardation,* 1975, 13, 33–36.

Gorham, K. A Lost Generation of Parents. *Exceptional Children,* 1975, 41, 521–525.

Graf, G. T., and Meyers, N. C. A Guideline for Social Action: Georgia's Community Services Act. *Mental Retardation,* 1973, 11, 23–25.

Guthrie, E. *Mental Retardation Guidelines for State Interagency Planning.* Washington, D.C.: U.S. Department of Health, Education and Welfare, 1964.

Hammill, D., and Wiederholt, J. *The Resource Room: Rationale and Implementation.* Philadelphia: Butterworth Farms, Inc., 1972.

Harris, W. J., and Mahar, C. Problems in Implementing Resource Programs in Rural Schools. *Exceptional Children,* 1975, 42, 95–99.

Hunter, B. *Coordination of Services for the Retarded.* Sacramento, California: Department of Mental Hygiene, State of California, 1963. With Burgener, W. Services and the Involvement of Elected Officials; Coleman, L. Restructuring the Status Quo; Merelman, J. Local Government and Services to the Retarded.

Illinois Association for Retarded Children. *How Does Your Community Rate?* Chicago: 1966.

Luckey, R. E., and Newman, R. S. The President's Panel Recommendations — Today. *Mental Retardation,* 1975, 13, 32–34.

McIntyre, R. Evaluation for Decision Making, in Meirhenry, W. (ed.). *Planning for the Evaluation of Special Education Programs.* Washington, D.C.: U.S. Office of Education, Bureau of Education for the Handicapped, 1969.

Meirhenry, W. What and When to Evaluate, in Meirhenry, W. (ed.). *Planning for the Evaluation of Special Education Programs.* Washington, D.C.: U.S. Office of Education, Bureau of Education for the Handicapped, 1969.

Neisworth, J., and Smith, R. An Analysis and Redefinition of Developmental Disabilities. *Exceptional Children,* 1974, 40, 345–347.

Mooring, I., and Currie, R. A Conceptualized Model for Community Services for the Mentally Retarded. *Exceptional Children,* 1964, 30, 202–205.

The President's Panel on Mental Retardation. *A Proposed Program for National Action to Combat Mental Retardation.* Washington, D.C.: U.S. Government Printing Office, 1962.

Reger, R., and Koppmann, M. The Child Oriented Resource Room Program. *Exceptional Children,* 1971, 37, 460–462.

Sellin, D., Clos, M., Deiter, J., Harris, G., Harrison, D., Peterson, A., Smith, R., and Zimmerman, H. Opinions Regarding Interagency Programming for the Mentally Retarded. *Mental Retardation,* 1974, 12, 24–28.

Sluyter, G. V., and Barbuto, P. Developmental Disabilities. *Mental Retardation,* 1972, 10, 38–39.

Stedman, D. State Councils on Developmental Disabilities, *Exceptional Children,* 1976, 42, 186–192.

Stedman, D. The State Planning Council on Developmental Disabilities. *Mental Retardation,* 1975, 13, 4–8.

Tarkington, L. W. Outreach: Delivery of Services to Rural Communities. *Mental Retardation,* 1971, 9, 27–28.

Tompkins, Mrs. Herbert. *How Would You Feel If No One Cared?* Lansing: Michigan Department of Mental Health, 1972.

Travelstead, C. Problems in the Education of Handicapped Children in Sparsely Settled Areas. *Exceptional Children,* 1960, 27, 52–55.

Yavorsky, D. K. *Discrepancy Evaluation: A Practitioner's Guide.* Charlottesville: University of Virginia, Evaluation Research Center, 1975.

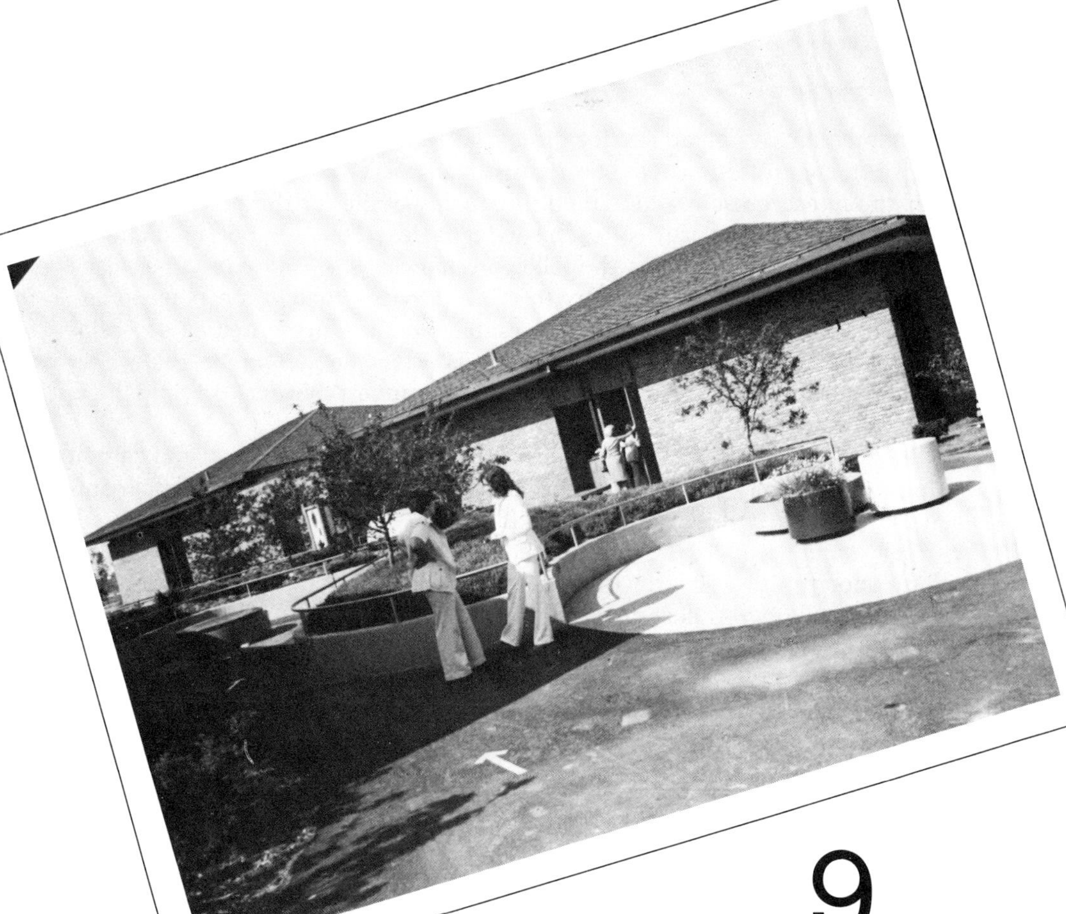

9

The Scope of Supportive Services

SYNOPSIS

This chapter surveys broad service groupings that realistically could be expected to exist at the community level. The term *supportive services* describes services designed to protect, enrich, and extend the quality of life for the retarded person and his or her family. The nature of each service is described and potential alternatives are listed. This chapter covers the following topics:

1. *Service management* refers to those services that locate persons so as to prevent the effects of neglect. Service management is presented as a possible solution to the problems of routing, diagnosis, placement, and the like. The service manager's role is ensuring continuing support beyond an initial contact and/or placement.

2. *Residential services* are discussed in the context of regional and community settings. Community residential alternatives that can make the regional center an even more specialized service are identified.

3. *Extended learnings* are described. This area of service is directed toward extending opportunities for growth and development for retarded persons.

4. *Guardianship* describes the management of resources to protect the rights and resources of the person and/or the family. Private and public resources are identified.

5. *The ARC movement* is described in terms of its role and mission. Special attention is given to its function in service development and outreach efforts.

OBJECTIVES

ATTITUDES

1 To have an open mind regarding the reactions of parents.
2 To be committed to prevention of service neglect of eligible persons.
3 To be willing to affiliate with the ARC movement as both a means of service as well as a source for one's own continuing inservice commitment.
4 To resolve to be a source of current and accurate information for parents.

UNDERSTANDINGS

1 To recognize service management as a consumer need.
2 To understand the function of follow-along services in service management.
3 To understand the regional mental retardation center as a community resource.
4 To recognize the full range of community alternatives for residential services.
5 To understand the concept of respite care in service delivery.
6 To view the retarded person as a franchised citizen.
7 To see the law as source of reduction of rights as well as conservator of rights.
8 To realize the values of extended learnings to the family and the retarded person.
9 To learn the evolutionary nature of the ARC movement.

SKILLS

1 To evaluate the needs of one's own community for development of supportive services.
2 To identify resources for supportive services.
3 To involve minorities in the mental retardation service system.
4 To outline the elements of guardianship and the life consultation needs of the retarded person and his or her family.
5 To specify examples of programs of special merit.
6 To identify standards of service which would be evidence of quality.

GUARDIANSHIP

Elements

According to Ogg (1973), guardianship involves the appointment of an agent to manage and oversee an individual legally ruled incompetent to function. Present guardianship provisions vary from state to state. Incompetence is defined by childhood (under age eighteen). For adults, legal incompetence can include the mentally retarded, the mentally ill, the epileptic, the elderly senile, and the alcoholic. The problem this diversity creates is that all are judged equally incompetent, without recognition for varying degrees of competence.

Legal guardianship involves protection of the person and protection of estate (financial resources). As protector of the person, the guardian is responsible for medical care, living arrangements, clothing, etc. Protection of the estate involves a *conservator* relationship in which the *ward's* property and financial resources are managed in the ward's best interests. It is not uncommon to have a bank or trust company, at the direction of the probate court and/or the parent, split guardianship. That is, a relative may be designated as guardian, while a bank would be the conservator. Ogg cited two significant problems with this typical arrangement. First, relatives may not outlive the ward, or siblings may be so mobile as to be unavailable. Second, commercial institutions may be unable to administer trusts under $50,000 in value. The cost of administration may be unprofitable to either the bank or to the person.

Guardianship Alternatives

The experience of the Massachusetts ARC and the New York ARC are described by Ogg as a possible solution to the problems of guardianship. In these states, it is possible for a group or organization to serve as guardian *and* conservator. The Massachusetts ARC Friendship Fund involves a yearly fee and may involve a sizable monetary bequest at the time the guardianship becomes active. If one parent dies, a social worker hired by the fund works with the surviving parent and a legal guardian as a resource person to make appropriate plans for the retarded person. The social worker assists in carrying out the plan and making periodic visits to evaluate progress. The New York ARC has set up a trust to manage donations for the benefit of a particular person. The New York system takes advantage of a state statute that permits standby guardians. Thus, younger persons may be designated to act after the death of parents. This ensures continuity of guardianship. Other features of the New York system deserve note. First, a nonprofit association such as an ARC can serve as a guardian. Second, the system recognizes partial conservatorship; the person can have freedom to spend sums up to $300 or a month's salary (whichever is greater).

The Human Relations Agency of California (1971) described a *public* concept of guardianship. This program contrasts with the private concept of Massachusetts and New York. Under the California plan, the state is divided into regions with a mental retardation regional service center operated by a board. The state director of public health can be nominated as guardian and/or conservator. The director performs these services with the assistance of regional centers.

Financial Resources for Guardianship

Parents will need to settle upon arrangements regarding *economic security* for their retarded offspring. The NARC Insurance Committee (1974) has summarized the scope of considerations. Their recommendations encompass provisions that can be established by parents and that use governmental benefits as well. Parents are urged to establish guardianship prior to age eighteen. Without this declaration, the retarded person *could be* considered ineligible for health insurance coverage as a family member and *might be* denied government benefits. Furthermore, the retarded person, not legally declared as nonresponsible for contracts, automatically would be left property that could be attached by the state as payment for institutional services. Consequently, the importance of a will and trust are stressed. The trust is an arrangement whereby one person administers assets on behalf of another according to the wishes of the person who set up the trust. The committee recommends that life insurance should be upon the wage-earner, not the retarded person.

The NARC Insurance Committee stresses the variability of laws regulating wills, trusts, guardianship and insurance. The parent is urged to seek the advice of trained persons for this type of life planning. In general, the extent of an estate should consider:

1 wage-earner's age, earnings, and number of years of anticipated earning power;
2 number and age of dependents;
3 extent of real and personal property;
4 benefits anticipated from Social Security;
5 the question of a will versus no will (the latter situation can be stark) and anticipation of "death" taxes; and
6 one's own philosophy of life concerning the present versus the future regarding self and dependents, and one's sense of responsibility to one's dependents, one's community, and society.

It was noted that the first five factors can be assessed by computer analysis, while the sixth is individual. The parent should seek advice and have a periodic review to update provisions. NARC does offer a relatively inexpensive insurance plan, with declining coverage as the parent grows older.

Health insurance, according to this report, varies from state to state. NARC and state ARCs are attempting to influence state insurance laws to cover the retarded person beyond age nineteen under family policies. This can be done only if the person's disability can be shown to exist before age nineteen. Relatively few companies offer direct coverage of the person.

Government Benefits and Guardianship

Federal benefits are in a constant state of change and flux. The parent or similar advocate for the family should seek out the local office of Social Security for current provisions under Social Security Supplemental Security Income (SSI), Medicaid, Veteran Benefits, and Railroad Retirement Benefits. According to the NARC committee, regardless of the federal program, the prudent parent will have preserved and have readily available the following documents: Social Security number of the wage-earner; marriage certificate of the parents in case of a stepchild; birth certificates of the children; names and addresses of person and facilities holding records concerning the retarded person; and name and address of wage-earner's employer for the past year and the last W-2 tax-withholding statement; and a copy of the last tax return if self-employed.

The Social Security Administration (1974) (1975) has provided orientation booklets to describe Social Security and Supplemental Security Income. SSI replaced the former federal programs of income maintenance for the aged, for the blind, and for the disabled. SSI constitutes a supplement to basic Social Security grants up to a maximum figure. All SSI recipients are eligible for Medicaid if medically indigent in most states and in some without indigence.

Another area of financial planning parents can consider is possible benefits under the federal income tax. The Michigan Association for Retarded Citizens (1976) prepared a guide concerning special income tax rulings related to mental retardation. Possible deductions include medical expenses for institutionalized persons, costs involved in chore services, and tuition fees, provided these are medically prescribed to alleviate the handicap. Expenses of mileage for visitations (but not meals and lodging) may be deducted if part of a required treatment. Similarly, mileage on behalf of an ARC and reasonably related expenses may be deducted.

Dimensions of Rights

The legal rights of the mentally retarded person, according to Ogg (1973), have progressed enormously since the colonial period in the United States, but civil rights and service rights still should be broadened.

Civil Rights

The urgency of civil rights protection is suggested by the reports of Marb, Friel, and Eissler (1975), Menolascino (1974), and Krishef (1972). The Marb et al. report observed that tests of criminal competence are based upon concepts of mental illness, not mental retardation. The incarcerated retarded person may be victimized. The retarded are placed in institutions or jails independent of the offense. They are perceived as less eligible for parole or probation. Menolascino observed that to be poor, retarded, and caught is an invitation to tragedy. He advocated a three-pronged approach: prevention, advocacy, and treatment. His recommendations are presented in an adapted form in figure 9–1. A particular merit of the Menolascino program is the emphasis upon prevention.

Figure 9–1 *A Model for Resolution of the Mentally Retarded Offender*

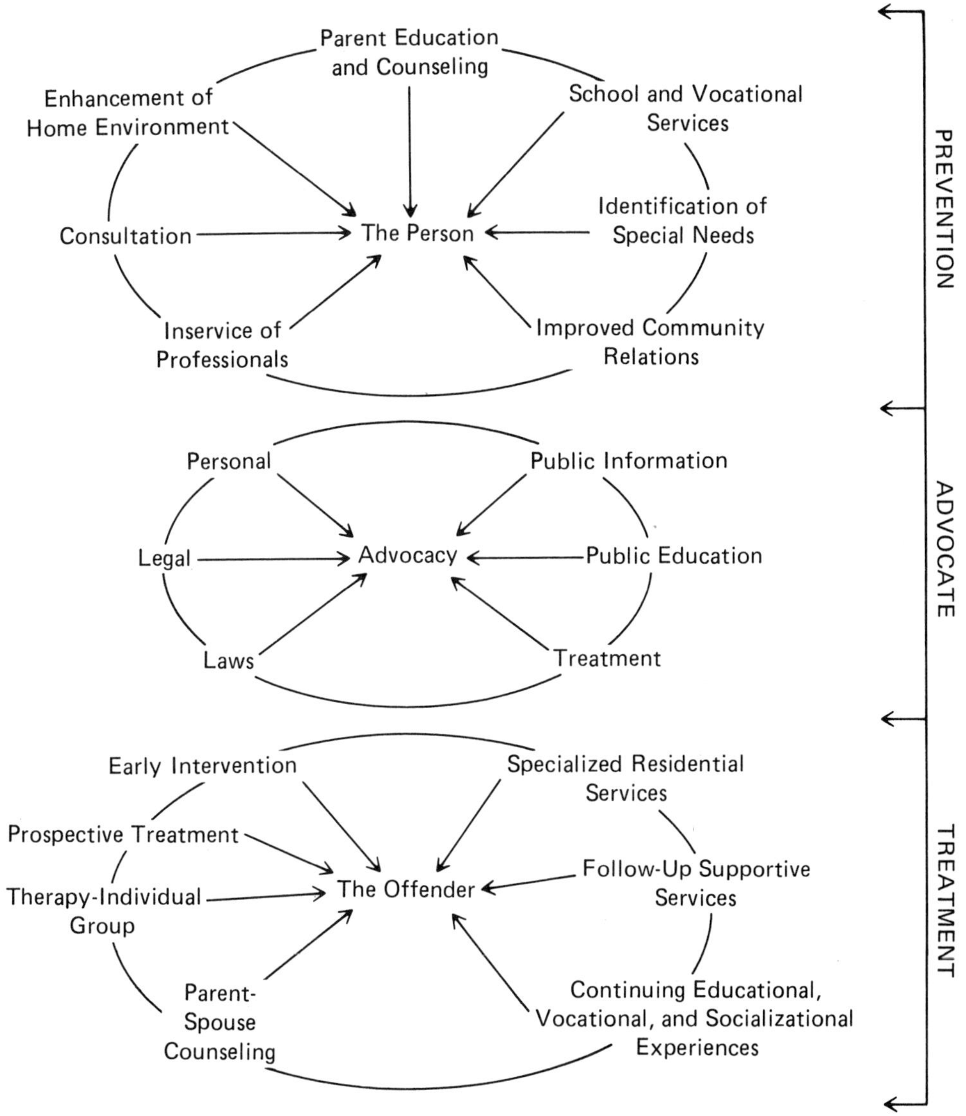

Krishef (1972) and Vaughan (1973) identified additional areas of concern. Krishef undertook a survey regarding laws related to sterilization and marriage. Fifty-one percent of the states have laws on both topics. Krishef discovered that legal standards of consent, authorization, and accountability lack clarity to protect either the person, the parent, or responsible administrators.

Service Rights

Turnbull and Turnbull (1975) affirm the Scheerenberger (1974) priority of legal safeguards associated with deinstitutionalization. These authors note the goal possesses merit, but legal concerns must be considered. The central problem is that advances in knowledge have progressed faster than has revision of antiquated statutes. Among the legal areas that require action, according to the Turnbulls, are:

1. *Due process.* This procedure was said to impact upon admission and discharge, especially voluntary admission (admittance without court procedures) and discharge (request to be released). Abuses of "false" incarceration were balanced against inappropriate dumping. These authors suggest an independent advocate to monitor the interests of the person; such an individual should not be prevented from participation.

2. *Professional liability.* The concept of malpractice might be extended to psychologists, administrators, and educators. The Turnbulls isolate low expectations and associated neglect as possible grounds for suit.

3. *Preparation.* This involves adequate training for community return. It also involves preparation of the family.

4. *Equivalency.* The Turnbulls challenge the assumption that any community is better than any institution. They cite "right to treatment" cases involving institutionalized persons. They suggest that right to treatment should continue with community placement.

5. *Transfer of rights.* Rights assigned to institutionalized persons may or may not transfer when the person becomes a community resident. The same rights available within the residential system should be available outside the system, especially in civil or criminal cases.

6. *State subsidy.* The problem targeted here is that deinstitutionalization from a public setting may shift costs to the private family in the community. While the state may save funds, the family is burdened to the point of harassment. Either the state must fund community services or agree to reimburse families for purchase of services.

7. *Right of voluntary discharge.* Here liability is a prime factor. The premise is that voluntary admission should be coupled with voluntary discharge. However, if the person is discharged upon his own request and is injured, can the administrator be held accountable? The Turnbulls suggest that the law is not clear.

8. *Parental custody and parental veto.* The courts assume that parents and the home are to be favored regardless. The Turnbulls suggest otherwise for the minority of instances in which the home environment is unfavorable for development or where pressure to institutionalize is for convenience. Again, the Turnbulls recommend an independent party as a neutral to function on the person's behalf.

9. *Truth in placement.* This concern involves disclosure of program and resources to parents and/or guardians prior to placement by the facility. This would facilitate an informed decision on placement by the consumer. This introduces a measure of future accountability. Rodriguez and Lombardi (1973) have recommended the application of this concept to placement factors in special education programs.

10. *Refining guardianship.* At present, guardianship in many states is either total or none. The Turnbulls advocate a system of partial protection for the person.

1 A given curriculum approach may not be equally applicable to all classrooms.
2 Testing and test results are not the exclusive criteria for inference.
3 Existing programs require periodic questioning, reevaluation, and implementation consistent with purpose.

Singer (1976) presents an example for the Turnbulls' discussion of truth in placement. A sample of secondary-level educators of the mildly mentally retarded were asked to identify their goals. Ninety percent listed vocational competency and social adjustment, while fifty percent listed academic competency. However, readiness to work was rated equal to academic readiness as transfer criteria from junior high to senior high. Ninety-five percent reported woodworking equipment as a principal mode of training, while office equipment and automotive repair was reported by 61 and 41 percent. Instructional time, measured in one hour or more per day, was divided among: academic (74 percent), social and occupational skills (51 percent), individual or group counseling (12 percent), and specific vocational training (40 percent). From an evaluation point of view, Singer concluded that academics, in practice, have higher emphasis than is reflected by stated goals.

EXTENDED LEARNINGS

This element recognizes that the retarded person has needs for companionship and contact in activities related to age-appropriate interests. Peers are a significant source, both normal and other retarded persons.

Sources of Peer Contact

The Division on Mental Retardation (1967) has identified three examples of assistance, or resources. The South Carolina Youth Task Force was enlisted by the Governor's Task Force on Mental Retardation. These young people organized statewide conferences to generate understanding of the retarded and to recruit camp staff for recreation programs. The SWEAT (Student Work Experience and Training) project, made possible by federal funding, enables high-school and junior-college persons to be actively involved in institution programs. This has been a national program. TARS (Teens Aid the Retarded) is a project of the Dallas ARC. This program features a "buddy system" between a TAR and a retarded person for friendship and mutual activities. All three programs feature an orientation process. United Cerebral Palsy Associations, Inc. (1959) utilizes a monitor program to interest, develop, and train persons of high-school age to care for cerebral palsied children in the home so that parents can share in a community and social life outside the home. A basic curriculum of feeding, physical care, and speech is a principal focus of training.

Two more recent organizations have emerged as participants in service to the retarded: YOUTH-ARC and SCEC. The YOUTH-ARC is an affiliate of the NARC. The letters denote Youth Organized and United To Help. Usually, a local ARC will sponsor a YOUTH-ARC chapter. An *Operations Handbook* (1969) developed by NARC describes some of the activities and projects engaged in by young people between junior-high and young-adult ages. The majority are within the high-school age level. Normalization for the retarded within the community is a prime goal. Activities include communications development (especially the idea that language can be fun), physical development (simple games as well as preparation for the Special Olympics), and public education. In this last area, the YOUTH member is encouraged to share his or her experiences with others, including peers and relatives. YOUTH-ARC has become a force to improve the quality of a retarded person's life, to inform the general public, and a means of career recruitment for talented young people.

Another organization of recent origin, SCEC (Student Council for Exceptional Children) (1975), is an affiliate of the Council for Exceptional Children. Its membership is centered around undergraduate college students. A SCEC chapter is sponsored by a college or university department of special education. Faculty members serve as advisors. Depending upon the individual chapter, the activities of the SCEC are a balance between professional development and community service. Among the former are planning and sponsoring professional meetings for self-development. Service activities include assisting or carrying out volunteer community services, sponsoring week-long campus activities to raise community awareness about exceptional children's needs and abilities, involvement in summer camps, sponsoring speakers for student National Education Association (NEA) groups, and participation in career days for high-school students.

Values of Extended Learnings

Pumphrey, Goodman, Kidd, and Peters (1970) have demonstrated some of the values of extended learnings for the mentally retarded. Their study describes forty-one persons ranging in age from six to nineteen with about half aged nine to eleven. Over a five-year period, a follow-up study was conducted. In general, the retarded persons reflected different social behaviors than their normal controls, but the participating retarded learners were superior to their retarded peers. Although recreation workers reported more positive incidents for the normal, the retarded participants were no different in negative incidents. When the retarded participants were compared to normals, the former were less likely to participate in all activities, to determine the group's choice of activities, to be chosen first in take-up-sides games, or to adapt to new situations; they were more likely to be upset by failure, to be easily frightened, and to require support from group leaders. Compared to their retarded peers, the normal were rated by their teachers as higher on effort, self-correction, memory, perseverance, ability, and adaptability to do a new task.

One of the most dramatic outcomes of an extended learning program was reported by *Mental Retardation News* (1973). Robert Busch, a retarded citizen, pitched in to give a heart attack victim mouth-to-mouth resuscitation so his supervisor could summon help. He had learned this technique as a member of the local ARC Boy Scout troop.

Spears (1967) has described one state's commitment to extended learnings at both community levels and for the residents of regional centers. Activities for the retarded included: bowling, swimming, music, arts and crafts, dancing, scouting, camping, and physical fitness. The Wildlife Resources Department and the mentally retarded can also help each other in: trail maintenance, tree planting, grounds maintenance, trout stream improvement, clearing wildlife openings, collection of pine cones for seedlings, and roadside park maintenance.

Religious Nurture

Zuk (1962) cites spiritual crisis as a factor in family reaction to retardation. He suggested that cultural beliefs influence the meaning of parenthood. The birth of a handicapped child can create disillusionment with religious values. The spiritual crisis is a search for meaning, particularly the meaning of the damaged child. The answer will prompt guilt or the spark of hope. For Zuk, the crisis can be a faith experience or an experience from which the family may never recover.

Petersen (1960) defines a threefold ministry to the mentally retarded as specialized responses to the person, to the family, and to the community. The first is directed toward the need to become a worthy and capable person. Parents can be assisted to work out the meaning of the experience, and the clergy can assist in seeking special help. The third ministry seeks an advocacy on behalf of the mentally retarded both as social action and as a counterweight to those beliefs, ascribed to religious tradition, which are dehumanizing to the retarded person.

Paralleling the Petersen discussion, Brockwell (1963) has outlined one state's concern for religious nurture. His report gives particular emphasis to social action by the religious community to encourage services for the retarded. Also outlined are examples from Catholic, Jewish, and Protestant ministries to the retarded and their families. Religious nurture is viewed as addressing itself to four basic needs: self-acceptance, acceptance by others, a feeling that the universe is benevolent, and the need for a positive engagement with life.

Shapiro (1964) has outlined the benefits of religious nurture as an experience of involvement with a living values system and of inclusion in a larger family. She also noted that parents have been appreciative of religious efforts and their feelings of isolation have been reduced. The parents' faith has been deepened by the enthusiasm of their children for the experience. Miller (1972) has affirmed the role of the chaplain as moral conscience. It is the duty of the chaplain, according to Miller, to call attention to program needs.

Theodore (1966) has outlined a sense of the meaning of the religious life for the retarded person, the family, and the larger community. She contends that religious nurture extends to the full range of mental retardation, including the severely retarded. She noted that religious nurture's central purpose is to offer the family a sense of purpose for the care of their child and to draw others into that circle of common purpose. Theodore leaves the rather strong impression that religious nurture for the retarded person becomes religious nurture for those who engage in it. The act of instruction, worship, and celebration deepen the faith of all involved.

Recreation

Singstock and Stein (1967) summarized helpful resources concerning recreation programming:

1. NARC, the National Association for Retarded Children (now Citizens), is supportive at local levels and a direct service in some communities. The national office sponsors a standing committee to marshall resources.

2. The American Association for Health, Physical Education, and Recreation (AAHPER) is devoted to leadership training, research, and materials preparation. Their publication, *The Journal of Health, Physical Education and Recreation,* features articles related to the mentally retarded.

3. The Joseph P. Kennedy Jr. Foundation is devoted to leadership training, research, and program standards. A continuing feature of the program has been acting as principal sponsor of the Special Olympics.

4. The National Recreation and Parks Association (NRPA) serves as a consult-

ing agency for private and public organizations and facilities. Increasingly, this organization sponsors evaluation projects to upgrade facilities.

5. The American Association on Mental Deficiency (AAMD) has established a section in recreation to serve as an informational resource for members.

6. The Boy Scouts of America has modified its program requirements for the retarded. An adapted manual is available.

7. Information Center — Recreation for the Handicapped (ICRH), located at Southern Illinois University, serves as a clearinghouse for both camping and recreation. Its publication, the *ICRH Newsletter,* describes materials and kits available to interested persons.

Witt (1971) has sketched the evolution of recreation for the mentally retarded. His analysis covers a time span from before World War I through the late 1960s. Recreation has progressed from the state of a luxury, to a method of control, to a teaching tool, to the status of a genuine discipline. At present, the author concludes, recreation is an allied partner along with education as a significant program component. Woods (1971), for example, has demonstrated that opportunity to participate in a recreation program can be a motivational incentive for both shaping socially acceptable behaviors as well as encouraging rewarding leisure experiences.

RESIDENTIAL SERVICES

Guidelines and Scope

The NARC Residential Services Committee (1971) defined guidelines for residential services:

1 The service should promote emotional maturity.
2 Attention should be given to the goals of retarded persons themselves.
3 Approaches in programming should emphasize "normalization," with emphasis upon drawing the retarded person *into* the mainstream of society.
4 Approaches should maximize all the human qualities of the retarded person.
5 Specific program goals should be tailored to increase complexity of behavior, to increase control over the environment, and to enable the person to acquire behaviors as normal as possible.

The scope of residential services identified by the NARC Residential Services Committee can be outlined as: individual alternatives, including adoption, foster home, and family living; group living alternatives, including the regional center; and community alternatives, such as group homes, apartments, and special units.

Influences for Placement

Jaslow and Stehman (1966) conducted an investigation of factors that influenced the selection of institutionalization by parents in a large, urban area. This study offers insight into efforts to assist persons in decision making. The sample consisted of four hundred families; three hundred had taken the legal step of commitment prior to the child's eleventh birthday, and one hundred families had not done so. Comparisons were made between the committed group and uncommitted group. The principal findings are:

1. The condition of the child is *not* a determinant of the decision. This finding held true regardless of IQ level as well as visibility of condition and for presence of secondary disabilities.

2. Parents who institutionalize are more frequently advised to do so than those who do not. Although the children of both groups were similar, the committed group received advice to commit in 50 percent of inquiries, while the other group received such advice in only 13 percent of their contacts.

3. Demographic and social-psychological characteristics of the family influence the probability of contact for advice. Three types of advisors were noted: medical, social agents, and schools. Seventy-five percent of whites had contact with medical sources, who were generally in private practice, while 50 percent of blacks saw this source, usually at general hospitals and clinics. Low-income families tended to use social agents more frequently.

4. Social agents (agencies, courts, relatives, and ARCs) will recommend commitment based upon certain characteristics of the family. The variables of influence for the social agent appeared to be immaturity of the mother, the mother's perception of the child as a handicap to the family, and the family's ability to cope. The investigators viewed the social agents as appropriate, although they did advise inservice efforts to lower the 40 percent rate of advice to commit.

5. Medical advisors suggested commitment about 50 percent of the time. They did not seem to discriminate on any variable, but reflected a generalized approach.

6. Socioeconomic conditions were associated with action taken after advice to commit. Blacks were overrepresented in the uncommitted group, and within the committed group they tended to commit later and appropriately. White-collar, professional, and college-trained tended to commit early and inappropriately. High-income groups committed inappropriately. Blue-collar workers tended to commit late.

7. Those who commit define their problem as a sense of helplessness. The uncommitted group reflect concern with the future and present practical problems.

8. Two-thirds of the committed group see the institution as a permanent solution, and one-third express belief that the child will eventually return. Those who commit late are more likely to reflect optimism.

9. About one-fourth of the committed group state that alternative community facilities might have altered their action.

10. Values are not a source of influence. Moral-religious values were not predictors. There were trends, however: emphasis on pleasure and status may expedite commitment, while family togetherness may discourage it.

11. Parents with high "ego-strength" are more likely to commit early, and to commit children of less problem.

12. Parents tend to be persuaded to commit rather than spontaneously seeking it.

The Mental Retardation Regional Center

Kirkland (1974) has discussed the limitations and the values of the residential facility. The mental retardation regional center is a program concept. The regional center is a state-funded facility serving a designated geographical area and responsible for all levels and ages of the retarded. Among the limitations of this type of environment are:

1. *The model for living.* The pace and demands, reduced to suit the retarded person, do not prepare the person for the speed and complexity of community living. Passive-dependent behavior tends to be encouraged. Segregation of the sexes is likely to compound later community adjustment rather than assist it.

2. *Conflict of mission.* Learning involves risk, which the facility may be obligated to prevent. For example, Kirkland notes that learning money management may involve "wasting it." This may be prohibited by law. Given group dynamics, the resident is expected to be a "child" with staff and a "sibling" with peers and never expected or encouraged to be an adult.

3. *Confusion of mission.* In multi-purpose facilities, the mild, moderate, and severe are pooled together. Kirkland suggests there is less difference between the mild and the normal and more difference between the mild and the severe in terms of basic abilities. Some facilities do not recognize these basic generalizations, and some do not take advantage of them. Some may exploit the abilities to create a "serf-like" state.

Among the possible values of the regional center, according to Kirkland, would be:

1. *Restoration of self-image.* The dependable routine and inflexible rules can be a source of help to the person who needs to experience stability and predictability. For the mildly retarded person, it may be helpful to experience capabilities not experienced in the "normal" world. In comparison to others, this person may discover new potentials for action.

2. *Economic efficiency.* It may be economic and efficient to assemble scarce personnel and equipment to bring to bear on target groups. Duplication of these resources could be prohibitive in expense, even if available.

3. *Protection.* Often the retarded person requires protection from exploitation from the normal, not the other way around. Typically, the institution has been able to offer services not historically found in the community, especially protective services.

4. *Care for the severely retarded.* It is argued that only a specialized facility can provide for the complex needs of the severely damaged person. Medical science has made it possible to maintain life to the extent that services will be required for age groups not previously demanding services. For example, Cleland, Powell, and Talkington (1971) found the mean of dying for the profoundly retarded to be 20.33, with a span of living to be 68 years.

Kirkland concluded her analysis with certain observations about the role of the regional center in a continuum of residential services. Her primary conclusion is that this option can be the treatment of choice for certain persons at certain times, but it is not for all retarded persons. The regional center is viewed by Kirkland as a resource to the community services program, and placement should *not* be permanent. Placement is for goal-oriented purposes. Eventual community placement is to be expected and is the norm. Among the resources the regional center might deliver would be diagnostic resources for rare conditions, surgical procedures for unusual conditions, behavior treatment, and services for the multihandicapped. Ideally, the center would be able to share its staff and its expertise with community programs.

Jaslow, Chatterton, and Sussman (1974) advocate the regional retardation center as a resource to the community. Their emphasis is upon integration of center services and community-level services.

The President's Committee on Mental Retardation (1970) issued a special report on residential services which mirrors the Jaslow et al. and Kirkland expositions. The committee reaffirmed that the concept of legal rights applies to the retarded person. Voluntary and involuntary commitments were singled out for special consideration. The guideline was advanced that commitment should be based on need, not on what is expedient or convenient. It is recommended that legal guardians be appointed for protection of individual rights. Given this basic protection for the person, the committee suggests these possible functions for the mental retardation center:

1. *Regional and community resource.* As a cooperative partner in the comprehensive service system, the center should coordinate its programs with community services. Among its resources, the regional center might offer: diagnostic and counseling services, outpatient services, special treatment services, and technical consultation. In turn, the community might offer participation of residents in educational, social, and recreational activities.

2. *Technical planning.* Staff personnel should be encouraged to participate in all levels of regional planning as well as to stimulate service development.

3. *Training of personnel.* A "career ladder" should be established to enable professionals and paraprofessionals to upgrade their skills and educational levels. The center could be a significant resource.

The committee established certain principles for construction. These would include: location of the center in close proximity to the community to provide for normal contacts with the community; living quarters that provide for privacy; structures designed in harmony with the program, not vice versa; size and type of facilities reflecting the need for a comprehensive program, not a simple orientation, and an annual budget that reflects a realistic allowance for plant maintenance.

As a resource to the center, the President's Committee recommended the establishment of an advisory committee. Appointees could be a blend of laypersons and professionals made by the responsible state department of operation. Obviously, appointments should be based upon broad knowledge of the field and demonstration of public service. The charge to the committee should leave no uncertainties as to its advisory role. It should be a consultative body, meeting directly with the appointing body to review progress and needs.

Status of Residential Centers

Scheerenberger (1976) summarized the status of public residential facilities (PRFs) in the United States. His report encompassed demographic data, population movement, resident programs, budgeting, and staffing. Eighty-two percent of such facilities responded to his survey form. Demographically, PRFs serve about as many males (53 percent) as females (47 percent). Fifty-five percent of residents were described as multihandicapped. The profound and severely retarded were the majority level served (71 percent). School-age persons, aged three to twenty-one, were the second largest age group (42 percent), while adults under age sixty-two were the largest group (53 percent). Children under three were less than 1 percent. PRFs constructed prior to 1964 were found to differ from those constructed afterwards. At the time of the study, newer facilities reflected a population decrease of nearly 9 percent, while the older PRFs reflected a 15.9 percent decrease. Of the reporting PRFs, there was a rated bed capacity of 148,160, as compared to a population of 141,522. The newer the PRF, the smaller the population; the range was from 10 to 3,094 persons, with a median of 585.

Population movement reflected a rate of about 8 percent. A majority (65 percent) of populations fall into the profound and severe range. Readmission ran at about 3 percent and was said to take place because of community rejection (22 percent), lack of local services (50 percent), adjustment (22 percent), and family (17 percent). Ninety-five percent of PRFs had a waiting list of less than twenty. Fifty-two percent of the superintendents estimated that 52 percent of the residents could be placed in the community, but because of lack of community services, only 10 percent would be.

Programming for residents reflected prescription by a team (99 percent) on an annual basis (77 percent). The major programs were formal education, language development, physical or occupational therapy, behavior management, and work activity or sheltered workshop. Ninety-five percent of the PRFs reported operating under some form of mandatory education laws. As such, residents could go off campus to school or receive education funds for on-campus programs. Eighty-eight percent of the PRFs indicated participation in community activities for their residents. Those PRFs that had work activity in sheltered workshops tended to be in compliance with labor standards.

Administrative data reflected per diem costs of $11.42 upwards to $79.29, with a median of $26.02. About one fourth of the budget came from federal sources such as Medicare/Medicaid and Titles I and III of the Elementary and Secondary Education Act. While gains have been made, only 11 percent of the PRFs had adequate staffing. Other administrative gains, according to Scheerenberger, were protection of resident rights, parent involvement, and collegiate involvement in research and/or practicum assignments. Less encouraging was the finding that some residents (percentages unspecified) were transferred to mental hospitals or county homes as a fiscal economy.

Trends

Ogg (1973) has noted that residential services have existed since colonial times. The common practice was to board retarded persons with private families or thrust them into jails. According to Ogg, there was no state acknowledgement of responsibility for the retarded until 1848.

Wolfensberger (1971A) suggests that the large, remote facility will "fade" or disappear rather than be abolished by legislation. The trends cited were: a declining birth rate; increase in health care services to high-risk groups; increased legalization and practice of abortion; improved health services; environmental betterment, especially in the reduction of poverty; and the impact of early childhood education. Wolfensberger (1971B) offers several ways to facilitate the establishment of community alternatives such as:

1. Boarding, or foster care placements.

2. *Family subsidy*. Given 1971 figures of between $100,000 to $300,000 for custodial care for a lifetime in an institution, a smaller investment for the family to hire a housekeeper, purchase an expanded washer and dryer, and/or expand living quarters might be a more humane and cost-effective decision.

3. *Adoption of a social systems process*. This procedure separates goals from ends. For example, we may say that a family needs counseling; a child needs special classes; and an adult needs to be institutionalized. Wolfensberger notes that these are means and suggests that the goal-oriented statements might be: the family should be prevented from an unwise placement; the child's behavior needs to be shaped; and the adult needs to live away from home. Systems theory can assist in choices if goals are defined; there may be a variety of alternatives.

4. *Purchase of services.* Medical and other technical services can be purchased by contract from existing facilities.

5. *New construction.* Wolfensberger contends that in 1971 institutional construction was about $40,000 per person as contrasted to about $3,500–$5,000 in the community. Community facilities should be homelike structures of family size, indistinguishable from other housing in the neighborhood. Furthermore, Wolfensberger notes that existing institution space is typically inadequate, and abandonment would not be financially extravagant in light of community costs.

The process of implementing alternatives in residential services has become known as "deinstitutionalization." This process involves three interrelated actions, according to Scheerenberger (1974): preventing admission through alternative community methods, return to community of residents who have been adequately prepared, and establishment of a residential environment that protects legal and civil rights. Scheerenberger feels these actions are desirable, feasible, and attainable. Five elements were identified as necessary to accomplish these three actions:

1. *Local boards.* These should be established for planning, coordination, and service. While the concept is not new, the recommendation is for legal accountability and statutory authority to discharge responsibility.

2. *Standard setting.* Scheerenberger advocates a statewide independent agency to set standards and review program quality. This agency would assist local boards, but it would retain enforcement of standards of quality of programming.

3. *Back-up services and support.* Technical consultation should be available to local boards on a demand basis. There should be a pooling of residential staff, university persons, and representatives from community agencies.

4. *Adequate financial resources.* Financial resources must accompany designated responsibilities, and local boards must have access to resources. Scheerenberger noted that programs, regardless of location, do require funding.

5. *Legal advocacy systems.* Scheerenberger identified three types: legal, agency, and citizen. Legal relates to protection of rights. Agency describes the operation of services on a client-centered basis that concentrates on a developmental approach to maintaining self-reliance and independence. Citizen advocacy was described as arranging for a mature citizen volunteer who represents the interests of a retarded citizen as if they were his own. Scheerenberger placed high priority on legal safeguards.

Group Living Alternatives

The NARC (1973) identified certain forms of community group living as an alternative to regional mental retardation centers. Pennsylvania was described as moving in this direction. The difficulties in expansion involve gaining zoning clearance and finding adequate housing. In Montgomery County, Maryland, the local ARC rents apartments for working retarded persons. A supervisor, who may hold another job, will come in at night, or a counselor may make periodic visits. In Wisconsin, a private, nonprofit foundation — New Concepts for the Handicapped Foundation — operates five group homes. The NCF uses private capital to build the homes, which are leased back, long term, to the unit for eventual repayment. The Proviso ARC of North Riverside, Illinois, operates a nine-apartment complex. Each apartment has two bedrooms, a living room, and a kitchen, each individually decorated and furnished. The twenty residents are eighteen years and older, mildly retarded, with minimal vocational and social handicaps. The state of Washington is lauded for its legislation to direct dollars to former residents of institutions. King County, Washington, which includes Seattle, is cited for its efforts. ARC and a mental retardation board, appointed by the county, collaborated on ten group homes involving 125 persons.

The San Diego ARC and the Salvation Army jointly operate a studio apartment complex. Each of the twenty-eight residents has an apartment. It is their first venture into independent living. A resident manager lives on the premises. At meetings the residents learn about shopping, working, budgeting, and transportation. Employment, at present, is at Goodwill Industries. There has been a conscious attempt to neither name nor publicize the complex so as to preserve the privacy of the persons.

Kemper (1973) has described one community's effort to provide a complete continuum of service to its retarded citizens: the Eastern Nebraska Community Office of Mental Retardation (ENCOR). At the time of this report, ENCOR served one thousand retarded persons with a budget of $3.5 million. A staff of 276 full-time and 84 part-time personnel covered a five-county area, with Omaha as the hub. This geographic area has a population base of 520,000, one third of the state's population and about half of its children. The emergence of ENCOR required over ten years of sustained effort and leadership. Great credit was given to Dr. Frank Menolascino and to Dr. Wolf Wolfensberger for their drive and leadership. ENCOR originated from a dissatisfaction with a remote state institution for adult care. The Greater Omaha ARC had begun some pioneer efforts in group living, and Menolascino had visited Sweden and observed normalization in practice. His observations of children dressed normally, being shown how to do bicycle and electrical assembly, and being treated with respect led him and others to attempt to duplicate the experience in Nebraska. Success was not instant. A citizens' study, led by Menolascino and Wolfensberger, persuaded people and organizations that change from institutional systems was desirable. The report was able to engineer basic maneuvers which were to have direct consequences for residential services. These include:

1 dispersal of services and the arrangement of "funding partnerships in county-multi-county levels with blending of public and private funds on a shared-cost basis";

2 proof that quality services can be *more* economical than custodial services;
3 dispersal of residential services across the state and within communities to facilitate integration;
4 facilities designed for special purpose rather than multipurpose;
5 emphasis upon programs rather than buildings; and
6 representation for the retarded person by a citizen advocate.

The residential component of ENCOR offers a continuum of possible placements, with each alternative constituting *increasing* independence for the retarded person. Another generalization from the ENCOR experience: when the person is ready and prepared, a living alternative is available. For example, the Developmental Maximization Unit combines educational and residential programs with medical support located within the county hospital. Another example is the Developmental Home, which provides foster care for children who cannot be in their natural homes. This arrangement permits retention in the community system. At adult levels, there are supervised training residences, leading to graduation to board-and-room small-group homes, then to coresident apartments, to controlled apartments, and finally to independent living arrangements.

Burchenal (1973) describes the concept of an *extended family* as an alternative in group living. The specific program was described as a protective boarding home designed to foster a family atmosphere among members and foster parents. Related to this concept of extended family was the concept of "extended family of services"; the facility did not exist in isolation but was integrated into rehabilitation, educational, and protective services, including medical supervision.

Subsidized Home Placements

Soeffing (1975) reports that thirty-seven states have some form of subsidy for placement of handicapped children in a setting other than an institution. The Soeffing report describes the experiences of several states and organizations regarding the use of homes rather than institutions to provide residential services. Examples of foster home and adoption arrangements are drawn from Maryland, Michigan, the District of Columbia, Kansas, New York, Tennessee, California, Virginia, and Pennsylvania. The motive for adopting retarded children is usually that the prospective parents have had previous experience with a handicapped child and are willing to share their family with a child with special need. The programs provide consultation to parents before and after adoption.

A particular problem in adoption is the matching of a child and a willing home. Soeffing identifies the following sources of help:

1. ARENA (Adoption Resource Exchange of North America) is sponsored by the Child Welfare League of New York. Since 1957, over 1,400 "hard to place" children have found adoptive homes. Agencies can place adoptable children on a central registry. Now ARENA is developing a computerized system to track children who should be adoptable.

2. AASK (Aid to Adoption of Special Kids) was founded in 1973. Between 1974 and 1975, 200 homes were found. This was founded by Dorothy and Robert DeBolts. The DeBolts have seventeen children (six to twenty-seven), eleven of whom are adopted and six of whom are handicapped. AASK serves as an intermediary between agency and seeking parents. In some instances, AASK can provide transportation visits to bring family and child together.

3. RIS (Retarded Infants Service), located in New York City, provides public education about adoption and supportive assistance. A special emphasis has been to place retarded infants with families of retarded children.

4. Project Memphis aims at early intervention of high-risk infants. Education and remediation techniques have enabled families to retain their children, although the project staff will facilitate adoption.

5. Georgetown University Hospital in Washington, D. C. emphasizes *crisis intervention* as a means of assisting the natural family and the child to remain together. In addition to supportive counseling and consultation, this facility arranges parent-to-parent counseling. The new parent is visited in the home by a parent with a similar problem to share experiences and receive help.

6. CAPS (Childcare Assistance Program) provides *respite* care for parents. A trained pool of persons is available to enter the home for from two hours to several weeks. It is described as providing a lifeline for parents. It enables the family to have time together. In cases of extreme physical disability and/or a chronic medical condition, a family's travel or vacation plans may be restricted. Families may be unwilling to leave the home even for a night's outing. The strain of this situation for years can be devastating. CAPS provides the alternative, and in cases of need will pay costs.

7. RISC (Reduce Institutionalization of Special Children), a Kansas project, provides another approach to *respite* care. Foster families are identified, trained, and have between one to three children live with them sometime during the year. Visits are arranged between foster and natural families prior to agreement.

8. Children's Bureau of the Department of Health, Education and Welfare, a federal agency, was identified by Soeffing as the principal federal resource. This agency offers technical assistance as well as financial support, especially in research and demonstration.

Montanari and Toussing (1973) suggest that community residential services using foster care offer "growth support" for foster parents. The focus should be upon what the retarded person can do, rather than on what the person lacks. Aside from philosophic considerations, they also allude to the cost-effectiveness of foster care compared to large, remote institutions.

Respite Care

Paige (1971) has described *respite care* as a short-term service on an individualized basis to assist the family or the retarded person to meet an emergency or scheduled need of temporary relief of the family from residential care, to restore the physical and mental well-being of the person, and to initiate training procedures. Respite care can be performed in or out of the home. Services within the home may be of three types: homemaker services, nursing services, and qualified baby-sitters. In the homemaker service, a trained person enters the home in times of crisis such as a death in the family or the birth of a sibling. The family finds relief from household duties. At another level, the homemaker may serve as a model and teacher to demonstrate methods of child care and home management. Nursing services are usually performed by a public health nurse or by the Visiting Nurses Association. The visitor provides limited nursing care and may also give instruction in self-help, nutrition, and infant stimulation. Trained baby-sitters are usually specially prepared to assist the handicapped person when other services are not needed. Paige notes that respite care service can have an active training component as well. She describes a growing trend among state residential facilities to send staff to families considering institutionalization. The home-training specialist assists the family to learn effective management skills. Paige also notes that out-of-home settings can range from the foster home, family-group home (four to six persons), group home (seven to twelve persons), halfway house (a bridge between sheltered and independent living), specialized nursing homes, and the mental retardation regional center.

SERVICE MANAGEMENT

Examples of Need

Consider these examples offered by Simonds (1970) of the needs of retarded persons that may be helped by service management.

1 A young woman asks for help in arranging care for aged mentally retarded brother who has been terminated from private group home.
2 A family is burned out of their home and the retarded child requires medical attention. The family requires immediate help for shelter, clothing, and furniture.

3 A retarded person asks help when indebtedness threatens eviction from the apartment where he lives with his wife and two children.

4 Hospitalized and disabled, a retarded woman desires to return to her supervised apartment. Its second-floor location and assumption of mobility appear to make return to her former situation unlikely.

5 A mother requests help for her retarded child who is on the verge of school exclusion for disruptive behavior.

The illustrations involve people who have encountered complex problems, perhaps beyond the resources of a single agency. The solutions could be:

1. The aged brother is found to require skilled nursing. A service manager arranges for enrollment in a nursing home. Outreach services maintain a continuing contact with both sister and brother. Also, explorations are initiated to determine eligibility for Medicare and SSI benefits.

2. In the case of the family burned out, a service manager calls in an emergency/crisis intervention worker, either staff and/or trained volunteer. Temporary relief is found, and immediate needs for clothing and furniture are met through service resources. Outreach contacts a local hospital for assistance.

3. For the debt-ridden parent, a service manager arranges for home and financial management guidance. Homemaker services are arranged. Legal services to protect the person's rights as a tenant and small claims court intervention are arranged.

4. A service manager arranges for outreach at the hospital to be in touch until discharge. Arrangement is made to initiate health care, rehabilitation, Medicaid, and the visiting nurse program. Home-delivered meals and transportation to and from her original apartment for physical therapy are arranged. Given therapy and meal assistance, she will be able to return home.

5. For the mother of the child about to be excluded, a service manager arranges for an outreach worker, either staff or trained volunteer, to get in touch with the school. A therapy unit arranges for a behavior therapy program to reverse school reasons for exclusion. The mother receives guidance from a parent unit.

Special Concerns

Sources of Parent Reaction to Diagnosis

Keim (1971) analyzed the shopping behavior of 218 families. Shopping behavior was defined as contacting a third clinic (the setting of this study) after having received two previous and definite assessments of mental retardation. Three percent of the families were found to fall within this definition. The remaining families were seeking additional advice for behavioral management *rather than* challenging a previous diagnosis.

Stone (1967) reported on the willingness of 108 families to institutionalize their Down's syndrome child. The decision not to institutionalize seems related to immediateness of diagnosis, adequate and realistic information, and counseling after diagnosis.

Cummings (1966) compared the personality traits of mothers of normal, mentally retarded, chronically ill, or neurotic children. Mothers of the mentally retarded compared favorably on measures of self-esteem with parents of normal children. The study concluded that the reaction to the child was based, in part, upon feelings of *competence* to fulfill the role of mother *rather than* a reaction to the child's condition.

Gath (1972) reported a survey of siblings of retarded persons. The author's conclusion was that siblings reflected the attitudes of their parents.

A study reported by Justice (1971) identified the reactions of 366 families. The major concerns were school-related achievement, health care, behavior and discipline, future supervision, and management of physical disabilities.

Need for Problem Focus

Avallone, Aron, Starr, and Breetz (1973) have isolated factors that appeared to influence decisions in routing and assignment of clients. Participants in this study (clinicians in a general-purpose mental health clinic) were given 109 cards concerning a specific problem which was to be assigned to various treatment modalities. A difference in recommendation was noted when a label was presented as contrasted to a problem statement. The label of mental retardation tends to influence the decision to refer elsewhere, to reject therapy for the child, and to reject family therapy.

Burton (1971) assessed the services of mental health clinics to retarded persons over a three-year period. The general finding was that 55 percent of the sample was terminated after diagnosis. The major service of these clinics appeared to be identification and routing rather than active consultation.

Need for Continuing Support

Hersh (1970) reported the reactions of fifteen families who institutionalized their child in a private facility. The major implication was that families require as much support *after* placement as before.

The importance of continuing follow-up beyond diagnosis is shown by Sigurdson and Evangelakes (1968). During the five-year period of their study, the authors described 638 persons diagnosed as mentally retarded. Of these persons, 284 were assisted to remain in the community through family support.

Need for Consumer Information

Anderson and Garner (1973) analyzed the reactions of mothers who used a developmental disabilities clinic (a facility eligible to serve epileptic, cerebral palsied, or mentally retarded persons). Mothers suspected a problem prior to diagnosis, and the longer the professional delayed in imparting the diagnosis, the more dissatisfied was the mother. The client also was less likely to regain positive feelings toward the clinic.

Skelton (1972) compared 98 families who institutionalized their child with 38 families who declined. The availability of services and knowledge of availability rather than the degree of retardation were predictors of decision to institutionalize. Respite care services were identified as significant.

Tasks of Service Management

Simonds (1970) reported on the need of retarded persons and their families for comprehensive services of identification, diagnosis, treatment/placement, follow-up, and management of economic and personnel resources. Service management is addressed to three major need areas: organization of services, involvement of the consumer in the system, and involvement of community agencies. The Simonds report proposes a structure for organizing and mobilizing services. The role of a *service manager* is stressed as a principal point of contact for the consumer. The service manager serves as the person's representative and broker for services (figure 9–2). The service manager may arrange for services within or outside the system of his or her employment. Within the service system, the *functional services* component constitutes direct services designed to alleviate, remediate, and/or ameliorate problems. The *social services* component allows for supportive services to the functional component. Finally, the *service facilitating* component permits environmental support as well as recognizing transportation as a key element.

The six illustrations identify three service goals for management: environment and housing, therapeutic-remediation, and problems associated with employment. The service manager, however, does not operate in a vacuum. A plan for organization and functioning for the best utilization of resources is required (figure 9–3). This figure summarizes a minimal list of agencies that could have a relationship to the consumer.

The Simonds concept of service manager requires access to information. Computerization of information has been found helpful. The state of Iowa has pioneered one application of this technology on behalf of the mentally retarded. This application, under the direction of Meyen (1965), was an attempt to apply the AAMD system of Heber (chapter 1) to information systems. The more recent Grossman report also contains a system for computerized record keeping. A computer system can save

Figure 9–2 *Four Major Elements of the Service Manager Consumer's Viewpoint*

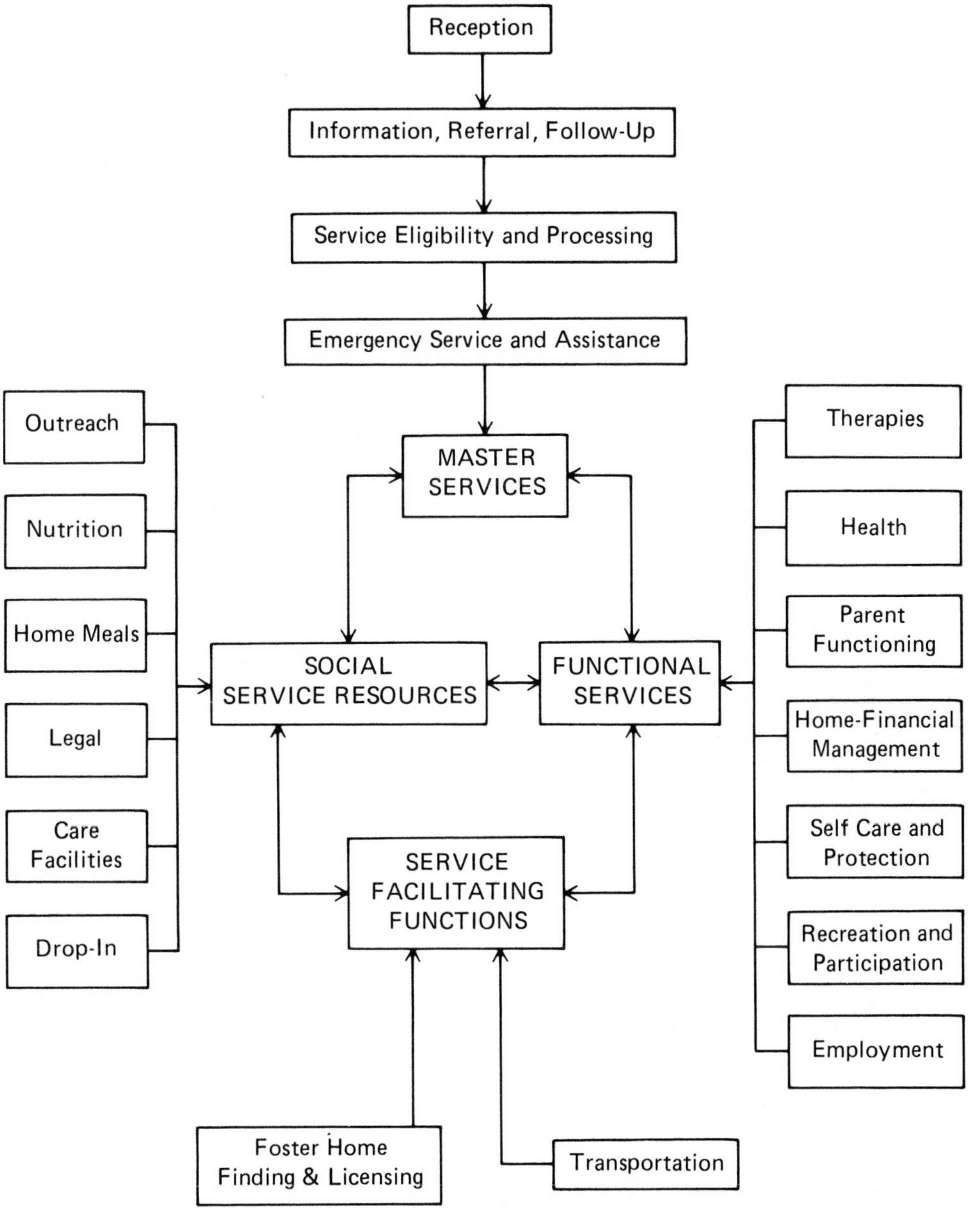

Figure 9–3 *Involvement of Community Agencies*

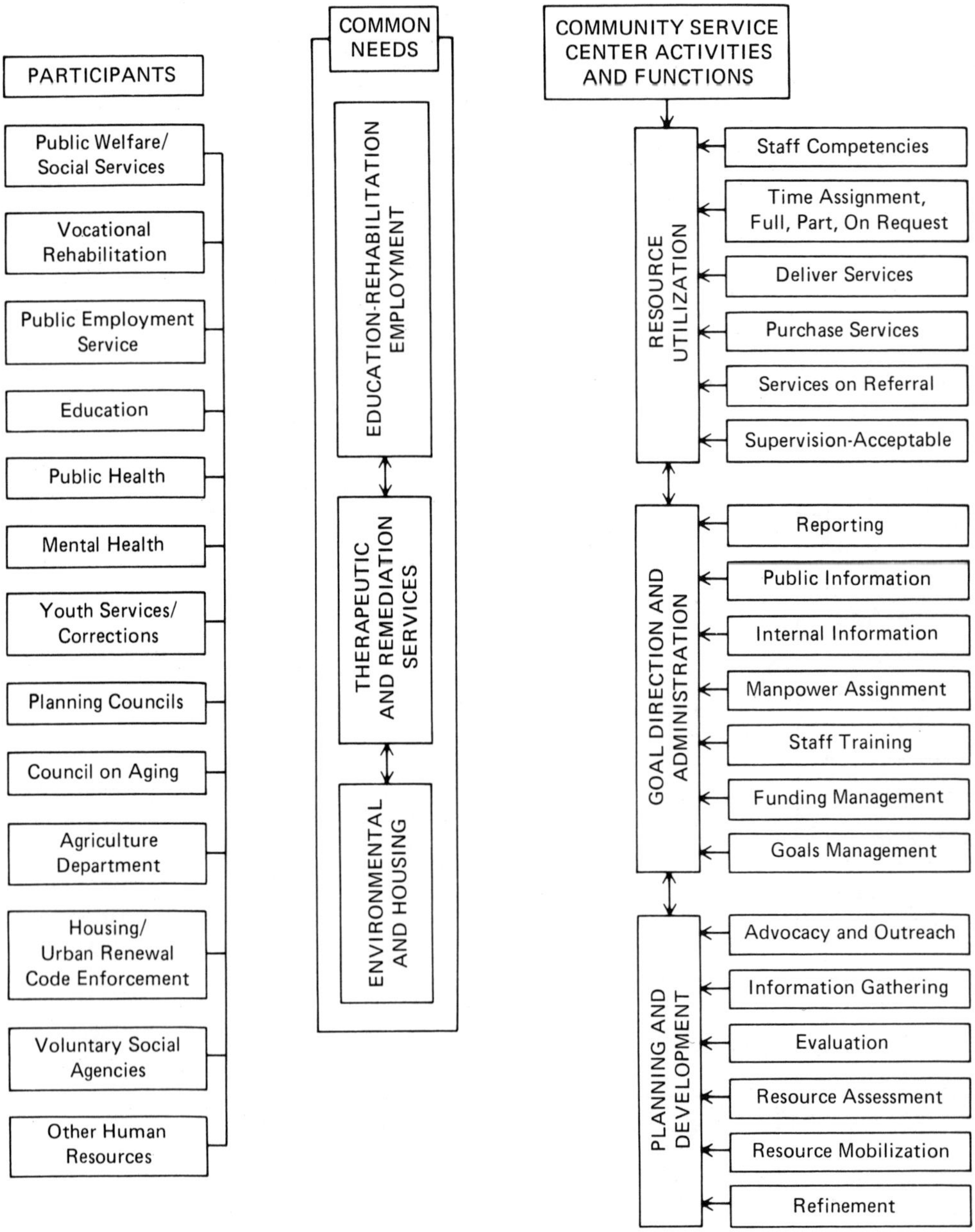

considerable time; for example, information can be entered once on a master file. Printouts can save great duplication of individual agency typing of forms. The Iowa experience was an attempt to gain interagency agreement on common data needs so as to speed the referral process.

Forms of Outreach

Beck (1969) has proposed the concept of the community service center (CSC) as a response to problems faced by consumers. Beck describes the CSC as a life consultation service which functions as a central point for information and referral for both consumer and the provider of services. The CSC can be a special categorical service for the mentally retarded or include the developmentally disabled. It can be a generic service. The Simonds report tends to favor the generic, with an avowed commitment to serve the retarded. Within a generic facility, advisors or specialists could be employed for unique situations.

It should be noted that the CSC arrangement does not imply one physical facility. The services could be dispersed, with an overall administrative structure. The dispersed arrangement would serve as a service broker, directing and coordinating the elements of diagnosis and treatment/management. In this role, follow-up and continuing contact with the parent and/or the person become the critical focus of the CSC. The direct service would be located elsewhere.

Rydell (1972) described a program called a follow-along service (FAS). The FAS is intended to extend a level of continuing supervision, consultation, and coordination of service to the retarded person and the family. The intent of the program is to structure a system of service delivery. Too often, Rydell noted, this function is left to the family, since agencies may feel little responsibility to contact one another. Using Developmental Disability funds, workers were employed outside and independent of any one particular agency and were thus able to function beyond agency limitations and impositions on behalf of the person and the family.

Brody, Esslinger, Casselman, McGlinchey, and Mitala (1975) offer one example of outreach by a staff. In their project, forty-eight severely retarded males in a cottage setting were identified as being in a state of near custodial care. A staff of five specialists developed an itinerant visiting team (IVT). The IVT had the mobility to move on site to demonstrate training procedures directly. As a result the team was able to decrease the need for custodial care in resident behavior. Subsequently, supervisory personnel became motivated and inspired to maintain the practices of the IVT. This concept can also be extended to the home to assist parents.

Perske and Marquis (1973) have identified the concept of the "live-in-friend" as a means of adult transition from institution to community life. The retarded persons had full-time jobs during the day and shared an apartment with a normal person who volunteered to serve in a supporting role. These volunteers were supervised by the community mental retardation agency. The retarded person was helped to function as an adult and assisted in dealing with everyday expressions such as "Come over sometime!" They needed to know that such expressions were not a literal invitation. Learning to shop was an instructional activity. A principal finding was that transition is not hampered by retardation but by inexperience in community living. Another key finding was that lay people can be helpful and derive pride from the accomplishments of their companions.

THE ARC MOVEMENT

In 1950, the National Association for Retarded Citizens (formerly Children), was formed. The NARC functions at national, state, and local chapter levels. It is a grass-roots movement to serve as an advocate for the retarded person. At national levels, public awareness has been a particular achievement. The NARC has been involved in research, job training, commendation of friends, and information dissemination through its official publication, *Mental Retardation News*. At national and state levels, another activity has been legislation and, more recently, litigation regarding civil rights and rights to services.

Evolutionary Nature of ARC

Wolfensberger (1973) has traced the three evolutionary stages of an ARC, which describe both historical and psychological processes.

In the first stage, younger parents organize to sponsor education programs not available to their children. As membership increases, there is the gradual recognition that a broader range of services is required. The parents experience four stages of growth: a self-centered concern; concern for the child, the spouse, and the family; a growing concern for all the retarded and their families; and the concern for all the handicapped and for human services in general. This period is also characterized by private sources of funding and use of private facilities such as churches and abandoned schools.

The second stage describes challenges and problems. The principal characteristic of this stage is the availability and use of public tax funds. One option is the use of public funds but continuation of program operation. The second option is to turn over the operation of the program to a public agency. Wolfensberger notes that the acceptance of public funds may be a short-range gain but a long-term loss; dependence on public funds creates both a bureaucracy to be maintained and a loss of independence to challenge policy. Conversely, when the struggle for services culminates in, for example, a public school system operating the school program, members feel a loss of mission. Membership may decline. The sense of zeal may be replaced by confusion and groping for make-do projects.

Stage three describes the demanding role of change agent. The change agent is obliged to monitor existing programs to ensure that agencies are adaptable to new knowledges and needs. Another responsibility involves safeguards for the retarded person, including: evaluation of quality of services, instituting grievance procedures within agencies, sustaining systematic membership education, and encouraging genuine integration between the membership and mentally retarded persons.

Wolfensberger concludes with an emphasis upon the self-renewal of mission, the change agent status, and the maintenance and encouragement of the retarded person's dignity. This emphasis is upon citizen advocacy. (Because of its magnitude and implications, the advocate relationship is discussed more fully in chapter 12.)

Outreach to Minority Groups

As an expression of its own third stage of development, the NARC has organized a Committee on Poverty and Mental Retardation. This committee has noted that you don't have to be poor to have a retarded child, but that poverty gives you a good head start. The NARC (1973) isolates the following factors of poverty for action:

1. *Malnutrition.* Even a proper diet in later life won't always reverse brain damage acquired in early critical periods of development.
2. *Poor medical care.* Lack of care and the resources to carry out instruction contributes to high rates of premature births.
3. *Cultural deprivation.* With basic survival as the goal, there may not be the resources and time left for stimulation.
4. *Lead poisoning.* Children from eighteen months to five years are vulnerable to this toxic substance in paints. Flaking paints are ingested and are dangerous.
5. *Health hazards.* The combined hazards of substandard housing and neighborhoods produce inadequate heating, shelter, water, and toilet facilities, which produce a high rate of infectious diseases.
6. *Isolation.* Families in low-income areas are often cut off from services, which are usually located outside of the area. Another result can be that families develop a sense of mistrust and often lack an effective voice to change the system.

The NARC Poverty and Mental Retardation Committee (1973) identified $4,200 per year for a family of four as a poverty line in 1973. (This figure is, of course, considerably higher now.) This was the upper limit. This means $350 per month for all expenses, including rent. The committee estimated that the "typical" welfare family of a mother and three children receives $115.78 per month. (This figure does not rise as fast as the poverty line.) This committee report outlines an action program that emphasizes demonstration in deed, not words, a message of commitment. The guidelines for involvement suggested by the committee are: cooperate, don't patronize; assist, don't demand; help, don't give; ask, don't tell; and show, don't say. The committee also suggested the following in dealing with low-income families:

1. The chapter must want to include members and recognize a different style of contribution.

2. Welcome both new families and low-income families at the same time to diffuse awkwardness. As much as possible, make the orientation a one-to-one, face-to-face process.

3. Give families time to adjust to "by-laws," committees, and the parliamentary system.

4. Transportation and babysitting will be problems. Frequently children will be brought to meetings. Car pools and pick-up services will be helpful. Planned activities for children can be helpful as well.

5. People respond to people. Make sure persons are greeted at meetings. Home visits may be helpful and encouraging. Language, especially among the Spanish-speaking, may be a problem. Some chapters have attempted to find interpreters.

SUMMING UP

This chapter has concentrated upon service elements designed to support or assist the family and/or the retarded person. The discussion of these services was viewed as consistent with concepts of service quality and need presented in the preceding chapter. Examples of special merit and proven worth were cited.

Service Management

1. This service element includes the prevention of service neglect as well as the consequences of excessive delay of services.

2. The review of literature cited suggests that identification and accurate routing are essentials for this service. Information appears a prime element.

3. Parents may be accused of guilt, denial, resisting advice, thwarting placement, and shopping behavior. A review of the literature suggests that these reactions may be the result of the behavior and practices of agencies.

4. Involvement of parents is a key element. Examples were cited as helpful illustrations.

5. The concept of the service manager was advanced as a positive solution. Examples of follow-along and service teams indicated the outreach nature of this service. The concept of the community service center was also discussed.

6. A major implication from the research literature is that a label is harmful when no helpful consequence follows. Quality of service may create a favorable response to special placements for both person and parent.

Residential Services

1. The residential facility as a regional mental retardation center was discussed. The RMRC should *not* be remote from the community but serve as a community resource and asset.

2. A status report of residential facilities was given. Size and years of operation are important variables in perception and discharge of mission.

3. Community alternatives for residential care were identified. The RMRC concept implies eventual community living. A sampling of community experiences from across the country was cited to suggest the variety of possible alternatives, including the supervised or sheltered apartment.

4. Retarded persons are being considered for adoption by families. This is perhaps the most dramatic evidence of public acceptance and understanding.

5. The concept of respite care was discussed and illustrated. This service element is essential to the preservation of the natural family's confidence in its ability to nurture their retarded child.

6. One notes that there seem to be more rewards and services (especially respite and intervention) for foster and adoptive families than for the natural family. If the family unit is to be encouraged to maintain the child, it would appear reasonable to extend the same level of help and support to the natural family as well.

Guardianship

1. The concept of the retarded person as a legal person was identified. This concept was presented as a logical outcome of the legal perspective presented in chapter 2. Special attention was given to the criminal justice system as well as to the concept of truth in placement.

2. Guardianship was discussed. Examples of enlightened guardianship laws were cited. "Enlightened" applies to a system that encourages independence of action.

3. Guidelines for using both public and private resources were identified. NARC guidelines were also presented. The need for expert advice was stressed, given the variety among the states as well as continuing revisions of federal programs.

Extended Learnings

Two elements of extended learnings were presented. Recreation was identified as a significant element beyond a mere emphasis upon leisure. Religious nurture was also discussed for its contributions to the person, the family, the community, and those involved in it.

ARC Movement

1. The ARC movement was discussed as both resource and forum. Not all ARC units are alike, because each unit will be in different stages of evolution.

2. The mission of the NARC and its local units to reach out to minority group families was discussed and examples of helpful approaches were cited.

3. The ARC movement represents an active partnership among parents and friends of the retarded. This movement has demonstrated that social action is no idle slogan. This will be especially true as each unit evolves into a change agent status.

ON LOCATION

This selection is included for several reasons. As preserved by Lowell (1957), this selection reminds the reader that siblings of retarded persons have needs as do the parents and the retarded person. It also pinpoints the concerns of the family for the future. Finally, the selection illustrates the power of the family to nurture.

Stairway to a Star

Johnny is fifteen. His sister Jane is eleven and mentally retarded. The other day I made an appointment with Johnny. I picked him up in my car, told him about *Span* [a publication of the then Michigan Association for Retarded Children] and asked if he would help me write about some of the problems of being the brother of a retarded child. He looked at me with a sort of amused suspicion and said, "Most of all, I think I get tired of people thinking I have a problem."

"You mean you don't think having a sister like Jane is a problem?" I asked.

"Sure it's a problem," said Johnny. "But then, all the kids I know have problems. My friend Bill has a brother who gets asthma. Jim has an older sister who's real bossy. And Barry worries because his face is broken out. I've got a mentally retarded sister. So what? I can't change it and neither can Mom or Dad, so why go on about it?"

This interview was not proceeding according to plan and I was silent. I think Johnny felt sorry for me, for he went on: "You see, people worry too much about Jane and me. My parents get all full of understanding and stuff because they think everything happens because Jane is retarded. It isn't that way at all. Sometimes Jane gets in my hair and I get mad and yell at her. She gets mad at me, too, and boy can she yell!

Well, what I mean is, all the kids I know get in fights with their brothers and sisters, but their parents don't make a production out of it."

"Do you and Jane do anything together except fight?" I asked.

Johnny grinned. "Sure," he said. "Jane's fun, and she's kind of restful. She doesn't ask you how you feel about stuff, and she thinks everything I do is wonderful. And sometimes I like to play with kid stuff like the little cars I used to be so crazy about. I gave 'em all to Jane, and now I play with her and everybody says how good I am to my sister, but sometimes it's just that I like to fool around with the little cars."

"No real worries, then?"

"Well," said Johnny. "I used to worry a lot about what made Jane retarded. I wondered if it had something to do with our family, and I didn't want to ask Mom and Dad in case it did. Well, I heard Mom tell somebody that Jane was brain-damaged, so I went to the library and read a lot of stuff. It took a long time, but I found out it didn't have anything to do with something you inherit. But I still think my family should have talked about it."

"You should have asked," I said.

"I guess so," said Johnny. "There's something else I wish they'd talk about. It's crazy, I guess, but I worry about what I'll do about Jane when we are grown up. My parents talk a lot about my going to college. Now, Dad doesn't make a lot of money. What I want is for them to take care of Jane so that I won't have to worry about her, and I'll manage for myself. With summer jobs, I'd get along. I don't mean I wouldn't help Jane if she needed it, but if the college money could send her to a special school or help her get started somewhere, I'd rather they used it that way. But when I talk about it, Dad just says, 'It will work out.' "

"I think maybe it will," I said.

Johnny smiled. "Sure," he said. "I guess you're right and Jane will be all right, too. Sometimes she surprises us. She's always been afraid of stairs. When she was little, we used to carry her up and down, and when she got bigger, one of us always held her hand. Well, last Christmas, we hung a big glittery star at the top of the stairs. We didn't do it for any reason. It just looked pretty there. Jane was crazy about it, and one day she just kept looking at that star and walked right upstairs, all by herself. When she got to the top, she just sat there under the star and looked down on us. I think she felt about nine feet tall."

I thanked Johnny and let him out of the car at the foot of the hill near his house. He waved and I sat watching him for a moment, a slim awkward figure climbing upward through the dusk. And suddenly I saw a long stairway with a sure star at the top and Johnny, too, feeling nine feet tall.

REFERENCES

Anderson, K., and Garner, A. Mothers of Retarded Children: Satisfaction with Visits to Professional People. *Mental Retardation,* 1973, 11, 36.

Avallone, S., Aron, R., Starr, P., and Breetz, S. How Therapists Assign Families to Treatment. *American Journal of Orthopsychiatry,* 1973, 43, 767–773.

Beck, H. *The Advantages of a Multi-Purpose Clinic for the Mentally Retarded.* Distributed by the National Association for Retarded Citizens, Arlington, Texas, 1969. Publication number 5M-2-69.

Brockwell, C. *Challenge and Opportunity for the Churches.* Columbia, South Carolina: Governor's Interagency Council on Mental Retardation, 1963.

Brody, J., Esslinger, S., Casselman, G., McGlinchey, M., and Mitala, R. The Itinerant Visiting Team: Variations on a Familiar Concept. *Mental Retardation,* 1975, 13, 38–42.

Burchenal, A. W. An Old Concept — A New Application: the Extended Family Concept Applied to the Provision of Comprehensive Services to the Mentally Retarded. *Mental Retardation,* 1973, 11, 14–17.

Burton, T. Mental Health Clinic Services to the Retarded. *Mental Retardation,* 1971, 9, 38–40.

Cleland, C., Powell, H., and Talkington, L. Death of the Profoundly Retarded. *Mental Retardation,* 1971, 9, 36.

Cummings, S. Effect of the Child's Deficiency on the Mother: A Study of Mothers of Mentally Retarded, Chronically Ill, and Neurotic Children. *American Journal of Orthopsychiatry,* 1966, 36, 595–608.

Division on Mental Retardation. *We Are Concerned — Three Youth Programs in Mental Retardation.* Washington, D.C.: U.S. Government Printing Office, 1967.

Gath, A. The Mental Health of Siblings of Congenitally Abnormal Children. *Journal of Abnormal Psychology,* 1972, 13, 211–218.

Hersh, A. Changes in Family Functioning Following Placement of a Retarded Child. *Social Work,* 1970, 15, 93 102.

Human Relations Agency, State of California. *Lanterman Mental Retardation Services Act.* Sacramento, California: State of California, 1971.

Jaslow, R., Chatterton, R., and Sussman, R. A Method for Community Involvement in the Institution. *Mental Retardation,* 1974, 12, 40.

Jaslow, R., and Stehman, V. *The Decision to Commit.* Lansing: Michigan Department of Mental Health, 1966.

Justice, R. Problems Reported by Parents of Mentally Retarded Children — Who Helps? *American Journal of Mental Deficiency,* 1971, 75, 685–691.

Keim, W. Shopping Parents: Parent Problem or Professional Problem. *Mental Retardation,* 1971, 9, 6.

Kemper, B. A Complete Continuum of Services. *Mental Retardation News,* 1973, 22, 8–9.

Kirkland, M. *Institutions for the Retarded: Their Place in the Continuum of Services.* Distributed by the NARC, Arlington, Texas. Publication number 5M-2-69, 1969, 1500-10-74.

Krishef, C. H. State Laws on Marriage and Sterilization of the Mentally Retarded. *Mental Retardation,* 1972, 10, 36–38.

Lowell, R. Stairway to a Star. *Span,* 1957, 1, 8–9.

Marb, R. L., Friel, C. M., Eissler, V. The Adult MR in the Criminal Justice System. *Mental Retardation,* 1975, 13, 21–25.

Menolascino, L. J. The Mentally Retarded Offender. *Mental Retardation,* 1974, 12, 7–11.

Meyen, E. *Computer Science Applied to the Improvement of Services for the Mentally Retarded Through Inter-Agency Participation.* Des Moines: Definitions Committee of Iowa's Comprehensive Plan to Combat Mental Retardation, 1965.

Mental Retardation News, Former Boy Scout's First Aid Saves a Life, 1973, 22, 4.

Michigan Association for Retarded Citizens. Guide for Parents of Retarded Citizens on 1975 Income Tax. *Focus,* January 1975, 1–7.

Miller, M. E. The Institutional Chaplain. *Mental Retardation,* 1972, 10, 41–42.

Montanari, A., and Toussing, P. Helping Troubled Children in a Strained Economy. *Exceptional Children,* 1973, 39, 559–563.

NARC. From Pennsylvania to California — Group Homes Are on the Rise. *Mental Retardation News,* 1973, 22, 4–5.

NARC Insurance Committee. *How to Provide for Their Future.* Arlington, Texas: NARC, 1974.

NARC Poverty and Mental Retardation Committee. *Plan for Everyone.* Arlington, Texas: NARC, 1973.

NARC Residential Services Committee. *Handbook for Residential Committees.* Arlington, Texas: NARC, 1971.

NARC. *You Don't Have to Be Poor to Have a Retarded Child . . . Poverty Just Gives You a Good Head Start.* Arlington, Texas: NARC, 1973.

Ogg, Elizabeth. *Securing the Legal Rights of Retarded Persons.* New York: Public Affairs Committee, Inc., 1973.

Paige, M. *Respite Care for the Retarded: An Interval of Relief for Families.* Washington, D.C.: U.S. Government Printing Office, 1971.

Perske, R., and Marquis, J. Learning to Live in an Apartment. *Mental Retardation,* 1973, 11, 18–19.

Petersen, S. *Retarded Children: God's Children.* Philadelphia: Westminster Press, 1960.

President's Committee on Mental Retardation. Residential Services for the Mentally Retarded — An Action Policy Proposal. Washington, D.C.: U.S. Government Printing Office, 1970.

Pumphrey, M., Goodman, M., Kidd, J., and Peters, E. Participation of Retarded Children in Regular Recreational Activities at a Community Center. *Exceptional Children,* 1970, 36, 453–458.

Rodriguez, J., and Lombardi, T. P. Legal Implications of Parental Prerogatives for Special Class Placement of the MR. *Mental Retardation,* 1973, 11, 29–31.

Rydell, C. A Follow-Along Service for the MR. *Mental Retardation,* 1972, 10, 12–14.

Scheerenberger, R. C. A Model for Deinstitutionalization. *Mental Retardation,* 1974, 12, 3–7.

Shapiro, H. Jewish Religious Education for Retarded Children. *Mental Retardation,* 1964, 2, 213–216.

Sigurdson, W., and Evangelakes, M. A Five Year Report on the Services of the Child Study Unit of the Kansas Neurological Institute. *Mental Retardation,* 1968, 22–27.

Simonds, S. *Building the Community Service Center.* Washington, D.C.: Community Services Administration, Social and Rehabilitation Services, U.S. Dept. of Health, Education, and Welfare, 1970.

Singer, S. Questionnaire Reveals Inconsistencies. *The Centerline,* 1976, Winter, 5–6.

Singstock, W., and Stein, J. Recreation for the Mentally Retarded: A Summary of Major Activities. *Exceptional Children,* 1967, 33, 491–497.

Skelton, M. Areas of Parent Concern about Mental Retardation. *Mental Retardation,* 1972, 10, 38–41.

Social Security Administration. *A Guide to Supplemental Security Benefits.* Washington,

D.C.: U.S. Dept. of Health, Education and Welfare, 1975.

Social Security Administration. *Social Security Information for Young Families.* Washington, D.C.: U.S. Dept. of Health, Education and Welfare, 1974.

Soeffing, M. Families for Handicapped Children: Foster and Adoptive Placement Programs. *Exceptional Children,* 1975, 41, 537–543.

Spears, R. *The Unused Swing: A Report on Recreation for the Mentally Retarded in South Carolina.* Columbia, South Carolina: Governor's Interagency Council on Mental Retardation Planning, 1967.

Stone, N. Family Factors in Willingness to Place Their Mongoloid Child. *American Journal of Mental Deficiency,* 1967, 72, 16–20.

Student Council for Exceptional Children. *An Opportunity for Professional Development.* Reston, Virginia: Council for Exceptional Children, 1975.

Theodore, Sister Mary. *The Retarded Child in Touch with God.* Boston: The Daughters of St. Paul, 1966.

Turnbull, H. R., and Turnbull, A. P. Deinstitutionalization and the Law. *Mental Retardation,* 1975, 13, 14–20.

United Cerebral Palsy Associations, Inc. *The Cerebral Palsy Monitor Program.* New York: U.C.P.A., 1959.

Vaughan, R. W. Community, Courts, and Conditions of Special Education Today: Why? *Mental Retardation,* 1973, 11, 43–46.

Witt, P. A. Historical Sketch of Recreation for the Mentally Retarded (1920–1968). *Mental Retardation,* 1971, 9, 50–53.

Wolfensberger, W. The Three Stages in the Evolution of Voluntary Associations for Retarded Persons. *Mental Retardation News,* 1973, 22, 2.

Wolfensberger, W. Will There Always Be an Institution? I. The Impact of Epidemiological Trends. *Mental Retardation,* 1971, 9, 14–20.

Woods, M. L. Development of a Pay for Recreation in a Token Economy. *Mental Retardation,* 1971, 9, 54–57.

YOUTH-ARC. *Operations Handbook.* Arlington, Texas: NARC, 1969.

Zuk, G. The Cultural Dilemma and Spiritual Crisis of the Family with a Handicapped Child. *Exceptional Children,* 1962, 28, 405–408.

10

Responsive Environments

SYNOPSIS

Certain environments facilitate the optimum development of the retarded person. Responsiveness is the interaction between the retarded person's need for maximized autonomy and the helping adult's capacity for acceptance. The ideal of a responsive environment implies the responsibility to deliver it.

Three particular environments are explored in this chapter: residence, schools, and job. A model for the design of a responsive environment is presented. Elements include assessment and the use of behavioral objectives. This approach, which is not unique, balances intra-individual variations against inter-individual ones. Awareness of these variations has implications for accountability.

This chapter is consistent with the provisions of the Individualized Education Plan (IEP) as prescribed by PL 94–142, the Education for All Handicapped Children Act. (See also chapter 14 for a discussion of PL 94–142.) The IEP concept, according to Cole and Dunn (1977), codifies the essentials of responsive services. These authors pointed out that the IEP provision provides encouragement, financial support, and legal sanction to those practitioners already engaged in responsive programming. MacMillan et al. (1977) noted that PL 94–142's IEP concept can provide a frame of reference for decision making regarding: assessment and testing (e.g. nondiscriminatory); goal setting (e.g. in performance criteria); parent and client involvement; selection of program (e.g. use of the least restrictive environment); and emphasis upon the person's *right* to service.

The chapter presents dimensions of accountability. The National Advisory Committee on the Handicapped (NACH) (1977) has identified accountability as an essential element of the IEP provision. Accountability is approached as a *shared* process which exists at various levels of service delivery. This view is consistent with the NACH presentation. Thus, accountability is beyond the pretesting versus posttesting of persons served by a program.

The IEP concept and its associated emphasis upon accountability could be of interest to other practitioners as well as educators. The validity of the concept could be applied to other settings as well. The NACH has noted that the IEP is valid because it represents sound practices derived from research and experience, not because PL 94–142 proclaims its validity.

This chapter extends the content of the discussion of residential services (chapter 9). It also serves as a preface to the subsequent chapter on educational and vocational services (chapter 11). The design and delivery of responsive environments can implement the promise of the IEP process.

OBJECTIVES

ATTITUDES

1. To develop a sense of responsibility for the implementation of a responsive environment.
2. To seek out additional information regarding positive examples of responsive environments.
3. To seek out additional information regarding procedures of implementation.
4. To approach legal and public policy matters in a spirit of constructive open-mindedness.

UNDERSTANDINGS

1. To describe the elements of performance analysis.
2. To describe the elements of a task analysis.
3. To define the elements of a behavior objective.
4. To program one's own work in a manner consistent with public law and policy.

SKILLS

1. To adopt a systematic approach to the design of a responsive environment.
2. To recognize a performance objective.
3. To apply evaluative procedures for creation of a responsive environment.
4. To compare and contrast types of assessment to the creation of a responsive environment.
5. To design and implement an "individual plan," educational or personal, for individual retarded persons.

DIMENSIONS

Directions

Ross (1964) has proposed a model that balances the needs of children/adolescents and the behaviors of significant adults (figure 10–1). The Ross model defines two

Figure 10–1 *A Model Depicting Responsive and Nonresponsive Environments*

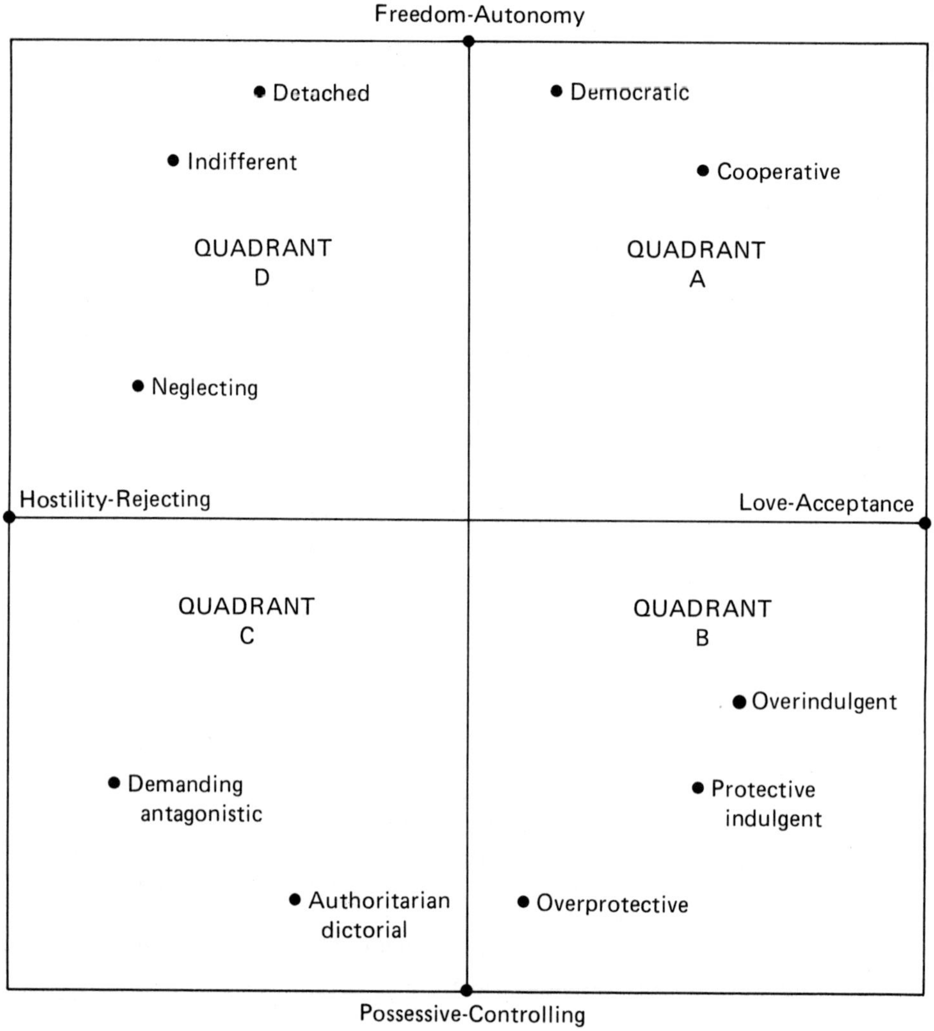

dimensions. The Love-Acceptance versus Hostility-Rejecting dimensions identify the *emotive* reactions of the adult, while the Autonomy-Freedom versus Controlling-Possessive dimensions describe the actual behavior of the adult. Consequently, four quadrants of environmental influences can be identified.

This model illustrates that the design of a responsive environment is directed toward freedom for the person's growth based upon an adult's acceptance. Normalization can be related to this model. Quadrant A suggests the target of normal, prudent risk to train for increased autonomy. Quadrant B defines overprotectiveness, which, though well intentioned, creates possessive restriction. Quadrants C and D describe patterns of potential abuse and neglect. These quadrants reflect a sense of direction and outcomes for services.

Physical Aspects

The Office of the Secretary of the Department of Transportation (1970) has prepared a helpful guide regarding the design of barrier-free environments for travel and recreation. Wolinsky and Walker (1975) have prepared an inventory for parents. Their procedure involves a checklist to survey the home. The involvement of handicapped persons to inspect plans and/or existing facilities for barriers has been described by Rusco (1974).

The Role of Structure

Nall (1970) defined structure in terms of benefits to the child and/or person. Structure serves to create a sense of limits, a sense of permanence, a sense of constancy, and a sense of dependability for performance. By specification of expectations based upon reasonable demands, Nall reasons, the learner is freed from distractors and inhibitors of action. It is the task of the sensitive practitioner to fade the structure as the learner's need for it fades. Structure is a point of origin, not an end point. Tawney, Middleton, and Cegelka (1973) have contrasted what a structured environment is *not* and what it *is* (table 10–1).

Characteristics of Responsive Environments

Martin (1972), and Garner (1976) have identified certain concepts associated with treatment and program environments. Their observations were advanced as guidelines for practice. A synthesis of these discussions suggests the following guidelines and qualities of a responsive environment:

1 The specification of goals (that which is desirable and/or of worth) requires clarification of the practitioner's intent.

Table 10–1 MISCONCEPTIONS REGARDING A STRUCTURED ENVIRONMENT

A Structured Environment	
IS NOT	*IS*
1. noncontingent	1. contingencies of positive, adversive, or ignoring to mold performance
2. M and Ms for everyone	2. the use of learned and unlearned incentives
3. punishment	3. an emphasis upon positives as first choice
4. expensive	4. the use of incentives readily available in the environment
5. inconsistent	5. consistent, dependable, and based upon observable behavior
6. a partial change in behavior	6. paying careful attention to what one does
7. restricted to deceleration of inappropriate behavior	7. equally concerned with the increase of positive behaviors
8. a dependency-producing technique	8. the eventual use of natural, learned, and/or secondary incentives to replace primary, tangible, and/or unlearned incentives
9. undocumented testimony	9. dependent upon accurate, precise records
10. a one-shot endeavor	10. a variety of projects to continue accelerate behavior
11. a teacher-dominated activity	11. the use of student involvement in goal setting, charting, etc.
12. always what you think you're doing	12. attention to maintaining target behavior without unwittingly maintaining undesirable behavior
13. restricted to one type of classroom or setting	13. applicable to the Cascade of Services (chapter 11)
14. restricted to social change	14. applicable to academic and vocational learnings
15. a highly complex system	15. acquired through practice

2 The adoption of goals for an environment requires involvement of consumers and providers of service.
3 Acquired goals should be of value to persons as well as to practitioners.
4 Structure should proceed from external controls to internal controls.
5 Emphasis should be upon active participation.
6 Employment and career education should be a priority concern.
7 Other disciplines should be engaged to enrich understanding of motivational and environmental influences.
8 Continued documentation and research should be encouraged.

Kidd (1974) has discussed the function of consequences as an index of responsiveness. His guidelines were that *positive* consequences should move from immediate, concrete, and external events to postponed, abstract, and internal events as the person progresses in age and complexity. *Neutral* responses, rather than negative consequences, would serve as a means to the extinguishing of behavior. *Adversive* consequences would favor noncorporal methods such as: time out, response cost, and failure to earn incentives. Corporal punishment would be stringently proscribed except as a last resort. For Kidd, the use of consequences is a *means* to a goal, not the goal itself.

Goals

Mason (1960) has examined a diversity of philosophical and research sources to identify persisting needs of persons. His discussion isolated four basic clusters of needs:

1. *Physical comfort*. These needs include sufficient nourishment, adequate dress, adequate shelter, and appropriate sexual expression. Attainment defines positive mental and physical health.

2. *Psychological stability*. This need describes security associated with work and income. It describes the need for feelings of significance and a sense of order and direction in one's life. It is the realization that life is immediate and that there is meaning to one's existence. Nonfulfillment of these aspirations produces bewilderment and sense of personal impotence. Also involved are needs for novelty, curiosity, and variation. Growth should be associated with a sense of adventure and opportunities for discovery of creativity. The alternatives would be a life of drudgery and monotony.

3. *Vocational adequacy*. This goal involves the acquisition of skills and knowledges necessary for work. The alternative is ignorance and psychological instability. A foundation for adequacy is said to be literacy skills.

4. *Social relationships*. This area relates to feelings of belonging, and a sense that one's efforts are appreciated by others. These feelings bring about a sense of

status and recognition. On an interpersonal level, one shares and is an active participant in life. The alternatives would be loneliness, indifference, and dominance by others.

The reader can see that "meeting the needs" is not a shallow slogan. If these needs of physical comfort, psychological stability, vocational adequacy, and social relationships are valid for the enrichment of human life, they would seem appropriate for retarded persons and a valid guide in defining the goals of a responsive environment.

DESIGN OF RESPONSIVE ENVIRONMENTS

A responsive environment possesses certain qualities. Raschke and Young (1976) have suggested clarity of intentions based on an individualized assessment, instructional/treatment, and evaluation. This section discusses the process of achieving clarity of purpose and individualized assessment. Subsequent sections will review implementation and dimension of evaluation. Evidence of design is defined, in the Raschke and Young sense, as program intent based upon knowledge of the person, not upon program convenience. The same would apply to assessment. The reader is advised to review the Stevens discussion in chapter 3 regarding the scope of diagnostic data.

Performance Objectives

One outcome of assessment is the formulation of objectives, sometimes labeled performance objectives, instructional objectives, behavioral objectives, etc. Regardless of the terminology, the intent and elements are the same. The Mager (1962) text is generally acknowledged to have popularized the process. It does not specify what objectives should be; it describes how to write them.

There are four intentions to objectives and three criteria by which to judge them. The intentions involve:

1. A method of *communication* of intentions. One "test" of an objective is that another person can convey to its author his or her expectations with accuracy.

2. A measure of *freedom* for the practitioner. Objectives convey the outcome, not implementation. In this sense, the practitioner is free to select a method so long as the objective is pursued.

3. A focus upon the *future*. Objectives focus upon what the person will be like. An objective states terminal behavior.

Objectives, as written statements, reflect three criteria. These criteria may be said to include conditions, act, and evaluation. The order of specifying the three elements is not as important as the scope. The specific elements are:

1. *Act* specifies what the person will be *doing*. Words that describe acts are preferred, such as *recite, select, discriminate, compare, list, identify, smile,* etc.

2. *Conditions* refers to the *circumstances* under which the act will be judged. These circumstances would include the materials to be used and the directions and/or prompts to be employed.

3. *Evaluation* refers to criteria for passing the objective so as to move to the next step. Criteria may be expressed in a variety of forms, such as percentages of rate of attainment, assembly, amount to be completed, etc.

Table 10–2 offers some examples of objectives. The three essentials are labeled to assist the reader in defining the language of the procedure.

Bloom, Hastings, and Madaus (1971), while commending the work of Mager, feel that preoccupation with objectives may result in the loss of long-range prescriptives. According to Bloom and his associates, goals are *general* statements of purpose

Table 10–2 EXAMPLES OF BEHAVIORAL OBJECTIVES

Given six nickels and six pennies and upon verbal direction of the teacher, "Please tell me the amount of money you have" (condition), the person will be able to say, "Thirty-six cents" (act and accuracy) (Frank, 1973).

Upon verbal direction of the teacher, "Please place the cards in alphabetical order" and when given individual flash cards with the words *stop, ask, diameter, name, boy, hat, purple,* and *vex* (condition), the person places the eight cards (act) in proper alphabetical order (evaluation) (Frank, 1973).

Given an empty aspirin bottle and ten pellets and the instruction, "First put three pellets in the bottle, then put four pellets in the bottle, and then three pellets in the bottle" (conditions), the student will respond by placing the pellets in the bottle (act) in the exact sequence of direction (evaluation) (Burke, 1975a).

Given three containers and twelve screws, five of similar size, four of smaller size, and three of larger size, upon the direction "Put the largest screws in one container, the smallest screws in another container" (condition), the person will select from among the screws (act) and put in two separate containers the three largest and the four smallest, leaving the five screws on the table with the third container empty (evaluation) (Burke, 1975a).

to excite the imagination and to influence policies. Specific statements enable practitioners to clearly define intention and the means to assess results. Thus, goals serve as an overall frame of reference to provide a context for specific objectives.

Assessment

Bloom and his associates identified two approaches to assessment: summative and formative. Summative involves interindividual differences of the person. This procedure is a comparison to other persons. It seeks to state the "what." Formative seeks to explain the "how." It is concerned with intraindividual differences. This procedure is more likely to use direct and systematic observation. Raschke and Young, among others, have noted a growing polarization between advocates of so-called norm-reference approaches and approaches of behavior analysis. These authors noted, in agreement with Bloom et al., that this polarization need not exist.

The literature of assessment relevant to the mentally retarded indicates that so-called norm-reference approaches — Wechsler Intelligence Scale for Children (WISC-R), Illinois Test of Psycholinguistic Abilities (ITPA) — can be compatible with criterion reference approaches.

The principles and procedures of an individualized assessment are usually associated with Mager (1970). Frequent references to the work occur in the literature of special education. These assessment elements are depicted in figure 10–2, which identifies assessment of discrepancy, values, attitude, environment, and skills as means to achieve an individualized statement of objectives.

Discrepancy Assessment

Discrepancy assessment involves recognizing a gap between the actual performance of the person and reasonable expectations. A gap exists if performance is either too much or too little. For example, acting-out behavior would be too much, and withdrawn behavior would be too little. At this level formal testing may be helpful to confirm existence as well as to specify exact dimensions.

Values Assessment

According to the Mager (1970) procedure, a value judgment is placed upon the discrepancy. The gap may be *important* to the person, parents, and/or practitioners, or a given gap may not be important, or the gap may be a low-priority problem in light of other problems. Thus, the value assessment judges the gap on a spectrum from important-high priority to nonimportant-low priority. Gaps are individual on a case-by-case situation. If the discrepancy is ultimately judged of a high priority, the procedure would continue.

Figure 10–2 *Elements of Individualized Assessment*

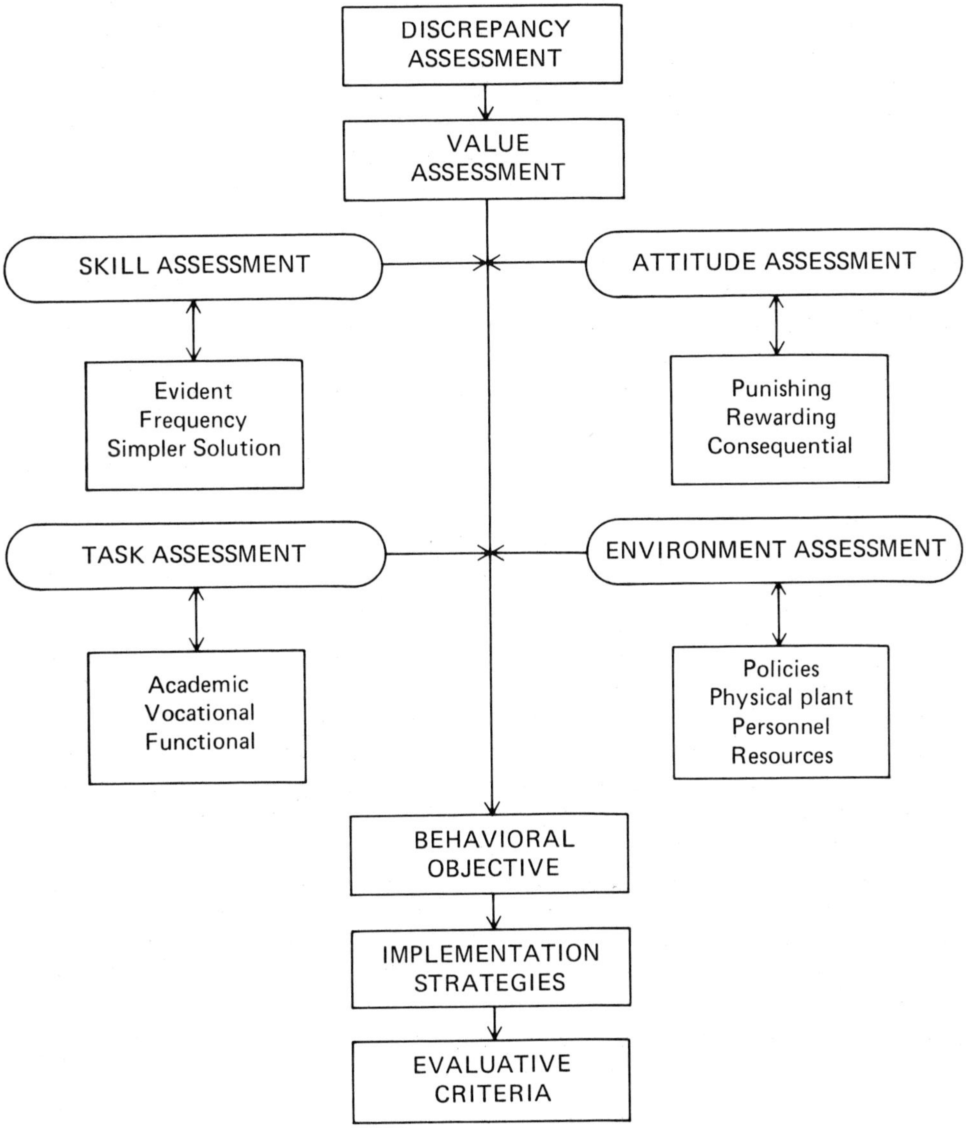

Attitude Assessment

Attitude assessment concentrates upon the person's reactions and/or past experience toward performance and performing. Mager (1970) suggested three essential inquiries, which concentrate upon the person's view of performance as punishing or nonconsequential, or nonperformance as rewarding. The practitioner may find that a discrepancy exists because performance has usually brought "extra" assignments for the person. Consequently, the person views doing as adversive. In certain instances, performance may fail to bring smiles, praise, or other acknowledgement. The person learns doing doesn't matter. Finally, consider the child among other children during a humid, hot day on a dusty playground. If the child soils herself or himself, he or she may be taken indoors, given a cool shower, and personal attention. Consequently, the child may learn that *not* being toilet-trained is a source of reward and being toilet-trained is punishing.

Skill Assessment

Skill assessment concentrates on abilities that may be present, but not evident because the skill has not been used sufficiently to stabilize it or the skill has been neglected through interfering experiences and/or attitudinal factors. A third possibility is that the skill is not required if a simpler solution is available. Loafers instead of laced shoes might be an example. Another example would be modification of job standard.

Assessment of the Environment

Environmental dimensions are variables, external to the person, which interfere with or inhibit performance. These external variables may discourage, distract, or diminish learning or contact with the learning-performance situation. According to Mager (1969), four dimensions of environment should be assessed.

1 *Practitioner* variables include adequate voice tones, use of developmentally appropriate activities, clarity of expectations, providing an appropriate model, promptness of feedback, and reflecting regard, respect, and interest in activities.
2 Variables in *instructional materials and devices* are clarity and appropriateness of visual and auditory elements, easy accessibility of materials, and relating of materials to goals.
3 *Physical environment* variables would be ample room size, adequate acoustics and lighting, and appropriate temperature and ventilation.
4 *Administrative rules or policies* variables can include inaccessible staff, discouraging use of materials, insistence that persons proceed at the

same rate, frequent interruptions of sessions by announcements or noise, not rewarding staff for achievement, initiative, and creativity, not rewarding successful practitioners differently than less effective ones, and ineffective monitoring of performance by administration.

Task assessment

If a least restrictive solution cannot be decided from attitude, environment, and/or skill assessment, the practitioner would proceed to task assessment. The literature does not endorse one approach, but rather reflects a variety of options depending upon focus. The focus options are: acquisition, specification, and evaluative.

Acquisition Focus

This focus is employed to identify particular points in the learning continuum. Burke (1975A and B), for example, concentrates on identification of the need for instructional prompts for the severely mentally retarded. These prompts were defined as visual or gesturing, physical (touching the person), demonstration (performing the act and requesting imitation) and physical (manipulation of the person through the act). In the Burke procedure, one attempts to specify which of these four prompts would be helpful.

Englemann (1969) offers another system of identification, which is oriented toward identifying the minimal essentials to be taught, identifying a necessary teaching sequence, and defining concepts for task mastery. The usefulness of his approach rests upon identifying a signal to the learner to perform, identifying the operations to be performed, assessing the complexity of directions required, and helping the learner to discriminate between when a response *does* apply and when it does *not* apply. The last two steps are especially critical so that a given skill does not become an isolated element.

Specification Focus

The scope and sequence of component elements necessary for task mastery may not be evident, available, or appropriate. Consequently, it may be necessary to develop a task analysis based upon observation to identify component elements. This approach, according to Mager and Beach (1967), involves direct observation of successful performers of the task. The procedure can be modified to compare beginners with veterans and/or efficient with inefficient performers. Observations are intended to isolate those events that define competence. These authors suggested *task listing* and *task detailing*. In task listing, these authors recommend identification of *all* of the behaviors necessary for performance. The function of task detailing is to describe what the person *does* (overt behaviors), describe what *is done* (criteria of success), and describe the sequence. Performance is defined in terms of the *person's* recognizing when to start and stop; selecting appropriate tools, cues, responses, etc.; safety; self-evaluation of actions; manipulation and coordination; and use of psychologically oriented behaviors of association, discrimination, recall, and choice. Consider this procedure applied to a typical task such as cleaning a chalk board. The resulting assessment could be:

1 Responds to request "Time to clean chalkboard" — *associative,* easy.
2 Locates source of water, sponge, and pail — *recall,* easy.
3 Erases board — *manipulation,* easy.
4 Fills pail and carries to board — *manipulation,* moderate to difficult without spillage.
5 Squeezes sponge of excess water — *manipulation* and *discrimination,* moderate.
6 Applies sponge evenly in up-and-down (or across) motions — *manipulation,* moderate.
7 Waits for drying to take place — *discrimination,* easy.
8 Checks quality of work (runs, streaks), and repeats process if necessary — *discrimination,* moderate to difficult.
9 Returns materials to appropriate storage — *recall,* easy to moderate.

Evaluative Focus

Frank (1973) and Mager (1972) suggested a group procedure in which participants write on separate cards their perceptions of what would cause them to conclude that a task has been accomplished. (In this procedure, the participants are presumed to be expert and/or familiar with the activities of the goal.) Cards are sorted into component piles as duplications are found. The *end product* is a statement of those behaviors judged essential for performance. A project reported by Cascapo (1972) illustrates this form of task analysis. The target was elimination of inappropriate classroom behaviors. The use of this cooperative procedure helped staff define their meanings of appropriate versus inappropriate behavior.

THE INDIVIDUALIZED EDUCATION PLAN

PL 94–142 has created a sense of urgency regarding the design of responsive environments. This federal law, which took effect in October 1977, has been described by Abeson and Zettel (1977) as a quiet revolution. Its most revolutionary provision and the keystone of the act is the Individualized Educational Plan (IEP). The IEP is the vehicle for responsive services in areas such as the rights to free education, nondiscriminatory testing, appropriate (least restrictive) alternative, and due process, including meaningful involvement of parents.

The IEP is also the mechanism for delivery of services to early childhood learners (ages three to eight). Fulfilling the vocational preparation mandate of PL 94–142 as well as provisions for career education involves another population between eighteen and twenty-one. Abeson and Zettel also noted that adapted physical education is also required. IEP does not imply that special services are restrictive, as such; the person's placement must be related to need, not the convenience of the service system.

The IEP involves both a written document, a process, and tasks for implementation.

The IEP as Written Document

The Council for Exceptional Children (CEC) (1976) cited four elements of the IEP as a *written* document. These elements were said to include: a statement of present educational functioning, a statement of goals, including short-term objectives, a listing of specific educational services, *including* the extent to which the child will be able to participate in the least restrictive educational alternative, and a projected time line. The time line involves specification of dates for: the initiation of the plan, the duration of services, the scheduling of evaluation procedures, and the scheduling at least annually of assessment of attainment objectives to be accomplished.

The criteria of a performance objective and assessment by both formative and summative procedures appears consistent with the National Advisory Committee on the Handicapped (1977) guidelines regarding nondiscriminatory testing and elements one and two of the CEC analysis. The discussion of educational alternatives in chapter 11 identifies alternatives for program selection. The alternatives identified for vocational and residential services provide a frame of reference for application of the least restrictive alternative principle.

The NACH (1977) has advocated that the listing of services should include *both* currently available resources and helpful resources *not* available. This latter listing could provide data and documentation for future resources.

The IEP as Process

As a written document, the IEP is the product of a cooperative process. According to the NACH (1977) the written plan is produced by a representative of the school system (e.g. the person's teacher), a qualified specialist in special education, the person's parent or guardian, and, when appropriate, the person. This committee specifically noted that these persons should be understood as a *minimum* listing to conform to the letter of the law. They urged that interdisciplinary efforts (inclusion of those who can make a substantial contribution) lie well within the spirit of the law.

Both Cole and Dunn (1976) and the NACH (1977) affirm the intent of PL 94–142 to set forth minimum expectations. This was done to allow maximum flexibility of implementation by the local educational units.

Development of the four elements of the IEP is at local option to devise. The NACH did suggest, however, certain considerations for the written IEP.

1. assessment of the person's *present* physical, emotional, intellectual development, and learning strengths (chapter 5);
2. consideration of relevant medical, environmental, or cultural considerations (chapters 3 and 4);
3. recommendations regarding placement, educational materials, and program procedures (chapter 11);
4. statement of the person's educational needs expressed as goals and specific objectives (see preceding discussion of design);
5. establishment of time frames for accomplishment, and
6. defining of responsibilities of members of the IEP team.

Implementation of the IEP

Cole and Dunn (1977) related the experience of Ohio in the organization of school services to comply with the spirit and letter of the IEP intent of PL 94–142. Their survey of local school district practices identified the following cluster of tasks for implementation:

1. *Involvement*. The school superintendent should establish an IEP task force that includes practitioners, consumers of services, and leaders. The process of involvement duplicates that regarding social action tactics described in chapter 8. The task force was strongly urged to designate an accountable person to supervise conformity to IEP mandates. A brochure could be helpful in orientation purposes.

2. *Information gathering*. Participants should be encouraged to attend conferences devoted to implementation of PL 94–142 and IEP provisions. Information should be sought from federal and state agencies as well as from advocate agencies such as the Council for Exceptional Children, the American Association on Mental Deficiency, and the National Association for Retarded Citizens. Visits to model school districts (as identified by state agencies) was also encouraged.

3. *Curriculum development*. Goals of instruction should be defined (chapter 11). These goals should then be translated into sequenced performance objectives which can be placed into an "objectives bank." Curriculum resources and materials

should be inventoried and placed in a central file. A related task would be to examine those texts used by both normal and handicapped learners. The intent would be to adapt text materials into shorter versions for the handicapped learner, supplemented by audiovisual materials.

4. *Inservice tasks.* The due process task force should receive intensive orientation to their tasks. Simulation of IEP procedures should precede the initiation of the process to allow for familiarization with role expectations. There should also be workshops to acquaint participants with assessment procedures, educational approaches, individualization procedures (see the discussion on the IGE movement which follows), and accountability methods.

5. *Reducing obstacles.* The Ohio experience suggested resistance to the IEP reflects neither a lack of sympathy to the spirit of the IEP concept nor a philosophic objection to a federal mandate imposed upon the states. Cole and Dunn recognized the gap between the initiation data of October 1, 1977 and availability of sufficient federal funding. It is estimated that it will require a five-year phase-in for federal appropriations. In the interval, the states and school districts will need to devise their own fiscal resources. Cole and Dunn have warned that the failure to comply with PL 94–142, including the IEP provision, places the district at risk of losing *all* Health, Education, and Welfare funding, not just those funds associated with PL 94–142. Cole and Dunn estimated that the IEP provision could save money for school districts in the more efficient use of resources. Another potential obstacle is the reaction of parents of normal children. These parents possibly will demand the equivalent of an IEP for their normal children. These authors suggested that individualization processes be extended to all children.

6. *Compliance.* Implementation of PL 94–142 and the IEP would be the high-priority goal for the future according to Cole and Dunn. (Dimensions of this implementation are considered in chapter 14.) Past experience affirms that vigilance is required to maintain the promise of legislation. Abeson and Zettel (1977) identified such vigilance as a special task for advocacy.

EDUCATIONAL ENVIRONMENTS

This is the first of three sections to offer illustrations and trends in implementation of responsive environments. One senses in the literature of both general and special education a common interest in individualization to match personal differences.

Historically, tracking systems based upon ability groupings originated in an effort to group with reference to a specific ability trait, usually measured intelligence. However, experience has led to a recognition that grouping by one trait may create greater variation in other developmental abilities. There has been a search within general and special education to identify alternatives to single-criterion groupings, including grouping by chronological age. This search has developed approaches of flexibility of staffing, grouping, instructional goals, and use of physical space. These variations have been termed open school, open classroom, alternative classrooms, schools without walls, street academies, free schools, and so forth. They do not specify curriculum or teaching method, but rather reflect certain beliefs regarding educational policy and practices and influences upon learning. The common term to express these beliefs is individually guided education (IGE). The point of commonality between special education and general education has been in cooperative efforts of mainstreaming, or inclusion of mildly retarded learners in alternatives to the self-contained classroom (chapter 11).

Sapp (1973) has offered an example of one school's use of an affirmative environment. This report detailed the operation of an *entire* school that has abandoned conventional grade levels for cross-age groupings. The staff was committed to insuring that each learner would receive tasks at his or her level based upon customized assessment, receive immediate and positive reinforcement based upon structuring tasks and unit teaching, and experience success with regular assignment of tasks within his or her capacity. These commitments are representative of the IGE model emerging in general education.

Gardner and Robinson (1974) and Robinson (1974) have presented one school's experience with inclusion of normal and exceptional learners which may serve to illustrate the use of the IGE concept. Both reports center around the experiences of staff and parents in transforming a typical school into an IGE-type school. The school had an enrollment of four hundred pupils plus seventy students certified as one of the following: orthopedic-multihandicapped, mildly mentally retarded, learning disabled, or hearing-impaired. The age range was from kindergarten through sixth grade. The eventual organizational pattern involved five units.

1. A primary unit was composed of 121 children between the ages of five through seven. An instructional team was composed of four teachers, one of whom was a certified teacher of the hearing impaired.

2. A middle unit was composed of 110 learners between the ages of seven through nine and four teachers. Two certified teachers of the hearing-impaired were available to this unit and to the upper unit.

3. An upper unit was composed of 106 children between the ages of nine and twelve, with four teachers. A certified teacher of the orthopedically impaired was assigned to all four units on a consultant basis.

4. A supportive services unit was composed of certified special education teachers, paraprofessionals, as well as physical, occupational, and physical therapists. This unit provided resource-room services for parts of the day and served as active consultant to other units.

5. A supportive help unit was composed of building personnel available within the school as well as school district specialists available to the building staff. Build-

ing personnel included art, music, and physical education teachers as well as library-media specialists. Teacher aides and parent volunteers were included in this grouping, as were custodial and secretarial staff. Out-of-school personnel were composed of personnel from school psychology, social work, English as a second language, and preprofessionals from various disciplines.

The four teachers of a given unit would be responsible for the learners but have a major responsibility for a subject area. Thus, preparations are fewer, so the teacher can concentrate on enrichment. This option of IGE enabled the specialization necessary to customize instruction. (In the typical self-contained classroom, the amount of different preparations for twenty-five to thirty students could defeat efforts to accommodate intraclassroom differences.) An interesting feature was that as the exceptional learners became introduced into units, the special educator became a part of the teaching team, teaching *both* normal and exceptional learners. The special educator would fade as the exceptional learner became incorporated.

Birch (1971) (1975) has examined the literature and inspected actual programs that included exceptional learners, including the mildly retarded, in regular classroom settings. The Birch documents identified ten characteristics of effective mainstreaming programs and seven pointers for planning, which are summarized in table 10–3 in adapted form. It would appear that the literature of the IGE movement could have application to special schools for the moderately and/or severely retarded. The elements of cross-variable groupings, instructor specialization, team teaching, customized assessment, etc. would possess certain merit.

Certain values and beliefs embedded in the Robinson and Birch documents are beyond mere technique. These include:

1. The teacher considers himself or herself a continuing learner in search of improved personal and professional competence.
2. There may be reasons for "failure," but no person should be considered a "failure."
3. It is unrealistic to ask all children at a given age, or in a given grade, to learn the same way or to do the same work in content areas.
4. Individualization does not seek a means of making all individuals alike, but it is a focus upon preserving personal uniqueness while personal improvement is carried on.
5. The right to quality education for children applies to the handicapped.
6. There must be readiness to cooperate with others and a willingness to participate in a team.
7. Parents have the right to be treated with respect.
8. Teaching styles must be flexible.
9. Social and personal development for learners are as valuable as academic skills.

Table 10–3 ELEMENTS AND POINTERS FOR EFFECTIVE MAINSTREAMING

Elements of Effective Programs	
	Subareas
Teacher Concerns	• classroom behavior of exceptional pupils • negative behavior of normal pupils • lack of professional preparation • negative reactions of adults • liability for accidents • special health problems • grading policies • family problems of children
Possible Solutions	• values clarification • inservice education • supportive and sensitive administration • emphasis on regular class placement • assessment and diagnosis a must • local autonomy for the local school • informed parents are helpful

Pointers for Planning	
Main Areas	*Subareas*
Curriculum	understanding the similarities between curricular goals for exceptional and normal learners degree of emphasis may vary
Methods of Teaching	need for continued experiment since structured methods and open methods have not been clearly "proven"; decision should be to specify the environment
Instructional Materials	emphasis is upon the logistics of ordering, sharing, and installing in advance
Organization of Physical Plant and Auxillary Services	emphasis is upon specifying what is to be taught and with what frequency and intensity as well as on evaluation methods; special needs for physical space adaptations and need for specialist must be considered
Community Resources	provisions for outreach to other helping agencies and to parents

Classroom Environments

Frank (1974) has described procedures for developing classroom *interest centers.* The interest center involves the use of materials, devices, games, and equipment that can be self-directed or used with a minimum of supervision. The utilization of the interest center involves prior diagnosis for prescription of activities to match goals to pupil readiness. This allows for a no-failure experience. As a classroom is organized into interest centers, pupils can be cycled through various centers to practice the teacher's instruction, enrich instruction, and refine needed skills. Obviously this arrangement can apply to groups as well as to individuals, assuming the practitioner can organize time, space, and materials.

Berkman (1974) has suggested the concept of the *activity center,* a procedure in which the classroom becomes a simulation environment. Thus, a high-school class can be transformed into an assembly-line operation to produce booster pins for the football team. An elementary schoolroom can become a store, with children exchanging roles of worker, manager, and customer.

Hansen (1973) has suggested *program slicing* as an approach to individualization. The procedure involves the use of standard, commercially available materials such as workbooks. Any given set of workbooks can be used, provided one's objectives for the series are consistent with the Mager criteria. Individual pages are examined in light of stated objectives to be cut and pasted. Thus, worksheets are formed consistent with one objective per page. The transformed pages can serve as diagnostic inventories, interest center materials, instructional activities, and/or as follow-up independent activities. Evaluation of the validity of the produced slices would be an index to pupil progress.

The concept of openness can also apply to areas of affect as well as to literary and vocational skills. Mersels (1974) described a procedure of individual contracting for considerate behavior. Billingsley and Smelser (1974) were interested in the same behavior, but they used a semicompetitive game to encourage its increase in children. The "teams" strove to demonstrate their behavioral awareness of consideration for one another.

Consumer Preferences

The preferences of parents of the moderately and severely retarded regarding school policies were investigated by Sellin and Gallery (table 10–4). Inspection of the responses suggests endorsement for involvement, general satisfaction with schools, and selectivity regarding sources of advice. Given the current emphasis upon parent involvement, it would seem appropriate to understand consumer reaction to program practices. The report did not allow parents to express preference as to reporting systems, only what they disliked. Ryan and Ryan (1973) have prepared a questionnaire for school districts to use to identify parent preferences.

Table 10–4 PARENT PRIORITIES FOR SCHOOL PRACTICES

School Practice	*Response*
1. Parents should have a say in the planning for their child.	SA
2. Professionals should listen to parent information about their child.	SA
3. Vocational planning should be begun while the child is in the primary grades.	SA
4. I would like to know my child's IQ.	SA
5. I think it is valuable to observe my child in the classroom.	SA
6. My child's report card should be like that used in the regular grades.	SD
7. My child should be present at parent-teacher conferences.	SD
8. I think my child should be compared to normal children of the same chronological age.	SD
9. Special education has done very little for my child.	SD
10. I think teachers ask too many personal questions.	SD
11. If parents do not attend parent-teacher conferences, the child should be terminated from school.	SD
12. Filling out questionnaires like this is a waste of time.	SD
13. I feel teachers are well informed about my child's conditions.	A
14. I think my child should be compared to other children of the same condition.	DK
15. The best source of advice is from a fellow parent.	DK
16. I prefer home visits to school conferences.	DK

SA = strongly agree
SD = strongly disagree
A = agree
DK = don't know

Grantham and Harris (1976) have described an application of the concept of problem ownership to accommodate consumer preferences in a school setting. Problems were seen as owned by staff, students, and administration as well as shared among them. Two outcomes were evident: the school could define *itself* as a cause of problems, and the principal's role could be more than that of a dispenser of punishments. Boyd and Bowers (1974) have described another use of problem ownership for staff and students. In this system, the principal is the pivot point. Problems referred for disposition must describe behaviors, not labels, define prior efforts, focus on why the referral was made, and recommend action. Based upon these data, the principal can design a plan for responsive action. Responsive action according to Dinkmeyer and Dinkmeyer (1976), strives to engage students in understanding logical consequences and in selecting alternatives. The former relates to helping students understand the effects of their actions (attention seeking, power, revenge, failure). The student is encouraged to become responsible for selection of a course of action to eliminate irresponsible actions.

VOCATIONAL ENVIRONMENTS

The concept of responsive environments can be extended to vocational preparation. This section covers both practice and process.

Career Education

Larkin (1975) has reviewed successful programs of career education at secondary levels. He noted that youth often lack exact knowledge for job choices and suggested that students should be informed regarding employment potential of occupations and the range of available occupations. Rumpf (1975) noted that information and practice of skills are required. Schools in the future must break out of the four walls and the nine-to-three schedule. Wuehle (1973) shared an example of a program emphasizing both information and practical opportunities. Among occupations encountered in this program were: radio announcing, electronic technology, meat cutting, produce management, sign painting, snowmobile repair, gas appliance repair, printing, and airport management. The school district has a demographic density of one student per mile and a half. Within a radius of forty miles there is no town of more than five thousand, and 70 percent of the land area of the district is state and federal forest — an unlikely setting for diversity of a program. The solution was to contract with local business and industry to provide the training site for an arranged fee. The costs averaged about the same as a conventional program but reflected more job placement after graduation.

Madlee (1973) has described a cluster approach beginning in kindergarten and extending through secondary levels. Clusters of instruction revolve around units that correlate skills and knowledge. For example, cooking classes for boys and girls include measurement concepts. Occupational units at early elementary units range from A (airport) to Z (zoo).

The integration of special education into career education is becoming increasingly evident. Some examples of responsiveness to employment needs would include:

1. A regular, district-wide high school can be modified. Adolescents, regardless of exceptionality, can be accommodated in a work-oriented setting (Colella, 1973).

2. A simulated work environment duplicating industrialized manufacture can be installed within a classroom. Punching a timeclock, learning about "breaks," and maintaining production levels on realistic tasks can be taught (Gray, 1973).

3. Rural areas can produce high-quality programs for retarded persons. The special educator and the guidance counselor can form the nucleus of a special team to engage community resources (Hayden, 1975).

4. Principles of behavior modification apply to employer and employee alike. Retarded persons can learn to use reinforcement principles to influence fellow employees and employers (Rosenberg, 1973).

5. Work-related concepts can be initiated at elementary levels. Emphasis can be placed upon work as dignified, fulfilling one's needs, having different rewards and satisfactions, getting along with others, fitting into the work of others, determining by where we live, and learning from watching others (Talagan, 1973).

6. Job-related concepts can be instituted at elementary levels. Emphasis would include that jobs are prepared for in school, require special training, are of many different types, produce goods or services, relate to families, and depend upon what we can do (Talagan, 1973).

7. Occupational information can be begun at early elementary levels. Choice can be influenced by interests, values, aptitudes, hobbies, information, and feelings of ability (Talagan, 1973).

8. Self-concept and occupational awareness can be taught at elementary levels. An experience-based approach involving observation of workers and reflection upon these experiences is stressed (Jackson and Peterson, 1973).

Vocational Rehabilitation-Habilitation

Kazden (1971) has reported on the involvement of clients in administration of incentives in a sheltered workshop setting. Target behaviors were verbal interaction and improved posture for moderately retarded persons. Tokens were used as incentives. In the Kazden procedure, the client passed out tokens to *other* clients for complimenting on posture and/or speaking. Thus, the client became a source of self-monitoring as well as demonstrated a growing capacity to engage in socially appropriate behavior.

The achievement of a responsive, vocation-oriented environment may require a rearrangement of practitioner values and orientation. Gold (1975), for example, has evolved the competence-deviance hypothesis. Persons may possess irremediable attributes that draw negative attention, such as physical disability, limited speech, etc. The Gold hypothesis, confirmed by his demonstration research, is that the more competent a person is, the more deviance will be tolerated. The Gold perspective implies a view of competence rather than an exclusive focus upon negative factors. Gold and Faur (1974) have advanced the "Train, Don't Test" principle. In essence, this approach suggests that the "test" of work ability is working. This requires deciding upon what should be done and finding a way to teach the objective. In the process of active involvement with the person, a great deal can be learned. Formal testing can be a barrier to formal opportunity. The Social Security Administration (1973) has described how benefits can be used to facilitate rehabilitation goals to minimize permanent dependence. These benefits are focused upon curbing unnecessary dependence upon others for support and maintenance.

Hemenway, Lemke, Hage, and Robertshaw (1972) reported an experiment to demonstrate the educational aspects of rehabilitation. The effort centered upon 200 moderate and mildly retarded persons whose IQ range was from 30 to 88, with a mean of 55. Of interest was the chronological age variable of eighteen to twenty-five. The overall results were that postschool retarded persons can indeed demonstrate significant gains in both academic areas and practical skills. These authors observed that adult education can be a normalizing experience for the retarded. Nibira and Nibira (1975) studied the adaptive behavior of 426 retarded persons who were formerly institutionalized. The results reflected adaptive behavior gains for adults denied access to community experiences during childhood. Length of institutionalization was not a predictor of gains or lack of gain. Rather, the availability of an expressive advocate was a critical factor, plus the initiative of the retarded persons themselves.

Vocational Preparation

The preparation of retarded persons for employment has attempted to keep pace with the strides being made in career education. Brolin (1974) investigated the competencies required by secondary-level teachers of the mildly retarded. His analysis identified educational, rehabilitation, and vocational clusters of competence. *Educational* competencies involved skills in programming for adolescents based upon curriculum, development, personality, guidance, and testing. The *rehabilitation* competencies included: job analysis, constructing work samples, vocational testing, counseling, behavior modification, in-school training, use of community resources, and job selection. *Vocational* competencies included: home and family living, food management, grooming, housekeeping, job tryouts, and supervision of out-of-school training sites. Muth and Singell (1975) have demonstrated the benefits of an effective program with reference to economic justifications alone. The authors compared a group of mildly retarded persons who participated in a program with an equated group whose school district did not provide such services. Over a three-year period of enrollment, the *excess* costs (beyond the costs involved for normal persons) for the group of thirty was found to be $157,077. The salary and employment differentials were found to be about $60,000 in the first year after graduation, favoring the special education group, and averaged about a $32,000 difference in five years after graduation. Differences were maintained by subsequent graduates in the special programs.

RESIDENTIAL ENVIRONMENTS

Residential refers to the natural home and alternatives to the natural home. Regardless of setting, the goals of responsive environments would be applicable.

Foster Parents

A project reported by Quick, Little, and Campbell (1973) was targeted toward development of skills of handicapped children in foster homes. The training program included areas of motor skills, language, perceptual-cognitive abilities, and parenting skills. The project showed gain in acquiring the skills of congruent communications described by Ginott and Gordon (chapter 13). Adoption of a retarded child, according to Kravik (1975), is becoming more frequent. Thirty-nine states and Washington, D.C. have some form of support services to facilitate this process. Persons who undertake adoption tend to perceive the child as a person first and his or her problem as secondary and to focus primarily on potential.

Krummel (1975) has described efforts to enable deinstitutionalized retarded persons to participate in the religious and social life of a church community. His article described the congregation's experience in "adopting" residents of a group-living home as members in their own right. This congregation discovered a reciprocal lesson: its members had opportunities to express and experience faith through outreach to others.

Residential Facilities

The comparison between the closing of orphanages for dependent children and the current deemphasis of institutions for the retarded has been summarized by Gula (1974). This report identified the need for careful planning among parents, community service systems, and residential facilities to create a helping experience. He credited the emergence of formal advocacy groups with facilitating the process. Both the Gula report and Payne (1976) have cited the potential for a backlash against community residential services. The former stressed the need for the involvement of staff and the person, while the latter report stressed the need for parent involvement to guarantee their encouragement. The decision of parents to institutionalize, according to Wolf and Whitehead (1975), is a function of lack of environmental support to assist parental management skills. Early intervention, according to Stone (1975), can strengthen the family's effectiveness in coping.

Oudenne (1974) has described one state's experience in the transformation of residential facilities. He noted that resident labor within the institution can run the risk of creating a form of peonage and/or a type of involuntary servitude. It was estimated that as high as 10 percent of a facility's labor force could be unpaid retarded workers. This labor force constituted such a significant contribution that normal workers were not required to perform their duties. The reported occupations held by these retarded workers were said to include: direct care of residents, food service, hospital, laundry, housekeeping, and general maintenance of the physical plant. The Oudenne report described how the residential facility can maximize its potential as a training site and escape the potential for peonage. The first step was to secure an agreement with fiscal officers of the executive and legislative branches of state government providing that for every resident released who performed equivalent labor, an equivalent normal worker would be hired. The agreement was honored and provided a genuine incentive for worker release. The second step was to create an institutional aide program (IAP). The wages paid to an IAP person would be an equivalent to the standard adopted for a community sheltered workshop. Residents were housed in halfway facilities to maximize eventual community return. A maximum of three years' enrollment was set for this program. Again agreement was sought with the state to provide wages appropriate for work efforts. These first two programs have reduced facility census by over seven hundred retarded persons. Currently there are two designations for retarded workers serving in work roles: "productive" worker and "handicapped" worker. In the former category, the person is paid the minimum wage and is of high priority for community release. In the latter category, the person is paid at a level approved by the U.S. Department of Labor.

The Natural Home

The major concern in residential environments remains the strengthening of the natural family.

1. Inner-city child-parent centers have been established as an alternative school sponsored by a school district. Preschoolers and early elementary learners receive individual attention and parents are actively engaged in teaching and modeling. Average academic achievement is about two to three grade levels superior to typical compensatory education programs (Mueller and Jennings, 1974; Bone, 1975).

2. Mothers of children in day centers are learning organizational tactics to improve services for their neighborhoods (Solnit-Sale, 1975).

3. The concept of family life education involves all family members to discover new learnings as an entire unit (Wagner, 1976).

4. The direct involvement of parents in preschool experiences for their handicapped child facilitates self-concept and achievement motivation for both parent and child (Hamilton, 1973).

5. A guidance program has been developed to assist fathers (frequently neglected) to deal with problems of acceptance, comparing children, coping with professionals, attitudes of the spouse and relatives, understanding development, and observation and evaluation (Erickson, 1974).

RESPONSIVE ENVIRONMENTS AND ACCOUNTABILITY

Jones (1973) views accountability as a *shared* process of goal accountability, in which a public board, elected or appointed, is held responsible to the public for selection of goals and objectives; program accountability, in which managers and administrators are responsible to the board for selection and/or development of instructional-management programs to implement objectives; and outcome/output accountability, in which teachers and staff are responsible to managers for performance attainments of learner-clients consistent with stated objectives.

Goal Accountability

Brolin (1973) has identified certain components of accountability for vocational programs. His model implied that job closures are not a complete measure of success. Vocationally oriented agencies must be concerned with the match among the worker's needs, the employer's needs, and the demands of the work task to be performed.

Kidd (1975) has shared examples relating to goal accountability. He cited the experience of his school program. The first example included the use of an annual survey of program graduates. The survey involves graduates of the last ten years. A chart displaying year of graduation and type of employment is prepared for release to the media. Second, Kidd advocates parent opinion as a measure of goal attainment. The parent questionnaire involves both a checklist and open-ended responses. The parent is asked to check satisfaction as either great, good, fair, or poor. Open-ended questions included the program areas least liked, best liked, and areas for recommended change. The results are tabulated and mailed to the superintendent of each local school district.

Program Accountability

The board of directors of the NARC (1975) adopted a series of policy statements regarding program operation and outcomes. Their focus was upon the school and nonschool agency; however, these statements would be applicable to residential environments. These statements were advanced for persons engaged in advocacy, planning, curricular, or evaluation roles.

1. *Cooperative relationships.* The plea was made for integration of school programs and the programs of habilitation agencies. There should be sufficient communications to affect orderly transition and transfer. Also involved in this process is the need for adequate feedback between training and preparation program and placement program. This feedback function can provide guidance to individual clients as well as provide data regarding program directions and practices.

2. *Relevance of training tasks.* There was a certain implied criticism of the "busy work" nature of simulated or artificial work environments. The emphasis should be upon tasks and skills that have direct work applications. It was also recommended that more attention be given to job tryouts in actual work situations.

3. *Program design.* The design of the program should reflect awareness of the career education movement, especially emphasizing early childhood years. Curriculum should also stress skills in choosing and holding a job in addition to its more traditional emphasis upon job placement. Attention also should be given to evaluation; it should be incorporated as an equal function of design.

4. *Program content.* There was a recognition that individuals and communities vary to such an extent as to confound a universal or uniform identification. Consequently, certain examples can serve as a possible model to be thoughtfully adapted.

Personal appearance was identified as attention to grooming, posture, mannerisms, clothing, and communication.

Social living skills were outlined as an emphasis upon use of recreation and leisure opportunities, consumer education, maintenance of personal possessions, meal preparation, and understanding of one's own emotional behavior.

Interpersonal relationships were involved as interactions with peers of the same or opposite sex, younger and older persons, persons in authority, use of social agencies, public transportation, public utilities, marriage and family living, and appropriate behavior in a variety of social groups.

Vocational skills were said to include physical dexterity, appropriate behavior for work situations, job selection, realistic expectations, training in securing and maintaining employment, and amenability to punctuality, supervision, persistence, and associated work behaviors.

Staff Accountability

MacMillan, Jones, and Myers (1976) have advanced certain guidelines for the behavior of staff with respect to:

1. *Change agentry*. This dimension involves the extent to which the program staff produce and/or influence change upon the system. The goal is to achieve responsiveness to the needs of the retarded person.

2. *Client advocacy*. A given approach is selected on the basis of what is best for the client, and this perspective is represented to others. A staff can be accountable for securing the best alternative and resisting expedient ones.

3. *Separate principle from program*. There may be the temptation to confuse a principle, such as normalization, with a particular program, such as resource room. Furthermore, a given principle should not become so ideologically paramount as to discourage objective evaluation.

4. *Staff training*. Another dimension is the extent to which a service system engages in orientation activities. Installation of a program without preparation may constitute considerable risk of failure. Inservice training also enhances communications among program staff.

Measurement and Accountability

The data base for inference of learner/client outcome has centered upon the use of normative test results versus the results obtained from mastery of performance objectives. Yesedale and Salvia (1974) term these options *normative reference measurement* and *criterion reference measurement*. In normative reference measurement, the person is compared (on the basis of test performance) to some norm appropriate for his or her group. Information about the person is communicated in terms of comparison to what is known about similar persons on the same test. From these data, training procedures in specific abilities can be instituted. Criterion reference measurement assumes that knowledge, skill, and/or attitude exists along a continuum or chain of prerequisites. Analysis of the task can identify the component parts needed to acquire the terminal behavior. Assessment of the person involves what she or he does and/or does not do. This essentially describes areas of assessment covered previously. From this procedure, activities are specified. The assessment becomes the criterion for movement to the next level. Both approaches have their limitations.

The difficulty of the norm reference measurement approach, according to Yesedale and Salvia, is that existing test procedures may not possess sufficient test-retest reliability for accurate evaluation. For example, a popular NRM test is reported to have test-retest coefficients of .66–.91, which could mean that improvement in *test* performance can range from 24.9 to 58.5 percent by chance or regression to the group mean. Accountability studies could be confounded by reliance on measures that have only modest reliability. Jones (1973) reported that the UCLA Center for Study of Evaluation assessed the measurement properties of 141 standardized reading tests currently available. One hundred and five possessed a reliability of less than .70 and had no alternate forms. Only seven had the traditional .90 figure required for confident judgment of gains.

Jones expressed reservation regarding the use of test scores as the principal means of accountability. He identified the limitations of normative reference measures as lack of norms on exceptional children and youth, little relationship of test content to the goals or objectives, and lack of instrumentation appropriate for secondary levels.

Criterion reference measurement (CRM) procedures have certain difficulties as well. The Jones article pointed out certain pitfalls in this system. For example, one state curriculum guide of twelve persisting life goals (for both elementary through secondary levels for the mildly mentally retarded) was found to contain seven thousand performance objectives. This is a stunning and awesome array to monitor. Also, Jones pointed out that CRM procedures have similar problems of validity and reliability as norm reference measurement (NRM) systems.

Jones suggested that accountability will be a permanent trend. CRM shows promise for the future, but research is required to manage the system, especially with respect to learner-client outcomes. Jones felt that research should focus upon validation of CRM objectives and understanding what circumstances facilitate attainments.

The reader should understand that both measurement approaches reflect areas of honest disagreement. Formal tests and criterion reference measures are perceived by the author to have their proper and respective places with respect to identification (finding), diagnosis (summary of current status), prescription (a treatment plan to be accomplished in relation to intentions), evaluation (accomplishment of attainments and appropriateness of prescription), and accountability (inferences about goals, program support, and outcomes management). Norm reference and criterion reference measurements can complement one another.

SUMMING UP

This chapter was concerned with the design of responsive environments. Such an environment was viewed as complementing the goals of an advocate relationship and of the helping relationship. A model of such an environment prizes autonomy for the person-protege and a caring-acceptance by the significant adult.

Residential environments can be either the natural home or community-based alternatives. Adoption, a promising trend, is chosen by those who see persons first and problems second. Emphasis is upon strengthening the family either as a unit or as individual members. Present education efforts appear directed toward the increase of skills and self-confidence.

Personal flexibility has emerged as a significant variable of program effectiveness in *educational* environments. Both general and special educators are engaged in cooperative efforts to establish the individual guided education model for the normal and retarded at school building levels. School staff, administration, and consumers of the schools can become responsible partners in implementing a concept of ownership of educational problems.

Vocational environments can originate during the early years of the school experience. Curricula are emerging with meaningful career content and emphasis. Schools are reaching out into the community to establish joint relationship for preparation. Information, in a form usable to consumers, is viewed as essential, as is job training. Special education has kept pace with career education trends in regular education. Competencies for school programs can be grouped into clusters of educational, rehabilitational, and vocational. The competence-deviance hypothesis based upon a "Train, Don't Test" model reflects great promise for vocationally oriented program.

Design of a responsive environment was couched in a problem-solving model. Dimensions of assessment included review of discrepancies, attitudes, skills, environmental influences, and task. The use of objectives as well as their construction was discussed as a phase of assessment. The model is viewed as consistent with the IEP provision of PL 94-142.

PL 94-142, Education for All Handicapped Children's Act (1975), creates a sense of urgency regarding the design of responsive environments in educational practice. The legislation mandates that all handicapped have the right to an economically and psychologically free and appropriate education. In turn, appropriate education can be defined as those practices based upon the Individual Education Plan (IEP). This provision calls for goals and objectives based on observation and formal procedures, identification of learning needs, selection of relevant methods and materials, use of normalized procedures as appropriate, and provisions for program accountability. An important outcome is the relationship of the design of responsive environments and accountability to the IEP process.

ON LOCATION

Lowell (1965, pp. 10–11) has presented a sensitive account of a lesson that took place in a residential facility. The selection was chosen to illustrate the responsiveness of an environment. Although the learners in this account are between severely and profoundly retarded, their enthusiasm for learning and desire to achieve is quite evident. Read on to discover how one teacher transforms the lives of her learners.

Big Potato, Small Potato

A small group of residents at Gaylord State Home and Training School eagerly looks forward to school each week. The program was initiated by a special education teacher from Alpena. Before leaving for an exchange year in England, she taught Mrs. Anita Cornish, an ex-teacher from the area, how to develop interest and response from her profoundly handicapped pupils. They are learning simple vocabulary, color coordination, group singing and other coordination skills.

The schoolroom is at the end of the corridor. Empty, it seems rather large, but in a matter of minutes it is full to overflowing.

We are never sure whether it is the appearance of the teacher that starts the rush or whether somebody says the magic word "school." For whatever reason, down the hall come the pupils — some in wheelchairs pushed by nurses, others powering their own chairs, some crawling or dragging themselves along the tiled floor, and, if all else seems too slow, they roll. It is a fantastic sight, this frantic rush to the end of the corridor — the lighted faces, the laughter, the eager joy — all for the privilege of sitting in that magic group with the attractive young woman and her brown paper bag.

What happens? The young woman opens the bag and holds up a potato. "What is it?" she asks. There is a long silence, and then Carrie, neck muscles straining, twisted limbs jerking with effort, gets out a low, hollow, unmistakable, "po-ta-doh." There is much nodding of heads, of repeating the word.

Out of the bag comes a big onion, a small onion, a banana. All are solemnly considered, passed from hand to hand, glances exchanged, and labels attached. Then, out of the bag comes an orange, a whole orange. Again there is an exchange of glances, a nervous twitching in chairs. Again the sidelong looks, the shoulder shrugs. Then Willie, more sophisticated than the others in the ways of the world, says it: "Orange." With a glad cry of recognition, Mamie says, "Juice." The strange has become familiar.

And then we realize that many of these homely common objects are, in their natural state, most uncommon to those who have all their lives, or for so long as they can remember, known a potato only as mashed, a banana only in a pudding, an onion only as a vague unidentified flavor. What is happening in this small room is more than the triumph of finding a label or sounding out a word. This is a voyage of great discovery, that the rough brown object is a potato and is related to the white mound on the noontime plate.

We are caught up, suddenly, by the unthinking ways in which we limit still further the limits of a limited mind when so simple a thing as potato appears on a plate from no predetermined ancestry. It might just as well have arrived from the moon. In this light, the common practice of attendants at Gaylord of pushing a wheelchaired patient before them as they go on errands from one part of the hospital to another becomes far more significant than just the giving of personal pleasure. It is rather the widening of a world. On such a trip, one might discover the kitchen magic that transforms orange into juice, brown potato into mashed, and the special alchemy that makes all the difference with an onion.

To the tune of "Home on the Range," we tiptoe out. Susie is still crooning "Big potato, small potato." It is a song of triumph.

REFERENCES

Abeson, A., and Zettell, J. The End of the Quiet Revolution: The Education for All Handicapped Children Act of 1975. *Exceptional Children,* 1977, 44, 114–128.

Berkman, G. Teachers Are Making It Work. *Teaching Exceptional Children,* 1974, 6, 126–133.

Billingsley, F., and Smelser, S. A Group Approach to Classroom Management: The Behavior Game. *Teaching Exceptional Children,* 1974, 7, 30–33.

Birch, J. W. Regular School Personnel and Programs. *Exceptional Children in Regular Classrooms.* Reynolds, M. and Davis M. (Ed.) Reston, Virginia: Council for Exceptional Children, 1975.

Birch, J. W. *Mainstreaming: Educable Mentally Retarded Children in Regular Classes.* Reston, Virginia: Council for Exceptional Children, 1971.

Bloom, B., Hastings, J., and Madaus, G. *Handbook on Formative and Summative Evaluation of Student Learning.* New York: McGraw-Hill, 1971.

Bone, J. They Get Them While They're Young. *American Education,* 1975, 11, 18–21.

Board of Directors of the NARC. *Vocational and Life Skills.* Arlington, Texas: NARC, 1975.

Boyd, J., and Bowers, R. Behavioral Analysis: The Principal and Discipline. *Clearing House,* 1974, 48, 420–426.

Brolin, D. Vocational Evaluation: Special Education's Responsibility. *Education and Training of the Mentally Retarded,* 1973, 8, 12–17.

Brolin, D. A New Model for Teacher Training: Secondary EMR. *TED Newsletter,* 1974, 10, 16–18.

Burke, D. *Reasoning and Problem Solving Training.* East Lansing, Michigan: College of Education, Michigan State University, 1975 A (with P. Hecht)

Burke, D. *Pre Vocational Skills.* East Lansing, Michigan: College of Education, Michigan State University, 1975 B (with P. Hecht)

Cascapo, M. Peer Models Reverse the "One Bad Apple Spoils the Barrel" Theory. *Teach Exceptional Children,* 1972, 5, 21–24.

Cole, R. W., and Dunn, R. A New Lease on Life for Education of the Handicapped: Ohio Copes with 94–142. *Phi Delta Kappan,* 1977, 59, 3–6.

Colella, H. Career Development Center. *Teaching Exceptional Children,* 1973, 5, 110–118.

Council for Exceptional Children, *Introducing PL 94-142.* Reston, Virginia: Council for Exceptional Children, 1976.

Dinkmeyer, D., and Dinkmeyer, D. Logical Consequences. *Phi Delta Kappan,* 1976, 57, 664–666.

Engleman, S. *Concept Learning.* Belmont, California: Fearon, 1969.

Erickson, M. P. Talking with Fathers of Down's Syndrome Children. *Children Today,* 1974, 3, 22–26.

Frank, A. R. Breaking Down a Learning Task: A Sequence Approach. *Teaching Exceptional Children,* 1973, 6, 16–19.

Frank, A. Centering Interest on the Student Interest Center. *Teaching Exceptional Children,* 1974, 7, 4–8.

Gardner, B., and Robinson, M. A School for All Children. *Illinois Principal,* 1974, 9–13.

Garner, H. G. A Truce in the War for the Child. *Exceptional Children,* 1976, 42, 315–320.

Grantham, M., and Harris, C. A Faculty Trains Itself to Improve Student Discipline. *Phi Delta Kappan,* 1976, 57, 661–663.

Gray, A. G. The Mini-Shop Approach in Career Education. *Teaching Exceptional Children,* 1973, 5, 145–146.

Gold, M., and Faur, P. *Train, Don't Test.* Urbana: Children's Research Center, University of Illinois, 1974.

Gold, M. *Vocational Training.* Urbana: Children's Research Center, University of Illinois, 1975.

Gula, M. Community Services and Residential Institutions for Children. *Children Today,* 1974, 3, 15–17.

Hamilton, A. Teaching Handicapped Children — and Their Parents. *American Education,* 1973, 9, 22–26.

Hansen, C. Program Slicing: A Tool for Individualization of Instruction. *Education and Training of the Mentally Retarded,* 1973, 8, 153–158.

Hayden, J. F. A Work Experience Program in Rural Areas. *Teaching Exceptional Children,* 1975, 7, 130–133.

Hemenway, R., Lemke, E., Hage, D., and Robertshaw, C. Three Curricula for Retarded Adults. *Mental Retardation,* 1972, 10, 13–15.

Jackson, A., and Peterson, M. Young Children and Self Awareness in the World of Work. *Teaching Exceptional Children,* 1973, 5, 119–123.

Jones, R. L. Accountability in Special Education: Some Problems. *Exceptional Children,* 1973, 5, 119–123.

Kazden, A. Toward a Client Administered Token Reinforcement Program. *Education and Training of the Mentally Retarded,* 1971, 6, 52–55.

Kidd, J. Accountability in Public School MR Programs. *Education and Training of the Mentally Retarded,* 1975, 10, 170–173.

Kidd, J. W. The ABC's of Behavior Modification — Skinner Applied. *Education and Training of the Mentally Retarded,* 1974, 9, 198–199.

Kravik, P. Adopting a Retarded Child. *Children Today,* 1975, 4, 17–21.

Krummel, C. The Mentally Retarded: God's Exceptional Children. *The Lutheran,* 1975, 13, 4–6.

Larkin, T. Improving our Rate of Passage. *American Education,* 1975, 11, 20–33.

Lowell, R. Big Potato, Small Potato. *Span,* 1965, 7, 10–11.

MacMillan, D. *Mental Retardation in School and Society.* Boston: Little, Brown, and Company, 1977.

MacMillan, D. L., Jones, R. L., and Myers, C. E. Mainstreaming the Mildly Retarded: Some Questions, Cautions, and Guidelines. *Mental Retardation,* 1976, 14, 3–10.

Madlee, D. Careers from A to Zoo. *American Education,* 1973, 9, 15–21.
Mager, R. Analyzing Performance Problems, or "You Really Oughta Wanna." Belmont, California: Fearon Publishing, 1970.
Mager, R. *Developing Attitudes Toward Learning.* Belmont, California: Fearon, 1968.
Mager, R. *Goal Analysis.* Belmont, California: Fearon, 1972.
Mager, R. F. *Preparing Instructional Objectives.* Belmont, California: Fearon, 1962.
Mager, R., and Beach, K. Jr. *Developing Vocational Instruction.* Belmont, California: Fearon, 1967.
Martin, E. W. Individualism and Behaviorism as Future Trends in Educating Exceptional Children. *Exceptional Children,* 1972, 38, 517–525.
Mason, R. *Educational Ideals in American Society.* Boston: Allyn and Bacon, 1960.
Mersels, L. The Student's Social Contract: Learning Social Competence in the Classroom. *Teaching Exceptional Children,* 1974, 7, 34–35.
Mueller, P., and Jennings, J. The Chicago Child-Parent Center Revisited. *Phi Delta Kappan,* 1974, 61, 51–53.
Muth, J., and Singell, L. Costs and Benefits of Training Educable Students: The Kansas Work-Study Project Reconsidered. *Exceptional Children,* 1975, 41, 334–335.
Nall, A. *What Is Structured?* Toronto, Canada: Ontario Association for Children with Learning Disabilities, 1970.
National Advisory Committee on the Handicapped, Implementing the IEP Concepts. *American Education,* 1977, 13, 608.
Office of the Secretary. *Travel Barriers.* Washington, D.C.: Department of Transportation, 1970.
Oudenne, W. Resident Labor: A Practical Solution in New Jersey State Institutions. *Mental Retardation,* 1974, 12, 17–19.
Payne, J. E. The Deinstitutional Backlash. *Mental Retardation,* 1976, 14, 43–45.
Quick, A., Little, T., and Campbell, A. A. *The Training of Exceptional Children and Their Foster Parents.* Memphis: Memphis State University, 1973.
Raschke, D., and Young, A. A Comparative Analysis of the Diagnostic-Prescriptive and Behavioral-Analysis Models in Preparation for the Development of a Dialectic Pedagogical System. *Education and Training of the Mentally Retarded,* 1976, 11, 135–145.
Robinson, M. *A Guide to Our School.* Champaign, Illinois: Champaign Public Schools, 1974.
Rosenberg, H. On Teaching the Modification of Employer and Employee Behavior. *Teaching Exceptional Children,* 1973, 5, 140–142.
Ross, A. O. *The Exceptional Child in the Family.* New York: Grune and Stratton, 1964.
Rumpf, T. The Voc Ed Breakthrough. *American Education,* 1975, 11, 22–25, 28.
Rusco, J. Are Your Facilities Suitable for the Handicapped? *American School and University,* 1974, 47, 25–32.
Ryan, S., and Ryan, R. Report Cards? Why Not Ask the Parents? *Teaching Exceptional Children,* 1973, 6, 34–36.
Sapp, A. Succeeding with Success Environments. *American Education,* 1973, 9, 4–10.
Social Security Administration. *Target Rehabilitation.* Washington, D.C.: Department of Health, Education, and Welfare, 1973.
Solnit-Sale, J. Family Day Care Center Mothers Work Together to Improve Services. *Children Today,* 1975, 4, 23–24.

Stone, N. A Plea for Early Intervention. *Mental Retardation,* 1975, 13, 16–17.

Talagan, D. Career of the Month. *Teaching Exceptional Children,* 1973, 5, 137–139.

Tawney, J., Middleton, D., and Cegelka, P. Behavior Modification Is Not. *Teaching Exceptional Children,* 1973, 5, 82–89.

Wagner, J. Toward Strengthening the Family. *American Education,* 1975, 12, 31–33.

Wolf, L., and Whitehead, P. The Decision to Institutionalize Retarded Children. *Mental Retardation,* 1975, 13, 3–7.

Wolinsky, G., and Walker, D. A Home Safety Inventory for Parents of Pre-School Handicapped Children. *Teaching Exceptional Children,* 1975, 7, 82–86.

Wuehle, E. Career Training by Contract. *American Education,* 1973, 9, 23–26.

Yesedale, J., and Salvia, J. Diagnostic-Prescriptive Teaching: Two Models, *Exceptional Children,* 1974, 41, 181–185.

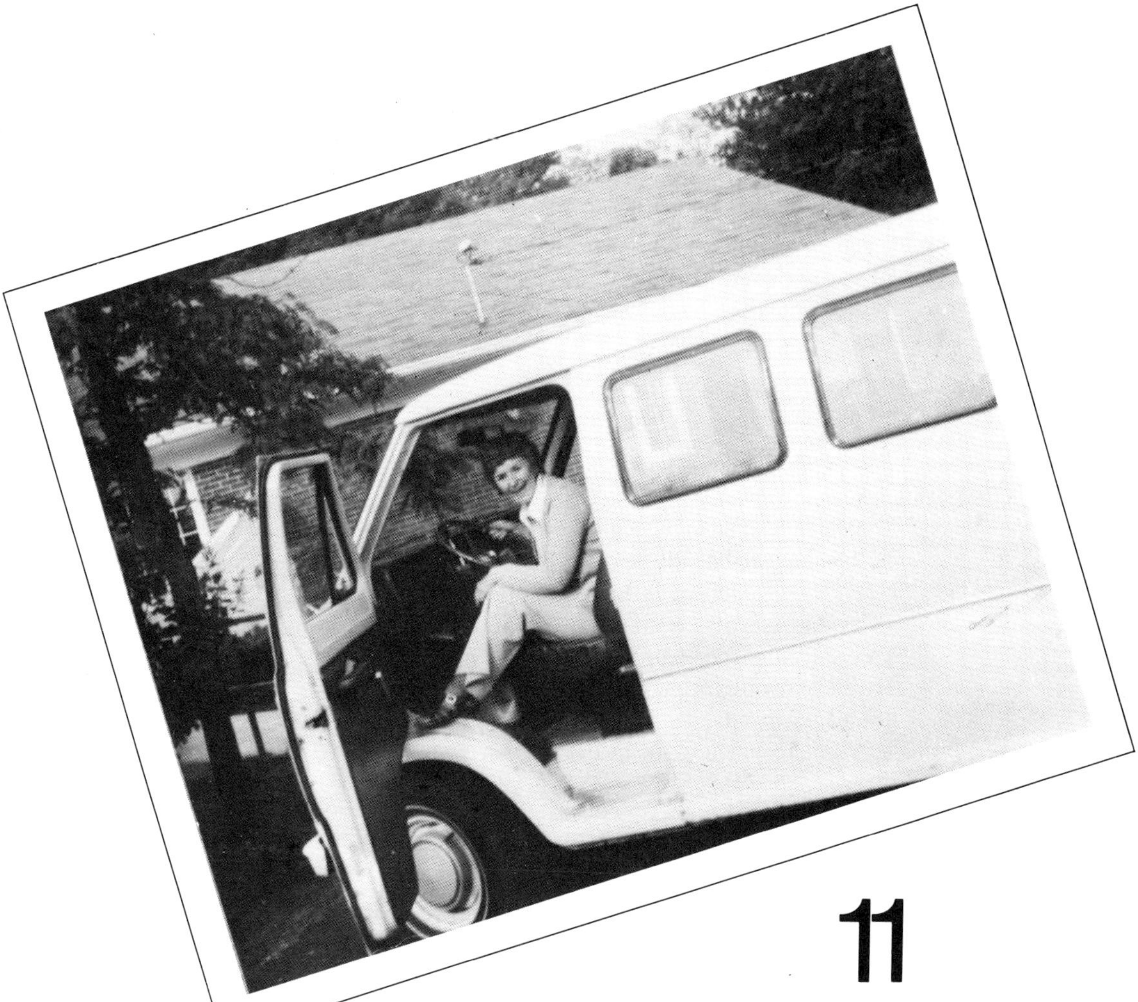

11

The Scope of Educational and Vocational Preparation Services

SYNOPSIS

This chapter examines the role of public schools and collaborative agencies in preparing retarded persons for adulthood. There is support in the literature for combining educational and vocational services. A primary concern of this chapter is an exposition of outcomes for the mentally retarded, which shape the intentions of this service system.

OBJECTIVES

ATTITUDES

1. To be aware that all persons who engage in deliberate efforts with the retarded person are indeed "teachers."
2. To recognize that education transpires inside and outside the school.
3. To see that career education neither begins nor ends at any specified age.
4. To feel an obligation to collaborate with other persons and agencies in life adjustment.
5. To want to participate in quality services.

UNDERSTANDING

1. To define alternatives of service.
2. To describe the basis for placement in program alternatives.
3. To define employment alternatives for the mentally retarded.
4. To describe alternative preparations for vocational adjustment.

SKILLS

1. To list the elements of curriculum design.
2. To list the elements of curriculum goals for mentally retarded citizens.
3. To list the competencies associated with an educationally oriented program of vocation preparation.

4 To describe standards by which to evaluate the functional validity of curriculum goals.

PREPARATION OUTCOMES

The Design of Preparation

Curriculum describes a system's aspiration for its learners, and it implies accountability to the learner, the family, and the community for intended outcomes. Curriculum, from its Latin origins, literally describes a race course to be traveled. Specifically, curriculum is a description of the content to be taught and the method, goals, and evaluation procedures.

Neisen (1967) has expressed this interdependence as a formula:

$$\text{Curriculum is: } \frac{\text{What} \times \text{When} \times \text{How}}{\text{Why}}$$

For Neisen, the *what* describes the content of attitudes, knowledges, and skills to be attained by learners. The *when* is descriptive of the application of principles of growth and development. This component suggests a rationale for the timing and sequencing of expectations. The *how* implies method based upon knowledge of the teaching-learning process. Also implied in this component are administrative considerations of physical facilities, teacher competencies, and educational placements. The *why* relates to a constellation of concerns; it represents the values or philosophical beliefs of the educator. The educator's values will influence the course of action with respect to the what, when, and how. The why also denotes a sense of obligation for evaluation of the integrity of the what, when, and how. The × in the numerator suggests interaction and interdependence. The position of the why denotes a consistent mediation among the three components.

The Education Committee of the National Association for Retarded Citizens (1971), under the leadership of W. Cegalka, has formulated a policy statement regarding the "appropriateness and scope of school curriculum."

> Present day curricula for mentally retarded persons frequently represents a simplified version of curricula originally intended for the average school student. Curricula for mentally retarded students should be designed with the intention of providing an individualized educational experience for all retarded persons.

The committee suggested that certain criteria of curricula adequacy can be applied regardless of level of retardation. Does the educational plan allow students to: increase the complexity of their behaviors, increase personal control over their environment, and attain behavioral characteristics that are culturally designated as normal? Are the classroom activities and teaching materials relevant to the chronological and social age of the child? Are curricula geared toward the practical aspects of daily living and effective integration into the community? Are they aimed at the effective use of leisure time via generic, community, recreational, and social outlets? Is there an early emphasis upon vocational skills?

The author, in preparing a curriculum guide, conducted a document analysis of twenty-four curriculum guides, randomly selected from a nationwide pool and about equally balanced between ones for the mildly and moderately mentally retarded. Eleven common areas constituted the elements of a curriculum guide.

1 *Acknowledgements* contains statements concerning personnel, time, and procedures used to develop the document and includes the sanctioners, such as school boards, parent groups, and state agencies, who "endorse" the guide.
2 *Philosophy* contains statements concerning beliefs about the role of the schools for services, the nature of learning, the nature of teachers, and includes group beliefs about how the guide is to be used.
3 *Populations to be served* contains legal and school code definitions of population to be served, defines levels of retardation to be served, with age ranges included, may also include procedures of identification, screening, placement, and also includes criteria for program termination.
4 *Goals and objectives*[a] should contain statements of intention of the schools for learners and should be couched in measurable performance terms.
5 *Instructional activities and experiences*[a] expresses the when and how of implementation of goals and objectives and should reflect a match between the two.
6 *Evaluation*[a] identifies formal and informal assessment procedures for pupil grouping and reporting to parents.
7 *Parent relationships* involves a statement of parent rights regarding admission and termination, policies regarding parent conferences, statements regarding reporting procedures, and also includes statements regarding parent involvement in school planning.
8 *Classroom management* contains statements regarding climate, control, and discipline, sample schedules, policies regarding discipline practices, school routines to be followed, recommended procedures for pupil behavior, and teacher responsibilities.

[a]May be combined into a separate curriculum program statement, such as *perceptual skill,* with subtopics under it.

9 *Administrative resources* identifies roles of administrators, supervisory-consulting-ancillary services, policies regarding ordering-purchasing of equipment, use of paraprofessionals, transportation, physical plant and equipment, provisions for teacher and community input for decision making, inservice training, staffing patterns and expectations, provisions of library and instructional material centers, and referral procedures to other agencies.

10 *Bibliographic resources* covers identification of periodicals, texts, catalogs, and films to which the teacher has access.

11 *Epilogue* defines procedures for continuous revision of the document and identifies resources not already covered for implementation.

Scope of Outcomes

More recent recommendations regarding curriculum goals have been advanced by Smith (1974) and Kolstoe (1970). Kolstoe identified areas such as communication skills (including language arts), arithmetic, social competencies, motor skills and recreation, esthetics (art and music), and vocational competencies. Smith (1974) recommended the broad areas of perceptual-motor performance, communication skills, reading skills, arithmetic skills, personal-social skills, gainful employment skills, and adult education. This listing appears compatible with the Grossman listing of adaptable behaviors (chapter 1). Specifically, the Smith and Kolstoe discussions identify five broad areas of curriculum outcomes:

Sensory-motor perception would be the foundation for subsequent learnings. Within the component would be motoric, visual, and auditory learnings built into assemblies of increasingly more complex skills. Processes of discrimination and association of stimuli would be emphasized. Goals would include directionality, contact, and body image. For older students the emphasis would be upon skills for recreation opportunities. A rigorous physical activity program would be geared toward producing the stamina required for work. Perceptual development would use motor areas as the basis for visual and auditory learnings. Special emphasis would be placed upon the concepts necessary for more formal areas of instruction, especially the vocabulary of classification, such as *same, different,* etc.

Communication-language would emphasize stimulation and motivation for language. Attention would be given to development of the mechanisms for articulation. Responding to external directions would be stressed. Exercises would be instituted toward strategies of memory and memory for sequence. A continuing theme would be concept formation as well as judgment/evaluation of choices. Opportunities for expression should be extended.

Literacy skills would range from functional skills of responding to signs of protection and the like to more formal skills. Listening skills would be emphasized as part of the communications program. Reading would build upon the base of vocabulary development and be a basis for word-attack skills. Comprehension would be the outcome, especially as applied to work situations. Written language would be emphasized, especially for social situations and work situations. Arithmetic would emphasize measurement skills. Special attention would be given to the metric system. Eventually there would be an emphasis upon money management.

Personal-self adjustment would build upon the base of perceptual development for an awareness of self known as body image. Communication instruction would stress one's name and personal pronouns such as *I, me, you, he,* etc. Both areas should establish a notion of self-existence, a recognition of being separate from others. Emphasis should be upon enabling the person to experience activities of cause and effect in order to establish feelings of accomplishment. Building feelings of a positive self-concept should be stressed through success experiences. A curriculum cannot build a protective shell, and the person will experience defeat and disappointment. At times aspiration will exceed capacity to respond. This area should assist the person to cope with and manage feelings. An essential element would be self-care, personal hygiene, and personal management. Eating, grooming, toileting, and management of emotions seem reasonable to help the child respond to cultural norms. Attention should be given to the topic of sexuality and education for sexuality. Given our cultural orientation toward parenthood and parenting, the retarded person should have the benefit of adult guidance in these life choices. As in communication, the best source for the learner will be the model presented by the teacher.

Social adjustment would be divided into two elements: environmental adaptation and career development. These would be continuing elements throughout the school experience. Environmental awareness would encompass traditional areas of science and social studies. Science instruction offers opportunities for developing skills of observation and inference. Units on living things can provide situations to draw analogues among families. The division of labor evident in insect colonies can be transferred to the interdependence of different occupations. Without resort to written materials, science can be highly visual and build complex skills. Nutrition can be a valid concern. Studies of the earth and the universe can be used to reinforce measurement of time and distance. Construction of scale models can be a functional use of arts and crafts, which in turn require measurement skills. (Similarly, music can be a reinforcement for subject areas.) Social studies should stress practical civics, especially identifying sources of help in times of crisis. Sources of recreation and use of leisure time also should be stressed. Participation in community events should be encouraged, especially culturally appropriate responses for holidays and special events. The ongoing endeavor of the school would be career education, discussed in some detail in this chapter. The reader is reminded that career education is a continuing emphasis throughout the school experience. Table 11–1 portrays curricular goals in an outline form. The intention is to provide a visual Gestalt.

Table 11–1 OUTLINE OF CURRICULUM CONTENT FOR MENTALLY RETARDED LEARNERS

I. Perceptual Development
  A. Motor
    1. Motor movement
    2. Laterality
    3. Directionality
    4. Body image
  B. Visual-Motor
    1. Figure-ground
    2. Eye-hand
    3. Perceptual constancy
    4. Orientation to space
  C. Auditory
    1. Discrimination
    2. Association
  D. Creative Activities
    1. Fine arts
    2. Physical activities
    3. Practical arts
    4. Physical education
II. Language and Cognition Skills
  A. Receptive
    1. Auditory
    2. Visual
  B. Inner
    1. Discovery-cognition
    2. Memory-retention
    3. Evaluation-judgment
    4. Reasoning-productive thinking
  C. Expressive
    1. Speech-articulation
    2. Oral language-syntax
    3. Language-gestural
III. Literacy Skills
  A. Reading
    1. Readiness
    2. Word attack
    3. Comprehension
    4. Functional
  B. Arithmetic
    1. Readiness
    2. Computation
    3. Problem solving
    4. Measurement
    5. Functional
  C. Language Arts
    1. Listening-speaking
    2. Writing-composition
    3. Spelling
    4. Literature
IV. Socialization
  A. Self Learnings
    1. Self-image concept
    2. Self-care
  B. Social Adjustments
    1. Relationships
    2. Vital choices
  C. Career Development
    1. Awareness of world of work
    2. Prevocational
    3. On-the-job training
  D. Environmental Awareness
    1. Home and family
    2. Communities
    3. Historical heritage
    4. Living things
    5. Earth and space
    6. Weather and seasons
    7. Machines

There would be many details to be ironed out in transforming these goals into an actual curriculum guide; especially for various ages and degrees of mental retardation. It is hoped that this presentation will enable the reader to begin this transformation.

Figure 11–1 *A Cascade System of Placement*

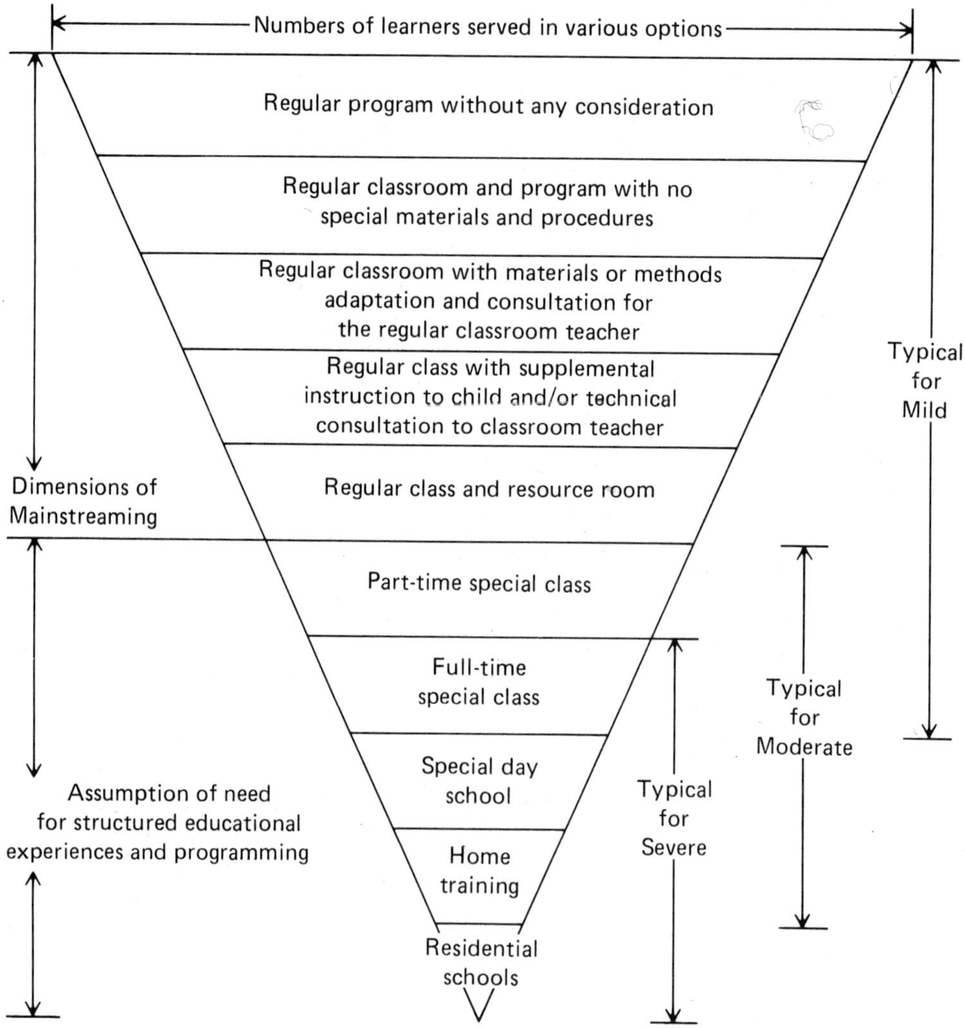

EDUCATIONAL ALTERNATIVES

A Cascade System

Caster (1976, p. 234) on behalf of the Council for Exceptional Children, has outlined a Cascade of Special Education Services. This system is depicted with adaptations in figure 11–1. This cascade emphasizes that a learner's need for specialized service, not a label, determines placement. Learner's needs can change, and so can placement. Learners can benefit from regular classroom placement. A close relationship between general and special education is necessary.

Principles for Selecting Alternatives

Abeson, Bolick, and Hass (1975) have provided an analysis of the legal implications of special education. The concept of *due process* was viewed as applicable to placement. The right to *least restrictive educational setting* has emerged as a condition of PL 93-380, quoted by Abeson et al.:

> Procedures insure that to the maximum extent appropriate, handicapped children, including children in public or private institutions or other care facilities, are educated with children who are not handicapped and that special classes, separate schooling, or other removal of handicapped children from the regular education environment occurs only when the nature of the severity of the handicap is such that education in regular classes with the use of supplementary aids and services cannot be achieved satisfactorily.

Caster (1975), on behalf of the Council for Exceptional Children, outlined the rights of parents and children regarding educational placement. Learners and/or their parents are entitled to:

1 the least restrictive educational placement;
2 appeal of any education decision that would alter program;
3 access to all information used by the school;
4 a neutral party to decide on program recommendations;
5 specification and evaluation of the benefits of a special program;
6 educational services, regardless of severity and handicap;
7 a variety of programs, not one option;
8 involvement in planning and notification of difficulties as early as possible;
9 a battery of information, not a single test, as the basis of decisions, which implies a team concept, not a single specialist; and
10 measurable objectives for programming, with periodic evaluation for progress.

Wirtz (1977) has recommended an educational ladder for selection of alternatives for the mentally retarded learner. The concept was formulated to identify age and overlapping abilities as principles for placement. This ladder, in adapted form, is presented in figure 11–2. The age and psychometric dimensions of this figure are shaded to convey that program boundaries (by age and IQ) need not be rigid. The Wirtz emphasis is upon behavioral functioning. He notes, for example, that certain groupings within the mild range may experience difficulties in adjustment to the open setting of the junior high with respect to locker combinations, moving from class to class, and participation in large physical education classes. The difficulty of implementing the Wirtz position is that state funding for mental retardation tends to follow psychometric groupings rather than adaptive behavior levels.

RESOURCE-ROOM ALTERNATIVES

The two main alternatives for the mildly retarded learner are the resource room and the special class. The former has gained a certain prominence, while the latter has encountered significant opposition. The resource-room alternative has become associated with the mainstreaming, normalization, and/or progressive inclusion movements. The reader should understand that the special class will be retained; however, its retention will be associated with greater precision of standards of quality of service.

Variations

Guerin and Szatlocky (1974) revealed four variations of resource rooms available to retarded persons.

1. *Programmed partial integration.* Students are assigned to special class and are programmed into regular class for blocks of time and for special subjects.

2. *Combination class.* Students are enrolled in a regular classroom whose enrollment is reduced. Materials and teacher aids are provided. (The funds normally spent on a special class may be used to employ aid(s) and/or materials.)

3. *Learning resources center.* Student is assigned to the regular program. The center teacher performs evaluation, prescription planning, and special tutorial assistance.

4. *Itinerant specialist.* Student is enrolled in a regular classroom. The itinerant specialist works with a small group for a specified time each day.

Jenkins and Mayhall (1973) confirm variation in the resource-room concept. They identified four common features and three elements of diversity. The common features include:

Figure 11–2 *An Educational Ladder*

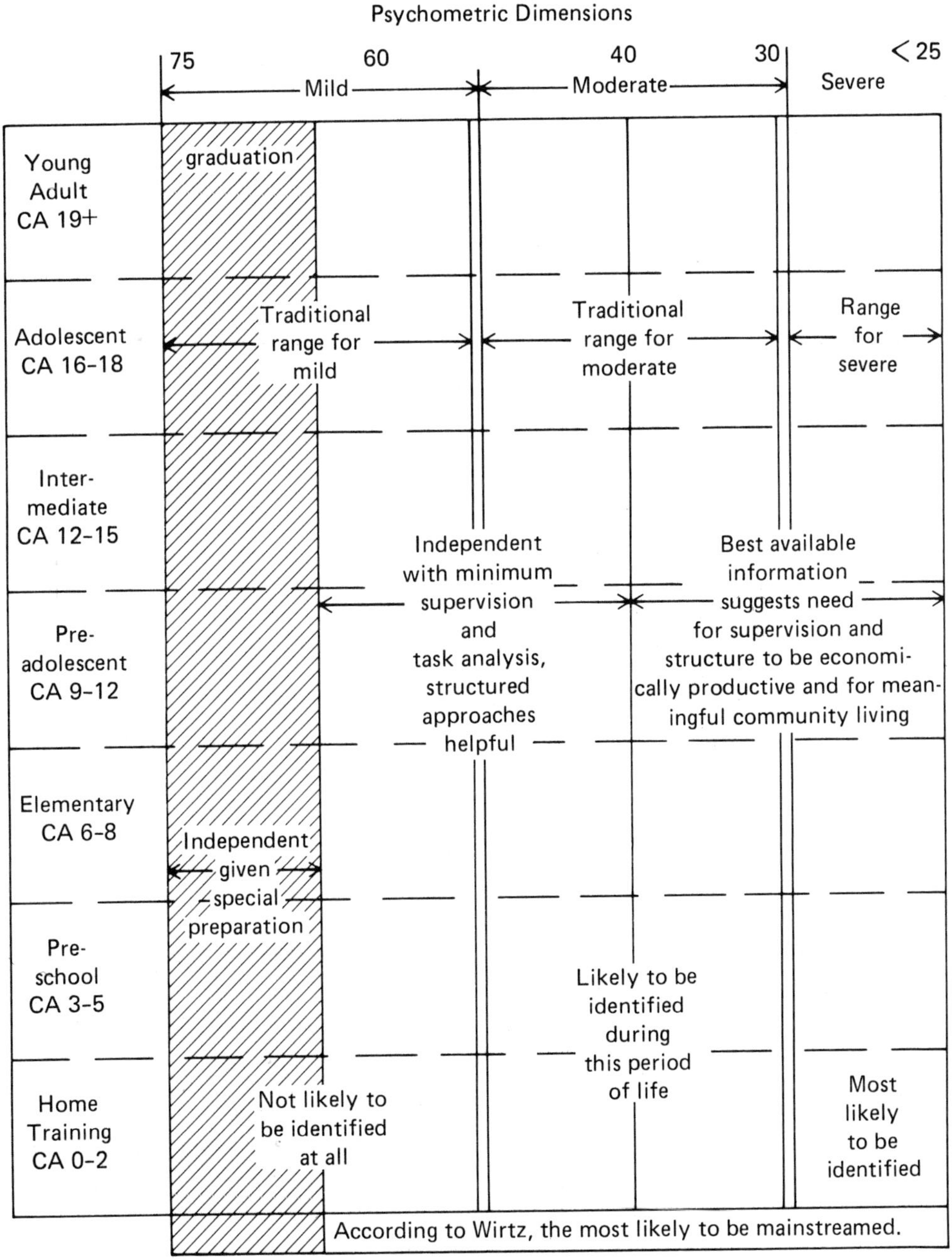

1. *Identified criterion performances.* Learners are not rejected because of handicap, but are accepted/rejected on the performance of classroom tasks. Thus, this program exists to maintain learners in the mainstream with appropriate support.

2. *Daily instruction and management.* Feedback and a consistent environment require a daily surveillance.

3. *Individual instruction.* One-to-one instruction would maximize instructional impact.

4. *Management of instruction.* These authors recommend the use of cross-age or peer tutors and other alternative means to manage instructional objectives.

The three areas of diversity were:

1. *Direct versus indirect service.* This option varies as to whether the child receives help from the resource room or from the regular classroom teacher, with the resource-room teacher as a consultant. The choice appears to depend on the accountability of the regular classroom teacher.

2. *Resident versus itinerant.* Is the specialist located in a school or employed on an itinerant basis.

3. *Skill/task versus ability orientation.* The ability orientation concentrates on central processes related to perception, motor, and/or psycholinguistic abilities. Prescriptions are based upon a differential diagnosis of these abilities. In the skill/task analysis, the focus is upon school-defined tasks. Prescriptions are based upon analysis of performance elements and subelements.

Rationale

The Jordan (1974) report justifies mainstreaming and resource rooms on the basis of the following assumptions:

1. Children are children, and handicapped children have needs and developmental tasks similar to others. Problems, as opposed to needs, require individual attention.

2. Public schools should be responsible and responsive to children.

3. Change is a way of life, and power determines, generates, and guides change. Planning can guide change into constructive channels, but without direction and surveillance, change becomes another fad without permanence.

4. More special children can be involved in school activities.

5. Schools become more child-centered if mainstreaming is present.

6. Individualization is becoming more common for normal children.

7. A team approach to assessment, program planning, and review is more likely.

8. School boards and central staff can be activated as enablers and serve as a power base for change.

9. Mainstreaming is not tokenism but meaningful inclusion.

Mainstreaming

Caster (1975B), on behalf of the Council for Exceptional Children, has defined the concept of mainstreaming according to what it is and what it is not. Mainstreaming is: a means to provide the least restrictive alternative; a focus upon need, not the label; creating alternatives that enable general and special educators to serve learners in the regular class setting; and using the skills of general and special educators to foster equal educational opportunity. Mainstreaming is *not:* placing children with special needs in regular classrooms without special support services; using a general education program as a substitute for a needed specialized program; an expedient to save costs at the expense of children; or an unplanned incorporation into regular education without orientation.

Davis (1974) has noted that the shift from self-contained classes to mainstreaming approaches should be accompanied by training for teachers. Former teachers of the self-contained class will require direction to help them function in the more open setting and role of the resource person. Psychological support can assist these former teachers to cope with criticism of past practices and to accept a new role definition.

Blum and Hewett (1971) have described an alternative that has gained attention as an approach to mainstreaming, the Madison Plan. According to Hewett, the Madison Plan *assumes* that: exceptionality is a secondary label; it is desirable to place as many exceptional learners as possible in a regular class setting; this alternative can do "more" than was done in the past; its costs are not beyond reasonable limits; and a total school-staff effort and responsibility will be gained for exceptional children. Implementation appears to depend on: communication between special and regular staff; the principal's willingness to serve as a focus for communication among parents, staff, and consultants; a willingness and readiness of staff to accept the premise that regular class placement *is* a good idea; staff competence which combines academic orientation and expectations with skills in psychological and remedial support; and availability of support systems and specialists for special needs.

The *framework* of the program involves learner variables and instructional organization (figure 11–3). Two teachers and two teacher aides were used in the Madison School in Santa Monica. One teacher and an aide staffed Preacademic I. Another teacher and aide shared Preacademic II and Academic I. Two adjacent classrooms with an adjoining door form the physical space. Hewett estimated that between 36 and 37 children can be served by this arrangement. The Madison Plan is not *the* alternative, but one possible approach. Its strength is in its use of planned, sequential flow from setting to setting.

Figure 11–3 *Components of the Madison Plan Program*

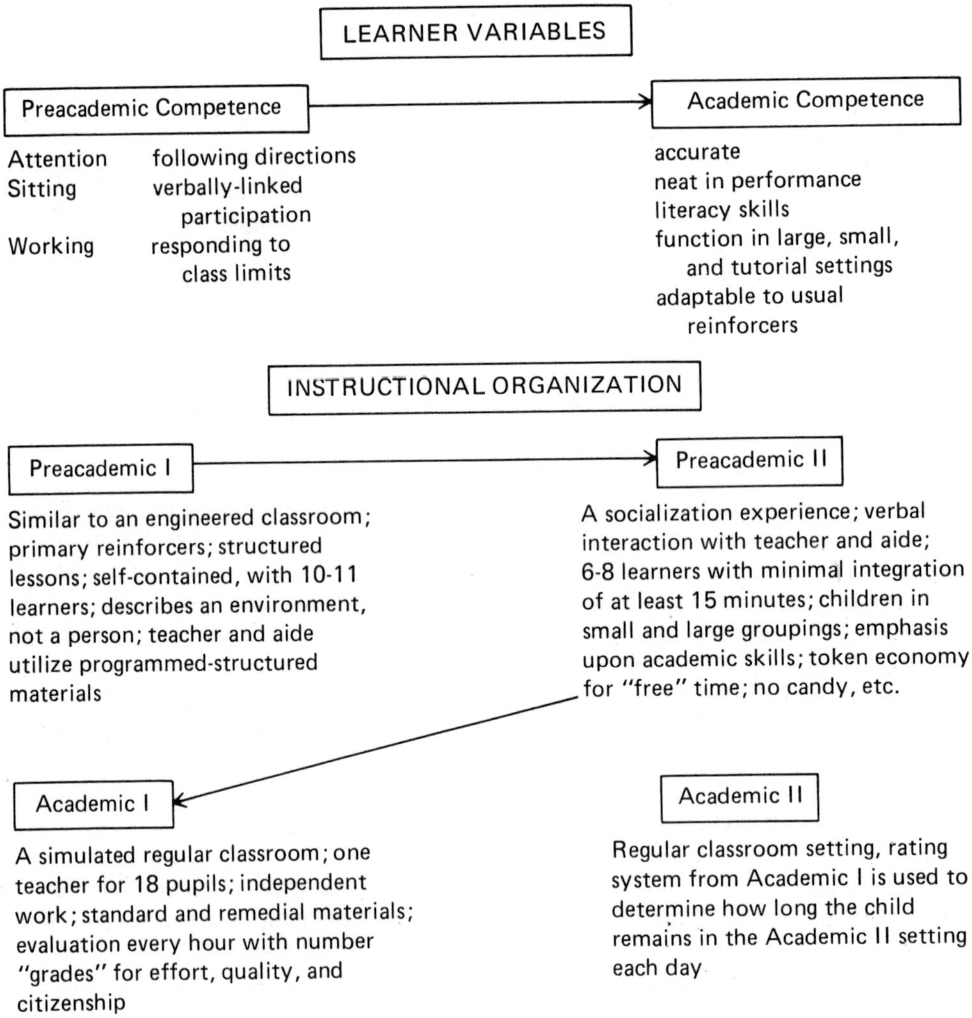

LEARNER VARIABLES
Preacademic Competence
Academic Competence
Attention following directions
Sitting verbally-linked participation
Working responding to class limits
accurate
neat in performance
literacy skills
function in large, small, and tutorial settings
adaptable to usual reinforcers
INSTRUCTIONAL ORGANIZATION
Preacademic I
Preacademic II
Similar to an engineered classroom; primary reinforcers; structured lessons; self-contained, with 10-11 learners; describes an environment, not a person; teacher and aide utilize programmed-structured materials
A socialization experience; verbal interaction with teacher and aide; 6-8 learners with minimal integration of at least 15 minutes; children in small and large groupings; emphasis upon academic skills; token economy for "free" time; no candy, etc.
Academic I
Academic II
A simulated regular classroom; one teacher for 18 pupils; independent work; standard and remedial materials; evaluation every hour with number "grades" for effort, quality, and citizenship
Regular classroom setting, rating system from Academic I is used to determine how long the child remains in the Academic II setting each day

Perspective

Martin (1974) has reflected concern over an apparent pell-mell and naive rush toward mainstreaming *without* recognition of the problems that must be overcome.

1. Training and experience orientation for regular educators must keep pace with efforts to mainstream.
2. Logistical movement from resource room to regular class requires management of schedules, dialogue, materials, etc.
3. Educational prescriptions for the resource and regular classroom experience must be drawn up.
4. Learner programs must be continuously assessed at least annually or semiannually.

THE SPECIAL CLASS

Present Status

Smith and Arkans (1974) have described the function of the special class as serving learners within the IQ range of 50 to 70/75 whose significant developmental discrepancy may preclude meaningful integration with normal learners. They express concern that school districts confused by least-restrictive environment rulings have tended to dismantle *all* their special classes.

Nelson and Schmidt (1974) have suggested that the controversies regarding special classes have lacked sufficient emotional detachment. Aspects of the problem have been: approaching services as either/or; viewing research as proving one method is "best"; engaging in a struggle for survival; viewing all special classes as the same treatment without regard to variations; assuming all resource rooms are alike; and failing to specify *why* alternatives were selected and *why* comparison was undertaken.

Jones (1974) polled *both* normal and mildly retarded students regarding their feelings about their school and schooling. Twelve junior-high schools provided the setting, and the sample was 341 special-class students and a random sample of 717 normal students. The measure was a seven-factor inventory regarding aspects of student morale about the school. (The full scale is reported within the article.) Differences between the retarded and nonretarded were the principal comparisons. In general, the Jones data did not support negative feelings of the retarded about special-class placement. Furthermore, some nonretarded students were negative about *their* regular class placement. Responses, for the most part, appeared to be related to a particular school. Jones concluded that mental retardation was not a homogeneous attribute with respect to attitudes toward placement. Jones also credited the special-class teachers, in both settings, with creating favorable learning environments, which students appeared to appreciate. With respect to stigma, Jones (p. 29) observed:

> One suspects that a confusion has resulted because of the leap from data on the stigmatizing effects of the label mentally retarded to the assumption that the effects generalize to all aspects of the school situation. This does not appear to be the case.

Jones concludes that alternative programs instituted as a reaction to the special class must be carefully evaluated.

Hammonds (1972) suggested that the decline of the self-contained class was more intense than even its critics intended. Hammonds urges that continued research be focused on identification of what groupings of learners are "best" served, and under what circumstances.

Definition

Stanback and Stanback (1975) have presented an updated concept of the needs to which the special class is directed. It is their conviction that a special class possesses certain characteristics:

1. *a skilled educator* who integrates the laws of learning into his or her response pattern;
2. *an individualized program* and individualized instruction;
3. *employment of materials* suited to the abilities of the learner;
4. *access* to related educational, medical, psychological, and social services;
5. *reduced class size* to meet the needs of students;
6. *pupil placement* based upon learning problems rather than on race, behavior disorders, or socioeconomic status;
7. *adequate planning time* for the teacher;
8. *strategies* for management of self-concept; and
9. *integration* of students into regular classes in *all* areas in which they can succeed.

The Stanbacks' study neither implied that the special class *is* the best, or that new alternatives should not be constructed. Their view was that the concept of the special class, as defined by them, has yet to be tested.

Perspective

Dunn (1968) and Johnson (1962) found little scientific evidence to justify the continuation of the special self-contained class. For Johnson, it was a scientific paradox that increased funding, reduced class size, and increased standards for teacher preparation did not seem to be associated with significant achievement and/or personal-social adjustment. For Dunn, six years later, this situation had evolved into a moral issue. Many of the Dunn recommendations of 1968 have become either realities or evident trends. Examples would be the diagnostic-prescriptive teacher, the resource room, the curriculum resource center, collaboration between regular and special education, ability training inventories, and mainstreaming.

Kolstoe (1972) has replied to the observations of Dunn and Johnson. Reviewing a similar body of research, Kolstoe identified the allegations, reviewed sources of evidence, and suggested solutions. Kolstoe (p. 51) states the motives for his study:

> The implications from these writings is that methods of identifying the retarded and programs for educating them actually impede their development. If this is true, it would be most difficult for those of us who work in educational programs for the educable mentally retarded to justify our positions. In view of the widespread criticism leveled at our efforts, it would seem important to examine some of the data used to support these charges.

Kolstoe analyzes the following assumptions:

1. *Labeling harms children.* The evidence is not clear. On the one hand, there are data to support the misuse of IQ testing with minority groups and evidence of using IQ as the exclusive indication of mental retardation. There is also evidence (cited in this text) that the person does not respond negatively in the presence of a quality program. Finally, the use of labels has made possible the channeling of funds and resources which nonlabeling might not have made possible.

2. *Special class placement is bad for the child's self-concept.* Kolstoe notes that the self-concept studies have used testing procedures whose reliability may be questioned. That is to say, changes may be due to measurement error rather than an internalized change.

3. *Segregated programs are fruitless.* The research in this area may be the most suggestive. Kolstoe used the Goldstein, Moss, and Jordan report (1965) as an example. The usual interpretation is that when comparison of general versus special placement shows no differences, general is "better." Kolstoe argues that general has not proven superior, and that research evidence has shown neither to be very effective for academic achievement. Comparison on measures of employability and self-management reflect a different pattern. He cited the studies of Porter and Milazzo (1958) and of Chaffin, Spellman, Regan, and Davison (1971) as typical of many. Both these citations reflect an average employment rate of 50 percent greater for the work-study special education program. Consequently, the effectiveness of special class may be beyond the immediate school years.

4. *General education is capable of dealing adequately with individual differences in the regular classroom.* Kolstoe remains doubtful. He noted surveys that uncovered an absence of course work and/or experience with exceptional learners for

preservice teachers and/or administrators. There was an apparent lack of interest in learning more.

5. *Standards of service quality are not available or known.* The crux of the Kolstoe case appears to focus upon administrative reform. Programs should be fitted to developmental needs of the learner. During the preschool and elementary grades the point-counterpoint between MA capabilities and CA social expectations requires careful management. The use of materials for *both* retarded and normal is still in dispute. The major index of effectiveness should be upon vocational effectiveness. If special programs produce an employment rate of eight out of ten, and nonspecial programs produce but two to three out of ten, this discrepancy requires attention.

A CONTINUING CHALLENGE: THE MODERATELY MENTALLY RETARDED

Renewed Interest

With significant attention focused upon the mainstreaming of the mildly retarded and the excitement generated by right to education for the severely retarded, the moderately mentally retarded learner should not be neglected. The Gearheart and Litton (1975) text indicates renewed interest in this matter. The most striking trend has been the acceptance by public schools of an educational responsibility. Among continuing issues, Gearheart and Litton isolated: effective means of normalization; the degree to which these persons can be economically self-supporting; the efficacy of behavior modification; the proper formula for community living, especially group living; and identification of effective alternatives in curriculum.

Program Emphasis

Bordwell (1974) has described a community involvement program based upon the premise that social learnings cannot be altogether confined to the classroom. The intent of the program was to enlarge the life experiences of these persons through visits and participation in community activities, especially recreation. The Bordwell report offered justifications for this out-of-classroom approach:

1 Frequent community exposure was viewed as a practical and realistic way to reinforce and practice both skills and behaviors developed in the class.

2 Within a relatively brief period of time, adolescents will be coping with community realities.

3 Normal citizens need to encounter retarded citizens, since both will be experiencing one another, given the trend toward community living.
4 School motivation is increased as learners seek to acquire community-living skills.

Bordwell identified certain helpful topics, or skill areas, for these learners:

1 appropriate appearance;
2 comprehension of printed words for information and protection;
3 crossing streets;
4 identifying and using stores, eating places, and sources of employment;
5 behavior appropriate for participation and visiting in another's home, party setting, and when unchaperoned;
6 writing name, address, phone number, age, and sex;
7 communication skills of discussing topics such as family, hobbies, school, as well as identifying themselves by means of an identification card or verbally; and
8 familiarization with action to be taken when lost or bothered by a stranger.

Goldberg (1971) has organized a conceptual frame of reference to describe the scope of education intent for the moderately retarded person. He endorses the Connor (1960) declaration of special education as: *enrichment* (enabling the pupil to interpret experience); *developmental* (tasks within the person's level of readiness); *evaluative* (diagnostic in assessment of strengths and areas for improvement), *preventive* (emphasis on the deletion of failure); *experimental* (testing of hypothesis and assessing "results"); *preparatory* (satisfaction of needs for independent living and vocational adjustment); *individualistic* (practice based on pupil's own diagnosis and prognosis); and *mobile* (providing for the learner wherever he or she resides and whenever it is required). The functions of special education, according to Goldberg, are fulfilled, in part, by three roles of the teacher of the moderately mentally retarded (figure 11–4). These roles describe the teacher as observer, instructor, and evaluator. These are complementary roles; observation formulates the basis of instruction, while evaluation provides the feedback necessary for validation.

A NEW FRONTIER: THE SEVERELY RETARDED

Stanback, Stanback, and Maurer (1976) have identified the education of the severely retarded as a new frontier for the public school. Four events account for the

Figure 11–4 *Suggested Competencies of Teachers of the Moderately Mentally Retarded*

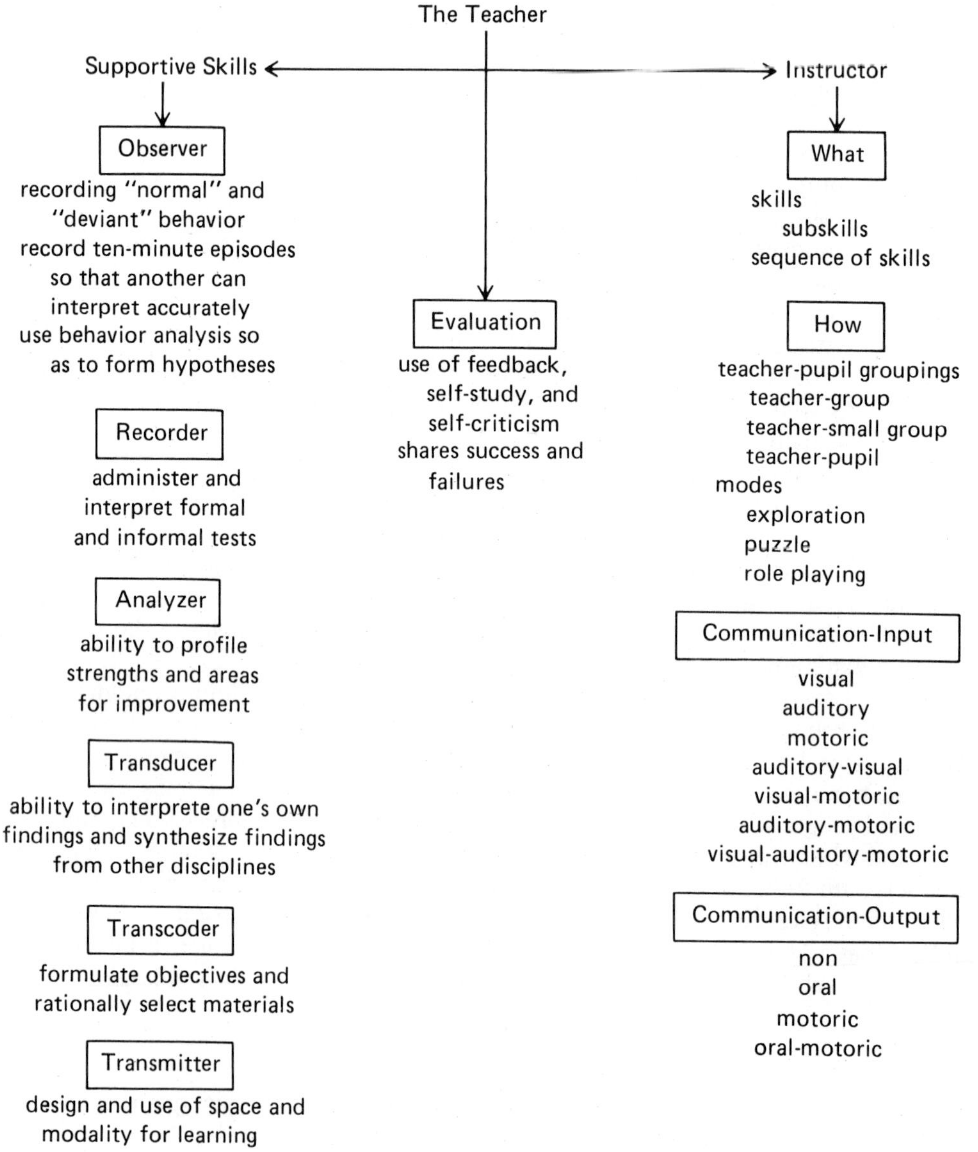
The Teacher
Supportive Skills
Instructor
Observer
recording "normal" and "deviant" behavior
record ten-minute episodes so that another can interpret accurately
use behavior analysis so as to form hypotheses
Recorder
administer and interpret formal and informal tests
Analyzer
ability to profile strengths and areas for improvement
Transducer
ability to interprete one's own findings and synthesize findings from other disciplines
Transcoder
formulate objectives and rationally select materials
Transmitter
design and use of space and modality for learning
Evaluation
use of feedback, self-study, and self-criticism
shares success and failures
What
skills
subskills
sequence of skills
How
teacher-pupil groupings
teacher-group
teacher-small group
teacher-pupil
modes
exploration
puzzle
role playing
Communication-Input
visual
auditory
motoric
auditory-visual
visual-motoric
auditory-motoric
visual-auditory-motoric
Communication-Output
non
oral
motoric
oral-motoric

adoption of the severely retarded as a public-school responsibility: the pioneering of behavioristic technology by Bensberg and the Pennsylvania Association for Retarded Citizens suit, which established the precedent for public-school involvement; the founding of the American Association for the Education of the Severely and Profoundly Handicapped by Haring; and a high national priority established by the Bureau for the Education for the Handicapped of the U.S. Department of Health, Education, and Welfare.

Program Approaches

Bokee, Burke, and Sontag (1974) have provided an overview of approaches to programming for the severely mentally retarded. Their articles outlined seventeen programs designed to extend services to learners as well as to constitute a preparation program for professional personnel. Common features included competency-based instruction with intensive practicum and rigorous evaluation. The University of Washington project, directed by Affleck and Haring, specified a rather complete curriculum for both the professional person and the retarded learner. The professional component included: educational needs; community resources; use of relevant data (legal rights, learning characteristics, family problems, etc.); assessing children's behavior at task entry; evaluating pupil progress daily; reporting progress to both administrators and parents; selection of materials and activities; and the use of appropriate strategies (modeling, imitating, instruction feedback, and contingency-management). The pupil curriculum included: language development; fine and gross motor skills; life skills (personal hygiene, time, and change); and prevocational and vocational development. Sailor, Guess, and Lavis (1975), as well as Smeets and Manfredini (1973), have described similar programs. Both reports utilized a residential facility as a demonstration station to encourage inspection and visits within their regional areas. Smeets and Manfredini organized their program around four skill centers through which pupils were rotated. Pupils would spend from one half hour to an hour and a half in each center. The four centers included motor skills, vocabulary, communication, and social behaviors. The content and activities described appear to parallel the focus of the TMR-Performance Profile and the Cain-Levine Social Competence Scale.

Professional Preparation

The Bradtke, Kirkpatrick, Rosenblatt, and Bannatyne (1975) report details an integrated approach to professional preparation and pupil services. Their program involves the following sequence:

1. *Orientation* outlines the aims and goals of the program and provides an overview of the training sequence.

2. *Observations* are of four types: specific positive behavior; child reaction to adult as expressed in attending; task analysis of child's response to a task, such as placing a ring on a stick; and child reaction to child, such as affective responses.

3. *Transitional activities* are discussions, written impressions, reading, and buzz sessions to reinforce and clarify what is being experienced.

4. *Simulation* activities involve examination of materials, role playing, and practice of reinforcement techniques.

5. *Classroom management* includes exposure to physical structure of the classroom, video-tapes showing operations, and finally participating in setting up a classroom.

6. *Prescriptive programming* involves developing a program for one observed child, including goals, materials, activity cards, and behavioral approaches.

7. *Individual conferences* allow time for discussion of progress.

8. *Rhythmitics* involves the reduction of anxieties, inhibitions about contact, and shyness. The attempt was to encourage freedom of movement. Examples may include being blindfolded and hobbled to imitate behaviors associated with impairment.

9. *Intensive play* constitutes the first physical contact with the child. The trainee selects the child, goals, and activity.

10. *Parallel teaching* is a modeling situation. The person selects a child and functions under the prescription and guidance of a staff person. Video-tapes are made.

11. *Solo teaching* is a kind of graduation. Although still under supervision, the trainee becomes increasingly responsible for all aspects of the child's program.

12. *Self-evaluation* involves viewing video-tapes to identify positive samples of mastery. A certificate is presented upon graduation.

Program Outcomes

Luckey and Addison (1974) have prepared a comprehensive (over one hundred references) summary regarding curriculum for the severely and profoundly mentally retarded. Based upon their review of the literature, these authors identified the following emphases in Preschool-Age curricula:

1 *Sensory-motor stimulation* involves encouraging sensory responses and providing an enriched environment.

2 *Physical development* involves basic motor skills of locomotion and movement.

3 *Pre self-care* involves passive-accepting responses to feeding, dressing, bathing, and toileting.
4 *Language stimulation* involves attending, vocalization, and responding.
5 *Interpersonal response* involves recognition of familiar persons, requesting attention, and engaging in brief play with toys.

In school-age curricula emphasis is on:

1 *Sensory-motor development* focuses upon identifying the names and sources of sounds, textures, weights, colors and odors.
2 *Physical mobility and coordination* involves walking, use of playground equipment, and track and field events.
3 *Self-care development* involves self-feeding, removing garments, and toileting with supervision.
4 *Language development* includes recognition of name, body parts, familiar objects, as well as imitating sounds, responding to simple commands, and using simple expressive language.
5 *Social behavior* includes requesting personal attention, using self-protective skills, and playing in parallel fashion.

The adult curriculum includes:

1 *Sensory-motor integration* involves sorting, inserting, pulling, folding, and transferring skills, as well as responding to music, making choices and discrimination of sizes, colors, temperatures, etc.
2 *Physical dexterity and recreation* should focus upon use of community parks and playgrounds, especially in swimming and game activities, as well as the use of pencil, scissors, pasting and cutting.
3 *Self-care* includes eating a varied diet, only partial supervision for dressing and bathing and occasional help in toileting.
4 *Language and speech* involves listening, directions, and use of phrases.
5 *Self-direction and work* involves a minimum of work-activity center participation, including skills in completing tasks, sharing, taking turns, and waiting for instructions.

The Bellamy, Peterson, and Close (1975) report provides an illustration of *vocational* competence. Inspired by Gold (1972) and with over fifty references, the report covers a project designed to train severely and profoundly retarded persons (some of the sample had measured IQs of 10) to assemble a nineteen-piece cam switch actuator. These authors report a fifty-one-step procedure to enable their clients to achieve a level of production equal to, and often exceeding, that of normal workers. They suggested that their results are similar to other reports in the literature: assembly of twenty-four-piece and twenty-six-piece printheads; a fifty-two-piece cam switch actuator; a fifteen-piece bicycle brake; constructing boxes; and soldering color-coded wires to a television plug, to name but a few. It is their contention that lack of work productivity is not an *intellectual* defect, but a defect in the *work environment*. The Bellamy et al. report identifies discrimination skills, reinforcement, and sequence of task as critical variables in the work environment.

VOCATIONAL PREPARATION AND EMPLOYMENT

Tasks

Community-based services will center upon employment opportunities for the mentally retarded person. The follow-up studies cited in this text have identified employment as a realistic goal. Employment requires preparation of the person *and* the community. The public schools will be a primary resource in this training and preparation. Associated with preparation will be identifying sources of employment, development of training sites, maintenance of supervision of trainees, as well as follow-up services.

Resources

Aside from the special education unit of a public-school district, the school's unit of vocational education will be a program resource. At county levels, a division of vocational rehabilitation (DVR) will assist in processing and assisting retarded persons during and after school years. A department of social services and welfare may be involved in job training for working mothers, either in training programs or in providing day-care facilities. Community mental health boards may sponsor subsidized activity centers for retarded persons unprepared or unable to engage in competitive employment. A department of labor will be involved in the certification of work conditions and standards for employment, and an employment security commission will monitor economic trends in the community and identify prospective employers. An ARC unit will serve as a catalyst for public awareness concerning employment needs and may also sponsor activity centers for retarded persons. The United Way Fund may be a principal sponsor of sheltered workshops and/or activity centers. Service groups and organizations may also constitute a source for employment as well as a source of contract work for sheltered workshops and activity centers. Given this array of potential resources for employment and training, it is evident that planning and coordination are vital.

A Cascade

Figure 11–5 constitutes a summary of vocational alternatives. The figure is intended to parallel the cascade concept associated with educational services. The probable levels for the retarded, based upon the Grossman report, are displayed. The Buddle and Menolascino (1971) report reflect the appropriateness of this cascade approach. They note that habilitation follows a sequence.

1 *Training readiness* involves work orientation and behavior management.
2 *Vocational exploration* involves critical social skills training and basic psychomotor training.
3 *Vocational training* involves job-related skills training, simulated job-task training, and on-the-job training.
4 *Vocational specialization* involves training in related social skills relevant to placement and specific skills required.
5 *Vocational habilitation* involves final placement based upon completion of the preceding four steps.

Their report identifies a type of employment noted in figure 11–5 as employment with *sheltered* adaptations. This category includes those who have sufficient skills to deserve wages comparable to the normal worker. However, this person may require modifications in work routine and complexity of duties. The person is a valued worker, and thus the employer may be willing to make certain adjustments in his or her job description.

Subsidized Settings

Certain persons may require a setting other than the standard, open, and competitive environment of business and industry. Fraenkel (1961) outlined these options as extended employment, work activity, and adult activity. These options differ as to the level of subsidy required for the work. In *extended* employment (formerly known as terminal employment), the facility accepts contracts. The worker is sufficiently capable to produce products with a minimum of supervision and is paid on a piecework basis. The facility usually operates on an income-equal-to expenses format. Consequently, the wages paid are an expense, not a subsidy. This type of facil-

Figure 11–5 *A Vocational Cascade*

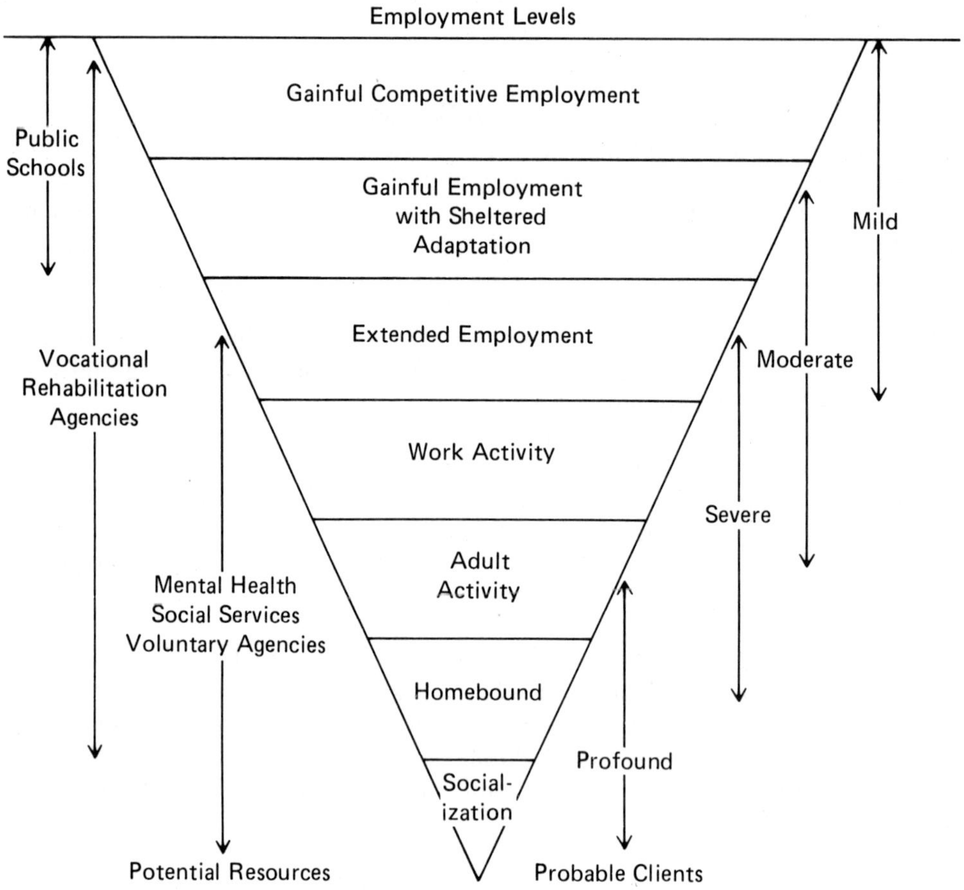

ity is termed a *sheltered workshop*. For some persons, the degree of supervision to complete a contract requires enough supervision to require a subsidy for the workers. Also, this type of program will emphasize continuing training in social and recreational skills, which also requires staffing. This type of facility is termed as an *adult activity center*. The concept of the *work activity center* has emerged in recent years as an option between extended employment and the adult activity center. In the work activity center deviations from minimum wage can be sought if special considerations of training and performance are justified. In actual practice, one will encounter a sheltered workshop providing all three options in one setting. Another typical pattern is for a combined work and adult activity center. The role of the sheltered workshop is changing to include a diagnostic and training function as well as an employment function. In some communities, employment in the home is possible. In this arrangement, the products are distributed through retail outlets and the worker is reimbursed. Simpson (1973) has identified the home as a possible career education site. She noted that television could be a useful training tool.

PERSPECTIVES

An Interface Perspective

Garrett (1970) has advocated an interface between the schools and rehabilitation services. His hypothesis is that preparation for vocational adjustment should begin in the early grades, and he suggests a *developmental* approach to encourage an orderly transition from school to work. Collaborative efforts may be more successful at local than at state levels. State education agencies are usually consultive and supervisory, while local rehabilitation agencies are direct service providers. Garrett suggests that local collaborative efforts can provide a long-term sequential program in keeping with the person's need for a more sustained period for training and practice of skills.

An Employment Perspective

The President's Committees on Mental Retardation and Committee on Employment of the Handicapped (1968) issued a collaborative analysis of employment for retarded persons. In consideration of employment trends for "today and tomorrow," the observation was made that the labor force is expanding and that automation is not associated with the evaporation of lesser-skilled jobs. This document cited the following situations:

1 A laundry owner has to hire 100 persons in one year to keep ten jobs filled.
2 An industrial plant has to go on a four-day week because of excessive Monday morning absenteeism.
3 A chain of restaurants has placed a standing order with local public employment offices for anybody. "If he's breathing, we'll hire him," says the manager.
4 A Labor Department survey of employment in eating places reflected a need for 65,000 jobs.

This report of the two committees urges that special emphasis be given to medical and social services to support education and training of the retarded. With respect to public awareness, a survey of one thousand persons selected in a scientific sampling procedure was reported. The following hypothetical case was presented:

> Thomas B: He is aged 20 and mentally retarded. Outwardly normal, he has the intelligence of an average 8-year-old. He can care for himself, do simple chores, and read and write at the third grade level. Should he and others like him be encouraged to work?

Sixteen percent thought the retarded person should be trained for regular employment side by side with normal workers. Thirteen percent thought work training should be undertaken only if strong desire were evident. Fifty-eight percent felt employment should be confined to sheltered workshops only, and ten percent felt there should be no employment at all.

The President's Committee on Employment of the Handicapped and the National Association for Retarded Citizens (1972) have prepared a manual regarding jobs for the mentally retarded. This manual reaffirms the availability of jobs despite general levels of unemployment. Among employers of note:

1. *Federal government* has employed about seven thousand retarded persons. In some instances the job has been reengineered to suit the specific abilities of the person by redefining the job situation.

2. *State governments* have opened significant opportunities. Examples would be the District of Columbia, Minnesota, New York, and North Carolina. Common features of these states is to identify the division of vocational rehabilitation as the source of referral and placement. Typical written exams are waived, and only the performance of the person is considered.

3. NARC, in cooperation with the U.S. Department of Labor, has provided employment training and placement within *private industry*. Employers have included: Hutzler's Department Store, Baltimore, Maryland; Iona Manufacturing Co., Manchester, Connecticut; Chicago Post Office; Johnson's Turkey and Sheep Ranch, Goldthwaite, Texas; Victor Wagner and Son, Cleveland, Ohio (box manufacturers); Lackland Military Training Center, Texas; RJR Foods, Duluth, Minnesota; San Francisco General Services Administration; American Industrial Safety Equipment Co., Cleveland; and the Mail and Messenger Branch, Department of HEW, Rockville, Maryland.

Work as Adjustment

Work has meaning to all persons beyond economic survival and/or materialistic comfort. Work means: adulthood, being grown up; feeling of being a part of society, not apart from it; a sense of internal growth, of confronting problems and meeting day-to-day situations; and the achievement of independence, a sense of freedom both in the present and the future, a control of one's own destinies.

Granat and Granat (1973) offer data to illustrate social adaptation as the prime criterion for defining mental retardation during adulthood. Nineteen thousand persons examined for induction into military service in Sweden were studied. Approximately 1.5 percent were found to fall within the psychometric criteria of mental retardation. The authors concluded that adaptability can mask intellectual level. Bunda and Mezzano (1968) have documented that a work experience program can reduce dropping out from school. Cantoni (1973) reported an investigation comparing an experimental work-experience program to a more conventional secondary program for the mildly retarded. The experimental program featured a self-contained building that included a simulated industrial work setting. The program also provided intensive diagnostic evaluation and counseling. The program also was a collaborative effort of public school, vocational rehabilitation, and social services. The comparisons reflected advancement for program graduates in job earnings and tenure. Also reported were gains in measured intelligence. The earnings of the graduates coupled with removal from the Aid to Dependent Children Program approached the cost of operation of the experimental program. Blue (1964) has demonstrated that the sheltered workshop can serve as an economic resource in a community. Industries may be swamped with production orders to which this type of facility can respond. Sheltered workshops also can engage in salvage and assembly production that normal workers would reject.

CAREER DEVELOPMENT AND EDUCATION

A new program emphasis in the mainstream of general education is career development and/or education. The theme of career education is to integrate career-related concepts as early as possible into the school experience. Consequently, awareness of work occurs in the *primary grades,* while exploration of "job families" constitutes *later elementary*. Prevocational examination of fairly specific vocational clusters may constitute the *junior-high* emphasis, while preparation for a particular career is the focus of the *high-school* period.

From a contemporary perspective, the Leland habilitation perspective (described in chapter 2) would appear to be highly complementary. From a historical standpoint, the concept of occupational education pioneered by Hungerford (1950) for mentally retarded persons also complements the current emphasis on Career Education. The common emphasis is upon introduction of career-related concepts early into the school experience. Occupational education centers upon the following:

Attitude formation. Here, stress is placed upon personal values necessary for work success. These may include dependability, responsibility, ability to accept criticism, and those values described in chapter 7 associated with successful job adjustment. Fulton (1975) reported that emotional maladjustment, as reflected in acting-out behaviors, differentiated between retained and terminated retarded workers. Factors such as IQ, academic achievement, and skills were not significant.

Related language concepts. The suggestion is made that work efficiency may center around certain language concepts. They include: words necessary for understanding signs and directions, signs necessary for self-protection, concepts of measurement, the language of application forms and personnel records, the language and structure of government benefits and record forms, and the language and customs of courtesy.

Job information. In this area the following topics would be covered: what jobs are available, the duties of jobs, the importance or significance of jobs, the necessity of "good" habits, the sources of jobs, and relating "academic" instruction to job performance. Cordier (1975) has noted the language of career education is confusing, even to professionals. She suggested certain clarifications. *Vocational* involves a sense of a need or motive to be productive. It is the feeling of identity one gains from usefulness and contribution. *Occupational* proceeds from this sense. Occupational, however, suggests a clustering of common attitudes, habits, and skills. Consequently, one may speak of service *occupations* such as food service, ground maintenance, small machine repair, etc. A *job* is conceived as a fairly specific task-related set of skills. Consequently, present efforts aimed at career education emphasize the vocational-motivational aspects as well as occupational and job-training aspects. Given the list of common topics, one might design topics as vocational for elementary, occupational for preadolescent and adolescent, and job-related for adolescent and adult. Cordier emphasized that the concept of career involves these elements of vocational, occupational, and job. That is to say, workers (including professionals), in theory, have a sense of viewing a career as a means of fulfillment of internal needs, possess knowledges and attitudes required for performance, and can display required skills. Given the Cordier discussion, one feels a sense of urgency if the implications of her suggestions are evident. If Career Education is deferred until the high-school period (ca 15 to 17), then vocational, occupational, and job must be covered in a compressed period. Contrast that to a career education period covering the full time span of schooling. Furthermore, the necessity of extending the school period *beyond* the traditional age for retarded persons becomes evident.

Job training. This element involves the acquisition of performance skills for a particular activity. Essential to this area is the opportunity to practice, under supervision, skills necessary for success. Kolstoe and Frey (1965) have emphasized the school as a job-training environment. The sequence may be thought of as: in class entirely, in class with in-school opportunities such as the cafeteria, in class and out-of-school exploration placements, in class with supervised placements in jobs, and out-of-school placement with supervision from the school. Tarkington and Overbeck (1975) offer data that reaffirms the importance of job satisfaction. Comparing satisfied and dissatisfied workers, these authors reported that certain traits discriminated between the two groups: responsible-irresponsible; helpful-nonhelpful; careful-careless; efficient-inefficient; pleasant-unpleasant; dependable-undependable; and interested-disinterested.

Program Scope

Drier (1975) has identified the school's responsibilities for career education as *needs assessment* of students, school resources, and economic conditions; *mobilization of resources* and development of related programs; and *evaluative procedures,* which must be developed to assess program validity and to evaluate new ways to either expand or improve programs. His emphasis is upon relating the person to the world of work and on an integration of school program and the community. Figure 11–6, an adaptation of Drier, suggests that schools and the community share mutual areas of interest, especially in the sharing of information between the two so that it is available and acted upon by the person.

Cohen's (1972) comments regarding rehabilitation-habilitation concepts for the retarded reinforce the Drier model. The Cohen model clusters around the responsibilities of practitioners, especially educators. These clusters are summarized as:

1 A life-space orientation about the retarded person. A focus on the range of life experiences, not merely upon the age span of one's clients.
2 Involvement in the team concept. The use of other disciplines, especially follow-up services.
3 Use of community resources and facilities. Emphasis is upon application of these resources for the person.
4 Viewing the retarded person as functioning within a family and a community. This involves the structuring of experiences that are meaningful to the person, not to the practitioner.

Guiding Principles

Cohen and Hungerford have stressed the importance of attitude regarding programming. Programs based upon relief, happiness, salvage, or busy-work concepts can only serve to limit opportunities and capabilities. For example, Gold (1973) contends there can be a discrepancy between what the retarded *do* vocationally and

Figure 11–6 *Summation of Emphasis of Career Education Programs*

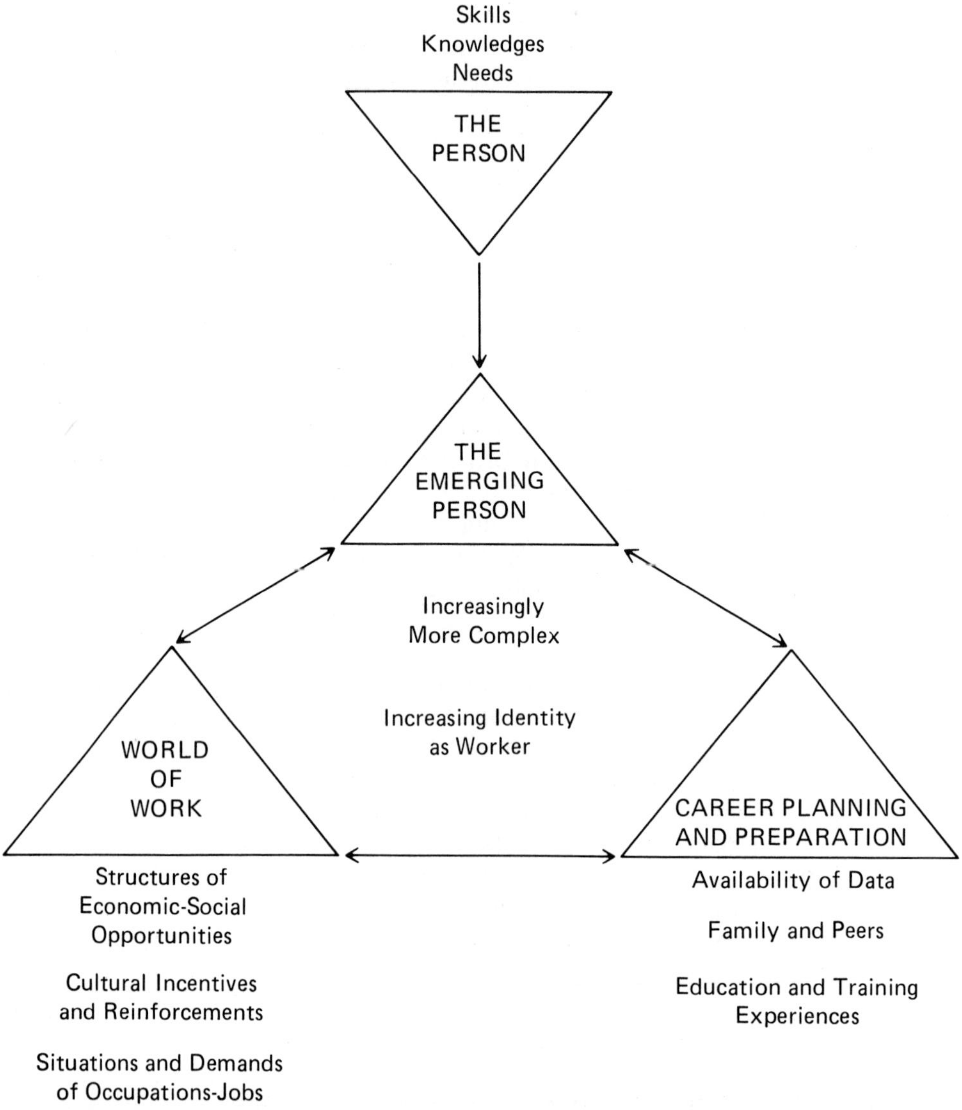

what they are *capable of doing*. Gold attributes this discrepancy, in part, to past experiences with professionals and to social expectations rather than to abilities of retarded persons. The Gold report utilized a sample of young adults within the moderately retarded range. The task was the assembly of a fourteen-piece bicycle brake. The report noted that these units were assembled at rates that matched or exceeded that for normal workers in both quantity (number assembled per hour) and quality (number accepted as error free). The training procedure used a task analysis to identify a sequential training procedure. Gold concluded that this study, typical of his project efforts, uncovered certain principles about job potential for the retarded.

1. Task complexity is more important than task difficulty in a work situation. A fourteen-piece assembly is difficult. Creating a sequential training program reduces complexity to a manageable level for the worker.

2. Attempts should be made to increase the level and economic value of work to be performed rather than evolving elaborate systems for reinforcing low-paying simple work. The fourteen-piece operation enabled these moderately retarded workers to be paid wages similar to those of the normal worker.

3. Reinforcement does not altogether depend upon money or praise. Completion of a complex task affords reinforcement to the person.

4. In the work situation, acquisition (time required for) of skill attainment is unrelated to production. Gold identified this as a key finding. It was his observation that certain persons may be "evaluated" as incapable and therefore denied access to training. It was Gold's conclusion that the best "test" is the training itself.

TRAINING AND PLACEMENT

Competencies

Brolin (1973) surveyed 281 persons directly responsible for career education of mildly retarded persons to identify the competencies required of personnel in this field. This report isolated thirty-one competencies: occupational (11); activities of daily living (ADL) (9); psychosocial (9); and academic (3). *Academic* competencies included teaching, organizing and evaluating, and literacy skills. *Psychosocial* areas included social behavior, self-concept, personal guidance, interaction with normal students, helping parents, independent thinking, aesthetic values, and functioning in the environment. *ADL* competencies involved care of personal needs, home management, communication skills, responsibility, use of community resources, leisure time, home mechanics, civic responsibilities, and use of transportation. *Occupational* areas included: work adjustment *and* job seeking, finding suitable job-tryout sites *and* suitable employment, conducting an evaluation program, providing guidance, using related community agencies *and* writing reports, coordinating postschool activities, and providing specific training and manual training. Occupational competencies were rated as more important than the other three areas. The respondents also recommended that the ADL area should be more fully provided by other school personnel rather than as an exclusive emphasis of the special educator. Coordination with out-of-school agencies was needed, and school programs should designate a responsible person for this task. An equally important need was for a prevocational placement and training specialist to coordinate intraschool programs. This role was viewed as monitoring both habilitative and academic efforts.

Flores (1975) has described behavioral analysis skills as helpful. A behavioral checklist for each student can be the criterion to demonstrate mastery. Its content should be based on skills rather than knowledges. Weisenstein (1975) has reported that audiovisual aids, such as a pictorial job training manual and slide presentation, were helpful in the acquisition of vocational skills. The goal was to prepare retarded persons to function as maids in hotels and motels.

Nonschool Settings

Borrelli (1972) has provided an overview of the relationship between public-school programming and the programming available from private agencies, especially the sheltered workshops. His focus was upon the involvement of the Social and Rehabilitation Services Administration (SRSA) of HEW, which includes vocational rehabilitation. For public-school programs, SRSA funds can be used to provide vocational rehabilitation counselors for students at age seventeen.

(It should be noted that many federal programs are permissive in nature. While a federal "benefit" may exist, it is left to the state to decide if it wishes to qualify. In turn, each community agency must decide if it wishes to accept federal and state standards.)

The SRSA response to sheltered workshops can be threefold.

1. *Evaluation.* One function is for assessment of job functioning and the other is extended evaluation. Both require evidence of disability sufficient to impair or limit vocational functioning. In general, mildly and moderately retarded persons would qualify. Estimates of job functioning may range from potential employment through extended employment. Borrelli took exception to the term *terminal employment* and advanced the concept of *permanent worker status.* If, after evaluation, the person is considered eligible for either gainful, sheltered-adaptive, or permanent-extended worker status, the person is referred for training. For persons for whom diagnosis is difficult, an extended evaluation is possible. Borrelli noted that acceptance does not bind the facility or SRSA funds for training. If not judged eligible, the person is referred to adult activity or work-activity programs. Borrelli identified the use of IQ as a prime indicator, although not the exclusive one. Itkin

(1972) has offered objections to the measure, as have Gold, Dybroad, and Leland. Their premise is that in a work situation, the "best" test is the training or work situation itself.

2. *Training*. This component of the sheltered workshop facility has three elements: work adjustment training (WAT), employment training, and extended evaluation. Following evaluation, SRSA will fund the facility for WAT. This element is devoted to basic work habits, socialization, and "motivation" to work for money. The second phase of WAT centers around rather specific skill training designed to increase productivity and/or skill proficiency. Extended evaluation may be made available to individuals who are judged by facility staff to be likely to benefit from further emphasis in areas covered under WAT. At present, extended employment may be for up to eighteen months. Following this period, a decision must be rendered.

3. *On-the-job training*. This phase involves a *supervised* placement in a competitive position. The person is afforded opportunities to practice and refine skills gained in training. In another arrangement, SRSA funds can be used to subsidize an on-the-job training placement. Initially, an employer pays 25 percent of the wages, then increases to 50 percent, and in the final phase, to 75 percent. (This "arrangement" may be available to public schools as well as sheltered workshops.) The employer has first option on the worker, but is not obligated to hire the person. The purpose of this program is to gain supervised training sites. Mention is made of the Post Office and Department of Defense as both employers and as training sites.

Garner (1972), Lacy (1972), and Greasy (1972) have advanced an analysis of the sheltered workshop movement as well as a projection regarding the future. Garner places the "first" workshop at the Perkins Institute in Boston around 1840. However, he noted that it was not until after World War I that the sheltered workshop gained prominence as a unique facility and program element. Garner concluded that sheltered workshops have possessed a dual tradition of a service to the handicapped *and* a means to fulfill perceived needs of social conscience. Lacy noted that at present a sheltered workshop facility can provide three elements of service: evaluation and work training, extended employment, and work activity. His observation was that while all three elements can exist under one roof, it may be more efficient to establish separate facilities (especially for training and evaluation) in order to focus upon specific program missions. Greasy has listed five program development considerations for multipurpose sheltered workshops.

1. *Single disability focus*. It was suggested that multidisability workshops (orthopedic, mentally restored, sensory disabled, mentally retarded, etc.) have certain advantages over a single disability facility. The prime advantage may be that a multidisability facility possesses a clientele of greater skills. It is possible to form an ability team of two disabled workers. For example, a retarded worker with motor skills can be paired with a physically impaired worker who can provide a degree of guid-

ance. The major problem in this arrangement is to protect the interests of the retarded worker. However, the ability team concept has the prime advantage of increasing the flexibility of the facility to accept contracts.

2. *Location of workshop.* The choice of site should be in areas of business and industry. It was suggested that location in industrial areas would increase availability of contracts and reduce unnecessary transportation costs.

3. *Community involvement.* This element involves the degree and extent of coordination of the facility in conjunction with other service elements. Also, the facility should be integrated into the economic life of the community to monitor sources of new jobs and new contract possibilities. The facility cannot passively await contracts but must assertively seek to publicize its mission. Regional cooperation among facilities was also stressed.

4. *Staffing.* Given the three possible elements of service, there are decisions regarding competencies of staff. For example, the recreational and leisure-time training elements of a work activity center dictate certain responsibilities. It was recommended that goals of the program should be a basis for selection of staff.

5. *New jobs.* A "task definer" could be employed by a single facility or by a consortium of facilities to investigate and examine industries to locate jobs potentially available for retarded workers. Negotiation with industry would involve establishment of equipment within the program site, or perhaps groups of workers could be located in the industry site.

The *residential facility* can also serve as both program and site for vocational preparation. Richardson (1975) has reported upon the status of vocational training for the retarded in state residential facilities. His report represented 146 such facilities. The Richardson survey isolated four basic generalizations.

1. Between 1957 and 1974, the populations of state facilities have changed, and this change is reflected in work-training programs. Actual residents in real-work conditions have dropped by 20 percent, and this mode of on-the-job training represented 64 percent of training modes.

2. The training-production conflict has been resolved. Facilities are either losing, training, and/or refusing to admit more capable persons. Those who remain are benefiting from professional recognition of the involuntary servitude aspects of production. Also, there is a recognition that "work-training" may constitute an exploitation of resident skills.

3. Resident pay is an issue. In 1957, about 31 percent of retarded workers received pay, while 90 percent currently receive pay. Of this portion, however, about 69 percent receive cash. Other payments constitute vouchers, tokens, treats, or privileges.

4. A need for planning remains. The transition to more extended employment and work-activity-oriented programs will require concentrated efforts.

Elements of Job Placement

Sigler and Kakaska (1971) have presented an outline of the elements of job placement. These authors assume that the practitioners responsible for vocational services must prepare for this assignment. While the outline does not guarantee success, attention to it would increase the chances.

1. *Hiring the retarded worker.* These authors stress that employers will respond to the benefits to the business or industry of hiring the retarded person more than to an appeal to social conscience. The authors identified certain traits, verified by research, which would be of interest to the world of commerce and industry. These were said to demonstrate the retarded worker as one who is able to do a variety of jobs and is a conscientious worker. These authors restated their suggestion that one should offer increased efficiency within the business.

2. *Qualifications of employers.* The suggestion is made that the business operation should be investigated *prior* to initial contacts. An analysis of types of jobs, skill levels of employees, work situations, etc. will save time and efforts in the future. There is little to be gained from employer contact if the work situation doesn't fit prospective employee abilities.

3. *Initial contacts. After* an initial appraisal has been made, employers may be contacted by three approaches: mail, telephone, or personal visitation. The most effective reception can be obtained through referral; there is a greater chance of obligating or obtaining time for an appointment. The purpose is to gain an appointment for a specific time and place. The mail mode may be a general information letter or a specific letter. The theme is to stress that one has persons in whom the employer *will* be interested because they fit the needs of the firm.

4. *Obtaining the interview.* This phase is the follow-up to the initial contacts. Initial contact must be pursued and specific time and place for the appointment secured.

5. *The appointment/interview.* The objective is to get the employer to say "Yes!" Sigler and Kakaska suggested the following rules and/or guidelines for the interview:

Keep the presentation short and direct.
Speak in terms relevant to the employer's needs and interests.
Sell the benefits of the worker. Share the evidence.
Concentrate on obtaining "Yes" answers. Maintain an atmosphere of positives.
Use trial closes. For example, if the person agrees that your workers are as reliable as his workers, move to when your client can start. If there is a negative response, move back to original point of agreement. One should not ignore negative answers.
Avoid sidetracks and digressions.

6. *Overcoming objections.* There may be objections. One should anticipate them and prepare for them. Some will originate from misconceptions. One should be honest and firm. Some may be valid. For example, an employer may observe that your clients aren't as "smart" as most. The practitioner will acknowledge that, but concentrate on the skills and benefits.

The Sigler and Kakaska discussion should *not* be understood as a set of "tricks" or "gimmicks" to persuade someone against their will. If a potential worker has certain potential problems, these should be identified and planned for. These authors reflected the principle of honesty. Placement and training personnel have a worthy cause to "sell." Promoting a partially prepared person as though she or he were trained only thwarts opportunities for others.

SUMMING UP

This chapter has been concerned with programs designed to prepare mentally retarded citizens for vocational roles. Among the concepts presented in this chapter, the following are selected for summation:

1. Educational services are a cascade which ranges from self-contained settings to mainstreaming in standard educational settings.

2. Standards of quality for educational and vocational services can be known and understood. Such standards can be a useful guide for practice.

3. There is no *one* model for the resource-room concept. There are variations to the goal of inclusion in the least restrictive alternative.

4. The stigma generally assumed with placement in a self-contained setting does not necessarily hold true. The quality of the program appears to be the significant factor to the person.

5. The moderately mentally retarded require continuing attention to insure program quality. Out-of-school experiences are to be fostered. Teachers need skills of observation, instruction, and evaluation.

6. The severely mentally retarded represent a new frontier for the public schools. There is a growing body of research literature and experience to guide practice.

7. The special class versus resource room illustrates the need for program standards. Just as the special class faded because of nonadherence to its program definition, a similar fate could befall the resource room.

8. The person's needs should dictate placement, not vice versa. The Madison Plan is *one* example of an approach that permits transition from a structured setting to open settings.

9. Schooling is designed to enable persons to acquire the attitudes, understandings, and skills associated with physical comfort, psychological stability, vocational adequacy, and social adequacy.

10. Specific outcomes for the mentally retarded can be identified. Elements would include perception, communication, literacy, personal adjustment, and social adjustment.

11. Vocational alternatives reflect a cascade of services. *Sheltered* employment (a restructuring of standard job tasks, but within a normal setting) reflects promise as an employment option.

12. Career education has become a prevalent program concept. Its emphasis begins in the early grades as an awareness effort and culminates with occupational entry.

13. Competencies of practitioners who assume vocational preparation roles can be known and understood. Such persons will have roles different from the traditional classroom setting.

14. The role of the sheltered workshop is changing. Aside from its emphasis upon noncompetitive employment, these facilities are also engaged in work evaluation, training, and employment.

15. Adult activity and work activity centers are becoming alternatives for adult retarded citizens.

16. Recent studies show that meaningful work and production are a possibility for even the most impaired of the retarded. The "best" test for work appears to be the work situation itself.

ON LOCATION

The observations of Wheeler (1976) offer certain insights into the reactions of an adaptable, career-oriented, twenty-five-year-old citizen to being mentally retarded. He is an alumnus of special education and rehabilitation. He is a positive example of a person who is enthusiastic about life and who possesses a sense of extending help to others.

> It is not easy to ask a retarded person how he feels about being retarded, but it is reassuring to hear one of them say, "*Oh, it doesn't bother me.*"
>
> Whether that is the whole truth or just a mask behind which the retarded individual has learned to hide his true feelings, it is not easy to decide.
>
> This question came up recently when *Mental Retardation News* was interviewing a young retarded man who appears to have a very well-adjusted life, working in Las Vegas. It had been suggested that reactions to the world in general, and his adjustments to his life in particular could be revealing.
>
> Wheeler first was an employee at the Opportunity Village (the Las Vegas Association for Retarded Citizens) button factory and he currently is employed at the Golden Nugget Casino, where he recently was promoted from packaging and wrapping to porter. He is married, his wife is pregnant for the first time, and from visible evidence, he has no regrets or bitterness about his life. In fact, he is a spirited citizen who is on the

board of directors of Nevada Advocates for the Mentally Retarded and attends all their board meetings and social functions. He also is a protege of advocate George Rogers, who brought him to talk with us.

Daniel appears to have a double mission in life, because he not only has his job and his marriage (to a girl he dated for five years after they met in a special education class in high school), but he himself acts as an advocate for several of his friends at the Opportunity Village Workshops.

"They are sometimes a little irresponsible," his advocate interjected, adding that part of Daniel's duty is to see that they get to the workshop on time, to the bus in time so they won't miss the ride when they are going on an outing, and he even helps to see that they get to church when they want to go.

Neatly dressed in a suit and tie and carrying his hat, Daniel spoke of his career in school.

"I didn't feel any different from anybody else," he stressed, "and all the students seemed to welcome me." He graduated from Sparks High School in Sparks, Nevada. "I just lived day-to-day and didn't worry about it."

Unlike many of his companions, Daniel has not been content to stay in what he refers to as their "square little world," referring of course to the dimensions and horizons, not a lack of sophistication.

"Too many of my friends just sit in a corner, and don't try to get involved in what's going on," he pointed out.

His hobbies include watching TV, playing records, and going to Sunday School. "That is," he adds, "when I get up in time." He also said, "The more I have my religion, the better life becomes."

He was raised in the Mormon faith by his mother and father, and he has three brothers and one sister, all of whom lead normal lives. It is one of his ambitions to better understand the gospel and be able to explain it to some of his friends, who may find it a bit difficult.

As to his relationship with his family, "I keep in close touch with them," he said. "My dad always tried to include me in everything, he never looked down on me."

Daniel's father has worked for the Southern Pacific railroad as an engineer in Arizona for twenty-two years and during the holidays it has been Daniel's advocate's Christmas present to let him and a couple of his other proteges talk to their parents long distance.

As to the future, Daniel doesn't know just what it holds for him, but he is hopeful. Currently he is working with his advocate on a plan for starting a business using retarded persons in yard maintenance, sweeping, cleaning and watering — something they could do after their workshop hours. He also is interested in art, and in studying cartooning, for which he has marked talent.

"I have also been making speeches," he told us, "going around to local organizations, and telling them how they can help retarded persons."

When applying as an advocate to the Nevada Advocacy group, he wrote the following:

This is what I think I can do. I can help the advocate board by my ability to talk on the level of the trainees and understand their problems. I also can understand and make some of the trainees understand what to do about their problems and hang-ups. I will learn and help in the best of my knowledge. This is what a trainee benefits from an advocate. A trainee has someone to turn to for advice when there is no one around to help. *They have someone to look up to when lonely or down.* The trainees have fun with an advocate by going places, doing many things with their advocate. *What is an advocate?* They are a group of people helping these trainees have a good time and give them advice on many things and problems they might have.

REFERENCES

Abeson, A., Bolick, N., and Hass, J. A Primer in Due Process: Education Decisions for Handicapped Children. *Exceptional Children,* 1975, 42, 68.

Bellamy, G. I., Peterson, L., and Close, D. Habilitation of the Severely and Profoundly Retarded: Illustrations of Competence. *Education and Training of the Mentally Retarded,* 1975, 10, 174–186.

Blue, M. Trainable Mentally Retarded in Sheltered Workshops. *Mental Retardation,* 1964, 2, 97–99.

Blum, E. P., and Hewett, T. The Madison Plan as an Alternative to Special Class Placement: An Interview with Frank Hewett. *Education and Training of the Mentally Retarded,* 1971, 6, 29–42.

Bokee, M., Burke, P. J., Sontag, E. W. Special Projects in Personnel Preparation — An Overview of Some Programs Designed to Train Personnel for the Education of Severely Retarded Children. *Education and Training of the Mentally Retarded,* 1974, 9, 169–176.

Bordwell, M. A Community Involvement Program for the Trainable Adolescent. *Teaching Exceptional Children,* 1974, 7, 110–114.

Borrelli, A. Occupational Training for Retarded Persons. *Mental Retardation,* 1972, 10, 15–17.

Bradtke, L. M., Kirkpatrick, W. J., Rosenblatt, K. P., Bannatyne, A. D. Training Institution and Community-Based Educational Staff to Work with Multiply Handicapped Children. *Education and Training of the Mentally Retarded,* 1975, 10, 51–55.

Brolin, D. Career Education Needs of Secondary Educable Students. *Exceptional Children,* 1973, 39, 619–624.

Buddle, J., and Menolascino, F. Systems Technology and Retardation: Applications to Vocational Habilitation. *Mental Retardation,* 1971, 9, 11–16.

Bunda, R., and Mezzano, J. The Effects of a Work Experience Program on Potential Dropouts. *The School Counselor,* 1968, 15, 272.

Cantoni, L. The Detroit S.E.V.R. Project. *The Journal for Special Educators of the Mentally Retarded,* 1973, 9, 182–185.

Caster, J. Teaching Children — Not Categories. *Exceptional Children,* 1976, 42, 234.

Caster, J. The Rights of Children and Their Parents. *Exceptional Children,* 1975A, 42, 114.

Caster, J. What is Mainstreaming? *Exceptional Children,* 1975, 42B, 174.

Chaffin, J., Spellman, C., Regan, C., and Davison, R. Two Follow-Up Studies of Former Educable Mentally Retarded Students from the Kansas Work Study Program. *Exceptional Children,* 1971, 37, 733–738.

Cohen, J. Vocational Rehabilitation Concepts in the Education of Teachers of the Retarded. *Education and Training of the Mentally Retarded,* 1972, 7, 189–194.

Connor, F. P. Guest Editorial, *Exceptional Children,* 1960, 27, 184.

Cordier, M. *Career Education.* Kalamazoo: College of Education, Western Michigan University, 1975.

Davis, W. The Changing Role of the Special Educator. *Mental Retardation,* 1974, 12, 40.

Drier, H. *K–12 Guide for Integrating Career Development into Local Curriculum.* Worthington, Ohio: Charles A. Jones Publishing Company, 1975.

Dunn, L. M. Special Education for the Mildly Retarded — Is Much of It Justified? *Exceptional Children,* 1968, 35, 5–22.

Flores, C. An Experiment in the Pre-Occupational Education of Mentally Retarded Students on the Junior High School Level. *Education and Training of the Mentally Retarded,* 1975, 10, 26–29.

Fraenkel, W. *The Mentally Retarded and Their Vocational Preparation.* New York: NARC, 1961.

Fulton, R. Job Retention of the Retarded. *Mental Retardation,* 1975, 12, 26.

Garner, R. E. An Historical View of Workshops. *Mental Retardation,* 1972, 10, 25.

Garrett, J. The Rehabilitation and Education Interface, in Cohen, J. (ed.). *The Proceedings of the Annual Spring Conference of the Institute for the Study of Mental Retardation.* Ann Arbor: University of Michigan Publications Distribution Service, 1970.

Gearheart, B., and Litton, F. W. *The Trainable Retarded: A Foundations Approach.* St. Louis: C. V. Mosby, 1975.

Gold, M. Factors Affecting Production by the Retarded: Base Rate. *Mental Retardation,* 1972, 11, 41–45.

Gold, M. Stimulus Factors in Skill Training of the Retarded on Complex Assembly Tasks: Acquisition, Transfer and Retention. *American Journal on Mental Deficiency,* 1972, 76, 517–526.

Goldberg, I. I. Toward a Systematic Approach to Educational Planning for the TMR. *Education and Training of the Mentally Retarded,* 1971, 6.

Goldstein, H., Moss, J., and Jordan, L. *A Study of the Effects of Special Class Placement on Educable Mentally Retarded Children.* Urbana: University of Illinois, 1965.

Granat, K., and Granat, S. Below Average Intelligence and Mental Retardation. *American Journal on Mental Deficiency,* 1973, 73, 27–32.

Greasy, R. Whither Are We Going? Problems and Possible Solutions. *Mental Retardation,* 1972, 10, 26–27.

Guerin, G., and Szatlocky, K. Integration Programs for the Mildly Retarded. *Exceptional Children,* 1974, 41, 173–179.

Hammonds, G. Educating the Mildly Retarded: A Review. *Exceptional Children* 1974, 38, 565–570.

Hungerford, R. *Vocational Rehabilitation of the Mentally Retarded.* Washington, D.C.: U. S. Government Printing Office, 1950.

Itkin, W. Needed: New Approaches to Evaluation and Training of the Retarded. *Mental Retardation,* 1972, 10, 35.

Jenkins, J., and Mayhall, W. Describing Resource Teacher Programs. *Exceptional Children,* 1973, 40, 35–36.

Johnson, G. O. Special Education for the Mentally Handicapped — A Paradox. *Exceptional Children,* 1962, 29, 62–69.

Jones, R. L. Student Views of Special Class Placement and Their Own Special Class Placement: A Clarification. *Exceptional Children,* 1974, 41, 22–29.

Jordan, J. Invisible College on Mainstreaming. *Exceptional Children,* 1974, 41, 31–32.

Kolstoe, O. Programs for the Mildly Retarded: A Reply to the Critics. *Exceptional Children,* 1972, 39, 51.

Kolstoe, O., and Frey, R. *A High School Work-Study Program for Mentally Subnormal Students.* Carbondale: Southern Illinois University Press, 1965.

Kolstoe, O. *Teaching Educable Retarded Children.* New York: Holt, Rinehart and Winston, 1970.

Lacy, G. Workshops Today. *Mental Retardation,* 1972, 10, 26.

Luckey, R., and Addison, M. P. The Profoundly Retarded: A New Challenge for Public Education. *Education and Training of the Mentally Retarded,* 1974, 9, 123–130.

Martin, E. Some Thoughts on Mainstreaming. *Exceptional Children,* 1974, 41, 150–153.

National Association for Retarded Children. *Policy Statement on the Education of Mentally Retarded Children.* Arlington, Texas: NARC, 1971, pp. 8–9.

Neisen, N. Organizing for the Effective Curricula for the Educable Mentally Retarded. *Education and Training of the Mentally Retarded,* 1967, 2, pp. 51–55.

Nelson, C. C., and Schmidt, L. The Question of Efficacy of Special Class. *Exceptional Children,* 1974, 37, 381–386.

Porter, R. B., and Milazzo, T. A Comparison of Mentally Retarded Adults Who Attended a Special Class with Those Who Attended Regular School Classes. *Exceptional Children,* 1958, 24, 410–412, 420.

President's Committee on Employment of the Handicapped/The National Association for Retarded Citizens. *About Jobs and Mentally Retarded People.* Washington, D.C.: U. S. Government Printing Office, 1972.

President's Committee on Mental Retardation/President's Committee on Employment of the Handicapped. *These, Too, Must Be Equal: America's Needs in Habilitation and Employment of the Mentally Retarded.* Washington, D.C.: U. S. Government Printing Office, 1968, 254–344.

Richardson, J. B. A Survey of the Present Status of Vocational Training in State Institutions for the M.R. *Mental Retardation,* 1975, 13, 16–19.

Sailor, W., Guess, D., and Lavis, L. Training Teachers for Education of the Severely Handicapped. *Education and Training of the Mentally Retarded,* 1975, 10, 201–203.

Sigler, G. R., and Kakaska, C. J. A Job Placement Procedure for the Mentally Retarded. *Education and Training of the Mentally Retarded,* 1971, 6, 161–166.

Simpson, E. The Home as a Career Education Center. *Exceptional Children,* 1973, 39, 626–630.

Smeets, P. M., and Manfredini, D. C. Skill Centers: A Model Program for Young Severely Retarded Children. *Education and Training of the Mentally Retarded,* 1973, 8, 124–127.

Smith, J. O., and Arkans, J. Now More than Ever: A Case for the Special Class. *Exceptional Children,* 1974, 40, 497–502.

Smith, R. M. *Clinical Teaching: Methods of Instruction for the Retarded.* New York: McGraw-Hill, 1974.

Stanback, S., and Stanback, W. A Defense of the Concept of the Special Class. *Education and Training of the Mentally Retarded,* 1975, 10, 91–93.

Stanback, S., Stanback, W., and Maurer, S. Training Teachers for the Severely and Profoundly Handicapped: A New Frontier. *Exceptional Children,* 1976, 42, 203–210.

Tarkington, L., and Overbeck, D. Job Satisfaction and Performance with Retarded Females. *Mental Retardation,* 1975, 15, 18–19.

Weisenstein, G. Use of a Pictorial Job Training Manual in an Occupational Training Program for High School EMR Students. *Education and Training of the Mentally Retarded,* 1975, 10, 30–35.

Wheeler, D. Oh, It Doesn't Bother Me. *Mental Retardation News,* 1976, 25, 8.

Wirtz, M. *An Administrator's Handbook of Special Education.* Springfield, Illinois: Charles C Thomas, 1977.

12

Advocacy

SYNOPSIS

The *advocate* relationship is characterized by *mutual* respect oriented toward increased independence as opposed to the more traditional role of *guardianship,* with its dependency emphasis. The advocate movement addresses itself to immediate advocacy and to the parents' ultimate concern: "What will happen to my child when I'm not here?" The implications of *normalization* are goals of the advocate relationship. There is some question if a provider of services can be a genuine advocate because of a potential conflict of interest, but this chapter suggests certain qualities of the professional as an advocate.

OBJECTIVES

ATTITUDES

1. To seek out opportunities for an advocate relationship.
2. To resolve one's own needs to be dominant with another person's needs for growth.

UNDERSTANDING

1. To distinguish between types of instrumental and expressive advocacy.
2. To identify normalization and mainstreaming as both compatible and conflicting goals.
3. To identify one's own potential as an advocate.
4. To identify special considerations associated with advocacy.

SKILLS

1. To identify, within one's own value structure, a respect for the advocate relationship.
2. To describe the scope of the advocate movement.

THE NATURE OF ADVOCACY

To place the advocate relationship in perspective, consider these episodes in the lives of retarded persons.

Elizabeth A. has been on community status for nine months. Twenty-three of her twenty-four years have been spent in a regional retardation center where she was placed on the advice of the family physician. The father is deceased, but the mother still lives in the community. Daughter and mother maintain telephone contact and visit together at least twice a month. The mother is pleased with Elizabeth's progress in the work activity center to which she commutes daily.

Elizabeth's first placement in a small group home was not altogether satisfactory. The eight residents were either mentally retarded or mentally ill. The mother reports that upon visiting the home it was difficult to tell the residents from the manager. The housekeeping was deplorable. The local office of client services was sympathetic, but the case worker indicated that close supervision was impossible. When the mother questioned how a color television in the home was paid for by resident "consent," the worker again repeated that supervision of managers was difficult and said that if the mother could locate another residence, the agency would consider a transfer. The mother took time from her employment and accomplished the transfer.

The mother's new concern is that the new manager has developed a back problem. He and his wife may have to give up their enterprise. Her constant concern is how her daughter's placement will be supervised should disability or death prevent her (the mother) from maintaining a continuing contact.

Philip W. was accused of threatening a woman in the community. She claimed some porch furniture worth twenty dollars was missing and alleged that Philip stole it. Philip, age twenty-seven, a deaf-mute with a mental age of four, vigorously denied the charge. Although able to communicate in sign language and employed as a kitchen helper, he was judged mentally incompetent to stand trial and was then committed to a state hospital until such time as he should "become competent." This amounts to a life sentence. An ironic twist is that the procedures for confinement to prison are more stringent than to facilities for the mentally retarded. What can be done on his behalf?

Mike M. is a thirteen-year-old moderately retarded boy who is mildly cerebral palsied but ambulatory. His two older siblings live away from home. He is transported some distance to his special school. His parents are very devoted, but they are aware that they cannot substitute as friends. He has no phone calls from friends. He is not invited to spend an overnight with other boys. He seems such a lonely person. He spends endless hours watching television or arranging his rock collection, which no one seems to notice. His parents know that he should be involved with boys his own age, but where can they turn?

John M., age twenty-seven, works as a baker's helper. He has a room in a modest home in a pleasant neighborhood. His life-style is an unbroken shuttle between his job and his room. His major source of recreation has evolved into watching some boys play baseball in the local park. He is too shy and awkward to participate, and he feels he is too "big" anyway. He enjoys the sunshine and the noisy chatter of the boys. When he returned to his room one evening, his landlord informed him that he must move out immediately. Certain neighbors have complained about John's "hanging around" the small boys. They hint at possible molestation, a groundless fear in John's case. John is bewildered. He believes that he must indeed move the next day. He is not sure where to turn. It is Friday and the social welfare office will not be open until eight o'clock Monday morning. What to do?

Andrew D. is a client in a sheltered workshop. He has been "employed" for three years, earning about the minimum wage, and is a prized employee. He is able to operate industrial laundry equipment with great skill. He is now under some pressure to be employed on the "outside." He feels caught in a psychological squeeze. He is aware that if he leaves and fails, he will have to go back on the waiting list to get his place back in the workshop. He has seen it happen. The staff appears bent on counseling him to accept the new job in a laundry firm on the other side of town. He is not sure. He doesn't know where to turn for advice.

Response to the personal difficulties expressed in these episodes may be a citizen advocate. Kolodziej (1974) estimates that there are over 125 programs of citizen advocacy in the United States. Communities pioneering in this venture were: Lincoln, Nebraska; Austin, Texas; Columbus, Ohio; Denver, Colorado; and New Jersey, starting between 1970 and 1971. This program and movement has become one of the major efforts of the NARC in collaboration with its state and local member units.

Definition

The Copeland et al. (1974, p. 8) report states:

> By definition, Citizen Advocacy for mentally retarded persons is basically a one-to-one relationship between a capable volunteer ("advocate") and a mentally retarded person ("protege") in which the advocate defends the rights and interests of the protege and provides practical or emotional reinforcement (or a combination of both) for him. All of this occurs within the framework of a structured advocacy system.

The concept of protege implies a growth potential, a friend, a partner concept not altogether implied by the term *client* or by the traditional guardianship systems described in chapter 9. Defending rights and interests involves acting as a spokesperson for the retarded individual, who is unable to speak for himself or herself. This role may take many forms. Practical guidance involves advice, instruction, and practice in daily activities. The intent is to increase the independence of the protege. Emotional reinforcement implies the role of a friend in providing attention and affection and letting the protege know someone cares.

The framework of a structured advocacy system is the citizen advocacy office. The citizen advocate office acts at state and local levels to recruit and train advocates, to match proteges with advocates, and to serve as a resource. Advocates do not necessarily exist alone. The experience of the citizen advocate movement suggests the need for supportive structures.

Sources of Advocacy

The Copeland et al. report noted that advocacy as such is not new. There is ample precedent of persons serving as spokespersons on behalf of others. Examples and sources of advocacy models cited were:

1. *Parents*. This has been a prime source and example. With increasing age, the parents may be unable to discharge their responsibilities effectively. Consequently, a citizen advocate (CA) program can be a reassurance.

2. *The ARC unit*. This source has been successful in obtaining services and in organizing collective effort, as well as in legislative and judicial efforts. The CA program offers new avenues for assistance.

3. *The ombudsman system*. This system was pioneered in Sweden in the 1800s. Copeland et al. reported that states such as Hawaii, Oregon, Iowa, Nebraska, and South Carolina have systems approximating the Swedish model. The ombudsman is a person (usually directing a staff) who is independent of administrative structure and reprisal. The role is to investigate complaints from citizens and to seek redress. This person has the power to secure documents. Systems vary as to the power of overruling or enforcing decisions. However, the role serves as a conscience and a reminder that government is to serve. This system does *not* decrease the need for the CA. First, the case load is so extensive that waiting lists can be lengthy. Second, the ombudsman is paid by government, while the CA is a free agent. Finally, the CA provides a one-to-one personal service.

4. *Residential facilities*. Progressive facilities are welcoming CA into staffings and planning for residents. The CA movement is being encouraged by such facilities as a means to guarantee the preservation of rights as well as opportunities for growth. In the absence of such encouragement, the CA will still persist on behalf of the protege.

5. *Protective Services*. A variety of governmental sources oversee the affairs of persons designated as requiring supervision, but Copeland et al. noted many serious

problems. In the legal sense, guardianship can create unnecessary dependence. Case loads outnumbering available staff is another problem. Governmental units may operate on rigid policies, such as a fixed workday. Consequently, problems that occur outside the eight-to-five schedule or on the weekends may not be resolved. Another problem can be conflict of interest when the needs of the person and of the agency clash. The agency may not be in the "best" position to render an impartial judgment. Finally, in the United States agencies are given the authority for self-evaluation of effectiveness. The agency can present data which has a "paper quality" but lacks substance.

Advocate Roles

Copeland et al. identified seven roles the CA might discharge. This definition of role is an "agreement" between the CA and the CA office. (A volunteer would not be asked to serve beyond reasonable expectations or venture into areas requiring legal competence.) These seven roles were defined as:

1. The advocate-*companion*. This form relates to friendship and emotional needs.

2. The advocate-*advisor*. This form may range from practical instruction to discussion of choice-problems such as dating, marriage, jobs, etc.

3. *Guardianship*. In certain instances, the CA may become a court-appointed guardian. The CA may function outside the protege's family. In some cases, the CA office may be a guardian (chapter 9).

4. *Conservator*. This is a legal role and involves management of the protege's assets. The concern will be management of an estate (chapter 9).

5. *Parent*. Although not a typical outcome, CA involvement can lead to either foster parenthood or adoptive parenthood. In the former, the protege lives with the CA, with some financial consideration given for his or her care. In the latter role, the protege is legally and formally made a member of the family.

6. *The YOUTH advocate*. YOUTH-ARCs have emerged as sources of expressive advocacy, especially in areas of practical guidance and emotional support. When a YOUTH-advocate attains legal majority, he or she may wish to expand the role.

7. *Standby advocates*. This role is provided on an emergency basis in times of crisis if the "regular" advocate is not available. This role can be helpful when legal infractions arise and the protege requires an immediate voice. Sometimes this role is termed an *associate advocate*.

Because of possible conflict of interest, a professional in mental retardation might not be an "ideal" advocate for a person directly under their supervision. As a technical advisor to a CA Office or as a CA for a protege served elsewhere, their knowledge and skill would be valued.

Competencies

Copeland et al. identified four broad areas of possible application of advocate roles: legal, social, educational, and employment. These areas imply certain competencies for the CA (table 12–1).

The Change Agent Nature of the Advocate

It will be recalled from chapter 8 that social action requires an actor known as a change agent. The Copeland et al. report notes that protege rights are opportunities for the change agent function. A process is documented in their report which suggests the advocate will use the skills contained in the section on social action

Table 12–1 INVOLVEMENTS OF THE CITIZEN ADVOCATE

Dimensions and Related Rights of the Protege			
Legal the right to	*Social the right to*	*Educational the right to*	*Employment the right to*
• vote • review of human and legal rights which is continuing and competent • use of the courts • enter into contracts and obtain credit • legal counsel, especially in institution-alizations • rights extended to citizens under federal and state law	• dignity • contribute in taxes • be of service • normal family living • marry and reproduce • make decisions and mistakes • suitable treatment • reject "opportunties" • acceptance by others	• choose goals • be in a normalized setting with contact with normal peers • have a teacher who values the learner's rights • be accepted at his or her learning level • be taught to be independent	• be trained for available jobs • have job described by dignified title rather than "low-level" • change job or job training • seek, gain, and hold employment to best of capabilities

(chapter 8). In practical terms, one of the functions of a CA office would be to assemble these data and serve as a resource for strategy formation.

Stages in the Advocate-Protege Relationship

Copeland et al. identified four stages. In the *beginning stages,* the CA will have attended orientation sessions. These sessions would be for those CAs who have been screened and matched to a specific protege. Additional sessions would be devoted to the uniqueness of the intended protege and his or her needs, expectations, and interests.

The *initial contact* and subsequent early contacts are recommended as friend-to-friend encounters. It was recommended that the CA *preplan* the time limits, location, and activities of the first few encounters. During this period, the CA will need to remind himself or herself to: give first allegiance to the protege; avoid overprotective reaction, for normal risks are part of the relationship; maintain the view of the protege as a friend; overcome possible reluctance to say No or to express disapproval of the protege's actions; remember what the protege *can* do (if possible, engage in activities in which the protege is equal or excels); remember the importance of listening as well as talking; recognize that the protege is first a person and only second a person labeled as mentally retarded; and remember to maintain contact with the CA office.

After the first six months, the *stabilization phase* emerges. The CA and protege may choose some goal activities consistent with the three roles described earlier or may concentrate on the rights aspects listed in table 12–1. Not all activities have to be goal oriented; simple companionship is often enough. The CA may still require time to assess his or her personal expectations. A critical factor during this time is the recognition of "crisis points," as Copeland et al. term them. These are painful events in the protege's life: the death of a parent, an insult from a stranger, or loss of a job. The advocate may feel doubts about his or her competence or may be disillusioned with the protege. The important thing is to recognize that these crisis points are a part of the process. The CA office can help, and the relationship may emerge as even stronger.

At some point, the relationship may *terminate* for sound reasons. Mobility is the most common reason. In some CA programs, a defined time limit of one to two years may be specified. The authors stressed that this experience can be profitable if handled properly.

1. The announcement should be made in advance and frequently to enable the protege to get used to the idea. A farewell celebration would be in order to give assurances of keeping in touch.

2. Neither the CA nor the protege should feel guilt. The protege should be helped to feel that losing was not his or her fault and that losing a friend is a part of life. The advocate should not be made to feel he or she has let the protege down.

3. The departing advocate can arrange a mutual meeting with the new friend. This can give the new relationship a solid initial contact. Furthermore, the protege can feel that his or her circle of friends is increasing rather than decide that one more person has found him or her to be a disappointment.

Involvement

The outcome(s) to the advocate in this relationship can be varied. Participation may enable the person to experience:

1 helping a protege to curb the effects of isolation;
2 helping in securing the rights and privileges due the protege;
3 observing another person gain a sense of personal worth;
4 gaining a new friend;
5 entrance on the ground floor of a movement that is socially activist; and
6 opportunities to learn firsthand about human problems and possible solutions.

The Structure of a Program

The CA and protege require a framework for the effort. Copeland et al. have prepared a manual that considers and reviews these organizational aspects. The reader will find this document a useful resource in the planning and operation of this type of service. In general the initial stages of development are similar to those presented in chapter 8.

A continuing function of the CA office is that of monitoring and evaluation. Each advocate is expected to compile or complete a monthly log of activities.

NORMALIZATION AND THE ADVOCATE RELATIONSHIP

Implications for Services

The application of the normalization principle to services for the retarded person, according to Nirji (1969) could be as follows:

1. A normal rhythm of the day. Examples of adherence would include getting dressed even if profoundly retarded, eating in a family atmosphere, allowing time to break away from the routine of the large group.

2. A normal routine of life. This component recognizes that most people live in one space, work in another, and have leisure in a variety of spaces. Work should be real and convey genuine purpose. There should be preparation for coping with leisure.

3. Experience of the normal rhythm of the year. Special emphasis is placed upon refreshment of mind and body. The concept of vacation should apply to the retarded person.

4. The opportunity to experience the life cycle. The cycle of childhood, school years, youth, and old age possess characteristics applicable to services. There should be stimulation in the environment. In most societies concessions are made to the young on the basis of maturation and readiness. The growth through adolescence requires careful nurturing of self-concept. The aged should be allowed to live and participate in settings *geographically* near the place where they have spent the majority of their years. These considerations should apply to retarded persons.

5. The choices, wishes, and desires of the retarded person should be respected, even if these cannot always be fulfilled.

6. Living in a bisexual world would mean staffing of facilities by both men and women. Facilities should be coeducational, with mixing of sexes, not restrictive separation.

7. Application of normal economic standards. The retarded person should be eligible for the same guarantees of economic security as all citizens. To promote learning experiences, the retarded person should have a reasonable amount of pocket money for private use.

8. The standards for physical facilities for retarded citizens should be the same as those applied to ordinary citizens. Geographical isolation of facilities should end. Additionally, the size of the population to be served should *not* exceed the numbers of persons the surrounding community can assimilate.

Soeffing (1974) has reported an interview with Dr. Wolf Wolfensberger, an acknowledged leader in the concept of normalization. This interview identified the dimensions of normalization as applied to human services. As the article points out, however, normalization is both a concept, a process, and a value system. Its major thrust is to shift power to the consumer. Its function is to assist the consumer in the skillful exercise of his or her rights. The interview concluded with a description of the l'Arche movement initiated by Jean Vanier. This movement involves a "community" of the handicapped and the nonhandicapped. The belief of l'Arche is that all persons have some degree of handicap, some more obvious than others. Consequently, people, the helpless and the helpers, live together on a near equal basis and share a common existence.

Throne (1975), citing a developmental perspective, suggests qualification for normalization as the total basis in programming for the retarded person. His developmental perspective suggests that the rate of development of the retarded person, by definition, is behind that of the normal person of similar age. Methods and procedures that treat the retarded as normal could perpetuate the difference. For Throne, the goal of normalization of enabling the retarded to live as normal lives as possible is not in question, only the treatment means. His plan is for the use of specialized procedures (e.g., behavior modification) that have proven efficiency in enabling the retarded to attain their fullest potential.

There appears agreement with respect to normalization in principle and viable options for achieving it.

Normalization and Mainstreaming

An educational equivalent of normalization has acquired the label of *mainstreaming*. Mainstreaming has commonly come to mean that an exceptional learner is placed in special services for specific, limited purposes and spends the remainder in the regular school setting. This approach has been widely popular for physically and sensory handicapped pupils. As a partial reaction against the alleged abuses of the self-contained class advanced by Dunn (1968) and Johnson (1962), the use of resource rooms has become an alternative to the use of self-contained programs.

Wolfensberger, as cited by Soeffing (1974), specifies that mainstreaming is not necessarily normalization. According to the normalization principle, integration of the retarded person is dependent upon two factors or circumstances. First, according to Wolfensberger normalization involves as much integration as the person can handle. The normalization principle suggests that not all persons can be fully integrated into a mainstream at all times or in all endeavors. Additionally, integration should be adaptive and successful. Integration is a continuum. Wolfensberger deplores the wholesale dumping of students into a pattern of either integrated or segregated programs.

Stephens (1975) has expressed certain reservations about mainstreaming en masse. His position is that a *variety* of delivery systems, including mainstreaming, should exist. Stephens's discussion implies the need for program standards.

The Dignity of Risk

Klein (1975) has isolated mainstreaming and deinstitutionalization as two prime concerns in normalization. He notes the discrepancy between the ideal and the reality and discusses the use of mainstreaming and deinstitutionalization as "magic words" to mask problems and realities. The central reality is the need for preparation of the community, of peers, of resources, etc. Without preparation, mainstreaming takes on the form of mainlining.

A central element in the reservations about normalization clusters around risk. The thoughtful advocate would not expose his or her protege to danger or traumatic failure. It appears to Conglon (1974) that the cause can become more important than the persons. This reservation is not opposition to normalization, but rather a concern about needless, unacceptable risk. Conglon's concern is the pretense of competence for retarded persons in the face of reality. His suggestion is to locate areas of performance functional to the retarded person and to society. Ignoring performance deficits does not lead to acceptance and may even discourage it.

Perske (1972) has summarized the Swedish and Danish experience as lessons of the risk involved. He noted that normalization in the Nirji sense did not emerge all at once. Rather, it was an evolutionary process based upon a recognition that mental retardation service systems had cleverly avoided all risk. The effect was to limit spheres of behavior and interaction with the community by an associative isolation. What has become popularized as normalization is the result of seeking alternatives to this isolation. For Perske, certain forms of risk are involved with certain constructive correlates; risk is a "normal" aspect of life and of socialization. The types of situations listed by Perske as normal risks include:

1. *Community experiences*. Already one observes alternatives to centralized facilities in this country based upon the Swedish and Danish models. Supervision is dependent on the person's need. Youth clubs can provide "hidden" social training for *both* the retarded and normal person.

2. *Industry*. The interest here is to perform the same tasks on the same equipment with the same safety and/or performance as the normal worker. To be sure, there are compensatory adaptations. For example, lathes give warning of impending breakage by fluctuations in sound; deaf-retarded persons are trained to be alert for visual signs.

3. *Heterosexual relationships*. Perske noted significant movement away from segregated facilities. Helping professionals were observed to provide support and guidance in establishing emotional ties. Should the relationship lead to marriage, the decision would be honored and respected.

4. *Building design*. In the past, "heavy duty" and "super safe" has been the theme. It is now recognized that a normalized environment enhances normalized behavior.

Perske concluded his analysis with an observation that the world, in general, is not safe. As a final observation, he noted that there can be dignity in risk, and there can be a dehumanizing indignity in safety.

Examples of Normalization

Hemenway, Lemke, Hage, and Robertshaw (1972) reported an experiment in educational intervention for two hundred moderately and mildly retarded persons whose IQ range was from 30 to 88, with a mean of 55. Of interest was the age variable of eighteen to twenty-five. The overall results were that postschool retarded persons can indeed demonstrate significant gains in both academic areas and practical arts. These authors observed that if lifelong learning and adult education are "normal" experience for the general population, this opportunity is appropriate for the retarded. Nibira and Nibira (1975) studied the adaptive behavior of 426 retarded persons who were formerly institutionalized. The results reflected gains in self-care, assistance on foster home chores, and appropriate behavior with peers and community neighbors. A sampling of typical incidents would include:

1 An eight-year-old severely retarded boy watched the home operators' baby being potty trained, started using it himself, and trained himself in several days.
2 A twenty-seven-year-old man went to night school for three years to earn his diploma without mentioning being retarded.
3 A nine-year-old moderately retarded boy learned to ride a tricycle when he felt nervous instead of rocking and hand twisting.
4 A thirty-one-year-old mildly retarded woman learned to run errands for an elderly resident on her own insistence.

The findings appeared to reflect gains across age, sex, and retardation levels. The overall impression left by the authors was one of concerned care by the operators and of increased potential for the persons.

Zisfein and Rosen (1973) have described a personal adjustment training (PAT) curriculum to prepare for normalized life. Its elements are directed toward functional skills of interest to advocates. These curricular elements can be summarized as:

1. *Self-evaluation.* The emphasis is upon self-concept and self-identity. Activities are directed toward grooming and general appearance and also toward the consequences of one's actions.

2. *Exploitation.* The goal is to enable the person to resist attempts at coercion or exploitation. Sample areas involve pill taking, paper signing, and financial areas.

3. *Assertiveness training.* The intent is to reduce helplessness, dependency, and passivity. Role playing and modeling are used. A specific emphasis is placed upon showing persons how behaviors invite dependent treatment.

4. *Heterosexual training.* The effort is to equip the person with appropriate responses in mixed settings. There is additional emphasis upon decreasing anxiety in heterosexual encounters.

5. *Independence training.* The target in this area is problem solving. Emphasis is focused upon self-reliant and initiated activity. Experience is provided for leadership experiences.

The authors allude to the use of role-playing scripts and prepared videotapes as instructional materials. Teaching procedures develop from awareness of appropriate and inappropriate episodes. Within the therapeutic session, the person is "graduated" toward practicing new skills. Eventually the person learns to practice these skills in "homework" assignments similar to Ellis's RT methods (chapter 13).

This discussion began with a consideration of reasonable reservations concerning the risk in normalization. Normalization, however, recognizes the possibility of risk.

DIMENSIONS OF INSTRUMENTAL ADVOCACY

A theme in the Copeland et al. reports was an emphasis on the advocate's protection of the protege's interests and rights. This dimension of advocacy was termed instrumental and can include guardianship, civil rights, equity from agencies, and the like. The instrumental role is required to preserve and protect the legal, civil, and regulatory interests of the protege. Frequently policies, rules, and even laws diminish the opportunity for growth of the retarded person and/or the family.

Rights

The dimensions of rights and the retarded person as a citizen with rights have been discussed elsewhere in this text. The purpose of this section is to identify certain guidelines for the advocate to consider as evidence of rights being protected.

Todd (1971) has identified the need for meaningful data to guarantee the right for individualization of treatment. Of special importance in light of the IEP requirement of 94–142 was the presence of work samples to augment normative data. The advocate may be in a particularly strategic position to offer helpful examples of his or her protege's performance.

Goldberg (1971) has offered three principles of *agency* behavior as indicators of protection of client rights. These are:

1. *Positive presumption.* This principle applics to denial of services. In effect, this principle requires sufficient cause to be shown for service denial. It suggests

that the absence of cause is not a justification, per se. The burden of proof is upon the agency rather than upon the person.

2. *Due process*. The abridgment of rights requires specificity. The mere label of mental retardation is not sufficient for denial, but essential details of the person must be considered.

3. *Instrumental protection*. This principle involves both protection and exercise of rights.

Roos (1974) has identified certain dimensions for advocates in monitoring services on behalf of proteges. These include:

1. Evidence that goals and objectives have been selected to reflect the values of the client. The concern is that agency goals may supercede, or be assumed to be similar to, client goals.

2. Program goals should be monitored systematically and on a continuing basis.

3. Program personnel should be willing to utilize community involvement to insure conformity with contemporary cultural values.

4. Program personnel and operations should reflect awareness of advances in scientific findings and new technologies. Also, there was the implication that program operators should undergo periodic evaluation.

5. Program means (methods) require differentiations from its end (goals). A given methodology does not always guarantee the values surrounding its use. Noble goals do not insure meritorious services. The advocate must learn to distinguish between ends and means.

6. The use of incentives requires attention. Employment of adversive consequences should be carefully examined with specification as to how such incentives will provide more effective outcomes than other alternatives; be clearly defined, as for example, the difference between seclusion and time out; be of value to the protege rather than to the advocate or agency; and be fully stated to the person so that informed consent can be given by the protege and/or the advocate.

Child Abuse and Neglect

Soeffing (1975, p. 126) cites PL 93–247 to define child abuse and neglect as:

> the physical or mental injury, sexual abuse, negligent treatment, or mistreatment of a child under the age of 18 by a person who is responsible for the child's welfare under circumstances which indicate that the child's health or welfare is harmed or threatened.

Soeffing noted that the Council for Exceptional Children (CEC) has affirmed that the abused and neglected children are exceptional children. After a review of the literature, she concluded that the susceptibility of exceptional children to abuse is more a risk concept than a cause-and-effect concept. The conclusion was advanced that the handicapped child is more at risk than the nonhandicapped child in the same family. Soeffing identified certain policies that child-care agencies, including the public schools, might adopt if these agencies feel a sense of advocacy. These guidelines include:

1. *Recognition of signs and symptoms of possible abuse and neglect.* The child's appearance and/or behavior may be signs of problems. Unexplained welts and bruises as well as clothing inappropriate for the weather may indicate abuse or neglect. Evidence of poor health and an unkempt attire may also reflect problems. Unusual behavior extremes of aggression and/or withdrawal may be the child's way of coping with abuse. Parental apathy and/or disinterest and defensiveness toward their child's attendance may also be symptoms. Neither Soeffing nor the author would suggest that this brief listing be understood as "evidence" against parents. The point is that *each* agency must develop specific indicators and nonindicators to guide practitioners.

2. *Policies regarding reporting of abuse and neglect.* All states have laws governing this topic. In some states there are penalties for *not* reporting. Each agency must have current knowledge regarding these legal implications. There also should be guidelines for the writing of information as well as designated responsibility for action.

3. *Services to the family.* Educators are critical for both prevention and identification. Examples of successful efforts to change family practices were reported. Again the necessity for routing families to helping resources was urged.

4. *Inservice training.* The preceding topics were suggested as the content of training for staff. It was recommended that special attention should be given to "warning" symptoms of neglect and abuse.

Sandgrund, Gains, and Green (1974) compared abused-neglected children with children free of this experience. The abused-neglected group were found to have significantly lowered IQ. The authors could not specify a cause-effect relationship, except to demonstrate the differences between the groups. They concluded that abuse and neglect are complicated in their origins and exceptionality is not necessarily the prompting cause.

Steele (1975), writing from a psychiatric perspective, confirms the complexity of causation. He estimates that less than 10 percent of abusing/neglecting parents would be classified and/or recognized as having serious psychiatric disorder such as schizophrenia, severe depression, or excessive phobias. Nagi (1975) estimated that 925,000 children could be reportable, with about 600,000 such instances actually reported. About 360,000 children are substantiated as abused or neglected, while the remainder reflect the symptoms. For this latter group, however, hard proof cannot be gathered. Moreover, the factor of proof leads persons in contact with children to shun involvement in reporting for fear of lawsuits. Hence, the recent legislative intent of creating penalties for failure to report. Reed (1975) reported that the feeling present in such parents is fear. This feeling takes the form of fear of what they're doing; what will happen if they don't get help; what will happen if they do get help; and going insane. She reported the emergence of Parents Anonymous, a parent self-help group. This group has 150,000 members in 150 chapters in the U.S. and Canada.

Davoren (1975) has outlined both causes and treatment-response. Her viewpoint, that of a social worker, is that such parents have learned their excessive responses; the pain inflicted upon the child is a measure of the pain imposed upon the parents when they were children. As children, Davoren observed, these parents learned from their own parents:

1. Survival depended upon conforming to their parents' wishes in such areas as not crying or reaching for anything.
2. They were expected to reassure and comfort their own parents — a reversal of the usual nurture, cuddling, and handling.
3. However much they conformed and comforted, they were no good and deserved to be hit.
4. Parents cannot be expected to understand the needs and feelings of children.
5. Having children is a way for adults to be taken care of and loved.
6. Children *must* be punished to achieve good results.
7. The day would come when they could release their stored up feelings without reprisal.
8. They must survive in order to grow up to have children.

Despite this cycle of repetition of abuse and neglect, the Davoren report is optimistic about interrupting this pattern. The outline of a full program would include:

1. homemaker services by a person who enters the home to demonstrate and/or model parent skills;
2. a hotline available around the clock, such as Parents Anonymous, which is based upon the AA model;
3. day care as one means to relieve the parent of constant care;
4. crisis nurseries to be used by the parents when tension builds;
5. emergency shelter care for all or part of the day to temporarily separate parent and child without a prolonged, imposed separation; and
6. emergency loans to provide cash for situations for which money is the only solution.

The last service gives a certain credibility to the program for parents. It is a demonstration to them of "real" help.

Treatment can take many forms. Young (1964), an early pioneer, advocated the use of Rogerian-type parent-centered therapy coupled with significant contingencies to curb abusive and neglecting practices. She called into question parents' rights to maintain children at the cost of the child's development. She challenged the assumption that the "best" home is the natural home and reported numerous instances of the child perceiving a foster parent as his or her "real" parent. In her treatment approach, after more "normal" procedures have been exhausted, the parent is confronted with the possible removal of the child from the home. The worker then outlines a detailed list of expectations. This may include controlling the family's budget and expenditures. At this point, the parents have a choice of conforming or losing their child. As treatment progresses, choices are widened and control is lessened as parent-child relationships stabilize.

Harris-Cohen, Shea-Ridge, and Collinghon (1975) have identified evaluation as a program essential. Their design format is similar to that presented elsewhere in this text and follows conventional guidelines. For the prospective advocate, this area will be most difficult. Observation of beaten and burned children arouses a response to be equally punitive. Obviously, children must be protected, even removed. The perspective, difficult to maintain, is that such parents are products of an unusual life experience.

Substance Abuse and Neglect

The long-term research of Bosco (1975) suggests the abuse of behavior-modifying drugs as another area for advocacy. His focus has been upon Menthylphenidate hydrochloride, or Ritalin. Patented in 1950, this drug falls under section II of the Controlled Substances Act, which restricts quantity and number of refills in order to monitor its use. Ritalin is thought to be helpful for school-age children with hyperkinesis syndrome, or excessive motor movement. For adults, it may be administered for drug-related lethargy, mild depression, and apathetic senile behavior. In the child, this stimulant drug, related to amphetamines, appears to accelerate brain function to the point where excessive and random motor activity appears to have a subduing effect. Bosco does *not* challenge the positive consequences of Ritalin, only its inappropriate use as a means to mask inadequacies in the environment, especially the school program. In order to prevent inappropriate uses, Bosco advanced the following recommendations:

1 Teachers must be informed regarding the laws of their state concerning the storage and administration of drugs.
2 Teachers should avoid statements such as: "I think Lucy's work would improve if she were on Ritalin."

3 The decision to administer Ritalin should be made only *after* there is reasonable assurance that the child's problem does *not* stem from boredom or inappropriate standards set by teachers.
4 When there is a suspicion of genuine hyperkinesis, a physician who specializes in learning and behavior problems (usually a pediatrician) should be consulted. Physicians who function to assuage teachers and parents are not helpful to the child.
5 Mechanisms should exist to open up communication among educators, parents, and physicians to monitor the prescription.
6 Finally, school administrators should be aware of the incidence of children being advised to seek drug treatment for learning problems. Unusually high referral rates may suggest an overreliance on drugs to solve classroom, rather than medical, problems.

Diagnosis and Placement

Chapter 3 identified the scope and sequence of identification and diagnosis. As this process involves human beings, there is bound to be human error. For example, Elonen, Polzien, and Zwarensteyn (1967) report the life histories of six children committed to an institution for the mentally retarded who were subsequently discovered to be *legally blind*. What saved these youngsters was that institutional staff extended themselves to visit the state school for the blind. The visits and subsequent personal appeal resulted in transfer.

Burke (1975) analyzed the placements of 180 black and white learners in a suburban school district with a population of 81,000. Whites were more frequently found in the learning disability program, while black learners were placed in classes for the retarded. This pattern was consistent for all grades, elementary through high school.

Neer, Foster, Jones, and Reynolds (1973) conducted a study of thirty-one graduate trainee psychologists. These persons were given similar case histories, except that socioeconomic status varied. Even with constant IQ, low sociometric status persons were perceived as mentally retarded, while persons of similar IQ but of middle to high status were not.

Hannaford, Simon, and Ellis (1975) utilized a simulation procedure to determine if school administrators, school psychologists, regular classroom teachers, and special-class teachers agree on diagnostic criteria for special education classes. Twenty-five case histories, varying on twelve variables, were presented to the four groups to rank for special-class placement. One variable was a teacher referral in which the person was rated retarded or nonretarded on the basis of the teacher's judgment. The following results were reported for the groups:

1. *Special education administrators* used the chronological age (CA), Wide Range Achievement Test (WRAT) reading score, WRAT math scores, Wechsler Intelligence Scale for Children (WISC) IQ, and teacher referral.
2. *School psychologists* attended to CA, WRAT reading, and WRAT math scores.
3. *Regular classroom teachers* used CA, WRAT reading, WRAT math, and teacher referral.
4. *Special education teachers* were found to use CA, race, WRAT reading, WRAT math, and teacher referral.
5. With all four groups combined, CA, WRAT reading, WRAT math, WISC IQ, and teacher referral were found to be the major variables.

The authors conclude that despite conflicting data within each of the twenty-five cases, different criteria are given more weight. It was also noted that the four groups responsible for diagnosis and placement do use different perceptions.

Prilman (1975) examined the placements of 7,427 children who were placed in primary and intermediate classes for the mildly mentally retarded. He concluded that children with an IQ above 75 are found in such classes; race and socioeconomic factors predict placement; placement is usually on the basis of a single psychometric score rather than a comprehensive assessment; special classes serve children with problems other than mild mental retardation; and children could be returned to regular grades if helping services were available.

Sabatino, Kelling, and Hayden (1973), based upon a review of research, concluded that cultural bias can be *prevented* in the process of diagnostic assessment and placement. Recommendations for changes in assessment procedures placed special emphasis on similarity of background between the examiner and the person being tested. Also recommended is specialized training of psychologists. Training, as viewed by these authors, should be prevention oriented.

The Loschen (1975) report offers additional help in the prevention of diagnostic and treatment errors. His hypothesis is that failure to deliver genuinely individualized programs originates from the lack of an individualized diagnostic procedure. One typical example, in his clinical experience, was a fourteen-year-old retarded person whose moderate hearing loss and slight orthopedic impairment was *never* considered in language treatment. He noted that diagnostic persons must have *firsthand* knowledge of programs recommended for placement. He cited the example of a young woman with an IQ of 110 without physical disability and labeled chronically mentally ill who was referred to a prevocational program. The referral source envisioned a controlled, behaviorally managed environment, but the facility existed to remediate visual-motor-perceptual problems. The young woman was most unhappy.

Special-class placement and special-education services need *not* be all negative. For example, Haring and Krug (1975) report a two-year project involving forty-eight mildly retarded learners between nine and ten years of age. Twenty-four persons were contrast subjects, and twenty-four were in a special class environment of twelve students each. The teaching program used structured methods and a token economy system. At the conclusion of the study, these "disadvantaged" learners were found to have maintained their gains in the regular grades after special-class placement.

Warner, Thrapp, and Walsh (1973) interviewed 369 learners between the ages of eight and seventeen years, with a mean IQ of 66. Sixty-one percent liked the special class, and 25 percent wanted to be somewhere else. Of the uncertain group, the preference was for a specific class such as driver education or home economics. When asked, "Why do you think you are in a special class?" 52 percent of the elementary-school learners had positive remarks, which declined to 34 percent for junior high, and 18 percent for senior high. By contrast, 68 percent of the junior-high students liked the academic work. The most disliked feature was the fighting behavior of classmates. The authors concluded that special-class placement was comfortable to the learners themselves.

Jones (1972) offers an insight into the reactions of retarded persons toward their placements. In a follow-up study of 405 persons who had been in two forms of special education programs, one group had been enrolled in a work-study program with an occupational emphasis, while the other group had been in a "general" special education program without specific or special direction. Both groups had subgroups of graduates and dropouts. Jones summarized the results of personal interviews with these four groups which should be understood as: Work-Study Graduate (WSG), Work-Study Dropout (WSD), Special-Education Graduate (SEG), and Special-Education Dropout (SED) (All participants were within the mild mental retardation range.) What follows are the questions and percentages reported by Jones.

1. Looking back, has being in a special class or work-study program been helpful to you? (Yes was declared by Jones to be positive) WSG 58.6%, WSD 49.3%, SEG 44.0%, SED 34.1%.

2. Has being in a special class or a work study program caused any problems for you? (A No answer was declared by Jones to be positive) WSG 62.9%, WSD 65.3%, SEG 52.0%, SED 48.7%.

3. Can schools help students get better jobs than they would get otherwise? (Yes) WSG 67.1%, WSD 65.3%, SEG 52.0%, SED 48.7%.

4. Did being in special education help you get along better with other people? (Yes) WSG 48.3%, WSD 44.0%, SEG 32.0%, SED 24.3%.

Jones notes that the dropout of a quality program is more positive in his or her recollection than the graduate of a lesser quality program. One inference might be that the reaction of a person to a label is more a function of perceived consequences than of the label itself. None of the participants was "free" of some negative reflection. However, negative effects can be prevented by quality program standards and if the program delivers a relevant service.

Sexism

Thomas-Cegelka (1976) has examined the possibility of sex biases in work experience programs for the mentally retarded. There were over 25 citations from the program and follow-up literature to identify differential treatment and upon which to formulate recommendations for reform. For example, Thomas-Cegelka reported that comparable weekly wages for work experience students was that normal females earn less than normal and retarded males do, and retarded females earn even less. Specifically, normal females earned 62 percent less than males (regardless of level), while retarded females earned 35 percent of what was earned by the two groups. Other indicators of discrimination included:

1. Fewer females than males were enrolled in work-study programs. Even allowing for sex incidence, there appears to be a factor in operation. Research data were presented which indicated that Anglo girls of equal IQ were less likely than boys to be placed.

2. Vocational training for females appeared to be oriented toward jobs of low or limited financial status, while boys were provided with training that encouraged job mobility.

3. Expectations for girls tend to be lower, in the sense that marriage or housekeeping (without marriage) appears to be a primary goal. Given a national average of between 25 to 40 percent for divorce, it would seem reasonable to prepare a person for a more stable employment future.

4. Lowered expectations are reflected in the follow-up literature, with detailed accounts of male workers and general categories of housewife, homemaker, etc. for women. There is rarely an attempt to specify "success" in these roles.

Possible solutions advanced by Thomas-Cegelka were:

1. *Admission to programs.* Admission should be based upon educationally relevant criteria, not upon sex or stereotypic thinking about "safe" occupations.

2. *Elimination of biases in curriculum and training opportunities.* Discrimination exists where there is evidence of differential patterns of employment in salary potential, job stability, and denied training opportunities are found to exist based upon sex.

3. *Program evaluation.* There should be specified criteria, which should be applied equitably to both sexes and for nonsalaried occupations.

The Thomas-Cegelka resumé alerts the potential advocate of a particular need for monitoring. This article clearly isolates the possibility that being retarded and female constitutes a dual handicap.

DIMENSIONS OF EXPRESSIVE ADVOCACY

Advocacy has its dimensions of affect. The Copeland et al. reports identified the need for the prevention of isolation and neglect. An associated role involves situations of practical guidance and the encouragement of self-worth. Situations in which the advocate-protege relationship might be applicable and needed could involve either the person and/or the family.

Marriage

Preparation for marriage will be a common topic of the advocate-protege relationship. Ginott (1969, 1971) offers practical guidance to parents of children and youth. While the knowledge of sexual reproduction is essential, preparation for the sexual role is critical. He recommends that parents and other adults emphasize the meaning of sexuality (roles of males and females, sexual expression, and responsibility) as well as the means of sexual reproduction.

As was seen in chapter 7, marriage is a possibility for the retarded person. Bowden, Spitz, and Winters (1971) and Androm and Sturm (1973) have offered studies that reflect the need for an advocate relationship for certain retarded persons. The Bowden et al. report detailed one couple's marriage after premarital counseling prior to discharge. There were lengthy intervals between contact and response from helping agencies, often as long as two months. The couple constantly needed money management and vocational assistance. The presence of an advocate would have made a tremendous difference. The Androm and Sturm report encompassed twelve couples in their early twenties to late thirties who were known to be retarded. Twenty-three of the respondents reported that married life was better than their previous isolation. Only one couple had children, for seven couples had been sterilized, three were naturally sterile, and one used birth control. All expressed a desire to have or adopt children. There was evidence of child substitutes. The seven sterilized couples voiced bitterness that they had not really understood the operation or had been told it was reversible. This reaction is borne out by a survey conducted by Whitcraft and Jones (1974) of 659 persons (either parents of retarded persons or professionals in the field of mental retardation). Approximately 85 percent expressed the attitude that sterilization is morally right. Sexual expression was accepted by the sample with equanimity, but they felt strongly that procreation should not be an accompaniment. Their recommendation was for voluntary sterilization, although only 6 percent believed that retarded persons would understand its implications.

These studies noted that the existence of informal advocates such as a relative, landlord, employer, or community service worker proved invaluable. Common problems were: health and care of one partner; money management; overindebtedness; erratic employment; legal difficulties, especially unscrupulous friends palming off stolen goods as bargains; involvement with demanding and difficult relatives; basic sex education; contraceptive information; and counseling regarding previous life experiences. The studies noted that certain programs and/or life experiences may preclude an adequate family model for a frame of reference. Certain programs may inadvertently encourage homosexual contacts and discourage heterosexual experiences. This can pose grave difficulties for expression of emotions, create vast misinformation, and thwart initiation of contacts with the opposite sex.

Sex Education

Perske (1973) has discussed sex education in both a historical and contemporary setting. Historically, there have been attempts to: de-sex the retarded (in some instances, literally), deny their sexuality, or treat them as if they were sexual monsters. The effect has been to rob the retarded person of responsibility for their own growth as well as to prevent initiating efforts early enough to prevent misinformation and stereotyped ideas. He also noted that in a rebound effort, some individuals "push" retarded persons together without regard for their preferences or readiness. Sex education is gradual and lifelong, not a short course, and ideally should be a parent responsibility. While sex education is no longer feared as arousing desire in holy innocents, sensitivity, tenderness, and confidence should be key elements of such preparation.

Vockell and Mattick (1972) identified certain problems, programs, and research regarding sex education for retarded persons. A central problem is that the physical development of the retarded person takes place at a normal pace, while the intellectual ability to interpret these changes may lag behind. Furthermore, it was pointed out that while physical development may be somewhat slower, there eventually is adequate reproductive functioning. The problem focus for sex education is to distinguish those retarded persons whose sexual development is unimpaired by personality problems from those retarded persons who find in sexual release a source of success denied them in other areas of life. The second group will require more extensive help to unlearn these behaviors. All retarded persons seem to share certain common problems in sex education. First, there is the prevalent American attitude of learning the facts of life from friends. For the retarded person this can be a significant source of misinformation. Second, the retarded person's need for guidance is greater and so is the helpful adult's need for planning learning experiences.

These authors placed great value upon the role of parents. Typical parent concerns about sex education were: their inability to answer the child's questions; excessive masturbation by the child; fear that the child is in sexual danger and will be sexually exploited; and problems of marriage. The authors suggested that without proper sex education these areas of concern are likely to become problems. Sexual stimulation can be a result of external forces; ill-fitting clothing and being put to bed when not tired encourage self-stimulation. With respect to marriage, the need for a helpful adult to provide guidance was stressed.

The responsibility of the schools was identified, especially if parents request such a role or if parents are unable or unwilling to fill it. The too frequent emphasis upon the biological and neglect of the psychosocial aspects of sex education was pointed out. The scope of the schools' responsibilities was seen as enabling the student to understand and deal with situations he or she will meet, protect oneself from harmful physical-mental consequences of the abuse of sex, express feelings about sexual choices, and acquire a value system to choose between alternatives in a time of changing attitudes. While three general approaches to sex education were discussed, the role of the teacher was seen as a critical link among parents, specialists, and pupils. Of importance is the teacher's attitude toward sex education. It was suggested that pupils will be affected by the teacher's own beliefs about family life. The need for training of preservice teachers was indicated. A survey within the article suggested present emphasis is meager and inservice education of present staff was advocated. This latter approach was viewed as the most promising. Meijin and Retish (1971) report that participants in such a workshop expressed satisfaction with its content and reported greater awareness regarding their role in this type of program. Goodman, Budner, and Lesh (1971) have outlined a similar approach targeted toward parents.

Parent Involvement

The initial reaction to a retarded child can be a traumatic experience. Parents can learn to master the crisis, but they vary in their abilities. Advocates may be required for the family. The process from mourning to compensation need not be a lonely struggle.

Rains (1975) has identified seven views of crisis in Western culture which exist along an implied continuum.

1. *Punitive, or retribution.* This view holds that there is a punishment inherent in the crisis or event itself. This view holds a rather specific view of the world as good versus evil. Thus, all good events are rewards and vice versa.

2. *Inevitable.* This view suggests a certain fatalistic resignation and, like the preceding one, offers little guidance for action, for it tends to accept the status quo as fixed and unchanging.

3. *Probationary, or testing.* This view constitutes a departure from the previous two in that the person senses the need to act. At this level the person is confronted with values rather than deeds.

4. *An awakening.* This view suggests that crisis possesses a purpose to return the person to awareness. This may be a return to spiritual values, a recognition of friends, and/or a resolve to cope.

5. *A purification.* This view involves a concept of *test,* a Middle English word meaning a vessel in which metal was assayed. This view holds that the experience has meaning, or at least the meaning will eventually become clear.

6. *Redemptive.* This view holds that crisis has a learning value from which the person senses a purpose. In a sense, it is a culmination of the previous two levels.

7. *Creative.* At this level the person concretely recognizes the limitations of "what if," "not me," or "yes, but." The person acts, not reacts. This person has a sense of trust that the future is within his span of control.

Rains suggested that crisis or disappointment can: divert us to something that proves better than an original aim; cause persons to seek less material gain and prize more humanistic values; be a means of ordering priorities; be a discovery of allegiance to persons similarly affected; and be a discovery of skills and competence. A Children's Bureau (1973) publication illustrates the progression from despair to action as learning to accept, learning where to seek help, and learning to cope, cooperate, and share. One mother's experience was cited to illustrate how the experience of a handicapped child had changed her perspective (pp. 6–7).

> Before I had Johnny I always thought of neighbors as just people next door to say hello to. One doesn't know what life is, just to go along taking everything for granted. It made me look at things differently. I have a better view of humanity. People mean more to me now because when they're nice to Johnny, they're even more than a neighbor — they're a friend.

Simches (1975) has noted that professionals need to reexamine their perceptions about parents and parent involvement. He recommended the partnership concept and identified three broad areas of involvement of parents. As *teachers,* parents were seen as continuing their traditional roles. Involvement in tutoring can also assist parenting skills. As *advisors,* parents were seen as offering antidotes and assisting in other ways in goal-setting priorities. As *advocates,* parents serve as monitors for their own children and as advocates for programs. Parents have proven roles, according to Simches, in increasing equal educational opportunity for all handicapped children, insuring a child's right to due process, and increasing accountability and standards of quality. Simches stressed that parents are not a threat, but rather an effective partner with whom to promote reform. Although the Simches exposition was directed toward educational agencies, there is reason to believe that service agencies, in general, could benefit from parent involvement.

Kingsley (1971) has recounted the experience of one school with the involvement of parents. His premise is that parents can reinforce the school program in everyday family life, and that parents and the school can reinforce one another's efforts. Karnes and Zehrbach (1972), as well as Benson and Ross (1972), have described methods of parent involvement within the school. The former stressed the need for training and orientation prior to involvement. Modeling and demonstration were the principal training methods. The need for frequent conferences was stressed. The benefits of such involvement were seen as: the chance for parents to teach one another, opportunities for individualized instruction, increased community support, and increase in availability of services. The Benson and Ross discussion focused upon the gains to the child as well as increases in community support of the school. In their project, and others, the parents are volunteers, but the recruiting of volunteers is not necessarily restricted to parents of handicapped children.

Consumer Orientation

Lanning (1973) has reported a procedure to obtain a consensus regarding priorities. Using a list similar to the Illinois ARC (chapter 8), community agency personnel (including consumer groups) generated rank-order priorities. The results generated a three-year timetable for implementation. The schedule called for: refinement of the timetable, specific service dimensions for service, possible curriculum and program guidelines, proposed budget and sources of funding, estimated numbers of clients to be served by 1975, and definition of standards.

Caccano (1974) summarized one local planning effort which avowed a consumer-oriented focus. One focus was to involve consumer ratings of services as a measure of satisfaction. The other focus was to obligate staff to work cooperatively with parents and persons as partners rather than clients.

Wolfensberger and Glenn (1975b) tend to exclude the dimension of client feelings of happiness and well-being on program evaluation. They argue the emphasis should be upon program and process and outcomes. They observed that normalization involves the dignity of risk in order to achieve higher levels of attainment, but such risk may bring temporary stress and trauma. Independence, self-sufficiency, and respect from others may be more significant indicators of quality than comfort. Wolfensberger and Glenn (1975a) have produced two documents, PASS and FUNDET, which are proposed for quantitative evaluation of human services. The premise of the Wolfensberger and Glenn (1975b) report is that normalization should be a guiding principle in decision making.

These specialists also commented on the politics of consumer-oriented involvement. Planning, evaluation, and social action are "political" in the sense that *political* means people. Consumers, advocates, agency directors, staffs, laypersons, funding sources, and regulatory agencies, among others, view decisions in emotional and rational ways. Planning and evaluation should be conducted, if possible, in a colleague spirit. The goal, process, and result should be assistance. The relationship becomes adversary when access to data is denied. Planning, as a scientific tool, can depoliticize funding. These specialists also suggest that analysis can include sources beyond the scope of PASS and FUNDET. The misuse of planning and evaluation arises when actions are taken on the basis of incomplete data. The procedure, the person, and the mission can become discredited.

Ethical Considerations

The regulation of ethical-moral behavior can range from direct, physical consequences associated with behavior to an ultimate recognition of behavior regulated by role reversal. That is to say, at one level, "good" is that which brings reward and avoids punishment, but on the highest level I respond to another person as I would want that person to respond should our situations be reversed. Here regulation is internal. For the advocate, ethics provide the basis for internal authority to guide human relationships. In this sense, ethics are not necessarily a dogmatic series of *don'ts,* but rather guidelines for quality of life.

Upon review of the material about advocacy, normalization, and the dignity of risk, one notes a need to balance risk and overprotection. The decisions are value-laden. Warren (1974) has presented an apocryphal account of admitted doubtful authenticity "authored" by Itard. The Itard letter is included to consider the values/ethical interplay among risk, knowing, and change.

July 14, 1803

Dr. Philippe Pinel
Professor of Pathology
Ecole de Medicine
Paris, France

Dear Professor Pinel,

Please permit me to congratulate you on your recent appointment, an honor well deserved. May I also take this occasion to relate to you a strangely disturbing dream I had recently? It concerned a patient you examined several years ago, a child who came to be known as "Victor, the Wild Boy of Averyon."

At the time of examination, it was your opinion that the child, who has been living wildly in the forests, was a hopeless idiot in need of confinement in some humane asylum. Despite this poor prognosis, I decided to attempt to treat the child, using the educational techniques we had developed for deaf children.

When we began work, he spoke not. His walk was that of the wolf and so were his manners. Frightened, snarling, vicious, unhappy child! It was months before our carefully planned efforts brought laughter, smiles and valiant effort to learn, but learn he did! He became a friendly, helpful, mute but joyous child, able to live in a civilized home and even to join me at dinner at the inn. But you will have read of this in the report I prepared for the Academy of Sciences. You will remember that we were unable to help him attain "normality" and that many, including myself, believed my five-year experiment to be a failure in that respect. Nevertheless, he did move.

I had hoped initially that by carefully recording the work I did with Victor I might serve other children by making the results of my work known to those teachers who came after me. In this effort, I have known success; several workers have reported to me that my techniques have been highly successful with other children. Nevertheless, a recent dream I had raised a number of ethical issues for me.

I dreamed that Victor came to me in a strange place, apparently at some far distant time. Outside the windows, carriages flashed by without horses! A cabinet by the wall had a window through which one could see and hear tiny people. Overhead, gigantic silver birds roared by trailing dark smoke. Victor stood mutely before me, holding in one hand the items we used to teach him and in the other hand a paper. His eyes begged me to teach him, but he would not give me the teaching materials until I read the paper. On it were listed numerous rules for the conduct of research and experiments.

Awakening in the chill grey dawns, I could remember from the paper only one phrase, "informed consent." And I remember Victor's eyes pleading that I teach him to write his name so that he could sign an "informed consent" paper. Both he and I seemed to know that the parents who had left him in the woods could not be found to sign papers for him . . . and that he could not write his name. He seemed to know that others would call my work with him "research" and that I would be in deep trouble if I did not follow these rules, which had obviously been intended to protect him, but were preventing me from helping him. What could I do? Refuse him? *Prende la lune avec aux dents?*

My dream dilemma was solved by awakening. But I am haunted by the dream. If we had such rules, I could not continue in my work here with deaf children. Like Victor, they can not comprehend "consent" and perhaps it is not needed for this type of work. What is your opinion? We do need guidelines to protect children, but I am not sure what they should be.

I look forward to your reply.

Your obedient servant,
Jean-Marc Gaspart Itard

One cannot but ponder the Itard dilemma. What is the definition of research? How much restriction is needed? How much risk is "acceptable" if one individual is placed in jeopardy for the sake of thousands of others. Some unborn? It is a nightmare which must be faced in the cold light of day.

SUMMING UP

This chapter has been a resumé of advocacy. The literature of citizen advocacy suggests that an inevitable conflict of interest may preclude the practitioner as citizen advocate for persons directly under his or her supervision and/or responsibility.

Practitioners can have an advocacy function provided they are sensitive to conflict of interest. Perhaps the best advocacy for service agencies would be to encourage the functioning of citizen advocates in their communities. Among the concepts presented within the chapter, the following are advanced for special emphasis:

1. The citizen advocate is emerging as a principal model of advocacy for retarded persons.

2. The roles of the CA can be divided into expressive functions of friendship, practical guidance, and normalization experiences, and instrument functions of protecting rights, gaining access to services, and guardianship.

3. The CA is a volunteer person available as needed and is not tied to the public-service system.

4. The essence of the retarded person's relationship with the CA is that of a protege. Regarding the retarded person as a protege implies a growth potential.

5. There is sufficient experience and literature available to suggest a permanence about the continuation of the CA program. The citizen advocacy office is a crucial element in the operation of the program.

6. The CA is a change agent. This program is a splendid example of both social action and of the willingness of persons to become involved. There appear to be benefits to the protege, the CA, and the larger society.

7. Parents as well as retarded persons may require advocates.

8. Certain topics encountered by advocates engaged in expressive advocacy were reviewed, with examples of helpful approaches. Among these topics were normalization, sexuality, sexism, parent involvement, rights, child abuse and neglect, and ethical considerations.

9. The intentions of normalization are not in dispute. Reservations toward mainstreaming and deinstitutionalization center around risk. There is a support from the research literature to suggest guidelines for normal risk. Examples of adult education and personal adjustment training suggest helpful examples of effectiveness training.

10. Sexuality was defined as knowledge of procreation and knowledge of sexual role. Marriage, as reflected in the research literature, appears to be a helpful experience for the retarded person, although the practical guidance of an advocate proves supportive. Sterilization appears to be an area where the practice is carried on without regard to its psychological consequences. Guidelines for a sex education curriuculum were identified, and current examples were cited.

11. Sexism appears evident. The trend appears to be for differential and preferential treatment for males in work-training programs. Guidelines to curb this trend were identified.

12. A concept of rights was explored. This discussion examined guidelines for advocates to use in assessing whether protege rights were important to the service agency.

13. Parents who engage in child abuse and neglect have learned these practices from their parents. Guidelines for identification of such children and examples of treatment programs were identified.

14. The advocate has many identities as well as varied roles. These were identified. The advocate can be distracted by his or her own perceptions, as well as rendered ineffective. Tactics are perceived to be within one's role definition. Possible sources of distraction and a variety of tactics were discussed.

ON LOCATION

This section utilizes two selections to illustrate both the need and response of advocacy. The first selection was a response written in longhand to *Children Limited*. The author, a retarded citizen, wrote to chide an article that described a week's experience of simulation of being mentally retarded. The author, Garrene (1967) expressed doubt that anyone could really experience these effects. The second selection was Posner's (1967) reply, which expresses a significant dimension of the subject matter of this chapter.

I Know What It's Like to be Retarded!

I have a story I want to tell all you folks it's about a good Christian family, the Mother, the father and 8 lovely children the youngest a girl (let's call her Sandy) well one day little Sandy only 18 mo. old toddled into the busy street and was hit by a car she was out 3 weeks had a busted head ect. the doctors had no hope and if by chance little Sandy lived she'd never be a normal human. but before the accident lets go back a little way and who do we see? a club footed infant this infant had a cast on her leg and finally the doc. correctored her foot it was normal. but guess who this baby was Yes, you're right it was Sandy all along. Well Sandy got well the accident left a mental block as far as mathmatics were conserned otherwise she was normal se had friends, loved ones ect. just like anyone else until she "got grown" Then it happened! people started wondering why Sandy would not have a steady job or why she'd droped out in thd 3rd grade. then all the neighbors realized Sandy was slightled retarded and so considered her insane and dangerious. roumers begin and got bigger and Bigger. although Sandy had a normal childhood she was rejected because of her handicapp. poor Sandy tried to explain to her "Best Friend" but soon found herself friendless and an outcast Was it her fault? after she realized she'd be lonely telling the truth she begin to lie and say she was a college graduate (but that only made hr consence act up) and she knew it'd be only a matter of time before her new friends found out. I want to tell you all Sandy is a Christian and she serves her Lord and Savior. there is no physical evidence of her condition yet her heart aches and her lonely life makes her sad. Sandy has come to this conclusion it is a cross she alone must bear. her beloved parents do every thing in the world to make her happy but they don't realize she's being talked about and pointed out as the - retarded nut. "oh, how it hurts her not being accepted but friends please listen, please don't judge others and if you know an unfortanate person who's life is a burden. I ask you please accept them and friends I know Sandy for she is me. this is a true story for friends it is My Story and my life. and I know where i stand *"Alone!*

A Reply from Bernard Posner

Dear Miss Garrene,

I agree with everything you said.

Certainly, I do not know what it's really like to be mentally retarded but I can sympathize with the way you feel since, as you said, you have been retarded for 23 years.

I had a reason for pretending to be retarded for one week. I wanted to make the rest of the world know that retarded people deserve as much of a chance in life as anybody else.

I want the rest of the world to know that really there isn't very much difference between mentally retarded people and people who are not retarded.

We are all human beings and we all have certain rights as human beings.

That was my reason for posing as a retarded person. I wanted, in my small way, to help people who are mentally retarded. I wanted to help them gain a better life.

I have read the article that you wrote and I think it's beautiful. One thing bothers me — at the end you say "I know where I stand 'alone!' "

I do not think you stand completely alone. I think many people want to help. As long as they do, the world isn't too bad a place to live in.

Bernard Posner,
Deputy Executive Secretary, President's Committee on Employment of the Handicapped

REFERENCES

Androm, L., and Sturm, M. L. Is I Do in the Repertoire of the Mentally Retarded? *Mental Retardation,* 1973, 11, 31–34.

Benson, J., and Ross, L. Teaching Parents to Teach Their Children. *Teaching Exceptional Children,* 1972, 5, 30–36.

Bosco, J. Behavior Modification Drugs and the Schools: The Case of Ritalin. *Phi Delta Kappan,* 1975, 51, 489–492.

Bowden, J., Spitz, H. H., and Winters, J. Follow-Up of One Retarded Couple's Marriage. *Mental Retardation,* 1971, 9, 42–43.

Burke, A. A. Placement of Black and White Children in Educable Mentally Handicapped Classes and Learning Disability Classes. *Exceptional Children,* 1975, 41, 438–439.

Caccano, J. M. Consumer Oriented Evaluation and Treatment Programs. *Mental Retardation,* 1974, 12, 48–49.

Children's Bureau. *A Handicapped Child in Your Home.* DHEW Publication No. (OCD) 73–29. Washington, D.C.: U.S. Dept. of Health, Education and Welfare, 1975.

Conglon, D. Cloak of Incompetence. *Mental Retardation,* 1974, 12, 29.

Copeland, S., Addison, M., and McCann, B. *Avenues to Change,* Books I–IV. Dallas: NARC, 1974.

Davoren, E. Working with Abusive Parents — A Social Worker's View. *Children Today,* 1975, 4, 2 and 38–43.

Dunn, L. M. Special Education for the Mildly Retarded — Is Much of It Justified? *Exceptional Children,* 1968, 35, 5–22.

Elonen, A., Polzien, M., and Zwarensteyn, S. The Uncommitted Blind Child: Results of Intensive Training of Children Formerly Committed to Institutions for the Retarded. *Exceptional Children,* 1967, 33, 301–307.

Garrene, S. I Know What It's Like to be Retarded. *Children Limited,* 1967, 16, 7.

Ginott, H. *Between Parent and Child.* New York: Avon, 1969.

Ginott, H. *Between Parent and Teenager.* New York: Avon, 1971.

Goldberg, I. I. Human Rights for the Mentally Retarded in the School System. *Mental Retardation,* 1971, 9, 3–7.

Goodman, L., Budner, S., and Lesh, B. The Parents' Role in Sex Education for the Retarded. *Mental Retardation,* 1971, 9, 43–45.

Hannaford, A. E., Simon, J., and Ellis, D. Criteria for Special Class Placement of the Mildly Retarded — Multidisciplinary Comparison. *Mental Retardation,* 1975, 13, 7–10.

Haring, N., and Krug, D. Placement in Regular Programs: Procedures and Results. *Exceptional Children,* 1975, 41, 413–417.

Harris-Cohen, A., Shea-Ridge, S., and Collinghon, F. Evaluating Innovative Treatment Programs in Child Abuse and Neglect. *Children Today,* 1975, 4, 10–12.

Hemenway, R., Lemke, E., Hage, D., and Robertshaw, C. Three Curricula for Retarded Adults. *Mental Retardation,* 1972, 10, 13–15.

Johnson, G. O. Special Education for the Mentally Handicapped — A Paradox. *Exceptional Children,* 1962, 29, 62–69.

Jones, R. L. Labels and Stigma in Special Education. *Exceptional Children,* 1972, 39, 553–564.

Karnes, M. B., and Zehrbach, R. Flexibility in Getting Parents Involved in the School. *Teaching Exceptional Children,* 1972, 5, 6–19.

Kingsley, L. Parents Can Help with School Difficulties. *The Exceptional Parent,* 1971, 1, 13–15.

Klein, S. Magic Words. *Exceptional Parent,* 1975, 5, 30–31.

Kolodziej, J. Citizen Advocacy: Speaking for Retarded Citizens. *Mental Retardation News,* 1974.

Lanning, J. W. Coordinating Services. *Mental Retardation,* 1973, 11, 46–47.

Loschen, E. L. Failures in Diagnosis and Treatment in Mental Retardation. *Mental Retardation,* 1975, 13, 29–31.

Meijin, E. L., and Rctish, P. Sex Education for the Mentally Retarded: Influencing Teacher's Attitudes. *Mental Retardation,* 1971, 9, 46–49.

Nagi, S. Child Abuse and Neglect. *Children Today,* 1975, 4, 13–17.

Neer, W., Foster, D., Jones, J., Reynolds, D. Socioeconomic Bias in the Diagnosis of Mental Retardation. *Exceptional Children,* 1973, 40, 38–39.

Nibira, L., and Nibira, K. Normalized Behavior in Community Placement. *Mental Retardation,* 1975, 13, 9–13.

Nirji, B. The Normalization Principle and Its Human Management Implications, in Kugel, R., and Wolfensberger, W. (eds.). *Changing Patterns in Residential Services.* Washington, D.C.: The President's Committee on Mental Retardation, 1969.

Perske, R. *New Directions.* New York: Abingdon Press, 1973.

Perske, R. The Dignity of Risk and the Mentally Retarded. *Mental Retardation,* 1972, 10, 24–26.

Prilman, D. An Analysis of Placement Factors in Classes for the Educable Mentally Retarded. *Exceptional Children,* 1975, 42, 107–108.

Posner, B. A Reply. *Children Limited,* 1967, 16, 7.

Rains, R. The Seven Biblical Views of Suffering. *Christian Herald,* 1975, 98, 24–27.

Reed, R. Working with Parents. *Children Today,* 1975, 4, 6–9.

Roos, P. Human Rights and Behavior Modification. *Mental Retardation,* 1974, 12, 3–6.

Sabatino, D., Kelling, K., Hayden, D. Special Education and the Culturally Different Child: Implications for Assessment and Intervention. *Exceptional Children,* 1973, 39.

Sandgrund, A., Gains, R., and Green, A. Child Abuse and Mental Retardation: A Problem of Cause and Effect. *American Journal of Mental Deficiency,* 1974, 79, 327–328.

Simches, R. The Parent-Professional Partnership. *Exceptional Children,* 1975, 41, 565–566.

Soeffing, M. Abused Children are Exceptional Children. *Exceptional Children,* 1975, 42, 126–133.

Soeffing, M. Normalization of Services for the Mentally Retarded — A Conversation with Dr. Wolf Wolfensberger. *Education and Training of the Mentally Retarded,* 1974, 9, 202–208.

Steele, B. F. Working with Abusive Parents — A Psychiatrist's View. *Children Today,* 1975, 4, 3–5 and 44.

Stephens, W. E. Mainstreaming: Some Natural Limitations. *Mental Retardation,* 1975, 13, 40–41.

Thomas-Cegelka, P. Sex Role Stereotyping in Special Education: A Look at Secondary Work Study Programs. *Exceptional Children,* 1976, 42, 323–328.

Todd, T. W. Supplying Meaningful Educational Data. *Mental Retardation,* 1971, 9, 10–11.

Throne, J. Normalization Through the Normalization Principle. *Mental Retardation,* 1975, 13, 16–18.

Vockell, E., and Mattick, P. Sex Education of the Mentally Retarded. *Education and Training of the Mentally Retarded,* 1972, 7, 129–134.

Warner, F., Thrapp, R., and Walsh, S. Attitudes of Children Toward Their Special Class Placement. *Exceptional Children,* 1973, 40.

Warren, S. A. Editorial-Nightmare. *Mental Retardation,* 1974, 12, 2.

Whitcraft, C., and Jones, J. P. A Survey of Attitudes of Sterilization of Retardates. *Mental Retardation,* 1974, 12, 30–33.

Wolfensberger, W., and Glenn, L. *Pass 3 Field Manual* (3rd ed.). Toronto, Canada: National Institute on Mental Retardation, 1973.

Wolfensberger, W., and Glenn, L. *Pass 3 Handbook* (3rd ed.). Toronto, Canada: National Institute on Mental Retardation, 1973.

Young, L. *Wednesday's Children, A Study of Child Neglect and Abuse.* New York: McGraw-Hill, 1964.

Zisfein, L., and Rosen, M. Personal Adjustment Training. *Mental Retardation,* 1975, 11, 16–20.

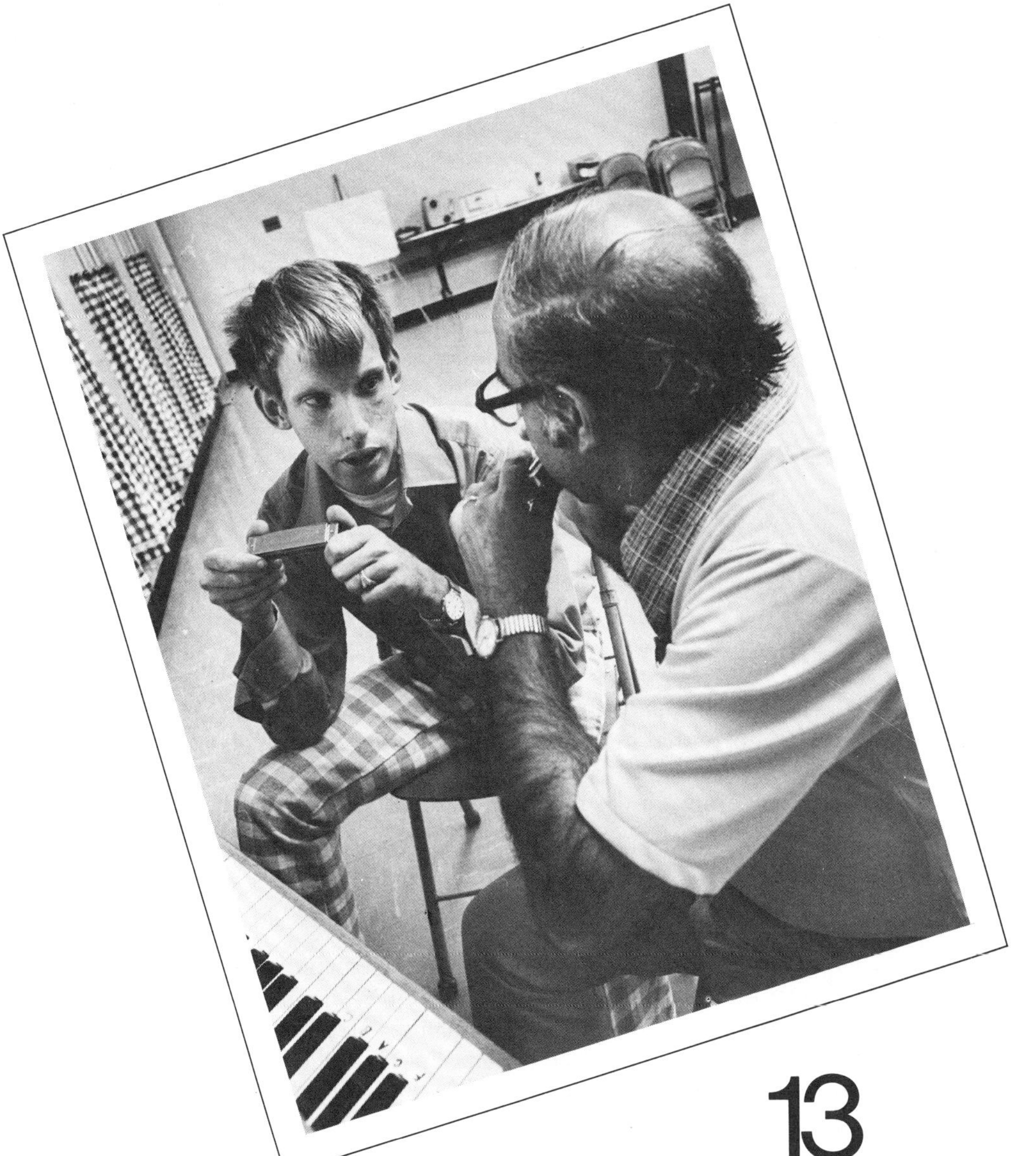

13

Helping Relationships

SYNOPSIS

This chapter explores approaches available for expressive advocacy. The term *helping relationship* was selected to substitute for traditional terms such as *counseling, guidance, therapy,* and the like. The concept of helping relationship conveys the nature of an advocate-protege relationship.

OBJECTIVES

ATTITUDES

1 To be open to opportunities for a helping relationship.
2 To recognize that in order to know another person, one must know one's inner needs.
3 To resolve one's own needs to be dominant to another person's needs for growth.

UNDERSTANDINGS

1 To distinguish between types of helping relationships.
2 To identify one's identity in the helping relationship.
3 To identify one's own potential qualities as a helper.
4 To identify the special considerations associated with listening, reflection, and problem solving.
5 To identify correlates of the helping relationship.

SKILLS

1 To practice skills of congruent communications.
2 To implement problem-solving approaches to situations requiring a helping relationship.
3 To identify, within one's own value structure, obstacles to the helping relationship.

4 To describe those circumstances where systems of helping relationships may be required.
5 To describe the compatibility between advocacy and systems of helping relationships.

FOUNDATION CONCEPTS

Nature

Gordon (1970) has expressed the helping relationship as a no-lose system. The concept of system does *not* imply a cold, impersonal mechanism. The notion of system assumes that certain principles can be known and understood with sufficient clarity to be acquired with a minimum of trial and error.

The concept of a no-lose system is presented in adapted form in figure 13–1. The notion is that human beings interact on an I-You basis. Unfortunately, the interaction can become a "contest," which implies winning or losing. Hence the four dimensions suggested in figure 13–1. Unfortunately, the relationship between practitioner and consumer can evolve into an I (practitioner) win — You (consumer) lose. Another alternative is I (practitioner) lose — You (consumer) win. For Gordon, this is destructive permissiveness.

Figure 13–1 *Dimension Personal Interactions*

		YOU	
		WIN	LOSE
I	WIN	Helping A Relationship	Autocratic B Overprotective
	LOSE	Destructive C Permissive	Detachment D Neglect

According to Gordon, it is the responsibility of the practitioner to arrange the elements necessary for the no-lose system and process. The professional person is, after all, prepared in these skills. Therefore, if a "client" has a need to lose, this trend should be reversed. Self-understanding can enable a practitioner to examine his or her own needs.

Outcomes

Rogers (1951) proposed outcomes for what he termed the helping relationship. Using research data and clinical experience, Rogers identified six outcomes resulting from the relationship. The client can/will be able to:

1 make statements about plans, identify the steps to be undertaken, and discuss outcomes — consequences of actions;
2 shift from "immature" self-centered behavior to "mature" behavior of planned purposeful activity;
3 reflect reduction of tension, even of physical tension evidenced in psychological symptoms;
4 decrease defensive behavior (distortion, denial, or escape from life's demands) and achieve an awareness-verbalization of the consequences of prudent behaviors;
5 increase tolerance for frustration, even in psychological terms and reactions; and
6 improve functioning in life tasks, which can be school achievement as well as job training and job performance.

Gordon (1951) has identified other examples of the behaviors of helpers which reflect an *internal* caring as opposed to concerns about one's performance or image. Table 13–1 summarizes a representative listing of these examples.

Dimensions

Ginott (1961) has identified a continuum along which the helping relationship might be charted (table 13–2). The continuum ranges from psychotherapy through guidance. From Ginott's perspective, psychotherapy, counseling, and guidance are dimensions of problem solving. The practitioner, especially the educator, will typically engage in guidance, with some incursions into counseling.

Table 13–1 INTERNAL VERSUS EXTERNAL CONCERNS

Internal Concerns	*External Concerns*
You're wanting to struggle toward. . . .	Why this interest?
It's hard for you to get started. . . .	We'll have to dig into those early days.
Decision making seems impossible. . . .	I feel sorry for anybody who. . . .
You want an answer, but it doesn't seem possible	He's an only child—I didn't know that
You feel yourself. . . .	The crying, the profanity; there must be repression
Being lonely has somehow had a feeling of sadness for you.	Why this reaction? What is the cause?
But it was the diagnosis which. . . .	I wonder if I shouldn't help him get started talking?
It is an experience which you. . . .	Is this anger a form of projective-reaction?
You are feeling ________?	Is the person/group going where I want?
You are saying ________?	I disagree with that.
If I understand ________	I wonder what they really think of me?
I'm not sure that I follow ________	How can I get others to talk?
I gather that you mean ________	That's an irrelevant remark.
You wish I would say ________	
I'm interested in hearing you ________	

Parent Preferences

Sellin and Gallery (1974), inspired by Patterson (1956), submitted a list of pointers for professionals to a leadership group of parents of retarded persons. The sample consisted of sixty-three members of a board of directors of a state association for re-

Table 13–2 DIMENSIONS OF HELPING RELATIONSHIPS

	Modes		
Elements	*Psychotherapy*	*Counseling*	*Guidance*
Goals	Restructure of the personality. Seeking permanent change and/or alteration.	Freedom from annoying symptoms. A mastery of reality. Attainment of a comfortable level of social adaptation.	Improvement of the everyday present and relationships. Sensitize parents to feelings and needs of others and of children.
Behaviors	Smothered by feelings and emotional behaviors. Hostility, anxiety, guilt are the principal ones. Drain off of energy and thought needed to cope.	Use of defenses to evade, escape, deny, or distort realities of the existence of a problem or the responsibility of one's actions and reactions.	Difficulties may be due to: ignorance, poor parent models, confused cultural standards, lack of information.
Treatment	Focus upon survival skills with progress toward coping. Encountering reality and its consequences. Open agenda.	Use of free-association techniques and of autobiographic recall. Resolution or reduction of defensiveness, countering transference and countertransference.	Use of the past *only* as it relates and affects the present, especially parent-child relationships. Awareness of the perspective of others. Learning to listen and question without finding fault. Learning to assert adult responsibilities.

Table 13–3 SUMMARY OF PARENT PRIORITIES FOR PATTERSON'S POINTERS FOR PROFESSIONALS

Pointer	*Parent Priority*
Tell us the nature of our problem as soon as you know the nature of the problem.	1
Always see both parents.	8
Watch your language. Avoid jargon. Use terms we can understand.	6
Help us to see this is *our* problem. (Do not take over for us.) Support our decisions. Help us to explore alternatives.	4
Help us to understand our problem—(give us information at our own pace which we need to deal with our problem)	2
Know your resources. (Have firsthand information about the people and agencies who help us.)	3
Never put us on the defensive. Do not make us justify our past actions. Help us to see our present and future tasks.	7
Remember, we parents are just people, neither saints, nor sinners.	11
We are parents, and you are professionals; regardless of how objective we may seem, remember, our loyalties are to our child.	9
Keep your professional biases and jealousies to yourself.	12
Remember the importance of attitude. Be objective about our problem, but respect our feelings.	5
Recognize our good intentions even though our actions may not meet your standards.	10

tarded citizens. This survey is summarized in table 13–3. These data reflect the priorities assigned by these parents to each pointer. These parents identified additional pointers, summarized in table 13–4. These data identified certain qualities of the advocate relationship as well as reasonable expectations for practitioners. The essence of the relationship is characterized by: honesty in sharing information, shared partnership in planning and programs, firsthand knowledge about resources and program consequences, and an informational approach, with emphasis upon sharing information with parents.

Table 13–4 ADDITIONAL POINTERS FOR PROFESSIONALS RECOMMENDED BY PARENTS

Additional Pointers	
Category	*Specific Pointer*
Additional Pointers Related to Patterson	1. Be honest. 2. Tell parents *all* of their child's problems as soon as they are known. 3. Refer parents to parent organizations. 4. Use common language. 5. Be human. Respect children for what they are. 6. Understand that parents are not necessarily retarded. 7. Don't make us feel guilty.
Additional Pointers	1. Doctors must be better informed about training for retarded. 2. Remember that retardates need to be trained, not stored away. 3. Communicate monthly with parents. 4. Know related problems of retarded. 5. Learn more about problems of retarded. 6. Involve parents in planning. 7. Interest public officials to meet needs of retarded.

Stages of Growth

Dembo et al. (1948), based upon research investigations, have offered a developmental schema of three stages in adjustment to disability: mourning, exhaustion, and compensation.

Mourning (reaction to recognition) includes evaluation of losses, idealization of normalcy, and viewing impairment as his or her basic trait. This evaluation and idealizing is the source and focus of activity, satisfaction, and a bereavement.

Exhaustion involves change and enlargement of values, seeking positive possibilities, seeking new values, and concentrating on what's available despite the impairment.

Compensation includes pride in doing old things in new ways, casting aside self-pity, healthy comparison with others "worse off," viewing his or her impairment as but another one of one's traits, and new involvement and challenges.

Helpful concepts for the nonexceptional and the nonparent include: mourning is required; reaction patterns stem *from* personality and values acquired *prior* to disability; reaction patterns seem more a response to limitations than to the disability itself; regression will occur; reaction patterns that become positive are dependent upon changes in values and value systems; and "understanding" a reaction pattern does not mean that the "helper" must excuse or tolerate unacceptable behavior.

Behmer (1976) offers a parallel resumé of reactions. Although the words vary, one observes similarities. She described initial reactions of *grief* (for the loss of perfection) and *shame* (guilt for feeling self-centered). Within this period tension occurs and with tension emerges frustration at seeming helplessness. Next comes a certain *matter-of-factness* and the emergence of *sense of humor*. This is a transitional stage similar to exhaustion in which the person or parent recognizes the disability as a condition shared by others and that there is potential in each person. Eventually there is realization of a *balanced life* and of *self-acceptance*. For parents this means recognizing that the family, as a whole, has a right to function and learning that to accept others one must accept oneself and one's imperfections. The stages of Dembo et al. or Behmer offer suggestions for assessing a parental/person's current level and identifying possible directions for the helping relationship.

FOUNDATION SYSTEMS

The historical origins of contemporary systems of helping relationships can be attributed to three persons: Rogers (1951), Perls (1969), and Ellis (1962). A comparison of these three systems is presented in table 13–5. The "historical" significance of these systems was a demonstration that Freudian concepts of sexuality, preoccupation with the past, life as shaped from without, and client dependence could be altered. These individuals were not anti-Freud, but sought different alternatives.

Client-Centered Therapy

In client-centered therapy, according to Rogers, the counselor provides both a model and active encouragement of self-actualization. As the client experiences acceptance, prizing, and nonpossessiveness from the helper, the client internalizes these qualities. As the client experiences an open, trusting, problem-oriented situation, these behaviors become acquired. A central feature of client-centered therapy is *reflective listening*. This type of listening serves as a communication check to test out accuracy of impressions as well as an opportunity for the client to experience being prized and understood.

Table 13–5 COMPARISON OF THREE INFLUENTIAL SYSTEMS OF HELPING

Dimensions	*Client-Centered Therapy*	*Gestalt Therapy*	*Rational-Emotive Therapy*
Counselor Goals	1. To understand the inner world of the client. 2. To enable the client to experience: being prized, being accepted, a nonpossessive love. 3. To display realness, openness, congruence, and transparency.	1. To create a "safe" emergency for the client to experience self-assertion. 2. To concentrate on nonverbal behaviors. 3. To avoid judgments, but to create opportunities to experience being understood by another person.	1. To learn client's process of self-indoctrination. 2. To uncover the catastrophising of the client. 3. To formulate therapeutic assignments to challenge the beliefs without affecting the person.
Client Outcomes	1. The ability to explore, discover, and to understand self. 2. Movement from remoteness about self to being immediate about self. 3. Ability to accept self with disappointments. To hypothesize rather than make rigid declarations.	1. To enable client to reclaim a "lost" potential. 2. To understand self-imposed obstacles to action. 3. To learn to exercise adult behavior.	1. To identify "sane" sentences. 2. To identify "insane" sentences. 3. To distinguish between *event* and subsequent judgment.
Mode of Treatment	1. As the client experiences the external model of the counselor, the client *internalizes* positive values about self.	1. Reference to discrepancies between words and actions, such as laughing when nervous.	1. To uncover concerns the counselor may have client list priorities, such as: "What bothers/hurts you?" "Let's talk about your. . . ."

	2. To enable the client to verbalize inner concerns, the counselor may say "I wish I could give you an answer" or "I can't answer for you, but I will help you to work toward. . . ." or "What do you wish I would say?" 3. To "convince" the client that the counselor is listening, the following might be used: "I hear it a little differently. . . ." "What I hear you say. . . ." "This may sound evasive, but. . . ." 4. To encourage choice behavior, one might say: "It's hard to. . . ." "I sense that. . . ." "It's risky to. . . ." "You sound. . . ."	2. Behavior and words in a congruent Gestalt such assertive gestures paired with verbal demands. 3. Create modified role-playing situations to practice skills of potential, such as: "How could you *show* me that?" "Go ahead, do it. What's stopping you?" "What would they do *for* you?" "Exactly, now we're getting somewhere."	2. To emphasize the catastrophising (the sane vs. insane) the counselor may say, "I hear the vote of no confidence. . . ." "Can that be so terrible? . . ." 3. Use of persuasion as feedback to client of capabilities. 4. Use of "assignments" outside of the session to practice skills.
Evaluation of Client Growth	1. Client reevaluation of inner experiences and feelings. 2. Moving from about me to me. 3. Source of authority from external to internal. 4. Moving from there and then to here and now.	1. Client "demands" respect and learns to expect it. 2. Casts aside "roles" and uses the self. 3. Defines and eliminates inconsistencies between childish and adult behavior.	1. Giving up of perfectionist behavior. 2. Ability to define sources of defeatist behavior. 3. Completion of assignments.

Gestalt Therapy

Gestalt therapy, according to Perls, is an assumption that persons are capable of action. Inaction is evidence of a "lost potential." The client is engaged in a recovery of the lost potential. Congruence of actions and inner feelings is stressed. Nonverbal behaviors may be the index of the person's inner world. Laughter when nervous, a "flat" voice tone accompanying endorsement, fidgeting hands associated with a declaration of agreement may be examples of a lack of congruence of the Gestalt between one's expressions and inner expressions. In Gestalt therapy, the person can give expression to inner feelings. One can practice what it would be like to express true feelings. One can examine obstacles that prevent action. For example, the reluctant parent may learn to effectively demand explanations, to seek out sources of services, and/or to express reservations about professional interpretations.

Rational-Emotive Therapy

Rational-Emotive Therapy is postulated upon self-indoctrination. According to Ellis, the concept of the "sane"-"insane" sentence is a critical foundation of the system. The counselor-client relationship is the identification of sane and insane statements. A sane sentence would be the statement "I'm unattractive"; the insane sentence would be "And therefore I'll never get what I want!" The sane sentence states an opinion, while the insane sentence states the catastrophic (a self-perception) result. Another key feature of the system is the assignment. The counselor will prescribe a task or activity to be performed prior to the session. The complexity of assignments is increased as the person's level of growth increases. For the "shy" person, the initial assignment may be nodding hello to strangers at a bus stop. A more complex assignment would be initiating a conversation. An appealing feature of rational-emotive therapy is out-of-session practice of exercises, the basis for subsequent sessions.

CONTEMPORARY SYSTEMS

The three foundation systems continue to influence current practices in the field of the helping relationships. This section will briefly describe four systems that have gained a certain prominence and met at least four of the following criteria: research validation, declared applicability to the disabled by its advocates, relevance to the nature of the helping relationship, suitablility for practitioners in the opinion of its advocates, consistency with Ginott's dimensions of guidance, and consistency with parent preferences.

Somatopsychology

Myerson, Stevens, and Guskin (cited in chapter 2 of the text) as well as Wright (1960) and Dembo, Ladieu, and Wright (1948) would be considered specialists in this area. This approach specifies the relationships among physique, adjustment, and environmental factors. The practitioner attempts to integrate knowledges regarding intrapersonal data (physique), interpersonal data (adjustment coping), and situational data (environmental) to make decisions regarding modification of: the person, his or her environment, situational aspects, and/or some combination of these three. These data can be translated into goals and prescriptions.

The treatment mode of somatopsychology would involve either Rogerian concepts of client-centered therapy *and/or* humanistic applications of behaviorism. While the combination of client-centered therapy and behaviorism may appear to be mutually exclusive, the reader is referred to an article by Rogers and Skinner (1956). Review of this paper identifies a certain compatible nature of the two systems. The essential agreement is that self-actualization is a behavior that can be encouraged and rewarded.

A central theme of somatopsychology is a distinction between disability (physique) and handicap (environmental demands and expectations). Shine (1971) has endorsed this distinction for parents. For parents, and for the person, disability should be viewed as an attribute, whereas handicap is perceived as a barrier to accomplishment of a particular goal. These authors recommended the term *disabled*, which implies the ability to master challenges. The term *handicap* implies severe or unsolvable limitation. *Handicap* has synonyms of *pity, charity, loneliness, isolation, emptiness, insecurity,* and *dependence*. By contrast, *disability* was viewed as associated with *participation, competence, independence, striving, confidence, respect,* and *achievement*. Shine conceded that this was an opinion. Of interest, however, was the reflection of values associated with somatopsychological constructs.

Values Clarification

Simon, Howe, and Kirschenbaum (1972) acknowledge that choice and decision making are difficult and often confusing. Every day, they noted, persons are required to make difficult choices about work, leisure time, family, sex and love, material possession, friends, aging and death, health, ideals, and authority. Typically, adults have employed three methods to guide young people toward happy and productive lives.

1. *Moralizing*. The target is values inculcation. This approach is based upon the premise that the adult's experience is a sufficient data base to be adopted by the

young person. The assumption is that the life experiences of the adult are "right" as a guide for the other person. The difficulty with this approach is that the person must decide for himself or herself without a procedure for doing so.

2. *Laissez faire.* This approach assumes that no one set of values is right. Consequently, the practice is nonintervention since the child must forge his or her own values and behavior eventually. The problem with this approach, according to Simon et al. is that young people do want *help,* but not indoctrination.

3. *Modeling.* The approach implies that the adult acts so that people will be motivated to emulate the behavior. This approach, for Simon et al., has the advantage of presenting a living example to imitate. The difficulty, however, is that many models compete for attention. Situations are encountered for which there is no model for imitation, especially in vocational choices.

Simon et al. acknowledge Rath's description of a *values clarification* method, which is founded upon the premise that behavior is a function of belief. The interest (within reason) is in the process of valuing rather than upon content of belief. Values clarification suggests that action is based upon beliefs that are consciously or unconsciously prized with reference to choice. Specifically, this approach follows a seven-step sequence:

Prizing Beliefs and/or Behaviors
1. cherishing
2. publicly affirming (when appropriate)

Choosing Beliefs and/or Behaviors
3. selection from alternatives
4. consideration of consequences
5. choosing freely

Acting on One's Beliefs and/or Behaviors
6. acting on a plan
7. action with consistency and repetition

As a system, this approach has developed and evolved exercises to engage people in personal clarification of that which is prized, cherished, and/or acted upon. The emphasis is on action based on information gained from the exercises. Without action, the exercises can become a "game" of Greenhouse. Some exercises may be structured to cover all seven steps, but usually they are targeted toward one of the three main areas of prizing, cherishing, and/or action.

Simon et al. reported that children exposed to this approach are less likely to be apathetic, flighty, conforming, and overdissenting and to be more zestful, energetic, critical-reflective thinkers and more likely to follow through on decisions. There is a suggestion that this approach has certain advantages in substance-abuse education programs.

Longhi, Follett, Bloom, and Armstrong (1975) reported the use of a values clarification approach with forty adolescent mildly mentally retarded adolescents. The topic was centered upon drinking and driving. The medium was a film produced by the authors and supplemented by discussions. The students "vowed" that they would not perform this act, but their reasons were fear of personal injury and possible legal consequences. The authors reflected a certain disappointment that these students focused upon the consequences of the act rather than the act itself. There had been, however, significant change from their initial perception of drinking and driving as not being a problem.

Transactional Analysis

Berne (1964) and Harris (1969) are generally credited with the popularization of this approach to the understanding and treatment of human behavior. The efforts of James and Jongeward (1971) also have increased the popularity of transactional analysis, or TA, as a model for child rearing. Berne and Harris have been emphatic that TA *is* applicable to the handicapped, including the mentally retarded.

TA specialists agree that life can be *beyond* games. Game-free living is more than role playing; it is the selection of a life position, or OKness. TA postulates that people are born to be winners, not losers. Game-free living is characterized by three attributes. *Spontaneity* (a freedom to respond to life's positives), *intimacy* (a relationship based upon trust and respect which is uncomplicated by analysis of motive), and *awareness* (freedom to perceive without being controlled by unexamined tradition) describe Berne's attributes of the quality of life. As a life position, the message is "I'm OK — You're OK" and as a value system the message is "I'm Important — You're Important." The initial life position through the preschool years is "I'm not OK — You're OK," with its correlate of "I'm not Important — You're Important." For a variety of explanations, people may adopt the other two possibilities of the abjectness of "I'm not OK — You're not OK" to the self-centered, irresponsible position of "I'm OK — You're not OK."

There are certain prerequisites, according to Harris, relating to the notions of TA:

1. While the concepts bear a certain similarity to Freudian theory, TA should *not* be understood as an adaptation. In fact, prior knowledge of Freud can create an initial negative transfer effect.

2. While labeled a "system," TA is also a philosophy of life. It does imply a morality about the nature of human existence.

3. TA, like other systems, can be intellectualized, rather than internalized. Consequently, it can become possible to play the ultimate game, transactional analysis.

4. TA can be a tool for understanding one's social interactions as well as a tool for self-understanding.

5. TA can be compatible with other systems. In the popular literature targeted for parents this trend is evident. The usual practice is to establish TA as a conceptual basis for assumptions about human behavior. One notes examples of this literary "marriage" between TA and such systems as client-centered Therapy, Gestalt therapy, and humanistic behaviorists.

6. TA is a partnership between client and helper. It is a growth system designed to foster independence. Client dependence is discouraged.

Kravas and Kravas (1974), as did Harris, suggest that the concept of ego states is an essential conceptual tool for understanding the system. TA postulates that within each human being there are three states of being: parent, adult, and child. Figure 13–2 attempts to illustrate the functions of each. Child refers to childlike

Figure 13–2 *Structure of Parent-Adult-Child*

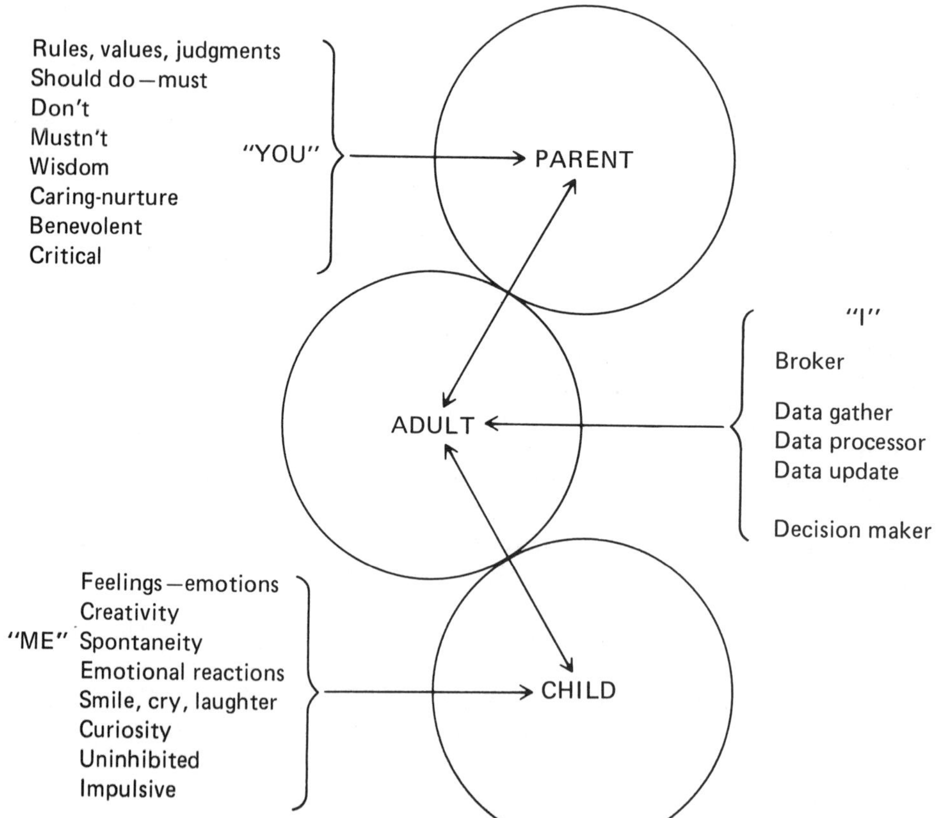

behavior, not childish. It speaks in the language of *me*. Child "records" feelings associated with learning. Parent is the knowing-value self. It can nurture and it can be critical. It speaks in the language of *you*. As can be seen from the figure, an adult is like a computer. It tests out the reality between child and parent data and it updates information. It speaks the language of *I*.

The concept of *transaction* describes the effects of ego state (parent, adult, child) stimulus and responses. Self-concept, for example, is the product of internal transactions between parent and child mediated by an adult. In self-devaluation, it is thought that critical parent dominates adaptive child. Helping relationships, in TA terms, would take the form of enabling an adult to program new tapes (a TA concept for internal conversations) to create self-worth.

TA postulates that human existence is a drive for social acceptance, status, and approval and the avoidance of neglect or isolation. Transactions (as a series of stimulus-responses) can take predictable forms. These forms are known as games. A game is "played" to gain certain outcomes. If the game leads to conflict, conformity, ulterior motives, and putting others at a disadvantage, it is a bad game, or "racket" in TA terms. A good game may have some of these elements, but it has none of the effects of disadvantagement to another person. Table 13–6 illustrates the good games played by adults and bad games played by troubled children (McCree, 1975).

The essence of TA, as a treatment system, is a teaching-learning system. The concepts possessed by the trained person are imparted to the person seeking help. The language of the system is neither technical nor mysterious.

Behaviorism as a Helping Relationship

The publication of the Bensberg (1965) text introduced the training of retarded persons by positive reinforcement. This text demonstrated that procedures of behavior modification could be applied to populations and settings that have been neglected by more conventional therapies and professionals. Self-care, language, and motor skills were the early demonstration targets. Behaviorism is not a "new" science, given Russian efforts at the turn of the century or its application to programmed instruction in the late 1950s. Forness and MacMillan (1970) have traced the origins of behavior modification from classical times through the late 1960s. They cited the Roman practice of placing eels in wine cups as a cure for excessive drinking. Their conclusion was that since the origins of behaviorism resulting from the efforts of Pavlov as well as Thorndike, the 1960s were a period of systematic application to exceptional children and youth. For these authors, the most evident trend was the shift from punitive approaches toward a structured inquiry into the uses of nonpunitive approaches. The historical achievement of the Bensberg effort is illustrated by the Ashbaugh report (1971), which compared the performance of attendant personnel trained in behavior modification procedures with those not so trained. The results indicated that the trained group was able to acquire and maintain these procedures. The Ashbaugh experiment, representative of many, confirms the Lindsley (1964) hypothesis that retardation is not necessarily inherent in the child but can be attributed to the practitioner's ability to design a responsive environment for such a child.

The language used to describe the principles (as opposed to the techniques) of behaviorism reflects an orientation toward a justification of system, distinguishing what behaviorism is, specifying available tactics, and elaborating on options. A common misconception is to view behaviorism as a unitary system. As with other systems, there are differences of opinion within the general framework. Smith (1971), Lovitt (1970) as well as Neisworth and Smith (1973), among others, have identified the essentials of agreement. Within these areas of broad agreement, however, certain

Table 13–6 COMPARISON OF GAMES

Helpful Examples	*Nonhelpful Examples*
They'll Be Glad They Know Me TBGTKM operates from repayment motive to return a kindness to someone who has been helpful. The original person can't be repaid, so the person helps others as a motive. TBGTKM may explain selection of a helping profession.	*Debate* This game involves argument to escape assignments or to avoid another failure.
Happy to Help Spontaneous response to persons in need. The person extends themselves to assist. Usually HTH operates without formal organization.	*Walk Out* This may be attention-getter, escape, or relief of tension. A symptom of deep trouble and conflict.
Busman's Holiday The giving of one's skills in a volunteer situation. Teacher Corps, Peace Corps, SWEAT, YOUTH-ARC would be examples.	*Disruption* Creation of distractions to gain attention to escape or to avoid expectations. In severe forms, the player may escalate to fighting.
Homey Sage The willingness to share experiences without offense if advice is not followed. Parent-to-parent counseling may be an example.	*Apathy* This game involves expectation. The person "finds" many good reasons (to him/her) to escape/avoid expectations and productivity
Cavalier The giving of praise without thought of return or acknowledgment.	*Horseplay* This will involve physical but rough "fun" contact. It is usually a group process to escape work.

differences exist as to options, approaches, techniques, etc. Areas of *common* agreement may be said to include:

1. *Individualization.* Human beings vary and are unique. A strong theme in these sources was the responsibility of the behaviorist to formulate a special plan for a particular person as opposed to a routine approach for all.

2. *Specification.* There is the need for defining behavior that requires changes by procedures similar to identifying performance objectives. The emphasis is on what the person does or does not do, not on the label or adjective. For example, according to Lovitt, to label a person as "crying" is not as precise as a description as a sound loud enough to be heard at fifty feet and more than ten seconds in duration.

3. *Measurement.* This area refers to collection of data regarding behavior: frequency, duration, and/or origins. This principle furnishes a baseline of behavior prior to intervention. During this period, there is the search for events or factors that appear to maintain current levels of behavior.

4. *Management.* This area reflects the most significant variation in application. The practitioner must decide between adding or withholding incentives and at what intervals of continuous or intermediate delivery.

5. *Inference.* The behaviorist is interested in understanding the validity of his or her management or intervention procedure. Comparing the performance of the person under baseline and intervention procedures may be a principal source of inference. However, in complex modification situations, the behaviorist will be concerned with identification of what circumstances led to positive results. Consequently, the pre and post comparisons may be insufficient. Therefore, one finds a recommendation for an A-B-A, or *reversal design.* In this procedure, A (antecedent condition of nonintervention) is compared to B (treatment), with a return to antecedent conditions. This procedure is felt to document the effectiveness of B. Others consider the A-B a sufficient documentation.

6. *Scientific.* Behaviorism is scientific to the extent that the individual practitioner is willing to specify intentions, procedures, and data to make his or her data believable. This willingness to be explicit and objective suggests the structured nature of the implementation of behaviorism.

The qualities of behaviorism as a helping relationship has been discussed by Edmonson (1974). She noted that behavioristic principles and procedures can produce change, but they can not suggest what to change. In the absence of guidelines, the dimensions of change may reflect program convenience rather than benefits to the person. Goodman advocated *competence* as the guideline, especially increased self-direction. Self-direction would mean behavior that frees the person from dependent care and enables the person to be of benefit to others. An additional guideline of competence, for Edmonson, is that of choice. Programming should prepare the person for making choices and for generating alternatives.

Ausman, Ball, and Alexander (1974) offer an example of promoting self-direction for a fourteen-year-old severely retarded boy who was self-destructive, did not chew his food, was unable to bathe or dress himself, and engaged in severe pica behavior (ingestion of inedible objects such as candy wrappers, string, rubber products, etc.). The boy's pica behavior was so severe as to have necessitated emergency surgery to prevent death by intestinal blockage. The report encompassed a nine-month period that utilized combinations of reward, time out, and a single electric shock (to curb self-abusive behavior). The eventual outcome was the elimination of negative behaviors. Self-care skills and appropriate mastication were also taught. Logan, Kinsinger, Shelton, and Brown (1971) have reported that the use of multi-reinforcers (praise and productivity charts) enable sheltered workshop clients to control their own productivity. Henderson (1971) utilized varied sensory reinforcements to increase the *ability* of a group of mildly mentally retarded adolescent boys to increase their use of descriptive language.

Principles and procedures of competence apply to adults as well. Fredericks, Baldwin, McDonnell, Hofman, and Harter (1971) have demonstrated the acquisition of competence is helpful in developing parental self-concept. These authors reported a parent-training curriculum organized around the concepts of *behavior* (described as the "thing" we want the child to either do or not do), *cue* (described as the equivalent of the Skinnerian Sd, or the antecedent events to response or behavior), and *reinforcement* (described as a consequence to strengthen-accelerate or weaken-diminish behavior). These three concepts were the foundations for parents to acquire skills of:

1 identification of cues preceding behavior;
2 breaking a complex task into component parts;
3 the use of component tasks to initiate chaining (or reverse chaining) to sequence subtask elements together;
4 shaping of successive approximations of a task into skill performance;
5 primary, secondary, and self-reinforcements;
6 use of rewards, extinction, and time-out procedures; and
7 charting of behavior responses.

Bendebba (1973) has suggested an on-site community homeworker program to encourage and reinforce parents in home management. The worker would be concerned with the establishment of a helping home environment. This worker would gradually phase out his or her activities as the child was introduced into the school situation, where the educator would be responsible for continued relationships.

Busse and Henderson (1972) offer an example of educational competence as a program guideline in a typical educational setting of one teacher to thirteen mildly retarded junior-high students. This report was an illustration of the principle that low-rate behavior can be accelerated if linked to a high-rate behavior. This study covered eighty-one school days. Low-rate behavior was reading, and high-rate behavior was defined as earned free time. There was a baseline period of ten days to determine initial achievement and the amount of time required to complete a lesson. During the management phase (fifty-five days) students earned free time for time spent in reading. Free time was spent in a variety of student-oriented activities. During the course of this period the amount of on-task behavior was increased for free time so as to provide significantly longer periods of time and delay of use of free time. A time-out procedure coupled with cancellation was used to deal with disruptive behavior. Then followed a five-day period during which the primary reinforcement of free time was faded. Praise and charting of performance were introduced. The remaining period operated on this basis. The final results indicated continued performance under secondary reinforcement and an average gain of two grade levels for the class from third grade to fifth grade.

Grieger (1976) utilized candy to eliminate name calling in an upper elementary classroom for mildly retarded learners. Jenkins and Gorrafa (1974) compared a *contingency contract* (a one-to-one agreement that for each performance there would be a consequence), a *token system* (consequences mediated by tokens to be exchanged for a consequence), and *no incentives*. Arithmetic achievement was the target area. The contract system was slightly more helpful than tokens, and the nonconsequence treatment was the least helpful. Alvord (1971) reported on his efforts to train parents to create a token system in a home setting. This report illustrated the feasibility of the procedure for environments and problems.

Programmed instruction represents yet another application of behavioristic principles to training for competence. Dezelle (1971) compared programmed instruction with conventional instruction for a sample of 132 mildly retarded junior-high pupils in arithmetic performance. The experimental materials were a programmed text characterized by small increments sequenced in a logical order which provided for immediate feedback. Experimental groups were not significantly different from controls in academic achievement *except* that the experimental group displayed significant gains in self-direction and self-discipline. Dezelle urged further research to isolate the possible salient benefits of programmed instruction. He speculated that this approach might help the retarded person in: acceleration of *rate* of learning, opportunities for overlearning, continuous positive reinforcement, providing extended practice, and adaptation to small-group situations.

Congruent Communications

This approach is a distillation of the systems previously discussed. Its proponents acknowledge a certain indebtedness to Rogers, Berne, and/or modifications of Skinner. The system, labeled congruent communications, acknowledges the OKness of TA, the client-centeredness of Rogers, and the supportive encouragement of humanistic behaviorism. Congruent communication emphasizes skills, especially of listening, reflection, and problem solving. These skills can be "inner," in the sense of resolving internal conflict, and can be observable as dialogue among people.

Definition

Ginott (1972) defiined congruent communications in terms of a match between our words/deeds and feelings. As a value system, this form of communication prizes the development of autonomy, self-esteem, self-confidence, and the decrease of anxiety, fear, frustration, rage and conflict. Ginott acknowledged that achieving this form of communications requires learning, rehearsing, and self-discipline. He stressed that adults cannot be artificial and effective. Skills divorced from genuineness are soon discredited. The reality of congruence is that one cannot pretend caring and respect. Consequently, congruent communications, in common with other systems of helping relationships, are not a bag of tricks.

Listening

Kroth (1975) has integrated the Gordon and Ginott systems into applications for parents of exceptional children and youth. Central to this application is listening. Active listening describes being involved with the person and being able to detect feelings. When the protege has a problem, the advocate must listen to capture how the person feels as well as to clarify the problem. Passive listening describes being physically present with the person to the point of nodding, smiling, and even the ability to render an accurate account of the conversation. Aside from lack of practice, Kroth identified six factors that inhibit active listening: fatigue (active listening *is* hard work); strong feelings (a desire to accomplish one's agenda to the exclusion of all else); words, such as labels, can blot out messages; monopoly (this involves structuring time so that another person has little time for his or her words); the environment (visual and auditory distractions, room temperature, furniture, etc.); and writing. Kroth suggested that taking notes may be distracting to some and a reflection of respect to others. Ginott suggests that parents take notes to have an accurate record to interpret to the child/adolescent, who may not be present.

Lichter (1976) stressed listening as an effective means of easing the isolation felt by parents. Active listening was described as a means of reflecting one's genuine understanding and acceptance of another. Lichter identified nonhelpful alternatives to active listening responses (table 13–7). Active listening, as interpreted by Lichter,

Table 13–7 NONHELPFUL ALTERNATIVES TO ACTIVE LISTENING RESPONSES

Response Type	*Sample Response*
Ordering	You must. . . .
Admonish	If you don't . . . then you'll. . . .
Exhorting	You shouldn't. . . .
Moralizing	It's your responsibility to. . . .
Preaching	You should show more respect for. . . .
Advising	Let me suggest that. . . .
Blaming	You're causing a *lot* of harm by. . . .
Psychoanalyzing	You're afraid to face. . . .
Ridiculing	You're acting like a little. . . .
Lecturing	Children need. . . .
Questioning	Why did you. . . .
Humoring	Maybe you'll be lucky and. . . .
Criticism	You're not behaving very. . . .
Persuading	Don't you realize that. . . .

recognizes feeling as the basis for encoding (speaking) as the stimulus of communication, while perceptions (empathy) and decoding (speaking in return) are the response of communication. This cycle of stimulus-response is summarized in figure 13–3. Note that the response is directed toward the feeling that prompted the question. A tempting response of "Yes" would likely close off the person's ability to explore the underlying sources of conflict. A response of "The future seems hopeless for Lucy if she won't be able to work" might be more likely to encourage further dialogue by the parent.

Reflection

Reflecting feelings are viewed by Gordon as door-openers to further conversation. Examples of reflective listening responses as adapted from Lichter are summarized

Figure 13–3 *Components of the Communication Cycle*

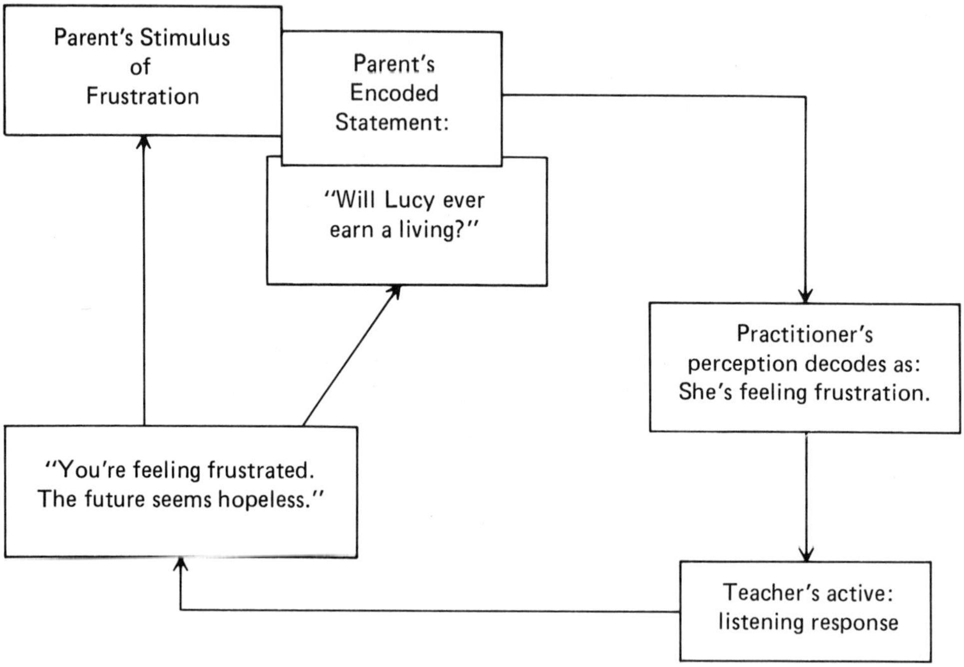

in adapted form in table 13–8. (The reader should be advised that active listening comes from practice. One should not feel mournful if merely reading about it doesn't help.)

Lichter listed four guidelines for decoding messages into helpful responses: listen for the basic message; restate a concise summary of content and/or feeling of the message; allow the speaker to confirm the accuracy of the comment and/or its helpfulness; and allow the speaker to correct the interpretation.

With any of these systems certain values are implied. Both Gordon and Ginott emphasize that permissiveness is not the outcome. (You win, I lose is permissiveness.) These systems allow adults to be adult. One can be accepting of feelings; it is actions which are the subject of assessment. Helping relationships allow for nonjudgmental acceptance of feelings, but actions are the concern. A child has the "right" to be jealous of a sibling, but hitting is not allowed. The child can be shown acceptable actions. A work trainee may feel resentment about work production, but cursing the boss is not permitted.

Table 13–8 EXAMPLES OF ACTIVE LISTENING RESPONSES

Stimulus	*Response*
I wish Philip were making as much progress as the other kids in this class.	You're feeling a little envious.
I don't understand. One day Mike really likes his workshop, and the next day he says he'll quit.	He really confuses you.
I'm really pleased how well Elizabeth is doing with her therapist. He always keeps us informed.	You really like him then.
It's so sad to see how hard John tries to learn to swim. His father and I work so hard.	It sounds like you're struggling with two conflicting emotions. One, what's the use, he can't learn, and two, learning to swim is so difficult.
Tell me this, and I want an answer. Should I send Andrew to camp? I know it's a good idea, but I'm not positive.	Sometimes it's hard to make choices. You feel uncertain. You wish I would say Yes or No. You wonder if all the effort will be worth it.

Problem Solving

Gordon (1970) described Parent Effectiveness Training (PET) in terms of problem solving. Central to the PET system are the skills of listening and reflection as antecedents for problem solving. The focus or outcome of these skills is the definition of problem ownership.

Ownership of a problem is a negotiated process. Real and honest persons recognize two feelings: acceptance of behaviors and nonacceptance of behaviors. Pretense of acceptance is unmasked. People vary in their definitions of acceptance and nonacceptance. Two persons can differ as to their acceptance levels. The relationship is probably confused by the mixed messages of acceptance versus nonacceptance expressed and received. (The mixed message pattern describes the lack of congruence cited by Ginott.) Acceptance of another's behavior means that one's own needs are being met and his or her actions do not interfere. Nonacceptance describes behavior perceived as interference with one's needs. Where both parties are in disagreement on behavior, there is a problem. Through negotiation and honest communication based upon listening both parties determine ownership of a problem. Gordon advised that classifying ownership of problems is a first step. Examples of a protege's owning a problem may include: lack of friends, indecision about making a vocational choice, taking skill lessons, losing a game or contest, shyness because of being too tall, doing poor work because of disliking a teacher or supervisor, and uncertainty about dating. Examples of an advocate's problems include: interruption of a conversation with a friend, feeling that others are not carrying a fair share of work, use of your tools without returning them, demanding excessive time for one's attention, excessive profanity, sensing impending damage to property, and failure to keep a promise. When the advocate "owns" the problem, she or he can modify the protege, the environment, and self. (Gordon noted that life-and-death situations require swift intervention.) Modifying one's self may involve values clarification to define one's sense of priorities. Modifying the protege and responding to the protege's ownership can utilize the skills of listening, reflection, and the use of a contract system.

SPECIAL TASKS OF THE HELPING RELATIONSHIP

The helping relationship oriented toward a no-lose growth experience can be directed to many tasks.

Group Procedures

Group procedures have received a certain attention in the literature as an approach in its own right and as a contrast to individual counseling. Berne, among others, has voiced distress that group procedures are viewed as merely an economical use of counselor time.

Gilmore (1971) compared the two approaches with respect to educationally oriented counseling of parents. The advantages of group procedures were found to be that parents learn from one another, modify their behavior to be acceptable to the group, inspire one another with their enthusiasm, encourage one another, and provide reinforcement when successes occur. Limitations can be that parents have difficulty sharing in a group setting, have difficulty in monopolizing group time, and have difficulty receiving specific help for lengthy, complex problems. Lewis (1972) demonstrated parents of moderately retarded children gain in expressed attitude and knowledge about mental retardation as a result of attending group discussions.

Group procedures can have a skill focus as well as an affective focus. Freeman and Thompson (1973) demonstrated gain for preschool retarded children in gross motor movement. Seitz and Terdal (1972) used modeling (the counselor demonstrating the skill while the parent observes and then practices under counselor's observation) to improve mother-child interactions. After intervention these mothers of moderately retarded children were: able to express interest in their child; more likely to be positive and rewarding in discipline; able to increase the child's compliance to mother's requests; likely to use praise to accompany compliance behavior; and able to increase their waiting time for child to respond. Mash and Terdal (1973) have demonstrated increase of play behavior of children within the moderately retarded range. Halperm, Philippa, and Butler (1968) have shown similar results with increasing communication skills of moderately retarded children. Duncan and Fitzgerald (1969) have demonstrated another outcome. Parents can learn to utilize school services more effectively through group processes. Specific outcomes appeared to favor experimental parents, for adolescents of these parents showed increased school attendance, reduction in dropout rate, reduction in referrals for disciplinary offenses, increased communications with their parents, and more appropriate schedule changes. Finally, the authors noted that these parents were more likely to continue their contacts with school staff.

Elements of approach to group procedures have received a certain attention. The following study is representative of many. Krauft and Bozarth (1971) compared leadership styles upon the behavior of twenty-one mildly and moderately retarded boys. The group was randomly assigned to one of three groups: authoritarian (complete direction from the adult leader); laissez faire (passivity from the leader); and democratic (facilitating choice and group planning). The theme was a "handicraft club" under these three interpersonal styles. Of fourteen variables, group-mindedness emerged as influenced by style. An authoritarian style was superior to laissez faire. Group-mindedness was defined as the incidence of use of the pronouns *we* or *us* in conversations. It is difficult to distinguish between one person's authoritarian environment and another's structured environment. The authors noted that laissez faire was less difficult to adopt as a style than democratic. However, purposeful activity seemed to be helpful.

Hillman (1968) has reported an experiment in group counseling in a public-school setting. The project specified ten weekly sessions of three hours each. The format generally followed one hour for small group discussion to identify parent problems, followed by a panel to discuss possibilities before the entire group. This was followed by the final hour of small-group problem solving to implement and clarify panel reactions. Parents involved in the project were compared to a nonintervention group. The former reported better feelings about themselves and about growth for their children. Larson (1972) has contrasted three approaches to methods of family management. Parents volunteered for assignments to one of three methods. One method stressed encounter techniques; one group involved behavior modification techniques; and the other approach stressed active listening and problem-solving skills. Over time, all three groups reflected improvement in family functioning, suggesting that time in group is helpful. For specific areas of parent concern, the encounter-confrontation group reflected less help than the other two methods. These other two methods appeared to have similar positive effects of improved parent self-concept and reduction of problems that had prompted enrollment in this parent education program.

IMPARTING DIAGNOSTIC DATA

Wolfensberger and Kurtz (1974) found parents of retarded children react to the label of mental retardation. Their conclusion was that parents can identify the behaviors associated with the term but have difficulty applying those behaviors to their own child. The major implication was that the term appears confused with mental illness. Their recommendation was that *initial* parent guidance should emphasize the distinction between the two conditions. Love (1971) found that parents with a retarded child were found to have more positive beliefs and accurate knowledge about the condition than parents without a retarded child. Guntz and Gubrium (1972) compared the reactions of fathers and mothers to *initial* diagnostic rendering. Fathers' and mothers' concerns were found to be future oriented. There were no differences in concerns with respect to job success and need for acceptance by others. Fathers were more concerned about financial management and security for the child. Mothers were found to be more concerned about their child having friends. The study suggested that interpretation should be couched in light of similarity and dissimilarities of parental concerns.

Stevens-Long (1973) found labeling, once understood through guidance sessions, had the effect of modifying harsh, punitive, and restrictive discipline. Strag (1972) has shown that parents of the severely mentally retarded were found to be more certain of their child's behavior than parents of learning disabled children. This author noted that parents of retarded children and parents of normal children were more accurate in estimating their own child's abilities than parents of learning disabled children. The accurateness of parental judgments has received a certain attention. The report of Heriot and Schmichel (1964), subsequently confirmed by VanderVeer and Schweld (1975), demonstrated that parents can be an accurate source of information regarding the learning potential of their retarded child. These reports reflect significant *agreement* between the developmental rate of the child reported by parents and subsequent IQ scores. One gains the impression that parents also can be a valid source of diagnostic data. A concern of the practitioner should be to arrange these circumstances of listening and reflection to gain parental insights. If the diagnostic interpretation is viewed as a one-way transaction to convince, the opportunity may be lost.

Assessment and the Helping Relationship

Ricks (1959) identified certain considerations in the interpretation of test scores to parents. These are summarized as two "commandments" and one verbal technique. The two commandments were:

1 *Parents have the right to know whatever the school knows about the abilities, the performance, and the problems of their children.*
2 *The school has the obligation to see that it communicates understandable and usable knowledge.*

To implement these "commandments" Ricks suggested these guidelines:

1 Telling a person information he or she does not understand does not increase communication.
2 Communication originates when the counselor knows the content he or she is trying to get across.
3 Content requires the what and how of communication. Ricks observed that numerical scores such as IQs, grade placement, standard scores, and percentiles can possess varying degrees of helpfulness. IQs may be understood by the parent as a fixed attribute, a final statement. Grade placement scores, especially arithmetic, may be more dependent upon what is taught than on what is known. Percentiles are viewed as more helpful *if* it is understood that these measures refer to a percent of people whose performance the parent's child is being compared to, *not* a percent of questions passed, and it is specified that the child is like those persons for whom the test was designed. Ricks questioned if numbers are really required. He suggested a verbal technique: "You score like people who . . ." or to a parent, "Your son (or daughter) scores like students who . . . ." This "script" is an open-ended sentence that imparts test results and their relationship to the possible future performance of persons who have taken the test. Ricks notes completing the sentence may put the school out on a limb. According to Ricks, this is as it should be.

Green (1975) has identified certain guidelines that he feels parents should know. He vigorously challenged the exclusive use of tests, especially IQ and academic achievement scores, for placement and tracking. He urged that parents and advocate-teachers should ensure that testing *improves* the person's chances for improvement rather than facilitates a stagnant placement, *enhances* talent, abilities, and values rather than restricts them, and *enables* people to *make* decisions rather than *impose* decisions. According to Green, parents and advocates should insist that testing policies reflect these guidelines.

Further implications for practitioners in the helping relationship have been identified by Klebanoff, Klein, and Schleifer (1972). These authors stress that parents have the right *not* to be intimidated by test scores and deserve understandable interpretation. These authors identified the concepts of *scatter analysis* and *process analysis* as helpful procedures to enrich the meaning of test scores. They cited an example of three children receiving equal scores on a hypothetical test composed of ten subtests. Each subtest could be worth from 0 to 20 points each. Child A received 20 points for subtests one through five and 0 on the rest, while Child B performed in an opposite fashion. Child C received 10 points for each test. *All* children "scored" 100 points. The interpretation of this different pattern was termed *scatter analysis.* The work and task of the test administrator is to communicate the meaning of scores to identify particular strengths and areas for improvement, specific procedures to be used, the direction for further evaluation, and the process used by the child to arrive at his or her responses. The examiner should be aware of research findings as a basis for understanding the meaning of the results, especially future planning. This four-part examination was termed *process analysis.*

Advocacy and Helping Relationships

Advocacy has been discussed by Kidd (1975) in the context of values orientation of the advocate. Advocacy itself does not guarantee that advocate-models are right or good. The value consensus of advocacy has been treated by Coleman (1975) as unsettling. His concern is that ideology can lead to an unwillingness to examine results that do not fit in a specific pattern. He, like Kidd, urges a continuing examination of ends and means of that which is being advocated.

The purpose of advocacy on behalf of the disabled can be distracted according to Shine (1971). Among these distractions can be these attitudes:

1. "My disability has more priority than your disability." The recognition should be that all disabled persons share common needs for helpful relationships.

2. "I shot a chairman into the air — and he went into orbit." This dynamic refers to the possibility of becoming so caught up in the organization mechanics that one forgets the original intent.

3. Management — Top and Middle. In advocacy, one may meet prominent persons, and these encounters with executives, leaders, and influence makers can

be very heady. There seems to be a getting along by going along. At other levels it may happen that the advocate has an empire complex about his or her relationships which precludes communications.

4. "If I can't take a poke at the person who hurt me, I will hit the friend who is near." There may be the temptation to direct one's frustrations away from the original source. Thus, if angered by a certain professional, it may be tempting to create distrust for all professionals. This can carry over to tarring the new professional person with the brush of "*You* professionals."

The role of advocate as counselor has its identity crisis as well, especially the professional as counselor. Pine (1975) noted that this crisis exists when one is caught between a therapeutic role and a role as executor of policy. He cited the need to revive an activist role on behalf of one's clients. This view of activism was endorsed by Klinkhamer (1973), who has favored greater assertiveness in adapting career education for exceptional learners.

A definition of advocacy and the helping relationship has been offered by Biklen (1976). The advocate must maintain autonomy so as to thwart conflict of interest. This trait requires a changing definition about helping relationships. The advocate must be able to: identify those conditions that make persons dependent; understand the protege's feelings, experiences, and needs; seek others as allies who want to assist proteges to participate in the mainstream; curb pity and use of anger at dehumanizing conditions to bring about change; and endure, if necessary, a certain disdain and criticism from persons and agencies that are questioned and examined. This last point suggests that change may be painful to those involved.

For those who have participated in the process, according to Biklin, there can be recognition for legislative, legal, and policy changes enabling more persons to obtain services; remediation of program exclusion and abuse; and new learnings about human services. The last would include thinking about rights rather than privileges and understanding the environment as a source of handicap. Also, parents, proteges, and friends have learned that one need not feel alone in the struggle for change.

SUMMING UP

Various systems of helping relationships compete for the attention of practitioners, but all these systems have certain common views.

1. Behavior is learned and can be relearned or unlearned.

2. It is a tension release to balance internal and external demands, drives, motives, etc.

3. It is repeated if linked to an incentive that has significance to the person, and diminished if not linked to an incentive that has significance to the person.

4. Behavior is sufficiently predictable to postulate consequences of action.

5. It is "owned" by the person for certain reasons of incentives. Consequently, being responsible for a behavior is a necessary step in *learning* to change it.

6. Perception of reality is defined by the person, by others, and by reality as it actually exists.

7. Behavior is the product of emotion and cognition. Learning has its emotional associations. It is *not* so much what happened to us in the past as *what* we learned from the experience which influences subsequent perceptions of ourselves.

8. Behavior is motivated by need for status, recognition, and approval. The complexities of twentieth-century life may be associated with feelings of loss of autonomy and loss of a sense of personal responsibility.

9. It is influenced by significant others, models, etc. in the person's environment. From exposure to these sources one gains feedback as to aspirations and capabilities. It is thought that from these origins arises the emergence of self-concept.

10. Personality today is viewed as a trinity related to long-term concerns, short-term concerns with a third aspect which mediates, directs, and supervises the first two.

11. Helpful behavior systems can be applied to the retarded person and his or her family.

Some additional summary statements:

1. The skills associated with a helping relationship are compatible with advocacy.

2. The helping relationship is founded upon a premise of an I win-you win relationship.

3. Outcomes can be known and inferred, and helpful procedures can be learned.

4. Certain systems, such as client-centered therapy, Gestalt therapy, and rational-emotive therapy have provided precedents for a contemporary emphasis upon helping relationships. These systems also continue as relevant approaches in their own right.

5. Somatopsychology offers a frame of reference for assessment of reaction or adjustment to disability. This system also suggests a values system to guide practice and choices.

6. Values clarification has emerged as a helpful system. Its intent is to enable persons to identify beliefs, select alternatives, and act upon choices. Also widely applicable, this approach has proven effective in areas of substance abuse, sex education, and career education.

7. Transactional analysis offers both understanding of self and others. It values spontaneity, awareness, and intimacy as essentials for game-free living. Its two major popularizers, Berne and Harris, have endorsed its applications to the mentally retarded.

8. Behaviorism can be a helping relationship, usually termed humanistic behaviorism. Self-direction and competence serve as dimensions for the nature of the relationship.

9. Congruent communications describe the fit between words and feelings. This fit describes a harmony and genuineness. This system uses listening and reflection as principal tools to establish ownership of problems.

10. Certain topics may be encountered by persons engaged in helping relationships. These topics include: use of group procedures, interpretation of diagnostic data, use of assessment data, and advocacy in the helping relationship.

ON LOCATION

Consider the following letter written by a nineteen-year-old Down's syndrome man preserved by Frank (1975, p. 25).

> Dear Mr. Frank:
>
> I received your letter and I thought your letter was very nice. I liked the trip very much and I thought it was very educational. I learned a lot from it. I liked the Wailing Wall a lot and was impressed when the elements tried to destroy the wall, it would not fall. It felt like it was my home and my temple. It made me feel like I was near God. I am also thinking about it right now. I felt bad when I left, I really miss Israel.
>
> Sincerely,
> *Marc*

Frank described Marc's helpfulness and eagerness throughout the trip, which he paid for from his wages. She also paid tribute to Marc's parents for their treatment and expectations and for their courage when counseling nineteen years ago was for institutionalization.

If the reader feels skepticism that this letter was written by a Down's syndrome person, then one problem of a helping relationship becomes apparent. While all such persons may not write letters, the theory of individual differences suggests the possibility. Marc has been fortunate to have a life experience to encourage his abilities.

REFERENCES

Alvord, J. The Home Token Economy: A Motivational System for the Home. *Corrective Psychiatry and Social Therapy,* 1971, 17, 6–13.

Ashbaugh, L. L. An Evaluation of an Attendant Training Program Based Upon Principles of Behavior Modification. *Dissertation Abstracts,* 1971, 32.

Ausman, J., Ball, T., and Alexander, D. Behavior Therapy of Pica with a Profoundly Retarded Boy. *Mental Retardation,* 1974, 12, 17–18.

Behmer, M. Coping With Our Children's Disabilities: Some Basic Principles. *The Exceptional Parent,* 1976, 6, 35–38.

Bendebba, M. Contingencies Management in Home and School Situations. *Mental Retardation,* 1973, 11, 34–37.

Bensberg, G. *Teaching the Mentally Retarded. A Handbook for Word Personnel.* Atlanta: Southern Regional Educational Board, 1965.

Berne, E. *Games People Play.* New York: Ballantine Books, 1964.

Biklen, D. Advocacy Comes of Age. *Exceptional Children,* 1976, 42, 308–313.

Busse, L., and Henderson, H. Effects of Contingency Management Upon Reading Achievement of Junior High Educable Mentally Retarded Students. *Education and Training of the Mentally Retarded,* 1972, 7, 67–73.

Coleman, J. S. Social Research and Advocacy. *Phi Delta Kappan,* 1975, 57, 166–169.

Dembo, T., Ladieu, G., and Wright, B. *Social Psychological Rehabilitation of the Physically Handicapped.* Final Report, Army Research and Development Board, Office of the Surgeon General, War Department W49-007-MO-325, Sup. 5, April 1948.

Dezelle, W. The Credibility of Programmed Material as an Instructional Technique with Mentally Retarded Pupils. *Education and Training of the Mentally Retarded,* 1971, 6, 16–19.

Duncan, W., and Fitzgerald, P. Increasing the Parent Child Communication Through Counselor-Parent Conferences. *The Personnel and Guidance Journal,* 1969, 47, 514–517.

Edmonson, B. Arguing for a Concept of Competence. *Mental Retardation,* 1974, 12, 14–15.

Ellis, A. *Rational-Emotive Therapy.* New York: Lyle Stewart, 1962.

Forness, S. R., and MacMillan, D. L. The Origins of Behavioral Modification With Exceptional Children. *Exceptional Children,* 1970, 37, 442–446.

Frank, J. L. Normalization — Marc, A Young Man I'll Never Forget. *Mental Retardation,* 1975, 13, 25.

Fredericks, H. D., Baldwin, V., McDonnell, J., Hofman, R., and Harter, J. Parents Educate Their Children. *Mental Retardation,* 1971, 9, 24–26.

Freeman, S., and Thompson, C. Parent Child Training for the MR. *Mental Retardation,* 1973, 11, 8.

Gilmore, J. Group or Individual Parent Counseling. *Journal of Education,* 1971, 54, 83–85.

Ginott, H. *Group Psychotherapy.* New York: McGraw-Hill, 1961.

Ginott, H., *Teacher and Child.* New York: Avon, 1972.

Gordon, T. *P.E.T.: Parent Effectiveness Training.* New York: Wyden, 1970.

Green, R. L. Tips on Educational Testing: What Teachers and Parents Should Know. *Phi Delta Kappan,* 1975, 57, 89–93.

Grieger, R. Behavior Modification With a Total Class. *Journal of School Psychology,* 1970, 8, 103–106.

Guntz, E., and Gubrium, J. Comparative Parental Perceptions of a Mentally Retarded Child. *American Journal of Mental Deficiency,* 1972, 77, 175.

Halperm, A., Philippa, M., and Butler, A. Verbal Expressivity as a Client Variable in Counseling the Mentally Retarded. *Exceptional Children,* 1968, 34, 693–700.

Harris, T. *I'm OK —You're OK.* New York: Harper and Row, 1969.

Henderson, L. J. Increasing Descriptive Language Skills in EMR Students. *Mental Retardation,* 1971, 9, 13–16.

Heriot, J., and Schmichel, C. Maternal Estimates of IQ on Children Evaluated for Learning Potential. *American Journal of Mental Deficiency,* 1964, 71, 920–924.

Hillman, B. The Parent-Teacher Education Center: A Supplement to Elementary School Counseling. *Elementary School Guidance and Counseling,* 1968, 3, 111–117.

James, M., and Jongeward, O. *Born to Win.* Reading, Massachusetts: Addison-Wesley, 1971.

Jenkins, J., and Gorrafa, S. Academic Performance of Mentally Handicapped Children as a Function of Token Economies and Contingency Contracts. *Education and Training of the Mentally Retarded,* 1974, 9, 183–186.

Kidd, J. W. Advocacy. *Education and Training of the Mentally Retarded,* 1975, 10, 2.

Klebanoff, L., Klein, S., and Schleifer, M. Psychological Testing — Part Two. *The Exceptional Parent,* 1972, 1, 30–33.

Klinkhamer, G. Career Education as a Philosophy and Practice. *Teaching Exceptional Children,* 1973, 5, 124–127.

Krauft, C., and Bozarth, J. Democratic, Authoritarian, and Laissez-Faire Leadership with Institutionalized Retarded Boys. *Mental Retardation,* 1971, 9, 7–10.

Kravas, K., and Kravas, C. Transactional Analysis in the Classroom. *Phi Delta Kappan,* 1974, 56, 194–197.

Kroth, R. *Communicating with Parents of Exceptional Children.* Denver: Love, 1975.

Larson, R. Can Parent Classes Affect Family Communications? *The School Counselor,* 1972, 19, 261–270.

Lewis, J. Effects of Group Procedures with Parents of MR Children. *Mental Retardation,* 1972, 10, 14–15.

Lichter, P. Communicating with Parents: It Begins with Listening. *Teaching Exceptional Children,* 1976, 8, 66–70.

Lindsley, O. Direct Measurement and Prosthesis of Retarded Behavior. *Journal of Education,* 1964, 147, 62–81.

Logan, D., Kinsinger, J., Shelton, G., and Brown, J. M. The Use of Multiple Reinforcers in a Rehabilitation Setting. *Mental Retardation,* 1971, 9, 3–6.

Longhi, P., Follett, R., Bloom, B., and Armstrong, J. A Program for Adolescent Educable Mentally Retarded. *Education and Training of the Mentally Retarded,* 1975, 10, 104–109.

Love, H. Attitudes and Knowledge of Parents Concerning Mental Retardation. *Journal for Special Educators of the Mentally Retarded,* 1971, 7, 168.

Lovitt, T. Behavior Modification: The Current Scene. *Exceptional Children,* 1970, 37, 85–91.

McCree, E. Games Children Play. *Teaching Exceptional Children,* 1973, 6, 20–22.

Mash, E., and Terdal, L. Modification of Mother-Child Interactions: Playing with Children. *Mental Retardation,* 11, 44–49.

Neisworth, J. T., and Smith, R. M. *Modifying Retarded Behavior.* Boston: Houghton-Mifflin, 1973.

Patterson, L. *Some Pointers for Professionals Children,* 1956, 3, 13–17.

Perls, F. *Gestalt Therapy: Verbatim.* LaFoyelle, California: Real People Press, 1969.

Pine, G. J. Quo Vadis School Counseling. *Phi Delta Kappan,* 1975, 56, 554–557.

Raths, L., Harmin, M., and Simon, S. *Values and Teaching.* Columbus, Ohio: Charles Merrill, 1966.

Rogers, C. *Client-Centered Therapy.* Boston: Houghton-Mifflin, 1951.

Rogers, C., and Skinner, B. F. Some Issues Concerning the Control of Human Behavior. *Science,* 1956, 124, 1057–1066.

Ricks, J. On Telling Parents About Test Results. *Test Service Bulletin,* 1959, 54, 1–4.

Seitz, S., and Terdal, L. A Modeling Approach to Changing Parent-Child Interactions. *Mental Retardation,* 1972, 10, 39–43.

Sellin, D., and Gallery, M. Pointers for Teachers as Counselors of the Moderately and Severely Retarded — Patterson Revisited. *Education and Training of the Mentally Retarded,* 1974, 9, 215–221.

Shine, V. Handicap or Disability. *The Exceptional Parent,* 1971, 1, 11–14.

Shine, V. Parent Power, *The Exceptional Parent,* 1971, 1, 6–8.

Simon, S., Howe, L., and Kirschenbaum, H. *Values Clarification. A Handbook of Practical Strategics for Teachers and Students.* New York: Hart Publishing Company, 1972.

Smith, R. M. *An Introduction to Mental Retardation.* New York: McGraw-Hill, 1971.

Stevens-Long, J. The Effect of Behavioral Context on Some Aspects of Adult Disciplinary Practices and Affect. *Child Development,* 1973, 44, 476–484.

Strag, G. Comparative Behavioral Ratings of Parents with Severe Mentally Retarded, Special Learning Disability, and Normal Children. *Journal of Learning Disabilities,* 1972, 5, 631–635.

VanderVeer, B., and Schweld, E. Infant Assessment Stability — Mental Functioning in Young Retarded Children. *American Journal of Mental Deficiency,* 1974, 78, 1–4.

Wolfensberger, W., and Kurtz, R. Use of Retardation-Related Diagnostic and Descriptive Labels by Parents of Retarded Children. *Journal of Special Education,* 1974, 8, 131–141.

Wright, B. *Physical Disability — A Psychological Approach.* New York: Harper and Row, 1960.

14

The Future

SYNOPSIS

This chapter is about what is known and understood, about the future. Its attempt is *not* to make exact predictions regarding the future, but to anticipate demands for adaptation. Past events and current trends can serve as the basis for *reasoned* anticipation. Toffler (1970) has altered thinking about time frames. His view of the future may be challenged and his data base may be in dispute, but his emphasis upon the need for a *balanced* sense of time — past, present *and* future — appears beyond dispute.

This chapter is directed toward the practitioner. Sellin (1971) pointed to the future of mental retardation, with 1984 as the reference point. He concluded that attitudes, understandings, and skills are the essentials for altering the gaps between aspiration and deed. This chapter discusses futureness and its application to attitudes, understanding, and skills. It is not a recitation of what these should be, but an attempt to identify genuine options. The chapter concludes with an agenda for action based on the perspectives of legal rights, leadership, and consumers.

The reader's attention is directed to the On Location selection. In the author's opinion, it captures the essence of a school commencement as a beginning, not an end. This is consistent with Blatt's (1971) view of learning as lifelong. He observed that effective practitioners possess an interest in people and in learning for its own sake. Such practitioners are likely to be *continuing* learners whose own excitement about learning is transferred to the learning of others. Thus, professional preparation is not a formal period, but an evolutionary process.

OBJECTIVES

ATTITUDES:

1. To anticipate the future and be eager to participate in it.
2. To speculate about the needs of the mentally retarded and their families in the year 2000.

UNDERSTANDINGS:

1 To define the sources of future shock.
2 To identify alternatives of services likely to be present in the future.
3 To describe the attitudes, understandings, and skills for the future.
4 To identify the structure and functions of human services.
5 To define information needs to prepare for the promise of the future.

SKILLS:

1 To choose one's vocational preferences for the future.
2 To appraise one's own personal capabilities to participate in the future.
3 To make intelligent selection of choices and options in the future.
4 To identify sources of potential helpfulness from a variety of perspectives.

OVERVIEW

The Concept of Future Shock

Any reader who has felt isolation and bewilderment in a new environment, can sense the feeling of future shock defined by Toffler (1970). Just as people experience "cultural shock" in the transition from a familiar setting into an "alien" culture, the pace and rate of change create uncertainty about the present and future in the oridinary lives of people. Toffler observed that change has always been associated with the human condition, but change now is explosive, as if human beings were being hurled into the future without sufficient time for preparation and adaptation. In the field of mental retardation, for example, the amount of time to develop residential facilities is in sharp contrast with the rapidity of deinstitutionalization. This rapidity also applies to the lengthy evolution of the special class as contrasted with the brief time for acceptance of the resource room. Consider the struggle for programs for the moderately retarded and the seemingly brief interval for the Pennsylvania decision on behalf of the severely retarded. Consider the Cleland et al. report and the Gardner and Selinger report (chapter 5), which estimates research articles in mental retardation doubled in five years. It is not change, but the pace of change which creates the sense of being a stranger in one's own field of interest and practice.

More specifically, Toffler describes future shock as an overload of the person's physical system, adaptive responses, and decision-making processes. The overwhelming affective response can be of crisis and distress. It is the reaction to overstimulation coupled with a feeling of loss of autonomy. Stimulation arises from several sources: loss of permanence, the increase of transience, and the array of novelty. Response to these sources can involve: denial of change, apathy, anxiety, hostility to outsiders, and even physical illness.

Impermanence, transience, and novelty are interrelated correlates of future shock. *Impermanence* is the trait of the throw-away society, the disposable culture. Nothing lasts or is preserved. Familiar landmarks, physical and psychological, are destroyed and replaced. *Transience* is made possible by mobility. The family unit is changing. The birth technology of *Brave New World* is a reality which could make biological parents obsolete. There is a loss of roots and heritage as nearly 30 million Americans become nomads because of job changes that require relocation. It is not that there is too little novelty, but that there is too much. Occupations change and increase. Value systems compete fiercely. The media imply that unless this or that is tried, one will have missed an opportunity. The new leisure creates an emptiness that Berne termed "stimulus and structure hunger." It is little wonder that there is mindless violence, a retreating from the mainstream, nostalgia, and a closing off of new ideas. Toffler asserted that these reactions are the responses of groups as well as of individuals.

Alternatives to Future Shock

Toffler is not a doomsday prophet. His data are meant to create a sense of urgency about preparation. As there are evasive responses toward the future, there can be adaptation. In fact, Toffler proposed a science of adaptation, which would assimilate and accommodate the knowledges currently available in psychology, neurology, communications theory, endocrinology, and other sources about adaptation.

The alternative to future shock, for Toffler, is coping and creative adaptation. The positive alternative suggests that persons can face the reality of change. Rational decisions can be made. The future can be anticipated with eagerness. The future can be managed with participatory ad-hocracy rather than planned bureaucracy.

The Family as Resource

Two social institutions were identified as possessing the possibilities of experiencing a "new" golden age: the family and the schools. The family can become a rediscovered resource. While change will continue, the family, though mobile, can provide the identity for humanization. Perhaps the results of persons such as Levinson et al. will contribute new insights and skills regarding the meaning of maturity.

Education as Resource

Toffler paid tribute to the American schools for their intentions and espoused values. He viewed the schools as the rallying centers for teaching "cope-ability" and "life know-how." The new curriculum for these skills would stress common skills, not common content. Literacy would be a common skill, as would learning, relating, and choosing. *Learning* involves adapting to changes in information. There could be specific learning environments for learning, then unlearning, and relearning; classifying and reclassifying; and the development of categories and new categories. *Relating* was described as the forging of human ties. Persons may need to learn helpful adaptation to accelerated relationships as well as to "tolerate" the absence of friendship over time. *Choosing* involves selection and autonomy. This common skill would involve exercising successive choices, using anticipatory information, and confronting alternatives. Choosing, for Toffler, involves choice, selection, and judgment consistent with a value system that facilitates a positive self-image of the person as a person as well as a positive self-image about the future.

Social Action as Resource

The arrangement of these circumstances will be no easy management task. Shane (1976) supports Toffler's goals and urges the schools to seek new partnerships with other social institutions, agencies, consumers, and influence sources for a united effort. This partnership among diverse elements around a common cause describes the Toffler process of ad-hocracy. This process involves social action, the skills of the change agent, and the determination of the advocate. Ad-hocracy is not necessarily fixed and static; people may merge and disband when problems are solved. Social action skills of the future may well be the skills of ad hoc rather than post hoc. Public institutions may adopt ad-hocracy's flexibility of management and operation, which is guided by the common skills of learning, relating, and choosing.

Thus, the future need not be shock. Freed from stress and disequilibrium about the future, attention can be directed toward the resolution of the present.

Cross-Cultural Resources

The essence of cross-cultural inquiries is to determine identification of possible solutions beyond one's frame of reference. Where problems and goals are similar, solutions may be suggested. The motivation for comparing one's culture to another has been discussed by Hechinger and Hechinger (1974). The incentive should neither be finding fault nor building pride, but simple curiosity and inquiry. Juul

(1974) has identified possible values to practitioners of studying problems in one's own culture from the perspective of another culture: exposure to new and different treatment methods, a new perspective of one's country and its strengths as well as its areas of needed improvement, a discovery of one's roots, and a discovery that treatment of the handicapped is indeed a reflection of values, history, tradition, and economic conditions.

The Juul report recounts programs and trends in Western Europe which have provided the models and the inspiration for the normalization movement in the U.S. Some illustrative examples might be:

1. Despite high unemployment and limited vocational training resources, the retarded should be viewed equally as any other citizen (Sen, 1975).

2. Testing should be based upon how much the child needs to know rather than on what adults need to teach (Nazzaro, 1973).

3. There are obstacles toward inclusion of retarded learners in the mainstream of comprehensive schools and effects from divided jurisdictions for service (Lippman, 1969).

4. Discipline at the kindergarten level should be built on the desire to persuade, not punish (Caldwell, 1974).

5. Vocational education should be available during unemployment and throughout life (Wanner, 1973).

GLIMPSES OF THE FUTURE

Hopeful Trends

A sense of future in America has been discussed by Shane (1976). He concluded that there is reason for cautious optimism, despite the continual existence of world political, economic, and ideological tension; continued crowding and planetary wear and tear; continuing and perhaps worsening world hunger; problems of debt and capital deficiency; changes in relative size of age groups in the population (despite our youth culture, the proportion of citizens over sixty-five will double by the year 2000); and changes in working styles. These problems require solution, but hopeful trends can be identified, such as a sense among people of interdependence; rediscovery of values; questioning of growth for the sake of growth without regard to consequences upon the quality of life; the emergence, although cautious, of education and the public schools to prepare young persons for an existence beyond mere survival. These larger trends will be of significance to the retarded citizen, his or her family, and practitioners.

Emerging Values Systems

The advent of advocacy and its organized efforts toward the elimination of isolation constitutes a hopeful signal. A model of the retarded person as citizen may emerge as the contribution of the last quarter of this century. The ideology of normalization and its emphasis upon the cycle of life may prove to be an enduring framework, not a rhetorical vogue. New insights in human physiology and a continued exploration of "inner" space can be the basis for prevention of etiological causes. There appears to be commitment to prevention of ecological causes as well. (Recall the discussions of these topics in previous chapters.)

Friedman (1974) has observed certain other indications. From his perspective as a student and teacher of social practice, the emergence of alternative schools, client-centered forms of participation in social services, community controlled development corporations, and reticulated work environments were viewed as examples of renewal. Strashower (1976) reported one community's effort to include retarded and normal youth in employment-bound programs, where adolescents encounter one another as future coworkers in training.

Early Medical Detection

While there may be no immediate breakthroughs on the etiologies of mental retardation, early detection efforts progress. Brandon (1975) has described computer-assisted detection of metabolic errors in the newborn. Guthrie (1972) has also described the use of automation for multiple screenings. This can be done without increased costs and with wider regional coverage. MacCready (1974) has documented the significant reduction in PKU by screening and treatment efforts, but he urges vigilance against efforts to dismantle early detection programs as too costly.

Education

Shane (1975) has noted that the future is becoming a force in the education of citizens. Alternatives and options in education exist as buffers against perceptions of a harsh reality that would limit the human condition. A model for the preparation of educators involved with both normal and exceptional learners has been described by Marsh (1974). The Teacher Corps is a federally structured partnership of a teacher preparation facility, a local school district, *and* consumers (within the school attendance area) engaged in a joint venture of preparation. Its emphasis upon collaborative functioning has the elements of ad-hocracy. It may have appeal to other areas of service delivery and practitioner preparation.

FUTURENESS AND ATTITUDE

The New Realism

Barry (1974) has outlined belief systems that influence actions toward the disabled, including the retarded. These include unwillingness to tolerate discrimination, perceiving differences among persons as relative rather than absolute, and willingness to become a competent professional. From the perspectives of futureness, the Barry description identifies certain goals for practitioners: engaging in activities designed to sensitize one to the needs of others, engaging in task-oriented training related directly to the needs of others, engaging in change processes designed to eliminate sources of prejudice held by "normal" populations, and using one's skills in individualized training and group procedures.

The quality of belief, according to Blatt (1971), arranges thought into dissent, wisdom, and conservatorship. Wisdom values tradition, not because it is convention, but because it allows for roots and the prizing of that which should be conserved. Dissent recognizes that change is an aspect of the human condition, but it does not prize mindless negativism or unreasoned reaction. Wisdom, for Blatt, is the belief that competence and truth are the deliverance from foolishness.

Equality of Life

The newborn and the aged focus attention upon the *meaning* of life itself. Stevens and Conn (1976) have observed and documented a growing acceptance of euthanasia of severely disabled infants with a fatal but correctable physical condition. O'Connor, Justice, and Warren (1970) have documented the myths that prevent the aged retarded citizen from community participation. From a social commentary perspective, Thimmesh (1973) has observed that the "acceptance" of life-death decisions has proceeded without appraisal or examination. Terms such as *therapeutic abortion, good death, death with dignity,* and *positive euthanasia* (suicide) are masks that hide the issues of life itself. Without a questioning of the motives involved, he warns that unlimited license for life-death decisions may introduce a new barbarism into American society. The public's threshold of permissiveness to practice the axiom that what is useful is good may be raised. The "rightness or wrongness" in the individual situation was not questioned, but rather the consequences for vulnerable groups. The following examples were cited: syphilitic men untreated for experimental purposes, demands for removal of the WHO's ban on drug experimentation with children and mentally incompetent persons, experimental drugs tested on free-clinic patients without their knowledge, and testimony before one state legislature that 90 percent of its institutionalized patients should be allowed to die. Perhaps the Thimmesh hypothesis is too stark, too alarmist, but his plea for surveillance, for honesty in terminology, and for respect for safeguards can help protect the vulnerable and those presently invulnerable.

The Stevens and Conn as well as the O'Connor et al. reports point to assumptions and/or beliefs that influence decisions to withhold medical intervention from the severely disabled and retarded. Belief about human potential is involved. The Stevens and Conn review also noted that decisions are usually couched as life with the parents or death without them. Recent trends in adoption and an increasing willingness for subsidy for families can provide more than the stark alternative. Research reflects a positive experience for families as a balance to the usual assumption of trauma. The O'Connor et al. report reflected that decisions about aged retarded persons may be founded upon assumptions that have little to do with the specific person. Their findings were that age, length of institutionalization, and IQ were not indicators of adjustment to community-living placements. Preparation of the person was the critical dimension, and age apparently is not related to adaptation.

The Stevens and Conn review revealed an absence of uniform standards to guide practice. The "arguments" justifying euthanasia and current indicators defining the quality and meaning of life were reviewed. Among the reported "indicators" to continue life were: can conceive of a self-identity; would choose to continue existence knowing self-identity; is capable of some form of human relationship; and biological symptoms reflect a potential for humanness. It is the parent's right to decide, but this raises a question of rights of the infant. The Stevens and Conn writing stressed the need for thoughtful citizens to demand standards. They also noted that thoughtful citizens should consider how a world can be created in which both the retarded and nonretarded would choose to live.

THE ROLE OF UNDERSTANDING

Planning Concepts

Planning, for Jordan (1973), involves securing a data base upon which to guide services of prevention, identification, intervention, and evaluation. Services are to be formulated upon the best estimates of the science of epidemiology. The suggestion was made that planning should follow five-to-ten-year cycles to provide sufficient balance between short-term and long-range goals, with provision for inclusion of new information and trends. Jordan also advocated that planning and services should follow life stages of gestation, infancy, sensory-motor, linguistic-sensory-motor, phenotypic, school entry, and formal skills. In Piagetian reference points, the first four stages would correspond to sensory-motor stages. The next two relate to concrete operations, with phenotypic constituting a transitional period.

Friedman (1974) presented a thoughtful essay that distinguishes the structure (what) and function (forms) of planning. His concentration was upon the theme of planning as problem solving, which raises fundamental questions of: What is a problem?, How does one define the existence of a problem? Who does the planning? The core of the Friedman presentation was addressed to a consideration of planning to achieve what purpose? He observed that past methods, although varied, have had a theme of: denial of a problem; raising thresholds of tolerance for injustice, violence, etc.; ritual cleansing of the problem symptoms, although the same events appear after clamor fades; dealing with symptoms to avoid a meaningful change; segregation of persons into special institutions, which absolves the larger community; and special commissions or investigative bodies to gather "facts." Friedman advanced the need for a science of social practice, a line of inquiry into the sources of alienation. In futureness terms, this proposed science would be to clarify the ways in which social structures create alienation and produce strategies to eliminate it. In this sense, the science of social practice is an example of Toffler's science of adaptation. In another sense it reflects the Jordan postulates for a broad perspective and the Barry concern of alienation between the normal and disabled, and may contribute to the Blatt sense of wisdom. Findings from these inquiries might contribute to the quality and equality of life.

Economics of Mental Retardation

World events have had great impact upon petroleum-related societies, especially the United States. This impact has had its consequences in services for the handicapped (Simches, 1975). The effect has "inflated" budgets without corresponding increases in either quantity, and/or quality of services. The economic base for quality of services must certainly create the feelings of future shock. Thomas (1973) warns that the problem of dwindling financial resources cannot be ignored or responded to in a sporadic fashion.

Mange (1975) has proposed criteria for the funding of special services which emphasize an integrated, coordinated approach. What might evolve would be allocation of resources based upon principles of:

1 equalization of resources to the person regardless of geographical residence;

2 coordination of federal, state, and local resources;
3 neither discouraging nor encouraging *one* service approach;
4 needs rather than labels as criteria;
5 support for actual expenditures, rather than "paper" overhead;
6 periodic reexamination of policies and practices; and
7 funding formulae comprehensible to legislators, citizens, and practitioners.

The impact of economics upon the mentally retarded and the family in human and financial terms has been detailed by Conley (1973). Neglect of services was shown to have consequences of loss, economic and human, in terms of misdiagnosis and its inflation of need for services, which draws resources from those persons in genuine need; loss of earning potential of retarded citizens; drain of family resources from the general economy; and the loss of human potential. The estimate was advanced that 400,000 retarded adults (out of a potential of 700,000) could be *gainfully* employed. These persons tend to be in an overlap population range between moderate and mild levels, with physical disabilities and secondary emotional impairment. A critical understanding was that neglect and inaction create waste, while financial support is an investment in the future. Specific understandings of the Conley theme of investment would be reflected and/or evaluated by increase of earning power for the retarded, reduction (not necessarily elimination) of dependency-orientation services; a redistribution of family resources among the general GNP mainstream, and encouragement of quality of services. There was a further observation that future generations could view our present efforts as cruel, incomprehensible, and outrageous.

THE ROLE OF SKILL

Role Expectations

As has been noted, the new curriculum insists on the process of literacy, learning, relating, and choosing. At present, the language of practitioner skill is expressed in competencies, or role expectation. Eisenbach (1975) has identified role expectation as the study of the relationship between practitioner performance to outcomes directly related to learner need. There was a proposal for increased accountability from those who administer programs and from those who prepare practitioners.

The presence of novelty and of the need for choosing skills, in the Toffler sense, is illustrated by the 1969 report of the Secretary's Committee on Mental Retardation. This report listed five major career fields in mental retardation, with thirty-four subspecialties, and specialization within each of these thirty-four components. While this report considered paraprofessional careers in institutions, it did not anticipate careers associated with community residential facilities. It did anticipate career roles in coordination and administration.

The concept of career education could well apply to the practitioner. While roles may change, there may be qualities or traits that will cut across varied careers in mental retardation. A 1966 report of the U.S. Bureau of Economic Security identified certain traits the practitioner might consider in appraisal of self in relation to role. These traits compliment the Eisenbach proposal for the match between practitioner role and learner, client, and/or protege outcomes. These traits may be said to be *at least* a minimum (table 14–1). It should be understood that these traits have more "weight" for certain occupations than others. The spirit of futureness suggests the need for research, refinement, and continuing evaluation.

Innovation

The implicit theme in the discussion on social action was upon change based upon perceived need. The advocate as change agent stresses innovation on behalf of the protege. The rise of the normalization movement is one example of innovation within the structure of social institutions and agencies. Normalization has set a tone for innovation.

As with planning, however, there must be consideration of the purpose of innovation. Certainly innovation will be a role expectation, but the practitioner may well ask, toward what end? Sarason (1971) provides a tentative view of the qualities of persons involved with decisions about change. *One* is the quality of here and now — an attribute of vigilance. A *second* is informality — a valuing of freedom and movement. A *third* factor was individualization — concern about the well-being of others. The *fourth* was autonomy — resistance to influences that would curb or decrease the first three.

With respect to innovation, Hobbs, Edgerton, and Matheny (1975) have proposed a set of priorities for the immediate future: support for parents; improved residential programs for children; help for children excluded from school; fairness to disadvantaged children, especially in the use of assessment procedures; and better organization and coordination of services. One might add the Conley emphasis upon employment opportunities for adult retarded citizens.

AN AGENDA FOR ACTION

As has been suggested, the future can be anticipated, and resources of attitude, understanding, and skill can be known and understood. This concluding section identifies, in an anticipatory way, the tasks that represent an agenda for action on behalf

Table 14–1 POSSIBLE TRAITS ASSOCIATED WITH MENTAL RETARDATION SERVICE CAREERS

Major Trait	*Component Trait*	*Related Traits*
Aptitudes (Depending on the job, there will be a range of variation.)	Intelligence	Reason, make judgments, verbal fluencies
	Verbal	Receive messages, relate to words and meanings, express ideas clearly
	Spatial	Think in visual terms and communicate visually
	Form Perception	Make visual comparisons and observe even subtle differences
	Clerical	Classify and especially check one's work accurately
	Motor Coordination	Eye-hand coordination with rapidity and accuracy
	Finger and Manual Dexterity	Relates to manipulation of occupationally related objects
Physical Demands (Not all demands are equally required or equally present. Each component can be further classified as sedentary, light, medium, heavy, and very heavy.)	Lifting, Carrying, Pushing/ Pulling	Raising from one level to another, exerting force, to or from the person
	Climbing, and Balancing	Ascending and descending. Maintaining equilibrium
	Stooping, Kneeling, Crouch-Crawl	Bending the body and parts of the body
	Handling, Reaching, Feeling	Coordination of the body to seize, grip, and release
	Talking and Hearing	Exchange of ideas by the spoken word

Table 14–1 (continued)

Major Trait	*Component Trait*	*Related Traits*
	Seeing	Qualities of vision such as: acuity, depth perception, field, accommodation, any color recognition
Interests (This area is both the demand of the job and the preference of the person)	Orientation	Preferences as to people-thing interactions, ambiguity vs. structure needs, and needs for internal vs. external rewards
	Temperament	Tolerance for change, order, and social contact aspects of work. Skills in interpreting feelings, responding to external evaluations, and responding to self-examination
Working Conditions	Inside	Protection from weather
	Outside	Performance in weather
	Both	Fifty percent of time is spent in both
	Temperature Variations	Preference and ability to tolerate extremes, changes in humidity and/or temperature
	Hazards	Situations that create risk in terms of personal safety and tolerance for such situations.
	Exposure	Specific situations including noise, fumes, odors, toxicity, dust, ventilation

of the retarded person and his or her family. Three sources were selected to identify a potential agenda: a legal-rights view, the views of leadership, and consumer perspectives.

Legal and Legislative Perspectives

Goodman (1976) has cited the enactment of PL 94-142 as a "blockbuster." This legislation, termed the Education for All Handicapped Children Act, transforms the ideal into the real. It provides for a fiscal partnership among federal, state, and local units to insure that *every* handicapped learner will have access to a free, public education. By the 1980s it is estimated that between \$3–5 billion will be available for distribution to state and local agencies. Among its key features, aside from fiscal resources, are requirements for: preschool programs, parent involvement, individualized plans for the learner, and delivery of educational services to every handicapped learner between the ages of three to twenty-one. According to the Goodman analysis, other innovative features of PL 94-142 include:

1 The prudent use of mainstreaming will be encouraged.
2 Testing for placement will be in the person's native language, and such testing will *not* be racially or culturally discriminatory.
3 Consultation of parents regarding placement will be required.
4 Location and identification of learners will be required. Additionally, attention must be given to quality of program.
5 Provision is made for inservice training of personnel in both general and special service systems.
6 Each state must appoint, through the governor, an advisory panel to monitor implementation.

The *Federal Register* (1976) affirms the Goodman analysis and targets the area of preschool programming as a special dimension of priority. Furthermore, it was noted that assessment and placement should be a team venture. One provision suggests that a representative from general education should be a focal member of the team.

The provisions of this act imply the application of evaluation and accountability as correlates to its implementation at all levels of local, state, and federal responsibility. The experience of implementation of the Developmental Disabilites legislation (chapter 8) should prove instructive.

PL 94-142 and its provisions list tasks, but Goldberg and Lippman (1974) noted that *implementation* of laws teaches that laws do not necessarily get children to school; statistical records are required to know if persons are indeed receiving services; and laws do not guarantee quality of education. The impact of right-to-education laws, according to Goldberg and Lippman, involves the following accommodations:

1. Learners not previously considered admissible to schools will be in school programs.
2. The parents of such children and youth may be more intense and troubled.
3. A zero-rejection model will operate which seeks to serve *every* learner.
4. All educators must deliver high-quality services.
5. Despite a current fiscal crisis in education, more funds than ever will be required.

The President's Committee on Employment of the Handicapped (1976) has prepared a *Handbook on the Legal Rights of Handicapped People.* The topics include:

1. architectural barriers,
2. benefits,
3. civil rights,
4. education,
5. employment,
6. hospital and medical matters,
7. housing,
8. insurance,
9. transportation,
10. vocational rehabilitation, and
11. sources of legal aid.

Each of its sections cites the federal source for law and identifies a specific contact office for further information. Table 14–2 conveys a representative sample of federal public laws applicable to mentally retarded persons. The listings in the committee's document and the adaptive listing in table 14–2 convey that there are resources available. The document does affirm the Goldberg-Lippman observation of the necessity for continuous monitoring to guarantee implementation of legislative provisions.

A Leadership Perspective

The President's Committee on Mental Retardation (1976) considered relevant trends, events, and conditions in the United States. From this perspective of the

Table 14–2 REPRESENTATIVE EXAMPLES OF RIGHTS OF HANDICAPPED PERSONS

Area of Concern	*Federal Law*	*Intent*
Architectural Barriers	90–480	Buildings involving federal funding must be accessible
	93–112	Both laws establish a compliance to review to oversee accessibility
	93–87	Provides for curb outs for access.
Civil Rights	93–112	Prohibits discrimination by any program that receives federal funds to a person because of handicap.
Education	93–380	States receiving federal funds must work toward a goal of education for all children. Parent participation is mandated and the concept of least restrictive alternative and the right to non-bias in testing are affirmed. (PL 94–142 extends this coverage.)
	92–420	Ten percent of Head Start shall be available to handicapped children
Employment	93–112	Mandares affirmative action employment of the handicapped by federal agencies and federal contractors.
	92–28	Special preference is given sheltered workshops in bids on federal contracts.
Housing	89–117	Allows HUD to assist families at certain income levels to receive rent supplements
Transportation	91–453	Designed to extend access of the handicapped to mass transportation.

Table 14–2 (continued)

Area of Concern	*Federal Law*	*Intent*
	93–87	Provides access to bus and motor transportation.
	93–503	Establishes adjusted fares for the handicapped through federal aid.
	93–140	Provides access to Amtrak facilities and transportation.
Vocational Rehabilitation	93–112	Outlines permissible services and training under vocational rehabilitation; requires an individualized plan for clients; annual review of plan is required; allows for appeal procedures for clients.
	91–517	Extends coverage to the developmentally disabled.

known, and of the promising, the committee generated a series of goals and objectives to provide a scientifically verified view of future demands. In general, the committee adopted a view of reasoned optimism similar to the viewpoints expressed earlier in this chapter. This document, *Mental Retardation: Century of Decision,* emerges as a helpful resource in anticipation of the future. The goals and principal objectives are presented in adapted form as items of an action agenda.

Full citizenship. As a goal, this means that rights are to be exercised in fact as well as in law. Objectives may be said to include assurances to the retarded person of maximum: freedom to exercise rights, independence, and access to a free and open community. The general theme of this goal area centered around concepts of guardianship and residential services.

The right to be well born. This goal is commitment to reduce the incidence of mental retardation by at least 50 percent by the year 2000. Objectives associated with this goal would include: commitment to achieve it, establishing a health care system which is accessible and reasonable in cost, continued emphasis upon research, and an assertive effort to publicize the known cause of this condition. The major theme of this goal was health care delivery, reduction of malnutrition and child abuse, and public awareness.

The right to a good start in life. This goal centered upon the reduction of ecological sources of mental retardation, especially poverty, to the lowest possible level. Associated objectives included: elimination of sources of discrimination, improvement of home and community environments, preservation of equal educational opportunities with emphasis upon nondiscrimination of culturally different groups, and provision for adequate control over allotments for public funds in order to protect minority groups. The theme of this goal clustered around protective safeguards and planned inclusion of minority persons.

Humane service systems. This goal implied availability of quality services to those in need. Associated objectives would include: availability of services in *all* sections of the United States, the exercise of free choice and decision in selection of services, availability of a personal representative for the retarded person who needs or desires one, opportunity to reside in a setting of one's choice, maintenance of standards of quality and standards of accountability, and utilization of research findings to influence program directions and preparation of practitioners. The persisting theme of this goal clustered around advocacy, described as a "personal representative" for the person. Attention was drawn to the need for both the volunteer system and for public systems.

Public attitudes. The themes of this goal involved acceptance of the retarded person as a citizen and as a member of the common community. Efforts should emphasize: the right to be different; understanding that humanized values can be achieved despite *seemingly* adverse economic trends; and gaining public support for prevention efforts (the right to be well born and the right to a good start in life). In this area, approaches similar to values clarification were called for with varied populations and settings.

Coordination. As a goal, services for the retarded should be equitable, coordinated, and use resources efficiently and effectively. Planning should be coordinated at federal, state, and local efforts; interagency efforts should reflect a genuine collaboration; and accountability should reflect *both* effectiveness and consumer interest. Private sector involvement should not be ignored.

The President's Committee also referred to cooperation and collaboration with other countries. Exchange of information should be encouraged.

Consumer Perspectives

The President's Committee on Mental Retardation (1975) reported the opinions of retarded persons regarding their unmet needs. Their concerns centered around leisure time, living conditions, education, and work.

With respect to *leisure time,* preference was expressed for small-group activities, sports, and exercise activities. There was also a willingness to participate with other persons of the same age. Finally, there was agreement that retarded persons should share in decision making.

The topic of *living conditions* reflected their perceived need for preparation for apartment living. They wanted courses in marketing, budgeting, cooking, etc. to fulfill this preparation. They affirmed their right to date and to marry and felt this right should extend to institutional living as well.

On *education,* there was a strong preference for inclusion in decision making. Curriculum, leisure time, and selection of materials were areas of concern.

Concerns about *work* centered on the right to more interesting jobs. There was the feeling that they should *not* be disadvantaged by perpetual assignment to the worst and most boring of tasks. They also identified the need for fellow workers to be informed of their handicap.

Commentary

It would appear that the future will not be lacking in tasks. Themes of rights, advocacy, prevention, service delivery, and dignity for the retarded person emerge as global agenda items. The advocate must be willing to participate fully, regardless of role and regardless of one's sphere of influence. Recall the essay of the "The Leaf and the Stone" in chapter 6. It is the efforts of imaginative people that fulfill an agenda of need.

SUMMING UP

This chapter identified the concept of futureness. The widespread popularity and credibility of Toffler's *Future Shock* has aroused an interest in futureness. Futureness is a balanced view of time among past, present, *and* future.

Futureness does not predicate absolutes, but it does attempt to anticipate beyond the present. Its emphasis is upon the *may* rather than the *will*. The history (futureness does not reject tradition) of mental retardation has been influenced by diverse informational sources. This chapter has cited a certain variety of illustrative sources. The history of mental retardation also reflects the significance of attitudes, understandings, and skills of the practitioner. This chapter attempted to present expert opinion and documented inferences regarding genuine options. Inferences about these future possibilities are a function of personal perspective.

1. Future shock describes the psychological and sense of physical distress that results from impermanence, transience, and/or novelty.

2. The alternative to future shock can be cope-ability and life know-how. These are based upon the common skills of literacy, learning, relating, and choosing which can be imparted.

3. The future can be managed by ad-hocracy. This approach involves the forging of partnerships that exist only so long as need persists. The tactics of the change agent and citizen as advocate may prove to be the model.

4. Cross-cultural studies may be useful for understanding the relationship between culture and practice.

5. There are glimpses of the future in present practice which encourage hope. These glimpses suggest an inclusion of the handicapped in normal work settings, automated technologies for early detection of genetic etiologies, and the future as a force in preparation.

6. A model of preparation among the institutions of higher education, the local school district, *and* the constituent community has evolved. Although found in education, the Teacher Corps model could have wider applicability.

Attitude

1. Futureness involves anticipatory belief as well as knowledge. Belief systems of practitioners will likely possess values regarding one's role as related to service as well as an emphasis upon change of existing patterns of stigma and isolation.

2. Valuing knowledge is an attitude, and wisdom is a focal point for conservatorship and dissent.

3. The practice of infant euthanasia and the quality of life for the aged retarded call into question beliefs about the equality of life. Equality involves valuing life based upon self-identity, the capacity to form human relationship, and choice to exist. These questions cannot be turned aside. There must be standards to protect parents and the person from misinformation.

Understanding

1. Planning, in ad-hocracy terms, should be guidelines. Cycles of five to ten years of attainments allow for allocation of activities and provide sufficient flexibility for new data and trends.

2. The components of planning may well incorporate understandings of epidimology, life stages, and intervention to form service goals.

3. Planning should consider planning for what purpose, and for what goals. Certain past practices have been directed toward confinement.

4. A worthy pursuit of understanding may well be clarification of sources of alienation among people.

5. Economic events have created alarm regarding availability of resources to meet needs. These events have consequences for the person and the practitioner.

6. Neglect and symptom funding are wasteful of human and economic potential. Services can be understood as an investment in the future.

Skills

1. Role expectations define the selection of competencies. Accountability between sources of service and preparation could prove helpful for practitioners.

2. The Toffler concept of novelty applies to careers in mental retardation.

3. Examination of careers by major traits of aptitudes, interests, physical demands, and working conditions as minimal indicators of self-appraisal and/or job descriptions were reviewed.

4. Innovation may well be a role expectation. Qualities of the here and now, individualization, informality, and autonomy reflect the essence of goals and of the person engaged in innovation.

Agenda

1. An agenda for action can be identified.
2. Implementation was defined as the master task.
3. Achievement of declared goals will require collaborative efforts.
4. Participation in the attainment of this agenda is a form of advocacy.

ON LOCATION

The selection chosen for this chapter originally was reported in *Mental Retardation News*. Bill Yore (1975), the author, is a graduate of a special education program. It seemed fitting that a very direct consumer of services be given an opportunity to share his views.

Commencement Address

STEVENSVILLE, MICH. When the seniors at Lakeshore High School had tryouts to choose three commencement speakers the seventh to try out was Bill Yore, a mentally retarded and physically impaired 19-year-old senior. His mother and teacher had both tried to discourage him, but he worked for weeks on his speech.

He had been in special education programs all of his life, but he had a message he felt impelled to impart. And it is one all persons teaching special education programs, as well as parents, employers — all of us need to hear. He hesitated, lost his place, stuttered, but he went on. No senior in the assembly moved.

Mr. Reilly, honored guest, ladies and gentlemen and members of the graduating class of 1974. I want to take this opportunity to convey appreciation to you for allowing me to express my feelings this evening.

Tonight represents a dream come true for my parents, friends and relatives. Tonight also represents the attainment of a goal for many interested and concerned teachers, counselors, and staff. Tonight also represents the downfall of a diagnosis that was made over fifteen years ago. Let me explain.

In 1958, a four-year-old boy was taken to the hospital for neurological examinations. After many hours of examinations, tests, X-rays, and waiting, a verdict and sentence was handed down by the university doctors. The parents were informed that their son was mentally handicapped and the best place for him was in an institution. "Your son, at best, may someday be able to sell papers on a street corner," the doctors informed the stunned couple. On the convictions of these parents, through the efforts of devoted teachers and the legislation of interested tax-payers like yourselves, this would-be resident of Coldwater's Home for the Mentally Handicapped was placed in our local school systems.

This boy was loved and cared for not only at home but also at school. Sure, there were hard and rough times. It isn't easy competing with other kids, even when you are normal, much less handicapped. But the love and the patience was there for nineteen long years. And, tonight I am proud to stand here and say that I am that boy — almost condemned to an institution. True, I am not an "A" student. But neither am I a dropout. I may never go to college, but I won't be on the welfare rolls, either. I may never be a great man in this world, but I will be a man in whatever way I am able to do it.

For tonight, I say thanks to my parents who prayed and worked so hard. I say thanks to you, my instructors and the staff, of Lakeshore High who had the patience and dedication to see me through. I say thanks to this audience for your work, your dollars, and your concern in providing me with an opportunity for an education. And, to you, my classmates, I also say thanks. I will always remember our years together and I hope that you will also.

Remember me as you search for a place in life, for there will be youngsters needing your help as you select a vocation in life. Remember me as you become paying members of our communities, because there will be children needing your financial support. And, remember me and others like me in your prayers, because in some cases there are not always parents, teachers, friends, and classmates like I have had at Lakeshore High School.

Thank You.

The senior class of Lakeshore High School stood in unison to give one of their classmates a standing ovation. He was their top choice for commencement speaker. A tribute? Yes. But even more — a message to all of us.

REFERENCES

Barry, M. The Exceptional Child Component and the Teacher Corps. *TED Newsletter,* 1974, 10, 17–21.

Blatt, B. Handicapped Children in Model Programs, in Reynolds, M., and Davis, M., (eds.). *Exceptional Children in Regular Classrooms.* Reston, Virginia: Council for Exceptional Children, 1975.

Blatt, B. On Dissent: Three Stages of Evaluation. *TED Newsletter,* 1971, 7, 2.

Brandon, G. R. Oregon Has Pioneered in Early Screening and Detection of Metabolic Disorders. *Bulletin: Oregon Health,* 1975, 53, 5 and 8.

Caldwell, B. The Little Apple — How China's Kindergartners Grow. *Instructor,* 83, 42–44.

Conley, J. *The Economics of Mental Retardation.* Baltimore: The Johns Hopkins University Press, 1973.

Eisenbach, J. J. Personnel Selection in Special Education, in *Research Needs Related to the Development of Personnel to Serve the Handicapped Proceedings.* Princeton: Educational Testing Service, 1975.

Federal Register. Education of Handicapped Children, Assistance to States, Proposed Rules. Monday, 29 November 1976, 52404–52407.

Friedman, J. Planning and the Good Society. *Fifteenth Anniversary Conference Papers.* Waltham, Massachusetts: Florence Heller School for Advanced Studies in Social Welfare, Brandeis University, 1974.

Goldberg, I. I., and Lippman, L. Plato Had a Word for It. *Exceptional Children,* 1974, 40, 325–344.

Goldman, R. Kibbutz Zafone, Northern Israel. *Children Today,* 1975, 4, 27–29.

Goodman, L. V., A Bill of Rights for the Handicapped. *Programs for the Handicapped,* 1976, 76–9, 15–21.

Guthrie, R. H. Mass Screening for Genetic Diseases. *Hospital Practice,* 1972, 14, 93–100.

Hechinger, G., and Hechinger, F. Are Schools Better in Other Countries? *American Education,* 1974, 10, 6–8.

Hobbs, M., Edgerton, J., and Matheny, M. Classification of Children. *Children Today,* 1975, 4, 21–25.

Jordan, T. E. Scope and Perspective in Special Education. *Education and Training of the Mentally Retarded,* 1973, 8, 116–123.

Juul, K. *Progressive and Innovative Programs for the Handicapped in Europe.* Carbondale: Southern Illinois University, 1974.

Lippman, L. England's Comprehensive Schools: Analogy for Special Education? *Exceptional Children,* 1969, 36, 279–281.

MacCready, R. Admissions of PKU Patients to Residential Institutions Before and After Screening Programs of the New Born Infant. *The Journal of Pediatrics,* 1974, 85, 383–385.

Mange, C. V., *Financial Support for Special Services.* East Lansing: Department of Elementary and Special Education, Michigan State University, 1975.

Marsh, O. D. Accomplishments: Outside Evaluations. *Journal of Teacher Education,* 1974, 26, 139–140.

Nazzaro, G. Mental Retardation in the Soviet Union. *Education and Training of the Mentally Retarded,* 1973, 8, 166–171.

O'Connor, G., Justice, R., and Warren, N. The Aged Mentally Retarded: Institution or Community Care? *American Journal of Mental Deficiency,* 1970, 75, 354–360.

President's Committee on Employment of the Handicapped. *A Handbook on the Legal Rights of the Handicapped.* Washington, D.C.: U. S. Government Printing Office, 1976.

President's Committee on Mental Retardation. *Mental Retardation: Century of Decision.* Washington, D.C.: U.S. Department of Health, Education, and Welfare, 1976.

President's Committee on Mental Retardation. *Mental Retardation: The Known and the Unknown.* Washington, D.C.: U.S. Department of Health, Education, and Welfare, 1975.

Sarason, S. *The Culture of the School and the Problem of Change.* Boston: Allyn and Bacon, 1971.

Secretary's Committee on Mental Retardation. *Career Opportunities in the Field of Mental Retardation.* Washington, D.C.: U.S. Department of Health, Education, and Welfare, 1969.

Sellin, D. Mental Retardation 1984: Will the Paradox End? *Mental Retardation,* 1971, 9, 34–38.

Sen, A. K. Mental Retardation in India. *Mental Retardation,* 1975, 13, 11–13.

Shane, H. G. America's Next 25 Years: Some Implications for Education. *Phi Delta Kappan,* 1976, 58, 78–83.

Shane, H. G. The Future as a Force in Educational Change. *Phi Delta Kappan,* 1975, 57, 13–15.

Simches, R. Economic Inflation: Hazard for the Handicapped. *Exceptional Children,* 1975, 41, 229–242.

Strashower, G. Mainstream in the Work World. *American Education,* 1976, 12, 9–13.

Stevens, H. A., and Conn, R. A. Right to Life/Involuntary Euthanasia. *Mental Retardation,* 1976, 14, 3–6.

Thimmesh, N. The Abortion Culture. *Newsweek,* July 9, 1973, 7.

Thomas, M. A. Finance: Without Which There is No Special Education. *Exceptional Children,* 1973, 39, 475–480.

Toffler, A. *Future Shock.* New York: Bantam Books, 1970.

U.S. Bureau of Employment Security. *Occupations in the Care and Rehabilitation of the Mentally Retarded.* Washington, D.C.: U.S. Department of Labor, 1966.

Wanner, R. Expanding on Career Education. *American Education,* 1973, 9, 11–13.

Yore, B. Commencement Address. *Mental Retardation News,* 1975, 24, p. 3.

Index